Street by Street

DERBY, LEICESTER NOTTINGHAM
BELPER, ILKESTON, LOUGHBOROUGH, RIPLEY

Beeston, Castle Donington, Coalville, Eastwood, Heanor, Hucknall, Long Eaton, Shepshed, Stapleford, West Bridgford

2nd edition November 2002

Published by AA Publishing (a trading name of Automobile Association Developments Limited, whose registered office is Millstream, Maidenhead Road, Windsor, Berkshire SL4 5GD. Registered number 1878835).

The Post Office is a registered trademark of Post Office Ltd. in the UK and other countries.

Schools address data provided by Education Direct.

One-way street data provided by:

Tele Atlas © Tele Atlas N.V.

Mapping produced by the Cartographic Department of The Automobile Association. A01532

A CIP Catalogue record for this book is available from the British Library.

Printed by G. Canale & C. S.P.A., Torino, Italy.

The contents of this atlas are believed to be correct at the time of the latest revision. However, the publishers cannot be held responsible for loss occasioned to any person acting or refraining from action as a result of any material in this atlas, nor for any errors, omissions or changes in such material. This does not affect your statutory rights. The publishers would welcome information to correct any errors or omissions and to keep this atlas up to date. Please write to Publishing, The Automobile Association, Fanum House (FH17), Basing View, Basingstoke, Hampshire, RG21 4EA.

Ref: MX087z

Key to map pages	ii-iii
Key to map symbols	iv-1
Enlarged scale pages	2-9
Street by Street	10-147
Index – towns & villages	148
Index – streets	149-184
Index – featured places	184-189

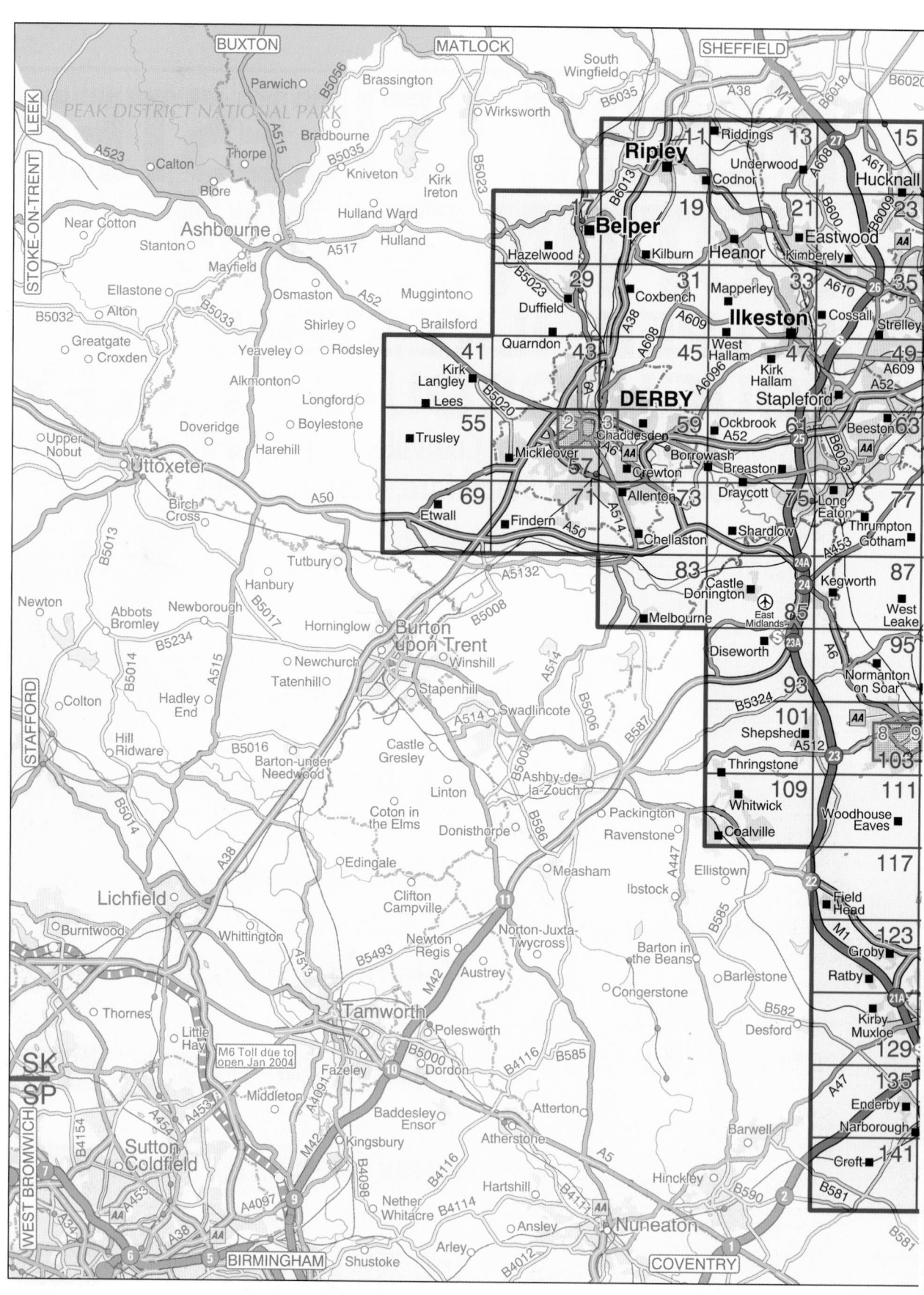

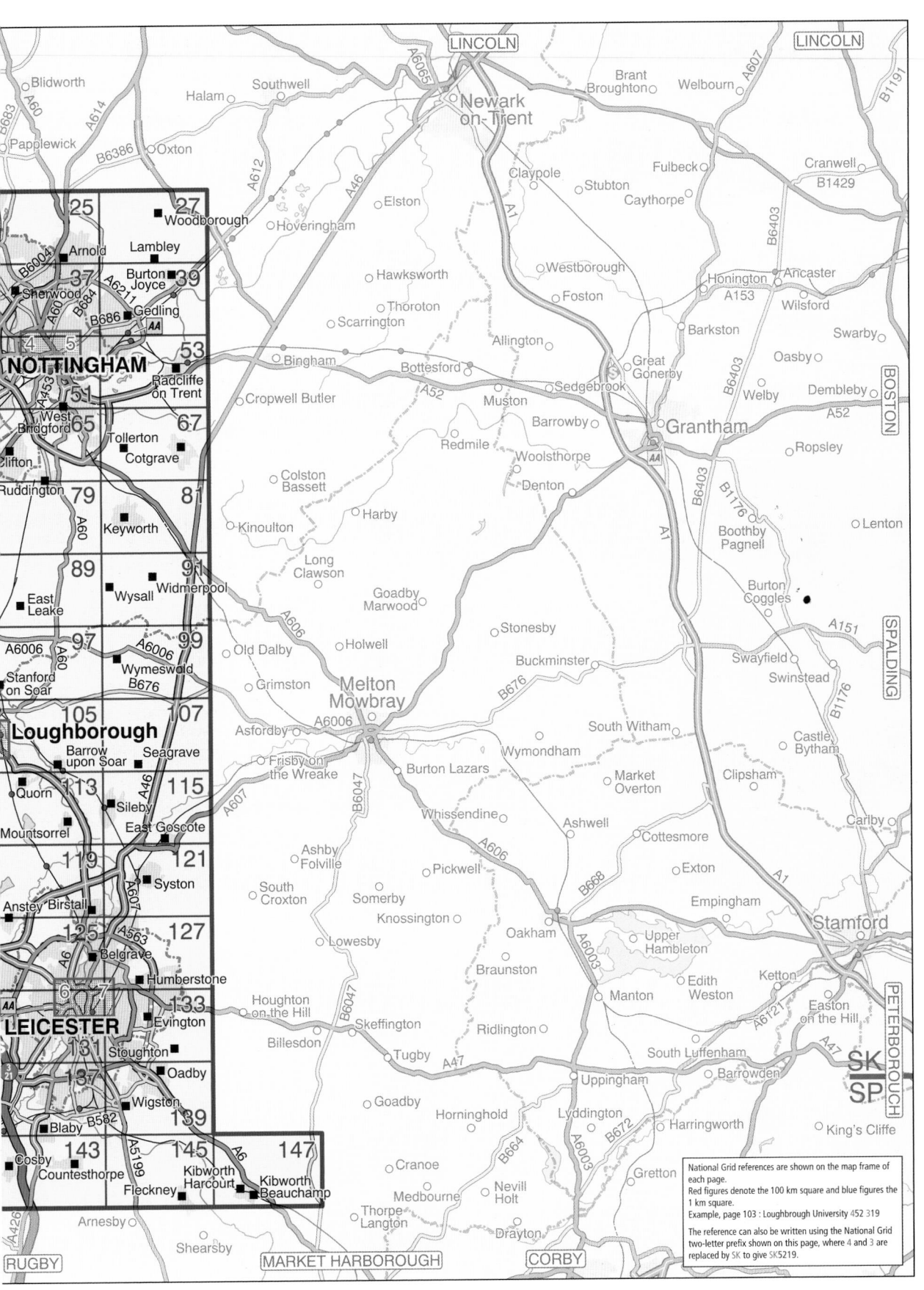

National Grid references are shown on the map frame of each page.
Red figures denote the 100 km square and blue figures the 1 km square.
Example, page 103 : Loughborough University 452 319

The reference can also be written using the National Grid two-letter prefix shown on this page, where 4 and 3 are replaced by SK to give SK5219.

3.6 inches to 1 mile   Scale of main map pages 1:17,500

0   1/2   miles   1

0   1/2   1   kilometres   1 1/2   2

iv

Junction 9	Motorway & junction
Services	Motorway service area
	Primary road single/dual carriageway
Services	Primary road service area
	A road single/dual carriageway
	B road single/dual carriageway
	Other road single/dual carriageway
	Minor/private road, access may be restricted
← ←	One-way street
	Pedestrian area
	Track or footpath
	Road under construction
	Road tunnel
AA	AA Service Centre
P	Parking
P+	Park & Ride
	Bus/coach station
	Railway & main railway station
	Railway & minor railway station

	Underground station
	Light railway & station
	Preserved private railway
LC	Level crossing
	Tramway
	Ferry route
	Airport runway
	County, administrative boundary
	Mounds
93	Page continuation 1:17,500
7	Page continuation to enlarged scale 1:10,000
	River/canal, lake, pier
	Aqueduct, lock, weir
465 ▲ Winter Hill	Peak (with height in metres)
	Beach
	Woodland
	Park
	Cemetery
	Built-up area

Featured building	Abbey, cathedral or priory
City wall	Castle
A&E Hosptial with 24-hour A&E department	Historic house or building
PO Post Office	Wakehurst Place NT National Trust property
Public library	Museum or art gallery
Tourist Information Centre	Roman antiquity
Petrol station Major suppliers only	Ancient site, battlefield or monument
Church/chapel	Industrial interest
Public toilets	Garden
Toilet with disabled facilities	Arboretum
PH Public house AA recommended	Farm or animal centre
Restaurant AA inspected	Zoological or wildlife collection
Theatre or performing arts centre	Bird collection
Cinema	Nature reserve
Golf course	Visitor or heritage centre
Camping AA inspected	Country park
Caravan site AA inspected	Cave
Camping & caravan site AA inspected	Windmill
Theme park	Distillery, brewery or vineyard

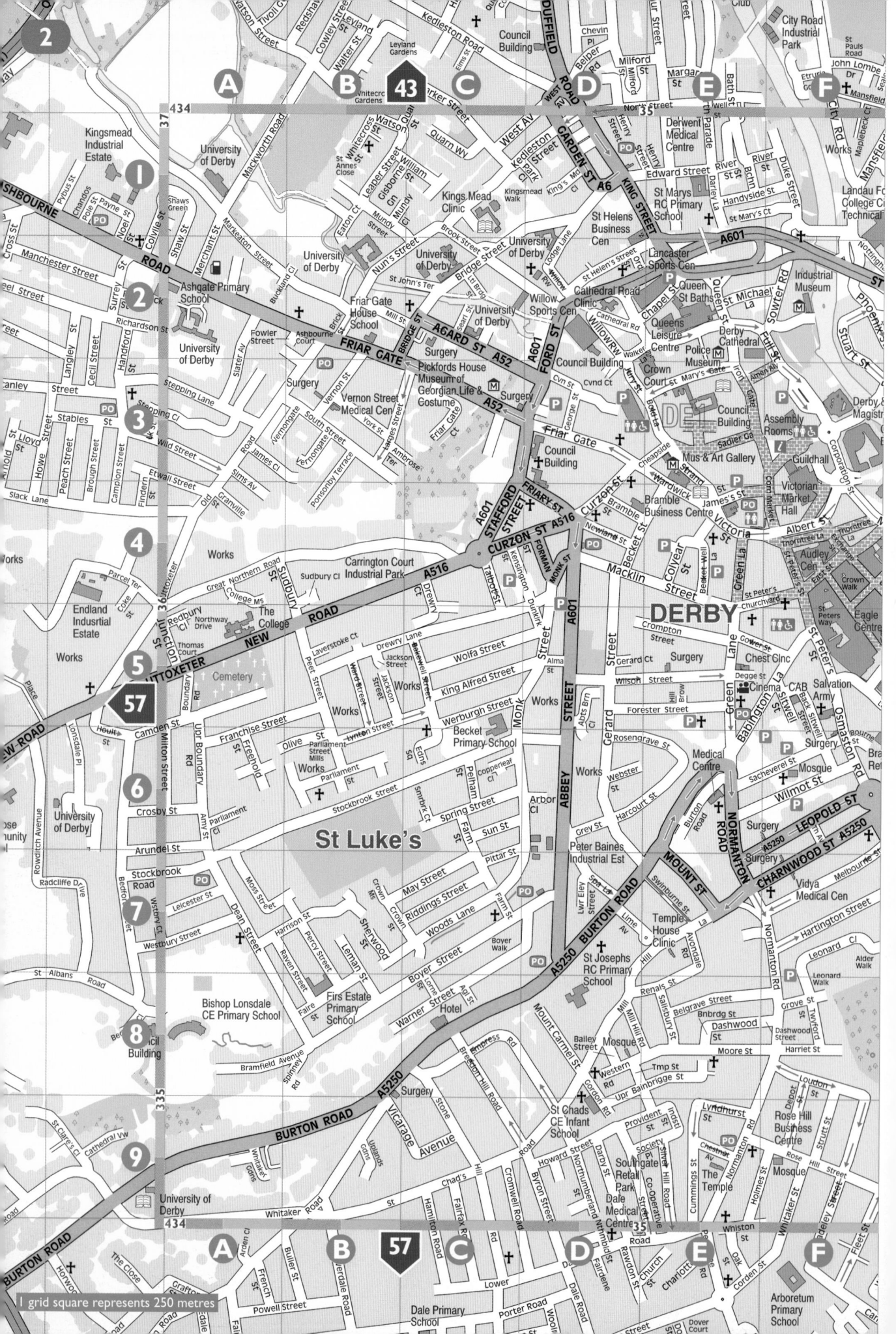

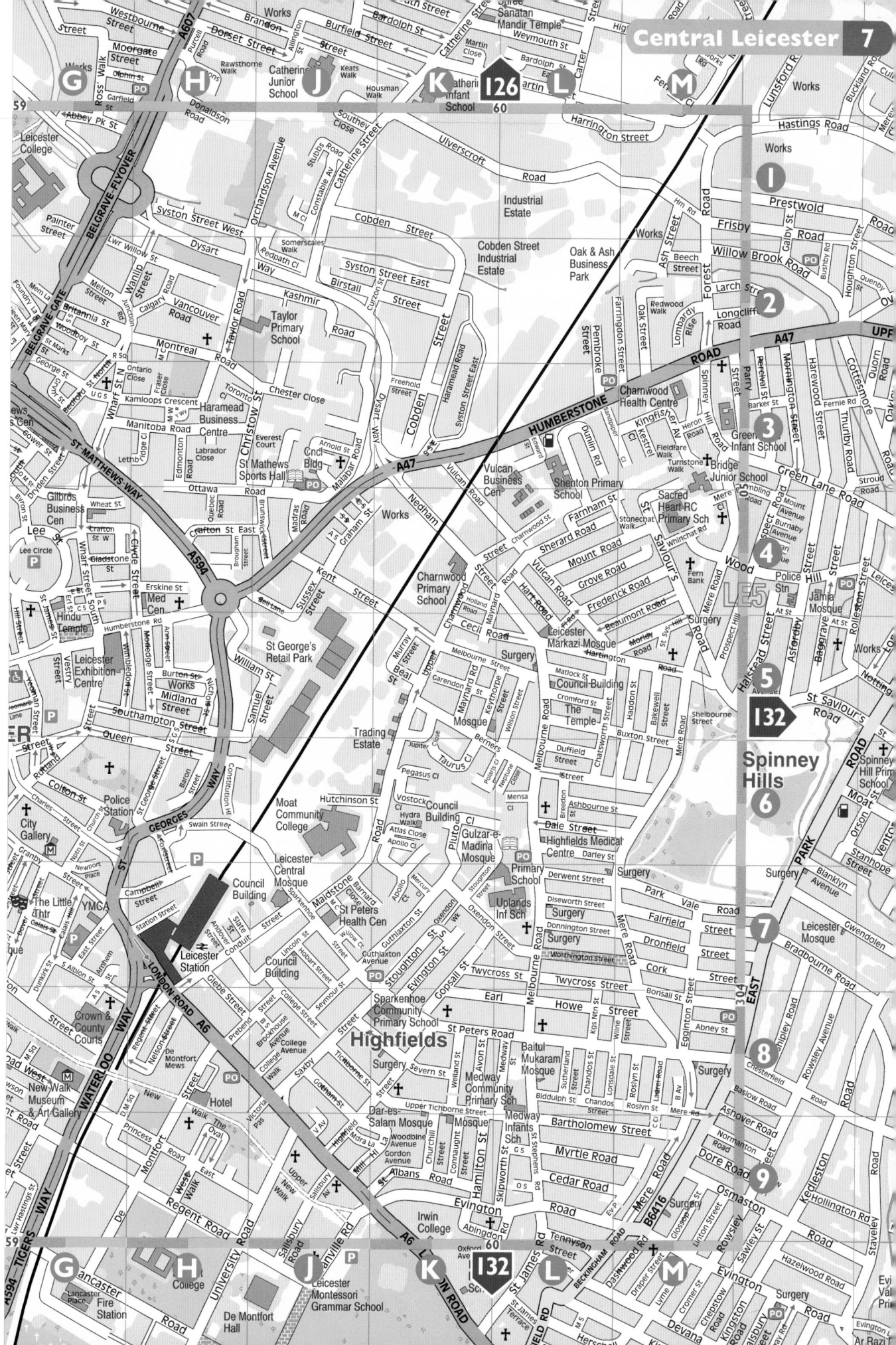

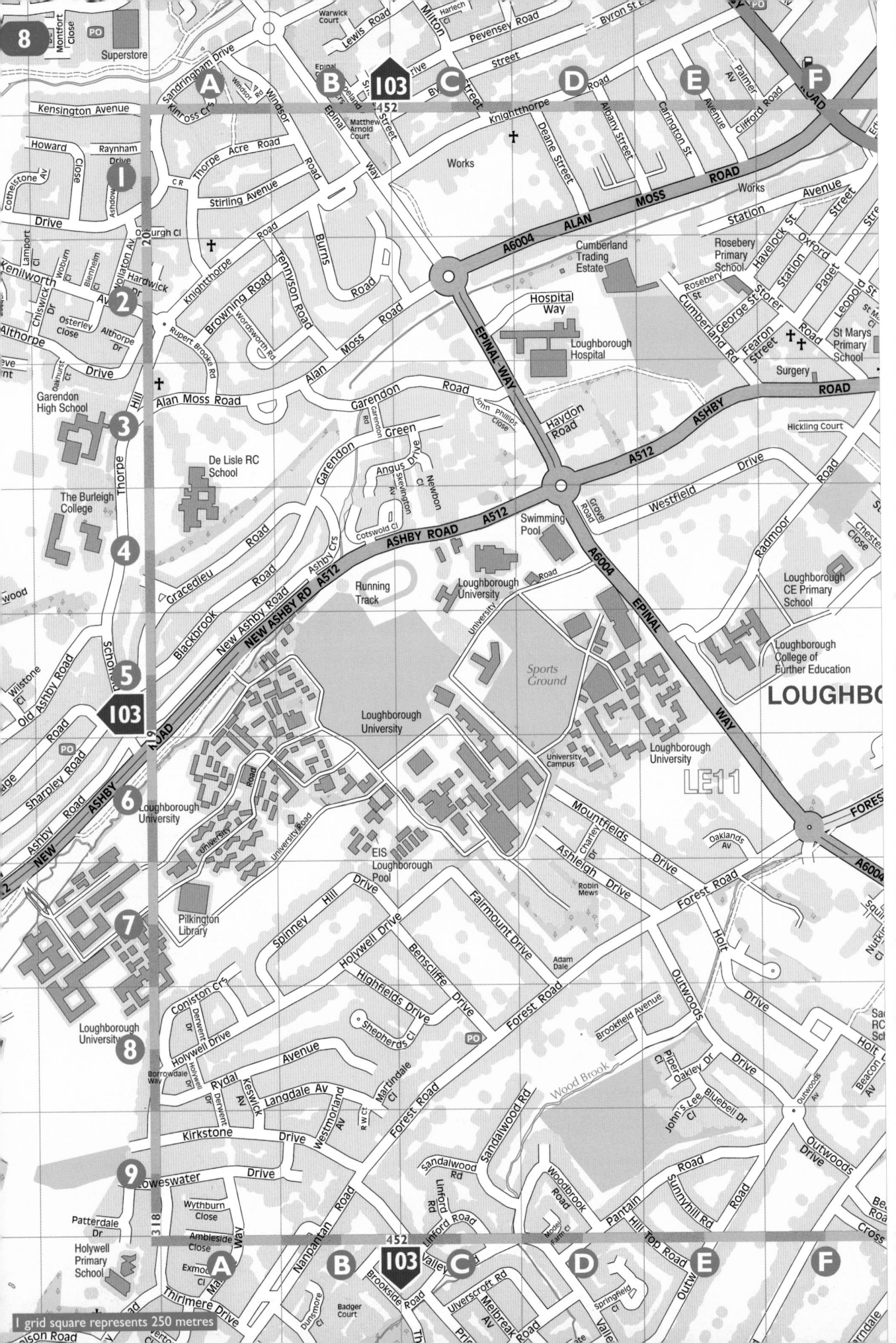

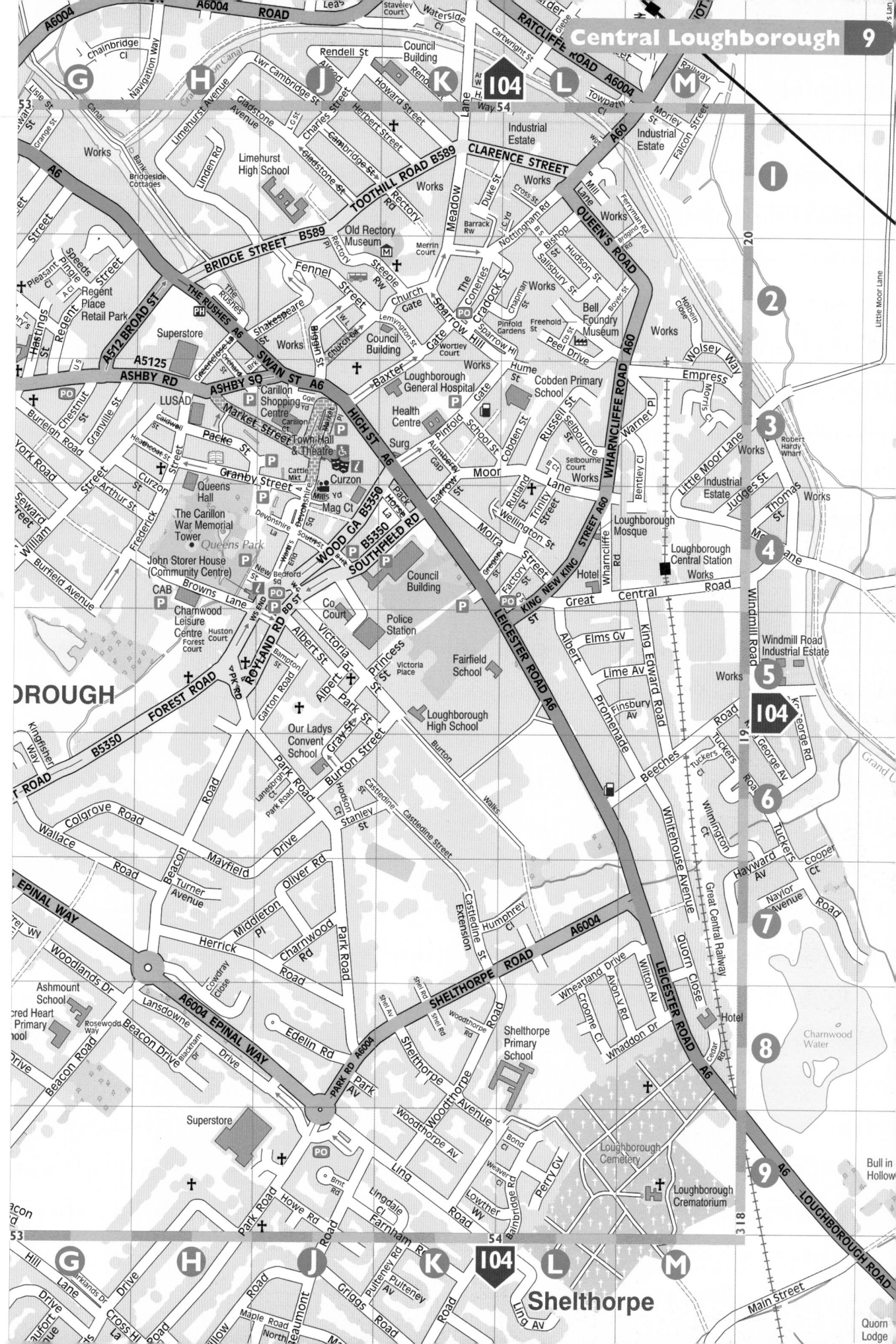

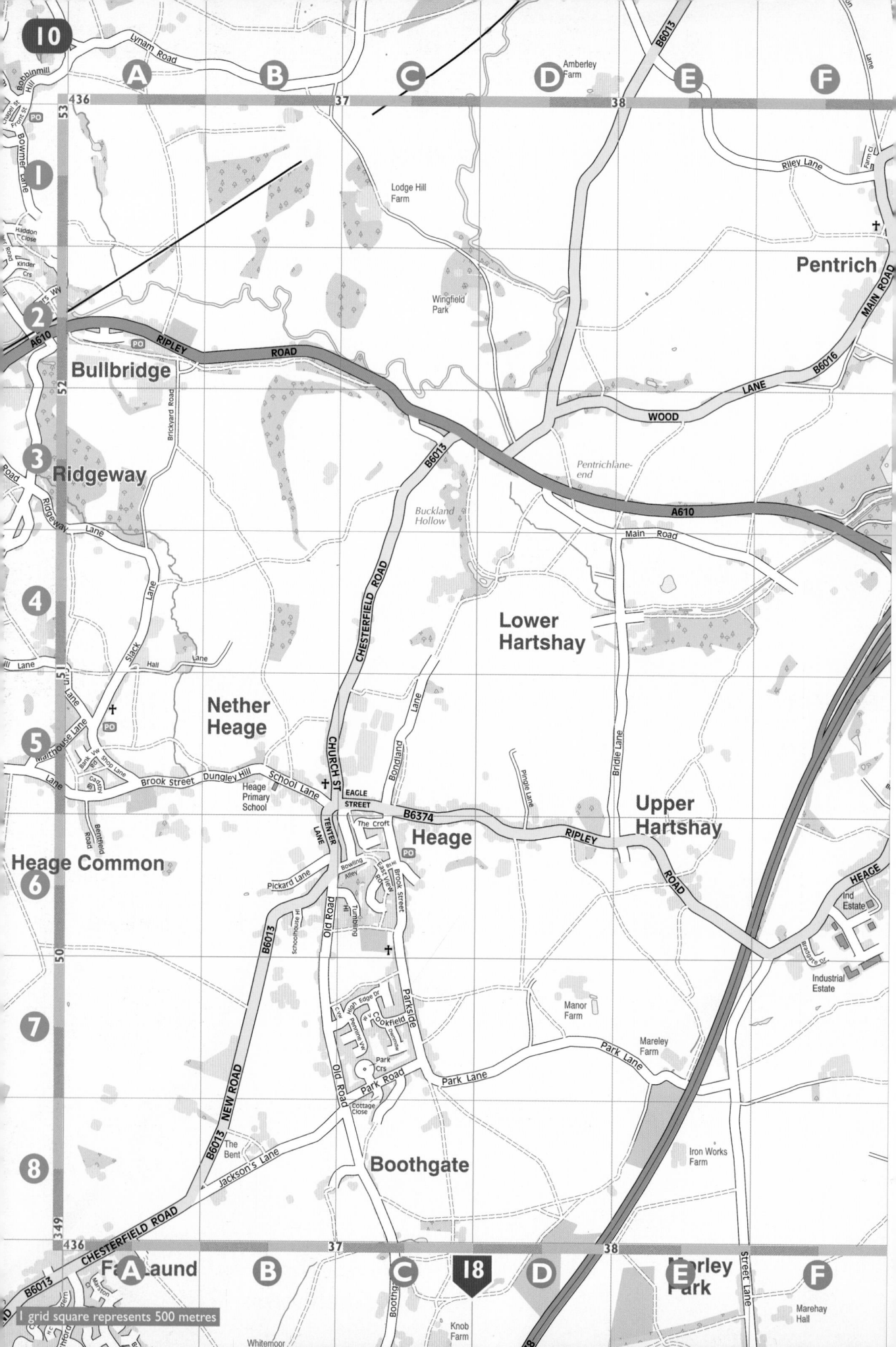

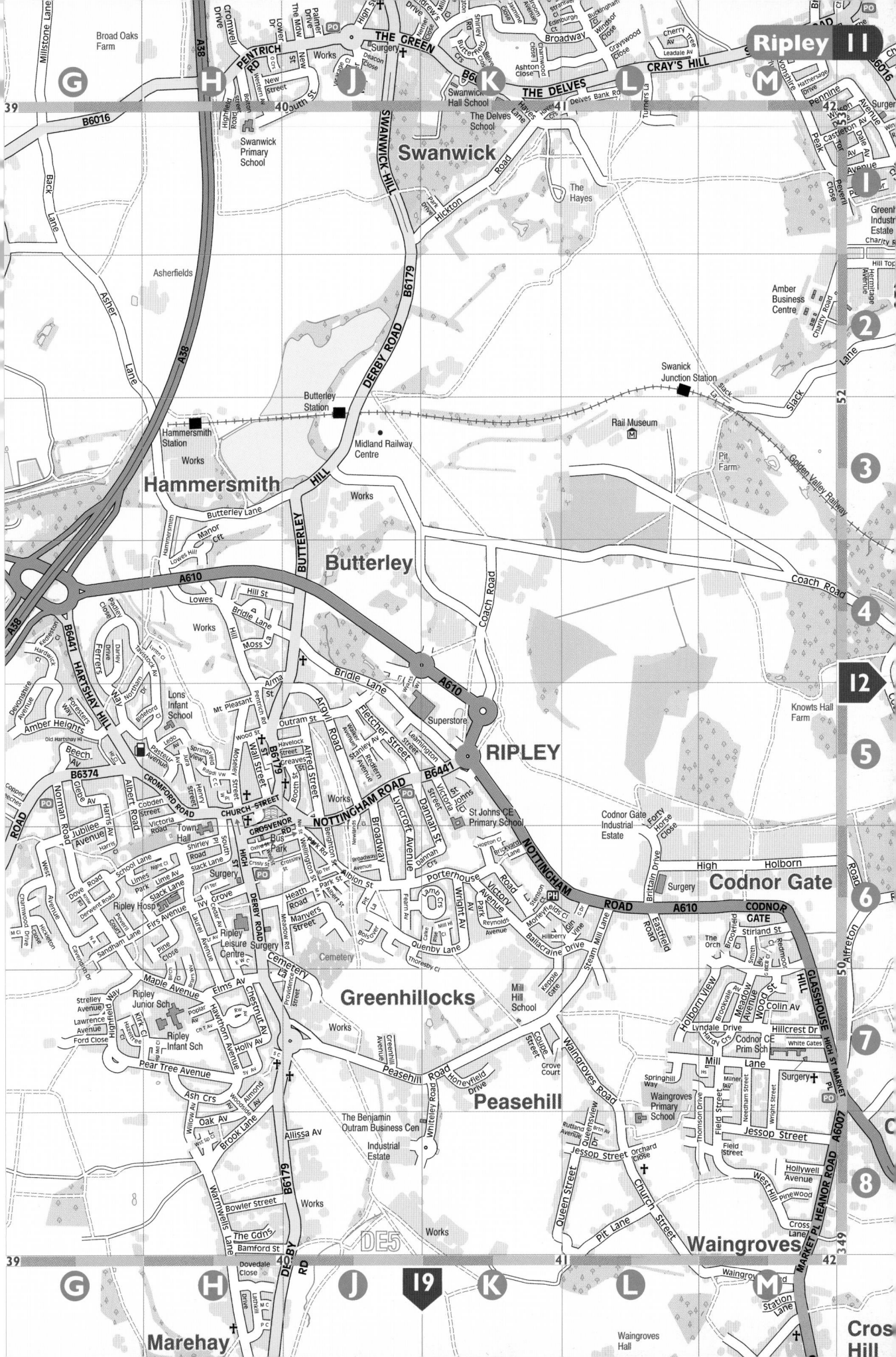

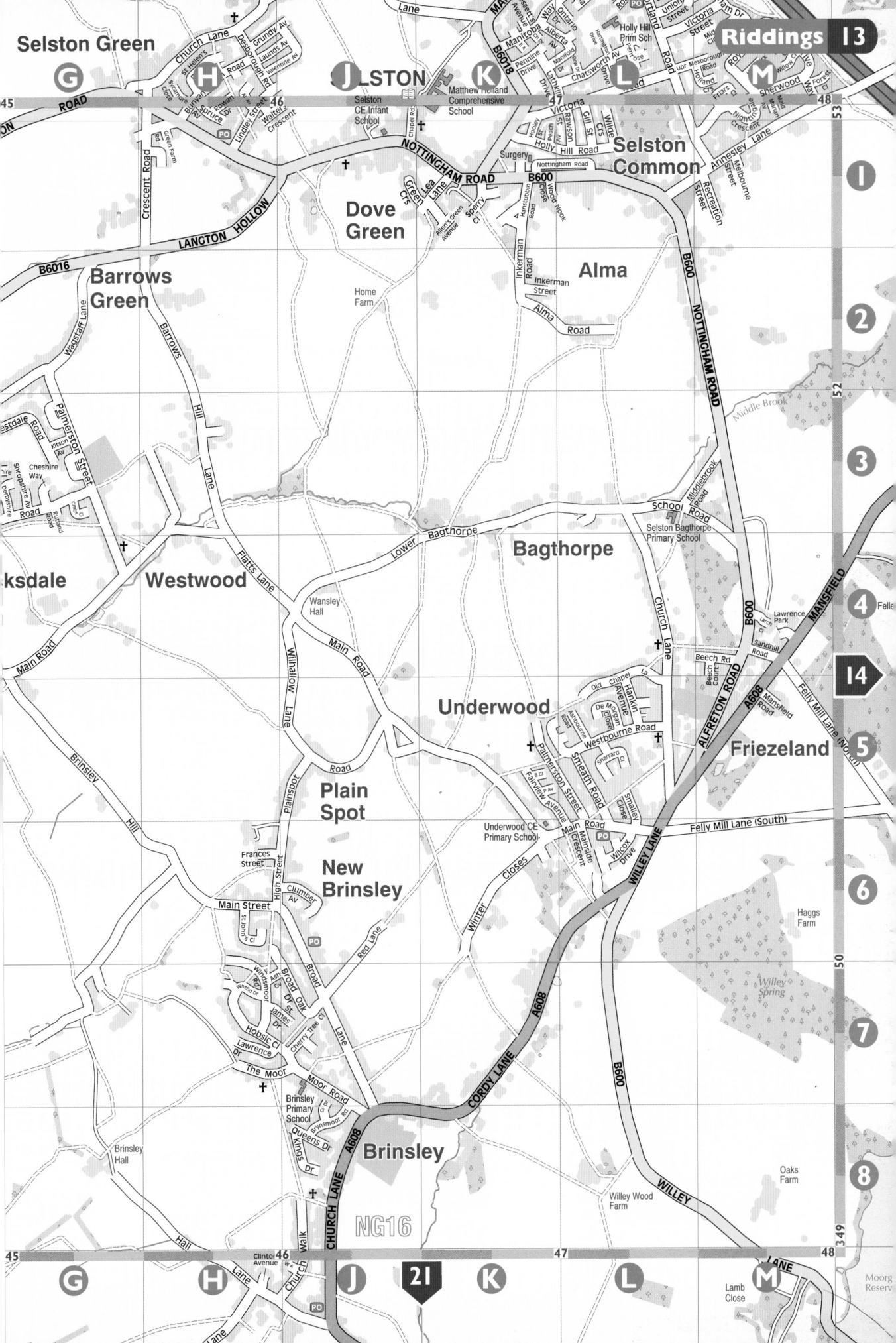

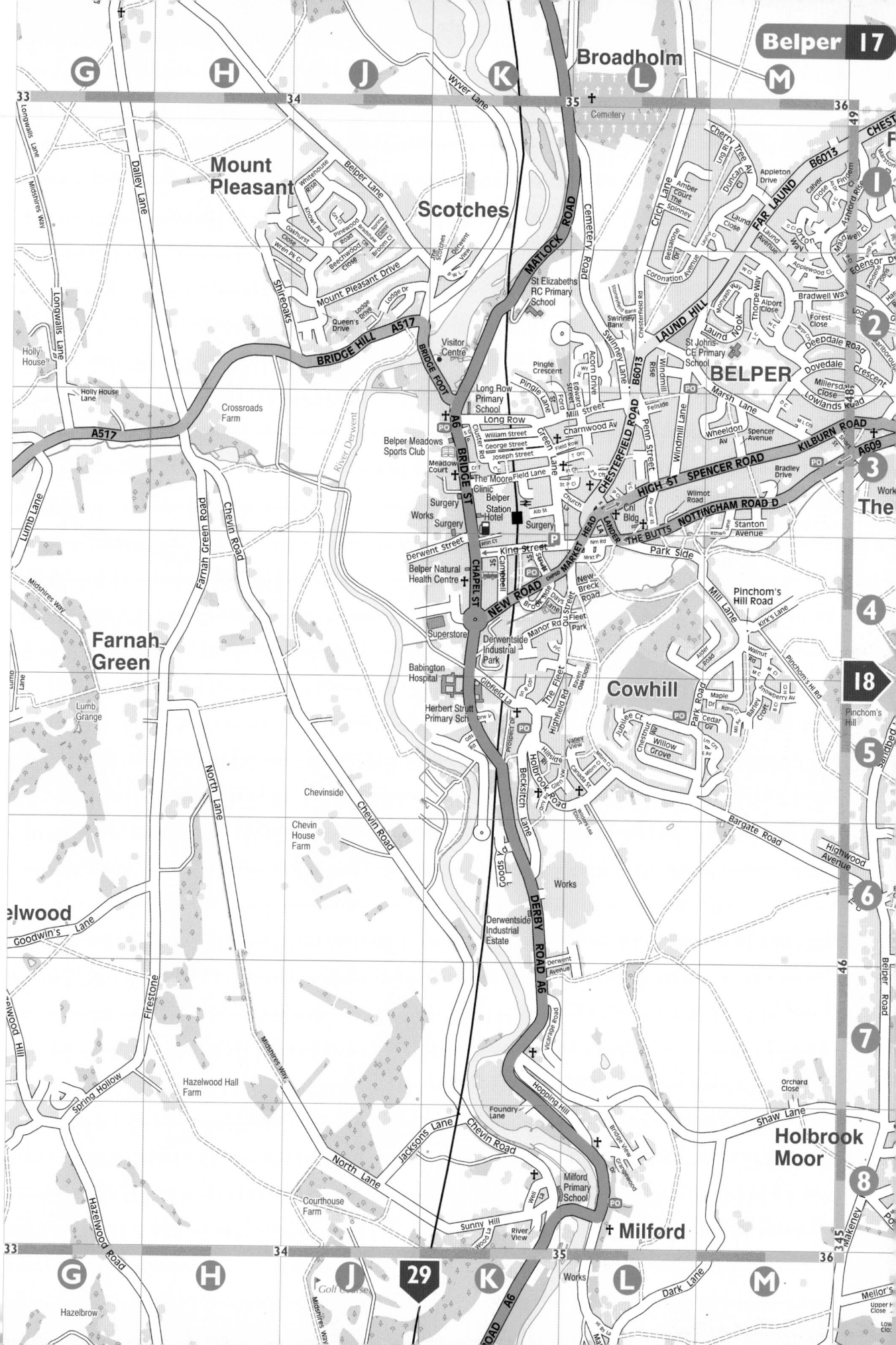

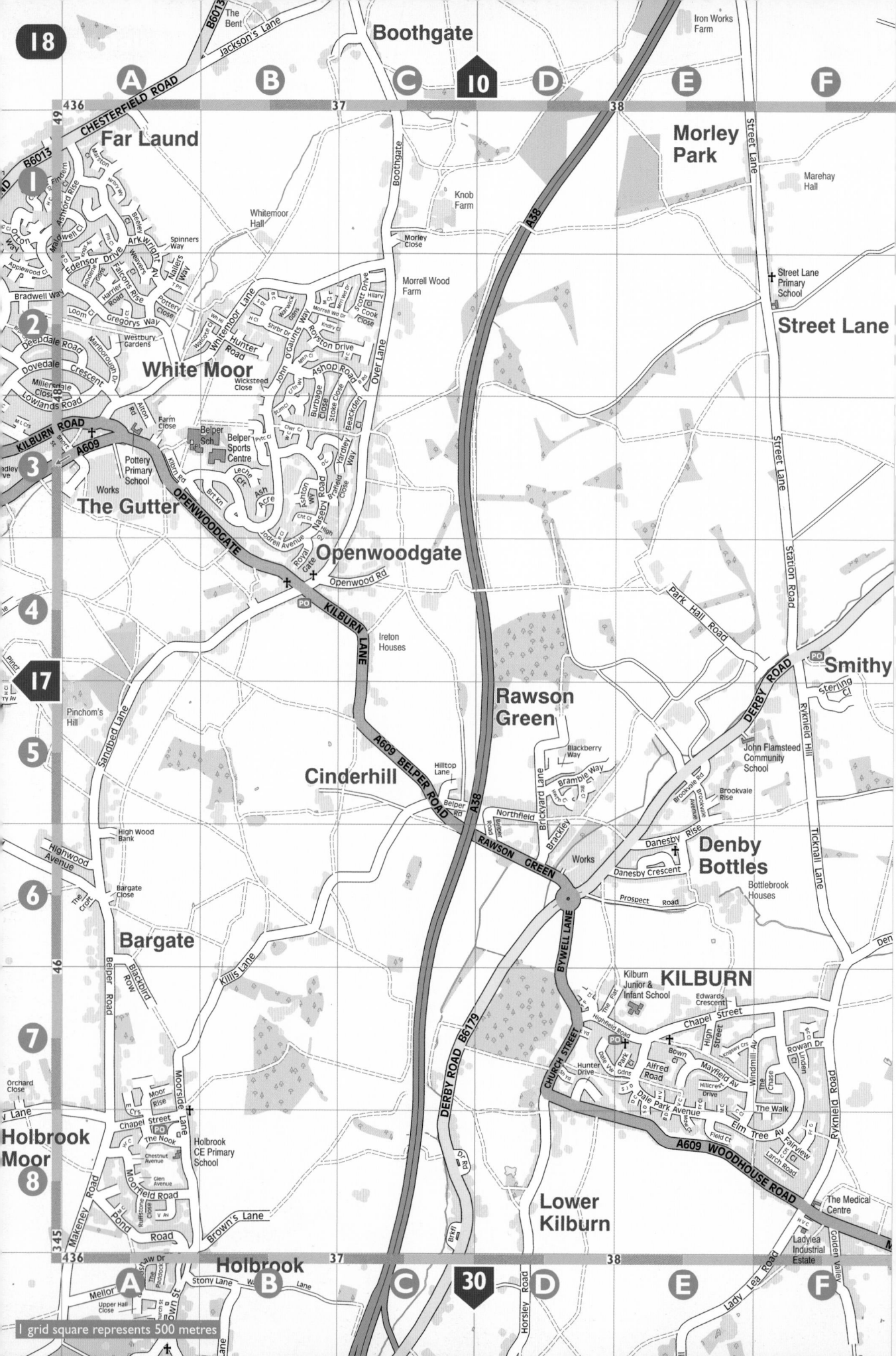

G H J | DE5 | II | K L M

Marehay

Bowler Street
The Gdns
Bamford St
Dovedale Close
Larkhill Drive
M C
P C
Upper Marehay Road
Belle Vue Avenue
PO
Lum Farm Leisure Centre

B6179 DERBY ROAD
Pottery Lane
Denby Pottery & Visitors Centre

Primrose Hill Farm

Waingroves Hall
Waingroves Road
Station Lane
Cemetery
Middleton Avenue
Cross Lane
Highfield Close
Springfield Avenue
Brook Street
Loscoe CE Prim Sch
Egreaves Avenue
Leniscar
Grm Av
Flamstead Avenue
Church View
Wilson Av
Flamstead Ave

Iss Hill

Codnor Breach
Cranmer Street
Welldon Street
Loscoe-Denby Lane
Heanor Road

Denby Common

Houses

Copper Yard
High Bank
Denby Common
Dumbles Lane

Parsons Groove
Lady Lane
Denby
Church Street
Flamstead Lane
Abells
Lane
PO
Denby Free CE Primary School
Hill Farm
Pippin Hill
Flamstead Dr
Flamstead House

Robey Fields Farm

Carr Farm

Redmoor Farm

Hirst Farm

HEANOR ROAD
Adale Rd
Marina Road
The Grange
The Beeches

Heanor
Heanor Gate Scho

The Crescent
C Rd
Chestnut Cl
Carr Fields
Fairfield Road
Meadow Close
Calladine
PO
IN STREET
CHURCH LANE
Horsley Woodhouse Primary School
Stainsby Avenue
A609
DOBHOLES
A608
Old Pit Lane
RC Dr
Kerry Drive
Dix Av
dford
Stafford
Holly Mount Farm

Horsley Woodhouse

G H J | 31 | K L M

2 3 4 20 5 6 7 8

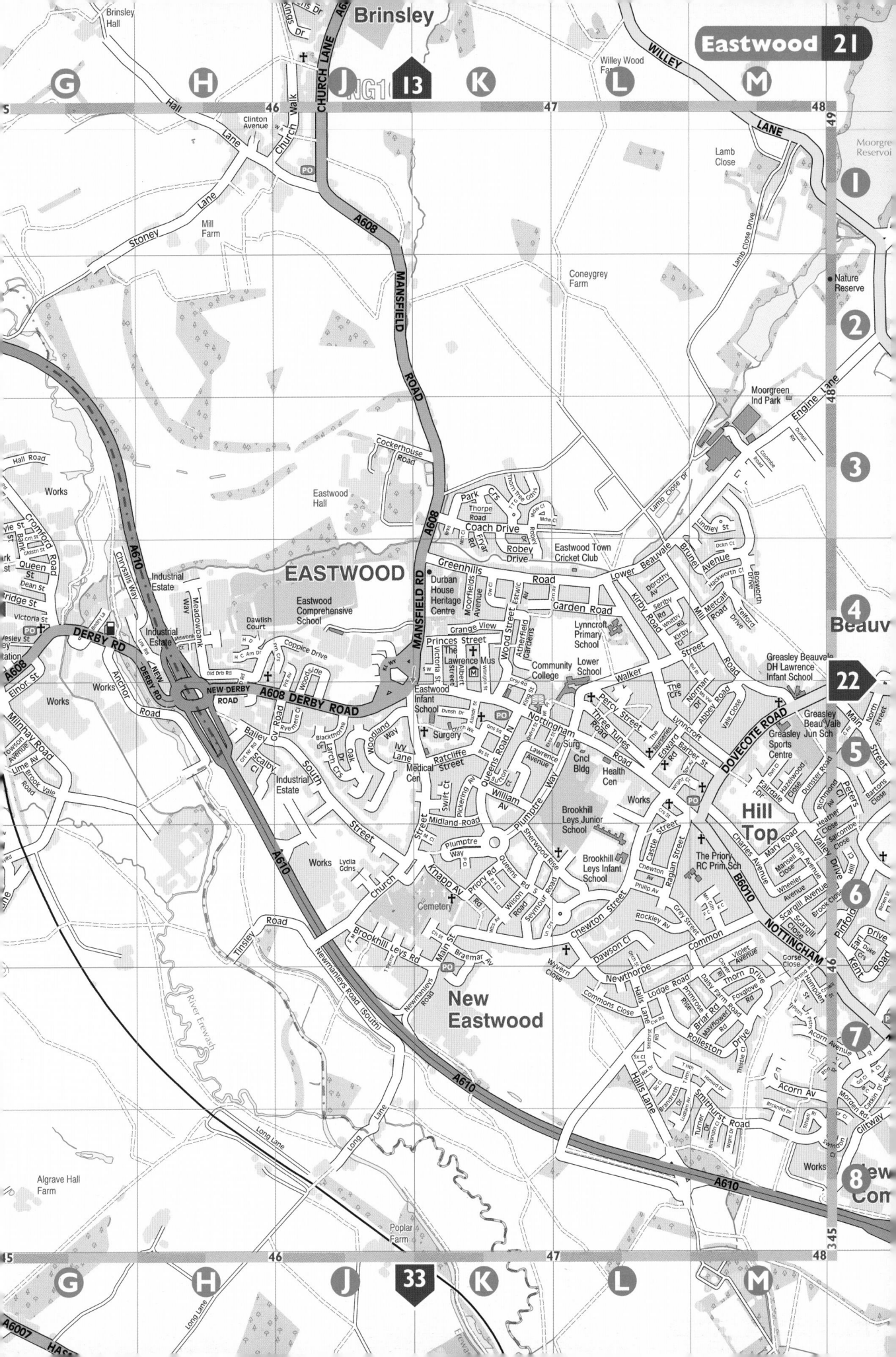

G   H   J   K   L   M

Moor Lane

Springwater Golf Club

Golf Course

Grimesmoor

Shelt Hill

Cemetery

Roe Hill

Ash Grove

Road

Sunningdale Drive

Dover Beck Dr

Aldene Way

Field Lane

Close

Roe Lane

Hawthorn Close

Woodborough

Shelt Hill

PO

Main Street

Pinfold Close

Pinfold Crs

Buckland Dr

Small's Croft

Holme Cl

Old Mnr

Ch Wy

Woods Foundation School

Manor Farm

Lowdham Lane

A6097

EPPERSTONE BY-PASS

Main Street

Church Lane

Chapel Lane

Neeps Cft

Epperstone

Bland La

Toad Lane

Parr Lane

PO

Lowdham Road

Dover Beck

Wash Bridge

EPPERSTONE BY PASS A6097

Old Epperstone Road

Gonalston

NG

Hagg Lane

Ploughman Wood

Lowdham Grange

HM Prison Lowdham Grange

The Green

Long Meadow Hill

Hill Syke

Hunters Hill Farm

Hill Farm

Lane

Bateman House

Harlow Wood Farm

Cocker Beck

Lambley Road

Park Lane

Church Street

Rise

Cocker Beck

Trinity Crs

W Cs

Street

PO

Grange Close

Ross Lane

Cemetery

Bulcote Wood

Lambley

G   H   J   K   L   M

Bridle Road

Stockhill Farm

39

Bulcote Lodge Farm

Hill Farm

Lodge

Bulcote

A345

I   2   3   4   5   6   7   8

Windley

A 430 45

B B5024 GUNHILLS LANE 31

C WINDLEY LA

16

D 32

E

F

Hall Farm

Yewtree Farm

Gunhills Lane

WIRKSWORTH ROAD

River Ecclesbourne

1

2 The Clouds

Windley Meadows

Cer

Gun Hills

Burland Green Lane 44

Moseyley

Gunhills Lane

Windleyhill Farm

WIRKSWORT

3 43

Ivyhouse Farm

Newlands

4

Farnah House Farm

Centenary Way

Champion Farm

Cocks-hut-hill

Woodfall Lane

Centenary Way

5

6 Weston Lodge 42

Hall Close

Cumberhills Cottages

Cumberhills Road

7 Ireton Farm

Beech Avenue

Park Nook

Kedleston Road

Kedleston Road

Kedleston

Mercaston Lane

Hay Wood

ersle

8 341

A 430 dge Lane

B 31

C 42

D 32

E Ke Park Golf

Inn Lane

F

Golf Course

Kedleston Park

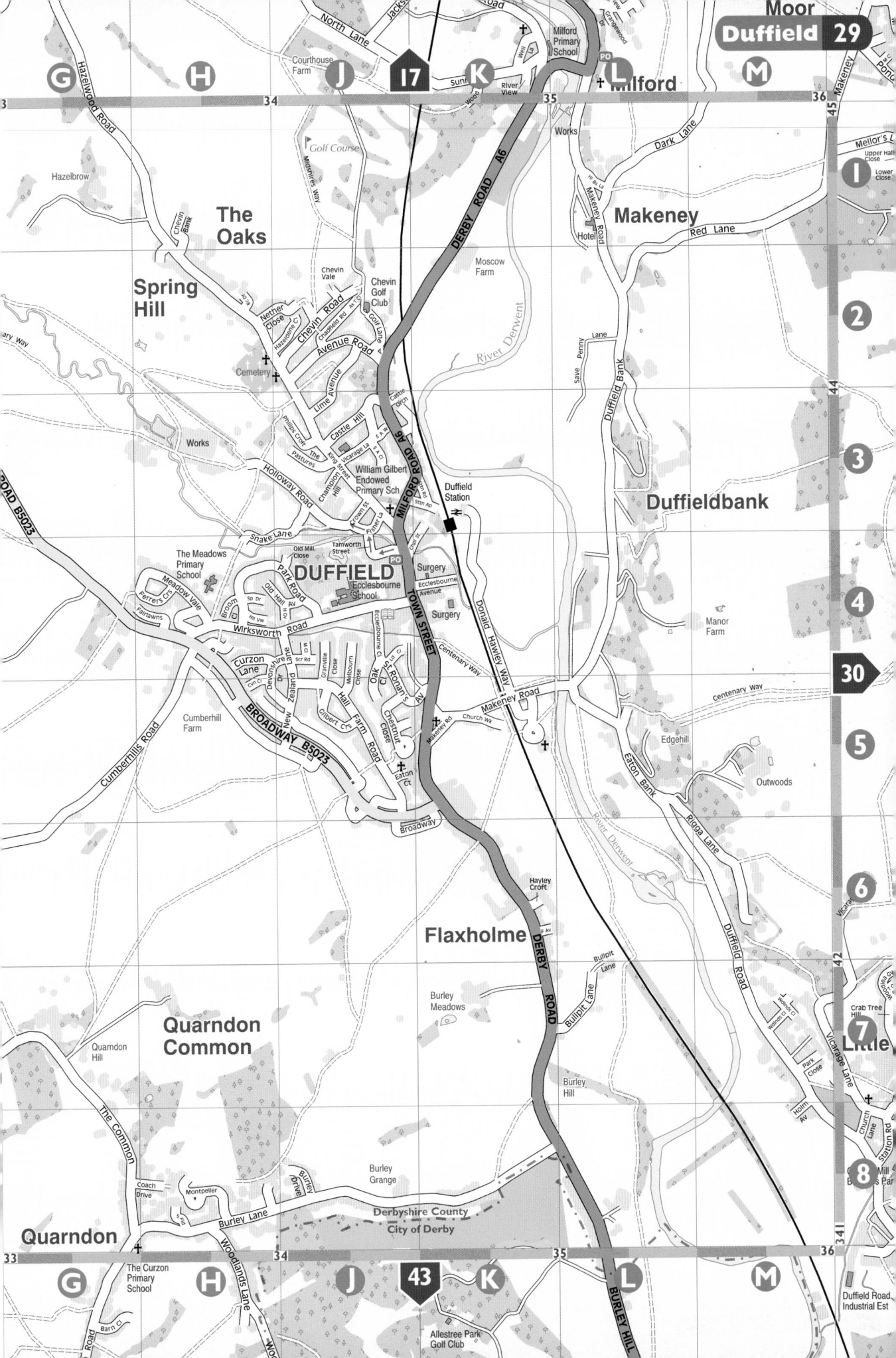

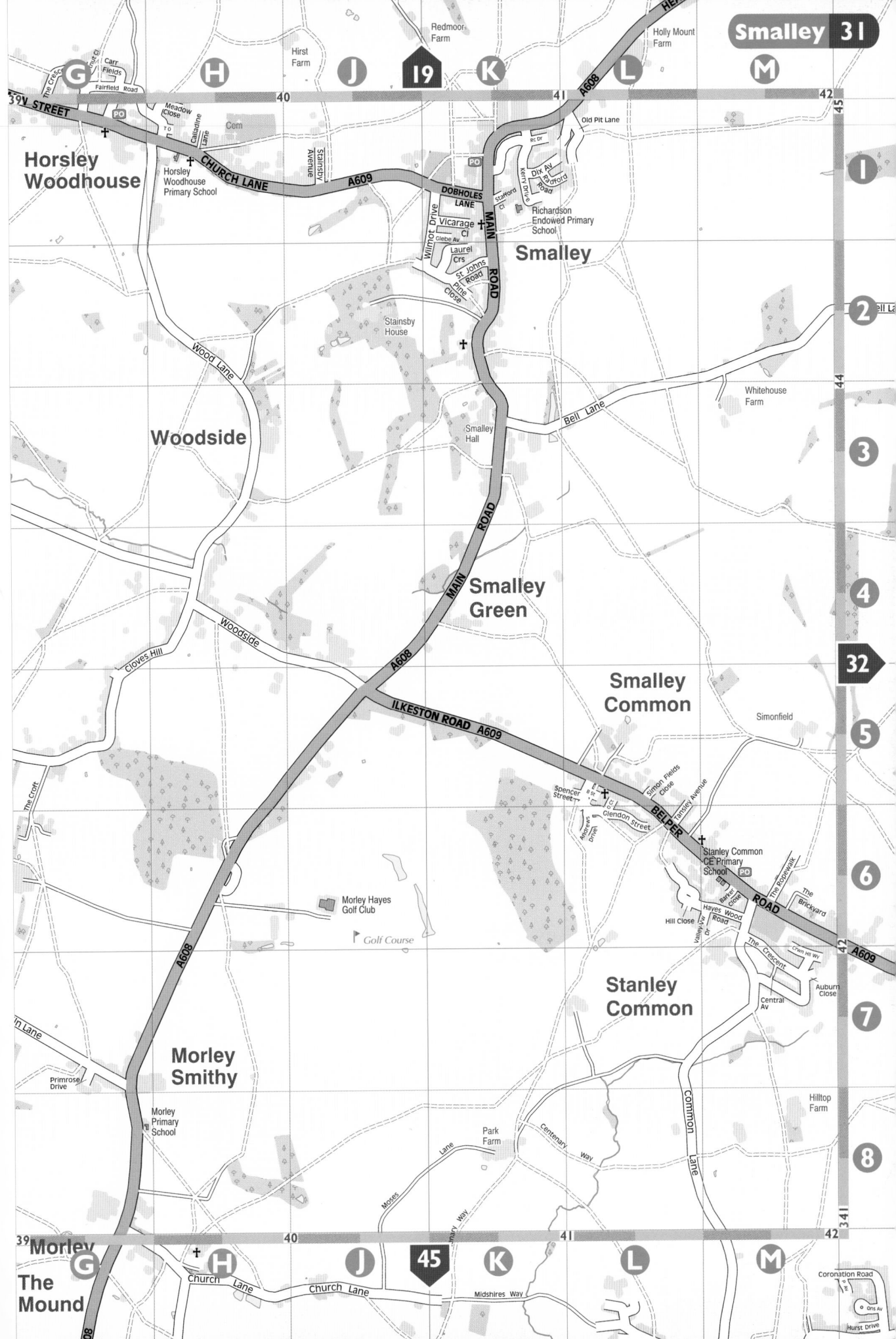

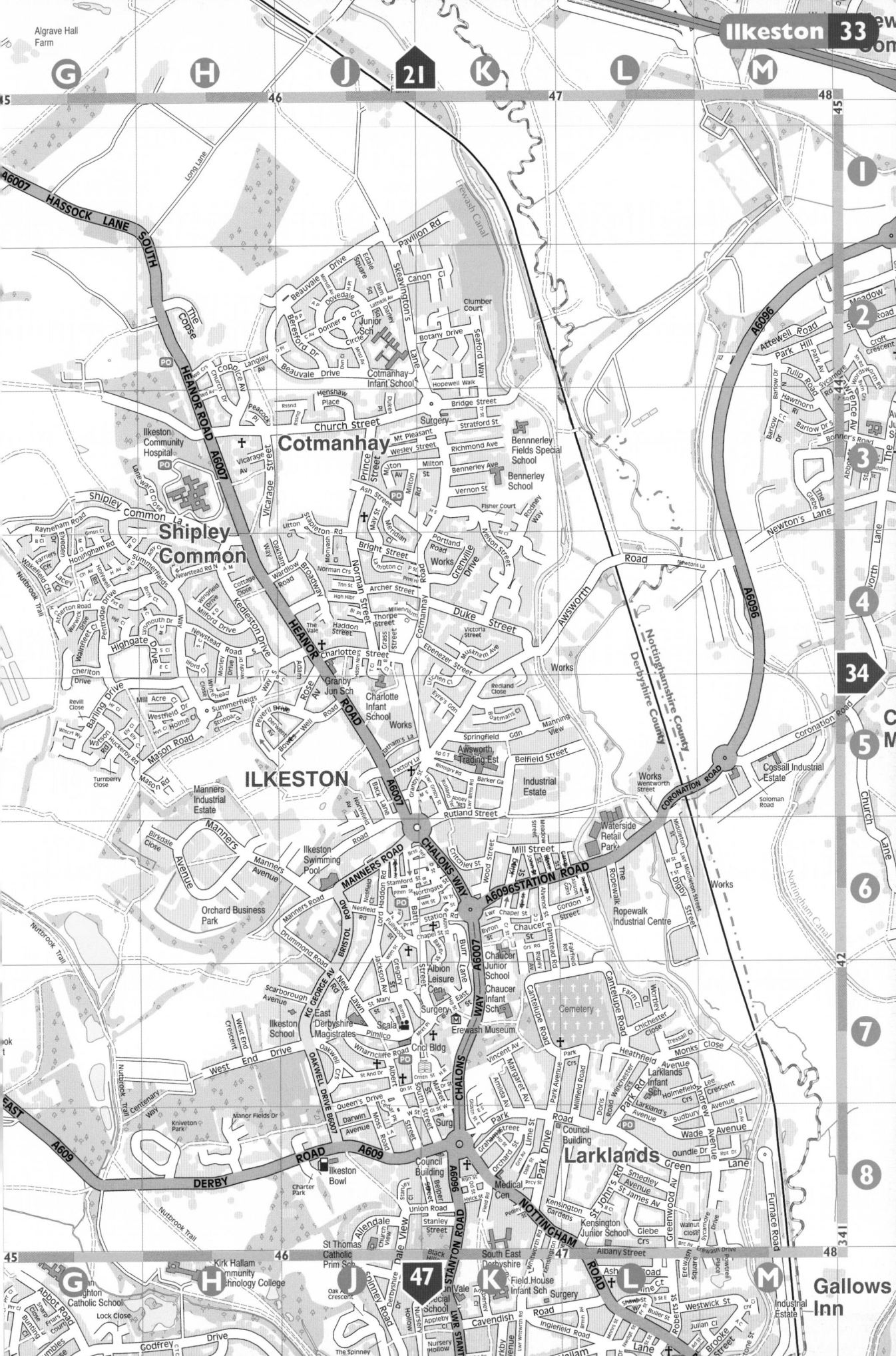

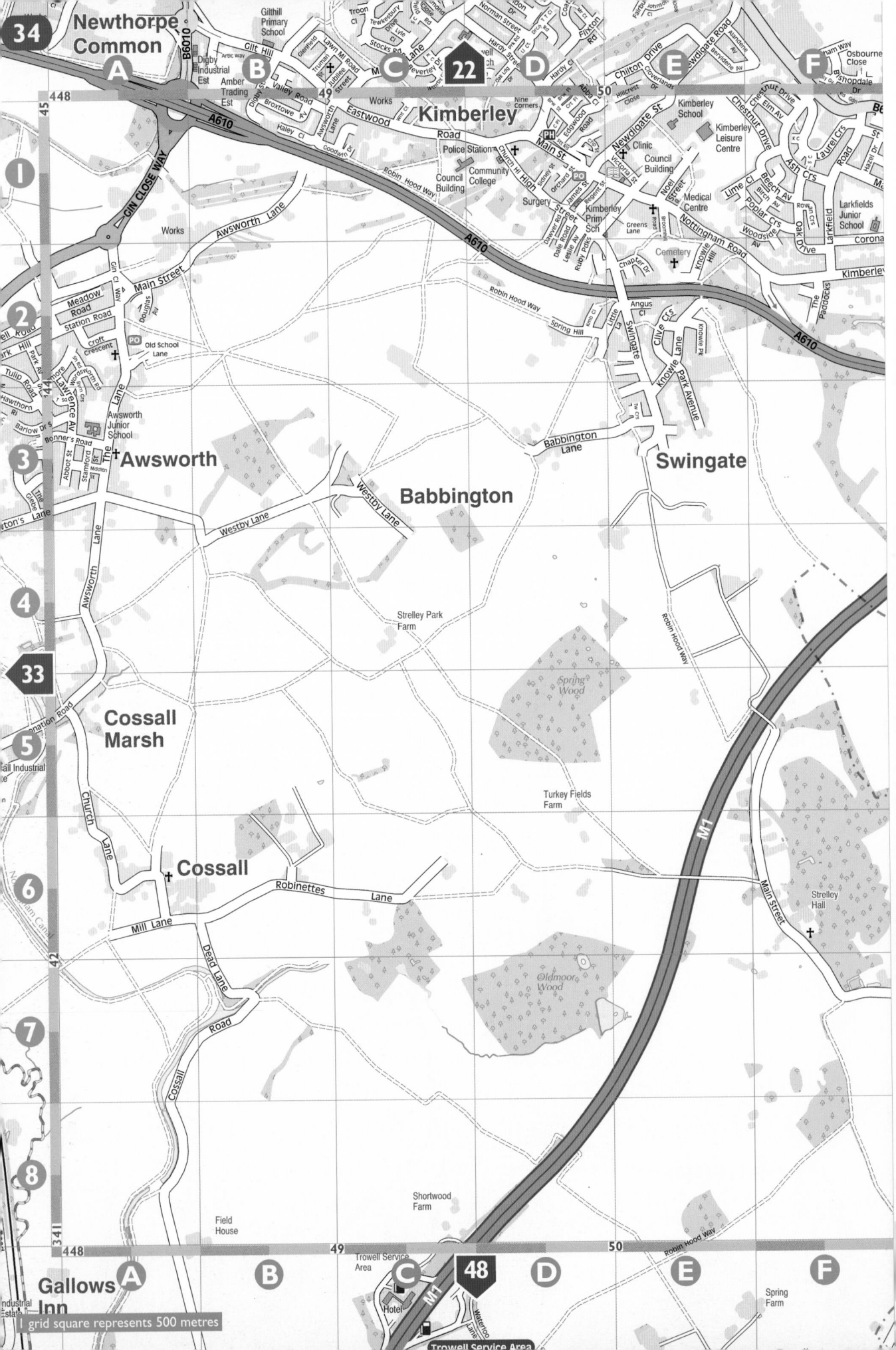

Newthorpe
Common

A B C D E F

22

Kimberley

Awsworth

Babbington

Swingate

33

Cossall
Marsh

Cossall

Gallows
Inn

A B C **48** D E F

1 grid square represents 500 metres

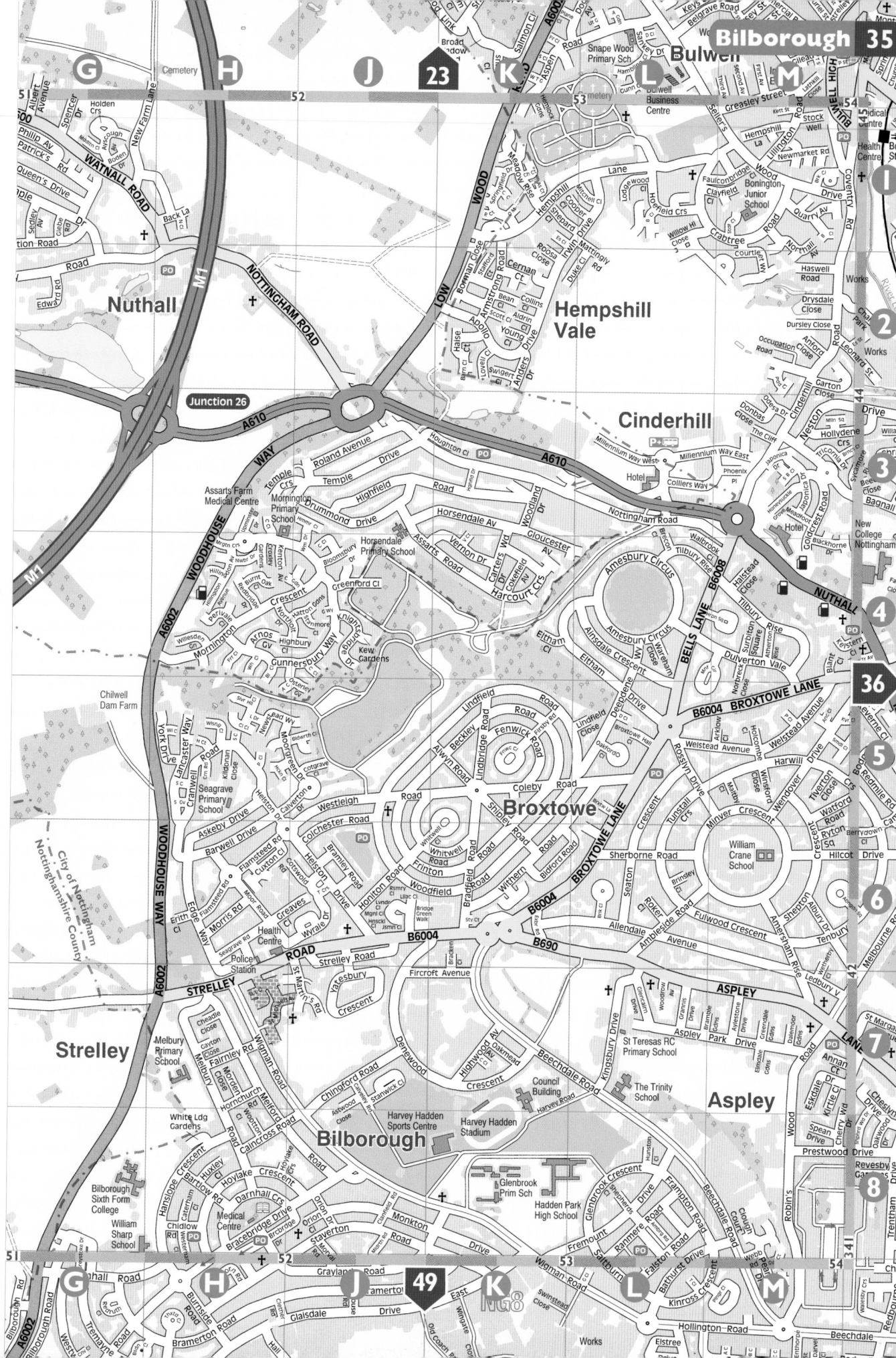

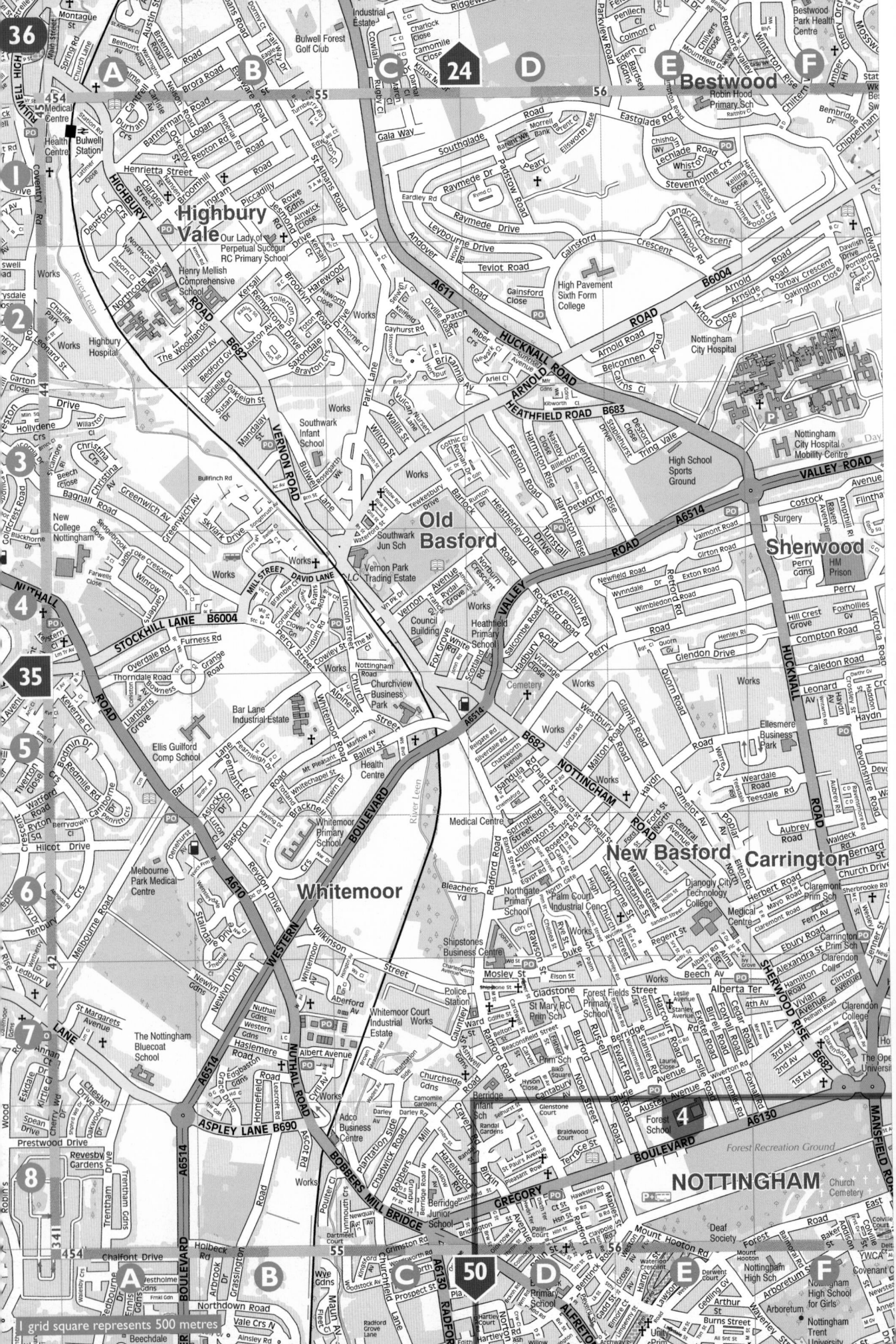

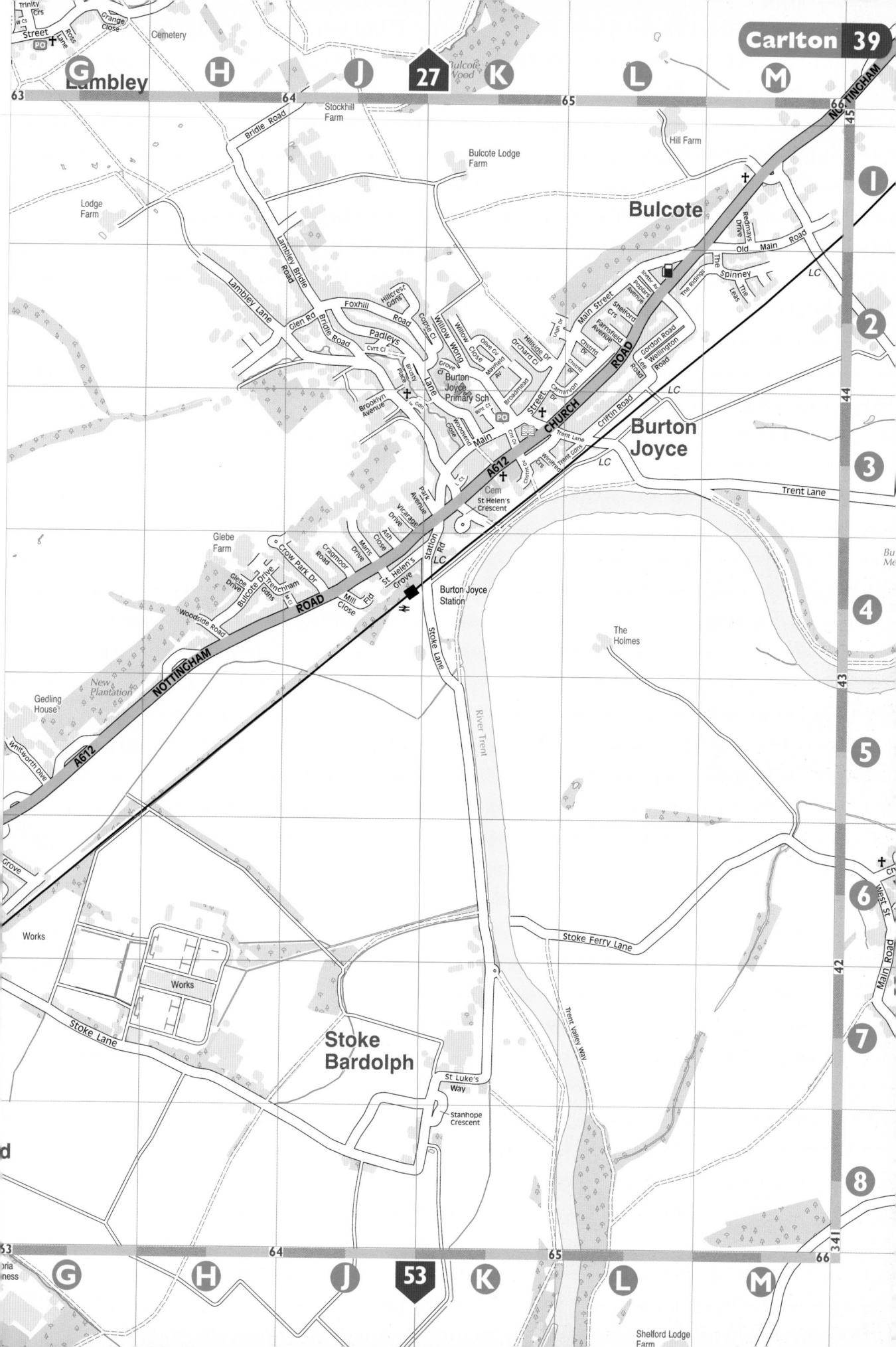

A B C D E F

Green

The Green

Brailsford CE Primary School

ROAD A52

Bullock Lane

Wood Lane

Centenary Way

424

41 25 26

I

Churchfields Farm

Pools Head

Hall Lane

2

Peatmoss Plantation

40

The Burma Rd

Snapes Farm

3

Culland Mount

Over Burrows

The Burma Road

Nether Burrows

4

Culland Hall

39

Bailsford Brook

5

Burrows Lane

Riddings Lane

Nunsfield

6

Longlane

Stoop Farm

Long Lane

Long Lane

Glebe Close

38

Long Lane CE Primary School

7

Thurvaston

Chapel Lane

Grange Fields Farm

8

Butt House

Bonnie Prince Charlie Walk

Lees

337

Trusleywood House

424

Osleston 25

A B C 54 D E F

Wildpark

G H J K L M

Kerston

27 28 29 30 41

Bucknazels Lane

Lodge Lane

Wildpark Lane

Buck
Hazels

1

Flagshaw Lane

Priestwood
Farm

Meynell Langley

ASHBOURNE ROAD A52

2

Windy
Arbour

40

Meyr
Lang

Hilltop
Farm

3

Lodge Lane

Lodge Farm

Langley
Hall

4

Flagshaw Lane

42

church Lane

Kirk Langley

PO

The Cannery

5

Helton Ct

Kirk Langley
CE Primary
School

ASHBOURNE ROAD A52

Bo
Fie

Petty Close Lane

The Green

Langley Green

MOOR LANE

6

38

Poyser Lane

B5020

The Pastures

Long Lane

Long Lane

Pole's Road

Adam's Road

Pimm's
Road

Wheathill
Farm

7

Brun Lane

**Langley
Common**

337

8

Radbourne
Common

27 28 29 30

Foxfields Farm

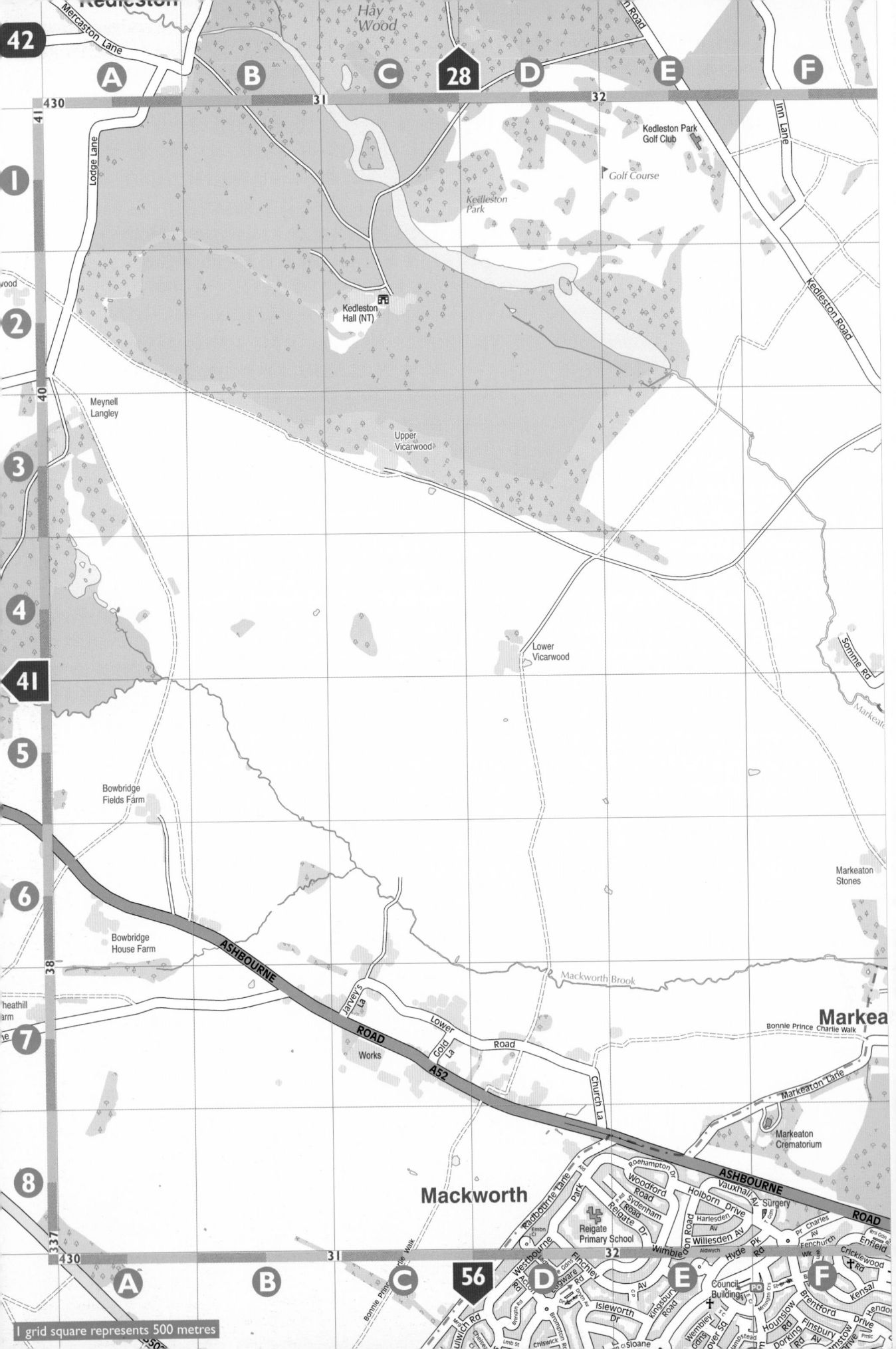

A   B   28   C   D   E   F

430   31   32

41   40

Hay Wood

Kedleston Park Golf Club

Golf Course

Kedleston Park

Kedleston Hall (NT)

Meynell Langley

Upper Vicarwood

Kedleston Road

wood

Lower Vicarwood

Somme Rd

Markeat

41

Bowbridge Fields Farm

Markeaton Stones

Bowbridge House Farm

ASHBOURNE

Mackworth Brook

Markea

heathill arm

Jarvey's La

Bonnie Prince Charlie Walk

ROAD   A52

Works   Gold La

Lower Road

Church La

Markeaton Lane

Markeaton Crematorium

ASHBOURNE

Mackworth

Radbourne Lane

Bonnie Prince Charlie Walk

Westbourne Park

Roehampton Dr

Woodford Road

Vauxhall

ROAD

Holborn Drive

Surgery

Reigate Primary School

Sydenham Reigate Dr

Pr Charles Av

Enfield

Kingsbury Road

Harlesden Av

Willesden Av

Fenchurch

Cricklewood

Finchley Rd

Wimbledon Road

Hyde Pk

PO

Brentford Drive

Council Buildings

Kensal

Isleworth Dr

Wembley Gdns

Hounslow Rd

Finsbury Rd

Dorking

337   430   31   32

A   B   56   C   D   E   F

1 grid square represents 500 metres

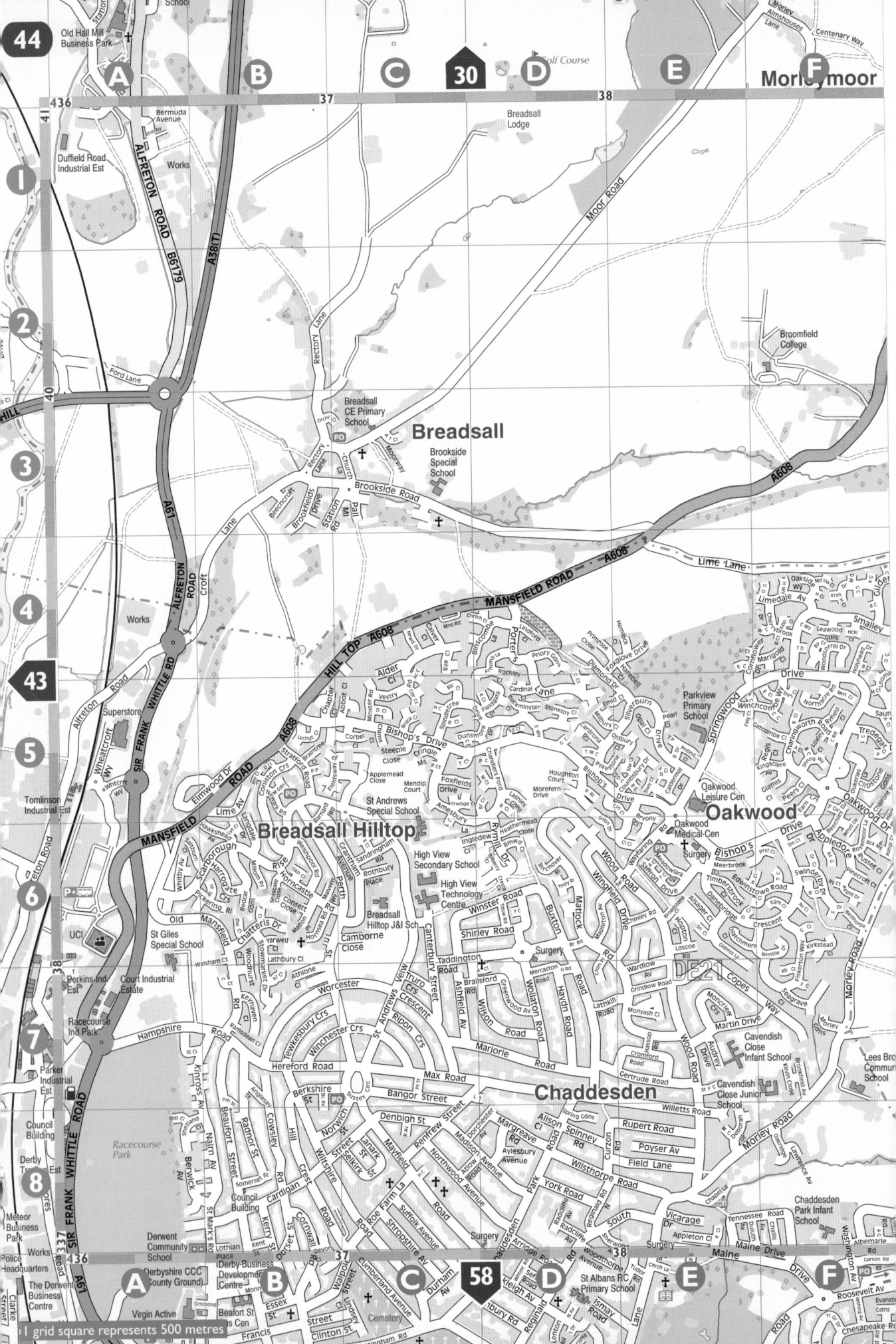

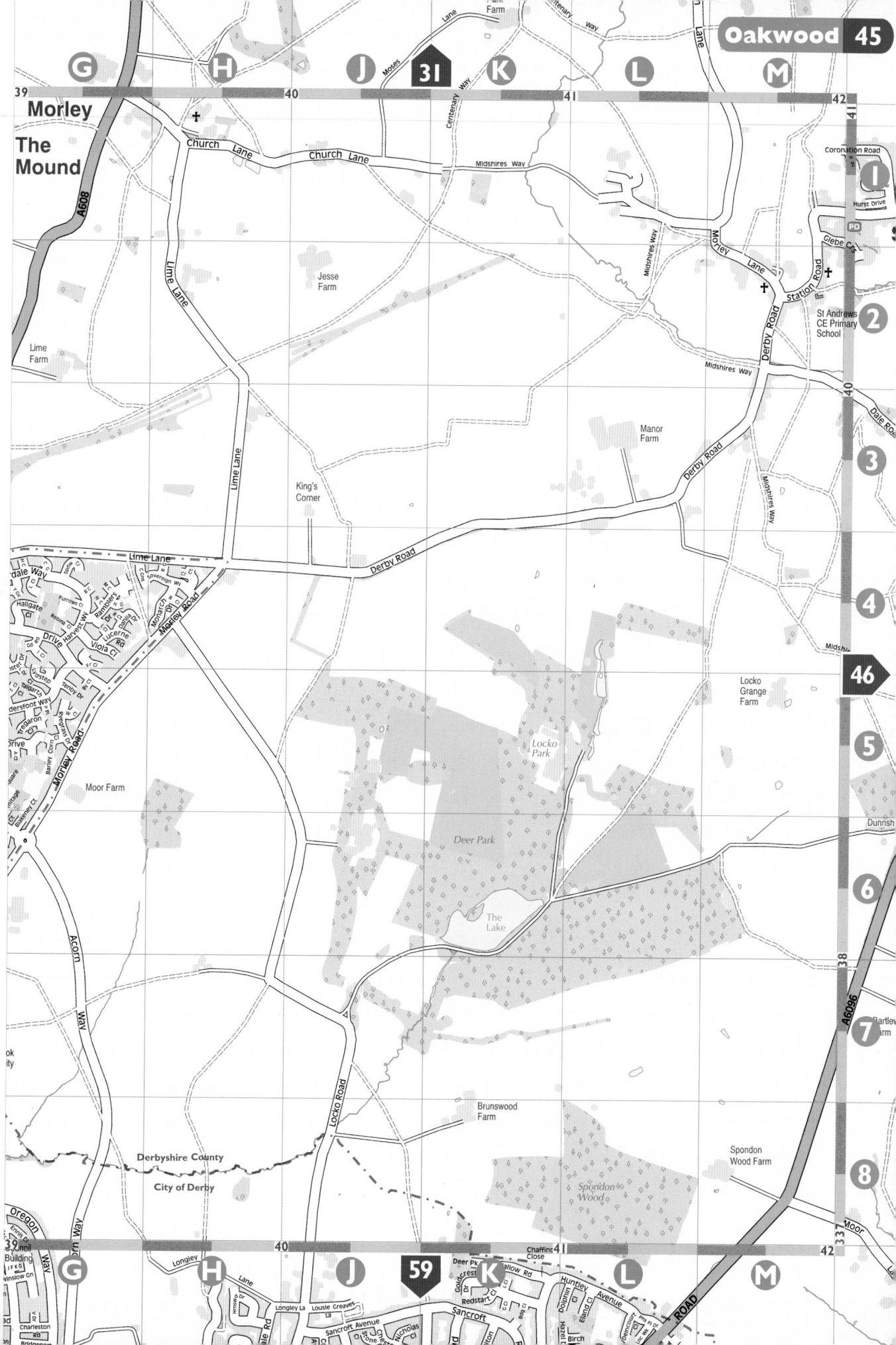

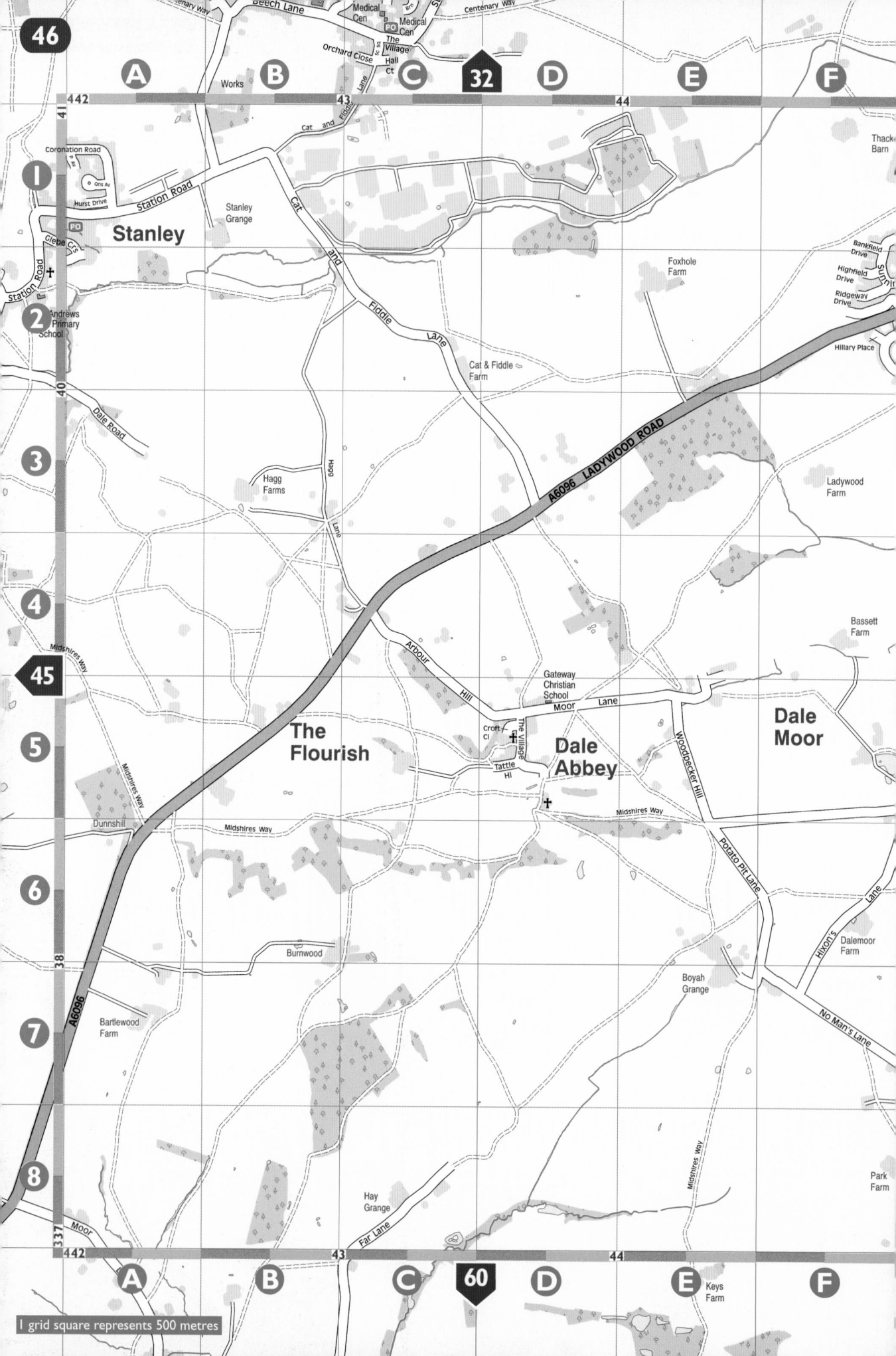

A **B** **C** **32** **D** **E** **F**

442
41 43 44

Thack
Barn

Coronation Road
1
Qns Av
Hurst Drive
Station Road
Stanley
Stanley
Grange

Bankfield
Drive
Highfield
Drive
Ridgeway
Drive

Foxhole
Farm

PO
Glebe Crs
Stanley

Cat and Fiddle Lane

Hillary Place

Station Road
2
Andrews
Primary
School

Cat & Fiddle
Farm

Dale Road
3

Hagg
Farms

A6096 LADYWOOD ROAD

Ladywood
Farm

Hagg Lane

4

Bassett
Farm

Midshires Way
45

Arbour Hill

Gateway
Christian
School

Moor Lane

**Dale
Moor**

Midshires Way
5

**The
Flourish**

Croft
Cl
The Village

**Dale
Abbey**

Woodpecker Hill

Dunnshill

Tattle
Hl

Midshires Way
6

Midshires Way

Midshires Way

Potato Pit Lane

Hixon's Lane

Dalemoor
Farm

Burnwood

Boyah
Grange

No Man's Lane

38
7
A6096

Bartlewood
Farm

Park
Farm

8

Midshires Way

337
Moor

Hay
Grange

Far Lane

442
43 44

A **B** **C** **60** **D** **E** Keys **F**
Farm

I grid square represents 500 metres

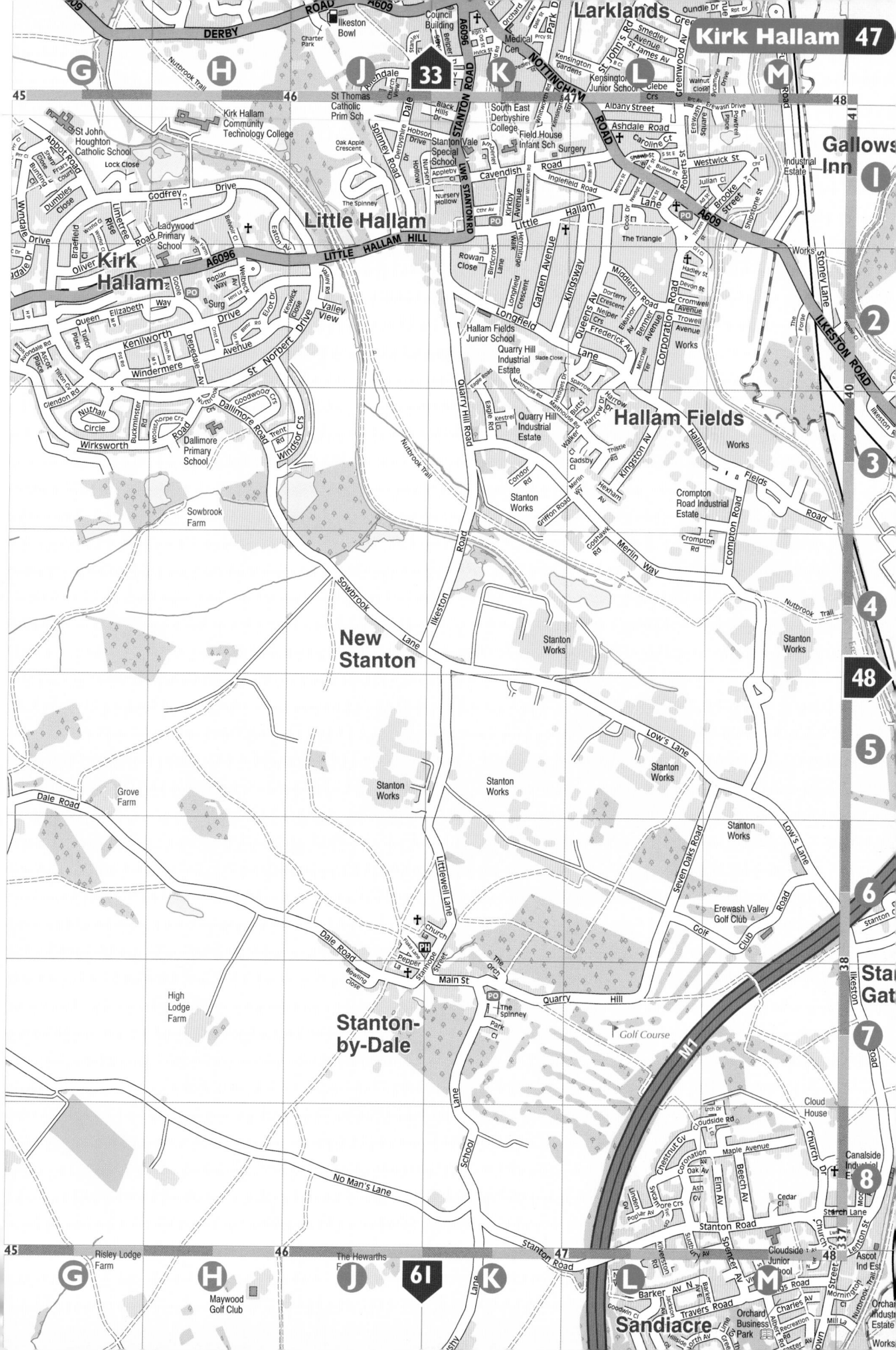

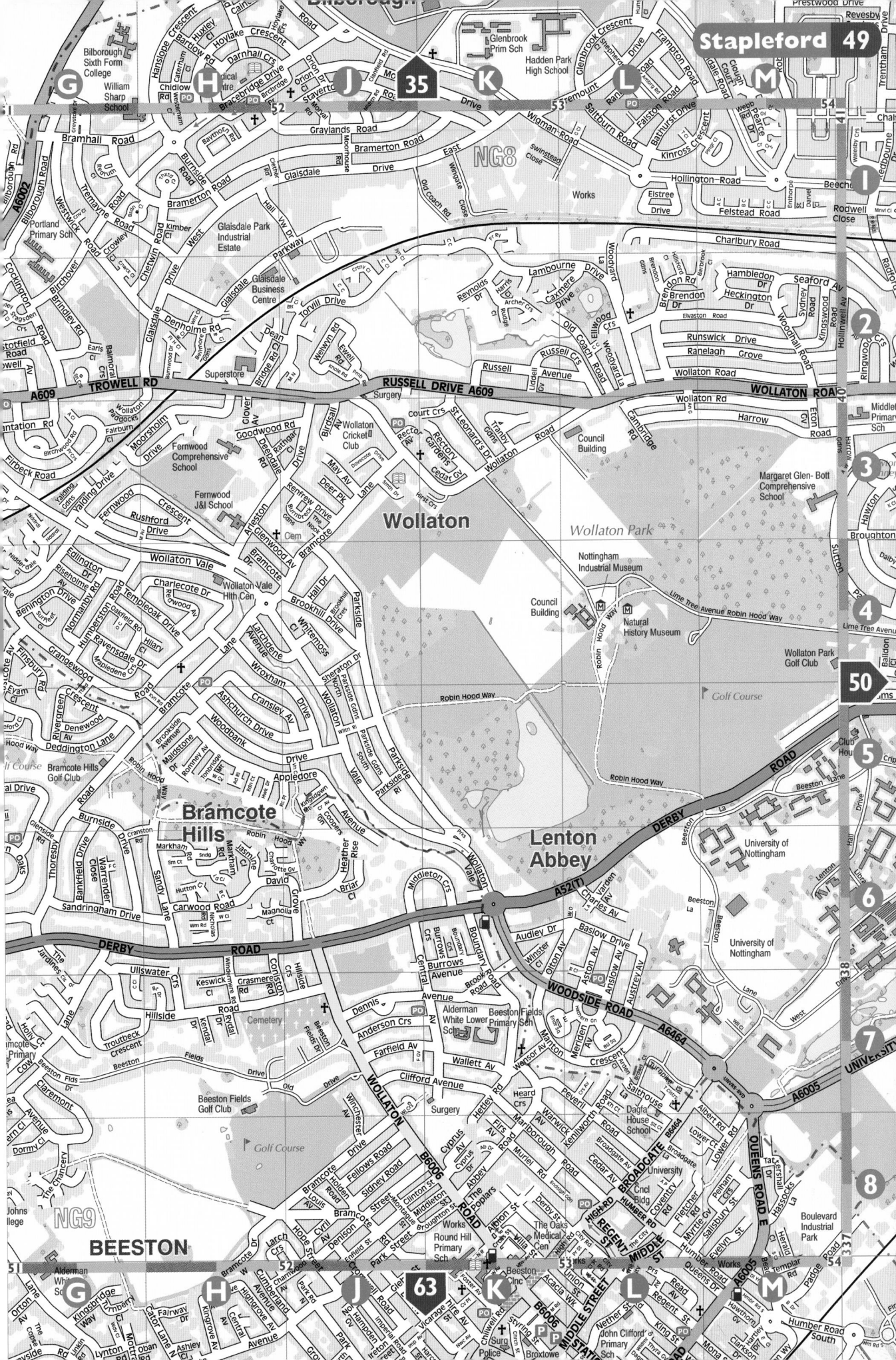

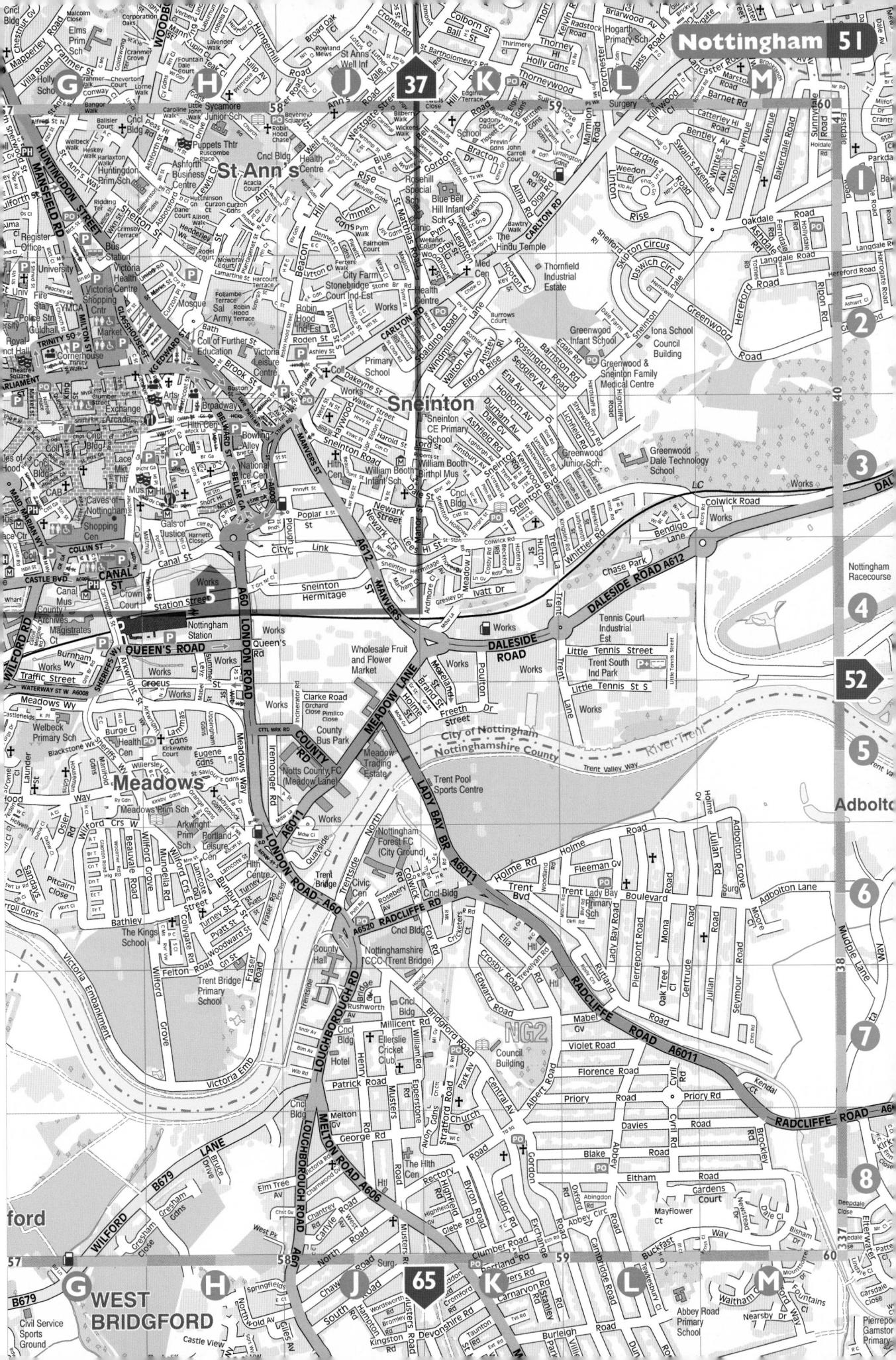

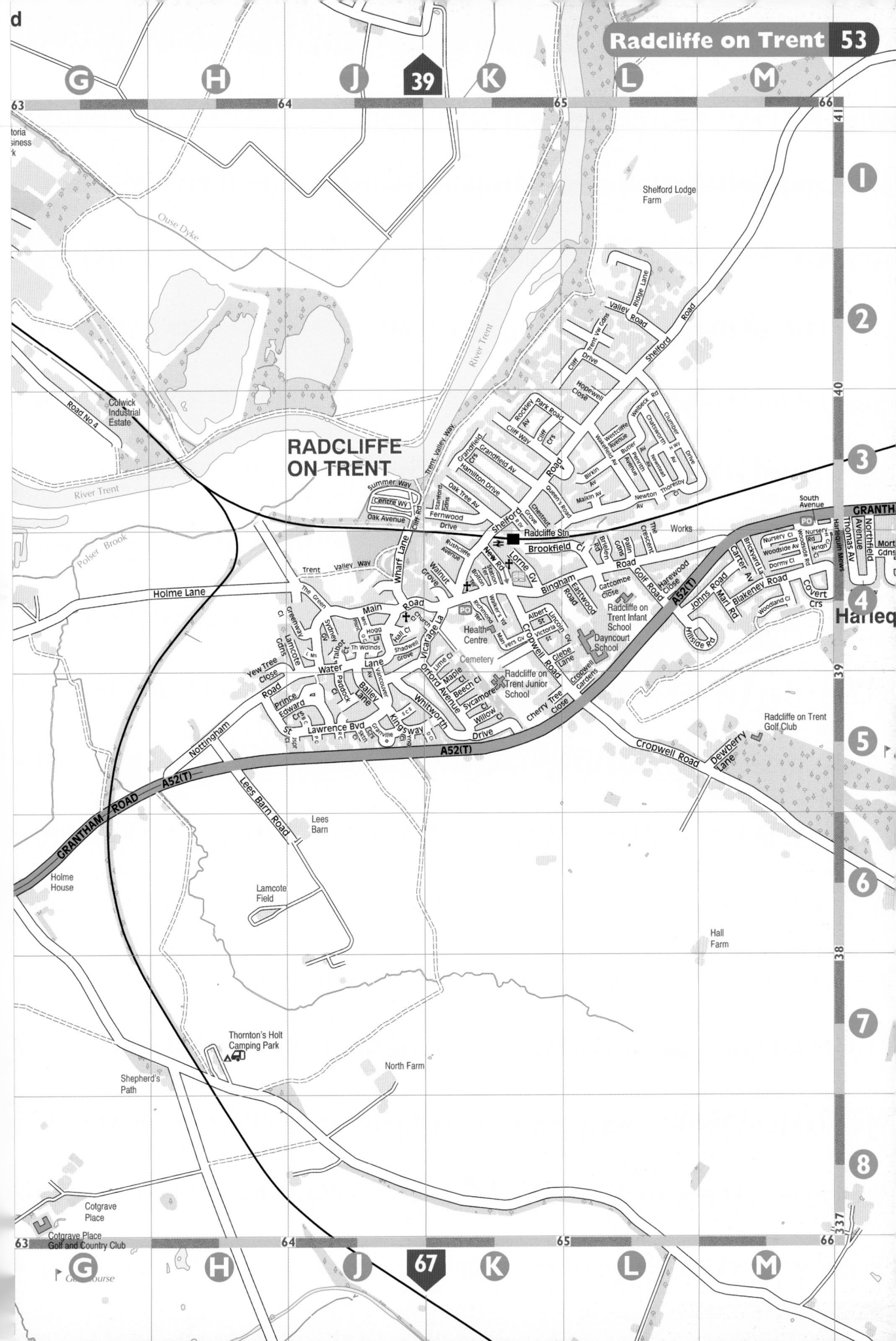

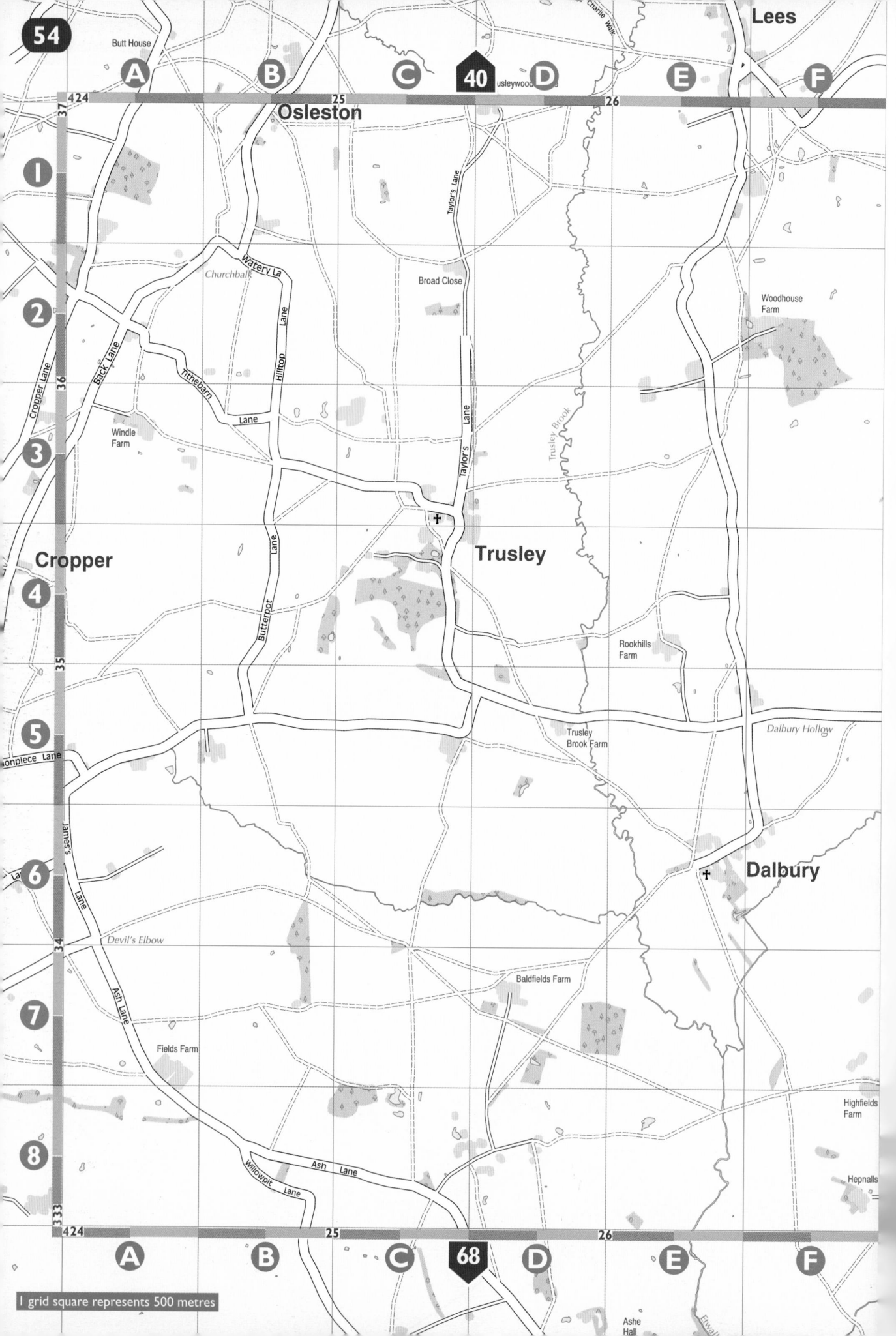

G H J 41 K L M

27 28 29 30 37

Foxfields Farm

I

2

Bonnie Prince Charlie Walk

Radbourne

Silverhill Farm

Bonnie Prnce Charlie Walk

Derbyshire County

36

3

Birch Wood

Potlocks Farm

Sandown Av

Naseby Close

Surg

Swayfield

4

56

5

Terrel Hays

Chertsey Rd

Glenfield Crs

Smerrills Farm

Bearwardcote Hall

Ladybank

6

Heage Lane

Bonehill Farm

34

Banneil's Lane

7

A516(T)

The Grange

ETWALL ROAD

Grassy Lane

Hospital Lane

Merlin Wy

Merlin Wy

8

Bearwardcote Farm

Merlin Wy

Wren Way

Merlin Wy

Sanderling Heath

Merlin Way

333

27 28 29 30

G H J 69 K L M

Heage Lane

A516

Oakdene Farm

Dee Lane

I grid square represents 500 metres

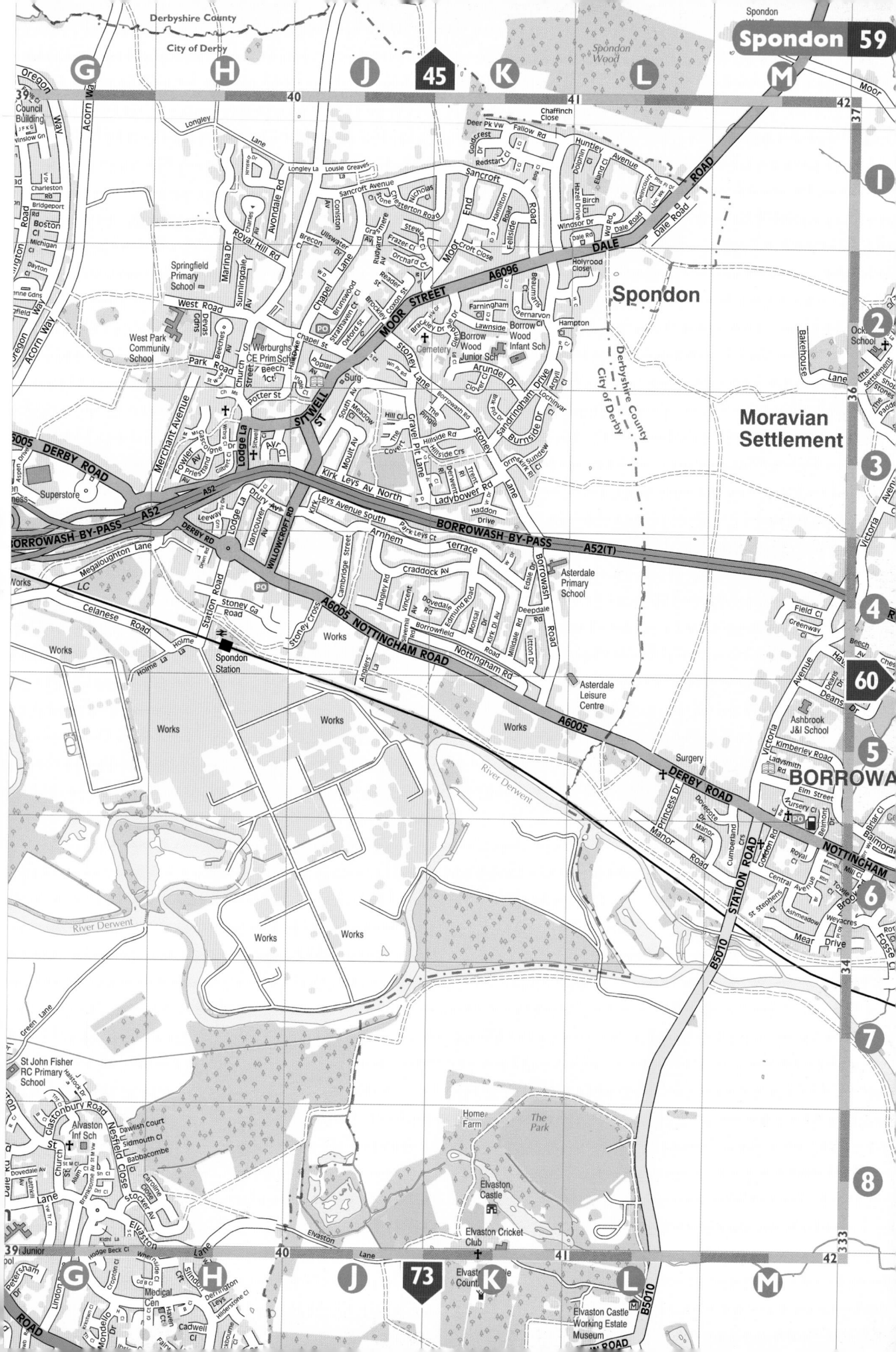

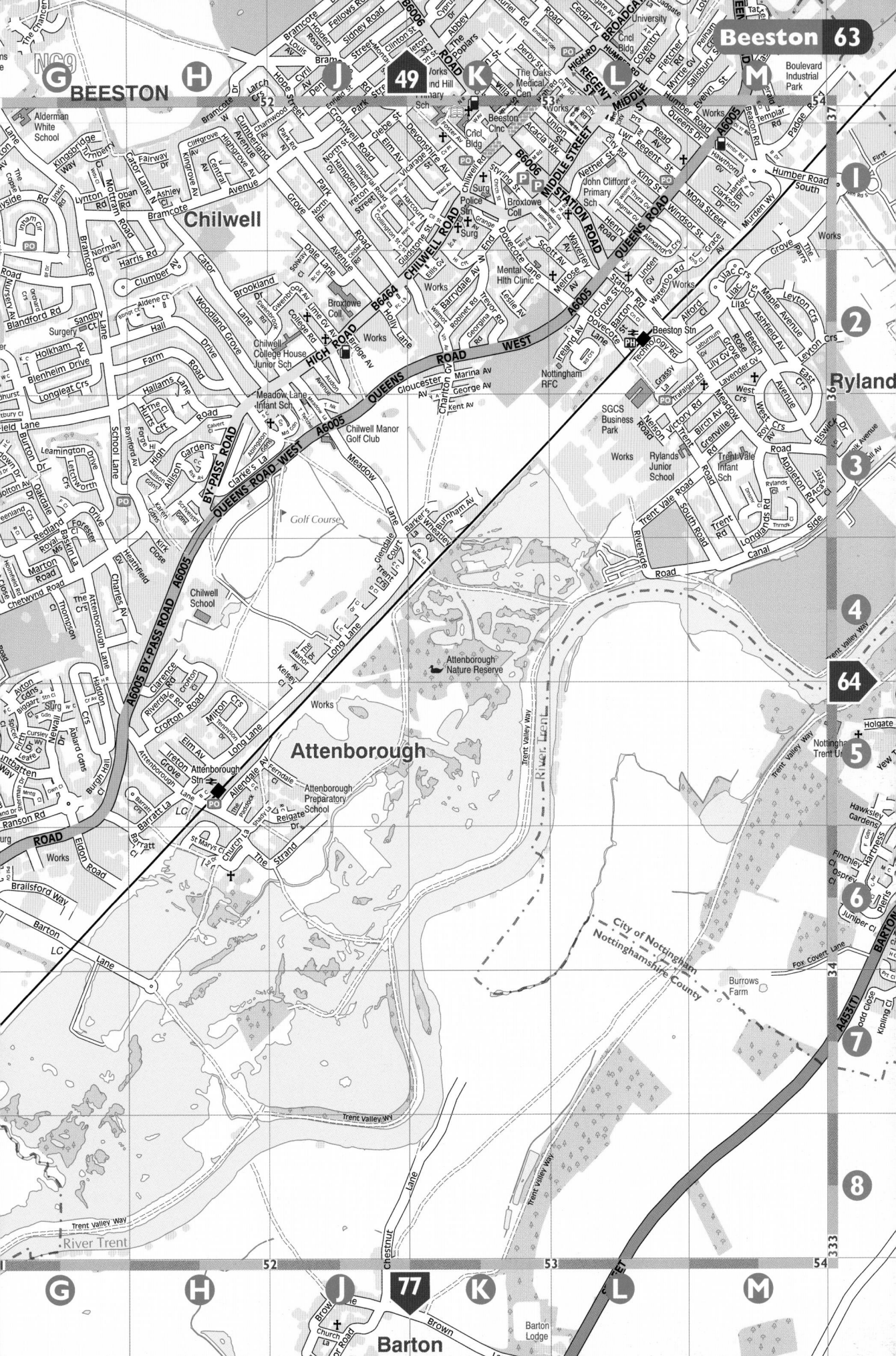

G H J **53** K L M

Cotgrave Place
Golf and Country Club

Golf Course

Peashill
Farm

Windmill
Hill

Grantham Canal (disused)

Hollygate
Industrial
Park

Business
Park

Hollygate Lane

Woodgate Lane

Main Road

Mill La

Morkinshire
Farm

The Old
Park

The
Park

Pinfold Cl

High Hazles Road

Cotgrave
CE Primary
School

Church
Lane

Bingham Road

Colston Gate

Rivermead

Cotgrave
Shppg Cntr

Health
Centre

Deanscourt

Avondale

Lingford

Greenbrook

Grassmere

Fir Dale

Crosshill

Cotgrave

Rectory Road

Hales
Close

Plumtree Road

Cherry Orch

Scrimshire Lane

Risegate
Risegate
Gardens

Candleby Lane

Cotgrave Close

Cotgrave
Infant Sch

Manvers Junior
School

Meadow

Spring

Willowdene

Thorntons

Baker's
Hollow

Mensing Av

Broad Meana

Forest

Furrows

White

Daisy Cl

Ash Lea
Special School

Owthorpe Road

Woodview

Ritchie Cl

Plough

Burhill

Flaxendale

Plumtree Road

Cotgrave Road

Barn

Manns

Toft Cl

Bonny Md

Miller's

Daleside

Westway

The Dial

Fox

Ring

Com

Flagholme

Cartbridge

Ring

Moor Leas

Brambleway

Cloverdale

Eastwold

Mattwood

Briar Ga

NG12

Gripps Com

Runcle

Saxon Way

Warwick
Gardens

Hickling
Way

A46(T)

Clipston

Gilliver La

Church Gate

Wolds Lane

Glebe
Farm

Owthorpe Road

Cotgrave
Wolds

Borders
Wood

I 2 3 4 5 6 7 8

-Wol

54

A B C D E F

Ash Lane
Willowpit Lane

Hepn

I

Hilton Fields

Park Farm

Ashe Hall

Etwall Brook

2

Sutton Lane

Willowpit Lane

A516

Sutton Lane

Church Hill

3

Burntheath

Sutton Lane

Derby Road

Hilton Road

Etw

Old Station Cl

The Bancroft

John Port School

Etwall Leisure Centre

Etwall Primary School

Main

Portland

Ash Va

DERBY RD

Chestnut Grove

4

A50

Hilton Industrial Estate

Dale End Lane

Sutton Lane

DERBY RD

Hilton Lodge

A516

A50

Eggington Road

5

West Avenue

Shd Cv

Cherry Tr

Derby Rd

Montgomery Close

DERBY A5132

Pegasus Way

Normandy Road

Lucas Lane

Blakeley Lane

Eggington Road

Main Street

PO

Hilton Primary School

Eggington Road

Peacroft Ct

New Road

A5132

Mulberry

Falaise Wy

Rodney

Halifax Cl

Enfield

6

Mill Lane

Back Lane

Bancroft Close

Field

Hawthorn Cl

Orchard Cl

Bloomfield Close

Peacroft Lane

Calder Close

Weland Road

Avon Wy

Wyston Brook

Rogers Brook

Marston Br

The Mease

Avon Way

Dale Br

Hntsp Rd

EGGINGTON ROAD

A5132

DE65

Hargate Manor

Blakeley Lodge

Eggington Road

7

The Hall

Avon Ryton Wy

Nene Way

Washford Road

The Mease

Oldfield Lane

LC

LC

8

329

424

25

26

Derby Airfield

HILTON ROAD

Etwall Road

Blacksmith's

A B C D E F

I grid square represents 500 metres

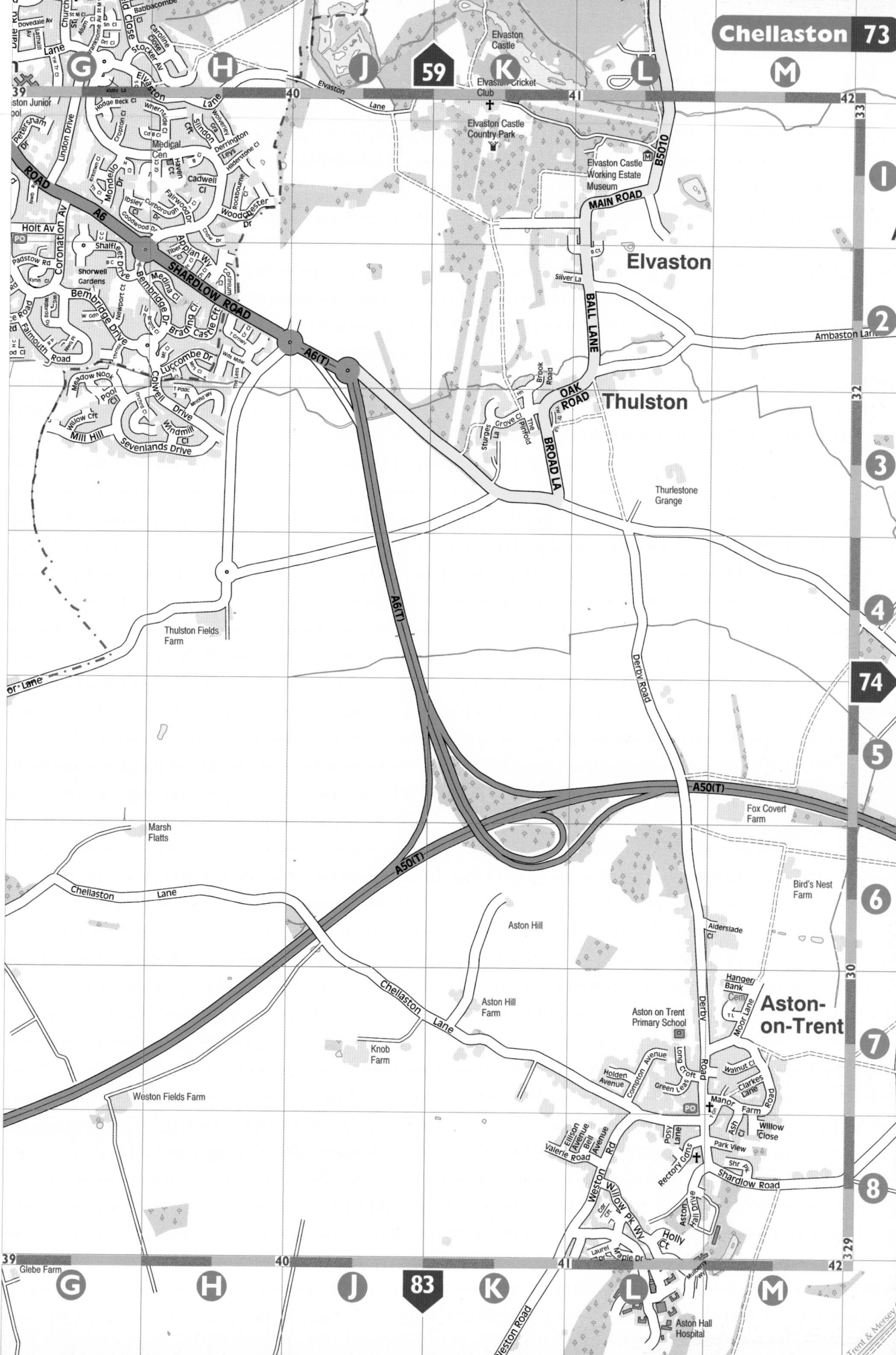

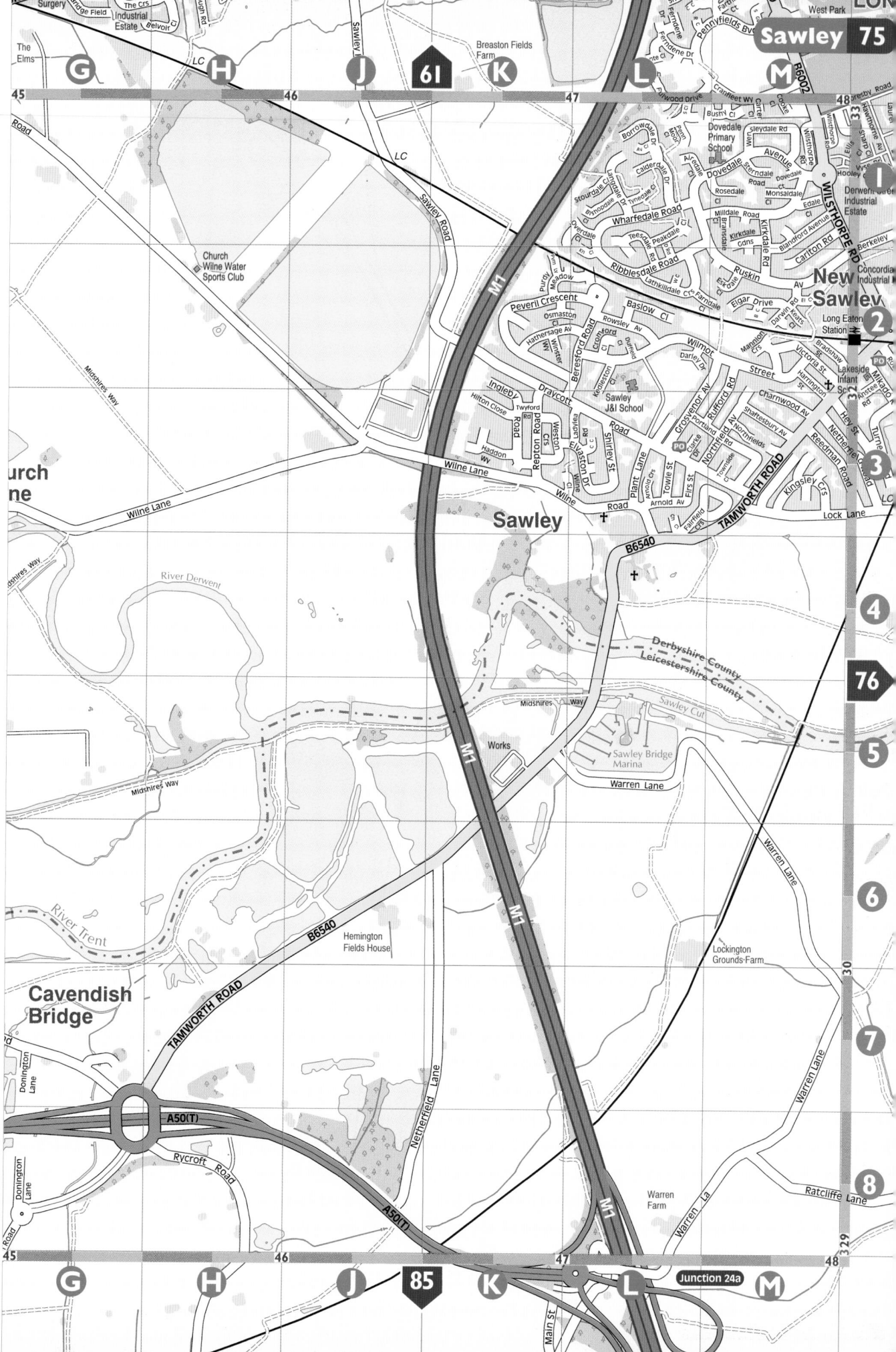

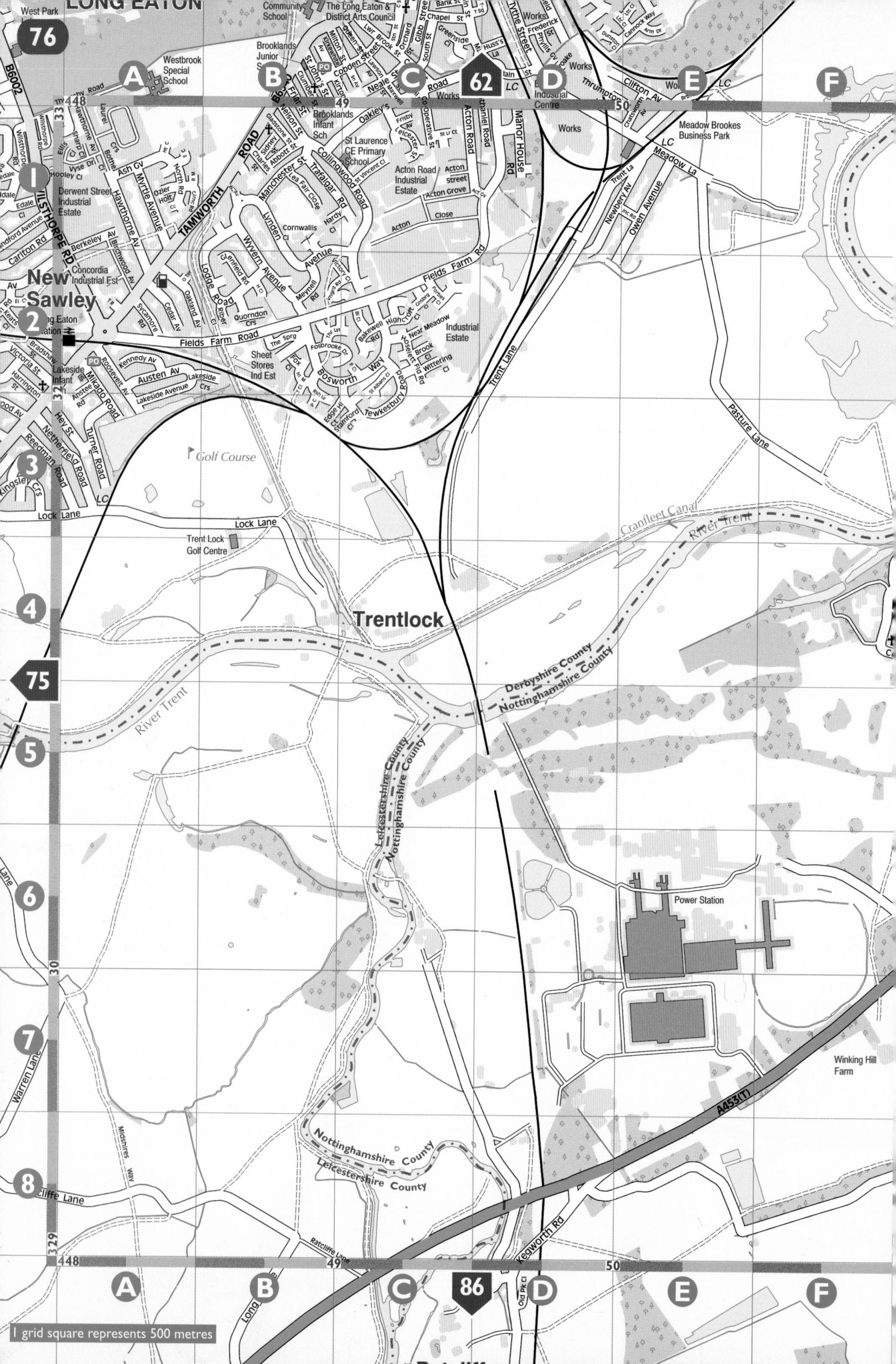

G   H   J   63   K   L   M

52   53   54   33

I

2

32

Barton Moor

3

4

78

NG11

5

Gotham

6

30

7

8

329

G   H   J   87   K   L   M

51   52   53   54

New

River Trent

Trent Valley Way

Brown Lane

Church La

Barton in Fabis

Ltl Lunnon

Manor Road

Manor Road

Brown Lane

Barton Lodge

GREEN STREET

CHESTNUT Lane

Barton Lane

A453(T)

Glebe Farm

Nottinghamshire County

Derbyshire County

Trent Valley Way

Thrumpton

Church Lane

PO

Barton Lane

A453(T)

Gotham Cricket Club

Surgery

Bidwell Crs

Wodenous Av

Nottingham Road

Grasmere Gdns

Industrial Estate

St Andrew Cl

Wallace St

Chaston Av

Fairham

East St

Ernest Av

Meadow

Home Farm Cl

Curzon St

PO

Naylor Av

The Rushes Cl

Leake Road

Malt St

Orchard St

Kegworth Rd

Tomlinson

Hall Drive La

Gotham Primary Sch

Pygall Av

Foredrift Cl

Cem

Monk's

Moor Lane

Kegworth Road

Road

West Leake Lane

Stonepit Farm

Kegworth Road

Wood Lane

Eyres Lane

Hill Road

Gypsum Way

British Gypsum Business Park

Cuckoo Bush Farm

Crownend

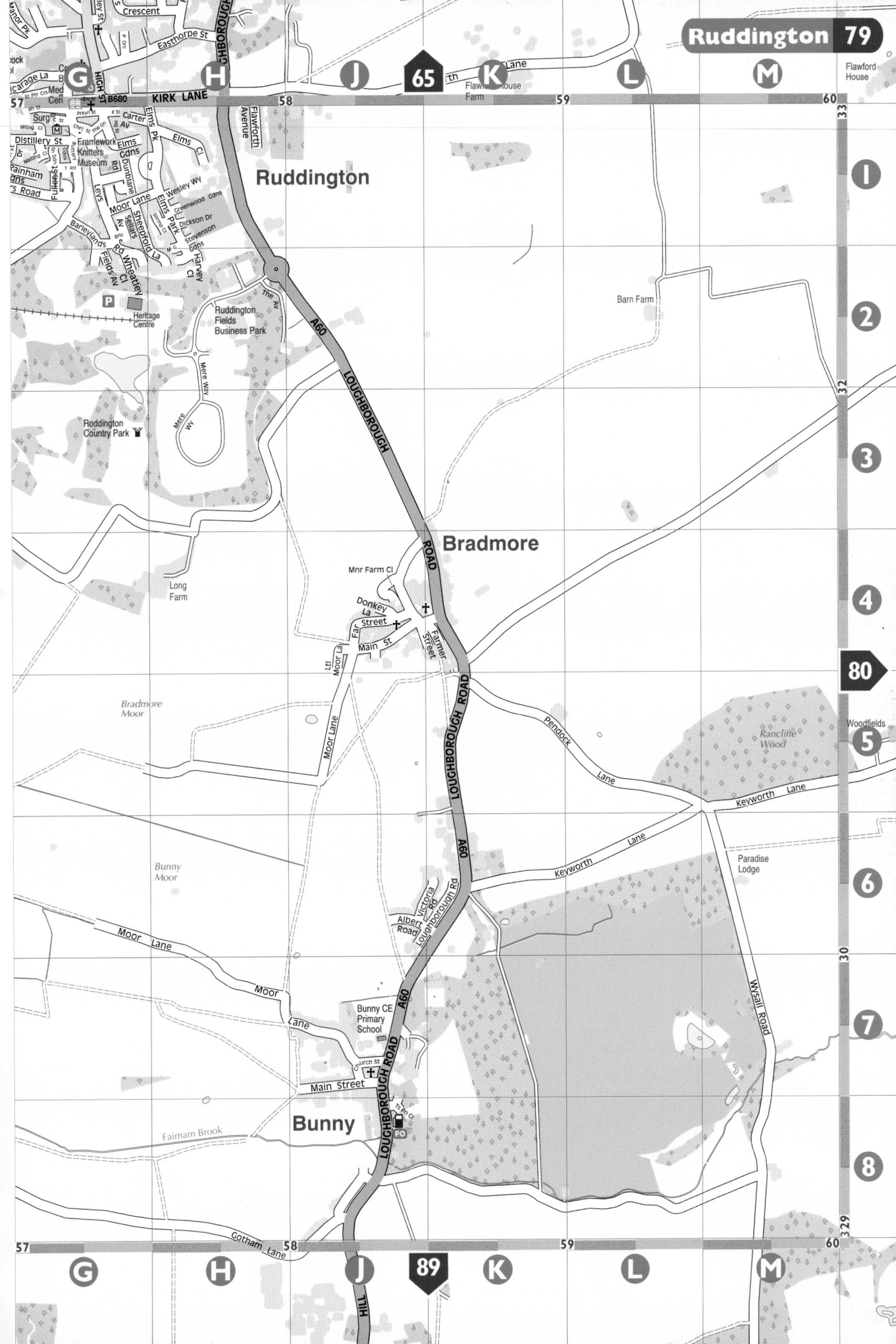

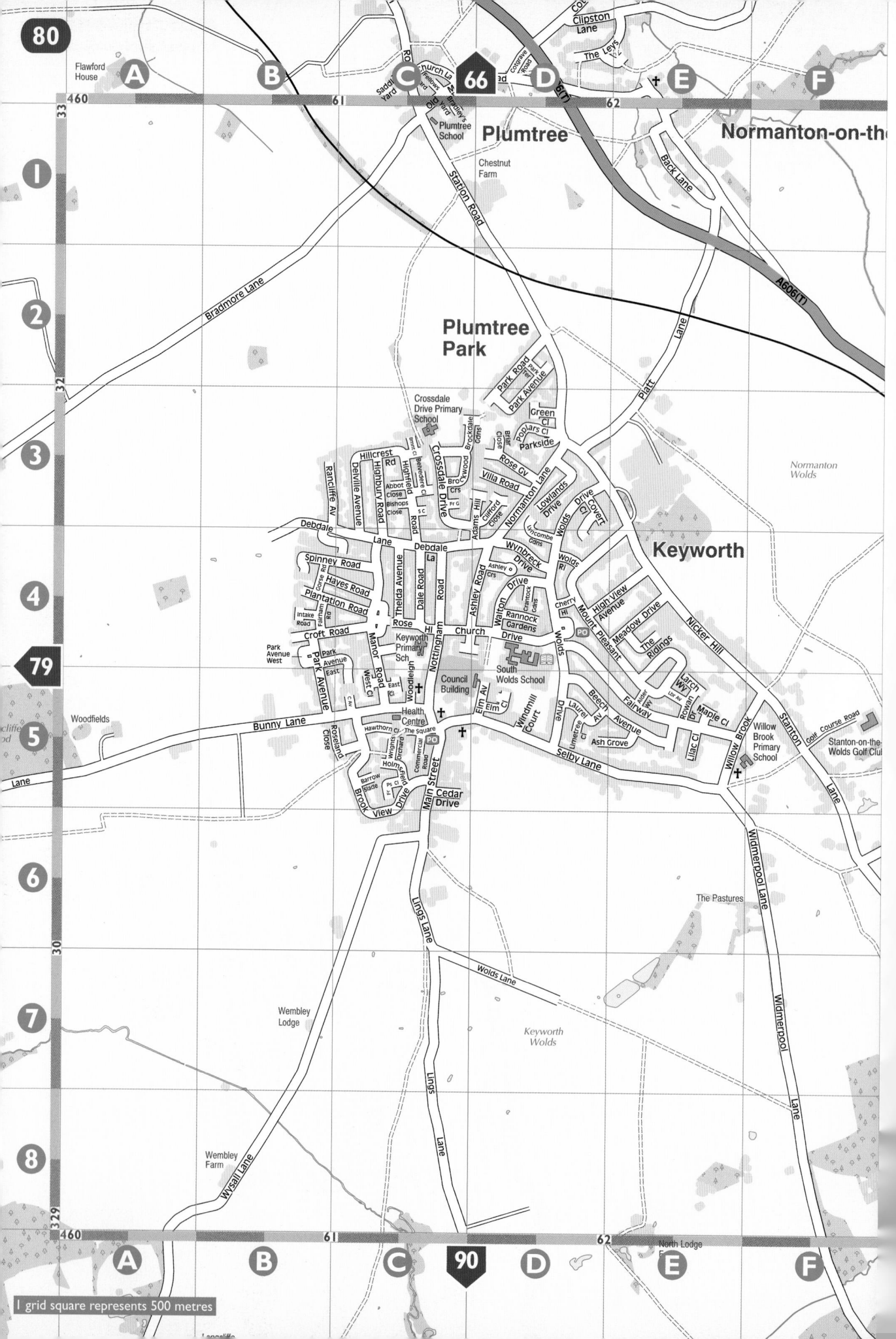

80

A B C **66** D E F

33 460 61 Saddl Yard 62

Plumtree **Normanton-on-the**

Flawford House

Plumtree School

Chestnut Farm

I

32

Bradmore Lane

Station Road

Platt Lane

A606(T)

2

Plumtree Park

Park Road
Park Avenue

Crossdale Drive Primary School

Normanton Wolds

3

Hillcrest Rd
Highbury Road
Delville Avenue
Rancliffe Av
Crossdale Drive
Brockdale Gdns
Abbot Close
Bishops Close
Belvedere La

Brocwood
Rose Gv
Villa Road
Normanton Lane
Green Cl
Poplars Cl
Parkside
Lowlands
Wolds Cl
Covert

Keyworth

Debdale Lane

Debdale La

Spinney Road
Thelda Avenue
Dale Road
Rose Hl
Hayes Road
Plantation Road
Intake Road
Farnham Rd
Croft Road

Adams Hill
Clifford Close
Wynbeck Drive
Ashley Road
Walton Drive
Rannock Gardens
Church Drive

Wolds Rd
Drive
Cherry Hl
High View Avenue
Mount Pleasant
Meadow Drive
The Ridings
Nicker Hill

4

79

Park Avenue West
Manor Road
Park Avenue
West Cl
East
Woodleigh
Keyworth Primary Sch
Nottingham Road
South Wolds School
PO
Larch Wy
Fairway
Maple Cl
Beech Avenue
Rowan
Willow Brook Primary School

Woodfields

5

Bunny Lane
Roseland Close
Hawthorn Cl
The Square
Commercial Road
PO
Health Centre
Elm Av
Windmill Court
Selby Lane
Laurel
Ash Grove
Lilac Cl
Willow Brook

Stanton Lane

Golf Course Road
Stanton-on-the-Wolds Golf Club

Lane

Barrow Blade
Holm
Brook View
Main Street
Cedar Drive
Lings Lane

Widmerpool Lane

6

30

The Pastures

Wolds Lane

7

Wembley Lodge

Keyworth Wolds

Widmerpool Lane

8

329

Wembley Farm

Wysall Lane

460 61 **90** 62 North Lodge

A B C D E F

I grid square represents 500 metres

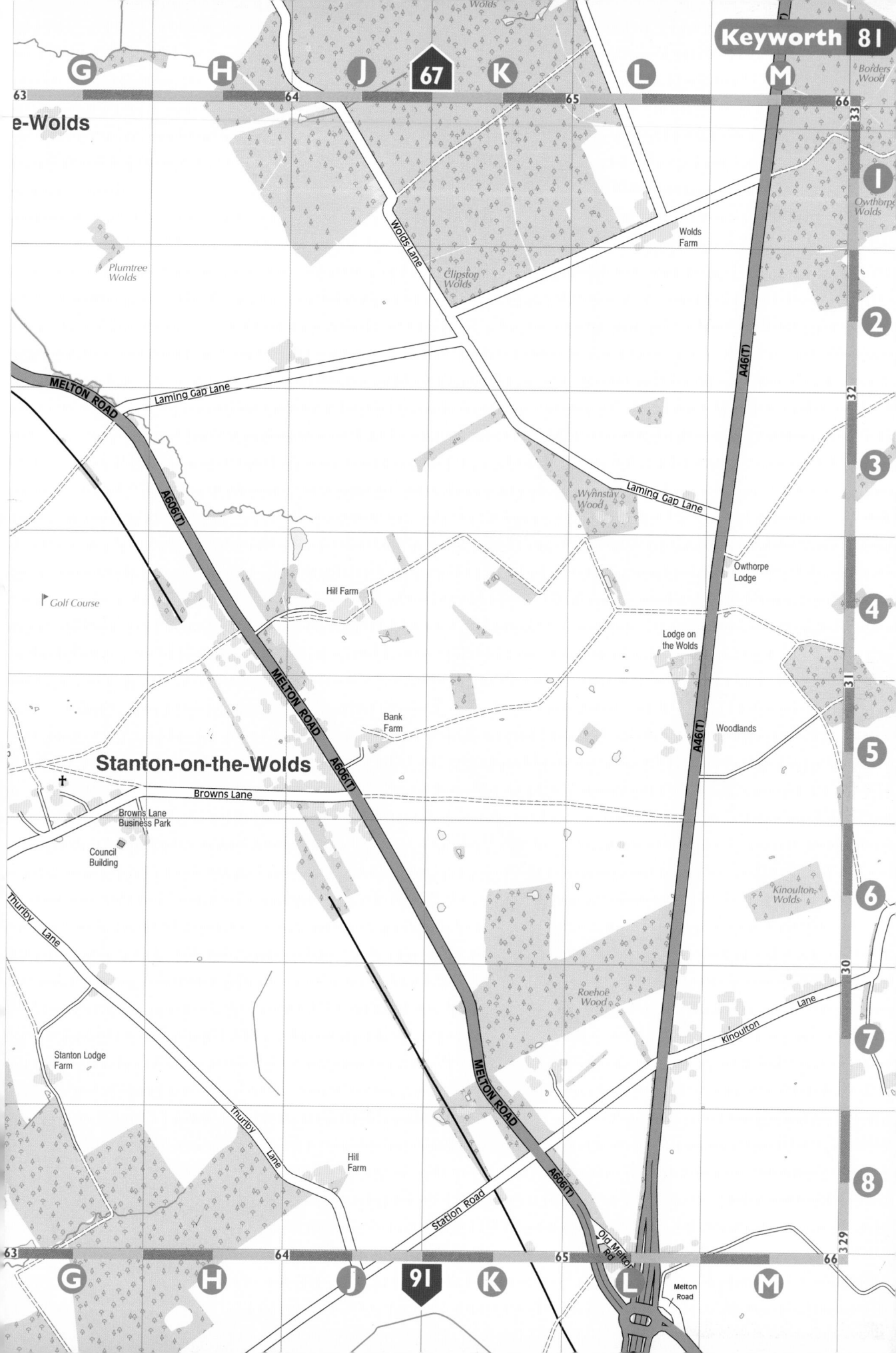

G H J 67 K L M

e-Wolds

Wolds

Borders Wood

1

Owthorpe Wolds

2

Plumtree Wolds

Clipston Wolds

Wolds Farm

Wolds Lane

MELTON ROAD

Laming Gap Lane

3

Laming Gap Lane

Wynnstay Wood

A46(T)

Owthorpe Lodge

A606(T)

4

Golf Course

Hill Farm

Lodge on the Wolds

Woodlands

MELTON ROAD

Bank Farm

5

Stanton-on-the-Wolds

A606(T)

Browns Lane

Browns Lane Business Park

Kinoulton Wolds

6

Council Building

Thurlby Lane

Roehoe Wood

Kinoulton Lane

7

Stanton Lodge Farm

Kinoulton

Thurlby Lane

Hill Farm

MELTON ROAD

8

A606(T)

Station Road

Old Melton Rd

Melton Road

G H J 91 K L M

329

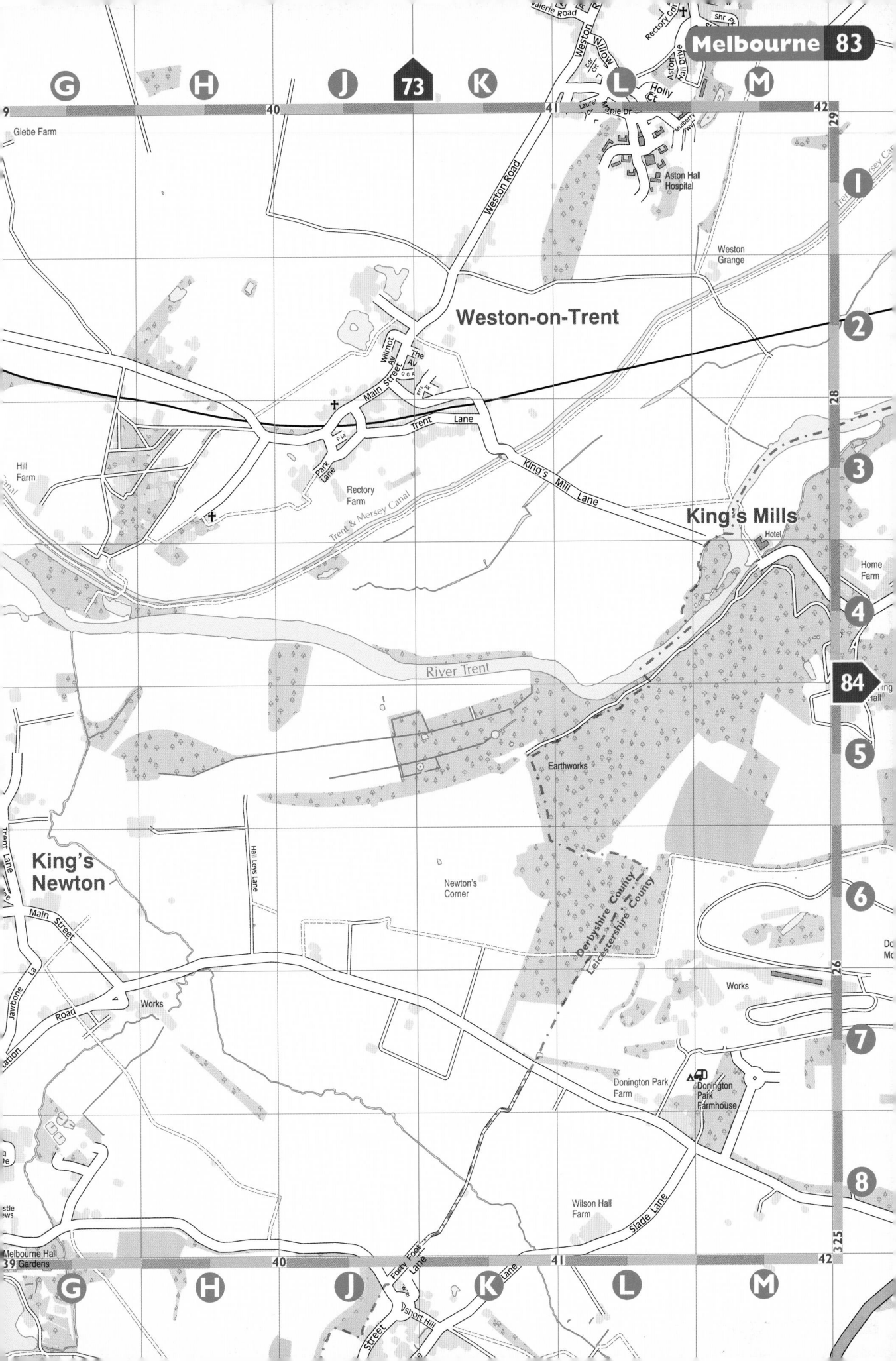

G H J **73** K L M

9 40 41 42

I
2
3
4
84
5
6
7
8

Glebe Farm

Weston Road

Weston Grange

Weston-on-Trent

Aston Hall Hospital

Willow

Holly Ct

Laurel Dr

Maple Dr

Mulberry Wy

Rectory Ct

Aston Hall Drive

Valerie Road

Wilmot Av

The Av

Main Street

Trent Lane

Park Lane

Rectory Farm

Hill Farm

Trent & Mersey Canal

King's Mill Lane

King's Mills

Hotel

Home Farm

River Trent

Earthworks

King's Newton

Main Street

Hall Leys Lane

Newton's Corner

Trent Lane

Derbyshire County

Leicestershire County

Works

Works

Donington Park Farm

Donington Park Farmhouse

Melbourne Hall Gardens

Wilson Hall Farm

Slade Lane

Forty Foot Lane

Station Road

Cambourne La

Castle Mews

39 Gardens

G H J K L M

40 41 42

Short Hill

Street

A B C **76** D E F

29 448   Ratcl 49 ne   Keg w   50

I

2

28

3

Junction 24

A453(T)

A6(T)

4

Side   Ley
85   Hotel
               Works

Windmill
Way

5

Sibson
Drive

Pep
Drive

Kegworth
Squash Club

Suthers
Road

Nine
Acres

Packington Hill

DERBY ROAD

Hotel
W Bank

Oldershaw
Av

Springfield

Lngly Dr

Broadhill Road

High Street

Pleasant Pl

Kegworth
Primary
School

Whatton Road

Foxhills

Shepherd
Wk

Kirby.
Drive

Sutton
Rd

St Andrew's R

Thomas
Road

Hillside

The Lodge

Cem

Bedford
Cl

Burley
Rise

Roberts
Close

Gerrard
Crescent

Brickyard
Lane

New

Works

Nottingham Road

Borough St

Mill La

Frederick

Trowell

Leathernlands

Moore
Av

Kirk Av

New Street

Station Road

Bridge Fields

The
Oslers

PH

Surg

PO

Kegworth
Museum

M

River Soar

KEGWORTH

Long Lane

Long Lane
Farm

Ratcliffe
on Soar

Kegworth Road

Kegworth Rd

Old Pk Cl

Kingston Lane

Station Road

Kingston
on Soar

Gotham Road

Station Road

Old Bull
Farm Cl

Station Road

Sutton
Fields
House

Melton Lar

College Road

6

26

LONDON ROAD

A6(T)

Soar   Lane

Landcroft La

Cemetery

7

Spring House
Farm

Marl   Pit Hill

Bollard's La

Buck's La

St Ann's
Manor

8

3 25 448

Whatton Road

Slade
Farm

49

River Soar

River Soar

Main Street

St Anne's

50

A B **94** C D E F

Devil's
Elbow

PO

Farm

G H J **77** K L M

52 53 54

29

New
Kingston

Cuckoo
Bush
Farm

I

Crownend
Wood

Midshires Way

2

28

Wossock Lane

Kingston Fields
Farm

3

Stocking La

Ash
Spinney

Kingston Brook

4

West Leake Lane

Scotland Farm

88

5

Dark Lane

Village Farm Cl

Main Street **West
Leake**

6

Pithouse Lane

Kingston Brook

West Leake Road

Melton Lane

PH

Landcroft Lane

Brickyard Lane

Manor Farm

26

Trowell Lane

Brickyard Lane

Midshires Way

7

California Farm

Hungary Lane

Hills Farm

8

Travell's Hill

325

52 53 54

G H J **95** K L M

Sutton
Bonington

Cold Harbour
Farm

REMPSTONE

A6006 ROAD

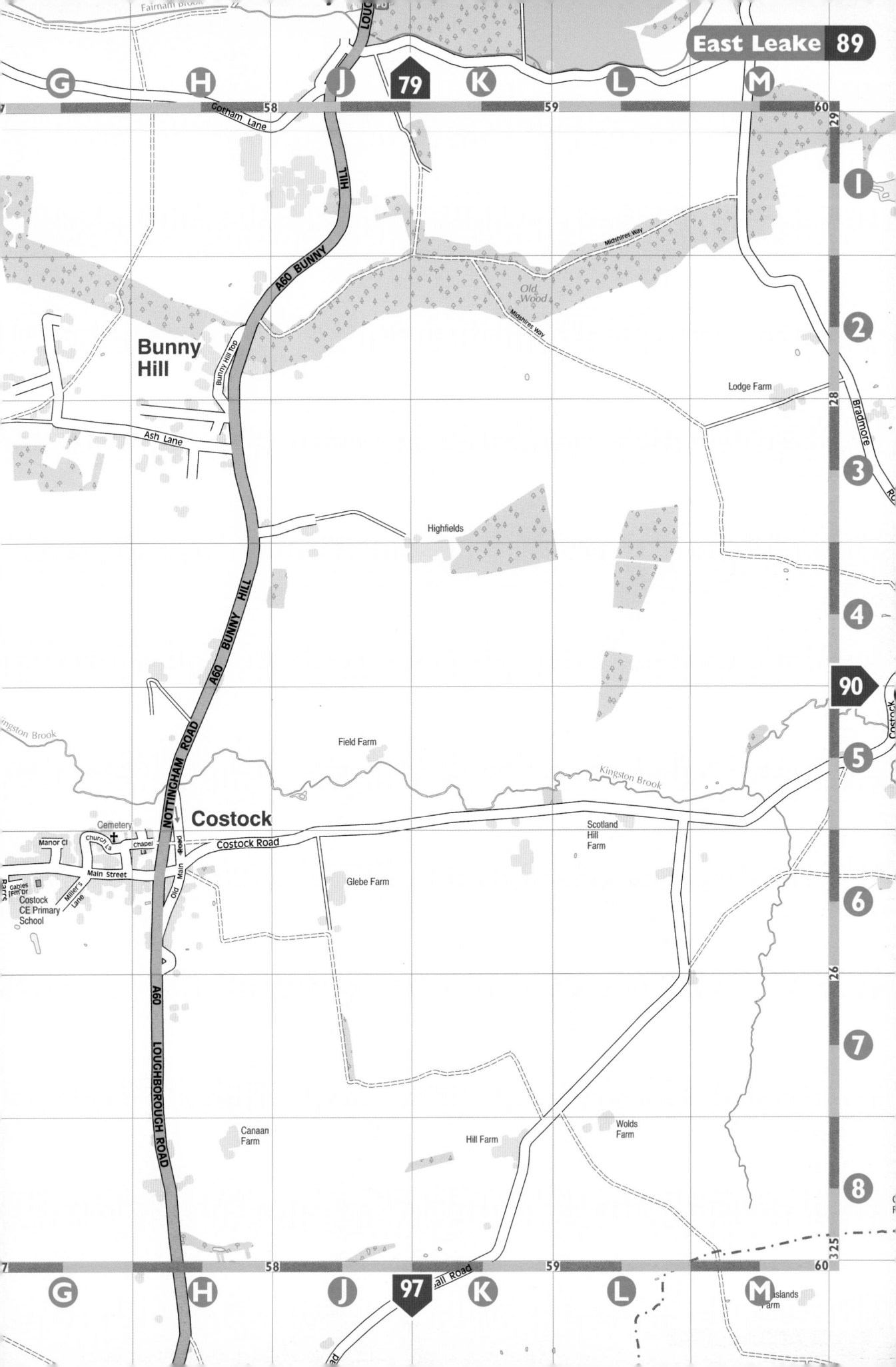

G H J 79 K L M

Gotham Lane 58 59 60 29

I

2

Midshires Way

Old Wood

Lodge Farm 28

3

Bradmore

A60 BUNNY HILL

Bunny Hill Top

Bunny Hill

Ash Lane

Midshires Way

Highfields

4

90

A60 BUNNY HILL

Kingston Brook

Field Farm 5

Kingston Brook

Costock

NOTTINGHAM ROAD

Costock

Cemetery

Manor Cl

church

chapel La

Old Main Road

Costock Road

Main Street

Gables Fm Dr

Miller's Lane

Costock CE Primary School

Glebe Farm

Scotland Hill Farm

6

26

7

A60 LOUGHBOROUGH ROAD

Canaan Farm

Hill Farm

Wolds Farm

8

3 25

58 59 60 3 25

G H J 97 K L M

Maslands Farm

all Road

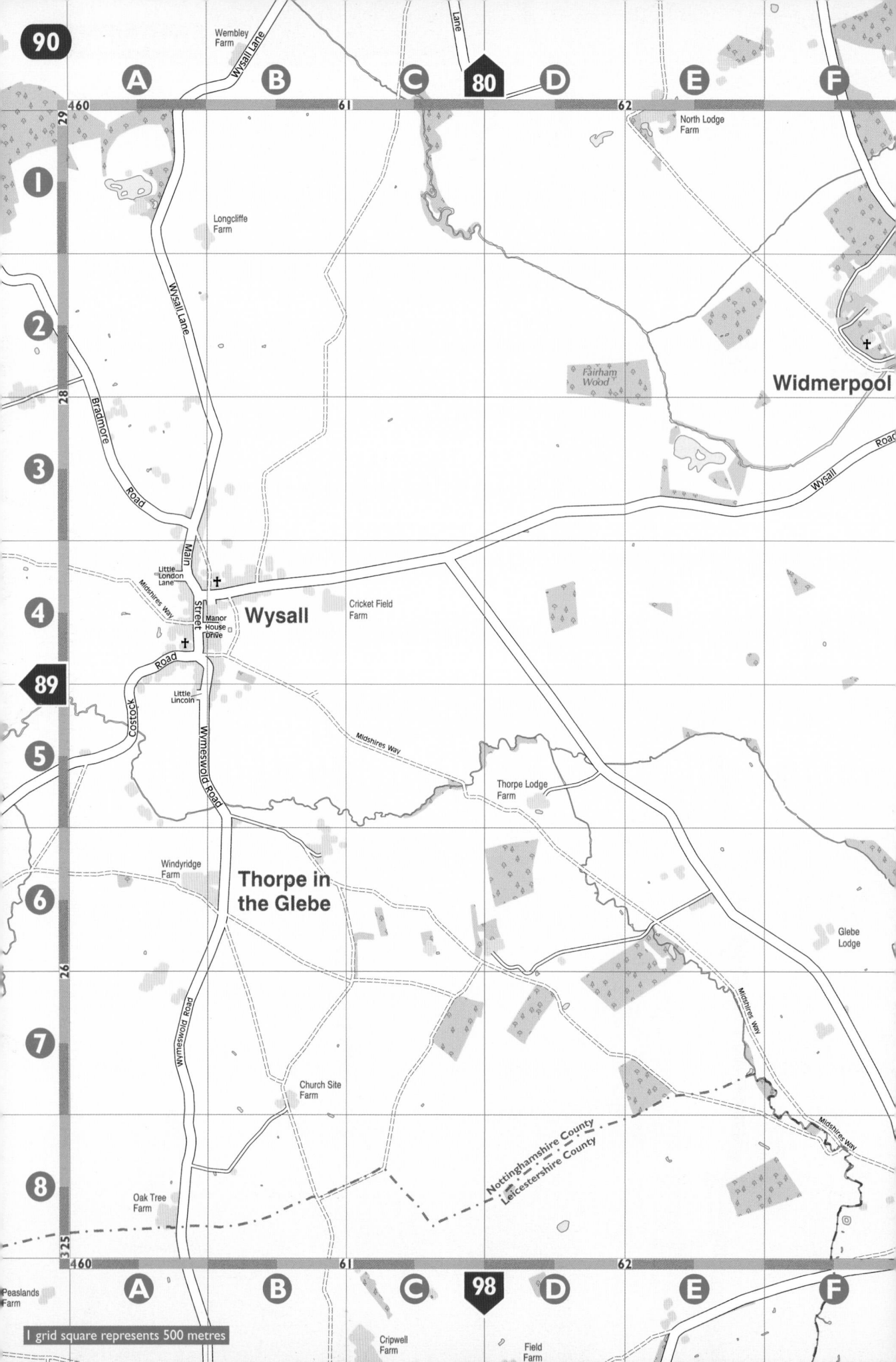

G   H   J   **81**   K   L   M

64   65   66   29

I

Hi
Pa

2

28

Hill
Farm

Station Road

Church
Lane

Keyworth Road

Brooklands

The
Grange

Pen Lane

London Lane

Green
Hill

Manor
Farm

Willoughby
Lodge

South
Lodge

Fields
Farm

A46(T)

Broughton Grange
Farm

Melton
Road

Old Melton
Rd

NOTTINGHAM ROAD A606

Manor
Farm

3

27

4

A46(T)

Wolds
Farm

5

Mill Lane

Fosse
Lodge

Manor Barn
Farm

26

6

Willoughby-
on-the-Wolds

Crosshill

Main Street

London Lane

Chapel Lane

Church Lane

Manor

PO

Willoughby Primary
School

Brook Farm

Main Street

Back Lane

Back Lane

A46(T)

Station Road

Manor
Farm

Star

7

Nottinghamshire County
Leicestershire County

Nottingham Lar

25

8

G   H   J   **99**   K   L   M

64   65   66   325

G   H   J   **85**   K   L   M

46   47   48   25

Bleak House

Windmill Farm   I

Donington Park Service Area

Hotel

Diseworth CE Primary School

Hyam's Lane

Junction 23a   2

Kegworth Road

Diseworth

Clements Gate

Gate   Hall

Page Lane   Orchard Cl   Brksd

Lady Gate

3

Kegworth Lane   24

Long Mere Lane

Wood Nook Farm   West   End   Main   Street   PO

Long Whatton   Long Whatton CE Primary School   4

Westmeadow   Lane

A42(T)

Crawsh

Smithy Lane

94

A42(T)

M1   5

Riste Farm

Dry Pot Lane   Glebe Farm   6

Smithy Lane

Piper Farm   22

ASHBY ROAD   7

B5324

Piper Wood

Highfields Farm

Woodlands Farm   8

B5324 **ASHBY ROAD**   Hallamford Road   Oakley   21   3

45   46   47   48

G   H   J   **101**   K   L   M

Grace Dieu   Black   Brook

G H J 87 K L M

52 53 54 25

Sutton
Bonington

Hungary Lane

Travell's Hill

Hills Farm

Cold Harbour
Farm

REMPSTONE

A6006

ROAD

1

Surgery

Willow Pool La

Shepherd's
Cl

Charnwood Av

Sutton
Cl

Charnwood
Rd

Hathernware
Industrial
Estate

The Cedars

2

A6006

Works

Grange Farm

24

3

Moor
Lane

Fat Lane

Tebbutt's
Farm

Normanton
on Soar

4

Butt Lane

Normanton
on Soar Primary
School

Stonehurst
La

Main Street

Barn Farm

96

PO

Bowley's Farm

5

Normanton

Stanford Road

Lane

Leake

River Soar

22

6

Black Brook

7

Meadow Lane

Industrial
Estate

Messenger
Cl

Summerpool
Road

Weldon Road

Bishop Meadow Road

Bakewell Road

Swinbridge Road

Kernan Drive

Hockey
Cl

Meadow Lane

8

Cotton
Wy

Industrial
Estate

DERBY ROAD A6(T)

52 53

Belton Road West

Festival
Dr

Bottleacre
Lane

North
Rd

321

Lawrence
Wy

Main Dr

Francis Dr

Durrell
Cl

Braddon
Rd

Newton
Cl

Alston Dr

Royatale Cl

Plumtree Cl

Oaks
Industrial
Estate

Works

G H J 103 K L M

Barsby Dr

Robert Bakewell
Primary School

Durham Rd

DERBY RD

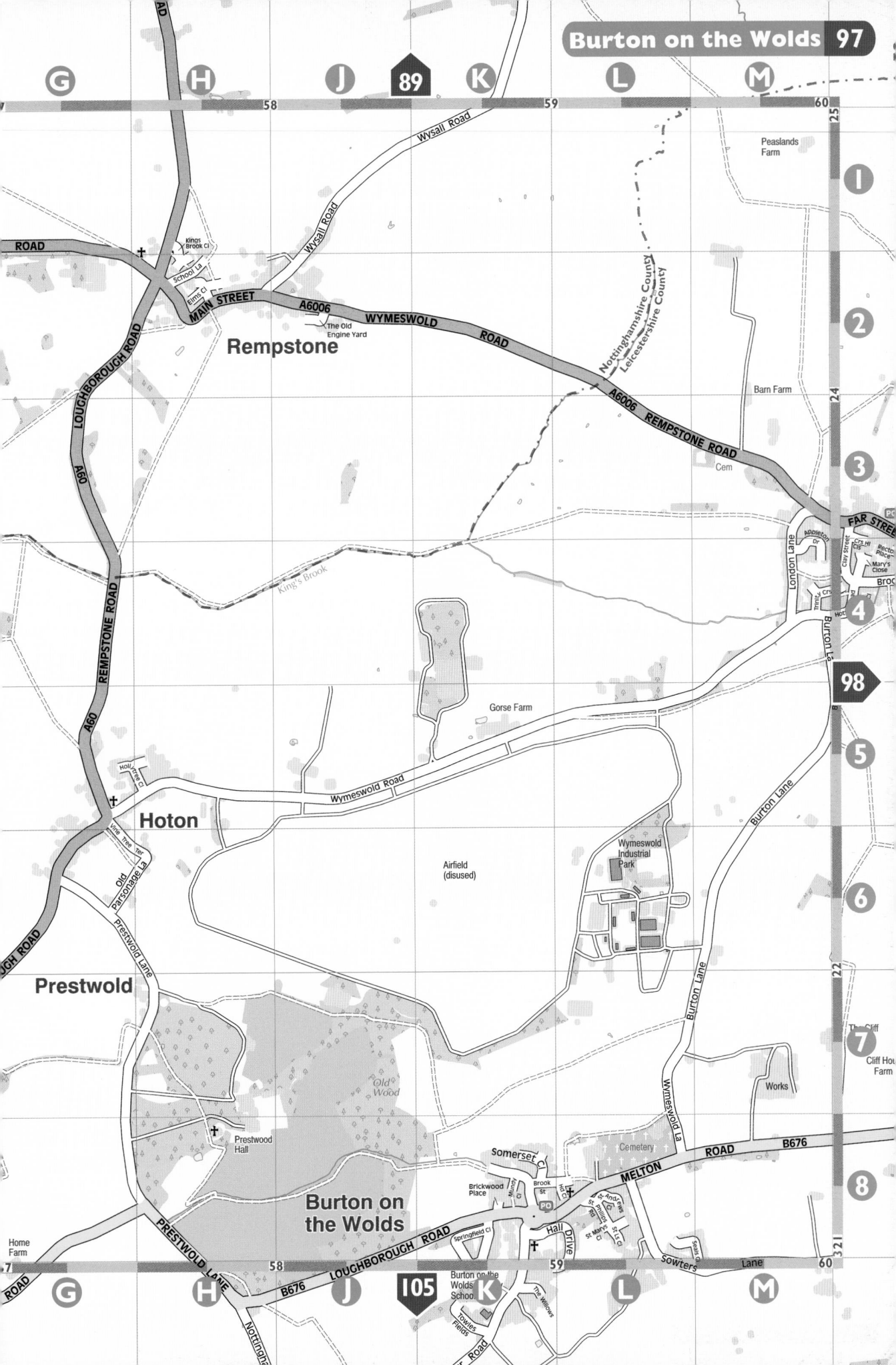

G H J 89 K L M

58 59 60 25

Peaslands
Farm

1

Wysall Road

ROAD

Kings
Brook Cl

School La

Elms Cl

MAIN STREET A6006 WYMESWOLD ROAD

Rempstone

The Old
Engine Yard

Nottinghamshire County
Leicestershire County

A6006 REMPSTONE ROAD

Barn Farm

2

24

LOUGHBOROUGH ROAD

A60

Cem

3

REMPSTONE ROAD

FAR STREET

London Lane

Appleton
Dr

Clay Street

Crs Hl
Trs

Rector
Place

Mary's
Close

Broo

King's Brook

Trinity Crs

4

A60

Burton La

98

Holt Vree Cl

Gorse Farm

Hoton

Wymeswold Road

Burton Lane

5

Vine Tree Ter

Old Parsonage La

Prestwold Lane

Airfield
(disused)

Wymeswold
Industrial
Park

6

22

UGH ROAD

Prestwold

Old
Wood

Burton Lane

The Cliff

7

Cliff Hou
Farm

Prestwood
Hall

Works

Wymeswold La

Somerset

Brickwood
Place

Brook
St

Cemetery

St And're

MELTON ROAD B676

8

Burton on
the Wolds

Springfield Cl

Hall Drive

St Mary's

St Ct Cl

Home
Farm

PRESTWOLD LANE LOUGHBOROUGH ROAD

Burton on the
Wolds School

Sowters Lane

ROAD

7 58 59 60

3 2 1

G H J 105 K L M

B676

Nottingha

The Willows

Fowles
Fields

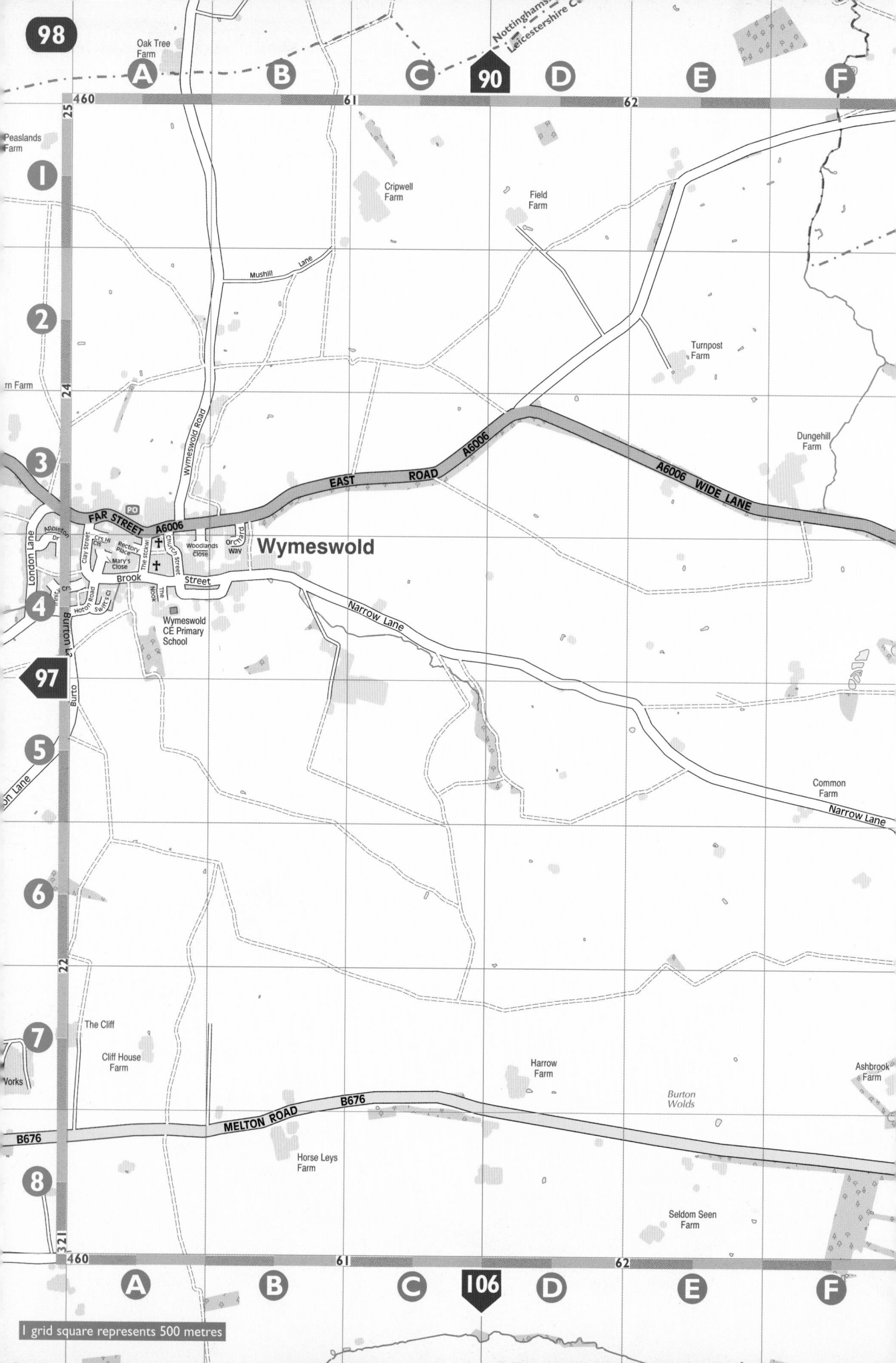

A B C 90 D E F

460 61 62
25

Oak Tree
Farm

Peaslands
Farm

I

Cripwell
Farm

Field
Farm

Mushill   Lane

2

24

Turnpost
Farm

rn Farm

Wymeswold Road

A6006 EAST ROAD A6006 WIDE LANE

Dungehill
Farm

3

PO

FAR STREET A6006

Appleton
Dr

London Lane

Clay Street
Crs.Hl
Cls
Rectory
Place
Woodlands
Close
Orchard
Way
The Stockwl

Mary's
Close
Church Street
The

Wymeswold

Brook   Street

Trinity
Crs
Horton Road
The
Nook
Swift's Cl

Narrow   Lane

4

Burton

Wymeswold
CE Primary
School

5

Common
Farm

Narrow Lane

6

22

7

The Cliff

Cliff House
Farm

Harrow
Farm

Ashbrook
Farm

Works

*Burton
Wolds*

MELTON ROAD B676

B676

8

Horse Leys
Farm

Seldom Seen
Farm

3 2 1
460 61 62

A B C 106 D E F

A   B   C   **92**   D   E   F

442   43   44

21

I

Breedon Brand Farm

Woodside Farm

Hillparks Farm

Lane

PO

Mill Lane
Works
The Toft
Presents
Church

Belton
Prim
Belto

School Lane
Long Street

Tylers Rd
De Verdun

Av
Wils
Slopes

ASHB

2

20

Breedon Lane

Greaveley Farm

Cemetery

Belton

B5324

Gracedieu La

3

West End

Osgathorpe

B5324

Dawson's Road

Armett's La

Hall Farm

Church   Lane

ROAD

Main

Street

Chapel La

Gracedieu   Lane

Low Woods Lane

Low Woods

4

ASHBY

Stordon Grange

Sparrow's

Road

Gracedieu   Lane

19

5

Stordon Lane

Abbey Ford Farm

6

A512

ASHBY ROAD

A512   ASHBY ROAD

Grace Dieu Priory

Spring Burrow Lodge

18

A512

Ivanhoe   Way

Lily Bank

Thringstone Primary School

Road

Heathfield

springfield

Grace Dieu Manor School

7

H RO

Ivanhoe Way

Henson's Lane

Main

Glebe

Tithe Cl

Rumsey Ct

Clover Pl

Priory Cl

Booth   Road

Kelso Ct

Melrose Rd

Homestead Rd

Loughborough   Road

Ash Dale

Bishop Dr

Grace Dieu Wood

Warren Lane

Thringstone

Warren   Lane

Turolough Road

Swannymore Road

8

Hill Lane

Talbot   Lane

Street

Field Close

John St

Swallow Dale

The Green

Brook La
PO

Grace

Whitwick Moor

Dieu

Carter

Crabtree

Car Hill Rd

Rosedale

High Sharpley

317

442

Swannington Common

Ivanhoe Way

Ivanhoe Way

A   B   C   **108**   D   E   F

43   44

Mossdale

Coverdale

Langton

Holcombe

Three

Loughborough   Road

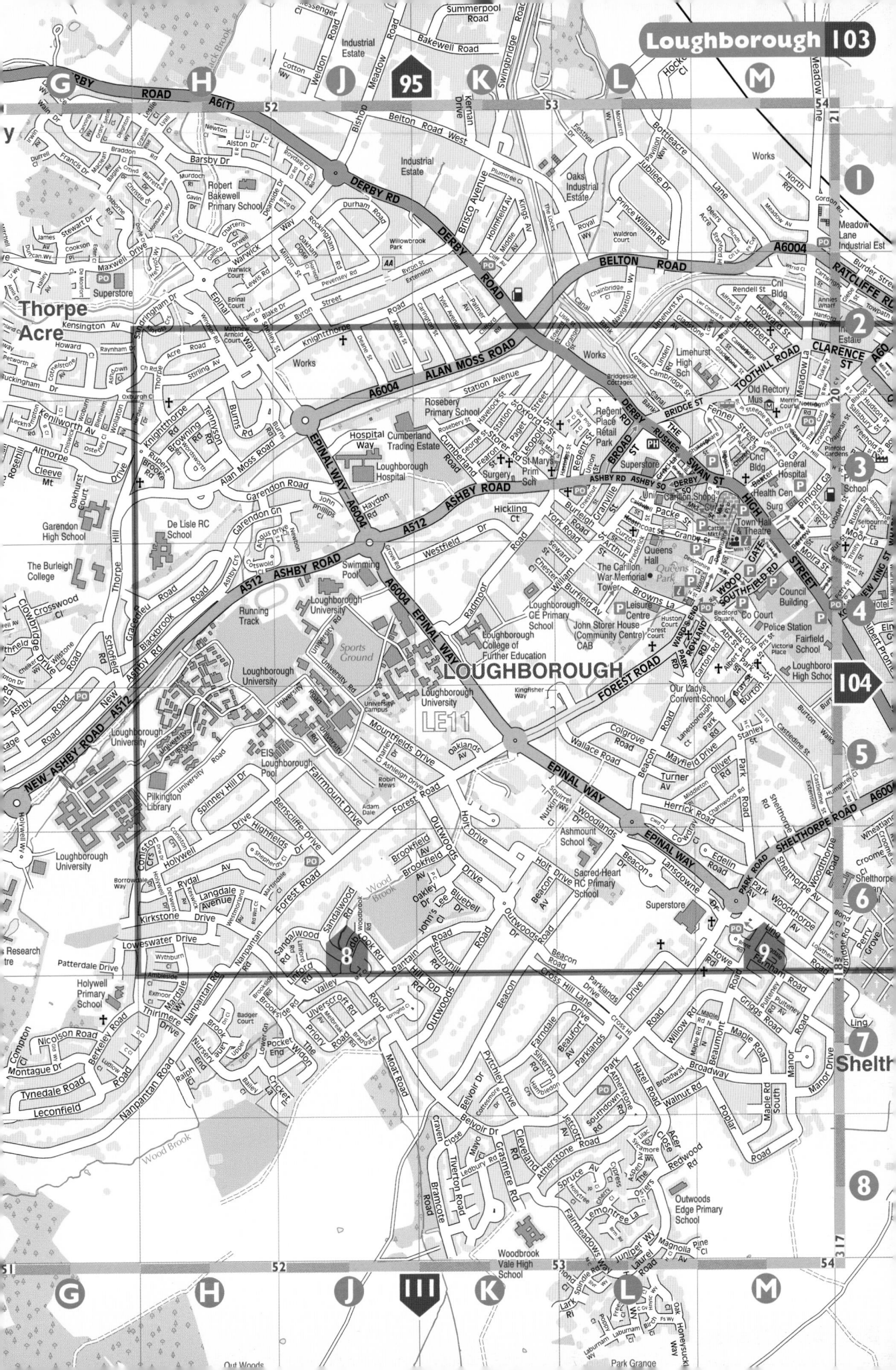

A B C **96** D E F

454 55 56

I

Cotes

Meadow Lane

Burton Bandalls

Meadow Av
Gordon Rd

Loughborough Station
Meadow Lane Industrial Est

A6004
Burder Street
RATCLIFFE RD
Cotes

LOUGHBOROUGH ROAD

A60 NOTTINGHAM ROAD   BARROW ROAD   B676

LOUGHBOROUGH

Cnl Bldg
Annies Wharf

Cotes Road

Railway

2

CLARENCE ST
Industrial Estate
A60
Falcon St
Industrial Estate

LC

Merrin Court

River Soar

3
Cobden Primary School
Empress
QUEEN'S ROAD
Works

Robert Hardy Wharf

Ryecroft Farm

Pinfold Gardens

WHARNCLIFFE RD

Little Moor Lane

Little Moor Lane

Loughborough Mosque
Loughborough Central Stn

Moor Lane

4
Council Bui
P
Police Station
Fairfield School
Victoria Place
Hotel
Elms Gv
Lime Av

Great Central

Windmill Road Industrial Est

9

Moor Lane

Loughborough Moors

103
Beeches

Kg George Rd
Windmill Rd
Kg George St

5
Castend
Extension

LEICESTER
A6004
Whitehouse

Hayward Av
Naylor Av
Cooper Ct

Grand Union Canal

Great Central Railway

SHELTHORPE ROAD

Woodthorpe Road

Wheatland Dr
Witton Av
Avon V
Croome Ct
Whaddon Dr

Hotel

Charnwood Water

Flesh Hovel La

6
Shelthorpe Primary School
Loughborough Cemetery
Loughborough Crematorium

Bull in the Hollow Farm

Lodge Farm

Pilling's Lock

Cemeter

Penny Grove
Ling Av

A6 LOUGHBOROUGH ROAD

7
Shelthorpe

Quorn Lodge Farm

Industrial Estate

Manor Drive
Main Street

A6

Barrow

8
317

Woodthorpe

Loughborough Road

Beacon View Farm

Quorn (Quorndon)

Huntsman's

454 55 56

A B C **112** D E F

Way
Pepper Dr
Alexande
Meynell

The Rawlins Community College

Soar Road

G   H   J   K   L   M

Home Farm

PRESTWOLD LANE

58   B676 LOUGHBOROUGH RD

Brickwood Place

Brook St

PO

Hall Drive

St Philips Cl

St Mary's Cl

Sowters Lane

59   **60**   **21**

Burton on the Wolds Primary School

Towles Fields

Springfield

Nottingham Road

Seymour Road

The Willows

1

Manor Lodge Farm

Barrow Road

2   **20**

Walton Grange

Strandals La

Walton Lane

Cemetery

Loughborough Road

New Lane

School Hi

PO

Poplar Hill

Walton on the Wolds

3

Black Lane

Foxhill Farm

Nottingham Road

4

106

Big

5

Tithe Farm

Lane

Strancliffe

Cream Lodge

Fishpool Brook

Quorn Park

Quorn Pk

Pawdy Lan

6   **18**

Cotes Road

Strancliffe Lane

Willow Rd

Ullswater Av

Birch

Coniston Rd

Elm's Gv

Ash

Fishpool

Nursery

Brook La

Brook La

Pawdy Farm

Humphrey Perkins High School

Thirlmere Road

Grasmere Cl

Ennerdale Road

Nottingham Rd

Babington

Morgans

Heron

Heron

Crebble

Melton Road

7

Beaumont Rd

Wycliffe

Beaumont Av

Woodgate

North St

Ellis Cl

Swan St

Bradcroft

Cave Rd

Newton Cl

Branston Av

Cl

3

Barrowcliffe Close

Cotes Road

The Rockery

Church St

Church Street

Highfields

The Banks

Barrow upon Soar

Road

8

17

Road

Barrow Health Centre

Crossley

High St

PO

Hall Orchard CE Primary School

Beveridge St

New St

Melton Road

London Rd

Lane

Bridge St

South Street

Warner St

Grove terrace

Breachfield Road

Cramps

Holcombe

Barrow-upon-Soar Station

Martin Av

Drive

Cherwell Rd

Avon Rd

Sileby Road

The Pastures

Hayhill

Lane

Slieby Road

River View

Mill Lane

Felland Road

58   **59**   **60**   **317**

57

G   H   J   **113**   K   L   M

A   B   C   98   D   E   F

460   61   62

98

21

I

20

2

Horse Leys
Farm

Seldom Seen

Shuttlewood's
Farm

Top
Farm

Walton
Thorns

Six   Hills   Road

3

Middle Farm

North Farm

Paudy Lane

4

The Lodge

105

Big Lane

Seagrave
Grange

5

Paudy Cross
Roads

Paudy Lane

18

6

Muckle Gate Lane

Green Lane

Berrycott Lane

Seagrave

Green Lane
Close

Water Lane

7

The Orchard

Big Lane

King   Street

Swan   Street

Church St

PO

Seagrave
Primary
School

Cemetery

Quebec
Farm

Seagrave Road

Pond St

Butchers
Lane

Hall Farm

8

317

Park Hill Lane

460   61   62

114

Park Hill
Golf Club

Belle

1 grid square represents 500 metres

G H B676 J 99 K SIX L HILLS M

3 MELTON ROAD 64 B676 65 66 21 20

Old Park
Farm

Six Hills

Paudy Lane

The Oaks
Farm

Wolds
Farm

Ragdale Wolds
Farm

Six Hills Road

Ragdale Hall

Seagrave
Wolds

A46(T)

A46

Bunker Hill
Farm

Charlton Gorse
Farm

19

Main Street

Thrussington
Grange

North Hill
Farm

18

Ox Brook

The Lodge
Farm

Motel

1
2
3
4
5
6
7
8

63 64 65 66 317

G H J 115 K L M

The
Elms

Hilltop

A   B   C   102   D   E   †   F

448   49   50

17

448

Woodhouse Lane

I

Lubcloud
Farm

Longcliffe
Lodge Farm

B591

Nanpantan Road

Wood Brook

16

2

3

Rock
Farm

Bawdon
Lodge

Dean's Lan

4

M1

109

Louella
Stud

*Charnwood
Forest*

Cha

B591

Hill
Farm

Bawdon Castle
Farm

Charley Road

5

6

Hall
Farm

14

M1

7

Bess
Bagley

B591

Ulverscroft
Lodge
Farm

8

313

448

don Drive

A   B   C   116   D   E   F

Whitcroft's Lane

49   50

*Poultney
Wood*

Golf Course

ONGLEBERRY   ROAD

M1

B591

N   an   Res   ir

Oak

G   H   J   103   K   L   M   117

52   53   54

I

2

116

3

Wood

4

112

5

6

114

7

313

8

G   H   J   117   K   L   M

52   53   54

Out Woods

Out Woods Farm

Charnwood Hall

Pocket Gate Farm

Blackbird's Nest

Woodhouse Lane

Brook Road

Brook Road

Brook Road

Golf Course

Breakback Road

Charnwood Forest Golf Club

Beacon Hill Country Park

Beacon Road

Beacon Road

Bird Hill Road

Herrick Rd

Tuckett Rd

Perry Cl

Main St

Windmill St

Paterson Dr

Paterson Dr

Rawlins Cl

Meadow Rd

Woodbrook Vale High School

Park Grange

Spruce Av

Almond Cl

Spindle Rd

Lark Ri

Laburnum Wy

Laburnum

Haddon

Atherstone

Fairmeadows

Lemontr

Juniper Wy

Laurel Road

Magnolia Av

Pine Cl

Honeysuckle Way

Edge Primary School

Beaumanor Hall

Council Building

Beaumanor Drive

May Tree La

Waterloo Spinney

School La

Briscoe Lane

Home Farm Cl

Forest Rd

Forest

Bea Cl

Woodhouse Eaves

Council Building

St Pauls CE Primary School & Community Centre

Leicestershire Round

Brand Lane

Brand Lane

PH

PO

The Dr

Hill Rise

Church Hill

Hastings Rd

Victoria Road

Charnwood Rd

Nannill Dr

Brand Hill

PH Hill

Mill Road

Upper Broombriggs

Maplewell Road

Maplewell Hall School

Joe Moore's Lane

Priory Lane

Benscliffe Road

Lingd Golf C

Golf Course

The Brand

Rensc

Woodthorpe

A   B   C   104   D   Quo(Quorndon) E   F

454   55   55   56

Woodthorpe

Beacon View Farm

Way

A6

Meynell Road

Quo(Quorndon)

Farley   Pepper Dr
Deeming Drive   Alexander
White Street   Barrow St   Thompson Cl   Turner   Seeman Wy
Beardsley Rd   Farnham St   Orchard Cl
Castledine   Swinfield Rd   Brown Av
Mansfield   Soar Road
Disraeli St   St   Freehold
Victoria Rd   Huntsman's
Catherines Cl

Loughborough Road

Woodhouse Road
Warwick Cl
Rumsey Cl   politeney
Woodhouse Avenue   The Sandhills   Silver Birches
St Bartholomews CE Primary School   Sutton Cl   Sanders Rd
Beacon Av   Spinney Dr   Wrights   Street   The Mills   Leicester Rd   Hotel
The Badgers Wk   Cradock Drive   Elms Dr   Meeting   Street   Council Building
Chaveney Dr   Road   Quorn House   Paddock Close
Wyvernhoe Dr
Toller Road   Northage Close
Chestnut Cl   Buddon Lane   Northage Close

The Rawlins Community College
Nursery La   Station   Stoop La   School Lane
Surgery
Leys   Armston Rd   Whall Cl   The Brinks   The Unitt Rd   Wood La   The Coppice   Selvester Dr   Giles Cl

Quorn & Woodhouse Station

Forest Rd

Home Farm Cl
Woodhouse
Vicary Lane

Beaumanor Drive   Beaumanor Gardens

Council Building
May Tree La   Waterloo Spinney
Briscoe Lane

Works

Buddon Wood

Great Central Railway

Leicestershire Round

Rushey Fields Farm

Swithland Reservoir

Rushey Lane

Kinchley Lane

Rothley Plain

Swithland

The Ridings

Main Street

Main street

Main Street

Swithland St Leonard CE Primary School

The Homestead

454   55   56

A   B   C   118   D   E   F

A B C **106** D E F

I

2

3

4

5

6

7

8

17 460   61   62   Park Hill Lane

Park Hill
Golf Club

Golf Course

Belle
Isle

Hanover
Lodge

Highgate
Primary
School

Highgate Farm

Jubilee Avenue

Greedon Rise

Homefield Road

Treedon Rd

Forest Cl

Barrasdale Av

St Mary's Road

Park Road

Seagrave Road

Albert St

Springfield Rd

Heathcote

Collingwood Drive

Weldon
Av

Brosfield

Newfield

Dickens Dr

Lanes
Drive

Ivy Close

Parsons Drive

Barnards
Drive

Stanage
Road

Ainsworth Dr

Redlands
Community
Primary School

Works

Marshall
Av

Rushin Way

Morton Dr

Haybrooke
Road

Wedding Dr

Hanover
Drive

Stuart Cl

Caldy

Caple Cl

Ha Rd

Barrow Road
Business Park

Barrow Road

Herrick

Highbridge

Swan Street

King Street

Back La

Works

PO

PH

Sileby
Station

Surgery

The Banks

Brook St

Ward Cl

St Cot Cl

Avenue Road

Highgate
Drive

Surgery

Wellbrook
Avenue

St Gregory's
Road

Sloper Cl

Finsbury Av

Leicestershire Way

Cncl
Bldg

High St

Works

Manor
Drive

Kendal
Road

Albion Road

Staveley Close

Phoenix St

Butler Way

SILEBY

Cemetery Rd

Cemetery

Peashill Close

Ratcliffe Road

Works

Rosminian Way

Ratcliffe
College

Preston
Close

Cossington Road

Charles Street

Milner
Close

Land Crescent

Kilbourne Rd

Sherrard
Dr

Charles
Street

West Orch

McO

Moynieux

Quaker Rd

Chalfont Drive

LC

Leicestershire Way

Glebe Lodge
Farm

Ratcliffe Road

Humble Lane

A46

PO

Cossington CE
Primary School

Fisher
Close

Homestead Close

Hall Cl

Bennett's Lane

Humble Lane

Blackberry Lane

Home Farm

Wreake House
Farm

River Wreake

Cossington

Main Street

Back Lane

Platts Lane

Middlefield
Road

Syston Road

A607 **SYSTON ROAD**

A607

**COSSINGTON
LANE**

Chestnut Farm

Lewin Bridge

Grange

13 313   460   61   62

A B C **120** D E F

G H J 107 K L M

64 65 66 117

I

2

116

3

4

115

Rearsby

5

Ratcliffe on
the Wreake

6

114

East
Goscote

7

113

8

Thrussington

Hilltop

Works

Motel

The
Elms

Thrussington
Lodge

Hoby Road

Leicestershire Way

Old Gate Road

Seagrave Road

Cleveland
Close

Rupert
Street

Cem

PO

The Green

Blacksmiths
Close

Ferneley
Rise

Back Lane

Church Lane

Church Lane

Works

Ratcliffe Road

Rearsby Road

River Wreake

Spinney Farm

Leicestershire Way

Thrussington
Road

LC

Wreake
Drive

Blackmoor
Close

Station Road

A607

MELTON ROAD

Church Leys
Avenue

station road

Leicestershire Way

LC

Main Street

Church La

Priory Farm

Rearsby House
Farm

Church
Lane

Brook St

Br H Cl

Brookside

PO

Rearsby St Michael &
All Angels CE Primary School

Mill Road

Orton Close

New Avenue

Weston
Close

A607

MELTON ROAD

Gaddesby Lane

Works

Broome Lane

LC

Golf Course

Badger's
Corner

Humsman's
Corner

The
Chase

Countryman's
Way

Squires
Corner

Broome Lane

Wayfarer
Dr

Greensward
Dr

The
Meadows

Grange Avenue

Weston
Close

Wetfield
Close

Beedles Lake
Golf Centre

Industrial
Estate

Long
Ridge

Squire's
Ride

Bracken Dale

Freeman's
Way

Ling Dale

T W

Foxglove
Close

Subedar Ln

Broome Avenue

Honeysuckle
Close

Meadow
View

The Warren

Cramsmans Wy

Woodman's
Chase

Cooper's
Way

Fletcher's
Way

Furrow

T Cr

Broomfield
Primary Sch

Cnl
Bldg

PO

Chestnut
Way

Lilac Wk

Saddlers'
Close

Farriers'
Way

Ploughman's Lea

Keepers'
Croft

Long Furrow

The Warren

A607

New Zealand La

Rearsby Rd

Rupert
Way

M Cl

Ervin
Wy

The Coppice

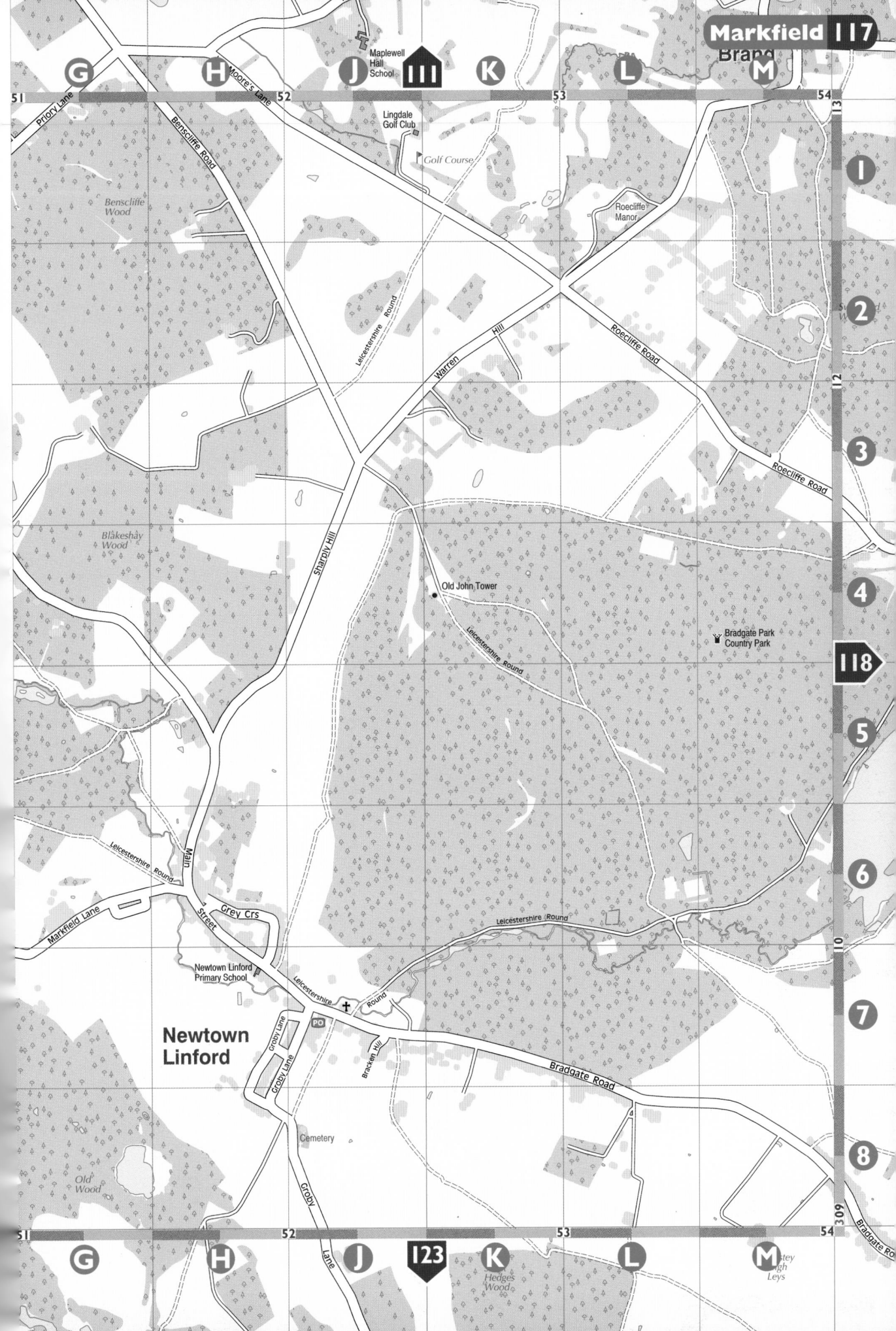

Brand

Maplewell Hall School

Lingdale Golf Club

Golf Course

Roecliffe Manor

Bens, Wood

Bensciffe Wood

Bensciffe Road

Leicestershire Round

Warren Hill

Roecliffe Road

Roecliffe Road

Blakeshay Wood

Sharpley Hill

Old John Tower

Leicestershire Round

Bradgate Park Country Park

118

Leicestershire Round

Main Street

Grey Crs

Leicestershire Round

Markfield Lane

Newtown Linford Primary School

Leicestershire Round

PO

Newtown Linford

Leicestershire Round

Groby Lane

Bracken Hill

Bradgate Road

Groby Lane

Cemetery

Old Wood

Groby Lane

Bradgate Ro

309

123

Hedges Wood

ey gh Leys

G H J K L M

I

2

3

4

5

6

7

8

13

12

11

10

309

51 52 53 54

G H J K L M

Swithland

118

A · Main · Street · B · Main Street · C · nd St Leo
CE Primary Scho · **112** · D · Main Street · E · F

454 55 56

1 · The Homestead

2 · Swithland Wood · Cropston Leys · Rothley Station

3 · Roecliffe Road · Swithland Road · Bybrook Lodge Farm

Bradgate Rd · Bradgate · Road · Station Road · Leicester Road · Lanesborough Close · Lanesboro Dr

4 · Reservoir · Lodge · Sandham Br Rd · Latimer Road · Cemetery · Mill Roa

117 · Guild Cl · Caudle Cl · PO · Stamford Rd · Thistle Cl · Waterfield Rd · Richard Hill CE Primary School · Memorial Hall · Hall Farm · All Saints Rd

Cropston Reservoir · Stamford Drive

5 · Causeway Lane · Lychgate Cl · Ridley · Waterfield Road · **Cropston** · **Thurcaston** · Rectory Lane · Anstey Lane

Cropston Road

6

10

7 · Anstey · Lane · Leicestershire County · City Of Leicester · A46

8 · Woolden Hill CP School · Woolgate · Broadway Furlong · Woodale · Castle Hill Country Park · Cherrybrook · St Mellion Close · Surgery

Martin High School · Netherfield Rd · Balladine Rd · Link Road · Broughton Cl · Charnwood Rd · Kitchener Street · Roseberry Rd · Andrew Road · Charles Drive · Anstey Nomads FC · Kingstear Lodge Rd · Beaumont Lodge Rd · Beaumont Primary Sc

The Close · James St · Dalby Road · Link Road · Forest Gate · Holloway Road · Stadon Road · Highfield St · Woodgon Rd · Princess · Edward Road · Albion Street · George St · Piper Ml · Cropston Rd

A · B · C · **124** · D · E · F

454 55 56 309

Anstey High Leys

Bradgate Rd

Ipswich Cl · Blackthor · Graywood · Sharpley · Phillips · Parkside · Plover Cl · Astill · Harley Cl · Swallowdale · The Poppins · Benmion Road · Linton Rd · Lipton Rd · Smthwaite · Cherryroyd

1 grid square represents 500 metres

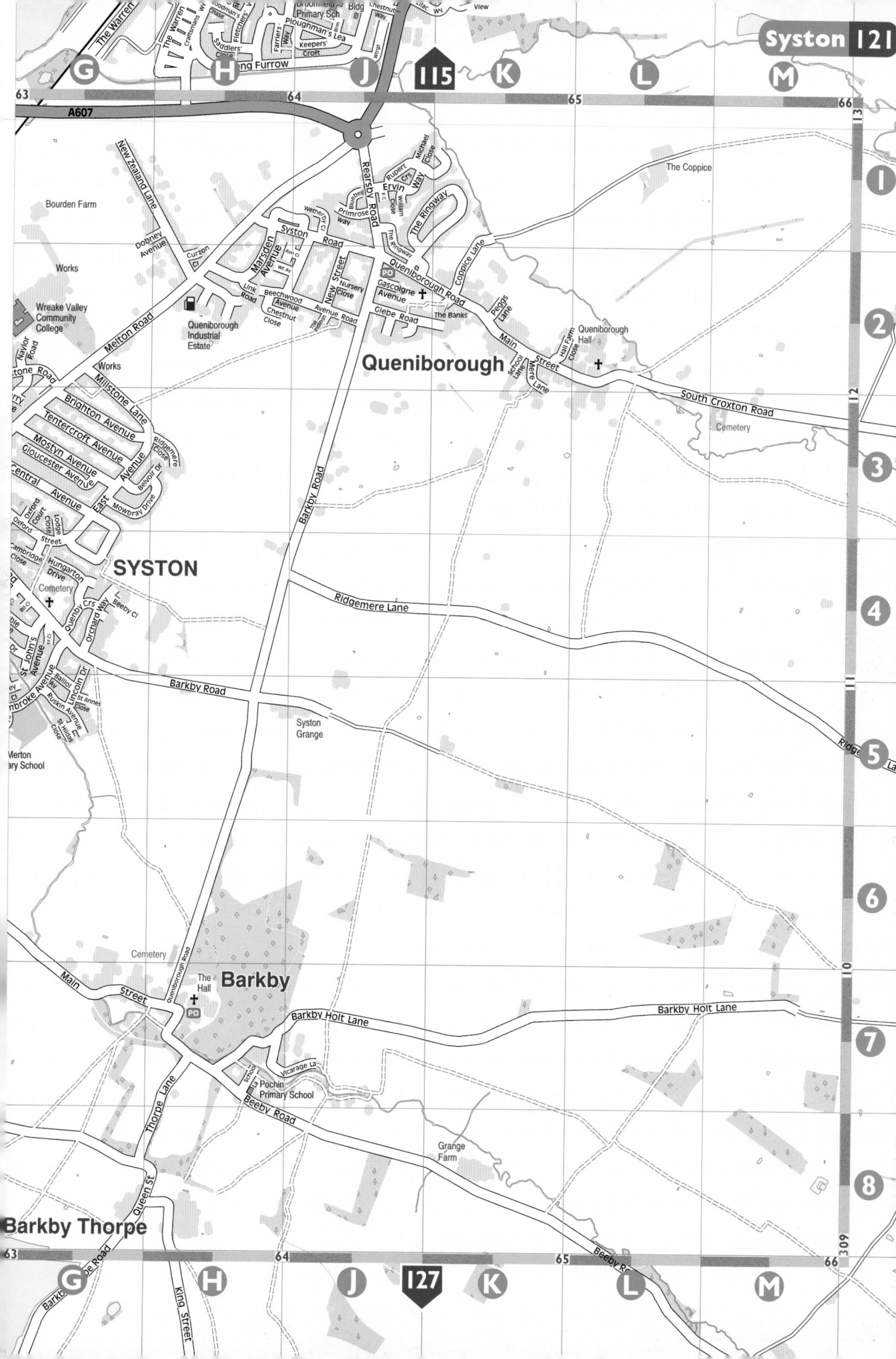

A607

63 64 65 66

G H J **115** K L M

I

2

3

4

5

6

7

8

The Warren
The Warren
Crattnabro W
Sadlers Chase
Fletchers
Farriers Way
Keepers Croft
Ploughman's Lea
ng Furrow
Broomfield Primary Sch
Bldg
Chestnut Way
Lilac Way
View

Bourden Farm

New Zealand Lane
Dobney Avenue
Curzon Cl

Works

Wreake Valley Community College

Works

Melton Road
Naylor Road
Millstone Road

Millstone Lane

Brighton Avenue
Tentercroft Avenue
Mostyn Avenue
Gloucester Avenue
Central Avenue
Oxford Court
Lodge Close
Orford Street
Cambridge Close
Hungarton Drive

SYSTON

Cemetery
Quenby Crs
Beeby Way
Orchard Way
Beeby Cl

Ridgemere Close
Belvoir Dr
Mowbray Drive
Ridgemere Close

Marsden Avenue
Syston Road
Ayn Cl
Wt Av
Link Road
Beechwood Avenue
Chestnut Close
New Street
Nursery Close
Avenue Road
Glebe Road
Rearsby Road
Rupert Crs
Michael Close
William Way
Ervin
Bluebell Close
Primrose Way
Wetherby Cl
The Ringway
The Ringway
Queniborough Road
Gascoigne Avenue
PO
The Banks
Coppice Lane
Pegg's Lane

Queniborough Industrial Estate

Queniborough

Main Street
School Lane
Mere Lane
Hall Farm Close
Queniborough Hall
Queniborough Hall

The Coppice

South Croxton Road

Cemetery

Barkby Road

Ridgemere Lane

Ridge La

Barkby Road
Balliol
St Annes Close
Ruskin Avenue
Lincoln Dr
Lins Cl
Pembroke Avenue
St John's Avenue
St Hildas Close

Merton Primary School

Syston Grange

Cemetery

Main Street
Queniborough Road
The Hall
PO
Barkby

Barkby Holt Lane
Barkby Holt Lane

Thorpe Lane
School La
Vicarage La
Pochin Primary School
Beeby Road

Grange Farm

Barkby Thorpe

Barkby Road
Queen St
King Street
Beeby Rd

63 64 65 66

G H J **127** K L M

309

13
12
10

A   B   C   **116**   D   E   F

448   49   50   BRADGATE

I

2

3

4

5

6

7

8

09
08
07
06
305
448

The Laurels
Birch
Chestnut Walk
The Blossoms
Pinewood Drive

Ratby
Ratby Lane

Thornton Lane

M1

The Oaks

Whittington Grange

Groby Park Farm

Markfield Road

Groby Lodge Farm

New Hayes Farm

Great Wood

Bondman Hays

Markfield Road

Cow Lane

M1

Markfield Lane

Forest Hill Golf Club

Old Hays Farm

Markfield Road

Bevington Cl
Ash Cl

▶ *Golf Course*

Ratby Burroughs

Burroughs   Road

06

Hunts Cl

Kirby Grange

Meadow View   Spinney Drive

Markfield Lane
Borcheston

The Woodlands

Desford Lane
Desford Lane

Road

Botc Aston

Main   Street   errington Cl
Borcheston

A   B   C   **128**   D   E   F

HILL

Bradg House

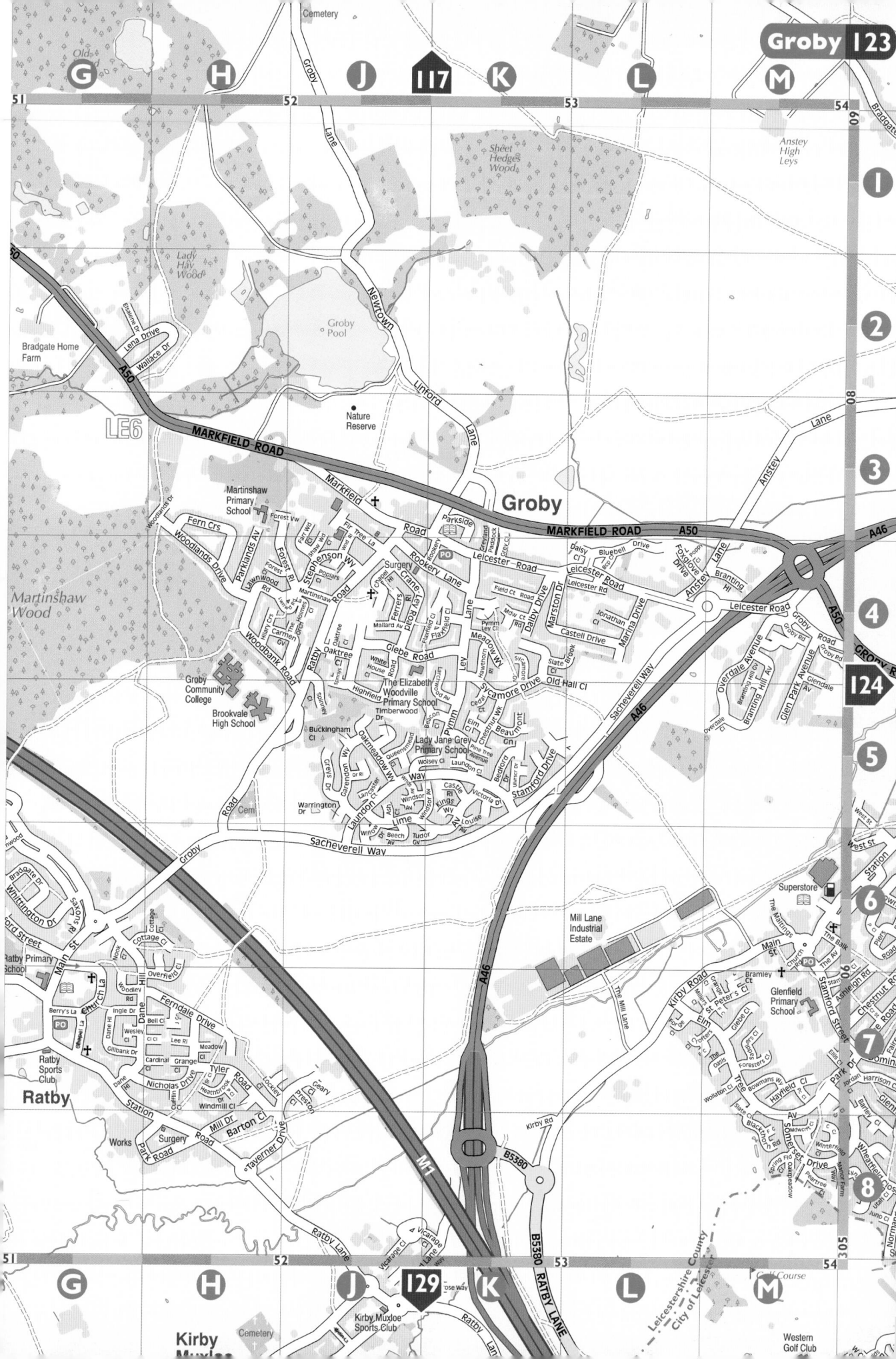

I grid square represents 500 metres

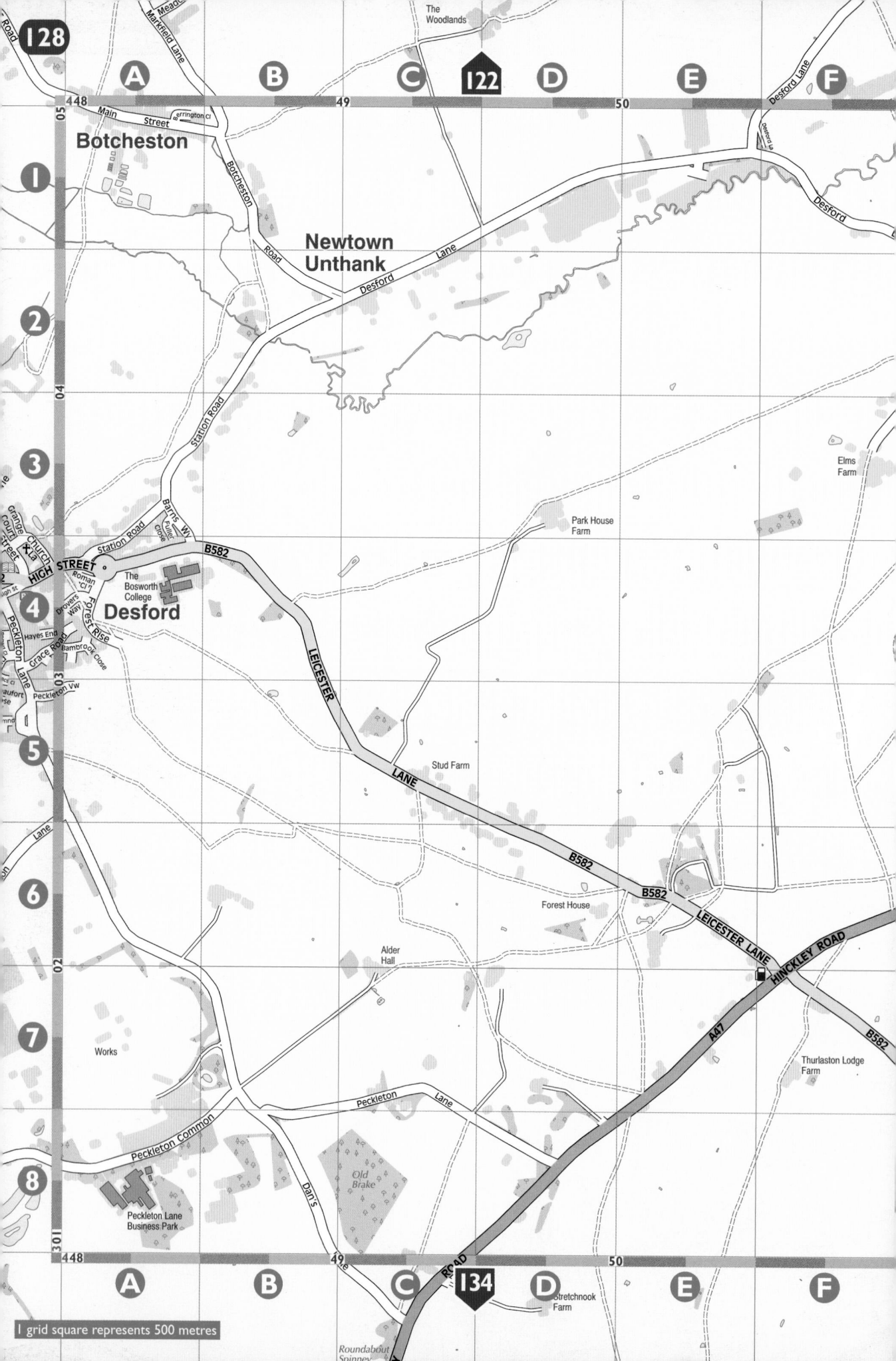

A   B   C   **122**   D   E   F

448   49   50   Desford Lane

Main   Street   Berrington Cl

Botcheston

1

Markfield Lane   Meadow

Botcheston   Road

Newtown Unthank

Desford   Lane   Desford

The Woodlands

2

04   Station Road

Elms Farm

3

Grange Court   Church Street   Barns Wy   Fuller Close

Park House Farm

HIGH STREET   Station Road   B582

The Bosworth College   Roman Cl

Desford   Drovers Way   Forest Rise

4   Peckleton Lane   Hayes End   Bambrook Close   Grace Road   Beaufort Cl   Peckleton Vw

LEICESTER

5   03   Stud Farm

LANE   B582

Lane

6   02   Forest House   B582   LEICESTER LANE   HINCKLEY ROAD

Alder Hall   B582

7   Works   A47   Thurlaston Lodge Farm

Peckleton   Lane

8   Peckleton Common   Dan's   Old Brake

Peckleton Lane Business Park

301   448   49   ROAD   50   Stretchnook Farm

A   B   C   **134**   D   E   F

Roundabout Spinney

G H J **123** K L M

52 53 54

05

Kirby Muxloe

Cemetery

Ratby Lane

Vicarage

Glenfield Lane

Primrose Way

Farley Way

Kirby Muxloe Sports Club

Desford Road

Hedgerow Lane

Barons Cl

The Huntings

Barns Cl

Ladysmith Rd

Pretoria Rd

Arnson Av

Garfit Av

Oakcroft Av

Main Street

Castle Rd

Church Rd

The Keep

Court Cl

Fox Lane

Barwell Rd

Kirby Muxloe Castle

Kirby Muxloe Primary School

Gullet Lane

Links Road

Lime Gv

Lime Gv

Lime Gv

Wishere Cl

Station Road

Princess Drive

Wentworth

Wentworth Gn

Station Cl

Station Dr

Kirby Muxloe Golf Club

Station Road

Station Drive

Towers Drive

Towers Dr

Portland Rd

Roundhill

Holmewood

Hastings Road

Forest Drive

Holt Dr

Rosedene

Stamford Road

Hewitt Dr

Hewitt Dr

Linden Lane

Walton

The Fairway

Kirby Fields

Beechwood Av

Kirby Lane

Priory Walk

Charnwood Dr

Charnwood

Rutland

Hotel

Ratby Lane

Junction 21a

B5380 Ratby Lane

Ratby Lane

Leicestershire County
City of Leicester

Golf Course

I 1

Western Golf Club

Scudamore Road

Wanstead Industrial Park

Wanstead Road

Wembley Road

Elland Rd

Carlow Service Centre

Braunstone Frith Industrial Estate

Murray

Road

Sunningdale

Sunning Industria Park

2

3

Packer Avenue

Churchill

Bignal Dr

Brightwell

Elliott Dr

Sylvan

PO

Surgery

Walsingham

Crs

Wardens

Holmfield Av

Park Drive

Batnes

4

130

Oaks Farm

Golf Course

Barry Cl

Mavrose Cl

Barry Cl

Cherry Tree Av

Avenue

Martin Av

Ellis Dr

Forest Rise

Stafford Leys

Boyers Wk

Kirloe Av

Regents

Rushmere Wk

Acres Rd

Kings Wk

Queens Dr

Kings Drive

South Av

Holmfield Primary School

Kings Wk

Chapel Gn

Kennedy Way

Hobill Close

Chapel Green

Baines La

Hotel

5

Shepherd Cl

Harene Crs

Mavtree Drive

Highland

Hawthorn

Pine Tree Gv

Valiean Crs

Barbara

Brickman Lane

Blue Pots Cl

Alder

Haven

St David's Cl

Seymour

Medical Cen

Stafford

Somerfield

Leys Community Primary School

Birchwood Cl

Galahad

Merlin

Lowland Av

Kings Wk

Lancelot

Leicester Forest East

Leicester Ivanhoe CC

Leicester

Brickman Lane

Pleasant Close

Kingcup Cl

Acacia Cl

Rose

Acacia Way

Pendragon Wy

Excalibur

Guinevere Wy

Tristram Cl

Leicester Forest East Service Area

Kingstand Farm

HINCKLEY ROAD

A47

Warren

Beggar's Lane

Mallard Wy

Woodpecker

Swallo

Lark

Carnation Cl

House

Teal Cl

Copse

Forest

Yew Close

Harvester Cl

Harrow

Old Warren Farm

6

DESFORD ROAD

Lawn Farm

Beggar's Lane

Enderby Lodge

Beggar's Lane

New House Farm

02

301

7

8

Huncote Grange

Hoefields

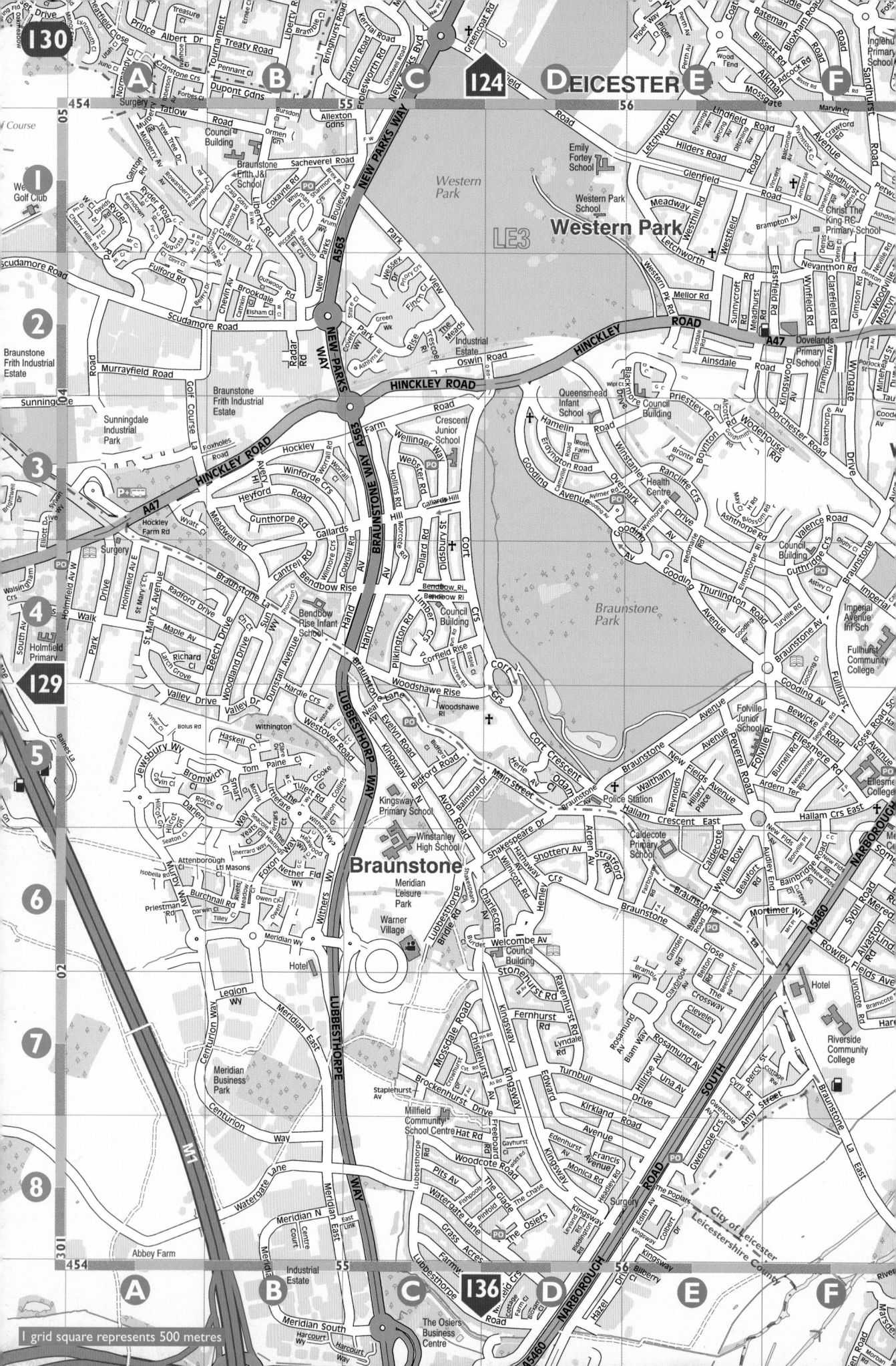

G H J **127** K L M

I

Bushby

2

Thurnby

3

4

5

6

Stoughton

7

Oadby

8

Great

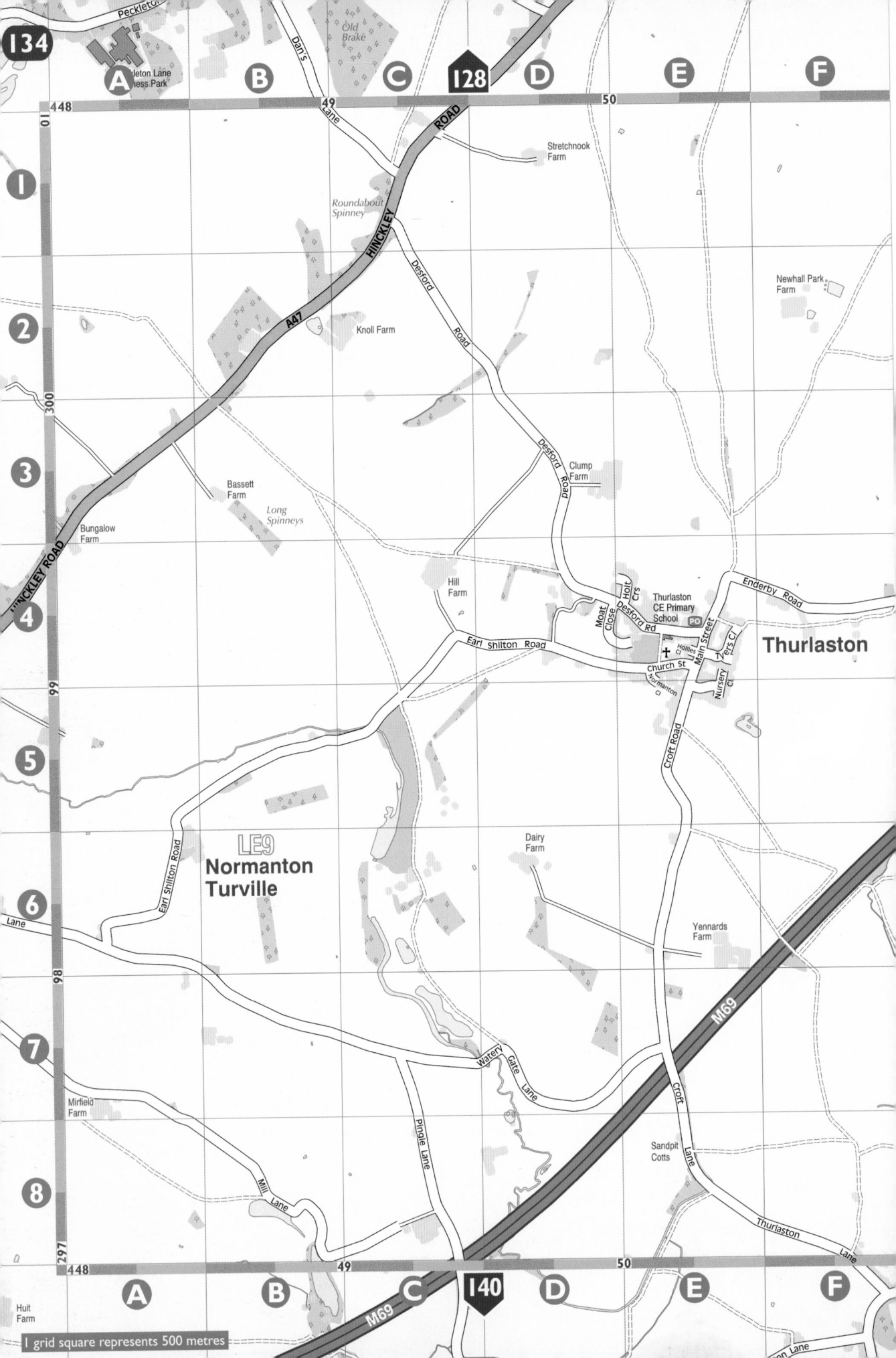

A · B · C · **128** · D · E · F

010
448
49 Lane
50
Peckleton
...deton Lane
...ness Park
Dan's

Old Brake

Stretchnook Farm

HINCKLEY ROAD

I

Roundabout Spinney

Newhall Park Farm

2

A47

Knoll Farm

Desford Road

300

3

Bassett Farm

Long Spinneys

Clump Farm

Desford Road

HINCKLEY ROAD

99

4

Bungalow Farm

Hill Farm

Earl Shilton Road

Moat Close
Holt Cl's
Desford Rd
Thurlaston CE Primary School
PO
Hollies Cl
Church St
Normanton Cl
Main Street
...yers Cl
Nursery Cl
Enderby Road

Thurlaston

5

Earl Shilton Road

Dairy Farm

Croft Road

98

6

Lane

LE9
Normanton Turville

Yennards Farm

M69

7

Mirfield Farm

Watery Gate Lane

Croft Lane

297

8

Mill Lane

Pingle Lane

Sandpit Cotts

Thurlaston Lane

448
49
140
50

Huit Farm

M69

...on Lane

I grid square represents 500 metres

G H J 129 K L M

52 53 54

Huncote Grange

Hoefields Farm

B582

DESFORD ROAD

Beggar's Lane

I

B582

MILL HILL

M69

Feldspar Cl

Warren Park Way

Harolds Lane

2

The Park

3

Forest Road

Thurlaston Lane

Works

Granite Cl

Mill Hill Industrial Est

Quarry La

Fcrones Cl

Moores La

Conwy Cl

Chapel St

High St

HALL WALK

Leicester Lane

Enderby

4

Cook's Lodge

Seine Lane

Enderby Road

Capers

Pope Crs

Drummond Rd

Sloane Cl

Gray

Blake Cl

Carter Rd

Jarrett

Adullie Ave

Mitchell

Alexander Av

Brook St

Broad St

Works

B582

Leisure Cen

PO

King St

Kng St

BLABY

136

Hardwicke Lodge Farm

Coleridge Drive

Herrick

Keats Cl

Sherdan

Shelley Rd

Equity Road

Jacob Cl

George St

John St

Rawson

Holyoake St

Mill Lane

Salt's Clsg

Danemill Primary Sch

Leisure Centre

Brockington College

5

The Pastures Primary School

Thornhills

Meadow Edge

Th

Kiplin Drive

Colerdge

Forest Road

Sourney Cl

West Street

Surg

The Rise

Ende Golf

Golf Course

Radnor Cl

Stainmore Av

Kielder Cl

Grizedale

GV

Meiller Cl

Camelot Wy

Stewart Av

6

Hemlock Close

Broom Wy

Ashlands

The Pastures

Buttercup

Milton

Browning St

Boswell St

Forest Rd

Woodland

Council Building

Pimpernel Cl

Speedwell Cl

Jasmine

Meadow Wy

Orchid Cl

Chaucer St

Tennyson St

Burns

KING EDWARD

Council Building

Narborough

Copt Oak Road

Alyssum Wy

Hornbeam Rd

Honeytop Cl

Pimro'n

The Pastures

Teasel Cl

Foxglove

Clove

Woodlands Day Hospital

Holland

7

G Sch

Hlth Cen

Cncl Bldgs

B4114

Red Hill

Marigold Wy

Hardwicke

Copt Oak Road

Red Hill Av

Langham Drive

Desford Rd

Canons

Huncote Cem

Huncote Leisure Centre

Sports Fld

Denman Rd

Langley Cl

Critchlow Rd

Hobill Cl

Bennett Rd

Huncote Community Primary Sch

Lodge Cl

Compton Dr

Cooper Cl

Woodside Cl

Greenhill

Blk Cl

Hillberry

Squire

Coltbeck Avenue

The Coppice

Callan

Homer

Woodhouse

Cutters Close

Park Road

Brief's

Coventry Rd

Cornfield

Cncl Bldgs

Church

8

Duncan

St James Cl

Charity Cl

Mill Cl

Eaney Cl

PO

The Gn

School Rd

Fitchley

Narborough Rd

Carey Drive

Ratcliffe

Main St

Brook Street

Huncote Road

Huncote Road

Works

Elms Farm

Finch Wy

Linnete Oaks Industrial Est

Acan Wy

Burrows Close

Mortimer Road

Thurlaston Brook

Huncote

52 53 54

South Knighton

132

I grid square represents 500 metres

134

A   B   C   D   E   F

448   49   50

97

M69

I

Huit
Farm

2

Thorney Fields
Farm

96

Potters
Marston

Works

Stanton Lane

Pingle Lane

3

Huncote Road

Stanton Lane

Cotts

Thurlaston
Lane

Marston Rd

Cem

Huncote Road

4

B581

Cadles
Close

Achurch
Close

Mays Farm Drive

Knights
Close

Ellson CI

Jms Str

George Hill
Close

Wgh Cl

Highfield

Huncote Road

The Fleet

John Bold Avenue

F R

M B C

Foxbank
Industrial
Estate

Works

Meadow
Close

Clint Hill Drive

Oak Lodge
Farm

95

5

Fisher
Close

Smithy Farm

Peter's
Close

Tansey
Crescent

Farndon Drive

Manorfield
CE Primary Sch

Surgery

Cem

Nock Verges

Church
Street

Long Street

Middleton
Close

Webbs
Way

New Road

PO

The
Oval

The Orch

Sapcote Road

South Drive

**Stoney
Stanton**

Port Hill
Farm

Broughton Road

6

George Mariott
Close

Hinckley   Road

Underwood
Close

Townsend

Carey   Hill   Road

Shadrack
Drive

Pixley

Martin
Drive

Howe
Close

Journey

Johnson Rise

Surgery

Lanes Hill
Grove

Road

Stoney
Cove

B581

94

7

Stanton   Lane

Road

Hinckley
Road

Frewen
Drive

Spa
Drive

Spa
Drive

Penfold

a c c

Stanton   Road

Buckwell Rd

Mnr Est

Sapcote   Road

Harecroft   Crescent

Underwood
Cres

Grace   Road

Stanton
Lodge

Coventry   Road

8

Livesey
Drive

Park   Road

Nevills
Smith
Close

Castle
Close

Church   St

A S C

Bassett Lane

Kirby
Close

Hucky
Close

PO

Mill
Close

Cook's Lane

Pougher
Close

Sharnfor

Wesley Cl

New Walk

Morley
Rd

Calver
Crescent

B4669   Leicester   Road

Sapcote

Brown's
Close

Works

Coventry Rd

All Saints CE
Primary School

Cem

293

448   49   50

A   B   C   D   E   F

B4114

1 grid square represents 500 metres

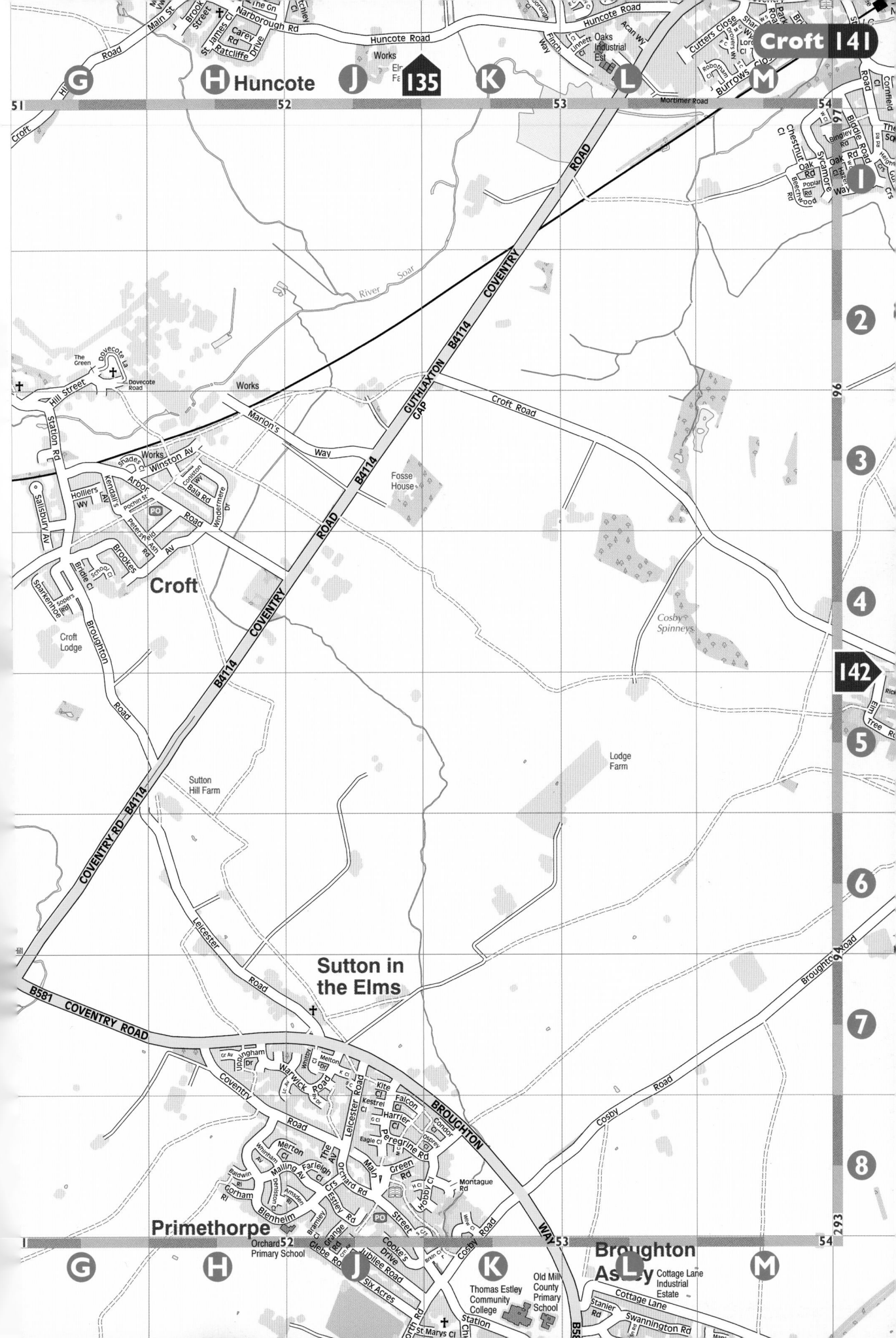

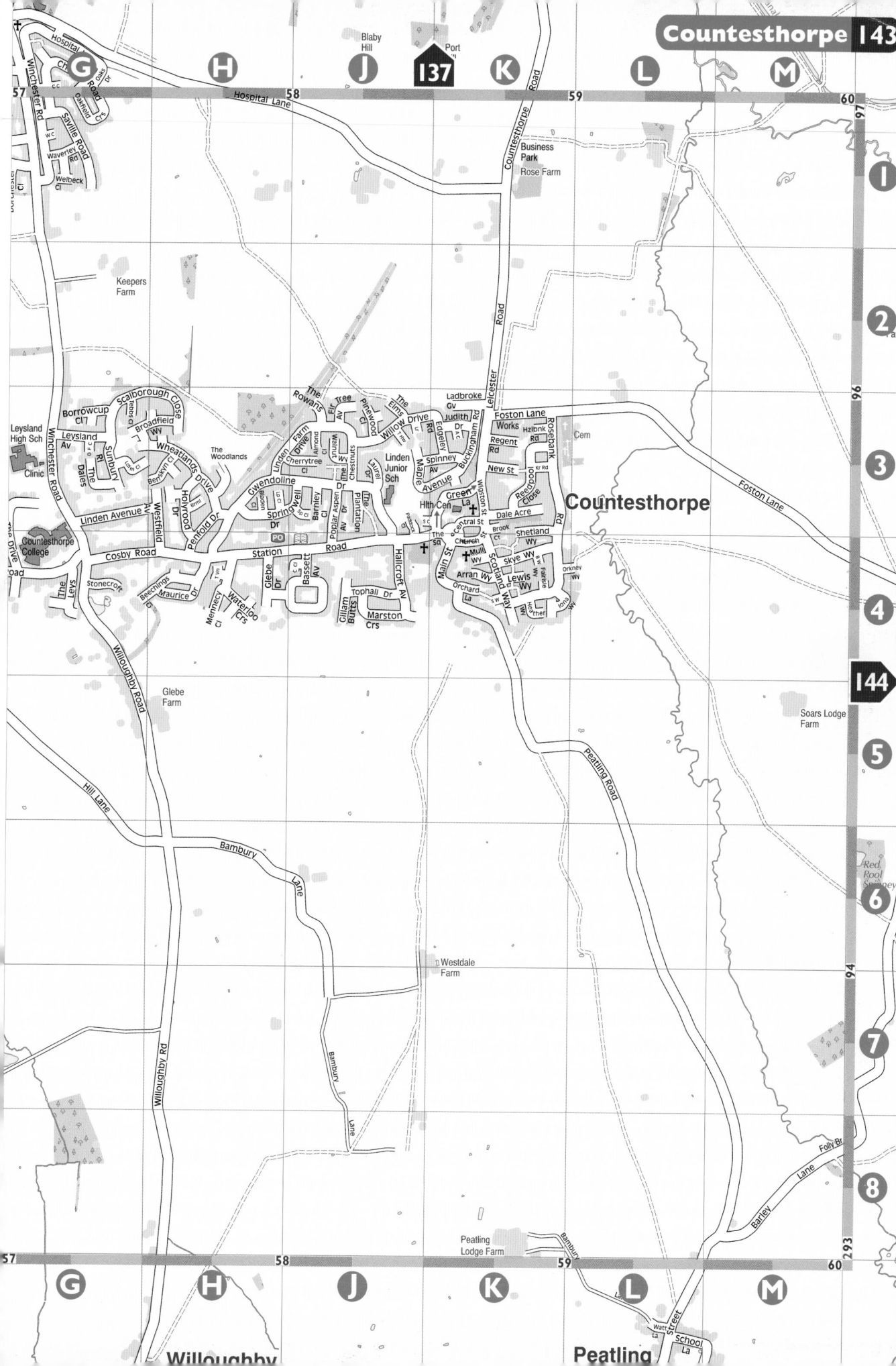

Port

Blaby Hill

Hospital Lane

58

59

60

Hospital Road

CR
CC

Oaks Dr

57

Winchester Rd

Saville Road

Oakfield Crs

Waverley Rd

WC

Welbeck Cl

Business Park

Rose Farm

Countesthorpe Road

Leicester Road

I

2

97

96

Keepers Farm

Leysland High Sch

Clinic

Borrowcup Cl

Scalborough Close

Broadfield Wy

Leysland Av

Sunbury

The Dales

Berwyn Cl

Wheatlands Drive

The Rowans

Linden Farm Drive

Fir Tree Av

Pinewood

The Elms

Willow Drive

Ladbroke Gv

Judith Dr

Foston Lane

Works

Hzlbnk

Regent Rd

Rosebank Rd

Cem

Foston Lane

3

Winchester Road

Holyrood Dr

Gwendoline Dr

Springwell

Cherrytree Cl

Chestnuts

Laurel Dr

Linden Junior Sch

Edgeley Rd

Spinney Av

Buckingham Rd

New St

Redpool Close

kr Rd

Countesthorpe

Countesthorpe College

Linden Avenue

Westfield

Penfold Dr

Barnley Cl

Poplar Aspen Av

The Plantation

Maple Avenue

Green

Hlth Cen

La

Dale Acre

Shetland Wy

The Sq

Woston St

Cosby Road

Station Road

Hallcroft Av

Main St

Church

Mull Wy

Skye Wy

Scotland Wy

Fairisle

Orkney Wy

4

Road

Stonecroft

Beechings

Maurice Dr

Mennecy Cl

Waterloo Crs

Gillam Butts

Glebe Dr

Bassett Av

Tophall Dr

Marston Crs

Central St

Arran Wy

Orchard La

Lewis Wy

Heather

Iona Wy

144

Glebe Farm

Willoughby Road

Soars Lodge Farm

5

Hill Lane

Bambury Lane

Peatling Road

Red Pool Spinney

6

94

Willoughby Rd

Bambury Lane

Westdale Farm

7

Folly Br

Barkby Lane

School La

8

293

57

58

59

60

Willoughby

Peatling

Peatling Lodge Farm

Bambury

Watt Street

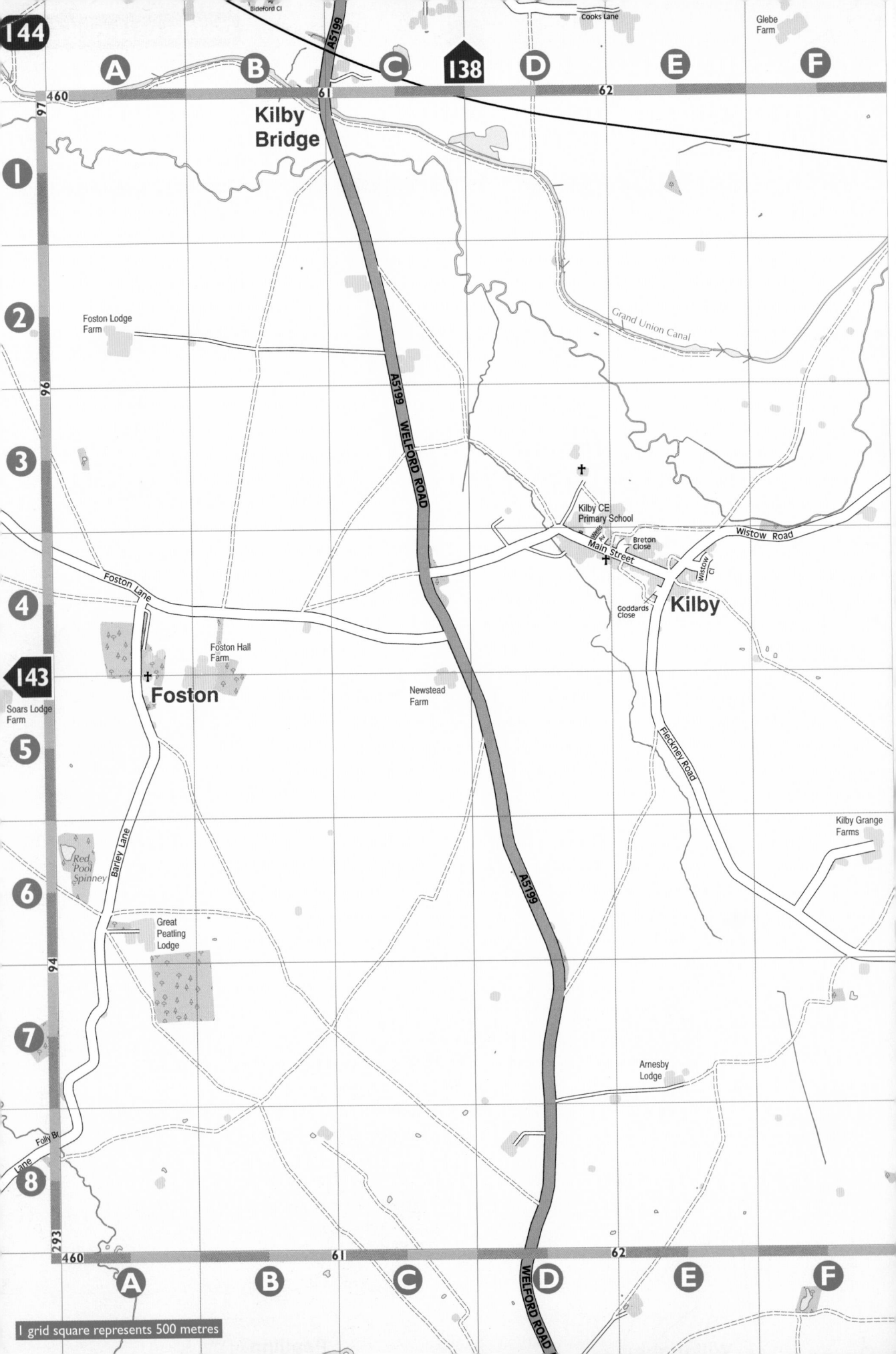

146

A · B · C · D · E · F

466
97
A6

1 · Stoneygate School

2 · Burton Lodge Farm · Burton Brook Farm

3

4

145

5 · Kibworth Bridge · Wistow Road · Westfield

Kibworth Harcourt

6 · Warwick Road · Hillcrest Avenue · Kibworth CE Primary School · The Leys · The Tithings · St Wilfrid's Close · Rectory Lane · The Lea · Cemetery

7 · Fleckney Road · Cricket Club · Gladstone St · Palmerston Cl · Peel · Dover Street · White Street · Prospect Road · Meadowbrook Rd · Elliot Cl · School Walk · Kibworth High Sch · School Rd · High Street · Surgery · Works · Rookery Cl · Brookfield Way · Larkswood · New Road · Links Road · Fairway

8 · Kibworth Road · Mill Lane · Smeeton Road · Health Morrison Court · Council Building · Springfield Crescent · Wentworth Close · Granary Close · Kibworth Golf Club · Kibw Beau

293
94
466 · 67 · 68

A · B · C · D · E · F

Mains Lane · Leicester Road · Main St · Albert St · Langton Road · Marsh Dr · Windmill Gdns · Marsh Avenue · Rochester Close · Hall Cl · Merton Way · Church Road · Carlton Road

Mill St · Bic La · Debdale Lane · Springfield Lane · Beaker Close · Saddington Road · Smeeton

The Paddocks Farm

1 grid square represents 500 metres

Carlton
Curlieu

Grange Road

Grange Rd

Kibworth Road

Mere Road

Kibworth Road

Kibworth
Hall

Sheepthorns
Spinney

Kibworth Road

Kibworth Road

Shangton

Main Street

The Hall

MELTON ROAD

B6047

Mere Road

SHANGTON ROAD

B6047

The Manor

Main Street

PO

PH

Cranoe Road

Tur
Langton

B6047

MELTON ROAD

HARBOROUGH ROAD

tive

West Langton Road

Golf Course

rth
hamp

Church
Langton

Langton
Hall

West Langton Road

G   H   J   K   L   M

70   71   72

97

1

2

96

3

4

95

5

6

94

7

293

8

Adbolton	51	M5
Agar Nook	108	F6
Aldercar	20	D3
Allenton	72	A3
Allestree	43	K4
Alma	13	L2
Alvaston	58	F8
Ambaston	74	A1
Anstey	124	C1
Arnold	25	L8
Aspley	35	M7
Aston-on-Trent	73	M7
Attenborough	63	J5
Awsworth	34	A3
Aylestone	137	H1
Aylestone Park	131	J8
Babbington	34	C3
Bagthorpe	13	K4
Bargate	18	A6
Barkby	121	H7
Barkby Thorpe	120	F8
Barrows Green	13	G2
Barrow upon Soar	105	J8
Barton in Fabis	77	J1
Bassingfield	52	E8
Beaumont Leys	124	F3
Beauvale	15	H8
Beauvale	22	A4
Beeston	49	G8
Belgrave	125	K6
Belper	17	M2
Belton	100	E2
Bestwood	24	E8
Bestwood Village	24	D2
Bilborough	35	J8
Birstall	119	L8
Blaby	136	F8
Blackbrook	16	F2
Bogend	22	D5
Bondman Hays	122	B4
Boothgate	10	C8
Borrowash	59	M5
Botcheston	128	A1
Boulton	72	E1
Boulton Moor	72	E4
Bradmore	79	K4
Bramcote Hills	49	H5
The Brand	111	M8
Braunstone	130	C6
Breadsall	44	C3
Breadsall Hilltop	44	B6
Breaston	61	G7
Brinsley	13	J8
Brook Hill	64	E7
Broomhill	23	M2
Broxtowe	35	K5
Bulcote	39	L1
Bullbridge	10	A2
Bulwell	23	L8
Bulwell Forest	24	B7
Bunny	79	J8
Bunny Hill	89	H2
Burnaston	69	K2
Burton Joyce	39	L3
Burton on the Wolds	97	J8
Bushby	133	M2
Butler's Hill	24	B2
Butterley	11	J4
Carlton	38	A6
Carrington	36	E6
Castle Donington	85	G5
Cavendish Bridge	75	G7
Chaddesden	44	D7
Chellaston	72	E6
Cherrytree Hill	58	E2
Chilwell	63	H1
Church Langton	147	M8
Church Wilne	74	F3
Cinderhill	18	B5
Cinderhill	35	L3
Clarendon Park	131	L6
Clifton	64	E5
Clipston	67	H6
Coalville	108	B8
Codnor	12	A8
Codnor Breach	19	L3
Codnor Gate	11	M6
Codnor Park	12	D4
Colwick	52	D2
Common Side	20	C7
Copt Oak	116	A1
Cosby	142	A4
Cossall	34	A6
Cossall Marsh	34	A5
Cossington	114	A7
Costock	89	H5
Cotes	104	D1
Cotgrave	67	M5
Cotmanhay	33	J3
Countesthorpe	143	K3
Cowers Lane	16	B4
Cowhill	17	L5
Crewton	58	D7
Croft	141	H4
Cropston	118	D5
Cross Hill	20	A1
Crown Hills	132	E2
Cumberhills Cottages	28	E6
Dalbury	54	F6
Dale Abbey	46	D5
Dale Moor	46	F5
Darley Abbey	43	L5
Daybrook	25	H8
Denby	19	G6
Denby Bottles	18	E6
Denby Common	19	L4
Derby	2	E5
Desford	128	A4
Diseworth	93	H1
Dishley	102	F1
Dorket Head	25	L3
Dove Green	13	J1
Draycott	60	D8
Drum Hill	30	D6
Duffield	29	J4
Duffieldbank	29	L3
Dunkirk	50	B5
East Goscote	115	J7
East Leake	88	C5
Eastwood	21	J4
Eaton Hill	30	A6
Edwalton	65	L4
Egginton Common	69	G8
Elvaston	73	L2
Enderby	135	M4
Epperstone	27	L2
Etwall	68	F3
Evington	132	E5
Eyres Monsell	137	H4
Far Laund	18	A1
Farnah Green	17	G4
Field Head	116	D7
Findern	70	B5
Flaxholme	29	K6
Fleckney	145	L7
The Flourish	46	B5
Foston	144	A1
Friezeland	13	M5
Gallows Inn	47	M1
Gamston	52	B8
Gedling	38	D5
Giltbrook	22	A7
Glenfield	124	A7
Glen Parva	136	F6
Golden Valley	12	A4
Gotham	77	M6
Greasley	22	C4
Great Stretton	139	L1
Great Wilne	74	F5
Greenhill	108	E7
Greenhillocks	11	J7
Groby	123	K3
Gun Hills	28	B2
The Gutter	18	A3
Hallam Fields	47	L3
Hathern	94	F6
Hammersmith	11	H3
Hazelgrove	23	L2
Hazelwood	16	F6
Heage	10	C6
Heanor	20	D4
Heanor Gate	20	A7
Heatherton	56	D7
Hemington	85	H2
Hempshill Vale	35	K2
Highbury Vale	36	A1
Highfields	7	J8
Hillcross	56	F8
Hill Top	21	M5
Hilton	68	B5
Holbrook	30	B1
Holbrook Moor	17	M8
Holme Lane	52	E7
Holme Pierrepont	52	F4
The Holmes	3	H4
Horsley Woodhouse	31	G1
Hoton	97	H5
Hucknall	15	H7
Humberstone	126	D8
Huncote	135	H8
Ilkeston	33	H5
Ironville	12	C3
Isley Walton	84	B8
Jacksdale	12	F4
Kedleston	28	A8
Kegworth	86	C5
Keyworth	80	E4
Kibworth Beauchamp	146	F8
Kibworth Harcourt	146	F5
Kilburn	18	E7
Kilby	144	E4
Kilby Bridge	144	B1
Kimberley	34	C1
King's Mills	83	L3
King's Newton	83	G6
Kingston on Soar	86	F3
Kirby Fields	129	K2
Kirby Grange	122	A7
Kirby Muxloe	129	H1
Kirk Hallam	47	G2
Kirk Langley	41	J5
Knighton	131	M8
Knighton Fields	131	K6
Lambley	27	G8
Langley	20	F5
Langley Common	41	M7
Langley Green	41	H6
Langley Mill	20	F4
Larklands	33	L8
Lees	40	F8
Leicester	6	F6
Leicester Forest East	129	L5
Lenton	4	A8
Lenton	50	E4
Lenton Abbey	49	K6
Linby	15	L4
Litchurch	3	J8
Little Chester	43	L8
Little Eaton	30	A7
Little Hallam	47	J1
Littleover	56	E7
Littlethorpe	142	A1
Lockington	85	K3
Long Eaton	62	A8
Longlane	40	C6
Long Whatton	93	M4
Loscoe	20	B3
Loughborough	8	F5
Lowdham Grange	27	K4
Lower Hartshay	10	D4
Lower Kilburn	18	D8
Mackworth	42	C8
Makeney	29	L1
Manor Park	64	F8
Mapperley	32	D4
Mapperley	37	J4
Mapperley Park	37	G6
Marehay	19	H1
Markeaton	42	F7
Markfield	116	A6
Marlpool	20	D7
Meadows	51	G5
Melbourne	82	C8
Mickleover	56	B5
Milford	17	L8
Moorgreen	22	B3
Moravian Settlement	59	M3
Morley	45	G1
Morleymoor	30	F8
Morley Park	18	E1
Morley Smithy	31	H7
Mount Pleasant	17	H1
Mowmacre Hill	125	J2
Nanpantan	102	F8
Narborough	135	J7
Nether Burrows	40	F4
Netherfield	38	F8
Nether Hall	127	H5
Nether Heage	10	B5
New Basford	36	D6
New Brinsley	13	J6
New Eastwood	21	K7
New Kingston	87	G1
Newlands	20	E6
New Parks	124	D8
New Sawley	75	M2
New Stanton	47	J4
Newstead	15	J1
New Swannington	108	B3
Newthorpe	22	A6
Newthorpe Common	22	A8
Newton Harcourt	145	J1
Newtown Linford	117	H7
Newtown Unthank	128	B1
Normanton	57	H8
Normanton on Soar	95	H4
Normanton-on-the-Wolds	80	E1
Normanton Turville	134	B6
North End	113	H3
North Evington	132	C1
Nottingham	4	D2
Nuthall	35	G2
Oadby	133	G8
Oaks in Charnwood	109	K2
The Oaks	29	H1
Oakwood	44	E6
Ockbrook	60	B2
Old Basford	36	C3
Openwoodgate	18	B4
Osgathorpe	100	B3
Osleston	54	B1
Osmaston	58	B8
Over Burrows	40	E3
Park Nook	28	E7
Pear Tree	57	C1
Peasehill	11	K7
Pentrich	10	F2
Plain Spot	13	J5
Plumtree	80	D1
Plumtree Park	80	C2
Porchester	37	M5
Potters Marston	140	D2
Prestwold	97	G7
Pride Park	58	C3
Primethorpe	141	H8
Pye Hill	12	E2
Quarndon	29	G8
Quarndon Common	29	H7
Queniborough	121	J2
Quorn	104	E8
Radbourne	55	H2
Radcliffe on Trent	53	J3
Radford	50	B2
Ratby	123	G7
Ratcliffe on Soar	86	C1
Ratcliffe on the Wreake	115	G6
Rawson Green	18	D5
Rearsby	115	K5
Redhill	25	J6
Red Hill	135	L7
Rempstone	97	H2
Riddings	12	B1
Ringing Hill	101	G6
Ripley	11	K5
Rise Park	24	C5
Risley	61	J3
Rose Hill	3	G9
Rothley	113	J8
Rothley Plain	112	F7
Ruddington	79	H1
Ruffs	23	J2
Rushey Mead	126	C3
Rylands	64	A2
St Ann's	5	K3
St Luke's	2	B5
Sandiacre	61	L1
Sapcote	140	C7
Sawley	75	K3
Scotches	17	J1
Scraptoft	127	J7
Seagrave	106	C5
Selston Common	13	L1
Shacklecross	60	B6
Shangton	147	L2
Shardlow	74	C5
Shelthorpe	104	A7
Shelton Lock	72	B4
Shepshed	101	L3
Sherwood	36	F4
Shipley	20	E8
Shipley Common	33	H4
Shottlegate	16	E4
Sileby	114	B4
Sinfin	71	J4
Six Hills	107	K1
Smalley	31	K2
Smalley Common	31	L5
Smalley Green	31	K4
Smithy Houses	18	F4
South End	113	J4
South Knighton	132	B8
South Wigston	137	K6
Spondon	59	L2
Spring Hill	29	H2
Stanford Hills	96	B3
Stanford on Soar	96	A6
Stanley	46	A1
Stanley Common	31	L7
Stanton by Bridge	82	B4
Stanton-by-Dale	47	J7
Stanton Gate	48	A7
Stanton-on-the-Wolds	81	G5
Stapleford	48	C8
Stenson	70	E7
Stocking Farm	125	H4
Stoke Bardolph	39	J7
Stoneyford	12	E8
Stoneygate	132	B6
Stoney Stanton	140	F5
Stoughton	133	H6
Street Lane	18	F2
Strelley	35	G7
Sunny Hill	71	H2
Sutton Bonington	95	G1
Sutton in the Elms	141	J7
Swanwick	11	J1
Swarkestone	82	C1
Swingate	34	E3
Swithland	112	B8
Syston	121	G4
Thorneywood	37	L7
Thorpe Acre	103	C2
Thorpe in the Glebe	90	B6
Thringstone	100	C8
Thrumpton	77	G4
Thrussington	115	J3
Thulston	73	L3
Thurcaston	118	E5
Thurlaston	134	F4
Thurmaston	120	E8
Thurnby	133	J3
Thurvaston	40	A7
Tollerton	66	B6
Top Valley	24	E7
Toton	62	E5
Trentlock	76	C4
Trowell	48	A4
Trusley	54	D4
Tur Langton	147	L6
Underwood	13	K5
Upper Hartshay	10	E5
Waingroves	11	L8
Walton on the Wolds	105	M3
Wanlip	120	A5
Watnall	22	E7
West Bridgford	65	C1
Westcotes	130	F3
West End	100	A4
Western Park	130	D1
West Hallam	32	D7
West Leake	87	K6
Weston-on-Trent	83	K2
Westville	23	J3
Westwood	13	H4
Whetstone	136	C8
White Moor	18	A2
Whitemoor	36	B6
Whitwick	108	E2
Widmerpool	90	F7
Wigston	138	A4
Wigston Magna	138	D5
Wilford	50	F8
Willoughby-on-the-Wolds	91	G7
Wilsthorpe	61	L7
Windley	16	B8
Wistow	145	H3
Wollaton	49	J3
Woodborough	27	H3
Woodhouse	112	A4
Woodhouse Eaves	111	L5
The Woodlands	145	L1
Woodlinkin	20	B1
Woodside	31	H3
Woodthorpe	37	J3
Woodthorpe	104	A8
Wymeswold	98	B4
Wysall	90	B4
Zouch	94	B4

USING THE STREET INDEX

Street names are listed alphabetically. Each street name is followed by its postal town or area locality, the Postcode District, the page number, and the reference to the square in which the name is found.

Standard index entries are shown as follows:

Aaron Cl *CFTN/RUD* NG11 ....**50** F8

Street names and selected addresses not shown on the map due to scale restrictions are shown in the index with an asterisk.

Aeneas Ct *MAPPK/POR/STA* * NG3........**36** F7

GENERAL ABBREVIATIONS

ACC	ACCESS	CH	CHURCH	CRS	CRESCENT	EST	ESTATE	GLN	GLEN
ALY	ALLEY	CHA	CHASE	CSWY	CAUSEWAY	EX	EXCHANGE	GN	GREEN
AP	APPROACH	CHYD	CHURCHYARD	CT	COURT	EXPY	EXPRESSWAY	GND	GROUND
AR	ARCADE	CIR	CIRCLE	CTRL	CENTRAL	EXT	EXTENSION	GRA	GRANGE
ASS	ASSOCIATION	CIRC	CIRCUS	CTS	COURTS	F/O	FLYOVER	GRG	GARAGE
AV	AVENUE	CL	CLOSE	CTYD	COURTYARD	FC	FOOTBALL CLUB	GT	GREAT
BCH	BEACH	CLFS	CLIFFS	CUTT	CUTTINGS	FK	FORK	GTWY	GATEWAY
BLDS	BUILDINGS	CMP	CAMP	CV	COVE	FLD	FIELD	GV	GROVE
BND	BEND	CNR	CORNER	CYN	CANYON	FLDS	FIELDS	HGR	HIGHER
BNK	BANK	CO	COUNTY	DEPT	DEPARTMENT	FLS	FALLS	HL	HILL
BR	BRIDGE	COLL	COLLEGE	DL	DALE	FLS	FLATS	HLS	HILLS
BRK	BROOK	COM	COMMON	DM	DAM	FM	FARM	HO	HOUSE
BTM	BOTTOM	COMM	COMMISSION	DR	DRIVE	FT	FORT	HOL	HOLLOW
BUS	BUSINESS	CON	CONVENT	DRO	DROVE	FWY	FREEWAY	HOSP	HOSPITAL
BVD	BOULEVARD	COT	COTTAGE	DRY	DRIVEWAY	FY	FERRY	HRB	HARBOUR
BY	BYPASS	COTS	COTTAGES	DWGS	DWELLINGS	GA	GATE	HTH	HEATH
CATH	CATHEDRAL	CP	CAPE	E	EAST	GAL	GALLERY	HTS	HEIGHTS
CEM	CEMETERY	CPS	COPSE	EMB	EMBANKMENT	GDN	GARDEN	HVN	HAVEN
CEN	CENTRE	CR	CREEK	EMBY	EMBASSY	GDNS	GARDENS	HWY	HIGHWAY
CFT	CROFT	CREM	CREMATORIUM	ESP	ESPLANADE	GLD	GLADE	IMP	IMPERIAL

149

IN INLET
IND EST INDUSTRIAL ESTATE
INF INFIRMARY
INFO INFORMATION
INT INTERCHANGE
IS ISLAND
JCT JUNCTION
JTY JETTY
KG KING
KNL KNOLL
L LAKE
LA LANE
LDG LODGE
LGT LIGHT
LK LOCK
LKS LAKES
LNDG LANDING
LTL LITTLE
LWR LOWER
MAG MAGISTRATE
MAN MANSIONS
MD MEAD
MDW MEADOWS
MEM MEMORIAL
MKT MARKET
MKTS MARKETS
ML MALL
ML MILL
MNR MANOR
MS MEWS
MSN MISSION
MT MOUNT
MTN MOUNTAIN
MTS MOUNTAINS
MUS MUSEUM
MWY MOTORWAY
N NORTH
NE NORTH EAST
NW NORTH WEST
O/P OVERPASS
OFF OFFICE
ORCH ORCHARD
OV OVAL
PAL PALACE
PAS PASSAGE
PAV PAVILION
PDE PARADE
PH PUBLIC HOUSE
PK PARK
PKWY PARKWAY
PL PLACE
PLN PLAIN
PLNS PLAINS
PLZ PLAZA
POL POLICE STATION
PR PRINCE
PREC PRECINCT
PREP PREPARATORY
PRIM PRIMARY
PROM PROMENADE
PRS PRINCESS
PRT PORT
PT POINT
PTH PATH
PZ PIAZZA
QD QUADRANT
QU QUEEN
QY QUAY
R RIVER
RBT ROUNDABOUT
RD ROAD
RDG RIDGE
REP REPUBLIC
RES RESERVOIR
RFC RUGBY FOOTBALL CLUB
RI RISE
RP RAMP
RW ROW
S SOUTH
SCH SCHOOL
SE SOUTH EAST
SER SERVICE AREA
SH SHORE
SHOP SHOPPING
SKWY SKYWAY
SMT SUMMIT
SOC SOCIETY
SP SPUR
SPR SPRING
SQ SQUARE
ST STREET
STN STATION
STR STREAM
STRD STRAND
SW SOUTH WEST
TDG TRADING
TER TERRACE
THWY THROUGHWAY
TNL TUNNEL
TOLL TOLLWAY
TPK TURNPIKE
TR TRACK
TRL TRAIL
TWR TOWER
U/P UNDERPASS
UNI UNIVERSITY
UPR UPPER
V VALE
VA VALLEY
VIAD VIADUCT
VIL VILLA
VIS VISTA
VLG VILLAGE
VLS VILLAS
VW VIEW
W WEST
WD WOOD
WHF WHARF
WK WALK
WKS WALKS
WLS WELLS
WY WAY
YD YARD
YHA YOUTH HOSTEL

POSTCODE TOWNS AND AREA ABBREVIATIONS

ALFN Alfreton
ARN Arnold
ASH Sutton in Ashfield/Kirkby in Ashfield
ASHB Ashbourne
BLWL Bulwell
BPR/DUF Belper/Duffield
BSTN/STPLFD Beeston/Stapleford
BWSH/BRSTN Borrowash/Breaston
CALV/BJ Calverton/Burton Joyce
CARL Carlton
CDON/KEG Castle Donington/Kegworth
CFTN/RUD Clifton/Ruddington
COAL Coalville
COT/KEY/RAD Cotgrave/Keyworth/Radcliffe on Trent
DERBY Derby
DERBYE Derby east
DERBYSE Derby southeast
DERBYW Derby west
END/NAR Enderby/Narborough
EWD/SEL/PNX Eastwood/Selston/Pinxton
GBY/RBY Groby/Ratby
HEANOR Heanor
HINC Hinckley
HUCK/RAV Hucknall/Ravenshead
ILK Ilkeston
LBORO Loughborough
LEI Leicester
LEIE Leicester east
LEIN Leicester north
LEIS Leicester south
LEIW Leicester west
LGEAT Long Eaton
MAPPK/POR/STA Mapperley Park/Porchester/St Ann's
MCKLVR Mickleover
MELB/CHEL Melbourne/Chellaston
MKTHBORO Market Harborough
NORM/LIT Normanton/Littleover
NOTT Nottingham
NOTTE Nottingham east
RDERBYSW Rural Derby southwest
RIPLEY Ripley
RLBORO Rural Loughborough
RLEINE/SYS Rural Leicester north & east/Syston
RLEIW/BAR Rural Leicester west/Barwell
RLEIS/BBY Rural Leicester south/Blaby
RMMWB Rural Melton Mowbray
WBRGFD West Bridgford
WGSTN Wigston
WOL/BIL/BRX Wollaton/Bilborough/Broxtowe

Index - streets

1st - Alv

1

1st Av *NOTTE* NG7 **36** F7
2nd Av *NOTTE* NG7 **36** F7
3rd Av *NOTTE* NG7 **36** F7
4th Av *NOTTE* NG7 **36** E7

A

Aaron Cl *CFTN/RUD* NG11 **50** F8
Abba Cl *EWD/SEL/PNX* NG16 **22** D8
Abberton Wy *LBORO* LE11 **102** E5
Abbey Br *NOTTE* NG7 **50** C5
Abbey Circ *WBRGFD* NG2 **51** L8
Abbey Cl *HUCK/RAV* NG15 **15** J8
Abbey Ct *LEIN* LE4 **125** K5
NOTTE NG7 **4** A8
Abbey Court Rd *LEIN* LE4 **125** K4
Abbey Dr *BSTN/STPLFD* NG9 **49** K8
LEIN LE4 **125** K4
Abbeyfield Rd *NOTTE* NG7 **50** D7
Abbeyfields Cl *DERBYW* DE22 **43** L5
Abbey Ga *LEIW* LE3 **6** C2
Abbey Gv *MAPPK/POR/STA* NG3 **37** K8
Abbey Hl *DERBYW* DE22 **43** M3
Abbey Hill Rd *DERBYW* DE22 **43** H5
Abbey La *DERBYW* DE22 **43** L6
LEIN LE4 **125** J5
Abbey Mdw *LEIN* LE4 **125** K6
Abbeymead Rd *LEIN* LE4 **125** K4
Abbey Park Rd *LEI* LE1 **125** K6
Abbey Park St *LEIN* LE4 **7** G1
Abbey Ri *LEIN* LE4 **125** K4
Abbey Rd *BSTN/STPLFD* NG9 **49** K8
COAL LE67 **109** H4
END/NAR LE19 **136** B6
EWD/SEL/PNX NG16 **21** M5
HUCK/RAV NG15 **15** J1
WBRGFD NG2 **51** L8
Abbey St *DERBYW* DE22 **2** D6
ILK DE7 **33** K5
LEI LE1 **6** F3
NOTTE NG7 **50** C5
Abbey Yd *DERBYW* DE22 **43** L6
Abbot Cl *COT/KEY/RAD* NG12 **80** C3
DERBYE DE21 **44** C5
Abbot Rd *ILK* DE7 **47** G1
Abbotsbury Cl *ARN* NG5 **24** B6
Abbots Cl *ARN* NG5 **37** H1
LEIE LE5 **126** F7
Abbots Dr *HUCK/RAV* NG15 **23** J1
Abbotsford Dr
MAPPK/POR/STA NG3 **5** K3
Abbotsford Ms *ILK* DE7 **33** H4
Abbotsford Rd *LEIE* LE5 **126** D8
Abbots Rd *HUCK/RAV* NG15 **23** J1
Abbot's Rd North *LEIE* LE5 **126** F7
Abbots Rd South *LEIE* LE5 **126** F7
Abbot St *EWD/SEL/PNX* NG16 **34** A3
Abbots Wy *WOL/BIL/BRX* NG8 **50** A3
Abbotts Barn Cl *DERBYW* DE22 **2** D5
Abbotts Cl *RLEINE/SYS* LE7 **120** D4
Abbott's Oak Dr *COAL* LE67 **108** F5
Abbott St *HEANOR* DE75 **20** C6
LGEAT NG10 **76** B1
Abells *RIPLEY* DE5 **19** G6
Abercarn Cl *BLWL* NG6 **23** M8
Aberdale Rd *LEIS* LE2 **137** M1
Aberdare Cl *DERBYE* DE21 **44** F5
Aberdeen St
MAPPK/POR/STA NG3 **5** L6
Aberford Av *WOL/BIL/BRX* NG8 **36** B7
Aber Rd *LEIS* LE2 **132** B6
Abingdon Dr *CFTN/RUD* NG11 **65** H7
Abingdon Gdns *ARN* NG5 **37** L2
BSTN/STPLFD NG9 **63** H3
Abingdon Rd *LEIS* LE2 **7** K9
WBRGFD NG2 **51** L8
Abingdon Sq *WOL/BIL/BRX* NG8 **35** M6
Abingdon St *DERBYSE* DE24 **58** A7
Ablard Gdns *BSTN/STPLFD* NG9 **63** G5
Abney Cl *MCKLVR* DE3 **56** D5
Abney St *LEIE* LE5 **7** M8
Acacia Av *LEIN* LE4 **119** M7
MCKLVR DE3 **56** C6
Acacia Cl *HUCK/RAV* NG15 **23** M2
LEIW LE3 **129** K5
Acacia Ct *MAPPK/POR/STA* NG3 **5** K4
Acacia Crs *CARL* NG4 **38** D7
Acacia Dr *MELB/CHEL* DE73 **82** E7
Acacia Gdns
EWD/SEL/PNX NG16 **22** D7
Acacia Wk *BSTN/STPLFD* NG9 **63** K1
Acan Wy *END/NAR* LE19 **135** L8
Acaster Cl *BSTN/STPLFD* NG9 **63** M3
Acer Cl *END/NAR* LE19 **135** L7
LBORO LE11 **103** L8
LEIN LE4 **125** G3
Acer Cft *DERBYE* DE21 **44** C5
Achurch Cl *RLEIW/BAR* LE9 **140** B4
Acle Gdns *BLWL* NG6 **23** M6
Acorn Av *EWD/SEL/PNX* NG16 **21** M7
Acorn Bank *CFTN/RUD* NG11 **64** F3
Acorn Cl *DERBYSE* DE24 **72** C4
LEIN LE4 **125** L1
Acorn Dr *BPR/DUF* DE56 **17** L2
CARL NG4 **38** E5
Acorn Pk *NOTTE* NG7 **50** C7
Acorn St *LEIN* LE4 **125** M5
Acorn Wy *BPR/DUF* DE56 **17** L2
DERBYE DE21 **45** G6
DERBYE DE21 **59** G2
WGSTN LE18 **138** C5
A'court St *NOTTE* NG7 **4** B3
Acrefield Wy *MELB/CHEL* DE73 **72** F5
Acre La *BWSH/BRSTN* DE72 **74** B8
Acres Rd *LEIW* LE3 **129** L4
Acton Av *BLWL* NG6 **36** B3
Acton Cl *LGEAT* NG10 **76** C1
Acton Gv *LGEAT* NG10 **76** C1
Acton Rd *ARN* NG5 **25** H7
DERBYW DE22 **56** D1
LGEAT NG10 **62** C8
Acton St *LGEAT* NG10 **76** C1
Adale Rd *HEANOR* DE75 **19** M7
Adam Dl *LBORO* LE11 **8** D7
Adams Cl *HEANOR* DE75 **20** B8
Adams Ct *ILK* DE7 **33** J4
Adams Hl *COT/KEY/RAD* NG12 **80** D4
NOTTE NG7 **50** A5
Adam's Rd *ASHB* DE6 **41** L7
Adam St *ILK* DE7 **47** L1
Ada Pl *HUCK/RAV* NG15 **15** M7
Adbolton Av *CARL* NG4 **38** C6
Adbolton Gv *WBRGFD* NG2 **51** M5
Adbolton La *WBRGFD* NG2 **51** M6
Adcock Rd *LEIW* LE3 **124** F8
Adderley Rd *LEIS* LE2 **131** M6
Addington Rd *NOTTE* NG7 **4** A3
Addison Dr *HUCK/RAV* NG15 **15** J7
Addison Rd *CARL* NG4 **37** M7
DERBYSE DE24 **57** M7
Addison St *NOTT* NG1 **4** F3
Adelaide Cl *BSTN/STPLFD* NG9 **48** D6
LEIN LE4 **119** G8
MCKLVR DE3 **56** C3
Adelaide Gv *ARN* NG5 **24** C7
Adelaide Wk
EWD/SEL/PNX NG16 **12** D3
Adel Dr *CARL* NG4 **38** C6
Adelphi Cl *NORM/LIT* DE23 **70** E1
Adenburgh Dr
BSTN/STPLFD NG9 **63** H6
Adler Ct *DERBY* DE1 **43** M8
Adlington Rd *LEIS* LE2 **139** G1
Admiral Cl *HEANOR* DE75 **20** B5
Adrian Cl *BSTN/STPLFD* NG9 **62** D6
Adrian St *DERBYSE* DE24 **72** B1
Adwick Cl *MCKLVR* DE3 **56** A5
Aeneas Ct
MAPPK/POR/STA * NG3 **36** F7
Aerial Wy *HUCK/RAV* NG15 **23** K2
Afton Cl *LBORO* LE11 **102** F4
Agard St *DERBY* DE1 **2** C2
Agar Nook La *COAL* LE67 **109** H6
Agar St *LEIN* LE4 **125** M6
Agnes Vls *MAPPK/POR/STA* NG3 **37** J5
Aikman Av *LEIW* LE3 **124** D7
Aikman Cl *LEIW* LE3 **124** E8
Aimploy Ct *NORM/LIT* DE23 **57** L6
Ainley Cl *DERBYSE* DE24 **58** D8
Ainsdale *RLEIW/BBY* LE8 **145** L8
Ainsdale Crs *WOL/BIL/BRX* NG8 **35** L4
Ainsdale Rd *LEIW* LE3 **130** E2
Ainsley Rd *WOL/BIL/BRX* NG8 **50** B1
Ainsworth Dr *NORM/LIT* DE23 **57** J8
RLBORO LE12 **114** C4
WBRGFD NG2 **50** F6
Aintree Cl *LEIE* LE5 **133** H3
Aintree Crs *LEIS* LE2 **138** D1
Aira Cl *WBRGFD* NG2 **66** B1
Airedale Cl *LGEAT* NG10 **75** L1
Airedale Ct *BSTN/STPLFD* NG9 **62** E3
Aisne Rd *WGSTN* LE18 **137** J4
Aitchison Av *HUCK/RAV* NG15 **15** K8
Alan Cl *LEIN* LE4 **125** M3
Alandene Av
EWD/SEL/PNX NG16 **22** E8
Alan Moss Rd *LBORO* LE11 **8** B3
Albany Cl *ARN* NG5 **25** J8
HUCK/RAV NG15 **23** G2
Albany Ct *BSTN/STPLFD* NG9 **48** C6
Albany Rd *DERBYW* DE22 **57** G3
NOTTE NG7 **36** E7
Albany St *ILK* DE7 **47** L1
LBORO LE11 **103** J2
Albemarle Rd *ARN* NG5 **37** H3
DERBYE DE21 **58** F1
Alberta St *LEIE* LE5 **7** J4
Alberta Ter *NOTTE* NG7 **36** E7
Albert Av *BSTN/STPLFD* NG9 **48** B8
CARL NG4 **37** M8
EWD/SEL/PNX NG16 **12** F3
EWD/SEL/PNX NG16 **35** G1
RLBORO LE12 **114** B3
WOL/BIL/BRX NG8 **36** B7
Albert Ball Cl *ARN* NG5 **24** D7
Albert Ct *RLEIW/BBY* LE8 **136** D7
Albert Crs *DERBYE* DE21 **58** F3
Albert Gv *NOTTE* NG7 **4** B6
Albert Pl *LBORO* LE11 **9** J5
Albert Prom *LBORO* LE11 **9** L5
Albert Rd *BSTN/STPLFD* NG9 **49** L7
BWSH/BRSTN DE72 **60** F8
CFTN/RUD NG11 **79** J6
COAL LE67 **108** B6
DERBYE DE21 **58** E2
LEIS LE2 **132** A5
LGEAT NG10 **61** M1
LGEAT NG10 **62** B8
MAPPK/POR/STA NG3 **37** H6
NOTTE NG7 **50** C4
RIPLEY DE5 **11** G5
WBRGFD NG2 **51** K7
Albert St *BPR/DUF* DE56 **17** K3
BSTN/STPLFD NG9 **48** B8
CARL NG4 **38** D6
COT/KEY/RAD NG12 **53** K4
DERBY DE1 **2** F4
EWD/SEL/PNX NG16 **21** K4
HUCK/RAV NG15 **15** M8
ILK DE7 **33** J7
LBORO LE11 **9** J5
NOTT NG1 **5** H8
RIPLEY DE5 **11** J6
RLEINE/SYS LE7 **120** F4
RLEIW/BBY LE8 **145** K7
RLEIW/BBY LE8 **146** E5
Albion Ri *ARN* NG5 **25** K6
Albion Rd *LGEAT* NG10 **62** C7
RLBORO LE12 **114** A4
Albion St *BSTN/STPLFD* NG9 **49** K8
ILK DE7 **33** K6
LEI LE1 **6** F7
LEIS LE2 **138** E2
NOTT NG1 **5** G9
RIPLEY DE5 **11** J6
RLEINE/SYS LE7 **120** F4
RLEINE/SYS LE7 **124** C1
WGSTN LE18 **137** K5
Albion Ter *ILK* * DE7 **33** K6
Albury Dr *WOL/BIL/BRX* NG8 **35** M6
Albury Sq *NOTTE* NG7 **4** C7
Alcester Dr *LEIE* LE5 **133** H3
Alcester St *NOTTE* NG7 **50** C7
Alcott Cl *LEIW* LE3 **130** E2
Aldeby Cl *END/NAR* LE19 **136** C4
LEIS LE2 **136** F3
Aldene Ct *BSTN/STPLFD* NG9 **63** H2
Aldene Wy *CALV/BJ* NG14 **27** G3
Aldercar La *EWD/SEL/PNX* NG16 **12** E8
EWD/SEL/PNX NG16 **20** F3
Alder Cl *DERBYE* DE21 **44** C5
LEIW LE3 **129** K5
Alderfen Cl *DERBYSE* DE24 **72** B4
Alder Gdns *BLWL* NG6 **23** L8
Alderleigh Rd *LEIS* LE2 **137** J6
Alderley Ct *DERBYE* DE21 **44** E5
Aldermens Cl *WBRGFD* NG2 **51** G5
Alderney St *NOTTE* NG7 **50** D4
Alder Rd *BPR/DUF* DE56 **17** L4
Alders Brook *RDERBYSW* DE65 **68** B6
Aldersgate *DERBYW* DE22 **42** D8
Alderslade Cl *BWSH/BRSTN* DE72 **73** M6
Aldersley Cl *RDERBYSW* DE65 **70** A6
Alderstone Cl *WGSTN* LE18 **138** A7
Alderton Cl *LEIN* LE4 **126** A2
Alderton Rd *ARN* NG5 **37** G2
Alder Wk *NORM/LIT* DE23 **2** F7
Alder Wy *COT/KEY/RAD* NG12 **80** E5
Aldgate Av *LEIE* LE5 **132** F4
Aldgate Cl *BLWL* NG6 **23** L8
Aldred's La *HEANOR* DE75 **20** E6
Aldridge Cl *BSTN/STPLFD* NG9 **62** C5
Aldrin Cl *BLWL* NG6 **35** K2
Aldworth Cl *ARN* NG5 **37** G1
Aldwych *DERBYW* DE22 **56** E1
Aldwych Cl *ARN* NG5 **24** E5
WOL/BIL/BRX NG8 **35** H5
Alexander Av *END/NAR* LE19 **135** L4
Alexander Cl *HUCK/RAV* NG15 **15** M6
Alexander Rd *NOTTE* NG7 **4** C8
RLBORO LE12 **104** D8
Alexander St *LEIW* LE3 **6** C5
Alexandra Crs
BSTN/STPLFD NG9 **63** L1
Alexandra Gdns
NORM/LIT DE23 **57** M5
Alexandra Pk
MAPPK/POR/STA NG3 **37** H7
Alexandra Rd *LEIS* LE2 **132** B6
LGEAT NG10 **62** B7
Alexandra St *ARN* NG5 **36** F7
BSTN/STPLFD NG9 **62** B1
END/NAR LE19 **136** A7
EWD/SEL/PNX NG16 **21** K5
LEIN LE4 **120** C7
Alexandre Cl *NORM/LIT* DE23 **71** H1
Alford Cl *BSTN/STPLFD* NG9 **63** L2
Alford Rd *WBRGFD* NG2 **65** M1
Alfred Av *MAPPK/POR/STA* NG3 **37** L5
Alfred Cl *MAPPK/POR/STA* NG3 **5** H3
Alfred Rd *BPR/DUF* DE56 **18** E7
Alfred St *ALFN* DE55 **12** B1
LBORO LE11 **103** M2
RIPLEY DE5 **11** J5
Alfred St Central
MAPPK/POR/STA NG3 **5** H3
Alfred St North
MAPPK/POR/STA NG3 **5** G3
Alfred St South
MAPPK/POR/STA NG3 **5** L5
Alfreton Rd *ALFN* DE55 **12** F1
DERBYE DE21 **30** B5
DERBYE DE21 **43** M7
DERBYE DE21 **44** A3
EWD/SEL/PNX NG16 **13** M5
NOTTE NG7 **4** B3
RIPLEY DE5 **12** A6
WGSTN LE18 **138** A3
Alice Gdns *RLEIW/BBY* LE8 **142** D2
Alice St *DERBY* DE1 **3** G2
Alison Cl *DERBYE* DE21 **44** D8
Alison Wk *MAPPK/POR/STA* NG3 **5** J4
Allan Av *NORM/LIT* DE23 **56** C7
Allandale Rd *HEANOR* DE75 **20** B5
LEIS LE2 **132** C5
Allen Av *RLBORO* LE12 **104** D8
Allendale *ILK* DE7 **33** J8
Allendale Av *BSTN/STPLFD* NG9 **63** H5
WOL/BIL/BRX NG8 **35** L6
Allen's Green Av
EWD/SEL/PNX NG16 **13** K1
Allen St *DERBYSE* DE24 **72** C2
HUCK/RAV NG15 **15** L7
Allen's Wk *ARN* NG5 **25** K7
Allenwood Rd *LEIS* LE2 **137** J3
Allerton Dr *LEIW* LE3 **124** E6
Allestree Cl *DERBYSE* DE24 **58** C7
Allestree La *DERBYW* DE22 **43** H5
Allestree St *DERBYSE* DE24 **58** C7
Allexton Gdns *LEIW* LE3 **130** B1
All Hallows Dr *CARL* NG4 **38** D5
Alliance Rd *LEIW* LE3 **124** A8
Allington Av *NOTTE* NG7 **4** B9
Allington Dr *RLEINE/SYS* LE7 **119** M7
Allington St *LEIN* LE4 **125** M7
Allinson Cl *LEIE* LE5 **132** E1
Allison Gdns *BSTN/STPLFD* NG9 **63** H3
ILK DE7 **33** L6
Allissa Av *RIPLEY* DE5 **11** J8
Alloway Cl *LEIN* LE4 **126** B3
All Saints Cl *RLEIW/BAR* LE9 **140** B8
All Saints Ct *MCKLVR* DE3 **56** A6
All Saints Rd *LEIW* LE3 **6** C5
RLEINE/SYS LE7 **118** F5
All Saints' St *NOTTE* NG7 **4** D4
All Saints Ter *NOTTE* NG7 **4** D4
Allwood Dr *CARL* NG4 **38** C7
Allwood Gdns *HUCK/RAV* NG15 **23** M1
Alma Cl *CARL* NG4 **38** E5
NOTT NG1 **5** G4
Alma Hts *MCKLVR* DE3 **56** C6
Alma Hl *EWD/SEL/PNX* NG16 **22** C7
Alma Rd *EWD/SEL/PNX* NG16 **13** K2
MAPPK/POR/STA NG3 **51** K1
Alma St *DERBYW* DE22 **2** D5
LEIW LE3 **131** G1
MELB/CHEL DE73 **82** E8
NOTTE NG7 **36** E6
RIPLEY DE5 **11** H5
Almond Av *RIPLEY* DE5 **11** H7
Almond Cl *EWD/SEL/PNX* NG16 **22** C8
HUCK/RAV NG15 **23** M2
RLBORO LE12 **111** K1
RLEIW/BBY LE8 **143** J3
Almond Rd *LEIS* LE2 **131** K4
Almond St *NORM/LIT* DE23 **57** K5
Almond Wk *CARL* NG4 **38** E5
Alnwick Cl *BLWL* NG6 **36** B1
Alpha Ter *NOTT* NG1 **4** F3
Alpine St *BLWL* NG6 **36** B5
Alport Cl *BPR/DUF* DE56 **17** M2
Alport Wy *WGSTN* LE18 **138** C5
Alsager Cl *DERBYE* DE21 **44** E6
Alston Dr *LBORO* LE11 **103** H1
Alstonfield Dr *DERBYW* DE22 **43** J6
Altar Stones La *COAL* LE67 **116** A5
Althorp Cl *LEIS* LE2 **136** F2
Althorpe Dr *LBORO* LE11 **103** G3
Althorpe St *NOTTE* NG7 **4** C6
Alton Av *CFTN/RUD* NG11 **64** F3
Alton Cl *CFTN/RUD* NG11 **65** G4
DERBYW DE22 **43** H4
Alton Rd *BPR/DUF* DE56 **18** A3
LEIS LE2 **137** J2
Alts Nook Wy
BWSH/BRSTN DE72 **74** C6
Alum Cl *DERBYSE* DE24 **59** G8
Alvaston Rd *LEIW* LE3 **130** F6
Alvaston St *DERBYSE* DE24 **58** F7

Alvecote Rd *LEIS* LE2................137 H2
Alvenor St *ILK* DE7........................33 K6
Alverstone Rd
  MAPPK/POR/STA NG3............37 G6
Alverton Cl *MCKLVR* DE3...........56 A6
Alvey Ter *NOTTE* * NG7...............50 C2
Alvis Dl *RLBORO* LE12................113 K7
Alward's Cl *DERBYSE* DE24.........72 A1
Alwards Ct *DERBYSE* * DE24.......72 E1
Alwood Gv *CFTN/RUD* NG11........64 B4
Alwyn Rd *WOL/BIL/BRX* NG8........35 K5
Alyssum Wy *END/NAR* LE19.......135 K6
Amadis Rd *LEIS* LE2...................124 E4
Amanda Cl *LEIS* LE2..................136 F3
Ambassador Rd
  CDON/KEG DE74.....................84 F8
  LEIE LE5..............................132 E1
Ambaston Rd
  BWSH/BRSTN DE72.................73 M2
Amber Cl *BPR/DUF* DE56...........17 L1
  HEANOR * DE75......................20 C6
Amber Dr *EWD/SEL/PNX* NG16....20 D7
Ambergate Dr *LEIN* LE4..............119 K7
Ambergate Rd
  WOL/BIL/BRX NG8...................35 L8
Amber Hts *RIPLEY* DE5...............11 G5
Amber Hl *ARN* NG5......................24 F8
Amberley Cl *ILK* DE7...................47 K1
  LEIN LE4.............................126 C1
Amberley Dr *DERBYSE* DE24.......71 K2
  LEIN LE4.............................126 C1
Amber Rd *DERBY* DE22................43 H6
Amber St *DERBYSE* DE24............58 A8
Ambervale Cl *NORM/LIT* DE23.....70 E1
Ambler Cl *WGSTN* LE18.............138 B6
Ambleside Cl *LBORO* LE11.........103 H7
  LEIS LE2.............................137 C4
Ambleside Dr
  EWD/SEL/PNX NG16.................21 H1
  LEIS LE2.............................137 C4
Ambleside Rd
  WOL/BIL/BRX NG8...................35 L6
Ambleside Wy *CARL* NG4.............38 F7
  LEIS LE2.............................137 C4
Ambrose Cl *LEIW* LE3................130 F1
Ambrose Ter *DERBY* DE1................2 E3
Amen Aly *DERBY* DE1....................2 E3
Amersham Ri
  WOL/BIL/BRX NG8...................35 M6
Amersham Rd *LEIN* LE4.............125 H6
Amesbury Circ
  WOL/BIL/BRX NG8...................35 L4
Amesbury La *DERBYSE* DE24......44 C5
Amesbury Rd *WGSTN* LE18.......138 A7
Amhurst Cl *LEIW* LE3.................124 D6
Amilda Av *ILK* DE7........................33 K7
Amis Cl *LBORO* LE11.................103 G2
Amos Rd *LEIW* LE3....................130 D1
Ampthill Ri *ARN* NG5....................36 F3
Amsden Ri *RLEIW/BAR* LE9........141 H8
Amyson Rd *LEIS* LE2..................133 C1
Amy St *DERBY* DE22.....................2 A6
  LEIW LE3.............................130 E8
Ancaster Gdns
  WOL/BIL/BRX NG8...................49 L3
Anchor Cl *RLBORO* LE12...............94 E7
  WOL/BIL/BRX NG8...................35 M5
Anchor Fold *NORM/LIT* DE23.........2 F9
Anchor La *RLBORO* LE12..............94 E6
Anchor Rd *EWD/SEL/PNX* NG16....21 K7
Anchor St *LEIN* LE4...................125 K5
Anders Dr *BLWL* NG6...................35 K2
Anderson Crs
  BSTN/STPLFD NG9...................49 J7
Anderson St *DERBYSE* DE24......58 D8
Andover Cl *WOL/BIL/BRX* NG8....49 M1
Andover Rd *ARN* NG5...................36 C1
Andover St *LEIS* LE2.....................7 H7
Andrew Av *ILK* DE7.......................33 L7
  RLEIW/BAR LE9......................142 B3
Andrew Cl *NORM/LIT* DE23.........56 C7
Andrewes Cl *LEIW* LE3..................6 A6
Andrewes St *LEIW* LE3..................6 A7
Andrewes Wk *LEIW* LE3................6 A7
Andrew Rd *RLEIW/SYS* LE7........124 C1
Andrews Dr
  EWD/SEL/PNX NG16.................20 E3
  ILK DE7..............................31 L6
Aneford Rd *LEIN* LE4..................126 C6
Anfield Cl *BSTN/STPLFD* NG9.....62 B1
Anford Rd *BLWL* NG6...................35 M2
Angela Cl *ARN* NG5......................25 J5
Angela Dr *LEIE* LE5....................132 F3
Angel Rw *NOTT* NG1.......................5 G7
Angel Rw West *NOTT* NG1.............4 F7
Anglers' La *DERBY* DE21..............59 J5
Anglesey Rd *WGSTN* LE18.........137 K4
Anglesey St *DERBY* DE21............44 B7
Angletarn Cl *WBRGFD* NG2.........66 A1
Angrave Cl *MAPPK/POR/STA* NG3....5 M2
Angrave Rd *RLBORO* LE12............88 C4
Angus Cl *ARN* NG5......................25 M6
  EWD/SEL/PNX NG16.................34 E2
  RLEIW/SYS LE7.....................133 K1
Angus Dr *LBORO* LE11...................8 B7
Anmer Cl *WBRGFD* NG2...............50 F6
Annan Ct *WOL/BIL/BRX* NG8.......35 M7
Anne Potter Cl
  BWSH/BRSTN DE72.................60 B2
Anne's Cl *MAPPK/POR/STA* NG3....37 L5
Annesley Gv *NOTT* NG1.................4 F4
Annesley La *EWD/SEL/PNX* NG16...14 C1
Annesley Rd *HUCK/RAV* NG15.....14 F2
  WBRGFD NG2........................51 K8
Annies Whf *LBORO* LE11...........103 M2
Ann St *LEIE* LE5............................7 H5
Ann's Wy *LEIS* LE2....................139 G2
Anslow Av *BSTN/STPLFD* NG9.....49 L7
Anson Rd *CDON/KEG* DE74..........84 F7
  RLBORO LE12.......................101 L4
Anstee Rd *LGEAT* NG10................76 A3
Anstey Ct *DERBYSE* DE21...........44 E6
Anstey La *GBY/RBY* LE6.............123 L4
  LEIN LE4.............................124 D3
  RLEIW/SYS LE7.....................118 D7
Anstey Ri *MAPPK/POR/STA* NG3....51 K2
Anthony Crs *DERBYSE* DE24.......72 D1

Anthony Dr *DERBYSE* DE24..........72 D1
  RLEINE/SYS LE7....................133 K2
Anthony Rd *LEIN* LE4.................125 H6
Anthony St *RLEINE/SYS* LE7......119 J1
Antill St *BSTN/STPLFD* NG9.........62 B1
Apiary Ga *CDON/KEG* DE74..........84 F4
Apollo Cl *LEIS* LE2.........................7 K6
Apollo Ct *LEIS* LE2........................7 K7
Apollo Dr *BLWL* NG6.....................24 E3
Appian Cl *BWSH/BRSTN* DE72.....60 A6
Appian Wy *DERBYSE* DE24..........73 H1
Appleby Cl *ILK* DE7......................47 K1
  LEIW LE3.............................130 A2
Appleby Ct *DERBYW* * DE21..........2 C8
Appleby Rd *LEIN* LE4..................120 E8
Applecross Ct *DERBYSE* DE24.....71 J4
Appledore Av
  WOL/BIL/BRX NG8...................49 H5
Appledore Dr *DERBYSE* DE21......44 F6
Appledorne Wy *ARN* NG5.............25 J5
Appledown Wy *NORM/LIT* DE23....70 E1
Applegate Cl *DERBYSE* DE21.......44 F4
Applemead Cl *DERBYSE* DE21.....44 C5
Appleton Av *LEIN* LE4................125 H3
Appleton Cl *DERBYSE* DE21.........44 E8
Appleton Dr *BPR/DUF* DE56.........17 M1
  RLBORO LE12.........................97 M3
Appleton Rd *BSTN/STPLFD* NG9....63 M3
Appletree Cl *BWSH/BRSTN* DE72...60 A6
Apple Tree Cl
  COT/KEY/RAD * NG12...............65 L3
Applewood Cl *BPR/DUF* DE56.....17 M2
Applewood Gv *ARN* NG5...............37 H4
The Approach *LEIE* LE5..............132 D3
Aquitaine Cl *END/NAR* LE19.......135 L4
Arbor Cl *DERBYW* DE22.................2 D6
Arboretum Sq *NORM/LIT* DE23......3 C8
Arboretum St *NORM/LIT* DE23.......3 C8
Arbor Rd *RLEIW/BAR* LE9..........141 C3
Arbour Hl *ILK* DE7.......................46 C4
Arbour Rd *LEIN* LE4...................125 M5
Arbrook Dr *WOL/BIL/BRX* NG8....50 B1
Arbury Dl *RLBORO* LE12.............102 A5
Arbutus Cl *CFTN/RUD* NG11........64 A6
The Arcade *WGSTN* * LE18.........138 B4
Archdale Rd *ARN* NG5.................37 G1
Archdale St *RLEINE/SYS* LE7......120 D5
Archeacon La *LEI* LE1...................6 F3
Archer Cl *LBORO* LE11................102 F1
  LEIN LE4.............................126 C3
Archer Crs *WOL/BIL/BRX* NG8.....49 K2
Archer St *BSTN/STPLFD* NG9.......62 C2
Archer St *DERBYSE* DE24............58 C5
  ILK DE7..............................33 J4
Archery Cl *RLEIW/BBY* LE8........143 K3
The Arches *RLBORO* LE12............88 C5
Archway Ct *NOTTE* NG7.................4 B4
Archway Rd *LEIE* LE5.................127 J6
Ardath Rd *LEIN* LE4...................126 A6
Arden Av *LEIW* LE3....................130 D5
Arden Cl *BSTN/STPLFD* NG9........49 L7
  HUCK/RAV NG15....................24 A2
  NORM/LIT DE23......................57 J5
Ardent Ter *LEIW* LE3..................130 E5
Ardleigh Cl *ARN* NG5..................24 B6
Ardmore Cl *WBRGFD* NG2.............5 M9
Ardsley Cl *HEANOR* DE75............20 E5
Argosy Rd *CDON/KEG* DE74.........85 J7
Argyle Cl *NOTTE* NG7....................4 B4
Argyle St *NOTTE* NG7....................4 B4
Argyll Cl *DERBY* DE21.................59 K2
Argyll Rd *RIPLEY* DE5..................11 J3
Ariel Cl *ARN* NG5.........................36 D2
Arkers Cl *BLWL* NG6....................36 B4
Arklow Cl *WOL/BIL/BRX* NG8.....35 M5
Arkwright Cl *BPR/DUF* DE56.......18 A1
Arkwright St *DERBYSE* DE24.......58 A8
  WBRGFD * NG2........................2 C8
Arkwright St North
  WBRGFD NG2........................51 G4
Arkwright St South
  WBRGFD NG2........................51 H6
Arkwright Wk *WBRGFD* NG2.......51 H6
Arleston Dr *WOL/BIL/BRX* NG8....49 H3
Arleston La *DERBYSE* DE24.........71 H6
Arleston St *NORM/LIT* DE23.........57 K8
Arlington Dr *DERBYSE* DE24........72 D1
  MAPPK/POR/STA NG3..............37 G6
Arlington Rd *NORM/LIT* DE23.......57 H6
Armadale Cl *ARN* NG5.................26 A7
Armadale Dr *LEIE* LE5................127 C7
Armett's La *RLBORO* LE12..........100 B3
Armfield Rd *ARN* NG5..................38 A1
Armitage Cl *LBORO* LE11...............9 G2
Armitage Dr *LGEAT* NG10............62 E8
Armscote Cl *DERBYSE* DE21.......44 F5
Armson Av *RLEIW/BAR* LE9........129 J2
Armson Rd *RLBORO* LE12...........112 E2
  RLEIW/BAR LE9......................142 B4
Armstrong Rd *BLWL* NG6.............35 K2
Arncliff Cl *WOL/BIL/BRX* NG8.....49 C3
Arncliffe Rd *LEIE* LE5.................127 C7
Arndale *WGSTN* LE18.................138 D6
Arndale Rd *ARN* NG5...................37 G2
Arnesby Crs *WGSTN* LE18..........137 K2
Arnesby Rd *NOTTE* NG7...............50 B4
Arnhem St *LEI* LE1........................7 G7
Arnhem Ter *DERBY* DE21.............59 J4
Arno Av *NOTTE* NG7.....................36 F7
Arnold Av *LGEAT* NG10................75 L3
  WGSTN LE18........................137 L6
Arnold Cl *RLEIW/BAR* LE9..........142 B5
Arnold Crs *LGEAT* NG10..............75 L3
Arnold La *MAPPK/POR/STA* NG3....36 D3
Arnold Rd *ARN* NG5.....................36 B3
Arnold St *DERBYW* DE22............57 H2
  LEI LE1...............................7 J3
Arno Gv *WOL/BIL/BRX* NG8........35 H4
Arno Hill Rd *ARN* NG5.................25 J8
Arno Vale Gdns *ARN* NG5...........37 K2
Arno Vale Rd *ARN* NG5...............37 K2
Arnside Cl *ARN* NG5....................36 F2
Arnside Rd *ARN* NG5...................36 E2

A Rd *BSTN/STPLFD* NG9..............64 A1
Arran Cl *BSTN/STPLFD* NG9.........48 C5
  DERBYSE DE24......................71 J4
Arran Rd *LEIN* LE4.....................126 B3
Arran Wy *RLEIW/BBY* LE8..........143 K4
Arreton Cl *LEIS* LE2...................132 A3
Arridge Rd *DERBYSE* DE21..........44 D8
Arthur Av *BSTN/STPLFD* NG9......48 D7
  NOTTE NG7.............................4 A8
Arthur Crs *CARL* NG4..................38 A4
Arthur Hind Cl *DERBYW* DE22.....43 K8
Arthur Mee Rd
  BSTN/STPLFD NG9...................62 C2
  CARL NG4.............................52 E1
  DERBY DE1............................43 J8
  LBORO LE11............................9 G4
  NOTTE NG7............................4 B3
Arthur St *BWSH/BRSTN* DE72......60 D8
  CARL NG4.............................52 E1
  DERBY DE21..........................43 J8
  MAPPK/POR/STA NG3................5 L6
Ashling St *WBRGFD* NG2.............51 J5
Ashlyn Rd *DERBYE* DE21...............3 J4
Ashlyns Ri *LEIW* LE3.................130 C2
Ashmead Crs *RLEINE/SYS* LE7....120 A6
Ashmeadow
  BWSH/BRSTN DE72.................59 M6
Ash Mount Rd
  EWD/SEL/PNX NG16.................20 F4
Ashness Cl *WBRGFD* NG2...........66 A1
Ashop Rd *BPR/DUF* DE56.............18 B2
Ashopton Av *NORM/LIT* DE23......57 K7
Ashover Cl *DERBYSE* DE21..........44 C7
  MAPPK/POR/STA NG3................37 J7
  RLEIW/BAR LE9.....................142 B3
Ashover Rd *DERBYSE* DE22.........43 H5
  NOTTE NG7............................4 C6
Ascot Av *EWD/SEL/PNX* NG16......22 C8
  COAL LE67...........................108 E7
  DERBYSE DE24......................58 B8
  HUCK/RAV NG15....................23 H2
Ascot Pl *ILK* DE7.........................47 G2
Ascot Rd *LEIN* LE4.....................125 M5
  WOL/BIL/BRX NG8...................36 B8
Ascott Gdns *WBRGFD* NG2..........64 F2
Asfordby St *LEIE* LE5..................132 B1
Ash Acre *BPR/DUF* DE56.............18 B3
Asha Margh *LEIN* LE4.................125 L5
Ashbourne Cl
  BSTN/STPLFD NG9...................48 E6
  DERBYW DE22..........................2 B2
Ashbourne Houses
  DERBY * DE21........................59 J3
Ashbourne Rd *ASHB* DE6.............41 G2
  BPR/DUF DE56.......................16 A5
  EWD/SEL/PNX NG16.................13 L5
  WGSTN LE18........................138 A3
Ashbourne St *LEIS* LE2..................7 L6
Ashbrook Av
  BWSH/BRSTN DE72.................60 A5
Ashbrook Cl *DERBYW* DE22.........43 C4
Ashburnham Av *NOTTE* NG7.........4 A7
Ashby Crs *LBORO* LE11.................8 B4
Ashby Gld *LEIE* LE5...................133 G2
Ashby Ri *RLEIW/BBY* LE8..........139 M6
Ashby Rd *CDON/KEG* DE74..........85 K8
  COAL LE67...........................100 A6
  COAL LE67...........................116 B5
  LBORO LE11............................8 B4
  RLBORO LE12.........................96 F2
  RLBORO LE12.......................100 F1
Ashby Rd Central
  RLBORO LE12.......................101 M6
Ashby Rd East *RLBORO* LE12.....102 B6
Ashby Rd West *RLBORO* LE12.....101 G6
Ashby Sq *LBORO* LE11...................9 H3
Ashby St *DERBYSE* DE24............72 C1
Ashchurch Dr *WOL/BIL/BRX* NG8....49 H5
Ash Cl *BWSH/BRSTN* DE72.........73 M8
  CALV/BJ NG14........................27 G2
  DERBYW DE22........................43 H3
  GBY/RBY LE6.......................122 F6
  RLBORO LE12.......................105 H6
Ashclose Av *LEIS* LE2................132 A8
Ashcombe Gdns *DERBY* DE21.....44 F6
Ash Ct *GBY/RBY* LE6..................123 J5
Ash Crs *EWD/SEL/PNX* NG16......34 E1
  RIPLEY DE5..........................11 H7
Ashcroft Cl *DERBYSE* DE24.........58 D8
Ash Dl *COAL* LE67.....................100 B8
Ashdale Av *HUCK/RAV* NG15......23 K2
Ashdale Rd *ARN* NG5..................25 L7
  ILK DE7..............................47 L1
  MAPPK/POR/STA NG3..............51 M1
Ashdene Gdns *BPR/DUF* DE56.....18 A2
Ashdown Av *LEIW* LE3...............130 F1
Ashdown Cl *CFTN/RUD* NG11......64 F1
  LBORO LE11.........................103 G2
Ashdown Rd *WGSTN* LE18.........138 B3
Ash Dr *RLEIW/SYS* LE7.............120 F5
  RLBORO LE12.........................25 M8
Ashe La *RDERBYSW* DE65..........68 E2
Ashe Pl *NORM/LIT* DE23.............57 K6
Asher La *CFTN/RUD* NG11..........78 E2
  RIPLEY DE5..........................11 G2
Ashfield Av *BSTN/STPLFD* NG9....63 M2
  DERBYSE DE21......................44 C7
Ashfield Dr *RLEINE/SYS* LE7......124 B2
Ashfield Rd *LEIN* LE4.................120 D7
  LEIS LE2.............................132 A4
  WBRGFD NG2........................51 K3
Ashford Cl *ILK* DE7.....................32 B7
Ashford Pl *ILK* DE7......................33 J2
Ashford Ri *BPR/DUF* DE56..........17 M1
  WOL/BIL/BRX NG8...................49 H5
Ashford Rd *COAL* LE67...............108 D2
  LEIS LE2.............................131 L6
Ashforth Av *HEANOR* DE75..........20 E6
Ashforth St
  MAPPK/POR/STA NG3................5 J3
Ashgate Rd *HUCK/RAV* NG15......24 A1
Ash Gv *BSTN/STPLFD* NG9..........62 B1
  CALV/BJ NG14........................27 G2
  COT/KEY/RAD NG12.................80 D5
  EWD/SEL/PNX NG16.................13 H7
  LGEAT NG10...........................47 L8
  LEIN LE4.............................76 A1
  RLBORO LE12.........................94 E5
  RLBORO LE12.......................113 J6
  RLEIW/BBY LE8.....................136 F7
Ashgrove Ct *DERBYSE* DE21.......44 F8
Ashington Cl *LEIW* LE3..............124 F7
Ashington Dr *ARN* NG5...............25 K5

Ashlands Wy *END/NAR* LE19......135 K6
Ash La *ASHB* DE6.........................54 A7
  RLBORO LE12.........................89 H3
Ash Lea *COT/KEY/RAD* NG12.......67 K5
Ashleigh Dr *LBORO* LE11.............72 D5
  MELB/CHEL DE73....................72 D5
Ashleigh Gdns *LEIW* * LE3.........131 G4
Ashleigh Rd *LEIW* LE3...............123 M7
  LEIW LE3.............................131 G3
Ashley Cl *BSTN/STPLFD* NG9......63 H1
Ashley Crs *COT/KEY/RAD* NG12....80 D4
Ashley Rd *COT/KEY/RAD* NG12....80 D4
Ashley St *DERBYSE* DE22...........57 G2
  MAPPK/POR/STA NG3................5 L6
Ashleigh Rd *LEIW* LE3...............131 G3
Attfield Dr *RLEIW/BBY* LE8.........136 E7
Attingham Cl *LEIE* LE5...............126 B7
Attlebridge Cl *DERBY* DE21.........44 E6
Attlee Wy *WGSTN* LE18.............137 K2
Atworth Gv *NORM/LIT* DE23........56 D8
Aubrey Av *WBRGFD* NG2...............5 M8
Aubrey Rd *ARN* NG5....................36 F6
Auburn Cl *ILK* DE7.......................31 M7
Auburn Rd *RLEIW/BBY* LE8........136 E7
Auckland Cl *MCKLVR* DE3............56 C5
  NOTTE NG7............................50 C2
Auckland Rd *HUCK/RAV* NG15....23 H2
Auden Cl *LEIN* LE4.....................124 F5
Audley Cl *ILK* DE7.......................33 H4
Audley Dr *BSTN/STPLFD* NG9......49 K6
Audley End *LEIW* LE3.................130 E6
Audon Av *BSTN/STPLFD* NG9.......63 J2
Audrey Dr *DERBY* DE21................44 E7
Augusta Cl *LEIW* LE3.................130 A1
Augusta St *NORM/LIT* DE23.........57 M5
Augustine Gdns *ARN* NG5............24 E6
Augustus Cl *RLEINE/SYS* LE7......120 A5
Aults Cl *RDERBYSW* DE65...........70 A5
Aumberry Gap *LBORO* LE11...........9 K3
Austen Av *LGEAT* NG10...............76 A2
  NORM/LIT DE23......................56 F7
  NOTTE NG7.............................4 C1
Austin Ri *LEIE* LE5.....................127 G6
Austin Rd *LEIN* LE4...................61 M3
Austin Sq *NORM/LIT* DE23...........57 K8
Austin St *BLWL* NG6.....................24 A8
Austrey Av *BSTN/STPLFD* NG9....49 L7
Austwick Cl *LEIN* LE4.................125 G4
Autumn Gv *DERBYE* DE21...........58 D2
Avalon Cl *BLWL* NG6...................24 A8
Avebury Wy *LEIN* LE4.................125 G6
Avebury Cl *CFTN/RUD* NG11........64 B8
Aveline Cl *ARN* NG5....................24 D7
The Avenue *BWSH/BRSTN* DE72....43 J7
  CFTN/RUD NG11......................79 H2
  DERBY DE1............................2 F6
  DERBYE DE21........................58 D2
  LEIS LE2.............................132 A5
  LEIW LE3.............................123 H6
  RLEIW/BAR LE9.....................141 J8
  RLEIW/BBY LE8.....................136 F7
Avenue A *NOTT* NG1....................5 K7
Avenue B *NOTT* NG1....................5 L7
Avenue C *NOTT* NG1....................5 L7
Avenue D *NOTT* NG1.....................5 L7
Avenue E *NOTT* NG1.....................5 L7
Avenue Gdns *LEIS* LE2..............132 A6
Avenue Rd *BPR/DUF* DE56..........29 J2
  COAL LE67...........................108 B7
  LEIS LE2.............................132 A6
  RLBORO LE12.......................114 B4
  RLEINE/SYS LE7....................121 H2
Avenue Rd Extension *LEIS* LE2....131 L6
Averham Cl *DERBYE* DE21...........44 F6
Averil Rd *LEIE* LE5.....................127 G6
Averton Sq *WOL/BIL/BRX* NG8....50 B4
Avery Dr *COAL* LE67...................116 B6
  RLEINE/SYS LE7....................120 F3
Avery Hl *LEIW* LE3.....................130 B3
Aviemore Cl *ARN* NG5.................25 M7
Aviemore Wy *DERBYSE* DE24......71 J3
Avis Av *HEANOR* DE75................20 D8
Avoca Cl *LEIE* LE5.....................132 F1
Avocet Ct *DERBYSE* DE21...........71 H3
Avocet Whf *WBRGFD* NG2...........50 D5
Avonbridge Rd *ARN* NG5.............26 A6
Avon Cl *DERBYSE* DE24..............58 C7
  LEIS LE2.............................139 G2
Avondale *COT/KEY/RAD* NG12......67 L4
Avondale Cl *LGEAT* NG10............75 L1
Avondale Rd *CARL* NG4...............52 B1
  DERBYE DE21........................59 H1
  ILK DE7..............................47 G2
  NORM/LIT DE23.......................2 E7
  WGSTN LE18........................138 B4
Avon Dr *RLEIW/BBY* LE8.............136 D8
Avon Gdns *WBRGFD* NG2............51 K8
Avonlea Cl *ILK* DE7......................47 M1
Avonmouyh Dr *DERBYSE* DE24....58 C7
Avon Rd *BSTN/STPLFD* NG9........49 L8
Avon Rd *CARL* NG4......................38 D5
  MAPPK/POR/STA NG3..............51 M2
  RLBORO LE12.......................113 H1
Avonside Dr *LEIE* LE5.................132 D2
Avon St *DERBYSE* DE24...............58 C7
  LEIS LE2.............................7 K8
Avon Vale Rd *LBORO* LE11............9 L7
Awsworth La
  EWD/SEL/PNX NG16.................34 A4
Awsworth Rd *ILK* DE7..................33 L4
Axbridge Cl *LEIN* LE4.................125 H6
Axford Cl *CARL* NG4....................38 D5
Aycliffe Gdns *DERBYSE* DE24......72 D8
Aylesbury Av *DERBY* DE21..........44 D8
Aylesham Av *ARN* NG5................37 K1
Aylestone Dr *LEIS* LE2...............137 H2
  WOL/BIL/BRX NG8...................35 M7
Aylestone La *WGSTN* LE18.........137 M3
Aylestone Rd *LEIS* LE2..............131 H8
Aylestone Wk *LEIS* LE2..............131 K4
Aylmer Rd *LEIW* LE3..................130 D3
Ayr Cl *DERBY* DE21.....................59 H3
Ayr St *NOTTE* NG7.......................4 C4
Ayscough Av
  EWD/SEL/PNX NG16.................35 G4
Aysgarth Rd *LEIN* LE4................125 G4
Ayston Rd *LEIN* LE4...................130 E6
Ayton Cl *WBRGFD* NG2...............50 F5
Ayton Gdns *BSTN/STPLFD* NG9....63 G5
Azalea Ct *EWD/SEL/PNX* NG16....22 M7

B

Babbacombe Cl *ARN* NG5............36 F1
  DERBYSE DE24......................59 C8
Babbacombe Wy
  HUCK/RAV NG15....................23 H1
The Babington *NOTTE* * NG7........50 C5

Babbington Crs CARL NG4 38 C5
Babbington La
EWD/SEL/PNX NG16 34 D3
Babingdon Rw LEIS LE2 137 L2
Babingley Dr LEIN LE4 125 H5
Babington Ct
BSTN/STPLFD NG9 63 G2
Babington La DERBY DE1 2 E6
Babington Rd RLBORO LE12 105 H7
RLEINE/SYS LE7 119 J1
Back La ASHB DE6 54 A3
CDON/KEG DE74 84 E1
COT/KEY/RAD NG12 80 E1
EWD/SEL/PNX NG16 35 H1
ILK DE7 33 J5
MELB/CHEL DE73 72 E5
RDERBYSW DE65 68 A5
RIPLEY DE5 11 G1
RLBORO LE12 91 G8
RLBORO LE12 96 C8
RLBORO LE12 114 A4
RLEINE/SYS LE7 114 B8
RLEINE/SYS LE7 115 K3
Back Sitwell St DERBY DE1 2 F5
Back Wyver La BPR/DUF DE56 17 K2
Bacon Cl EWD/SEL/PNX NG16 21 L7
Bacton Av BLWL NG6 23 M7
Bacton Gdns BLWL NG6 23 M7
Baddely Dr WGSTN LE18 137 M3
Baden Powell Rd WBRGFD NG2 51 L3
Baden Rd LEIE LE5 132 C4
Bader Rd CFTN/RUD NG11 50 F8
Badger Cl CARL NG4 38 C7
DERBYE DE21 59 K1
END/NAR LE19 135 L8
HUCK/RAV NG15 23 G1
Badger Ct LBORO LE11 103 H7
Badger Dr RLEIW/BBY LE8 142 D2
Badgers Bank RLEINE/SYS LE7 113 J8
Badger's Cnr RLEINE/SYS LE7 115 H7
Badgers Holt LEIS LE2 138 E3
Badgers Wk RLBORO LE12 112 C2
Badmington Rd LEIN LE4 126 B2
Badminton Rd RLEINE/SYS LE7 120 F2
Baggrave St LEIE LE5 132 B1
Bagley Cl LBORO LE11 103 G1
Bagnall Av ARN NG5 25 G8
Bagnall Rd BLWL NG6 36 A3
Bagot St ILK DE7 32 A7
Bagshaw St DERBYSE DE24 58 C7
Bagthorpe Cl ARN NG5 36 E4
Baildon Cl WOL/BIL/BRX NG8 50 A4
Bailey Brook Crs
EWD/SEL/PNX NG16 20 E3
Bailey Brook Dr
EWD/SEL/PNX NG16 20 D3
Bailey Cl ARN NG5 25 H8
LBORO LE11 103 H7
Bailey Grove Rd
EWD/SEL/PNX NG16 21 H5
Bailey La COT/KEY/RAD NG12 53 J5
Bailey St BLWL NG6 36 C5
BSTN/STPLFD NG9 62 A1
CARL NG4 38 E8
NORM/LIT DE23 2 D8
Bainbridge Rd LBORO LE11 104 A7
LEIW LE3 130 F6
WGSTN LE18 138 C6
Bainbridge St NORM/LIT DE23 2 E8
Baines La LEIW LE3 129 M5
Bains Dr BWSH/BRSTN DE72 60 B6
Bainton Gv CFTN/RUD NG11 64 D6
Bakeacre La RDERBYSW DE65 70 C4
Bakehouse La
BWSH/BRSTN DE72 59 M2
Baker Av ARN NG5 25 L6
HEANOR DE75 20 D8
Bakerdale Rd
MAPPK/POR/STA NG3 51 M1
Baker Rd EWD/SEL/PNX NG16 22 A7
Bakers Hl BPR/DUF DE56 10 C6
Baker's Hollow
COT/KEY/RAD NG12 67 J4
Baker St COAL LE67 108 A5
DERBYSE DE24 58 D7
HUCK/RAV NG15 15 L8
ILK DE7 33 K6
NOTT NG1 4 F2
Bakery Cl RLEIW/BAR LE9 142 B5
Bakewell Av CARL NG4 38 C6
Bakewell Cl MCKLVR DE3 56 B4
Bakewell Dr ARN NG5 24 C8
CDON/KEG DE74 84 E5
Bakewell Rd LBORO LE11 95 K8
LGEAT NG10 76 C2
WGSTN LE18 138 A3
Bakewell St COAL LE67 108 C6
DERBYW DE22 2 C5
LEIS LE2 7 M5
Balaclava Rd NORM/LIT DE23 57 L8
Bala Dr ARN NG5 24 E8
Bala Rd RLEIW/BAR LE9 141 H3
Balcombe Av LEIW LE3 130 F1
Balderstone Cl LEIE LE5 132 E2
Baldwin Av WGSTN LE18 137 L6
Baldwin Ct NOTTE NG7 4 B6
Baldwin Ri RLEIW/BAR LE9 141 H8
Baldwin Rd WGSTN LE18 137 M2
Baldwin St EWD/SEL/PNX NG16 22 A6
NOTTE NG7 4 C5
Bale Rd LEIN LE4 126 C6
Balfour Rd BSTN/STPLFD NG9 62 B1
NORM/LIT DE23 57 L7
NOTTE NG7 4 B6
Balfour St LEIW LE3 6 A2
Balisfire Gv LEIN LE4 124 F4
Balisier Ct MAPPK/POR/STA NG3 5 H3
The Balk LEIW LE3 123 M6
Ballacraine Dr RIPLEY DE5 11 K6
Balladine Rd RLEINE/SYS LE7 118 C8
Ballantrae Cl ARN NG5 25 M7
Ballards Cl LEIN LE4 124 F4
Ballards Wy BWSH/BRSTN DE72 60 B6
Ballater Cl DERBYSE DE24 71 J3
LEIE LE5 133 H4
Balleny Cl DERBYE DE21 44 D5
Ballerat Crs ARN NG5 24 C7
Balliol Av RLEINE/SYS LE7 121 G5
Ball La BWSH/BRSTN DE72 73 L2
Ball St MAPPK/POR/STA NG3 37 K8
Balmoral Av RLBORO LE12 101 L5
WBRGFD NG2 51 J7
Balmoral Cl HEANOR DE75 20 A6
LEIS LE2 132 A8
LGEAT NG10 61 M4
NORM/LIT DE23 56 F5
Balmoral Crs WOL/BIL/BRX NG8 49 G2
Balmoral Dr BSTN/STPLFD NG9 48 F5
LEIW LE3 130 C5
Balmoral Gv HUCK/RAV NG15 15 M7
Balmoral Rd BWSH/BRSTN DE72 60 A6
CARL NG4 52 D1
COAL LE67 108 D7
ILK DE7 47 H2
NOTT NG1 4 E2
RLBORO LE12 113 H6
Bamburgh Cl DERBYE DE21 59 H3
Bambury La RLEIW/BBY LE8 143 H6
Bamford Av NORM/LIT DE23 57 J7
Bamford St RIPLEY DE5 11 H8
Bamkin Cl HUCK/RAV NG15 23 M1
Bampton Cl WGSTN LE18 138 B7
Bampton Ct WBRGFD NG2 52 A8
Bampton St LBORO LE11 9 J5
Banbury Av BSTN/STPLFD NG9 62 D4
Banbury Dr RLBORO LE12 101 K4
The Bancroft RDERBYSW DE65 68 F3
Bancroft Cl RDERBYSW DE65 68 B5
Bancroft Dr DERBYW DE22 43 G3
Bancroft St BLWL NG6 24 A8
Bandalls La RLBORO LE12 105 G3
Bangor St DERBYE DE21 44 C7
Bangor Wk
MAPPK/POR/STA NG3 5 H2
Bankart Av LEIS LE2 132 C6
Bank Ct DERBYW DE22 43 J7
Bankfield Dr BSTN/STPLFD NG9 49 G6
Bank Field Dr DERBYE DE21 59 K3
Bankfield Dr ILK DE7 46 F1
Bank Hl CALV/BJ NG14 26 D4
Bankholmes Cl DERBYSE DE24 71 J5
Bank Pl NOTT NG1 5 H7
The Banks RLBORO LE12 105 H7
RLBORO LE12 114 A4
RLEINE/SYS LE7 121 K2
RLEIW/BAR LE9 142 B5
Banksburn Cl HEANOR DE75 20 A6
Banks Cl ARN NG5 37 M2
RLBORO LE12 114 A4
Bank Side DERBYW DE22 43 J5
Bankside LEIE LE5 127 J7
Banks Rd BSTN/STPLFD NG9 62 C5
LEIS LE2 131 H8
Bank St EWD/SEL/PNX NG16 21 G3
LGEAT NG10 62 C8
Bank View Rd BPR/DUF DE56 10 A5
DERBYW DE22 43 K7
Bankwood Cl WOL/BIL/BRX NG8 35 L6
Bannell's La MCKLVR DE3 55 K7
Bannels Av NORM/LIT DE23 56 F8
Bannerman Rd BLWL NG6 36 A1
LEIE LE5 132 B4
Bantlam La END/NAR LE19 135 M4
Banwell Cl MCKLVR DE3 56 A4
Barbara Av LEIE LE5 126 F8
LEIW LE3 129 J4
Barbara Cl END/NAR LE19 135 L4
Barbara Rd LEIW LE3 130 F6
Barbara Sq HUCK/RAV NG15 15 K6
Barber Cl ILK DE7 33 J4
Barber St EWD/SEL/PNX NG16 21 L5
Barbrook Cl WOL/BIL/BRX NG8 49 M2
Barbury Dr CFTN/RUD NG11 64 B8
Barcheston Cl DERBYE DE21 44 F5
Barclay Ct ILK DE7 33 H4
Barclay St LEIW LE3 131 G3
Barden Cl LBORO LE11 102 F4
Barden Dr DERBYW DE22 43 K5
Barden Rd ARN NG5 37 L3
Bardfield Gdns ARN NG5 24 B6
Bardney Dr BLWL NG6 23 L7
Bardolph St LEIN LE4 125 M7
Bardolph St East LEIN LE4 126 A7
Bardon Cl COAL LE67 108 E8
Bardon Rd COAL LE67 108 C7
Bardsey Ct DERBYE DE21 44 F4
Bardsey Gdns ARN NG5 24 E8
Bare La BWSH/BRSTN DE72 60 A2
Barent Cl ARN NG5 36 D1
Barent Wk ARN NG5 36 D1
Barf Cl MCKLVR DE3 56 C6
Barfoot Cl RLEIW/BBY LE8 145 J6
Barfoot Rd WGSTN LE18 137 K2
Barford Cl WGSTN LE18 138 A7
Bargate Cl BPR/DUF DE56 18 A6
Bargate Rd BPR/DUF DE56 17 M5
Barge Cl WGSTN LE18 137 L7
Barkby Holt La
RLEINE/SYS LE7 121 J7
Barkby La RLEINE/SYS LE7 120 F6
Barkby Rd LEIN LE4 126 C5
RLEINE/SYS LE7 120 F4
RLEINE/SYS LE7 127 M1
Barkby Thorpe La
RLEINE/SYS LE7 120 C6
Barkbythorpe Rd LEIN LE4 126 D3
Barker Av EWD/SEL/PNX NG16 12 F3
Barker Av East LGEAT NG10 61 M1
Barker Av North LGEAT NG10 61 L1
Barker Cl ILK DE7 31 M6
Barker Ga ILK DE7 33 K5
NOTT NG1 5 K7
Barker's La BSTN/STPLFD NG9 63 J3
Barker St LEIE LE5 126 B8
Barkford Cl LEIE LE5 127 J6
Barkla Cl CFTN/RUD NG11 64 A7
Bar La WOL/BIL/BRX NG8 36 A5
Barley Cl DERBYE DE21 30 A7
LEIW LE3 124 A7
Barley Corn Cl DERBYE DE21 45 G5
Barley Cft BPR/DUF DE56 17 M5
MELB/CHEL DE73 72 D6
WBRGFD NG2 65 G3
Barley Dale Dr
BSTN/STPLFD NG9 48 B5
Barleylands CFTN/RUD NG11 79 G1
Barley La RLEIW/BBY LE8 143 M8
Barley Wy RLEINE/SYS LE7 113 J8
Barling Dr ILK DE7 33 G5
Barling Rd LEIE LE5 126 D7
Barlock Rd BLWL NG6 36 C3
Barlow Dr EWD/SEL/PNX NG16 33 M3
Barlow Dr North
EWD/SEL/PNX NG16 33 M3
Barlow Dr South
EWD/SEL/PNX NG16 33 M3
Barlow St DERBY DE1 3 H8
Barmouth Av LEIS LE2 137 L1
Barnard Cl LEIS LE2 7 J7
Barnard Rd DERBYE DE21 44 B6
Barnards Dr RLBORO LE12 114 C3
Barnard Wy RLBORO LE12 113 H6
Barnby Av WGSTN LE18 138 A3
Barnby Wk ARN NG5 37 G2
Barn Cl BLWL NG6 35 K2
CDON/KEG DE74 84 E4
COT/KEY/RAD NG12 67 J5
DERBYW DE22 43 G1
RDERBYSW DE65 70 B5
WGSTN LE18 138 C7
Barn Cft BSTN/STPLFD NG9 62 F1
Barndale Cl WBRGFD NG2 65 G4
Barnes Cl LEIN LE4 126 C2
RLEIW/BBY LE8 146 D7
Barnes Heath Rd LEIE LE5 132 E2
Barnes Rd ARN NG5 24 D7
Barnet Cl LEIS LE2 138 E4
Barnet Rd
MAPPK/POR/STA NG3 37 M8
Barnfield CFTN/RUD NG11 64 F3
Barnfield Cl RLBORO LE12 93 M3
RLEIW/BBY LE8 139 M6
Barngate Cl LEIN LE4 119 K7
Barnhill Gv NORM/LIT DE23 56 E8
Barnley Cl RLEIW/BBY LE8 143 J3
Barns Cl RLEIW/BAR LE9 129 G2
Barnsdale Rd LEIN LE4 124 D2
Barnsley Ter WBRGFD NG2 51 G6
Barnstaple Cl DERBYE DE21 44 E5
WGSTN LE18 138 B7
Barnstaple Rd LEIE LE5 133 H4
Barnston Rd WBRGFD NG2 51 K2
Barns Wy RLEIW/BAR LE9 128 A3
Barn Wy COAL LE67 116 C7
Barnwell Av LEIN LE4 125 K3
Barnwood Cl MCKLVR DE3 56 A5
Baron Cl DERBYE DE21 45 H4
Baronet Wy LEIE LE5 127 J6
Barons Cl CARL NG4 38 C6
RLEIW/BAR LE9 129 G2
Baron St LEI LE1 7 H6
Barons Wy RLBORO LE12 113 J4
Barrack La NOTTE NG7 4 B7
Barrack Rw LBORO LE11 9 K1
Barradale Av RLBORO LE12 114 A3
Barra Ms WBRGFD NG2 50 F5
Barratt Cl BSTN/STPLFD NG9 63 H6
LEIS LE2 132 B5
Barratt Crs BSTN/STPLFD NG9 63 H5
Barratt La BSTN/STPLFD NG9 63 H6
Barr Crs COAL LE67 108 D3
Barrett Dr LBORO LE11 103 H1
Barrett St DERBYSE DE24 58 E8
Barrhead Cl ARN NG5 24 C6
Barrie Dr DERBYSE DE24 71 K2
Barrington Cl
COT/KEY/RAD NG12 53 J5
Barrington Rd LEIS LE2 132 C6
Barrique Rd NOTTE NG7 50 C6
Barrons Ct BWSH/BRSTN DE72 73 L2
Barron's Wy BWSH/BRSTN DE72 60 A6
The Barroon CDON/KEG DE74 84 F4
Barrowcliffe Cl RLBORO LE12 105 G7
Barrow Cl WGSTN LE18 138 D6
Barrow La MELB/CHEL DE73 82 A1
Barrow Rd RLBORO LE12 104 D1
RLBORO LE12 105 J2
RLBORO LE12 112 D1
RLBORO LE12 114 A4
Barrows Hill La
EWD/SEL/PNX NG16 13 H2
Barrow Slade
COT/KEY/RAD NG12 80 C5
Barrow St LBORO LE11 9 K4
Barrs Hl RLBORO LE12 89 G6
Barry Cl LEIW LE3 129 J4
Barrydale Av BSTN/STPLFD NG9 63 K2
Barry Dr LEIW LE3 129 J4
RLEINE/SYS LE7 120 F3
Barry Rd LEIE LE5 127 H6
Barry St BLWL NG6 23 M8
Barsby Dr LBORO LE11 103 H1
Barston St LEI LE1 6 E3
Bartholomew St LEIS LE2 7 L9
Bartlow Rd WOL/BIL/BRX NG8 35 H8
Barton Cl CFTN/RUD NG11 78 F1
GBY/RBY LE6 123 H8
WGSTN * LE18 138 A6
Barton Knowle BPR/DUF DE56 18 B3
Barton La BSTN/STPLFD NG9 63 G6
CFTN/RUD NG11 64 A6
CFTN/RUD NG11 77 G6
CFTN/RUD NG11 77 L2
Barton Rd LEIW LE3 125 G7
LGEAT NG10 62 E8
Bartons Cl EWD/SEL/PNX NG16 22 A5
Barton St BSTN/STPLFD NG9 63 L2
Barwell Dr WOL/BIL/BRX NG8 35 H6
Barwell Rd RLEIW/BAR LE9 129 H2
Basa Crs ARN NG5 24 D7
Basford Rd BLWL NG6 36 B6
Basildon Cl DERBYSE DE24 72 D2
Baskin La BSTN/STPLFD NG9 63 G3
Baslow Av CARL NG4 38 B6
Baslow Cl LGEAT NG10 75 L2
Baslow Dr BSTN/STPLFD NG9 49 L6
DERBYW DE22 43 K4
Baslow Rd LEIE LE5 7 M8
Bassett Av RLEIW/BBY LE8 143 J4
Bassett Cl EWD/SEL/PNX NG16 22 C8
ILK DE7 33 G4
Bassett La RLEIW/BAR LE9 140 B8
Bassett Rd EWD/SEL/PNX NG16 22 C8
Bassett St LEIW LE3 6 A3
WGSTN LE18 137 K6
Bassford Av HEANOR DE75 20 D5
Bassingfield La
COT/KEY/RAD NG12 52 C8
Bassingham Cl DERBYE DE21 44 F6
Bass St DERBYW DE22 57 H1
Bastion St NOTTE NG7 50 C2
Batchelor Rd RLEIW/BBY LE8 145 K7
Bateman Gdns NOTTE NG7 4 A1
Bateman Rd LEIW LE3 124 E8
RLBORO LE12 88 B5
Bateman St DERBY DE1 3 J9
Bath Cl RLEIW/BAR LE9 140 B7
Bath La LEIW LE3 6 C5
Bathley St WBRGFD NG2 51 G6
Bath Rd MCKLVR DE3 56 C5
Baths La HUCK/RAV NG15 15 M8
Bath St DERBY DE1 43 L8
ILK DE7 33 J6
LEIN LE4 125 L4
NOTT NG1 5 K6
RLEINE/SYS LE7 120 E3
Bathurst Dr WOL/BIL/BRX NG8 49 L1
Bathurst Rd LEIE LE5 133 H3
Battenberg Rd LEIW LE3 131 G1
Batten St LEIS LE2 131 J6
Battersbee Rd LEIW LE3 124 C7
Battersbee Wy LEIW LE3 124 C7
Baulk La BSTN/STPLFD NG9 48 D8
Baverstock Cl MELB/CHEL DE73 72 D4
Bawtry Wk
MAPPK/POR/STA NG3 51 K1
Baxter Ga LBORO LE11 9 J3
Baxters Cl LEIN LE4 124 F5
Baxter Sq NORM/LIT DE23 71 K1
Baycliff Cl LEIW LE3 124 F7
Bayham Cl LEIE LE5 132 F2
Bayleaf Crs DERBYE DE21 44 F4
The Bayley NOTTE * NG7 50 C5
Bayliss Cl RLBORO LE12 104 D8
Bayliss Rd CARL NG4 38 B4
Baysdale WGSTN LE18 138 D5
Baysdale Rd LEIS LE2 131 J4
Bay St LEI LE1 6 D3
Bayswater Cl DERBYW DE22 56 D1
Bayswater Dr LEIS LE2 137 H6
Bayswater Rd
EWD/SEL/PNX NG16 22 D8
Baythorn Rd WOL/BIL/BRX NG8 49 H1
Beackden Cl BPR/DUF DE56 18 C3
Beacon Av LBORO LE11 8 F8
LEIN LE4 120 D8
RLBORO LE12 112 C2
Beacon Cl COAL LE67 116 C6
GBY/RBY LE6 123 K5
LEIN LE4 124 E1
Beacon Crs COAL LE67 108 F7
Beacon Dr LBORO LE11 9 G8
Beacon Hill Dr HUCK/RAV NG15 23 G2
Beacon Hill Ri
MAPPK/POR/STA NG3 5 L5
Beacon Rd BSTN/STPLFD NG9 63 M1
LBORO LE11 8 F9
RLBORO LE12 111 G6
Beaconsfield Rd LEIW LE3 131 G3
Beaconsfield St LGEAT NG10 62 C8
NOTTE NG7 36 D7
Beal St LEIS LE2 7 K5
Beamwood Cl DERBYE DE21 44 D6
Bean Cl BLWL NG6 35 K2
Beardall St HUCK/RAV NG15 23 M1
Beardmore Cl DERBYE DE21 44 D5
Beardsley Gdns WBRGFD NG2 50 F5
Beardsley Rd RLBORO LE12 104 D8
Beardsmore Gv
HUCK/RAV NG15 15 K6
Beast Market Hl NOTT NG1 5 G7
Beatrice Rd LEIW LE3 124 F8
Beatty Av LEIE LE5 126 C8
Beatty Rd LEIE LE5 126 C8
RLEINE/SYS LE7 120 F3
Beatty St DERBYSE DE24 58 D7
Beauchamp Rd
RLEIW/BBY LE8 146 D7
Beauclerk Dr ARN NG5 24 C7
Beaufort Av LBORO LE11 103 L7
Beaufort Cl LEIS LE2 139 H3
Beaufort Ct CFTN/RUD NG11 65 G4
Beaufort Dr BSTN/STPLFD NG9 63 G2
Beaufort Gdns DERBYE DE21 3 L1
Beaufort Rd DERBYSE DE24 71 G5
LEIW LE3 130 E6
Beaufort St DERBYE DE21 44 B7
Beaufort Wy LEIS LE2 139 H3
Beaulieu Gdns WBRGFD NG2 65 G2
Beaumanor Dr RLBORO LE12 112 A3
Beaumanor Gdns RLBORO LE12 112 A3
Beaumanor Rd LEIN LE4 125 K5
Beaumaris Ct DERBYE DE21 59 K2
Beaumaris Crs RLBORO LE12 101 K5
Beaumaris Dr
BSTN/STPLFD NG9 62 F3
CARL NG4 38 F6
Beaumaris Rd RLBORO LE12 113 G7
Beaumont Cl BSTN/STPLFD NG9 48 C6
COT/KEY/RAD NG12 80 C3
Beaumont Ct LBORO * LE11 103 L1
Beaumont Gdns WBRGFD NG2 65 H3
Beaumont Gn GBY/RBY LE6 123 K5
Beaumont Leys La LEIN LE4 125 G2
Beaumont Lodge Rd LEIN LE4 124 F1
Beaumont Rd COAL LE67 108 E3
LBORO LE11 9 J9
LEIE LE5 7 L5
RLBORO LE12 105 G7
Beaumont St LEIS LE2 138 E1
WBRGFD NG2 5 L8
Beaumont Wy LEIN LE4 124 E2
Beaurepaire Crs BPR/DUF DE56 17 M2
Beaureper Av DERBYW DE22 43 H4
Beauvale EWD/SEL/PNX NG16 22 A5
Beauvale Crs HUCK/RAV NG15 23 H1
Beauvale Dr ILK DE7 33 J2
Beauvale Ri
EWD/SEL/PNX NG16 21 L4
Beauvale Rd HUCK/RAV NG15 23 J1
WBRGFD NG2 51 G6
Beauville Dr LEIN LE4 124 E4
Beaver Cl RLEIW/BBY LE8 142 D2
Becher St NORM/LIT DE23 57 L6
Beck Cl LEIS LE2 136 E4
Beckenham Rd NOTTE NG7 4 A3
Beckenham Wy DERBYW DE22 56 F1
Becket St DERBY DE1 2 D4
Beckett Rd LEIE LE5 126 C7
Becket Well La DERBY DE1 2 E4
Beckford Rd WBRGFD NG2 51 K4
Beckhampton Rd ARN NG5 24 E8
Beckingham Rd LEIS LE2 132 A4
Beckitt Cl DERBYSE DE24 58 E7
Beckley Rd WOL/BIL/BRX NG8 35 K5
Beckside COT/KEY/RAD NG12 66 A3
Becksitch La BPR/DUF DE56 17 K5
Beck St CARL NG4 38 C7
NOTT NG1 5 J6
Bedale Cl COAL LE67 108 A7
Bedale Ct BSTN/STPLFD * NG9 62 E3
Bedale Dr LEIN LE4 125 H2
Bedale Rd ARN NG5 37 G2
Bedarra Gv NOTTE NG7 50 C3
Bede-Ling WBRGFD NG2 65 G1
Bede St LEIW LE3 6 B8
Bedford Cl CDON/KEG DE74 86 B6
DERBYW DE22 57 H4
Bedford Ct BSTN/STPLFD NG9 48 C6
NOTTE * NG7 36 D7
Bedford Dr GBY/RBY LE6 123 K5
Bedford Gv BLWL NG6 36 B2
Bedford Rd WGSTN LE18 137 L4
Bedford Rw NOTT NG1 5 K6
Bedford Sq LBORO LE11 9 J4
Bedford St DERBYW DE22 57 H4
LBORO LE11 9 J5
Bedford St North LEI LE1 7 G3
Bedford St South LEI LE1 6 F4
Bedlington Gdns
MAPPK/POR/STA NG3 37 J6
Beeby Cl RLEINE/SYS LE7 121 G4
Beeby Rd LEIE LE5 132 B1
RLEINE/SYS LE7 121 H7
RLEINE/SYS LE7 127 L7
Beecham Av
MAPPK/POR/STA NG3 37 K8
Beech Av BSTN/STPLFD NG9 63 M2
BWSH/BRSTN DE72 60 A4
BWSH/BRSTN DE72 61 K7
CARL NG4 52 D1
COT/KEY/RAD NG12 80 D5
DERBYSE DE24 58 F8
DERBYW DE22 28 E7
EWD/SEL/PNX NG16 34 F1
GBY/RBY LE6 123 J6
HUCK/RAV NG15 15 L8
LGEAT NG10 47 M8
LGEAT NG10 62 C6
MAPPK/POR/STA NG3 37 L3
MELB/CHEL DE73 82 F2
NOTTE NG7 36 E7
RIPLEY DE5 11 G5
RLBORO LE12 88 B7
Beech Cl BLWL NG6 36 A3
BPR/DUF DE56 18 F7
COAL LE67 116 C7
COT/KEY/RAD NG12 53 K5
COT/KEY/RAD NG12 65 L3
Beech Ct DERBYE DE21 59 H2
EWD/SEL/PNX NG16 13 M5
Beechcroft ILK DE7 44 B3
Beechcroft Av LEIW LE3 130 E7
Beechcroft Rd LEIS LE2 132 A6
Beechdale Rd
WOL/BIL/BRX NG8 35 K7
Beech Dr DERBYW DE22 43 K7
LEIW LE3 130 B4
RDERBYSW DE65 69 G3
RDERBYSW DE65 70 C6
RLEINE/SYS LE7 120 F5
The Beeches HEANOR DE75 20 A7
Beeches Av DERBYE DE21 59 H2
RLBORO LE12 113 J5
Beeches Rd LBORO LE11 9 M6
Beechfield Av LEIN LE4 119 L8
Beechfield Cl RLEIW/BBY LE8 139 M6
Beech Gdns DERBYSE DE24 58 F8
Beechings Cl RLEIW/BBY LE8 143 G4
Beech La ILK DE7 32 B8
Beechley Dr DERBYE DE21 44 F6
Beech Rd EWD/SEL/PNX NG16 13 L4
LEIS LE2 138 E2
RLEIW/BBY LE8 136 F8
Beech St LEIE LE5 7 M2
Beech Tree Cl RLEIW/BBY LE8 146 E5
Beech Tree Rd COAL LE67 108 E7
Beech Wk NORM/LIT DE23 57 H6
Beechwood Av LEIN LE4 126 C1
RLEINE/SYS LE7 121 H2
RLEIW/BAR LE9 129 K3
Beechwood Cl BPR/DUF DE56 17 J2
LEIE LE5 133 G2
Beechwood Crs NORM/LIT DE23 57 G7
Beechwood Rd ARN NG5 25 L7
END/NAR LE19 141 M1
Bee Hive La LBORO LE11 9 J4
Beeley Cl BPR/DUF DE56 18 A1
DERBYW DE22 43 H5
Beeston Ct BLWL NG6 24 B8
Beeston Cl BLWL NG6 24 C3
Beeston Fields Dr
BSTN/STPLFD NG9 49 G7
Beeston La NOTTE NG7 49 L6
Beeston Rd NOTTE NG7 50 B6
Beggar's La LEIW LE3 129 J5
Begonia Cl LEIW LE3 129 K5
Beighton St RIPLEY DE5 11 J6
Belconnen Rd ARN NG5 36 D2
Belfield Rd RDERBYSW DE65 69 G4
Belfield St ILK DE7 33 K5
Belfield Ter RDERBYSW * DE65 69 G4
Belford Cl BLWL NG6 23 K7
Belfry Cl MCKLVR DE3 56 D6
Belfry Dr LEIW LE3 130 A2
Belfry Wy COT/KEY/RAD NG12 66 A3
Belgrave Av LEIN LE4 125 L4
Belgrave Bvd LEIN LE4 125 G2
Belgrave Cl BPR/DUF DE56 17 M2
COAL LE67 109 G6

Belgrave F/O LEI LE1......7 G2
Belgrave Ga LEI LE1......6 F4
Belgrave Ms CFTN/RUD NG11......65 G4
Belgrave Rd BLWL NG6......23 L8
  LEIN LE4......125 L7
Belgrave St NORM/LIT DE23......2 E8
Bellamy Cl LEIS LE2......136 E4
Bellar Ga NOTT NG1......5 K7
Bell Av BWSH/BRSTN DE72......73 L8
Bell Cl GBY/RBY LE6......123 H7
Belle-Isle Rd HUCK/RAV NG15......23 L1
Belleville Dr ARN NG5......24 E7
  LEIS LE2......139 C1
Belle Vue Av LEIN LE4......125 J5
  RIPLEY DE5......19 G1
Bellevue Ct
  MAPPK/POR/STA NG3......5 L3
Bellflower Rd LEIE LE5......126 F5
Bellholme Cl LEIN LE4......125 M4
Bellingham Ct DERBYW DE22......43 G5
Bell La CFTN/RUD NG11......50 F8
  END/NAR LE19......136 A8
  ILK DE7......31 L5
  LEIE LE5......7 J4
Bellmore Gdns
  WOL/BIL/BRX NG8......49 H2
Bells La WOL/BIL/BRX NG8......35 L4
Bell St CARL NG4......38 B7
  WGSTN LE18......138 B4
Bell Vw END/NAR * LE19......136 A7
Belmont Av BLWL NG6......24 A8
  BWSH/BRSTN DE72......61 J7
  HUCK/RAV NG15......23 L3
Belmont Cl BSTN/STPLFD NG9......62 F3
Belmont Dr
  BWSH/BRSTN DE72......59 M6
Belmont St LEIW LE3......131 H8
Belmont Wy LBORO LE11......102 E5
Belper Av CARL NG4......38 B6
Belper Cl LEIS LE2......138 E3
  WGSTN LE18......137 L7
Belper Crs CARL NG4......38 B6
Belper Houses DERBYE * DE21......59 J4
Belper Rd BPR/DUF DE56......18 A6
  DERBY DE1......43 K8
  ILK DE7......31 L6
  NOTTE NG7......4 B2
Belper St ILK DE7......33 K8
  LEIN LE4......125 M6
Belsay Rd ARN NG5......24 E8
Belsford Rd EWD/SEL/PNX NG16......22 E7
Belsize Cl DERBYW DE22......56 D1
Belton Cl COAL LE67......109 G6
  LGEAT NG10......61 M3
  WGSTN LE18......137 K2
Belton Dr WBRGFD NG2......64 F3
Belton Rd LBORO LE11......103 L2
  LEIW LE3......130 E7
Belton Rd West LBORO LE11......103 J1
  NOTTE NG7......36 D7
  RLBORO LE12......101 M3
Belvedere Av NOTTE NG7......36 D7
Belvedere Cl
  COT/KEY/RAD NG12......80 C3
  MCKLVR DE3......56 B4
Belvoir Cl BWSH/BRSTN DE72......61 G8
  ILK DE7......47 H1
  LEIS LE2......139 G3
  LGEAT NG10......76 C2
  RLBORO LE12......113 H7
Belvoir Dr LBORO LE11......103 K8
  LEIS LE2......137 G1
  RLEINE/SYS LE7......121 G3
Belvoir Dr East LEIS LE2......137 H1
Belvoir Hl WBRGFD NG2......51 K3
Belvoir Rd CARL NG4......38 E8
  COAL LE67......108 A6
  WBRGFD NG2......51 L6
Belvoir St HUCK/RAV NG15......15 K7
  LEI LE1......6 F7
  MAPPK/POR/STA NG3......37 K5
  NORM/LIT DE23......57 K5
Belvoir Wy RLBORO LE12......101 L5
Belward St NOTT NG1......5 K7
Belwood Cl CFTN/RUD NG11......64 D5
Beman Cl LEIN LE4......126 C2
Bembridge Cl LEIW LE3......125 H7
Bembridge Ct
  BSTN/STPLFD NG9......48 E7
Bembridge Dr ARN NG5......36 F1
  DERBYSE DE24......73 G2
Bembridge Rd LEIW LE3......125 G2
Bemrose Rd DERBYSE DE24......58 C8
Benbow Av MELB/CHEL DE73......82 E7
Bencroft Cl RLEINE/SYS LE7......124 B1
Bendall Gn NORM/LIT DE23......71 G2
Bendbow Ri LEIW LE3......130 C4
Bendigo La WBRGFD NG2......51 L4
Benington Dr
  WOL/BIL/BRX NG8......49 G4
Ben Mayo Ct NOTTE NG7......4 A4
Benmore Ct DERBYE DE21......44 F4
Benner Av ILK DE7......47 L2
Bennerley Av ILK DE7......33 K3
Bennerley Rd BLWL NG6......23 K7
Bennett Ri RLEIW/BAR LE9......135 J7
Bennett Rd
  MAPPK/POR/STA NG3......37 L4
Bennett's La RLBORO LE12......114 B7
Bennett St DERBYSE DE24......72 B2
  LGEAT NG10......61 M1
  LGEAT NG10......62 A5
  MAPPK/POR/STA NG3......37 L3
Bennett Wy WGSTN LE18......137 L5
Benneworth Cl HUCK/RAV NG15......23 K2
Bennion Rd LEIN LE4......124 E3
  RLEINE/SYS LE7......133 L3
Benscliffe Dr LBORO LE11......8 C7
Benscliffe Rd GBY/RBY LE6......117 H1
Benskins Ov LEIN LE4......119 G3
Benskyn Cl RLEIW/BAR LE9......143 H3
Bensley Cl MELB/CHEL DE73......72 E4
Benson St DERBYSE DE24......58 C8
  LEIE LE5......132 C2
Ben St NOTTE NG7......4 A3
Bentfield Rd BPR/DUF DE56......10 A6

Bentinck Av
  COT/KEY/RAD NG12......66 B6
Bentinck Ct WBRGFD NG2......5 L7
Bentinck Rd CARL NG4......38 A5
  NOTTE NG7......4 B3
Bentinck St HUCK/RAV NG15......15 K7
Bentinghouse Rd LEIS LE2......137 H3
Bentley Av
  MAPPK/POR/STA NG3......51 L1
Bentley Cl LBORO LE11......9 M4
Bentley Rd CDON/KEG DE74......84 D3
  LEIN LE4......119 L7
  RDERBYSW DE65......69 H3
Bentley St DERBYSE DE24......72 C1
Bentwell Av ARN NG5......25 L8
Beresford Dr DERBYE DE21......59 J3
  ILK DE7......33 J2
Beresford Rd LGEAT NG10......75 L2
Beresford St NOTTE NG7......50 C2
  MAPPK/POR/STA NG3......37 G7
Berkeley Av LGEAT NG10......76 A2
  MAPPK/POR/STA NG3......37 G7
Berkeley Cl LEIS LE2......139 H2
  NORM/LIT DE23......57 H8
Berkeley Rd LBORO LE11......103 C3
Berkley St LEI LE1......6 D3
Berkshire Rd LEIS LE2......131 H8
Berkshire St DERBYSE DE21......44 B7
Berle Av HEANOR DE75......20 C4
Bermuda Av DERBYE DE21......44 A1
Bernard Av HUCK/RAV NG15......15 M6
Bernard St ARN NG5......36 F6
Berners St LEIS LE2......7 K5
Berridge Dr LEIS LE2......138 F3
Berridge La LEIN LE4......125 M4
Berridge Rd NOTTE NG7......36 C8
Berridge Rd West NOTTE NG7......36 C8
Berridge St LEI LE1......6 E6
Berriedale Cl LEIN LE4......26 A7
Berrington Cl LEIE LE5......126 C7
  RLEIW/BAR LE9......128 A1
Berrisford St COAL LE67......108 A7
Berrycott La RLBORO LE12......106 E7
Berrydown Cl
  WOL/BIL/BRX NG8......35 M6
Berry Hill Gv CARL NG4......38 C5
Berry Park Cl DERBYW DE22......43 J6
Berry's La GBY/RBY LE6......123 G7
Berwick Av DERBYE DE21......44 A8
Berwick Cl ARN NG5......37 C1
  DERBYSE DE24......72 F2
Berwick Dr DERBYSE DE24......71 H4
Berwin Ct LGEAT NG10......61 L6
Beryldene Av
  EWD/SEL/PNX NG16......22 E8
Besecar Av CARL NG4......38 C5
Besecar Cl CARL NG4......38 C5
Bessalone Dr BPR/DUF DE56......17 L2
Bessell La BSTN/STPLFD NG9......62 A2
Best Cl WGSTN LE18......137 K6
Besthorpe Cl DERBYE DE21......44 E5
Bestwick Av HEANOR DE75......20 F6
Bestwood Av ARN NG5......25 J7
Bestwood Cl ARN NG5......25 J7
Bestwood Lodge Dr ARN NG5......25 G6
Bestwood Park Dr ARN NG5......24 F7
Bestwood Park Dr
  West ARN NG5......24 B6
Bestwood Rd BLWL NG6......24 B7
  HUCK/RAV NG15......24 A1
Bestwood Ter BLWL NG6......24 B7
Beth-El NORM/LIT DE23......138 A7
Bethel Gdns HUCK/RAV NG15......23 C2
Bethulie Rd NORM/LIT DE23......57 L7
Betula Cl CFTN/RUD NG11......64 A6
Bevan Rd LEIN LE4......119 C8
Beveridge St RLBORO LE12......105 H8
Beverley Av LEIN LE4......125 M6
Beverley Cl LEIN LE4......120 C8
  WOL/BIL/BRX NG8......48 F3
Beverley Dr
  EWD/SEL/PNX NG16......22 C8
  RLEIW/BAR LE9......141 J7
Beverley Gdns CARL NG4......38 D6
Beverley Rd CDON/KEG DE74......85 H7
Beverley Sq
  MAPPK/POR/STA NG3......5 L2
Beverley St DERBYSE DE24......58 B5
Bevington Cl GBY/RBY LE6......122 F6
Bewcastle Gv LEIN LE4......125 H2
Bewcastle Rd ARN NG5......24 D5
Bewdley Rd MELB/CHEL DE73......72 E4
Bewick Dr
  MAPPK/POR/STA NG3......52 A2
Bewicke Rd LEIW LE3......130 F5
Bexhill Ri LEIE LE5......127 J8
Bexwell Cl CFTN/RUD NG11......64 C7
Biam Wy LEIW LE3......130 E7
Biant Cl WOL/BIL/BRX NG8......35 M4
Bicester Av DERBYSE DE24......71 C5
Bickley Moss DERBYE DE21......44 F6
Biddle Rd END/NAR LE19......142 A1
  LEIW LE3......124 F8
Biddulph Av LEIE LE5......7 M8
Biddulph St LEIS LE2......7 L8
Bideford Cl RIPLEY DE5......11 C5
  WGSTN LE18......138 B8
Bideford Rd DR NORM/LIT DE23......71 H1
Bidford Cl LEIW LE3......130 C5
Bidford Rd LEIW LE3......130 C5
  WOL/BIL/BRX NG8......35 K6
Bidwell Crs CFTN/RUD NG11......77 M5
Biggart Cl BSTN/STPLFD NG9......63 G5
The Biggin CDON/KEG DE74......84 F4
Biggin Hill Rd LEIE LE5......132 F4
Bigg's Cl RLBORO LE12......101 L4
Biggs Cl RLBORO LE12......106 A5
Bignal Dr LEIW LE3......129 M3
Biko Sq NOTTE NG7......36 D7
Bilberry Cl DERBY DE21......44 D6
Bilberry Wk
  MAPPK/POR/STA NG3......5 M3
Bilborough Rd
  WOL/BIL/BRX NG8......48 F2

Bilby Gdns
  MAPPK/POR/STA * NG3......51 K2
Billesdon Dr ARN NG5......36 D3
Billington Cl LEIN LE4......125 J4
Bilsdale Rd WGSTN LE18......138 D6
Bindley La RLEIW/BBY LE8......139 L6
Bingham Rd ARN NG5......37 G5
  COT/KEY/RAD NG12......53 K4
  COT/KEY/RAD NG12......67 K4
Bingham St DERBYSE DE24......72 C1
Bingley Cl WOL/BIL/BRX NG8......49 M1
Bingley Rd END/NAR LE19......141 M1
Binscombe Cl DERBYE DE21......44 D4
Birch Av BSTN/STPLFD NG9......63 M3
  CARL NG4......38 B8
  COAL LE67......108 E3
  EWD/SEL/PNX NG16......34 F1
  ILK DE7......33 L8
  RLBORO LE12......105 H6
Birch Cl COAL LE67......122 C1
  DERBYE DE21......59 L1
  LEIN LE4......126 B6
  RIPLEY DE5......11 H7
  RLBORO LE12......111 L1
Birchdale Av HUCK/RAV NG15......23 C2
Birches Rd DERBYW DE22......43 H4
Birchfield Cl COAL LE67......116 B7
Birchfield Cl MELB/CHEL DE73......72 D5
Birchfield Pk HEANOR DE75......20 D8
Birchfield Rd ARN NG5......25 L6
Birch Lea ARN NG5......25 H7
  RLBORO LE12......88 B6
Birchover Pl ILK DE7......33 J2
Birchover Ri DERBYE DE21......44 D6
Birchover Rd
  WOL/BIL/BRX NG8......49 G2
The Birches CDON/KEG * DE74......93 G1
Birch Tree Av RLEINE/SYS LE7......119 L6
Birchtree Rd WGSTN LE18......138 B3
Birchview Cl BPR/DUF DE56......17 M5
Birchwood HEANOR DE75......20 A3
Birchwood Av
  BWSH/BRSTN DE72......61 K8
  LGEAT NG10......76 A1
  NORM/LIT DE23......71 H1
Birchwood Cl LEIW LE3......129 K5
  RLEINE/SYS LE7......121 G4
Birchwood Rd
  WOL/BIL/BRX NG8......49 G3
Bircumshaw's Rd
  HEANOR DE75......20 C5
Birdcage Wk DERBYW DE22......56 D1
Birdcroft La ILK DE7......47 K2
Bird Hill Rd RLBORO LE12......111 K5
Birdie Cl RLEIW/BBY LE8......146 F7
Birdsall Av WOL/BIL/BRX NG8......49 J3
Birds Nest Av LEIW LE5......124 D7
Birdwood St NORM/LIT DE23......57 K6
Birkdale Av LEIS LE2......132 B6
Birkdale Cl COT/KEY/RAD NG12......65 L5
  ILK DE7......33 H6
  MCKLVR DE3......56 D5
Birkdale Rd RLEINE/SYS LE7......124 A1
Birkenshaw Rd LEIW LE3......124 E6
Birkin Av BSTN/STPLFD NG9......63 G7
  CFTN/RUD NG11......65 G7
  COT/KEY/RAD NG12......53 L3
  NOTTE NG7......4 A2
Birkland Av
  MAPPK/POR/STA NG3......37 L3
  NOTT NG1......5 H3
Birley St BSTN/STPLFD NG9......62 B2
Birling Cl BLWL NG6......23 J8
Birrell Rd NOTTE NG7......36 E7
Birsmore Av LEIN LE4......126 B3
Birstall Av LEIN LE4......125 L2
Birstall St LEI LE1......7 K2
Bistow Crs LEIN LE4......125 H2
Biscay Ct DERBYE DE21......45 G5
Bisham Dr WBRGFD NG2......51 M8
Bishop Dl COAL LE67......100 B8
Bishopdale Cl LGEAT NG10......75 L1
Bishopdale Dr
  EWD/SEL/PNX NG16......22 F8
Bishopdale Rd LEIN LE4......125 G4
Bishop Meadow Rd
  LBORO LE11......103 J1
Bishops Cl COT/KEY/RAD NG12......80 C3
Bishops Ct MELB/CHEL DE73......82 F8
Bishop's Dr DERBYE DE21......18 D5
Bishop St EWD/SEL/PNX NG16......21 K5
  LBORO LE11......9 L2
  LEI LE1......6 F6
Bishops Wy HUCK/RAV NG15......15 M6
Bisley St LEIW LE3......131 H4
Bispham Dr BSTN/STPLFD NG9......62 D4
Blaby By-Pass RLEIW/BBY LE8......136 E8
Blaby Cl NORM/LIT DE23......71 H1
Blaby Rd END/NAR LE19......135 M4
  WGSTN LE18......137 L6
Blackberry La RLEINE/SYS LE7......114 C7
Blackberry Wy BPR/DUF DE56......18 D5
Blackbird Av LEIN LE4......125 H7
Blackbird Rd LEIN LE4......125 H7
Blackbird Rw BPR/DUF DE56......18 A6
Blackbrook Cl RLBORO LE12......101 L4
Blackbrook Dr COAL LE67......108 F7
Blackbrook Rd LBORO LE11......8 A5
Blackburn Hl ILK DE7......33 H4
Blackett Av LEIW LE3......124 E7
Blackfriars Cl WOL/BIL/BRX NG8......35 H5
Blackfriars St LEI LE1......6 A2
Blackham Rd LBORO LE11......9 H8
Blackhill Dr CARL NG4......38 D7
Blackmore Dr LEIW LE3......130 E2
Blackmore St NORM/LIT DE23......57 L8
Blackmount Ct DERBYSE DE24......71 H4
Blackrod Cl
  BSTN/STPLFD * NG9......62 E5
Blacksmiths Av RLBORO LE12......102 A2
Blacksmiths Cl RLEINE/SYS LE7......115 L4
Blackstone Wk WBRGFD NG2......5 L7
Blackthorn Cl DERBYE DE21......44 C5
  MELB/CHEL DE73......82 E8

Blackthorn Dr LEIN LE4......124 D1
  RLEINE/SYS LE7......120 C4
Blackthorne Cl BPR/DUF DE56......18 D5
Blackthorne Dr BLWL NG6......35 M4
  EWD/SEL/PNX NG16......21 J5
Blackthorn La LEIS LE2......132 F5
Blackthorn Rd LEIS LE2......123 M8
Blackwell Cl WGSTN LE18......138 C6
Blackwell La MELB/CHEL DE73......82 F8
Blackwood Cl COAL LE67......108 B5
Bladen Cl RLEIW/BBY LE8......143 H3
Bladon Cl MAPPK/POR/STA NG3......37 J5
Bladon Rd CFTN/RUD NG11......64 F5
Blagreaves Av NORM/LIT DE23......71 G2
Blagreaves La NORM/LIT DE23......57 G8
Blair Cl RLBORO LE12......113 C7
Blairmore Rd LEIE LE5......130 A1
Blaise Cl CFTN/RUD NG11......64 C7
Blaise Gv LEIN LE4......126 B6
Blakebrook Dr
  MELB/CHEL DE73......72 E4
Blake Cl ARN NG5......25 L8
Blake Ct END/NAR LE19......135 L4
  LGEAT NG10......75 M2
Blake Dr LBORO LE11......103 H2
Blakeley La RDERBYSW DE65......68 F5
Blakelow Dr RDERBYSW DE65......68 F4
Blakemore Av MELB/CHEL DE73......82 F7
Blakeney Rd
  COT/KEY/RAD NG12......53 M4
Blakenhall Cl END/NAR LE19......135 K7
Blakenhall Rd LEIE LE5......132 C2
Blake Rd BSTN/STPLFD NG9......62 C1
  WBRGFD NG2......51 L8
Blakesley Rd WGSTN LE18......138 D4
Blake St ILK DE7......33 K6
  LEI LE1......6 E4
Blanch Cft MELB/CHEL DE73......82 F8
Blandford Cl LGEAT NG10......75 M2
Blandford Cl DERBYSE DE24......73 H1
Blandford Rd
  BSTN/STPLFD NG9......63 G2
Bland La CALV/BJ NG14......27 L2
Bland Rd LEIW LE3......124 D7
Blanford Gdns WBRGFD NG2......65 G2
Blankley Dr LEIS LE2......132 B6
Blanklyn Av LEIE LE5......132 D4
Blankney Cl DERBYSE DE24......71 H5
Blankney St BLWL NG6......36 C3
Blantyre Av ARN NG5......24 C6
Blaydon Cl LEIW LE3......124 F7
Bleaberry Cl WBRGFD NG2......66 A2
Bleachers Yd NOTTE NG7......36 E6
Bleakmoor Cl RLEINE/SYS LE7......115 L4
Bleasby Cl LEIN LE4......126 E3
Bleasby St WBRGFD NG2......51 K3
Bleasdale Cl CARL NG4......38 C5
Blencathra Cl WBRGFD NG2......66 A2
Blencathra Dr MCKLVR DE3......56 C4
Blenheim Av
  MAPPK/POR/STA NG3......38 A5
Blenheim Cl CFTN/RUD NG11......64 F7
  LBORO LE11......103 G3
  WGSTN LE18......137 K7
Blenheim Ct BPR/DUF DE56......18 C3
Blenheim Crs RLEINE/BAR LE9......141 H8
Blenheim Dr BSTN/STPLFD NG9......63 G2
  DERBYW DE22......43 G4
Blenheim La BLWL NG6......23 K6
Blenheim Ms
  RDERBYSW * DE65......69 G3
Blenheim Pde DERBYW DE22......43 J3
Blenheim Rd LEIN LE4......119 M7
Blenheim Wy LEIN LE4......125 J3
Bley Av RLBORO LE12......88 D3
Blidworth Cl WOL/BIL/BRX NG8......35 J3
Blind La BWSH/BRSTN DE72......61 H7
Blissett Rd LEIW LE3......124 F4
Blithe Cl RDERBYSW DE65......68 C6
Blithfield Av LBORO LE11......102 F4
Blithfield Gdns
  MELB/CHEL DE73......72 E4
Bloomfield Cl DERBY DE1......3 H8
  RDERBYSW DE65......68 B6
Bloomfield Rd LEIS LE2......131 K8
Bloomfield St DERBY DE1......3 H8
Bloomsbury Dr
  EWD/SEL/PNX NG16......35 J4
Bloomsgrove Rd ILK DE7......33 K5
Bloomsgrove St NOTTE NG7......4 B3
Blossom Rd LEIW LE5......130 E3
The Blossoms COAL LE67......122 C1
Blount Rd LEIN LE4......126 D1
Bloxams Cl LEIW LE3......136 D1
Bloxham Rd LEIW LE3......124 F8
Blue Banks Av LEIS LE2......136 E4
Bluebell Cl DERBYSE DE24......71 G5
  EWD/SEL/PNX NG16......13 K5
  HUCK/RAV NG15......23 G1
  RLEINE/SYS LE7......121 J1
  RLEIW/BAR LE9......129 K1
Bluebell Dr GBY/RBY LE6......123 L4
  LBORO LE11......8 E5
  WGSTN LE18......137 K3
Blue Bell Hill Rd
  MAPPK/POR/STA NG3......5 M3
Bluebell Wy HEANOR DE75......20 F6
Bluebird Ct DERBYSE DE24......71 H3
Bluecoat Cl NOTT NG1......5 G4
Bluecoat St NOTT NG1......5 G4
Blue Gates Rd LEIN LE4......124 D2
Blue Granite Pk
  RLBORO * LE12......113 G5
Blue Pots Cl LEIS LE2......129 J5
Blundell Cl
  MAPPK/POR/STA NG3......37 K7
Blundell Rd LEIE LE5......132 C4
Blunt's La WGSTN LE18......138 D5
Blunt St ILK DE7......33 L5
Blyth Gdns
  MAPPK/POR/STA NG3......37 J3
Blyth Pl DERBYE DE21......44 B6
Blyth St MAPPK/POR/STA NG3......37 J6
Blyton Wk ARN NG5......24 D7
Boat La EWD/SEL/PNX NG16......12 C8

Boatmans Cl ILK DE7......33 K5
Boatswain Dr HUCK/RAV NG15......15 M7
Bobbers Mill Br NOTTE NG7......36 B8
Bobbers Mill Rd NOTTE NG7......36 C8
Boden Dr EWD/SEL/PNX NG16......35 J1
Bodenham Cl WGSTN LE18......138 A7
Boden St NORM/LIT DE23......3 C9
  NOTTE NG7......4 B5
Bodicoat Cl RLEINE/BBY LE8......142 D2
Bodmin Av HUCK/RAV NG15......23 C2
  WGSTN LE18......138 A7
Bodmin Cl DERBYSE DE24......71 H4
Bodmin Dr WOL/BIL/BRX NG8......36 A5
Bodnant Av LEIE LE5......132 C4
Body Rd BSTN/STPLFD NG9......62 F4
Bohem Rd LGEAT NG10......62 A4
Bold Cl BLWL NG6......23 M7
Bold La DERBY DE1......2 E3
Bolero Cl WOL/BIL/BRX NG8......49 J2
Bolingey Wy HUCK/RAV NG15......23 G2
Bollard's La RLBORO LE12......86 E8
Bollington Rd LEIS LE2......139 C1
  LEIE LE5......132 C1
Bolton Av BSTN/STPLFD NG9......63 G3
Bolton Cl WBRGFD NG2......51 L8
Bolton Rd LEIW LE3......131 G2
Bolton Ter COT/KEY/RAD NG12......53 K4
Bolus Rd LEIW LE3......130 A5
Bonchurch Cl COAL LE67......108 D2
  DERBYSE DE24......73 G2
Bonchurch St LEIW LE3......6 A2
Bond Cl DERBYE DE21......9 L9
Bondgate CDON/KEG DE74......84 F4
Bondland La BPR/DUF DE56......10 C5
Bond Rd RLEINE/SYS LE7......113 G5
Bondman Cl LEIN LE4......125 J3
Bond St ARN NG5......25 J7
  WBRGFD NG2......51 M5
Bonetti Cl MAPPK/POR/STA NG3......38 A2
Bonington Cl BLWL NG6......35 L1
Bonington Dr ARN NG5......25 K8
Bonington Rd
  MAPPK/POR/STA NG3......37 K3
Bonner Cl LEIS LE2......139 H3
Bonner Hl CALV/BJ NG14......26 D1
Bonners La LEIS LE2......6 D8
Bonner's Rd
  EWD/SEL/PNX NG16......33 M3
Bonney Rd LEIS LE2......124 E6
Bonnie Prince Charlie Wk
  DERBYW DE22......56 C1
Bonnington Crs ARN NG5......37 G3
Bonnington Rd LEIS LE2......131 M6
Bonny Md COT/KEY/RAD NG12......67 J6
Bonnyrigg Dr DERBYE DE21......44 E5
Bonsall Av NORM/LIT DE23......57 H7
Bonsall Dr MCKLVR DE3......56 C4
Bonsall St LEIS LE2......62 C7
  LGEAT NG10......62 C7
Bonser Cl CARL NG4......38 C8
Bonville Pl LEIW LE3......130 F6
Booth Cl LEIE LE5......132 F2
  MAPPK/POR/STA NG3......5 J5
Boothgate BPR/DUF DE56......18 C1
Booth St DERBYSE DE24......58 D8
  RIPLEY DE5......11 J5
Bordeaux Cl END/NAR LE19......135 L4
Border Crs DERBYSE DE24......72 F3
Border Dr LEIN LE4......125 J3
Borlace Crs BSTN/STPLFD NG9......62 C1
Borlace St LEIW LE3......6 A4
Borman Cl BLWL NG6......35 K2
Borough St CDON/KEG DE74......84 F4
  CDON/KEG DE74......86 B5
Borrowash By-Pass
  DERBYE DE21......58 F4
Borrowash Rd DERBYE DE21......59 K4
Borrowcup Cl RLEIW/BBY LE8......143 G3
Borrowdale Cl WBRGFD NG2......66 B1
Borrowdale Dr LGEAT NG10......75 L1
Borrowdale Wy LBORO LE11......103 G6
Borrowell CDON/KEG DE74......86 A4
Borrowfield Rd DERBYE DE21......59 J4
Borrowfields
  BWSH/BRSTN DE72......59 M6
Boscastle Rd DERBYSE DE24......72 F1
Bosden Cl WOL/BIL/BRX NG8......49 G5
Bosley Sq BSTN/STPLFD NG9......49 L8
Bostock's La
  BWSH/BRSTN DE72......61 K3
Boston Cl DERBYE DE21......59 G1
Boston Ms ARN * NG5......36 D4
Boston Rd LEIN LE4......124 D3
Boston St NOTT NG1......5 K7
Boswell Sq NORM/LIT DE23......57 K8
Boswell St END/NAR LE19......135 L6
  NOTTE NG7......50 C2
Bosworth Av NORM/LIT DE23......71 J1
Bosworth Dr
  EWD/SEL/PNX NG16......21 M4
Bosworth Rd CDON/KEG DE74......84 D4
  LEIE LE5......6 A5
Bosworth Wy LGEAT NG10......76 C2
Botany Av
  MAPPK/POR/STA NG3......37 J7
Botany Cl CFTN/RUD NG11......65 G4
Botany Dr ILK DE7......33 K2
Botcheston Rd GBY/RBY LE6......128 B1
Bothe Cl LGEAT NG10......76 A1
Bottleacre La LBORO LE11......103 L1
Botts Wy COAL LE67......108 D8
Boulder La LEIE LE5......137 K1
Boulter Crs WGSTN LE18......138 B4
Boulton Ct LEIS LE2......139 J3
Boulton Dr DERBYSE DE24......72 E1
Boulton La DERBYSE DE24......72 D2
Boundary Crs
  BSTN/STPLFD NG9......49 K6
Boundary La
  EWD/SEL/PNX NG16......21 M4
Boundary Rd BSTN/STPLFD NG9......49 K6
  DERBYW DE22......2 A5
  LEIS LE2......131 H6
  RDERBYSW DE65......69 H3

RLBORO LE12 113 H6
WBRGFD NG2 65 J3
Boundary Wy RLBORO LE12 102 A2
Bourne Cl BSTN/STPLFD NG9 49 H6
Bourne Cottages ILK * DE7 33 J6
Bourne Ms CARL NG4 52 E1
Bourne Sq BWSH/BRSTN DE72 61 J7
Bourne St CARL NG4 52 E1
DERBY DE1 2 F6
Bournmoor Av CFTN/RUD NG11 64 C6
Bourton Crs LEIS LE2 139 G2
Bovill St NOTTE NG7 4 B4
Bowbank Cl NORM/LIT DE23 70 E1
Bow Br LEIW LE3 6 B6
Bowbridge Av NORM/LIT DE23 71 G2
Bowden Dr BSTN/STPLFD NG9 63 M1
Bowers Av MAPPK/POR/STA NG3 5 J1
Bower St DERBYSE DE24 58 D7
Bowes Well Rd ILK DE7 33 J5
Bowhill Gv LEIE LE5 133 J1
Bowland Cl
MAPPK/POR/STA NG3 37 L8
MCKLVR DE3 56 C6
Bowlees Ct NORM/LIT DE23 56 C8
Bowler Ct LBORO LE11 9 L3
Bowler Dr BPR/DUF DE56 18 E8
Bowler St RIPLEY DE5 11 H8
The Bowley CDON/KEG DE74 92 F2
Bowling Aly BPR/DUF DE56 10 C6
Bowling Cl ILK DE7 47 J7
Bowling Green St LEI LE1 6 F6
Bowlwell Av ARN NG5 24 D7
Bowmans Wy LEIW LE3 123 M7
Bowmars La LEIW LE3 6 C3
Bowmer Rd DERBYSE DE24 58 C6
Bown Cl BPR/DUF DE56 18 E7
Bowness Av BLWL NG6 36 A5
Bowness Cl WBRGFD NG2 52 A8
Bowscale Cl WBRGFD NG2 66 A2
Boxley Dr WBRGFD NG2 65 H3
Boxmoor Cl NORM/LIT DE23 56 D8
Boyce Gdns
MAPPK/POR/STA NG3 37 K6
Boycroft Av
MAPPK/POR/STA NG3 37 K7
Boyd Cl ARN NG5 25 M6
Boyd Gv MELB/CHEL DE73 72 E7
Boyer St DERBYW DE22 2 C8
LBORO LE11 9 L2
Boyers Wk LEIW LE3 129 K4
Boyer Wk DERBYW DE22 2 C7
Boylestone Rd NORM/LIT DE23 71 G2
Boynton Dr
MAPPK/POR/STA NG3 37 K6
Boynton Rd LEIW LE3 130 E3
Brabazon Cl LEIS LE2 138 D2
Brabazon Rd LEIS LE2 138 D1
Bracadale Rd ARN NG5 24 D6
Bracebridge Dr
WOL/BIL/BRX NG8 35 H8
Bracey Ri WBRGFD NG2 65 J4
Bracken Cl CARL NG4 38 B5
LEIE LE5 132 F3
LEIW LE3 129 K5
LGEAT NG10 61 M6
WOL/BIL/BRX NG8 35 K6
Bracken Dl RLEINE/SYS LE7 115 J8
Brackendale Av ARN NG5 25 K7
Brackenfield Dr
EWD/SEL/PNX NG16 21 M7
Brackenfield Wy LEIN LE4 120 D7
Bracken Hl GBY/RBY LE6 117 J7
Bracken Rd LGEAT NG10 61 M6
Brackens Av DERBYSE DE24 72 D1
Brackensdale Av DERBYW DE22 56 F2
Bracken's La DERBYSE DE24 72 D1
Brackenthwaite LEIN LE4 126 B4
Bracken Wy COAL LE67 116 C6
Brackley BPR/DUF DE56 18 D6
Brackley Dr DERBYE DE21 59 J2
Brackley Ga ILK DE7 30 E5
Bracknell Crs WOL/BIL/BRX NG8 36 B6
Bracknell Dr DERBYSE DE24 72 E2
Bracton Dr
MAPPK/POR/STA NG3 51 K1
Bradbourne Av CFTN/RUD NG11 64 E2
Bradbourne Ct DERBYW * DE22 2 B8
Bradbourne Rd LEIE LE5 132 B2
Bradbury Cl BWSH/BRSTN DE72 60 A6
RLEIW/BAR LE9 142 B4
Bradbury St WBRGFD NG2 51 L3
Braddock Cl NOTTE NG7 50 C3
Braddon Av BSTN/STPLFD NG9 48 C6
Braddon Rd LBORO LE11 103 G1
Bradfield Cl LEIE LE5 132 C3
Bradfield Rd WOL/BIL/BRX NG8 35 K6
Bradgate Av LEIN LE4 120 D8
Bradgate Cl LGEAT NG10 61 M3
RLEINE/SYS LE7 133 J2
Bradgate Ct NORM/LIT DE23 71 J1
Bradgate Dr COAL LE67 108 F7
GBY/RBY LE6 123 G6
RIPLEY DE5 10 F6
WGSTN LE18 137 M2
Bradgate Hl GBY/RBY LE6 116 E8
Bradgate Rd COAL LE67 116 C6
GBY/RBY LE6 117 K7
LBORO LE11 103 J7
NOTTE NG7 36 D7
RLEINE/SYS LE7 118 C4
Bradgate St LEIN LE4 6 B1
Brading Cl DERBYSE DE24 73 H2
Brading Rd LEIW LE3 125 G7
Bradley Dr BPR/DUF DE56 17 M3
Bradley St DERBYW DE22 43 J7
LGEAT NG10 62 A2
Bradley's Yd
COT/KEY/RAD NG12 66 C8
Bradley Wk CFTN/RUD NG11 64 C7
Bradman Gdns ARN NG5 37 M1
Bradmoor Gv MELB/CHEL DE73 72 F5
Bradmore Av CFTN/RUD NG11 65 G7
Bradmore La
COT/KEY/RAD NG12 80 B2
Bradmore Ri ARN NG5 37 G3
Bradmore Rd
COT/KEY/RAD NG12 90 A3
Bradshaw Av ALFN DE55 12 B1
LEIS LE2 137 G4
Bradshaw Cft BPR/DUF DE56 17 J1
Bradshaw Dr BPR/DUF DE56 30 A1
Bradshaw St LGEAT NG10 75 M2
Bradshaw Wy DERBY DE1 3 G6
Bradston Rd LEIS LE2 137 J2
Bradwell Cl EWD/SEL/PNX NG16 22 A7
MCKLVR DE3 56 C6
Bradwell Dr ARN NG5 24 E7
Bradwell Wy BPR/DUF DE56 17 M2
Braefell Cl COT/KEY/RAD NG12 66 B2
Braefield Cl ILK DE7 47 G2
Braemar Av
EWD/SEL/PNX NG16 21 K6
Braemar Cl DERBYSE DE24 71 H4
RLBORO LE12 113 H7
Braemar Dr CARL NG4 38 F6
LEIN LE4 126 A3
Braemar Rd BLWL NG6 24 A8
Brafield Cl BPR/DUF DE56 18 B3
Braidwood Ct NOTTE NG7 4 B1
Brailsford Rd DERBYE DE21 44 C7
NOTTE NG7 50 C6
WGSTN LE18 137 M3
Brailsford Wy
BSTN/STPLFD NG9 63 G6
Braintree Cl DERBYE DE21 44 B5
Braithwell Cl DERBYW DE22 43 K5
Bramall Ct LEIE LE5 126 C7
Bramall Rd LEIE LE5 126 B8
Bramber Cl LEIN LE4 126 C1
Bramber Gv CFTN/RUD NG11 64 C8
Brambleberry Ct DERBYE DE21 44 F4
Bramble Cl BLWL NG6 36 B4
BSTN/STPLFD NG9 63 H5
LEIE LE5 127 H5
LEIW LE3 124 B8
LGEAT NG10 61 M6
Bramble Dr
MAPPK/POR/STA NG3 37 L8
Bramble Gdns
WOL/BIL/BRX NG8 35 M7
Bramble Ms MCKLVR DE3 56 B6
Bramble St DERBY DE1 2 D4
Bramble Wy BPR/DUF DE56 18 D5
Brambleway
COT/KEY/RAD NG12 67 L5
Bramble Wy LEIW LE3 130 E6
Bramblewick Dr
NORM/LIT DE23 70 E1
Brambling Crs MCKLVR DE3 55 L8
Brambling Rd LEIE LE5 7 M4
Brambling Wy LEIS LE2 138 E3
Bramcote Av BSTN/STPLFD NG9 63 H1
Bramcote Dr BSTN/STPLFD NG9 49 J8
WOL/BIL/BRX NG8 49 H4
Bramcote Dr West
BSTN/STPLFD NG9 63 H1
Bramcote La BSTN/STPLFD NG9 63 G1
WOL/BIL/BRX NG8 49 H5
Bramcote Rd
BSTN/STPLFD NG9 49 J8
LBORO LE11 103 K8
LEIW LE3 130 F7
WGSTN LE18 138 A4
Bramcote St NOTTE NG7 50 C2
Bramcote Wk NOTTE NG7 50 C2
Bramerton Rd
WOL/BIL/BRX NG8 49 H1
Bramfield Av DERBYW DE22 2 A8
Bramhall Rd WOL/BIL/BRX NG8 49 G1
Bramham Cl LEIW LE3 124 E6
Bramley Cl DERBYE DE21 45 G4
RLEIW/BAR LE9 141 J8
Bramley Ct LEIW LE3 123 M7
Bramley Orch RLEINE/SYS LE7 133 L2
Bramley Rd LEIN LE4 119 M8
LEIW LE3 131 G2
WOL/BIL/BRX NG8 35 J6
Brampton Av HEANOR DE75 20 E5
LEIW LE3 130 E1
Brampton Cl MCKLVR DE3 56 A4
Brampton Ct BPR/DUF * DE56 18 B3
Brampton Dr BSTN/STPLFD NG9 62 C2
Brampton Wy LEIS LE2 138 D1
Brancaster Cl BLWL NG6 35 M3
LEIN LE4 125 H5
Brandelhow Ct DERBYE DE21 44 F4
Brand Hl RLBORO LE12 111 L7
Brandish Crs CFTN/RUD NG11 64 B6
Brand La RLBORO LE12 111 M7
Brandon St LEIN LE4 125 L7
Brandreth Av
MAPPK/POR/STA NG3 37 K7
Brandreth Dr
EWD/SEL/PNX NG16 21 L8
Brand St WBRGFD NG2 51 J4
Branklene Cl
EWD/SEL/PNX NG16 22 C8
Branksome Av DERBYSE DE24 59 G8
Bransdale Cl LGEAT NG10 75 M1
Bransdale Rd CFTN/RUD NG11 64 B7
WGSTN LE18 138 D5
Branston Av RLBORO LE12 105 J7
Branston Gdns WBRGFD NG2 65 H3
Branston Wk ARN NG5 37 G3
Brantford Av CFTN/RUD NG11 64 D6
Branting Hl GBY/RBY LE6 123 M4
Branting Hill Av LEIW LE3 123 M5
Branting Hill Gv LEIW LE3 123 M5
Brassington Cl
EWD/SEL/PNX NG16 21 M8
ILK DE7 32 C7
Brassington Rd DERBYE DE21 44 D6
Bratmyr RLEIW/BBY LE8 145 K6
Braunstone Av LEIW LE3 130 E5
Braunstone Cl LEIW LE3 130 D6
Braunstone Ga LEIW LE3 6 B7
Braunstone La LEIW LE3 130 B4
Braunstone La East LEIW LE3 130 F7
Braunstone Wy LEIW LE3 130 C4
Braunton Cl HUCK/RAV NG15 23 H1
Braybrooke Rd LEIN LE4 126 C6
Brayfield Av NORM/LIT DE23 57 H7
Brayfield Rd NORM/LIT DE23 57 G7
Braymish Cl RLEIW/BBY LE8 146 F7
Brayton Crs BLWL NG6 36 B2
Brazil St LEIS LE2 131 J4
Breachfield Rd RLBORO LE12 105 H8
Breach La MELB/CHEL DE73 82 C6
Breach Rd COAL LE67 108 B8
HEANOR DE75 20 E7
RIPLEY DE5 19 K3
Breadcroft La RLBORO LE12 105 H7
Breadsall Ct ILK * DE7 33 K4
Breakback Rd RLBORO LE12 111 H4
Breaston La BWSH/BRSTN DE72 61 H3
Brechin Cl ARN NG5 25 M6
Breck Hill Rd ARN NG5 37 J3
Breckswood Dr
CFTN/RUD NG11 64 C8
Brecon Cl DERBYE DE21 59 J1
LGEAT NG10 61 L7
WGSTN LE18 137 K5
WOL/BIL/BRX NG8 35 L3
Bredon Cl LGEAT NG10 61 L7
Breech Hedge RLEINE/SYS LE7 113 H8
Breedon Av NORM/LIT DE23 71 H2
WGSTN LE18 138 A4
Breedon Hill Rd NORM/LIT DE23 2 C8
Breedon La RLBORO LE12 100 B2
Breedon St LEIS LE2 7 L6
LGEAT NG10 61 M5
Brendon Cl RLBORO LE12 102 A6
Brendon Ct
BSTN/STPLFD * NG9 48 F7
Brendon Dr
EWD/SEL/PNX NG16 22 D8
WOL/BIL/BRX NG8 49 L2
Brendon Gdns
WOL/BIL/BRX NG8 49 L2
Brendon Rd WOL/BIL/BRX NG8 49 L2
Brendon Wy LGEAT NG10 61 L6
Brentcliffe Av
MAPPK/POR/STA NG3 37 L8
Brentford Dr DERBYW DE22 56 F1
Brent Knowle Gdns LEIE LE5 133 H2
Brentwood Rd LEIS LE2 131 L6
Bren Wy RDERBYSW DE65 68 C5
Bressingham Dr
CFTN/RUD NG11 65 G4
Bretby Rd LEIS LE2 137 J1
Bretby Sq NORM/LIT DE23 71 G2
Breton Cl WGSTN LE18 144 E4
Brett Cl HUCK/RAV NG15 23 J3
Brettell Rd LEIS LE2 137 H3
Bretton Av NORM/LIT DE23 57 G5
Bretton Cl LEIN LE4 125 J4
Bretton Rd BPR/DUF DE56 18 C2
Brewer Cl LEIN LE4 126 C2
Brewery St EWD/SEL/PNX NG16 34 D1
Brewsters Rd
MAPPK/POR/STA NG3 37 K7
Brex Ri LEIW LE3 130 B1
Breydon Cl DERBYSE DE24 72 B3
Brian Rd LEIN LE4 125 H6
The Brianway LEIE LE5 126 D8
Briar Av LGEAT NG10 61 L4
Briarbank Av
MAPPK/POR/STA NG3 37 L7
Briar Cl BSTN/STPLFD NG9 49 J6
BWSH/BRSTN DE72 60 A6
COT/KEY/RAD NG12 80 D3
DERBYE DE21 58 F2
HUCK/RAV NG15 23 H2
LEIS LE2 138 F3
Briarfield Dr LEIE LE5 127 J6
Briar Ga COT/KEY/RAD NG12 67 L5
LGEAT NG10 61 L5
Briargate Dr LEIN LE4 119 J7
Briar Lea Cl DERBYSE DE24 71 K3
Briar Meads LEIS LE2 138 F4
Briar Rd EWD/SEL/PNX NG16 21 M7
LEIE LE5 127 H8
Briarsgate DERBYW DE22 43 H5
Briars Wy RIPLEY DE5 11 H7
Briar Wk LEIS LE2 138 F3
Briarwood Av
MAPPK/POR/STA NG3 37 L8
Briarwood Wy NORM/LIT DE23 71 G1
Brickcliffe Rd RLBORO LE12 88 D5
Brickenell Rd CALV/BJ NG14 26 D1
Brickkiln La ILK DE7 30 F7
Brick Kiln La RLBORO LE12 101 L6
Brickley Crs RLBORO LE12 88 D6
Brickman Cl LEIW LE3 129 J5
Brick Rw DERBYW DE22 43 L6
Brick St DERBY DE1 2 B2
Brickwood Pl RLBORO LE12 97 K8
The Brickyard ILK DE7 31 M6
Brickyard Dr HUCK/RAV NG15 24 A2
Brickyard La BPR/DUF DE56 18 D6
COT/KEY/RAD NG12 53 M4
RIPLEY DE5 11 K6
RLBORO LE12 87 K7
Brickyard Rd BPR/DUF DE56 10 A3
Bridevale Rd LEIS LE2 137 J2
Bridge Av BSTN/STPLFD NG9 63 J2
Bridge Cl LEIN LE4 120 D7
Bridge Ct HUCK/RAV NG15 23 L2
Bridge Farm La
CFTN/RUD NG11 64 C5
Bridge Fld BWSH/BRSTN DE72 61 G8
Bridge Flds CDON/KEG DE74 86 C4
Bridge Foot BPR/DUF DE56 17 J2
Bridge Gv WBRGFD NG2 51 J7
Bridge Hl BPR/DUF DE56 17 J2
Bridgeland Rd LBORO LE11 9 L2
Bridgend Cl BSTN/STPLFD NG9 62 B2
Bridgeness Rd NORM/LIT DE23 70 D1
Bridge Park Rd LEIN LE4 120 B8
Bridgeport Rd DERBYE DE21 59 G1
Bridge Rd COAL LE67 108 B7
LEIE LE5 126 B8
WOL/BIL/BRX NG8 49 H2
Bridgeside Cottages
LBORO LE11 9 G1
Bridge St BPR/DUF DE56 17 K3
DERBY DE1 2 C2
EWD/SEL/PNX NG16 21 G4
ILK DE7 33 K3
LBORO LE11 9 H2
LGEAT NG10 62 A2
LGEAT NG10 62 B6
RLBORO LE12 101 M3
RLBORO LE12 105 G8
Bridge Vw BPR/DUF DE56 17 L8
Bridgewater Dr
RLEIW/BBY LE8 139 M6
Bridge Wy RLEIW/BBY LE8 142 D1
Bridgford Rd WBRGFD NG2 51 K7
Bridgnorth Dr CFTN/RUD NG11 64 C5
Bridgnorth Wy
BSTN/STPLFD NG9 62 C4
Bridgwater Cl DERBYSE DE24 59 G8
The Bridle LEIS LE2 136 F3
Bridle Cl MELB/CHEL DE73 72 E6
RLEIW/BAR LE9 141 G4
Bridle La BPR/DUF DE56 10 E5
RIPLEY DE5 11 H4
Bridle Rd BSTN/STPLFD NG9 48 F7
CALV/BJ NG14 39 H1
COAL LE67 108 A4
Bridlesmith Ga NOTT NG1 5 H7
Bridlespur Wy LEIN LE4 125 J2
Bridlington St NOTTE NG7 36 C8
Bridport Av WOL/BIL/BRX NG8 50 B2
Bridport Cl WGSTN LE18 138 A6
Brielen Rd COT/KEY/RAD NG12 53 L4
Brierfield Av CFTN/RUD NG11 64 F3
Brierfield Rd RLEIW/BAR LE9 142 B5
Brierfield Wy MCKLVR DE3 56 C7
Brierley Ct RIPLEY * DE5 11 L8
Brierley Gn CARL NG4 38 E8
Briers Cl END/NAR LE19 135 M8
Briers Wy COAL LE67 108 C2
Brigden Av DERBYSE DE24 58 C8
Brige Green Wk
WOL/BIL/BRX NG8 35 J6
Brightmoor Ct NOTT * NG1 5 J7
Brightmoor St NOTT NG1 5 J7
Brighton Av RLEINE/SYS LE7 121 G3
WGSTN LE18 138 A2
Brighton Cl WGSTN LE18 138 A2
Brighton Rd DERBYSE DE24 58 D7
LEIE LE5 126 B7
Brightside Rd LEIE LE5 132 C4
Brightstone Cl DERBYSE DE24 73 G2
Bright St DERBYW DE22 57 G2
ILK DE7 33 J4
Brightwell Dr LEIW LE3 129 M3
Brigmore Wk DERBYW * DE22 57 H2
Brindley Ct DERBYSE * DE24 72 C1
Brindley Ri LEIE LE5 127 J6
Brindley Rd WOL/BIL/BRX NG8 49 G2
Bringhurst Rd LEIW LE3 124 B8
Brington Cl WGSTN LE18 138 C5
Brinkhill Crs CFTN/RUD NG11 64 D4
The Brinks RLBORO LE12 112 F2
Brinsley Cl WOL/BIL/BRX NG8 35 L6
Brinsley Hl EWD/SEL/PNX NG16 13 G5
Brinsmead Rd LEIS LE2 131 M8
Brisbane Dr ARN NG5 24 C7
BSTN/STPLFD NG9 48 C6
Brisbane Rd MCKLVR DE3 56 C3
Brisco Av LBORO LE11 103 K1
Briscoe La RLBORO LE12 111 M3
Briset Cl DERBYSE DE24 71 J5
Bristol Av LEIN LE4 125 H6
Bristol Dr MCKLVR DE3 56 C5
Bristol Rd ILK DE7 33 J6
Britannia Av BLWL NG6 36 C2
RIPLEY DE5 11 L8
Britannia Cl
EWD/SEL/PNX NG16 22 E8
Britannia Rd LGEAT NG10 62 B6
Britannia St LEI LE1 7 G2
RLBORO LE12 101 M3
Britannia Wy RLEINE/SYS LE7 120 C6
Britford Av WGSTN LE18 137 M7
Briton St LEIW LE3 6 A9
Brittain Dr RIPLEY DE5 11 L6
Britten Gdns
MAPPK/POR/STA NG3 51 K1
Brixham Dr WGSTN LE18 137 L2
Brixham Rd HUCK/RAV NG15 23 H2
Brixton Rd NOTTE NG7 50 C2
Brixworth Ri LEIE LE5 133 J1
B Rd BSTN/STPLFD NG9 64 B1
Broad Av LEIE LE5 132 D2
Broad Bank DERBYW DE22 43 J7
Broadbent Cl RLEIW/BBY LE8 136 D8
Broad Cl CALV/BJ NG14 26 F3
Broad Eadow Rd
EWD/SEL/PNX NG16 23 K8
Broadfields Cl DERBYW DE22 43 K7
Broadfield Wy RLEIW/BBY LE8 143 G3
Broadford Cl LEIN LE4 126 B3
Broadgate BSTN/STPLFD NG9 49 L8
Broadgate Av
BSTN/STPLFD NG9 49 L8
Broadgate Cl LEIN LE4 119 L7
Broadgate La
BSTN/STPLFD NG9 49 L8
Broadhill Rd CDON/KEG DE74 86 A5
Broadholme St NOTTE NG7 50 D4
Broadhurst Av
WOL/BIL/BRX NG8 36 B5
Broadhurst St LEIN LE4 125 M5
Broadlands LGEAT NG10 61 M3
Broad La BWSH/BRSTN DE72 73 K3
EWD/SEL/PNX NG16 13 J7
Broadleaf Cl DERBYE DE21 44 C5
Broadleigh Cl CFTN/RUD NG11 65 G4
Broadmead CALV/BJ NG14 39 K3
Broad Meadow WGSTN LE18 138 C6
Broadmead Rd RLEIW/BBY LE8 142 E1
Broad Meer COT/KEY/RAD NG12 67 J4
Broad Oak Cl
MAPPK/POR/STA NG3 5 L2
Broad Oak Dr
BSTN/STPLFD NG9 62 B1
EWD/SEL/PNX NG16 13 H7
Broadstairs Rd
BSTN/STPLFD NG9 62 D5
Broadstone Cl DERBYE DE21 44 E6
WBRGFD NG2 65 G2
Broad St COAL LE67 108 B7
END/NAR LE19 135 M4
LBORO LE11 9 G2
LGEAT NG10 62 B8
NOTT NG1 5 J6
RLEINE/SYS LE7 120 E4
Broad Valley Dr BLWL NG6 24 C3
Broad Wk BLWL NG6 36 A4
The Broadway LEIS LE2 132 E7
Broadway BPR/DUF DE56 29 H5
DERBYW DE22 43 J7
HEANOR DE75 20 C6
ILK DE7 33 J4
LBORO LE11 103 L7
NOTT NG1 5 J8
RIPLEY DE5 11 J5
RLEINE/SYS LE7 120 E4
Broadway Av RIPLEY DE5 11 J6
Broadway Ct RIPLEY * DE5 11 J5
Broadway East CARL NG4 52 B1
Broadway Furlong
RLEINE/SYS LE7 118 C8
Broadway Park Cl
DERBYW DE22 43 J7
Broadway Rd LEIE LE5 132 B5
Broadwood Ct BSTN/STPLFD NG9 49 L7
Broadwood Rd ARN NG5 24 F7
Brockdale Gdns
COT/KEY/RAD NG12 80 C3
Brockenhurst Dr LEIW LE3 130 C7
Brockhall Ri HEANOR DE75 20 E6
Brockhole Cl WBRGFD NG2 66 B2
Brockhurst Gdns
MAPPK/POR/STA NG3 51 K1
Brocklesby Wy LEIE LE5 127 J7
Brockley DERBYE DE21 59 J2
Brockley Rd WBRGFD NG2 51 M8
Brocks Hill Cl LEIS LE2 138 F3
Brocks Hill Dr LEIS LE2 138 E2
Brockwood Crs
COT/KEY/RAD NG12 80 C3
Bromfield Cl
MAPPK/POR/STA NG3 38 A8
Bromhead St LBORO LE11 9 L1
Bromley Cl BLWL NG6 35 M1
Bromley La RLBORO LE12 92 F8
Bromley Pl NOTT NG1 4 F7
Bromley Rd WBRGFD NG2 65 J1
Bromley St DERBYW DE22 43 J8
Brompton Cl ARN NG5 24 E5
Brompton Rd DERBYW DE22 56 D1
Brompton Wy CFTN/RUD NG11 65 G4
Bromwich Cl LEIW LE3 130 A5
Bronte Cl LEIW LE3 130 E3
LGEAT NG10 61 L8
Bronte Pl NORM/LIT DE23 56 F7
Bronze WGSTN LE18 138 D6
Brook Av ARN NG5 25 L7
Brook Cl BLWL NG6 35 M1
DERBYW DE22 43 G3
EWD/SEL/PNX NG16 21 M6
LGEAT NG10 76 C2
RDERBYSW DE65 70 B6
Brook Ct RLEIW/BBY LE8 143 K3
Brookdale Ct ARN NG5 37 H2
Brookdale Dr NORM/LIT DE23 70 E2
Brookdale Rd LEIW LE3 130 B2
Brookes Av RLEIW/BAR LE9 141 G4
Brooke St ILK DE7 47 M1
LGEAT NG10 61 M2
Brook Farm Ct RLBORO LE12 91 G8
Brookfield Av DERBYE DE21 44 F7
HUCK/RAV NG15 23 L2
LBORO LE11 8 D8
NORM/LIT DE23 71 H1
RLEINE/SYS LE7 120 F3
Brookfield Cl
COT/KEY/RAD NG12 53 K4
RIPLEY DE5 11 M6
Brookfield Ct WBRGFD * NG2 51 G5
Brookfield Ri LEIS LE2 137 K1
Brookfield Rd ARN NG5 25 K8
Brookfields BPR/DUF DE56 18 C8
Brookfields Dr ILK DE7 44 B3
Brookfield St RLEINE/SYS LE7 120 F4
Brookfields Wy RLBORO LE12 88 C5
Brookfield Wy HEANOR DE75 20 F6
RLEIW/BBY LE8 146 F7
Brook Gdns ARN NG5 25 L7
LEIS LE2 136 F4
Brookhill Crs WOL/BIL/BRX NG8 49 J4
Brookhill Dr WOL/BIL/BRX NG8 49 J4
Brookhill Leys Rd
EWD/SEL/PNX NG16 21 J6
Brookhill St BSTN/STPLFD NG9 62 B2
Brookhouse Av LEIS LE2 7 J8
Brook House Cl
RLEINE/SYS LE7 115 L6
Brookhouse St DERBYSE DE24 72 B2
LEIS LE2 7 J8
Brookland Dr
BSTN/STPLFD NG9 63 H2
Brookland Rd LEIS LE2 131 L6
Brooklands COT/KEY/RAD NG12 91 G3
Brooklands Av HEANOR DE75 20 D5
Brooklands Cl RLEIW/BBY LE8 142 D1
Brooklands Crs CARL NG4 38 E6
Brooklands Dr CARL NG4 38 E6
NORM/LIT DE23 57 G7
Brooklands Rd
MAPPK/POR/STA NG3 37 M8
RLEIW/BAR LE9 142 B3
Brook La COAL LE67 100 B8
LBORO LE11 103 H7
RIPLEY DE5 11 H8
RLBORO LE12 105 J7
Brooklyn Av CALV/BJ NG14 39 J3
Brooklyn Cl BLWL NG6 36 B2
Brooklyn Rd BLWL NG6 36 B2
Brook Rd BSTN/STPLFD NG9 49 K7
BWSH/BRSTN DE72 59 M6
BWSH/BRSTN DE72 73 K2
LEIE LE5 127 H8
RLBORO LE12 111 H3
Brooksby Dr LEIS LE2 138 E2
Brooksby La CFTN/RUD NG11 64 D3
Brooksby St LEIS LE2 131 J6
Brook Side BPR/DUF DE56 17 K4
Brookside CDON/KEG DE74 93 G2
EWD/SEL/PNX NG16 21 K3
LBORO LE11 9 H3
RLBORO LE12 88 C7
RLEINE/SYS LE7 115 L5
RLEINE/SYS LE7 120 E3

Brookside Av
BSTN/STPLFD NG9 .....49 H5
RLBORO LE12 .....88 B6
Brookside Cl DERBYW DE22 .....43 J8
LGEAT NG10 .....61 M7
RLBORO LE12 .....101 M5
RLBORO LE12 .....105 H6
Brookside Dr LEIS LE2 .....139 G2
Brookside Gdns
CFTN/RUD NG11 .....64 F7
RLEIW/BBY * LE8
Brookside Rd CFTN/RUD NG11 .....64 F7
ILK DE7 .....44 C3
LBORO LE12 .....103 H7
Brooks La COAL LE67 .....108 B2
Brook St BPR/DUF DE56 .....10 A5
DERBY DE1 .....2 C1
END/NAR LE19 .....135 M4
HEANOR DE75 .....19 M2
LEIN LE4 .....120 B8
NOTT NG1 .....5 J6
RLBORO LE12 .....97 K8
RLBORO LE12 .....98 A4
RLBORO LE12 .....101 M3
RLBORO LE12 .....114 A4
RLEINE/SYS LE7 .....115 L6
RLEINE/SYS LE7 .....120 E3
RLEIW/BAR LE9 .....135 H8
RLEIW/BBY LE8 .....136 D8
Brookthorpe Wy
CFTN/RUD NG11 .....64 E3
Brookvale La RIPLEY DE5 .....11 M7
RIPLEY DE5 .....18 E5
Brookvale Ri RIPLEY DE5 .....18 E5
Brook Vale Rd
EWD/SEL/PNX NG16 .....21 G5
Brookvale Rd RIPLEY DE5 .....18 E5
Brook View Ct
COT/KEY/RAD * NG12 .....80 C5
Brook View Dr
COT/KEY/RAD NG12 .....80 C5
Brookwood Crs CARL NG4 .....38 A6
Broom Av RLBORO LE12 .....103 L8
Broom Cl BPR/DUF DE56 .....17 J2
BPR/DUF DE56 .....29 H4
DERBYSE DE24 .....71 H5
MELB/CHEL DE73 .....72 D5
Broome Av RLEINE/SYS LE7 .....115 J3
Broome La RLEINE/SYS LE7 .....115 G6
Broomfield RLEINE/SYS LE7 .....115 J8
Broomfield Cl LGEAT NG10 .....61 L2
Broomhill Av ILK DE7 .....47 L5
Broomhill Cl MCKLVR DE3 .....56 B4
Broomhill Rd BLWL NG6 .....36 A1
EWD/SEL/PNX NG16 .....34 E1
HUCK/RAV NG15 .....23 L2
Broomhills Rd END/NAR LE19 .....135 K7
Broomleys RLEIW/BBY LE8 .....143 H3
Broom Leys Av COAL LE67 .....108 C2
Broom Leys Rd COAL LE67 .....108 C7
Broom Wy END/NAR LE19 .....135 K6
Brora Rd BLWL NG6 .....24 B8
Brougham St LEI LE1 .....7 H4
Brough St DERBYW DE22 .....2 A7
Broughton Av NORM/LIT DE23 .....57 H6
Broughton Cl ILK DE7 .....33 H5
LBORO LE11 .....103 G3
RLEINE/SYS LE7 .....118 C8
Broughton Dr
WOL/BIL/BRX NG8 .....50 A4
Broughton Fld WGSTN LE18 .....138 C7
Broughton Rd LEIS LE2 .....137 J1
RLEIW/BAR LE9 .....140 C5
RLEIW/BAR LE9 .....141 G4
RLEIW/BAR LE9 .....141 M7
Broughton St
BSTN/STPLFD NG9 .....49 J8
COAL LE67 .....108 C7
Broughton Wy RLEIW/BAR LE9 .....141 K8
Brown Av RLBORO LE12 .....112 E1
Brownhill Crs RLEINE/SYS LE7 .....118 F2
Browning Av ARN NG5 .....25 H3
Browning Rd LBORO LE11 .....8 A2
Browning St END/NAR LE19 .....135 L6
LEIW LE3 .....131 G3
NORM/LIT DE23 .....57 K8
Brown La CFTN/RUD NG11 .....77 K1
Brownlow Dr BLWL NG6 .....24 B6
Brown Meadow Rd NOTTE NG7 .....36 C7
Brown's Cl RLEIW/BAR LE9 .....140 C7
Browns Cft BLWL NG6 .....36 B4
Brown's Flats
EWD/SEL/PNX NG16 .....34 D1
Brown's La BPR/DUF DE56 .....18 B8
COT/KEY/RAD NG12 .....81 H5
LBORO LE11 .....9 H4
Browns Rd LGEAT NG10 .....62 C7
Brown St NOTTE NG7 .....4 A2
Brown's Wy RLEIW/BBY LE8 .....142 E2
Broxburn Cl LEIN LE4 .....126 B3
Broxfield Cl LEIS LE2 .....138 E4
Broxtowe Av
EWD/SEL/PNX NG16 .....34 B1
WOL/BIL/BRX NG8 .....36 A5
Broxtowe Dr HUCK/RAV NG15 .....15 K6
Broxtowe Hall Cl
WOL/BIL/BRX NG8 .....35 L5
Broxtowe La WOL/BIL/BRX NG8 .....35 L6
Broxtowe St ARN NG5 .....37 G5
Bruce Cl WBRGFD NG2 .....51 H5
Bruce Dr WBRGFD NG2 .....51 H8
Bruce St LEIW LE3 .....131 H4
Bruce Wy RLEIW/BBY LE8 .....142 C2
Bruin St LEIN LE4 .....125 L6
Bruins Wk LEIS LE2 .....138 D2
Brunel Av EWD/SEL/PNX NG16 .....21 L4
LEIW LE3 .....124 C6
Brun La ASHB DE6 .....41 M7
Brunswick Dr
BSTN/STPLFD NG9 .....62 C2
Brunswick St LEI LE1 .....7 J4
NORM/LIT DE23 .....57 K6
Brunswood Cl DERBYE DE21 .....59 J2
Brunton Cl MCKLVR DE3 .....56 A6
Brushfield Av RLBORO LE12 .....114 B3
Brushfield St NOTTE NG7 .....36 C8
Brussells Ter ILK DE7 .....33 J6
Brusty Pl CALV/BJ NG14 .....39 J2

Bruxby St RLEINE/SYS LE7 .....120 D4
Bryan Cl RLBORO LE12 .....105 H7
Bryan's Cl RLBORO LE12 .....108 D1
Bryngarth Crs LEIE LE5 .....126 F8
Brynsmoor Rd
EWD/SEL/PNX NG16 .....13 J8
Bryony Cl DERBYE DE21 .....44 E5
Bryony Rd LEIE LE5 .....127 H5
Buchanan St DERBYW DE1 .....2 E1
Buchan St DERBYSE DE24 .....58 B8
Buckfast Wy RLEIW/BAR LE9 .....132 D4
WGSTN LE18 .....138 A6
Buckfast Wy WBRGFD NG2 .....65 L1
Buckford La RDERBYSW DE65 .....70 C7
Buckhaven Cl LEIN LE4 .....126 B3
Buckhazels La ASHB DE6 .....41 L1
Buckingham Av DERBYE DE21 .....44 B7
HUCK/RAV NG15 .....15 M7
Buckingham Cl LGEAT NG10 .....61 L4
Buckingham Ct LGEAT NG10 .....61 L4
LEIS LE2 .....136 F2
Buckingham Dr LBORO LE11 .....103 G2
LEIS LE2 .....136 F2
Buckingham Rd ARN NG5 .....37 J2
COAL LE67 .....108 C7
LGEAT NG10 .....61 L4
RLEIW/BBY LE8 .....143 K3
Buckingham Wy
EWD/SEL/PNX NG16 .....22 F8
Buckland Cl DERBYW DE22 .....2 A2
Buckland Dr CALV/BJ NG14 .....27 G3
Buckland Rd LEIE LE5 .....126 B7
Bucklow Cl WOL/BIL/BRX NG8 .....36 B6
Buckminster Cl DERBYE DE21 .....44 D5
Buckminster Rd ILK DE7 .....47 G3
LEIW LE3 .....125 G7
Buck's La RLBORO LE12 .....86 E8
Buckwell Rd LEIW/BAR LE9 .....140 B7
Budby Ri HUCK/RAV NG15 .....15 M8
Buddon La RLBORO LE12 .....112 C3
Bude Dr LEIW LE3 .....124 A6
Bufton Dr GBY/RBY * LE6 .....128 B1
Bulcote Dr CALV/BJ NG14 .....39 H4
Bulcote Rd CFTN/RUD NG11 .....64 C4
Bullace Rd
MAPPK/POR/STA NG3 .....5 M2
Bull Close Rd NOTTE NG7 .....50 C7
Buller Rd LEIN LE4 .....125 L6
Buller St ILK DE7 .....47 L1
NORM/LIT DE23 .....57 J5
RLEIW/BBY LE8 .....146 D7
Buller Ter ARN NG5 .....37 H4
Bullfinch Rd BLWL NG6 .....36 B3
Bull Head St WGSTN LE18 .....138 B5
Bullins Cl ARN NG5 .....25 G6
Bullivant St
MAPPK/POR/STA NG3 .....5 J3
Bullock La ALFN DE55 .....12 C2
Bullpit La BPR/DUF DE56 .....29 L7
Bulrush Cl DERBYE DE21 .....113 K6
Bulstode Pl CDON/KEG DE74 .....86 A5
Bulwell High Rd BLWL NG6 .....35 M1
Bulwell La BLWL NG6 .....36 B3
Bulwer Rd LEIS LE2 .....131 M6
NOTTE NG7 .....4 A6
Bunbury St WBRGFD NG2 .....51 H6
Bunny Hl RLBORO LE12 .....89 H4
Bunny Hill Top RLBORO LE12 .....89 H2
Bunny La COT/KEY/RAD NG12 .....80 B5
RLBORO LE12 .....88 C2
Bunting Cl ILK DE7 .....47 C1
MCKLVR DE3 .....56 E4
Buntings La CARL NG4 .....38 A8
Bunting St NOTTE NG7 .....50 C6
Bunyan Green Rd
EWD/SEL/PNX NG16 .....13 H1
Burbage Cl BPR/DUF DE56 .....18 B3
LBORO LE11 .....103 J1
Burbage Pl DERBYSE DE24 .....58 D8
Burchnall Rd LEIW LE3 .....130 A6
Burcot Cl ILK DE7 .....32 C7
Burder St LBORO LE11 .....104 A2
Burdet Cl LEIW LE3 .....130 C6
Burdett Wy LEIN LE4 .....125 H3
Burdock Cl DERBYE DE21 .....44 C5
LEIE LE5 .....127 H5
Burfield Av LBORO LE11 .....9 G4
Burford St LEIN LE4 .....125 M7
Burford Dr NOTTE NG7 .....36 D7
Burgass Rd
MAPPK/POR/STA NG3 .....37 L8
Burge Pl WBRGFD NG2 .....51 J5
Burgess Rd COAL LE67 .....108 A7
LEIS LE2 .....137 J1
Burgess St LEI LE1 .....6 D3
WGSTN LE18 .....138 B4
Burgh Hall Cl
BSTN/STPLFD NG9 .....63 C5
Burghley Cl MELB/CHEL DE73 .....72 D5
Burghley Wy NORM/LIT DE23 .....70 C1
Burgin Rd RLEINE/SYS LE7 .....124 B2
Burhill COT/KEY/RAD NG12 .....67 L5
Burland Green La ASHB DE6 .....28 A2
Burleigh Av WGSTN LE18 .....138 A3
Burleigh Rd CARL NG4 .....38 D8
Burleigh Dr DERBYW DE22 .....43 K7
Burleigh Rd LBORO LE11 .....9 J3
WBRGFD NG2 .....65 K1
Burleigh St ILK DE7 .....33 K6
Burley Cl RLEIW/BAR LE9 .....142 B4
Burley Dr DERBYW DE22 .....29 J8
Burley Hl DERBYW DE22 .....43 L1
Burley La DERBYW DE22 .....29 H8
Burleys F/O LEI LE1 .....6 F3
Burleys Wy LEI LE1 .....6 E3
Burlington Cl
BWSH/BRSTN DE72 .....61 H7
Burlington Rd ARN NG5 .....37 G4
CARL NG4 .....38 D7
DERBYW DE22 .....56 D1
LEIS LE2 .....132 A6
Burlington Wy MCKLVR DE3 .....56 B6
The Burma Rd ASHB DE6 .....40 E2
Burnaby Av LEIE LE5 .....132 B1
Burnaby St BLWL NG6 .....36 B3
DERBYSE DE24 .....58 D7

Burnaston Rd LEIS LE2 .....137 J1
Burnbank Cl WBRGFD NG2 .....66 B2
Burnbreck Gdns
WOL/BIL/BRX NG8 .....49 J3
Burncroft ILK DE7 .....32 C8
Burndale Wk ARN NG5 .....24 C7
Burnell Rd LEIN LE4 .....130 F5
Burneston Wy WGSTN LE18 .....138 C5
Burnet Cl LEIS LE2 .....127 G5
Burnham Av
BSTN/STPLFD NG9 .....63 K3
ILK DE7 .....32 B7
WGSTN LE18 .....138 B8
Burnham Dr LEIS LE2 .....125 H5
MCKLVR DE3 .....56 A5
RLEIW/BBY LE8 .....142 D1
Burnham St ARN NG5 .....37 G5
Burnham Wy WBRGFD NG2 .....51 G4
Burnmoor St LEIS LE2 .....131 J5
Burns Av NOTTE NG7 .....4 A4
Burns Cl NORM/LIT DE23 .....56 F7
Burnside DERBYSE DE24 .....71 H4
Burnside Dr BSTN/STPLFD NG9 .....49 G5
DERBYE DE21 .....59 K3
Burnside Gv
COT/KEY/RAD NG12 .....66 A6
Burnside Rd LEIS LE2 .....137 L1
WBRGFD NG2 .....65 J2
WOL/BIL/BRX NG8 .....49 H1
Burnside St DERBYSE DE24 .....58 E7
Burns Rd LBORO LE11 .....8 L1
Burns St END/NAR LE19 .....135 L6
HEANOR DE75 .....20 B5
ILK DE7 .....33 J7
LEIS LE2 .....131 L7
NOTTE NG7 .....4 C4
Burnt House Rd HEANOR DE75 .....20 B6
Burnt Oak Cl
EWD/SEL/PNX NG16 .....35 H4
Burnwood Dr
BSTN/STPLFD NG9 .....49 H2
Burr La ILK DE7 .....33 K6
Burroughs Rd GBY/RBY LE6 .....122 E6
The Burrows END/NAR LE19 .....135 K7
RLBORO LE12 .....88 C5
Burrows Av BSTN/STPLFD NG9 .....49 K6
Burrows Cl END/NAR LE19 .....135 M8
Burrows Ct
MAPPK/POR/STA NG3 .....51 K2
Burrows Crs BSTN/STPLFD NG9 .....49 K6
Burrows La ASHB DE6 .....40 D5
Burrows Wk DERBY DE1 .....2 F5
Bursdon Cl LEIW LE3 .....130 B1
Bursom Rd LEIN LE4 .....124 F1
Burtness Rd CFTN/RUD NG11 .....64 B6
Burton Av CARL NG4 .....37 M7
Burton Cl CARL NG4 .....38 E7
LEIS LE2 .....139 H3
Burton Dr BSTN/STPLFD NG9 .....63 G3
Burton La RLBORO LE12 .....97 M4
Burton Rd CARL NG4 .....38 E7
DERBY DE1 .....2 B6
NORM/LIT DE23 .....57 H5
RDERBYSW DE65 .....69 K8
Burton St HEANOR DE75 .....20 C5
LBORO LE11 .....1 J6
LEI LE1 .....7 H5
NOTT NG1 .....5 G6
Burton Wk RLBORO LE12 .....88 C7
Burton Wks LBORO LE11 .....9 K6
Burwell St NOTTE * NG7 .....4 A2
Buscot Cl LEIN LE4 .....126 B7
Bushby Rd LEIS LE2 .....126 B8
Bush Cl ARN NG5 .....24 D7
Bushey Cl LEIN LE4 .....135 M7
Bush Lock Cl WGSTN LE18 .....137 L7
Bushloe End WGSTN LE18 .....138 A5
Bushy Cl LGEAT NG10 .....75 L1
Butchers La RLBORO LE12 .....106 E8
Butcombe Rd LEIN LE4 .....125 H6
Bute Av NOTTE NG7 .....4 A7
Bute Wk DERBYE * DE21 .....44 A8
Butler Av COT/KEY/RAD NG12 .....53 L3
Butler Cl LEIN LE4 .....126 C1
Butlers Cl HUCK/RAV NG15 .....24 A2
Butler Wy RLBORO LE12 .....114 B5
Butt Cl WGSTN LE18 .....138 C6
Butt Close La LEI LE1 .....6 E4
Buttercup Cl END/NAR LE19 .....135 L6
GBY/RBY LE6 .....123 L4
RLBORO LE12 .....113 K5
Buttercup Dr COAL LE67 .....108 E8
Butterley Dr LBORO LE11 .....102 F5
Butterley Hl RIPLEY DE5 .....11 J4
Butterley La RIPLEY DE5 .....11 H3
Buttermead Cl
BSTN/STPLFD NG9 .....48 B5
Buttermere Cl LGEAT NG10 .....61 L5
WBRGFD NG2 .....52 A8
Buttermere Ct ARN NG5 .....37 G5
Buttermere Dr
BSTN/STPLFD NG9 .....48 F7
DERBYW DE22 .....43 J4
Buttermere St LEIS LE2 .....131 J4
Buttermere Wy RLBORO LE12 .....105 G6
Butterpot La ASHB DE6 .....54 B4
Butterton Cl ILK DE7 .....33 L8
Butterwick Cl NORM/LIT DE23 .....71 J2
Butterwick Dr LEIN LE4 .....125 G3
Buttery Gdns CFTN/RUD NG11 .....79 G1
Butthole La RLBORO LE12 .....102 A3
Butt La MELB/CHEL DE73 .....95 H4
Buttonoak Dr MELB/CHEL DE73 .....72 E4
The Butts BPR/DUF DE56 .....17 L4
Butts Cl ILK DE7 .....47 L3
Butt St LGEAT NG10 .....61 M2
Buxton Av CARL NG4 .....38 B6
HEANOR DE75 .....20 D8
Buxton Cl RLEIW/BBY LE8 .....136 D8
Buxton Dr DERBYE DE21 .....30 A5
Buxton Gn HEANOR * DE75 .....20 D8
Buxton Houses DERBYE * DE21 .....30 B3
Buxton Rd DERBYE DE21 .....44 D6
Buxton St LEIS LE2 .....7 L5
Byard La NOTT NG1 .....5 H7
Byfield Cl DERBYE DE21 .....44 F5

NOTTE NG7 .....4 A4
Byfield Dr WGSTN LE18 .....138 C4
Byford Cl DERBYE DE21 .....59 J5
Byford Rd LEIN LE4 .....125 J5
Byland Wy LBORO LE11 .....102 F2
Byley Rd WOL/BIL/BRX NG8 .....48 F3
Byng Av NORM/LIT DE23 .....57 K8
Byrne Ct ARN NG5 .....37 M2
Byron Av LGEAT NG10 .....61 M4
Byron Cl END/NAR LE19 .....135 L5
RLEIW/BBY LE8 .....145 L5
Byron Ct BSTN/STPLFD NG9 .....48 C6
WBRGFD * NG2 .....5 L7
Byron Crs EWD/SEL/PNX NG16 .....34 A2
Byron Gv ARN NG5 .....37 G4
Byron Rd WBRGFD NG2 .....51 K8
Byron St ARN NG5 .....25 H8
HUCK/RAV NG15 .....15 H1
HUCK/RAV NG15 .....23 L1
ILK DE7 .....33 K6
LBORO LE11 .....103 J2
LEI LE1 .....7 G4
NORM/LIT DE23 .....2 D1
Byron St Extension
LBORO LE11 .....103 J2
Byway Rd LEIE LE5 .....132 C3
Bywell La BPR/DUF DE56 .....18 D7

C

Cabin Leas LBORO LE11 .....103 M2
Caddaw Av HUCK/RAV NG15 .....23 L1
Cadeby Ct ALFN DE55 .....12 A1
Cademan Cl LEIS LE2 .....131 M8
Cademan St COAL LE67 .....108 D2
Cadgwith Dr DERBYW DE22 .....43 J5
Cadlan Cl ARN NG5 .....24 E8
Cadles Cl RLEIW/BAR LE9 .....140 B4
Cadwell Cl DERBYSE DE24 .....73 H1
Caerhays Ct DERBYSE DE24 .....71 H4
Caernarvon Cl DERBYE DE21 .....59 K2
RLBORO LE12 .....101 L5
RLBORO LE12 .....113 H7
Caernarvon Pl
BSTN/STPLFD * NG9 .....62 F3
Caesar St DERBY DE1 .....43 M8
Caincross Rd WOL/BIL/BRX NG8 .....35 H8
Cairngorm Cl LEIS LE2 .....131 K8
Cairngorm Dr ARN NG5 .....24 F5
DERBYSE DE24 .....71 H4
Cairns Cl ARN NG5 .....36 E2
MCKLVR DE3 .....56 A6
Cairnsford Rd LEIS LE2 .....137 M1
Cairnsmore Cl LGEAT NG10 .....61 L4
Cairo St NOTTE NG7 .....36 D6
Caister Rd CFTN/RUD NG11 .....64 C7
Calais Hl LEI LE1 .....7 G7
Calais St LEI LE1 .....7 G7
Caldbeck Cl WBRGFD NG2 .....52 A8
Caldbeck Wk ARN NG5 .....24 F8
Caldecote Rd LEIW LE3 .....130 E6
Caldecott Cl WGSTN LE18 .....138 C7
Calder Cl DERBYW DE22 .....43 J4
RDERBYSW DE65 .....68 B6
Calderdale WOL/BIL/BRX NG8 .....48 F4
Calderdale Dr LGEAT NG10 .....75 L1
Calderhall Gdns ARN NG5 .....25 G7
Caldermill Dr DERBYE DE21 .....44 E5
Calder Rd LEIE LE5 .....125 G4
Caldwell St LBORO LE11 .....9 H3
Caledine Rd LEIW LE3 .....124 D7
Caledon Rd ARN NG5 .....36 F5
Calgary Rd LEI LE1 .....7 H2
California Gdns DERBYW DE22 .....57 G3
Calke Ri RIPLEY DE5 .....11 K6
Calladine La BPR/DUF DE56 .....16 A2
ILK DE7 .....31 H1
Calladine Rd HEANOR DE75 .....20 B5
Callan Cl END/NAR LE19 .....135 L4
Callaway Cl WOL/BIL/BRX NG8 .....49 J2
Callow Hill Wy NORM/LIT DE23 .....56 D8
Caloe Cl DERBYE DE21 .....114 C4
Calstock Rd ARN NG5 .....37 J2
Calveley Rd WOL/BIL/BRX NG8 .....35 J7
Calver Cl BPR/DUF DE56 .....17 M1
DERBYE DE21 .....44 C4
WOL/BIL/BRX NG8 .....50 A3
Calver Hey Rd LEIN LE4 .....124 E4
Calvert Cl BSTN/STPLFD NG9 .....63 H4
Calvert Crs RLEIW/BAR LE9 .....140 C8
WGSTN LE18 .....138 A3
Calverton Cl BSTN/STPLFD NG9 .....62 E5
DERBYSE DE24 .....72 C4
GBY/RBY LE6 .....123 H7
Calverton Dr WOL/BIL/BRX NG8 .....35 H5
Calverton Rd ARN NG5 .....25 L6
Calvert St DERBY DE1 .....3 J6
Calvin Cl DERBYSE DE24 .....72 E2
Camberley Ct BLWL NG6 .....23 L7
Camberley Rd BLWL NG6 .....23 L7
Camberwell Av DERBYW DE22 .....56 E1
Camborne Cl DERBYE DE21 .....44 C6
WGSTN LE18 .....138 A6
Camborne Dr
WOL/BIL/BRX NG8 .....36 A5
Cambria Ms
MAPPK/POR/STA NG3 .....5 H2
Cambrian Cl RLEIW/BAR LE9 .....142 B5
Cambridge Cl RLEINE/SYS LE7 .....120 F4
Cambridge Crs
BSTN/STPLFD NG9 .....48 B5
Cambridge Gdns ARN NG5 .....37 G5
Cambridge Rd RLEIW/BAR LE9 .....142 B4
WBRGFD NG2 .....51 J8
WOL/BIL/BRX NG8 .....49 J3
Cambridge St CARL NG4 .....38 C7
COAL LE67 .....108 C6
DERBYE DE21 .....59 J4
LBORO LE11 .....103 J2
LEIW LE3 .....131 G3
NORM/LIT DE23 .....57 L5
RLBORO LE12 .....101 M5

Camden Cl WBRGFD NG2 .....5 M7
Camden Rd LEIW LE3 .....130 E6
Camden St DERBYW DE22 .....57 H3
LEIE LE3 .....7 G4
Cameford Rd COAL LE67 .....108 A8
Camelia Av CFTN/RUD NG11 .....64 A6
Camelia Cl RLEIW/BAR LE19 .....135 K6
MCKLVR DE3 .....56 B4
Camelot Av LEIE LE4 .....126 C1
Camelot Crs CFTN/RUD NG11 .....64 F7
Camelot St CFTN/RUD NG11 .....64 F7
Camelot Wy END/NAR LE19 .....135 L6
Cameo Cl CARL NG4 .....52 D1
Cameron Av LEIN LE4 .....125 M4
Cameron Rd NORM/LIT DE23 .....57 K7
Cameron St ARN NG5 .....37 G5
Camfield Ri LEIS LE2 .....137 H3
Camomile Av LEIE LE4 .....126 C1
Camomile Gdns NOTTE NG7 .....36 C7
Campbell Av LEIN LE4 .....126 C1
Campbell Dr CARL NG4 .....38 A7
Campbell Gdns ARN NG5 .....26 A6
Campbell Gv
MAPPK/POR/STA NG3 .....5 K4
Campbell St BPR/DUF DE56 .....17 K4
DERBYSE DE24 .....72 B1
EWD/SEL/PNX NG16 .....21 G4
LEI LE1 .....7 G7
MAPPK/POR/STA NG3 .....5 G7
Campden Gn CFTN/RUD NG11 .....64 C5
Campion Cl END/NAR LE19 .....135 L6
Campion Hl CDON/KEG DE74 .....84 E3
Campion St ARN NG5 .....25 J7
DERBYW DE22 .....57 H2
Campsie Ct DERBYSE DE24 .....71 H4
Camp St DERBY DE1 .....43 L8
Camrose Cl WOL/BIL/BRX NG8 .....35 K8
Camville Rd LEIW LE3 .....130 D3
Canada St BPR/DUF DE56 .....17 K4
Canal Bank BWSH/BRSTN DE72 .....74 E6
LBORO LE11 .....103 L2
Canal Side BSTN/STPLFD NG9 .....63 M4
MELB/CHEL * DE73 .....72 C4
Canal St DERBY DE1 .....3 H7
ILK DE7 .....33 L6
LEIN LE4 .....120 B7
LEIS LE2 .....131 G8
LGEAT NG10 .....61 M2
NOTT NG1 .....5 H9
WGSTN LE18 .....137 K7
Canberra Cl BSTN/STPLFD NG9 .....48 C5
MCKLVR DE3 .....56 C5
Canberra Crs WBRGFD NG2 .....65 H4
Canberra Gdns WBRGFD NG2 .....65 H4
Candleby Cl COT/KEY/RAD NG12 .....67 K4
Candleby La
COT/KEY/RAD NG12 .....67 K4
Candle Meadow WBRGFD NG2 .....52 B3
Cank St LEI LE1 .....6 E5
Cannam Cl RLEIW/BBY LE8 .....142 E2
Canning Pl LEI LE1 .....6 E3
Canning St LEI LE1 .....6 E3
Canning Ter NOTT NG1 .....4 D6
Canning Wy LBORO LE11 .....103 L2
Cannock St LEIN LE4 .....126 E4
Cannock Wy LGEAT NG10 .....62 E8
Cannon St ARN NG5 .....37 G4
LEIS LE2 .....138 F3
Canon Cl ILK DE7 .....33 J2
Canons Cl END/NAR LE19 .....135 M7
Canonsleigh Rd LEIN LE4 .....125 J4
Canon St LEIN LE4 .....125 M5
Canon's Wk DERBYW DE22 .....43 K5
Cantelupe Rd ILK DE7 .....33 K7
Canterbury Cl BPR/DUF * DE56 .....29 J4
EWD/SEL/PNX NG16 .....35 H2
Canterbury Rd
WOL/BIL/BRX NG8 .....50 B2
Canterbury St DERBYE DE21 .....44 C6
Canterbury Ter LEIW LE3 .....130 F4
Cantley Av CARL NG4 .....38 C5
Cantley Rd ALFN DE55 .....12 A1
Cantley Ct DERBYSE DE24 .....72 B4
Cantrell Rd BLWL NG6 .....36 A1
LEIS LE3 .....130 B4
Canver Cl WOL/BIL/BRX NG8 .....49 G1
Canvey Cl WGSTN LE18 .....138 D4
Canwick Cl WOL/BIL/BRX NG8 .....49 G2
Capers Cl END/NAR LE19 .....135 L4
Capesthorne Cl LEIE LE5 .....126 B7
Caporn Cl BLWL NG6 .....36 A2
Carbery Cl LEIS LE2 .....139 H3
Cardale Rd
MAPPK/POR/STA NG3 .....51 L1
Cardales Cl RDERBYSW * DE65 .....70 B5
Cardean Cl DERBY DE1 .....43 M8
Cardigan Dr WGSTN LE18 .....137 K5
Cardigan St DERBYE DE21 .....44 B8
Cardinal Cl DERBYE DE21 .....44 D5
GBY/RBY LE6 .....123 H7
MAPPK/POR/STA NG3 .....5 M3
Cardinals Wk LEIE LE5 .....127 G7
Cardington Av ARN NG5 .....24 C6
Cardrona Ct DERBYE DE21 .....44 D5
Cardwell St NOTTE NG7 .....36 D7
Carew Rd CFTN/RUD NG11 .....64 C5
Carey Cl WGSTN LE18 .....138 B7
Carey Hill Rd RLEIW/BAR LE9 .....140 D3
Carey Rd BLWL NG6 .....24 A7
RLEIW/BAR LE9 .....135 H8
Careys Cl LEI LE1 .....6 D6
Carfax Av LEIS LE2 .....132 C4
Car Hill Rd COAL LE67 .....100 C8
Carillon Ct LBORO LE11 .....9 J3
Carington St LBORO LE11 .....103 K2
Carisbrooke Av
BSTN/STPLFD NG9 .....49 L7
CARL NG4 .....38 F6
LEIS LE2 .....132 A8
MAPPK/POR/STA NG3 .....37 G5
Carisbrooke Dr
MAPPK/POR/STA NG3 .....37 G6
Carisbrooke Gdns LEIS LE2 .....132 A7
NORM/LIT DE23 .....71 G1
Carisbrooke Pk LEIS LE2 .....132 A8
Carisbrooke Rd LEIS LE2 .....132 A7
RLBORO LE12 .....113 C7

Carlile Rd *CARL* NG4 ....38 C7
Carlin Cl *BWSH/BRSTN* DE72 ....61 J7
Carlingford Rd *HUCK/RAV* NG15 ...15 L8
Carlin St *BLWL* NG6 ....23 M8
Carlisle Av *BLWL* NG6 ....24 A8
  NORM/LIT DE23 ....56 F7
Carlisle St *LEIW* LE3 ....130 F2
Carl St *LEIS* LE2 ....137 G1
Carlton Av *DERBYSE* DE24 ....72 C3
  END/NAR LE19 ....136 A7
Carlton Cl *HEANOR* DE75 ....20 E4
Carlton Crs *RLBORO* LE12 ....88 D5
Carlton Dr *DERBYSE* DE24 ....72 C3
  WGSTN LE18 ....138 A4
Carlton Fold *WBRGFD* NG2 ....51 K4
Carlton Gdns *DERBYSE* DE24 ....72 C3
  RLEINE/BBY LE8 ....139 M8
Carlton HI *CARL* NG4 ....38 B8
Carlton Ms *CARL* NG4 ....38 A8
Carlton Rd *LGEAT* NG10 ....75 M2
  MAPPK/POR/STA NG3 ....51 K1
  NORM/LIT DE23 ....57 H6
  RLEIW/BBY LE8 ....146 F4
Carlton St *LEI* LE1 ....6 E8
  NOTT NG1 ....5 J7
Carlton Vale Cl *CARL* NG4 ....38 B6
Carlyle Ct *WBRGFD* NG2 ....65 J1
Carlyle Rd *WBRGFD* NG2 ....51 J8
Carlyle St *DERBYSE* DE24 ....71 K2
  HEANOR DE75 ....20 B4
Carman Cl *EWD/SEL/PNX* NG16 ...22 F7
Carmel Gdns *ARN* NG5 ....37 K1
Carmen Gv *GBY/RBY* LE6 ....123 H4
Carnarvon Dr *CALV/BJ* NG14 ....39 K2
Carnarvon Gv *CARL* NG4 ....38 B7
Carnarvon Rd *WBRGFD* NG2 ....65 K1
Carnarvon St *CARL* NG4 ....52 D1
Carnation Cl *LEIW* LE3 ....129 K5
Carnation St *LEIW* LE4 ....125 K5
Carnegie St *NORM/LIT* DE23 ....57 L7
Carnforth Cl *BSTN/STPLFD* NG9 ...62 B2
  MCKLVR DE3 ....56 C6
Carnival Wy *CDON/KEG* DE74 ....84 F3
Carnoustie Cl *MCKLVR* DE3 ....56 D5
Carnoustie Rd *LEIW* LE3 ....130 F1
Carnwood Rd *ARN* NG5 ....36 E1
Carol Crs *DERBYE* DE21 ....58 D3
Caroline Cl *DERBYSE* DE24 ....59 G8
Caroline Ct *ILK* DE7 ....47 L1
  LEIS LE2 ....137 J1
Caroline Wk
  MAPPK/POR/STA NG3 ....5 J2
Carpenter's Cl *LEIW* LE3 ....123 M8
Carpe Rd *LEIN* LE4 ....126 B6
Carradale Cl *ARN* NG5 ....26 A7
Carrfield Av *BSTN/STPLFD* NG9 ...62 D6
Carr Flds *ILK* DE7 ....19 G8
Carriers Rd *RDERBYSW* DE65 ....69 G8
Carrington Ct *ARN* NG5 ....37 G6
Carrington St *DERBY* DE1 ....3 H1
  NOTT NG1 ....5 H9
Carrock Av *HEANOR* DE75 ....20 F6
Carroll Gdns *WBRGFD* NG2 ....50 F6
Carron Cl *DERBYSE* DE21 ....71 J3
Carrow Rd *LEIW* LE3 ....129 M2
Carrs Cl *CDON/KEG* DE74 ....84 E4
Carsington Crs *DERBYW* DE22 ....43 H6
Carsington Ms *DERBYW* DE22 ....43 H6
Carson Rd *DERBYSE* DE21 ....58 F1
Cartbridge *COT/KEY/RAD* NG12 ...67 K5
Carter Av *CFTN/RUD* NG11 ....79 C1
  COT/KEY/RAD NG12 ....53 M4
Carter Cl *END/NAR* LE19 ....135 L4
  LGEAT NG10 ....61 M8
Carter Dl *COAL* LE67 ....108 B1
Carter Ga *NOTT* NG1 ....5 K8
Carter Rd *BSTN/STPLFD* NG9 ....62 D5
Carter St *DERBYSE* DE24 ....72 B1
  LEIN LE4 ....126 A7
Carters Wood Dr
  EWD/SEL/PNX NG16 ....35 K4
Cartland Dr *LBORO* LE11 ....103 G1
Carts La *LEI* LE1 ....6 E5
Cartwright Dr *LEIS* LE2 ....138 E2
Cartwright St *LBORO* LE11 ....103 M2
Carvers Cnr *LEIS* * LE2 ....136 F4
Carver St *NOTTE* NG7 ....36 D7
Carwood Rd *BSTN/STPLFD* NG9 ...49 H6
Cascade Gv *NORM/LIT* DE23 ....56 E8
Cashmore Vw *LEIW* LE4 ....125 H3
Casson Av *DERBYSE* DE24 ....72 E1
Casson St *EWD/SEL/PNX* NG16 ...12 C3
Castellan Ri *ARN* NG5 ....25 G7
Casterton Rd *ARN* NG5 ....24 F7
Castings Rd *NORM/LIT* DE23 ....57 M7
Castle Bvd *NOTT* NG1 ....5 G9
  NOTTE NG7 ....50 E4
Castle Bridge Rd *WBRGFD* NG2 ...50 E5
Castle Cl *BWSH/BRSTN* DE72 ....60 B1
  RLEIW/BAR LE9 ....140 B8
Castlecraig Ct *DERBYSE* DE24 ....71 J3
Castle Cft *DERBYE* DE24 ....73 H2
Castledine Av *RLBORO* LE12 ....104 C8
Castledine St *LBORO* LE11 ....9 K6
  RLBORO LE12 ....112 C1
Castledine St Extension
  LBORO LE11 ....9 K7
Castle Dr *RIPLEY* DE5 ....12 F7
Castlefields *EWD/SEL/PNX* NG16 ...12 C3
Castlefields *WBRGFD* NG2 ....50 F5
Castleford Rd *LEIW* LE3 ....130 C4
Castle Gdns *NOTTE* NG7 ....50 D4
Castlegate Av *LEIN* LE4 ....119 K7
Castle Gv *NOTTE* NG7 ....4 C9
Castle HI *BPR/DUF* DE56 ....29 J3
  CDON/KEG DE74 ....84 D7
  RDERBYSW DE65 ....70 B6
  RLBORO LE12 ....88 D7
  RLBORO LE12 ....113 J5
Castle La *EWD/SEL/PNX* NG16 ...12 C5
  MELB/CHEL DE73 ....82 F8
Castle Marina Rd *WBRGFD* NG2 ...50 E5
Castle Meadow Rd *WBRGFD* NG2 ...5 F8
Castle Ms *MELB/CHEL* DE73 ....82 F8
  NOTTE NG7 ....4 C9

Castle Mills *MELB/CHEL* DE73 ....82 F8
Castle Orch *BPR/DUF* DE56 ....29 J3
Castle Pk *WBRGFD* NG2 ....50 F5
Castle Quay *NOTTE* NG7 ....50 F4
Castlerigg Cl *WBRGFD* NG2 ....66 A2
Castle Ri *GBY/RBY* LE6 ....123 K5
Castle Rd *NOTT* NG1 ....5 G8
  RLBORO LE12 ....113 H6
  RLEIW/BAR LE9 ....129 H2
Castle Rock Dr *COAL* LE67 ....108 C5
Castleshaw Dr *NORM/LIT* DE23 ...56 C8
Castle St *DERBY* DE1 ....3 G5
  EWD/SEL/PNX NG16 ....21 L6
  LEI LE1 ....6 D7
  WBRGFD NG2 ....51 K3
Castle Yd *LEI* LE1 ....6 D7
Castleton Av *ALFN* DE55 ....11 M1
  ARN NG5 ....25 K8
  CARL NG4 ....38 C6
  ILK DE7 ....33 J2
  NORM/LIT DE23 ....57 K7
Castleton Cl
  EWD/SEL/PNX NG16 ....35 K1
Castleton Rd *WGSTN* LE18 ....138 A3
Castle Vw *EWD/SEL/PNX* NG16 ...20 E3
  LEI LE1 ....6 D7
  WBRGFD NG2 ....65 H1
Caswell La *LEIN* LE4 ....125 H3
Caterham *WOL/BIL/BRX* NG8 ...35 H8
Caters Cl *RLEINE/SYS* LE7 ....124 B1
Catesby St *LEI* LE3 ....6 A7
Cat & Fiddle La *ILK* DE7 ....46 B1
Catfoot La *CARL* NG4 ....26 B7
Cathedral Rd *DERBY* DE1 ....2 D2
Cathedral Vw *NORM/LIT* DE23 ...57 H5
Catherine Av *ILK* DE7 ....47 K1
Catherine La *BLWL* NG6 ....23 L8
Catherines Cl *RLBORO* LE12 ....112 F1
Catherine St *LEIN* LE4 ....7 J1
  NORM/LIT DE23 ....57 M5
Cathkin Cl *LEIW* LE3 ....130 B2
Catkin Dr *EWD/SEL/PNX* NG16 ...22 A8
Catlow Rd *ARN* NG5 ....25 G7
Cator Cl *CARL* NG4 ....38 B4
Cator La *BSTN/STPLFD* NG9 ....63 H2
Cator La North
  BSTN/STPLFD NG9 ....63 G1
Catriona Crs *ARN* NG5 ....25 L5
Catterick Dr *MCKLVR* DE3 ....56 A6
Catterley Hill Rd
  MAPPK/POR/STA NG3 ....51 M1
Cattle Market *LBORO* LE11 ....9 J3
Cattle Market Rd *WBRGFD* NG2 ...51 H5
Catton Rd *ARN* NG5 ....25 L7
Cauby Cl *RLBORO* LE12 ....114 C4
Caudle Cl *RLEINE/SYS* LE7 ....118 D4
Caulton St *NOTTE* NG7 ....4 B3
Caunton Av
  MAPPK/POR/STA NG3 ....37 J6
Causeway *DERBYE* DE21 ....58 F3
Causeway La *GBY/RBY* LE6 ....118 D5
  LEI LE1 ....6 D4
Causeway Ms *WBRGFD* NG2 ....50 F5
Cavan Cl *CFTN/RUD* NG11 ....64 B5
Cavell Cl *CFTN/RUD* NG11 ....64 B5
Cavendish Av *CARL* NG4 ....38 B5
  BWSH/BRSTN DE72 ....74 E5
  CDON/KEG DE74 ....84 E5
  HUCK/RAV NG15 ....24 A2
Cavendish Ct
  BWSH/BRSTN DE72 ....74 E6
  DERBY DE1 ....2 D3
Cavendish Cl *BPR/DUF* DE56 ....29 H5
Cavendish Crs
  BSTN/STPLFD NG9 ....48 B5
  CARL NG4 ....38 A5
  COAL LE67 ....108 A8
Cavendish Crs North *NOTTE* NG7 ...4 C7
Cavendish Crs South *NOTTE* NG7 ...4 C9
Cavendish Dr *CARL* NG4 ....38 C7
  RIPLEY DE5 ....11 G6
Cavendish Ms *NOTTE* NG7 ....4 D9
Cavendish Pl *BSTN/STPLFD* NG9 ...63 K1
  NOTTE * NG7 ....4 D9
Cavendish Rd *CARL* NG4 ....38 A5
  ILK DE7 ....47 K1
  LEIS LE2 ....131 J7
  LGEAT NG10 ....62 A5
Cavendish Rd East *NOTTE* NG7 ...4 D7
Cavendish Rd West *NOTTE* NG7 ...25 J7
  DERBY DE1 ....2 D3
  NOTTE NG7 ....50 D7
Cavendish V *ARN* NG5 ....37 H4
Cavendish Wy *MCKLVR* DE3 ....56 C5
Cave Rd *RLBORO* LE12 ....105 H7
Caversfield Cl *NORM/LIT* DE23 ...56 E7
Caversham Rd *LEIS* LE2 ....137 G4
Caversham Wy *ILK* DE7 ....32 B7
Cawsand Rd *WGSTN* LE18 ....138 A6
Cawston Gdns *BLWL* NG6 ....23 M7
Caxmere Dr *WOL/BIL/BRX* NG8 ...49 K2
Caxton Cl *CARL* NG4 ....38 E8
Caxton Ct *NORM/LIT* DE23 ....71 J1
Caxton St *NORM/LIT* DE23 ....57 K5
Caythorpe Crs *ARN* NG5 ....37 G4
Caythorpe Ri *ARN* NG5 ....37 G3
Cecilia Rd *LEIS* LE2 ....131 M5
Cecil Rd *LEIS* LE2 ....7 K5
Cecil St *DERBYW* DE22 ....57 H2
  WBRGFD NG2 ....51 K3
Cedar Av *BSTN/STPLFD* NG9 ....49 L8
  LEIN LE4 ....119 L3
  LGEAT NG10 ....76 A2
  RIPLEY DE5 ....11 H6
  RLBORO LE12 ....88 B7
  WGSTN LE18 ....138 B6
Cedar Cl *LEIW* LE3 ....124 C6
  LGEAT NG10 ....47 M8
  RLEIW/BBY LE8 ....146 D7
Cedar Ct *GBY/RBY* LE6 ....123 K5
Cedars End/Nar LE19 ....135 M8
Cedar Cft *BPR/DUF* DE56 ....18 F8
  BWSH/BRSTN DE72 ....73 L8
Cedar Dr *BWSH/BRSTN* DE72 ....60 A3

Cedar Ldg *NOTTE* * NG7 ....4 D7
  COT/KEY/RAD NG12 ....80 C5
  RLEINE/SYS LE7 ....120 F5
  BPR/DUF DE56 ....17 L5
  HUCK/RAV NG15 ....23 M2
  RLBORO LE12 ....113 J6
  WOL/BIL/BRX NG8 ....49 K3
Cedar Gv *ARN* NG5 ....25 M7
Cedar Pk *ILK* DE7 ....33 J7
Cedar Rd *BSTN/STPLFD* NG9 ....63 J2
  CDON/KEG DE74 ....84 F5
  LBORO LE11 ....9 M8
  LEIS LE2 ....7 L9
  NOTTE NG7 ....36 E7
  RLEIW/BBY LE8 ....142 F1
Cedars *LEIS* LE2 ....131 M8
Cedars Ct *LEIS* LE2 ....132 A5
Cedar St *DERBYW* DE22 ....43 J8
Cedar Tree Rd *ARN* NG5 ....24 F6
Cedarwood Cl *LEIN* LE4 ....126 B6
Cedarwood Ct *DERBYE* DE21 ....44 C5
Celandine Cl *ARN* NG5 ....24 D5
  DERBYE DE21 ....44 D5
  RLBORO LE12 ....113 K5
Celandine Rd *DERBYE* DE21 ....44 D5
Celia Dr *CARL* NG4 ....38 B8
Cello Cl *COAL* LE67 ....108 C2
Celt St *LEI* LE1 ....6 B4
Cemetery Hill (Nottingham Rd)
  DERBYSE DE21 ....3 M2
Cemetery La *RIPLEY* DE5 ....11 H6
Cemetery Rd *BPR/DUF* DE56 ....17 L1
  BSTN/STPLFD NG9 ....48 C8
  RLBORO LE12 ....114 B4
  RLEIW/BBY LE8 ....136 D8
Centenary Wy *ASHB* DE6 ....28 B5
  BPR/DUF DE56 ....29 M5
  ILK DE7 ....33 G8
Central Av *ARN* NG5 ....25 K8
  BSTN/STPLFD NG9 ....48 C7
  BSTN/STPLFD NG9 ....49 J6
  BSTN/STPLFD NG9 ....63 H1
  BWSH/BRSTN DE72 ....59 M6
  HUCK/RAV NG15 ....23 L1
  ILK DE7 ....31 M7
  LEIS LE2 ....132 A5
  LGEAT NG10 ....61 M1
  MAPPK/POR/STA NG3 ....37 L3
  NOTTE NG7 ....36 E6
  RLBORO LE12 ....101 M4
  RLEINE/SYS LE7 ....120 F3
  WBRGFD NG2 ....51 K7
  WGSTN LE18 ....138 A5
Central Cl *RLEIW/BBY* LE8 ....136 D7
Central Ct *COAL* * LE67 ....108 B7
  NOTTE NG7 ....50 D6
Central Rd *COAL* LE67 ....108 B8
  LEIS LE2 ....6 A2
Central St *MAPPK/POR/STA* NG3...5 M3
  RLEIW/BBY LE8 ....143 K4
Centre Ct *DERBY* DE1 ....3 H8
  END/NAR LE19 ....130 B8
Centre Wy *COT/KEY/RAD* NG12 ...53 J3
Centurion Wy *END/NAR* LE19 ...130 B7
  NOTTE NG7 ....50 E7
Century Ct *LEI* LE5 ....133 C1
Cernan Ct *BLWL* NG6 ....35 K2
Cerne St *NORM/LIT* DE23 ....64 C7
Chaceley Wy *CFTN/RUD* NG11 ...64 E4
Chadborn Av *CFTN/RUD* NG11 ...77 M6
Chadderton Cl *LEIS* LE2 ....131 L8
Chaddesden Av
  MAPPK/POR/STA * NG3 ....5 G1
Chaddesden La *DERBYE* DE21 ...58 D2
Chaddesden Park Rd
  DERBYE DE21 ....58 D1
Chadfield Rd *BPR/DUF* DE56 ....29 J2
Chad Gdns *ARN* NG5 ....24 E5
Chadwell Rd *LEIW* LE3 ....124 C8
Chadwick Av *DERBYSE* DE24 ...72 C2
Chadwick Rd *NOTTE* NG7 ....36 C8
Chaffinch Cl *DERBYE* DE21 ....59 K1
  LEIN LE4 ....124 E1
Chainama Cl *LEIW* LE3 ....130 A1
Chainbridge Cl *LBORO* LE11 ....103 L2
Chain La *MCKLVR* DE3 ....56 E5
  NOTTE * NG7 ....50 C6
Chale Rd *LEIN* LE4 ....125 K5
Chalfield Cl *CFTN/RUD* NG11 ...64 B6
Chalfont Dr *RLBORO* LE12 ....114 A6
  WOL/BIL/BRX NG8 ....50 A1
Chalfont Sq *DERBYSE* DE24 ....44 F5
Chalkley Cl *DERBYSE* DE24 ....58 D3
Challis Av *DERBYE* DE21 ....44 F8
Chalons Cl *ILK* DE7 ....33 K6
Chalons Wy *ILK* DE7 ....33 K7
Chalvington Cl *LEIS* LE5 ....133 C4
Chamberlain Ct *CFTN/RUD* NG11...64 A6
Chambers Av *ILK* DE7 ....33 M8
Chambers Cl *COAL* LE67 ....116 D7
Chambers St *DERBYSE* DE24 ...58 C7
Champion Av *ILK* DE7 ....33 G4
Champion Cl *LEIE* LE5 ....132 F2
Champion HI *BPR/DUF* DE56 ....29 J3
Chancel Pl *DERBYW* DE22 ....2 D7
Chancel Rd *LEIN* LE4 ....119 H7
The Chancery
  BSTN/STPLFD NG9 ....49 G8
  CFTN/RUD NG11 ....64 E1
Chancery Pl *LEI* * LE1 ....6 E5
Chancery St *LEI* LE1 ....6 E7
Chandlers Ford *DERBYE* DE21 ...44 D5
Chandos Av *CARL* NG4 ....38 E7
Chandos Pole St *DERBYW* DE22 ...57 H1
Chandos St *CARL* NG4 ....38 E8
  LEIS LE2 ....7 L8
  MAPPK/POR/STA NG3 ....5 M1
Chandres Ct *DERBYW* DE22 ....43 J3
Chandwick Ct *DERBYSE* DE24 ...71 H4
Chantrey Cl *BSTN/STPLFD* NG9 ...63 H3
Chantrey Rd *WBRGFD* NG2 ....51 J8
Chantry Cl *LGEAT* NG10 ....75 J3
  MCKLVR DE3 ....56 A6
  RLEIW/BAR LE9 ....135 C7
Chapel Bar *NOTT* NG1 ....4 F7
Chapel Cl *RLEINE/SYS* LE7 ....118 F4
  RLEINE/SYS LE7 ....120 E3

Chapel Gn *LEIW* LE3 ....129 M5
Chapel HI *GBY/RBY* LE6 ....123 J4
Chapel La *ARN* NG5 ....25 J7
  CALV/BJ NG14 ....27 L1
  CARL NG4 ....26 F8
  COT/KEY/RAD NG12 ....67 K4
  DERBYE DE21 ....44 B8
  DERBYE DE21 ....59 J2
  GBY/RBY LE6 ....123 G7
  LEIS LE2 ....131 M8
  MELB/CHEL DE73 ....72 E6
  RLBORO LE12 ....89 H6
  RLBORO LE12 ....91 M8
  RLBORO LE12 ....100 C4
  RLEINE/BAR LE9 ....142 B5
Chapel Mews Ct
  BSTN/STPLFD * NG9 ....48 F7
Chapel Rd *EWD/SEL/PNX* NG16 ...13 J1
Chapel Rw *BWSH/BRSTN* DE72 ...59 M6
Chapel Side *DERBYE* * DE21 ....59 J2
Chapel St *BPR/DUF* DE56 ....17 K4
  BPR/DUF DE56 ....18 A8
  BPR/DUF DE56 ....18 E7
  BPR/DUF DE56 ....29 J4
  BSTN/STPLFD NG9 ....48 F7
  CFTN/RUD NG11 ....79 G1
  DERBY DE1 ....2 D2
  DERBYE DE21 ....59 J2
  END/NAR LE19 ....135 L4
  EWD/SEL/PNX NG16 ....21 K6
  EWD/SEL/PNX NG16 ....34 C1
  HEANOR DE75 ....20 E7
  ILK DE7 ....33 J6
  LEIS LE2 ....138 E2
  LGEAT NG10 ....62 C8
  MELB/CHEL DE73 ....82 F8
  RIPLEY DE5 ....11 H5
  RLBORO LE12 ....101 M2
  RLEINE/SYS LE7 ....120 F5
  RLEIW/BBY LE8 ....136 H6
Chaplin Ct *LEIW* LE3 ....130 B4
Chapman Av *DERBYSE* DE24 ...72 F1
Chapman St *LBORO* LE11 ....9 L2
Chapmans Wk *ARN* NG5 ....24 F1
Chappell Cl *LEIN* LE4 ....120 C8
Chapter Cl *DERBYE* DE21 ....44 B5
Chapter Dr *EWD/SEL/PNX* NG16 ...34 C1
Chardlace Wk *NOTT* NG1 ....5 K4
Chard St *NOTTE* NG7 ....36 D5
Charing Ct *DERBY* DE1 ....43 M8
Charingworth Rd *DERBYE* DE21 ...44 F5
Chariot Cl *DERBYSE* DE24 ....73 H2
Charity Rd *ALFN* DE55 ....11 M2
Charlbury Ri *NORM/LIT* DE23 ...56 F7
Charlbury Ct
  BSTN/STPLFD * NG9 ....48 F3
Charlbury Rd *WOL/BIL/BRX* NG8 ...49 M1
Charlecote Av *LEIW* LE3 ....130 C6
Charlecote Dr
  WOL/BIL/BRX NG8 ....49 K4
Charlecote Park Dr
  WBRGFD NG2 ....65 G3
Charles Av *BSTN/STPLFD* NG9 ...48 D7
  BSTN/STPLFD NG9 ....49 L6
  BSTN/STPLFD NG9 ....63 G4
  DERBYE DE21 ....59 H1
  EWD/SEL/PNX NG16 ....21 H4
  LGEAT NG10 ....61 M1
Charles Cl *CARL* NG4 ....38 C5
  ILK DE7 ....47 M1
Charles Dr *RLEINE/SYS* LE7 ....124 C1
Charles Pk *BLWL* NG6 ....36 A2
Charles St *ARN* NG5 ....25 J8
  CFTN/RUD NG11 ....65 G8
  HUCK/RAV NG15 ....15 L8
  LBORO LE11 ....9 J1
  LEI LE1 ....6 F4
  LGEAT NG10 ....76 B1
  RLBORO LE12 ....114 A6
Charles Wy *RLEIW/BBY* LE8 ....142 F6
Charlesworth Av *NOTTE* NG7 ...36 C7
Charley Dr *LBORO* LE11 ....8 D7
Charley Rd *RLBORO* LE12 ....101 J6
  RLBORO LE12 ....110 E6
Charlock Cl *ARN* NG5 ....24 C8
Charlotte Cl *ARN* NG5 ....25 J5
Charlotte St *ILK* DE7 ....33 J4
Charlton Av *LGEAT* NG10 ....62 D7
Charlton Cl *RLEIW/BBY* LE8 ....142 E1
Charlton Gv *BSTN/STPLFD* NG9 ...63 K3
Charnborough Rd *COAL* LE67 ...108 F6
Charnia Gv *RLBORO* LE12 ....118 D1
Charnock Av *WOL/BIL/BRX* NG8 ...50 A4
Charnor Rd *LEIW* LE3 ....124 C7
Charnwood Av *BPR/DUF* DE56 ...17 K3
  BSTN/STPLFD NG9 ....63 H1
  BWSH/BRSTN DE72 ....60 A5
  CDON/KEG DE74 ....85 G4
  COT/KEY/RAD NG12 ....80 C5
  LEIN LE4 ....120 D7
  LGEAT NG10 ....61 J3
  NORM/LIT DE23 ....75 M3
  RLBORO LE12 ....95 G2
  RLEIW/BBY LE8 ....136 D7
Charnwood Dr *COAL* LE67 ....116 D7
  LEIW LE3 ....129 L4
  RIPLEY DE5 ....11 G6
  RLEIW/SYS LE7 ....133 K2
Charnwood Flds *RLBORO* LE12 ...95 G2
Charnwood Gv *HUCK/RAV* NG15 ...15 J8
  WBRGFD NG2 ....51 J8
Charnwood La *ARN* NG5 ....37 L1
Charnwood Ri *RLBORO* LE12 ....111 K2
Charnwood Rd *RLBORO* LE11 ....9 H7
  RLBORO LE12 ....101 M4
  RLEINE/SYS LE7 ....118 D4
Charnwood St *COAL* LE67 ....108 C7
  DERBY DE1 ....2 E3

  LEIW LE5 ....7 L4
Charnwood Wy *CALV/BJ* NG14 ...27 H3
Charterhouse Cl *DERBYE* DE21 ...44 C4
Charteris Cl *LBORO* LE11 ....103 H1
Charterstone La *DERBYW* DE22 ...43 J3
Charter St *LEI* LE1 ....6 F2
Chartley Rd *LEIW* LE3 ....131 G4
Chartwell Av *CFTN/RUD* NG11 ...64 F8
Chartwell Dr *DERBYE* DE21 ....3 K3
  WGSTN LE18 ....137 L5
Chartwell Gv
  MAPPK/POR/STA NG3 ....38 A2
The Chase *BPR/DUF* DE56 ....18 F7
  COAL LE67 ....116 C7
  DERBYE DE21 ....30 B5
  DERBYSE DE24 ....71 K3
  LEIS LE2 ....130 D8
  RLEINE/SYS LE7 ....115 H7
Chase Cl *MELB/CHEL* DE73 ....72 F5
Chase Pk *WBRGFD* NG2 ....51 L4
Chater Cl *LEIE* LE5 ....127 H8
Chatham St *BPR/DUF* DE56 ....18 B3
  LEI LE1 ....6 F7
  NORM/LIT DE23 ....57 L7
  NOTT NG1 ....5 G3
Chatsworth Av
  BSTN/STPLFD NG9 ....63 G5
  CARL NG4 ....38 C7
  COT/KEY/RAD NG12 ....53 L3
  LGEAT NG10 ....76 E1
  NOTTE NG7 ....36 E5
  WGSTN LE18 ....137 L6
Chatsworth Cl *LGEAT* NG10 ....61 M3
  RLBORO LE12 ....101 L4
Chatsworth Ct *ILK* DE7 ....32 C7
Chatsworth Crs *DERBYW* DE22 ...43 K5
Chatsworth Dr *DERBYE* DE21 ...30 B5
  HUCK/RAV NG15 ....23 L1
  MCKLVR DE3 ....56 C1
  WGSTN LE18 ....120 D4
Chatsworth Pl *ILK* DE7 ....46 F2
Chatsworth Rd *LBORO* LE11 ....8 A1
  WBRGFD NG2 ....51 M7
Chatsworth St *LEIS* LE2 ....7 L6
  NORM/LIT DE23 ....57 J6
Chatteris Av *LEIE* LE5 ....133 H4
Chatteris Dr *DERBYE* DE21 ....44 B6
Chaucer St *END/NAR* LE19 ....135 L6
  ILK DE7 ....33 K6
  LEIS LE2 ....132 A4
Chaveney Ct *RLBORO* LE12 ....112 C2
Chaveney Rd *RLBORO* LE12 ....112 C2
Chaveney Wk *RLBORO* LE12 ....112 C2
Chaworth Av
  EWD/SEL/PNX NG16 ....22 D6
Chaworth Rd *CARL* NG4 ....52 D1
  WBRGFD NG2 ....65 J1
Cheadle Cl
  MAPPK/POR/STA NG3 ....37 M5
  NORM/LIT DE23 ....56 F6
  WOL/BIL/BRX NG8 ....35 H7
Cheam Cl *DERBYW* DE22 ....56 C1
Cheapside *BPR/DUF* DE56 ....17 K4
  DERBY DE1 ....2 D3
  RLBORO LE12 ....102 A3
Checketts Cl *LEIN* LE4 ....125 M5
Checketts Rd *LEIN* LE4 ....125 M4
Checkland Rd *LEIN* LE4 ....120 C8
Cheddar Rd *CFTN/RUD* NG11 ...64 C7
  WGSTN LE18 ....138 C4
Chedington Av
  MAPPK/POR/STA NG3 ....38 B1
Chediston V *ARN* NG5 ....24 F7
Chedworth Cl
  MAPPK/POR/STA NG3 ....51 K2
Chedworth Dr *DERBYSE* DE21 ...73 H1
Cheer Cl *RLEIW/BBY* LE8 ....142 D3
Chelker Wy *LBORO* LE11 ....103 G4
Chellaston La *MELB/CHEL* DE73 ...73 G6
Chellaston Park Ct
  MELB/CHEL DE73 ....72 D6
Chellaston Rd *DERBYSE* DE24 ...72 C6
  WGSTN LE18 ....138 A3
Chelmarsh Cl *MELB/CHEL* DE73...72 E6
Chelmsford Cl *MCKLVR* DE3 ....56 A4
Chelmsford Rd *NOTTE* NG7 ....36 D5
Chelsbury Ct *ARN* NG5 ....25 J8
Chelsea Cl *DERBYW* DE22 ....56 C1
  EWD/SEL/PNX NG16 ....35 J4
  LEIS LE2 ....137 H6
Chelsea St *NOTTE* NG7 ....36 E6
Cheltenham Cl
  BSTN/STPLFD NG9 ....62 D5
Cheltenham Rd *LEIN* LE4 ....125 G5
Cheltenham St *BLWL* NG6 ....36 C5
Chelwood Rd *DERBYSE* DE73 ...72 D5
Cheney End *RLEINE/BAR* LE9 ...135 H7
Cheney Rd *LEIN* LE4 ....126 C2
Chennel Nook
  COT/KEY/RAD NG12 ....67 L5
Chepstow Rd *CFTN/RUD* NG11 ...64 C7
  LEIS LE2 ....132 A4
Chequers La *DERBYE* DE21 ....3 L3
Chequers Rd *DERBYE* DE21 ....3 K3
Cherhill Cl *CFTN/RUD* NG11 ....64 B8
Cheriborough Rd *CDON/KEG* DE74...84 F5
Cheriton Dr *ILK* DE7 ....33 G4
Cheriton Gdns *NORM/LIT* DE23 ...56 C8
Cheriton Rd *LEIS* LE2 ....137 H2
Cherry Av *HUCK/RAV* NG15 ....23 M2
Cherrybrook Cl *LEIE* LE4 ....118 F6
Cherrybrook Dr *DERBYE* DE21 ...44 F4
Cherry Cl *ARN* NG5 ....25 M6
  BWSH/BRSTN DE72 ....61 J7
  LBORO LE11 ....9 L8
Cherrydale Rd *NORM/LIT* DE23 ...70 E1
Cherry Dr *RLEINE/SYS* LE7 ....133 K2
Cherry HI *COT/KEY/RAD* NG12 ...80 D4
Cherry Hills Rd *DERBYE* DE21 ...130 A1
Cherryleas Dr *LEIW* LE3 ....131 G3
Cherry Orch
  COT/KEY/RAD NG12 ....67 J4
Cherry Orchard Mt *ARN* NG5 ....24 E4
Cherry Rd *RLEIW/BBY* LE8 ....136 F8
Cherry St *WGSTN* LE18 ....137 M5

Cherry Tree Av BPR/DUF DE56 ......17 L1
LEIW LE3 ......129 J4
RIPLEY DE5 ......11 H7
Cherry Tree Cl
BWSH/BRSTN DE72 ......61 K3
COT/KEY/RAD NG12 ......53 K5
EWD/SEL/PNX NG16 ......13 J7
ILK DE7 ......47 H1
RDERBYSW DE65 ......68 B5
Cherrytree Cl RLEINE/SYS LE7 ......124 B2
RLEIW/BBY LE8 ......143 H3
Cherry Tree Gv END/NAR LE19 ......135 L4
Cherry Tree La
COT/KEY/RAD NG12 ......65 M4
Cherry Tree Ms DERBYE DE21 ......58 F3
Cherry Wood Dr
WOL/BIL/BRX NG8 ......35 M8
Cherrywood Gdns
MAPPK/POR/STA NG3 ......37 L7
Chertsey Cl
MAPPK/POR/STA NG3 ......37 K6
Chertsey Ct ILK DE7 ......32 B7
Chertsey Rd MCKLVR DE3 ......56 A5
Cherwell Ct BLWL NG6 ......35 K1
Cherwell Rd RLBORO LE12 ......105 H8
Chesapeake Rd DERBYE DE21 ......58 F1
Chesham Dr ARN NG5 ......36 F5
BSTN/STPLFD NG9 ......48 F4
Cheshire Dr WGSTN LE18 ......137 K4
Cheshire Gdns LEIS LE2 ......131 H8
Cheshire Rd LEIS LE2 ......131 H8
Cheshire St DERBYSE DE24 ......72 B2
Cheshire Wy
EWD/SEL/PNX NG16 ......13 G3
Chesil Av WOL/BIL/BRX NG8 ......50 B2
Cheslyn Dr WOL/BIL/BRX NG8 ......36 A7
Chester Av DERBYW DE22 ......43 M2
Chester Cl LBORO LE11 ......8 F4
LEI LE1 ......7 J3
RLEIW/BBY LE8 ......137 G8
Chesterfield Av CARL NG4 ......38 B5
LGEAT NG10 ......62 D8
Chesterfield Dr CALV/BJ NG14 ......39 L2
Chesterfield Houses
DERBYE * DE21 ......59 J4
Chesterfield Rd BPR/DUF DE56 ......10 C4
BPR/DUF DE56 ......17 L3
LEIE LE5 ......132 B3
Chesterfield St CARL NG4 ......38 B8
Chesterford Ct NORM/LIT DE23 ......70 D1
Chester Gn BSTN/STPLFD NG9 ......62 C5
Chester Green Rd DERBY DE1 ......43 L8
Chesterman Cl
EWD/SEL/PNX NG16 ......33 M3
Chester Pk DERBYE * DE21 ......43 M7
Chester Rd RLEIW/BBY LE8 ......137 G8
Chesterton Av NORM/LIT DE23 ......57 J8
Chesterton Rd DERBYE DE21 ......59 J1
Chestnut Av ALFN DE55 ......12 B2
BPR/DUF DE56 ......17 L5
BPR/DUF DE56 ......18 A8
BSTN/STPLFD NG9 ......63 K1
LEIE LE5 ......127 G6
LEIS LE2 ......138 D2
MAPPK/POR/STA NG3 ......37 M5
MCKLVR DE3 ......56 C4
MELB/CHEL DE73 ......72 D4
NORM/LIT DE23 ......2 E9
RIPLEY DE5 ......11 H7
Chestnut Cl BPR/DUF DE56 ......29 J5
END/NAR LE19 ......141 M1
ILK DE7 ......19 G8
RLBORO LE12 ......102 A4
RLBORO LE12 ......112 C3
RLEINE/SYS LE7 ......120 F5
RLEINE/SYS LE7 ......121 H2
Chestnut Dr
EWD/SEL/PNX NG16 ......34 E1
LEIS LE2 ......139 K5
RLEINE/SYS LE7 ......133 L3
Chestnut Gv ARN NG5 ......25 L7
BWSH/BRSTN DE72 ......60 A4
CALV/BJ NG14 ......39 K3
CARL NG4 ......38 D6
COAL LE67 ......108 F7
COT/KEY/RAD NG12 ......53 K3
HUCK/RAV NG15 ......23 M3
LGEAT NG10 ......47 L8
MAPPK/POR/STA NG3 ......5 G1
RDERBYSW DE65 ......68 F3
WBRGFD NG2 ......51 H8
Chestnut La CFTN/RUD NG11 ......77 J1
Chestnut Rd
EWD/SEL/PNX NG16 ......20 E4
LEIW LE3 ......124 A7
The Chestnuts LGEAT NG10 ......61 L7
MAPPK/POR/STA NG3 ......37 K6
RLEIW/BBY LE8 ......143 J3
Chestnut St LBORO LE11 ......9 G3
Chestnut Wk COAL LE67 ......122 C1
GBY/RBY LE6 ......123 K5
Chestnut Wy RLEINE/SYS LE7 ......115 J8
Chettle Rd LEIW LE3 ......124 E8
Chetwin Rd WOL/BIL/BRX NG8 ......49 H2
Chetwynd Rd
BSTN/STPLFD NG9 ......62 E5
Chevely Ct DERBYE DE21 ......44 B7
Cheverton Cl DERBYSE DE24 ......73 H2
Cheverton Ct
MAPPK/POR/STA NG3 ......5 H2
Chevin Av BWSH/BRSTN DE72 ......60 A5
LEIW LE3 ......130 B2
MCKLVR DE3 ......56 D5
Chevin Bank BPR/DUF DE56 ......29 H1
Chevin Gdns ARN NG5 ......24 E6
Chevin Pl DERBYW DE22 ......43 K8
Chevin Rd BPR/DUF DE56 ......17 H3
BPR/DUF DE56 ......29 J2
DERBYW DE22 ......43 K8
Chevin Side BPR/DUF * DE56 ......17 K6
Chevin V BPR/DUF DE56 ......29 J2
Chevin Vw BPR/DUF * DE56 ......17 K3
Cheviot Av EWD/SEL/PNX NG16 ......12 D4
Cheviot Cl ARN NG5 ......24 F5
Cheviot Dr BLWL NG6 ......23 K7
RLBORO LE12 ......102 A4
Cheviot Rd LEIS LE2 ......131 K8
LGEAT NG10 ......61 L6
Cheviot St DERBYW DE22 ......57 G2
Chewton Av
EWD/SEL/PNX NG16 ......21 L6
Chewton St
EWD/SEL/PNX NG16 ......21 L6
Cheyenne Gdns DERBYE DE21 ......58 F2
Cheyne Wk HUCK/RAV NG15 ......15 M7
Cheyny Cl WBRGFD NG2 ......51 G6
Chichester Cl ARN NG5 ......24 C8
ILK DE7 ......33 L7
LBORO LE11 ......103 G7
Chichester Dr
COT/KEY/RAD NG12 ......67 J3
Chidlow Rd WOL/BIL/BRX NG8 ......35 H8
Chigwell Cl WOL/BIL/BRX NG8 ......35 J4
Chilcombe Cl LEIN LE4 ......125 J4
Chillon Wy HUCK/RAV NG15 ......23 H1
Chilson Dr MCKLVR DE3 ......56 A4
Chiltern Av RLBORO LE12 ......102 B4
RLEIW/BAR LE9 ......142 B5
Chiltern Cl ARN NG5 ......24 F5
Chiltern Dr ILK DE7 ......32 C7
Chiltern Gdns LGEAT NG10 ......61 L6
Chiltern Gn LEIS LE2 ......137 L1
Chiltern Wy ARN NG5 ......36 F1
Chilton Dr EWD/SEL/PNX NG16 ......22 E8
Chilvers Cl ARN NG5 ......24 E8
Chilwell Ct BLWL NG6 ......24 B8
Chilwell La BSTN/STPLFD NG9 ......49 G8
Chilwell Rd BSTN/STPLFD NG9 ......63 K1
Chilwell St NOTTE NG7 ......50 D4
Chime Cl DERBYE DE21 ......44 C5
Chingford Ct DERBYW DE22 ......56 F2
Chingford Rd
WOL/BIL/BRX NG8 ......35 J7
Chinley Rd DERBYE DE21 ......44 E6
Chippendale St NOTTE NG7 ......50 D4
Chippenham Rd ARN NG5 ......36 F1
Chisbury Gn CFTN/RUD NG11 ......64 B8
Chisholm Wy ARN NG5 ......36 E1
Chislehurst Av LEIW LE3 ......130 C7
Chiswick Cl DERBYW DE22 ......56 D1
Chiswick Dr LBORO LE11 ......103 G3
Chiswick Rd LEIS LE2 ......131 K6
Chitterman Wy COAL LE67 ......116 C7
Chorley Wood Rd LEIE LE5 ......133 H3
Chrisett Cl LEIE LE5 ......132 F1
Christchurch Rd
HUCK/RAV NG15 ......23 H3
Christie Dr LBORO LE11 ......103 G1
Christina Av BLWL NG6 ......36 A3
Christina Crs BLWL NG6 ......36 A3
Christopher Cl RLEIW/BBY LE8 ......143 J4
WOL/BIL/BRX NG8 ......49 K1
Christopher Dr LEIN LE4 ......126 D3
Christow St LEI LE1 ......7 H3
Chrysalis Wy
EWD/SEL/PNX NG16 ......21 G4
Church Av ARN NG5 ......25 J8
LEIW LE3 ......131 G2
Church Cl ARN NG5 ......25 H8
BSTN/STPLFD NG9 ......48 A3
COT/KEY/RAD NG12 ......53 J4
MAPPK/POR/STA * NG3 ......5 H3
MELB/CHEL DE73 ......72 E6
MELB/CHEL * DE73 ......82 B4
RLBORO LE12 ......88 C6
RLEINE/SYS LE7 ......120 F3
RLEIW/BBY LE8 ......146 E6
Church Ct RIPLEY * DE5 ......19 H6
Church Crs ARN NG5 ......25 H8
BSTN/STPLFD NG9 ......62 E3
Church Cft RIPLEY DE5 ......11 H5
WBRGFD NG2 ......51 K7
Churchdale Av
BSTN/STPLFD NG9 ......48 C6
Churchdown Cl DERBYE DE21 ......44 F5
Church Dr East ARN NG5 ......25 J8
Church Dr ARN NG5 ......25 H8
ARN NG5 ......25 J8
ARN NG5 ......36 F6
COAL LE67 ......116 B7
COT/KEY/RAD NG12 ......80 C4
HUCK/RAV NG15 ......15 L8
ILK DE7 ......33 H2
LGEAT NG10 ......47 M8
WBRGFD NG2 ......51 K8
Churchfield La NOTTE NG7 ......50 C1
Church Ga COT/KEY/RAD NG12 ......67 G7
LBORO LE11 ......9 K2
LEI LE1 ......6 E5
RLBORO LE12 ......102 A3
Church Gv NOTTE NG7 ......50 C4
Church Hl EWD/SEL/PNX NG16 ......34 D1
LEIN LE4 ......125 M1
RDERBYSW DE65 ......68 F2
RLBORO LE12 ......111 L7
RLEINE/SYS LE7 ......127 K7
Church Hill Rd LEIN LE4 ......120 C8
RLBORO LE12 ......113 H6
Churchill Cl ARN NG5 ......37 K1
BWSH/BRSTN DE72 ......61 H7
LEIS LE2 ......138 E2
Churchill Dr BSTN/STPLFD NG9 ......48 C7
CFTN/RUD NG11 ......64 F8
LEIW LE3 ......129 M3
RDERBYSW DE65 ......68 C5
Churchill St LEIS LE2 ......7 K9
Churchlands LBORO LE11 ......103 M1
Church La ARN NG5 ......25 K6
ASHB DE6 ......41 J5
BLWL NG6 ......24 A8
BPR/DUF DE56 ......17 K3
BSTN/STPLFD NG9 ......49 B8
BSTN/STPLFD NG9 ......63 H6
CALV/BJ NG14 ......27 L1
CDON/KEG DE74 ......84 F4
CFTN/RUD NG11 ......76 F4
CFTN/RUD NG11 ......77 J1
COT/KEY/RAD NG12 ......66 C8
COT/KEY/RAD NG12 ......67 J4
COT/KEY/RAD NG12 ......91 G2
DERBYE DE21 ......30 A8
DERBYE DE21 ......58 E1
DERBYW DE22 ......42 D7
DERBYW DE22 ......43 L5
END/NAR LE19 ......136 A7
EWD/SEL/PNX NG16 ......13 L4
EWD/SEL/PNX NG16 ......21 J1
EWD/SEL/PNX NG16 ......34 A5
GBY/RBY LE6 ......123 G7
HUCK/RAV NG15 ......15 M6
ILK DE7 ......31 H1
ILK DE7 ......44 C3
ILK DE7 ......45 H1
ILK DE7 ......47 J6
LEIN LE4 ......120 B8
LEIS LE2 ......131 M8
LEIS LE2 ......133 J6
RLBORO LE12 ......89 G6
RLBORO LE12 ......91 G8
RLBORO LE12 ......100 C3
RLBORO LE12 ......105 H7
RLBORO LE12 ......112 D1
RLEINE/SYS LE7 ......115 G5
RLEINE/SYS LE7 ......115 K3
RLEINE/SYS LE7 ......115 L5
RLEINE/SYS LE7 ......124 B1
RLEINE/SYS LE7 ......133 K3
RLEIW/BBY LE8 ......136 D7
RLEIW/BBY LE8 ......145 K8
Church La Little RLBORO LE12 ......114 A4
Church La North DERBYW DE22 ......43 K4
Church Leys Av
RLEINE/SYS LE7 ......115 L5
Church Ms DERBYE DE21 ......59 H3
WBRGFD NG2 ......51 H6
Church Nook WGSTN LE18 ......138 B4
Church Rd BLWL NG6 ......24 C8
CALV/BJ NG14 ......39 K3
DERBYW DE22 ......43 G1
EWD/SEL/PNX NG16 ......22 B4
LEIE LE5 ......132 F5
LEIS LE2 ......137 G1
LEIW LE3 ......123 M6
MAPPK/POR/STA NG3 ......5 K2
RLEINE/SYS LE7 ......120 A5
RLEIW/BAR LE9 ......129 H2
RLEIW/BBY LE8 ......139 L7
RLEIW/BBY LE8 ......146 E7
Church Side RLBORO LE12 ......102 A3
Churchside Gdns NOTTE NG7 ......36 C7
Churchside Wk DERBYW * DE22 ......2 C6
Church Sq NOTTE * NG7 ......4 A9
Church St ALFN DE55 ......12 B1
ARN NG5 ......25 K7
BLWL NG6 ......36 C5
BPR/DUF DE56 ......10 B5
BPR/DUF DE56 ......18 D7
BPR/DUF DE56 ......30 A1
BSTN/STPLFD NG9 ......48 B8
BSTN/STPLFD NG9 ......48 F7
BSTN/STPLFD NG9 ......63 K1
BWSH/BRSTN DE72 ......60 A3
CARL NG4 ......27 G7
CARL NG4 ......38 C8
CDON/KEG DE74 ......85 K3
CFTN/RUD NG11 ......79 J7
CFTN/RUD NG11 ......79 G1
DERBYE DE21 ......30 D2
DERBYE DE21 ......59 H3
DERBYSE DE24 ......59 G8
EWD/SEL/PNX NG16 ......21 J6
HEANOR DE75 ......20 D6
ILK DE7 ......33 J3
LEI LE1 ......7 G6
LEIN LE4 ......126 B1
LEIS LE2 ......138 E2
LGEAT NG10 ......47 M8
MELB/CHEL DE73 ......82 F8
NORM/LIT DE23 ......57 G6
NORM/LIT DE23 ......57 L5
NOTTE NG7 ......50 C4
RIPLEY DE5 ......11 H5
RIPLEY DE5 ......11 L8
RIPLEY DE5 ......19 G6
RLBORO LE12 ......94 E6
RLBORO LE12 ......98 A4
RLBORO LE12 ......100 F1
RLBORO LE12 ......101 M3
RLBORO LE12 ......105 H7
RLBORO LE12 ......106 D7
RLEINE/SYS LE7 ......119 K1
RLEIW/BAR LE9 ......134 E4
RLEIW/BAR LE9 ......140 B5
RLEIW/BAR LE9 ......140 B8
RLEIW/BBY LE8 ......137 G7
RLEIW/BBY LE8 ......143 K4
Church Vw BWSH/BRSTN DE72 ......61 J8
END/NAR LE19 ......136 A7
HEANOR DE75 ......19 M3
ILK DE7 ......33 J8
Church View Cl ARN NG5 ......24 F6
Churchview Ct WBRGFD * NG2 ......51 J8
Church Wk ALFN DE55 ......12 C1
BPR/DUF DE56 ......29 K5
EWD/SEL/PNX NG16 ......21 J1
EWD/SEL/PNX NG16 ......21 K5
Churchward Av LEIN LE4 ......125 G3
Churnet Cl CFTN/RUD NG11 ......64 C3
Churston Ct
BSTN/STPLFD * NG9 ......63 L1
Cinder Bank
EWD/SEL/PNX NG16 ......12 D3
Cinderhill Gv CARL NG4 ......38 C5
Cinderhill Rd BLWL NG6 ......35 M3
The Circle DERBYSE DE24 ......71 J3
LEIE LE5 ......132 D3
Citadel St NOTTE NG7 ......50 C2
The City BSTN/STPLFD NG9 ......49 L8
City Link WBRGFD NG2 ......5 L9
City of Dan COAL LE67 ......108 D3
City of Three Waters COAL LE67 ......108 C1
City Rd BSTN/STPLFD NG9 ......49 L8
BSTN/STPLFD NG9 ......63 L1
DERBY DE1 ......43 L8
NOTTE NG7 ......50 B6
Clandon Dr ARN NG5 ......36 F5
Clanfield Rd WOL/BIL/BRX NG8 ......35 J8
Clapgun St CDON/KEG DE74 ......84 F4
Clapham St NOTTE NG7 ......50 C2
Clara Mount Rd HEANOR DE75 ......20 E6
Clarborough Dr ARN NG5 ......37 L1
Clarefield Rd LEIW LE3 ......130 F2
Clare Gv LEIW LE3 ......130 B5
Clarehaven BSTN/STPLFD NG9 ......62 C2
Claremont Av
BSTN/STPLFD NG9 ......49 G7
HUCK/RAV NG15 ......23 L2
Claremont Dr CFTN/RUD NG11 ......65 G4
Claremont Rd ARN NG5 ......36 F6
Claremont St LEIN LE4 ......125 L4
Clarence Dr COAL LE67 ......108 D7
Clarence Rd BSTN/STPLFD NG9 ......63 H5
END/NAR LE19 ......136 B5
LGEAT NG10 ......76 A1
NORM/LIT DE23 ......57 J6
Clarence St LBORO LE11 ......9 K1
LEI LE1 ......6 F5
MAPPK/POR/STA NG3 ......5 M5
Clarendon Pk ARN NG5 ......36 F7
Clarendon Park Rd LEIS LE2 ......131 L6
Clarendon St LEIS LE2 ......6 D9
NOTT NG1 ......4 E5
Clare St NOTT NG1 ......5 H6
Clare Va NOTTE NG7 ......4 E8
Clarewood Gv CFTN/RUD NG11 ......64 C8
Clarges St BLWL NG6 ......36 A1
Clark Cardens RLEIW/BBY LE8 ......136 E7
Clarke Av ARN NG5 ......25 K7
HEANOR DE75 ......20 A5
Clarke Cl COAL LE67 ......108 D3
Clarke Dr LGEAT NG10 ......75 L3
Clarke Gv LEIN LE4 ......125 L1
Clarke Rd COAL LE67 ......109 G7
WBRGFD NG2 ......51 J5
Clarke's La BSTN/STPLFD NG9 ......63 H3
BWSH/BRSTN DE72 ......73 M7
Clarkes Rd WGSTN LE18 ......137 M5
Clarke St DERBY DE1 ......3 H1
LEIN LE4 ......125 M4
Clarkson Dr BSTN/STPLFD NG9 ......63 M1
Claude St NOTTE NG7 ......50 C6
Clawson Cl LBORO LE11 ......103 H1
Claxton St HEANOR DE75 ......20 B5
Claxton Ter HEANOR DE75 ......20 B5
Clay Av MAPPK/POR/STA NG3 ......37 L4
Claybrook Av LEIW LE3 ......130 E7
Claydon Rd LEIE LE5 ......126 C7
Claye St LGEAT NG10 ......62 C8
Clayfield Cl BLWL NG6 ......35 L1
Claygate MAPPK/POR/STA NG3 ......37 L8
Clay La HEANOR DE75 ......20 D5
Claymill Rd LEIN LE4 ......126 D3
Claypole Rd NOTTE NG7 ......4 B2
Clay St BWSH/BRSTN DE72 ......60 E8
RLBORO LE12 ......98 A4
Clayton Ct NOTTE NG7 ......4 B6
Clayton Dr LEIN LE4 ......126 D1
Clayton Gv HEANOR DE75 ......20 A3
Claytons Dr NOTTE NG7 ......50 C5
Cleeve Mt LBORO LE11 ......103 G3
Clematis Cl LEIN LE4 ......124 E2
Clement Av LEIN LE4 ......125 L4
Clement Rd ILK DE7 ......19 G8
Clements Ga CDON/KEG DE74 ......93 G1
Clether Rd WOL/BIL/BRX NG8 ......49 H1
Cleve Av BSTN/STPLFD NG9 ......62 C4
Clevedon Crs LEIN LE4 ......126 C7
Cleveland Av
BWSH/BRSTN DE72 ......60 D8
DERBYE DE21 ......58 F2
LGEAT NG10 ......62 D7
Cleveland Cl NOTTE NG7 ......50 C2
Cleveland Rd LBORO LE11 ......103 K8
WGSTN LE18 ......138 B3
Cleveleys Av LEIW LE3 ......130 E7
Cleveleys Rd BSTN/STPLFD NG9 ......62 C4
Clevely Wy CFTN/RUD NG11 ......64 C4
The Cliff BLWL NG6 ......35 M3
Cliff Av LBORO LE11 ......103 K2
Cliff Bvd EWD/SEL/PNX NG16 ......22 D8
Cliff Crs COT/KEY/RAD NG12 ......53 K3
Cliff Dr COT/KEY/RAD NG12 ......53 L2
Cliffe Hill Av BSTN/STPLFD NG9 ......48 B8
Cliffe House Ms
RLEIW/BBY LE8 ......136 D8
Cliffe Rd LEIN LE4 ......125 K1
Cliffgrove Av BSTN/STPLFD NG9 ......63 H1
Cliffmere Wk CFTN/RUD NG11 ......64 B6
Clifford Av BSTN/STPLFD NG9 ......49 J7
Clifford Cl COT/KEY/RAD NG12 ......80 D3
LGEAT NG10 ......75 L3
Clifford Ct NOTTE NG7 ......4 B5
Clifford Rd LBORO LE11 ......8 E1
Clifford St DERBYSE DE24 ......58 B5
LEIW LE3 ......6 A5
LGEAT NG10 ......62 C8
NOTTE NG7 ......4 B4
WGSTN LE18 ......137 K5
Cliff Rd CARL NG4 ......52 B1
COT/KEY/RAD NG12 ......53 J3
NOTT NG1 ......5 J8
Cliff Wy COT/KEY/RAD NG12 ......53 K3
Cliffwood Av LEIN LE4 ......119 K8
Clifton Av CFTN/RUD NG11 ......65 G7
LGEAT NG10 ......62 E8
Clifton Bvd NOTTE NG7 ......50 B5
Clifton Br CFTN/RUD NG11 ......64 E1
Clifton Crs BSTN/STPLFD NG9 ......63 J4
Clifton Dr MCKLVR DE3 ......56 C4
WGSTN LE18 ......137 L7
Clifton Gv CARL NG4 ......38 C5
Clifton La CFTN/RUD NG11 ......64 B7
CFTN/RUD NG11 ......64 E7
Clifton Rd CFTN/RUD NG11 ......64 F8
CFTN/RUD NG11 ......65 G8
DERBYW DE22 ......43 H4
LEIS LE2 ......131 J7
Clifton St BSTN/STPLFD NG9 ......63 L1
DERBY DE1 ......3 J8
Clifton Ter NOTTE NG7 ......4 D9
Clint Hill Dr RLEIW/BAR LE9 ......140 C5
Clinton Av ARN NG5 ......36 F7
EWD/SEL/PNX NG16 ......21 H1
Clinton Ct NOTT NG1 ......5 G4
Clinton St BSTN/STPLFD NG9 ......49 J8
DERBYE DE21 ......3 M2
Clinton Ter NOTTE * NG7 ......4 C6
Clipper Rd LEIN LE4 ......126 D4
Clipstone Av
MAPPK/POR/STA NG3 ......37 L3
NOTT NG1 ......4 F3
Clipstone Cl WGSTN LE18 ......138 C5
WOL/BIL/BRX NG8 ......35 H5
Clipstone Gdns DERBYE DE21 ......44 F5
WGSTN LE18 ......138 C5
Clipston La COT/KEY/RAD NG12 ......66 D8
Clive Crs EWD/SEL/PNX NG16 ......34 E2
Cliveden Gn CFTN/RUD NG11 ......64 B6
The Cloisters BSTN/STPLFD NG9 ......49 L7
Cloisters Ct DERBYE DE21 ......44 D4
Cloister St NOTTE NG7 ......50 C5
The Close ARN NG5 ......37 G4
BSTN/STPLFD NG9 ......63 H3
DERBYW DE22 ......43 K5
END/NAR * LE19 ......135 L5
NORM/LIT DE23 ......57 H5
RLEINE/SYS LE7 ......118 B8
Close Quarters
BSTN/STPLFD NG9 ......49 G7
Cloud Av BSTN/STPLFD NG9 ......48 D8
Cloud Lea RLBORO LE12 ......113 J7
Clouds Hl CFTN/RUD NG11 ......64 C7
Cloudside Rd LGEAT NG10 ......47 L8
Cloudwood Cl NORM/LIT DE23 ......56 F6
Clough Ct WOL/BIL/BRX NG8 ......35 M8
Clovelly Rd LEIE LE5 ......132 D3
LEIW LE3 ......124 B7
Clover Cl DERBYE DE21 ......59 K2
END/NAR LE19 ......135 L7
Clover Ct BWSH/BRSTN DE72 ......74 C5
Cloverdale COT/KEY/RAD NG12 ......67 L5
Cloverdale Dr DERBYSE DE24 ......71 K5
Cloverdale Rd LEIE LE5 ......127 G5
Clover Gn BLWL NG6 ......36 B4
Clover Lands CFTN/RUD NG11 ......65 G4
Cloverlands Dr
EWD/SEL/PNX NG16 ......22 E8
Clover La RLBORO LE12 ......113 K6
Clover Pl COAL LE67 ......100 B7
Clover Ri EWD/SEL/PNX NG16 ......21 M6
Cloverslade RDERBYSW DE65 ......70 A6
Cloves Hl ILK DE7 ......31 G5
Clowbridge Dr LBORO LE11 ......103 G4
Clumber Av ARN NG5 ......36 F7
BSTN/STPLFD NG9 ......63 H2
CARL NG4 ......38 E8
EWD/SEL/PNX NG16 ......13 J6
MAPPK/POR/STA NG3 ......37 L3
Clumber Cl RLEINE/SYS LE7 ......120 F2
Clumber Ct ILK DE7 ......33 K2
Clumber Crs North NOTTE NG7 ......4 C8
Clumber Crs South NOTTE NG7 ......4 C9
Clumber Dr COT/KEY/RAD NG12 ......53 L3
Clumber Rd LEIE LE5 ......132 C2
WBRGFD NG2 ......65 K1
Clumber Rd East NOTTE NG7 ......4 D8
Clumber Rd West NOTTE NG7 ......4 C8
Clumber St LGEAT NG10 ......62 B8
NOTT NG1 ......5 H6
Cluster Ct BPR/DUF * DE56 ......17 K3
Cluster Rd BPR/DUF DE56 ......17 K3
Clusters Ct BPR/DUF DE56 ......17 K3
Clutsom Rd COAL LE67 ......108 A8
Clyde St LEI LE1 ......7 H4
Coach Dr DERBYW DE22 ......29 G8
EWD/SEL/PNX NG16 ......21 K3
Coachmans Ct RLBORO LE12 ......102 A2
Coachmans Cft
WOL/BIL/BRX NG8 ......49 L2
Coach Rd RIPLEY DE5 ......11 K4
Coachways ILK DE7 ......32 C4
Coalbourn Cl LEIN LE4 ......125 J3
Coales Av RLEIW/BBY LE8 ......142 E2
Coatbridge Av LEIN LE4 ......126 B4
Coates Av HUCK/RAV NG15 ......15 K6
LEIW LE3 ......124 E8
Coatsby Rd
EWD/SEL/PNX NG16 ......22 D8
Cobden St DERBYW DE22 ......57 H2
LBORO LE11 ......9 L3
LEI LE1 ......7 K3
LGEAT NG10 ......62 B8
NOTTE NG7 ......50 C2
RIPLEY DE5 ......11 G5
Cobham Cl DERBYSE DE24 ......71 H4
Cobthorn Dr DERBYW DE22 ......43 G3
Coburn Pl DERBY * DE1 ......2 D4
Cobwells Cl RLEIW/BBY LE8 ......145 L8
Cockayne Cl LGEAT NG10 ......61 M4
Cockayne St North
DERBYSE DE24 ......72 C1
Cockayne St South
DERBYSE DE24 ......72 C1
Cocker Beck CARL NG4 ......27 G8
Cockerhouse Rd
EWD/SEL/PNX NG16 ......21 J3
Cockington Rd
WOL/BIL/BRX NG8 ......49 G2
Cockleys LGEAT NG10 ......76 A1
Cockshut La MELB/CHEL DE73 ......82 D8
Cod Beck Cl DERBYSE DE24 ......73 G1
Codnor-Denby La RIPLEY DE5 ......19 L2
Codnor Ga RIPLEY DE5 ......11 M6
Codnor La ALFN DE55 ......12 A5
Coe Av LBORO LE11 ......102 F2
Cohen Cl ARN NG5 ......37 M2
Cokayne Rd LEIW LE3 ......130 B1
Cokefield Av WOL/BIL/BRX NG8 ......35 K4
Coke St DERBYW DE22 ......57 H3
Colbert Dr LEIW LE3 ......130 E8
Colborn St
MAPPK/POR/STA NG3 ......37 K8
Colby Dr LEIN LE4 ......126 E1
Colby Rd LEIN LE4 ......126 D2
Colchester Rd LEIE LE5 ......132 F1
WOL/BIL/BRX NG8 ......35 J6
Colebrook Cl LEIE LE5 ......132 C4
Coleby Av NOTTE NG7 ......50 C5
Coleby Rd WOL/BIL/BRX NG8 ......35 K5
Coledale WBRGFD NG2 ......66 A1
Coleford Rd LEIN LE4 ......126 E2
Cole La BWSH/BRSTN DE72 ......60 A3
Coleman Cl LEIE LE5 ......126 D8
Coleman Rd LEIE LE5 ......126 D8
RLEIW/BBY LE8 ......145 J7
Coleman St DERBYSE DE24 ......58 C8
Coleraine Cl DERBYE DE21 ......58 F3
Coleridge Crs ARN NG5 ......25 H8
Coleridge Dr END/NAR LE19 ......135 L5
Coleridge St NORM/LIT DE23 ......57 K8

NOTTE NG7 ....4 A4
Colesbourne Rd
CFTN/RUD NG11 ....64 D5
Coles Cl LE4 ....126 E3
Colgrove Rd LBORO LE11 ....9 G6
Colin Av RIPLEY DE5 ....11 M7
Colindale Av LEIN LE4 ....119 L7
Colindale Gdns
EWD/SEL/PNX NG16 ....35 H4
Colin Grundy Dr LEIE LE5 ....126 F6
Colinwood Av ARN NG5 ....24 C6
Collaton Rd WGSTN LE18 ....138 A6
Colledge St ALFN DE55 ....12 A1
College Av LEIS LE2 ....7 J8
College Dr CFTN/RUD NG11 ....64 B5
College Ms DERBY DE1 ....2 A4
College Rd BSTN/STPLFD NG9 ....63 J2
RLBORO LE12 ....86 E6
RLEINE/SYS LE7 ....120 F4
RLEIW/BBY LE8 ....136 D7
College St LEIS LE2 ....7 J8
LGEAT NG10 ....61 M4
NOTT NG1 ....4 E7
College Wk LEIS LE2 ....7 J8
Collett Rd LEIN LE4 ....125 G3
Colleymoor Leys La
CFTN/RUD NG11 ....64 D5
Collier La BWSH/BRSTN DE72 ....60 A3
Colliers Wy EWD/SEL/PNX NG16 .....35 L3
Colliery Cl WBRGFD NG2 ....50 F6
Collin Av LGEAT NG10 ....61 M3
Collingham Gdns DERBYW DE22 ....56 C3
Collingham Rd LEIW LE3 ....131 G5
Collin Gn ARN NG5 ....37 H3
Collington St BSTN/STPLFD NG9 .....63 J1
Collington Wy WBRGFD NG2 ....65 H3
Collingwood Dr RLBORO LE12 ....114 B3
Collingwood Rd LGEAT NG10 ....76 B1
Collin Pl LEIN LE4 ....126 A5
Collins Cl BLWL NG6 ....35 K2
LEIW LE3 ....130 E5
Collins Homes
BSTN/STPLFD * NG9 ....49 J6
Collin St BSTN/STPLFD NG9 ....63 K1
NOTT NG1 ....5 H9
Collis Cl DERBYSE DE24 ....58 C8
Collison St NOTTE NG7 ....4 A3
Collumbell Av
BWSH/BRSTN DE72 ....60 A2
Collygate Rd WBRGFD NG2 ....51 H6
Colmon Cl ARN NG5 ....24 E8
Colne Cl LEIS LE2 ....139 H2
Colombo St NORM/LIT DE23 ....57 M6
Colonsay Cl BSTN/STPLFD NG9 ......48 B4
Colsterdale Cl LEIN LE4 ....125 H2
Colston Crs WBRGFD NG2 ....65 H3
Colston Ga COT/KEY/RAD NG12 ......67 L4
Colston Rd BLWL NG6 ....24 A8
Coltbeck Av END/NAR LE19 ....135 L8
Colthurst Wy LEIS LE2 ....133 L1
Colton St LEI LE1 ....7 G6
Coltsfoot Dr DERBYSE DE24 ....71 K5
Coltsfoot Rd LEIE LE5 ....127 G5
Columbia Cl END/NAR LE19 ....135 L4
LEIW LE3 ....130 C5
Columbine Rd LEIE LE5 ....126 F4
Colville Cl DERBYW DE22 ....57 H1
Colville Ct NOTT NG1 ....4 F2
Colville St NOTT NG1 ....4 F3
Colville Ter NOTT NG1 ....4 F3
Colville Vls NOTT NG1 ....4 F3
Colwell Dr DERBYSE DE24 ....73 H2
Colwell Rd LEIE LE5 ....6 A1
Colwick Loop Rd CARL NG4 ....52 C2
Colwick Manor Farm CARL NG4 ......52 C2
Colwick Park WBRGFD NG2 ....52 C2
Colwick Rd WBRGFD NG2 ....51 J6
Colwyn Av NORM/LIT DE23 ....57 H6
Colyear St DERBY DE1 ....2 E4
Combe Cl LEIW LE3 ....125 G7
Comery Av
MAPPK/POR/STA NG3 ....37 J8
Comet Cl LEIW LE3 ....124 F8
Comet Wy COAL LE67 ....108 A5
Comfrey Cl ARN NG5 ....24 C8
NORM/LIT DE23 ....70 D1
Commerce Sq NOTT NG1 ....5 J8
Commerce St DERBYSE DE24 ....58 D7
MELB/CHEL DE73 ....82 E6
Commercial Av
BSTN/STPLFD * NG9 ....63 J5
Commercial Rd BLWL NG6 ....23 M8
COT/KEY/RAD NG12 ....80 C5
Commercial Sq LEIS LE2 ....131 K5
Commodore Gdns
WOL/BIL/BRX NG8 ....36 A5
The Common DERBYW DE22 ....29 G7
LEIE LE5 ....132 E4
Common La
BSTN/STPLFD NG9 ....62 F1
EWD/SEL/PNX NG16 ....22 E8
HUCK/RAV NG15 ....23 H1
ILK DE7 ....31 L8
Common Piece La
RDERBYSW DE65 ....70 C6
Commons Cl
EWD/SEL/PNX NG16 ....21 L7
Compass Rd LEIE LE5 ....127 G8
Compton Acres WBRGFD NG2 ....64 F1
Compton Av
BWSH/BRSTN DE72 ....73 J7
Compton Cl DERBYSE DE24 ....73 G1
LBORO LE11 ....103 G7
Compton Dr RLEIW/BAR LE9 ....135 H7
Compton Rd ARN NG5 ....36 F4
LEIS LE2 ....131 G5
Comyn Gdns
MAPPK/POR/STA NG3 ....5 J4
Conaglen Rd LEIS LE2 ....136 F1
Condon Rd RLBORO LE12 ....105 J8
Condor Cl RLEIW/BAR LE9 ....141 K8
Condor Rd ILK DE7 ....47 K3
Conduit Cl WBRGFD NG2 ....51 G5
Conduit St LEIS LE2 ....7 H7
Cone La LEIS LE2 ....132 K3
The Coneries LBORO LE11 ....9 G4

Conery La END/NAR LE19 ....135 L4
Coneygrey RLEIW/BBY LE8 ....145 K6
Coney Wk ARN NG5 ....24 D7
Conifer Cl LEIE LE5 ....7 M9
Conifer Crs CFTN/RUD NG11 ....64 C8
Coningsby Gdns East ARN NG5 ....37 K3
Coningsby Rd ARN NG5 ....37 K2
Coningswath Rd CARL NG4 ....38 A5
Coninsby Cl LEI LE1 ....130 F6
Conisborough Ter WBRGFD NG2 .....51 G6
Conisbrough Av CARL NG4 ....38 F6
Coniston Av BLWL NG6 ....36 A5
DERBYE DE21 ....59 J1
LEIS LE2 ....131 J4
Coniston Cl WBRGFD NG2 ....52 A8
Coniston Crs DERBYE DE21 ....44 B5
LBORO LE11 ....8 A8
Coniston Dr ILK DE7 ....47 H2
Coniston Rd BSTN/STPLFD NG9 ......49 H6
HUCK/RAV NG15 ....15 K7
LGEAT NG10 ....61 L5
RLBORO LE12 ....105 H7
Coniston Wy RLEIW/BAR LE9 ....141 H3
Connaught Rd DERBYW DE22 ....57 G3
Connaught St LEIS LE2 ....7 K9
Connelly Cl ARN NG5 ....38 A1
The Connery HUCK/RAV NG15 ....15 L7
Connery Ms BSTN/STPLFD NG9 ......62 F6
Consett Cl DERBYE DE21 ....44 B6
Consort Gdns DERBYE DE21 ....45 G4
Constable Av DERBYW DE22 ....57 G4
LEIN LE4 ....7 J1
Constable Rd LEIE LE5 ....132 B2
Constance Rd NOTTE NG7 ....36 E6
Constitution Hl LEI LE1 ....7 H6
Convent Cl COAL LE67 ....108 B7
Convent St NOTT NG1 ....5 J6
Conway Av BWSH/BRSTN DE72 ....60 B5
CARL NG4 ....38 E8
Conway Cl LBORO LE11 ....102 F2
MAPPK/POR/STA NG3 ....5 H2
Conway Crs CARL NG4 ....38 E7
Conway Dr RLBORO LE12 ....101 K5
Conway Gdns ARN NG5 ....37 K1
Conway Rd CARL NG4 ....38 E8
HUCK/RAV NG15 ....23 H4
LEIS LE2 ....132 B4
NOTTE NG7 ....36 E6
RLBORO LE12 ....113 H6
Conway St LGEAT NG10 ....62 D7
Conway Wk
MAPPK/POR/STA NG3 ....5 H2
Cooden Av LEIW LE3 ....130 F3
Cook Cl BPR/DUF DE56 ....18 C2
Cook Dr ILK DE7 ....47 L1
Cooke Cl LEIW LE3 ....130 B5
LGEAT NG10 ....61 M8
Cookfield Cl BPR/DUF DE56 ....10 C7
Cookham Cl MCKLVR DE3 ....56 A5
Cooks Av CDON/KEG DE74 ....84 E4
Cook's La RLEIW/BAR LE9 ....140 B8
WGSTN LE18 ....138 D8
Cookson Av CARL NG4 ....38 B5
Cookson Pl LBORO LE11 ....103 G1
Coombe Cl RLBORO LE12 ....102 A5
WOL/BIL/BRX NG8 ....50 A4
Coombe Pl LEIS LE2 ....138 F3
Coombe Ri LEIS LE2 ....139 G4
Coombe Rd
EWD/SEL/PNX NG16 ....21 M3
Co-operation St
END/NAR LE19 ....135 M4
Co-operative Av
HUCK/RAV NG15 ....15 M7
Co-operative St LGEAT NG10 ....62 C8
NORM/LIT DE23 ....2 D9
Cooper Cl ARN NG5 ....38 A1
BLWL NG6 ....35 K1
COAL LE67 ....108 B2
LEIS LE2 ....137 G1
RLEIW/BAR LE9 ....135 H7
Cooper Ct LBORO LE11 ....104 B5
Cooper Gdns LEIS LE2 ....139 H3
Coopers Cl BWSH/BRSTN DE72 ....46 B8
Coopers Gn WOL/BIL/BRX NG8 ....49 J5
Cooper's Nook RLEINE/SYS LE7 .....115 H8
Cooper St CARL NG4 ....52 E1
DERBYE DE22 ....57 G1
LEIN LE4 ....125 L6
Copdale Rd LEIE LE5 ....132 C2
Copeland Av BSTN/STPLFD NG9 ......48 C7
LEIE LE5 ....124 E6
Copeland Crs LBORO LE11 ....103 H2
Copeland Rd LEIN LE4 ....125 K1
Copeland St DERBY DE1 ....3 G5
Cope St NOTTE NG7 ....4 A4
Copes Wy DERBYE DE21 ....44 E7
Copinger Rd LEIS LE2 ....131 K8
Coplow Cl RLEINE/SYS LE7 ....132 C5
Coplow Crs RLEINE/SYS LE7 ....120 E5
Copper Beeches RIPLEY DE5 ....10 F5
Copperleaf Cl DERBYW DE22 ....2 C6
Copper Yd RIPLEY DE5 ....19 K5
The Coppice BPR/DUF * DE56 ....17 L4
COAL LE67 ....116 C7
END/NAR LE19 ....135 L7
LEIN LE4 ....120 E8
RLBORO LE12 ....112 F3
Coppice Av ILK DE7 ....33 H2
Coppice Cl BPR/DUF DE56 ....18 E7
DERBYW DE22 ....43 K6
Coppice Ct HEANOR * DE75 ....20 D8
Coppice Dr EWD/SEL/PNX NG16 ......21 J4
HEANOR DE75 ....20 D8
Coppice Ga ARN NG5 ....25 K7
Coppice Gv
MAPPK/POR/STA NG3 ....37 K5
Coppice Rd RLEINE/SYS LE7 ....121 K2
ARN NG5 ....25 K7
Coppicewood Dr
NORM/LIT DE23 ....56 E6
Copplestone Dr
MAPPK/POR/STA NG3 ....38 A1
The Copse BSTN/STPLFD NG9 ....63 G1
HUCK/RAV NG15 ....24 A1
ILK DE7 ....33 H2

Copse Cl CALV/BJ NG14 ....39 J2
COAL LE67 ....108 A8
LEIS LE2 ....133 G8
LEIW LE3 ....129 J6
Copse Gv NORM/LIT DE23 ....56 E8
RLBORO LE12 ....111 L1
Copseside Cl LGEAT NG10 ....61 L7
Copthorne Cl LEIW LE3 ....130 B2
Copt Oak Rd END/NAR LE19 ....135 K6
Corah St LEIW LE3 ....6 C7
Coral St LEIN LE4 ....125 L6
Corbel Cl DERBYE DE21 ....44 C5
Corben Gdns BLWL NG6 ....23 K8
Corbet Cl LEIN LE4 ....124 F4
Corbridge Gv NORM/LIT DE23 ....56 E8
Corby Cl DERBYSE DE24 ....72 D2
Corby Rd MAPPK/POR/STA NG3 ....37 J6
Cordelia Cl DERBYE DE21 ....44 C5
Cordell Rd LBORO * LE11 ....103 H1
Corden Av MCKLVR DE3 ....56 E5
Corden St NORM/LIT DE23 ....57 L5
Cordery Rd LEIE LE5 ....132 F4
Cordville Cl DERBYE DE21 ....58 F2
Cordwell Cl CDON/KEG DE74 ....84 D4
Cordy La EWD/SEL/PNX NG16 ....13 K8
Corfe Cl NORM/LIT DE23 ....71 H1
Corfield Av HEANOR DE75 ....20 D8
Corfield Ri LEIW LE3 ....130 C4
Corinium Dr DERBYE DE24 ....73 H2
Corinth Rd CFTN/RUD NG11 ....64 C4
Corinth St LEIS LE2 ....136 E5
Corn Cl COT/KEY/RAD NG12 ....67 J5
Corncrake Av BLWL NG6 ....36 B4
Corncrake Dr ARN NG5 ....26 A8
Cornell Dr ARN NG5 ....26 A7
Cornfield Cl END/NAR LE19 ....135 K6
Cornfield Rd
EWD/SEL/PNX NG16 ....22 C8
The Cornfields ARN * NG5 ....24 F7
Cornflower Dr DERBYE DE21 ....44 E5
Cornhill DERBYW DE22 ....43 K3
Cornhill Rd CARL NG4 ....37 M7
Corn Market DERBY DE1 ....2 F3
Cornmill Cl DERBYSE DE21 ....73 H2
Cornwall Av BSTN/STPLFD NG9 ....64 A3
Cornwallis Av LEIN LE4 ....124 F5
Cornwallis Cl LGEAT NG10 ....76 B1
Cornwall Rd ARN NG5 ....25 C8
DERBYE DE21 ....3 M1
LEIN LE4 ....137 K5
WGSTN LE18 ....137 K5
Cornwall St END/NAR LE19 ....135 M4
Coronation Av BPR/DUF DE56 ....17 L2
CFTN/RUD NG11 ....50 F7
DERBYSE DE24 ....73 C2
LGEAT NG10 ....47 L8
WGSTN LE18 ....137 M5
Coronation Cl MELB/CHEL DE73 ......82 F7
Coronation Cottages
BWSH/BRSTN * DE72 ....74 F2
Coronation Rd BLWL NG6 ....24 C3
EWD/SEL/PNX NG16 ....34 F2
HUCK/RAV NG15 ....15 K7
ILK DE7 ....33 L5
ILK DE7 ....45 M1
MAPPK/POR/STA NG3 ....37 K3
Coronation St ILK DE7 ....33 J7
NORM/LIT DE23 ....57 M7
Coronation Wk CARL NG4 ....38 E6
Coronet Ct DERBYE DE21 ....45 H4
Corporation Oaks
MAPPK/POR/STA NG3 ....5 H1
Corporation Rd ILK DE7 ....47 L2
LEIN LE4 ....125 K5
Corporation St DERBY DE1 ....2 F3
Corsham Gdns
MAPPK/POR/STA NG3 ....37 L8
Corshaw Wk LEIE LE5 ....126 B7
Cort Crs LEIW LE3 ....130 C3
Cosby Rd END/NAR LE19 ....142 A1
RLEIW/BAR LE9 ....141 L8
RLEIW/BBY LE8 ....142 F4
WBRGFD NG2 ....51 K4
Cossall Rd BSTN/STPLFD NG9 ....34 A7
Cossington La RLEINE/SYS LE7 ....114 E8
RLEINE/SYS LE7 ....119 L1
Cossington Rd RLBORO LE12 ....114 A5
Cossington St LEIN LE4 ....125 M6
Costock Av ARN NG5 ....36 F3
Costock Rd RLBORO LE12 ....88 D6
RLBORO LE12 ....89 H6
Cotes Rd RLBORO LE12 ....104 D2
Cotes Yd LBORO LE11 ....104 A2
Cotgrave Av CARL NG4 ....38 D5
Cotgrave Cl WOL/BIL/BRX NG8 ....35 J5
Cotgrave La
COT/KEY/RAD NG12 ....66 E5
Cotgrave Rd
COT/KEY/RAD NG12 ....66 D8
Cothelstone Av LBORO LE11 ....103 G2
Cotley Rd LEIE LE5 ....125 G2
Cotmanhay Rd ILK DE7 ....33 K4
Coton Cl CFTN/RUD NG11 ....64 E4
Cotswold Av RLEIW/BAR LE9 ....142 B5
Cotswold Cl LBORO LE11 ....8 A4
LGEAT NG10 ....61 M7
NORM/LIT DE23 ....56 E8
Cotswold Rd WOL/BIL/BRX NG8 ......35 H6
Cottage Cl BPR/DUF DE56 ....10 C8
GBY/RBY LE6 ....123 G6
ILK DE7 ....33 H4
RLBORO LE12 ....88 D4
Cottage Farm Cl LEIW LE3 ....136 D1
Cottage Garden La
HEANOR DE75 ....20 B5
Cottage La COAL LE67 ....116 A4
Cottage Meadow CARL NG4 ....52 D6
Cottage Rd WGSTN LE18 ....138 C6
Cottage Rw LEIW LE3 ....130 C5
Cottagers Cl WGSTN LE18 ....137 J2
Cottage Ter NOTT NG1 ....4 D6
Cottam Dr ARN NG5 ....24 D7
Cottam Gdns ARN NG5 ....24 D7
Cottesbrooke Cl WGSTN LE18 ....138 B5

Cottesmore Av LEIS LE2 ....139 G3
Cottesmore Dr LBORO LE11 ....103 K7
Cottesmore Rd LEIE LE5 ....126 B8
NOTTE NG7 ....4 A7
Cottisford Cl NORM/LIT DE23 ....56 E7
Cotton Brook Rd
NORM/LIT DE23 ....57 M7
Cotton Cl LEIN LE4 ....126 E1
Cotton Cft DERBYSE DE24 ....101 M5
Cotton La DERBYSE DE24 ....57 M7
Cotton Wy LBORO LE11 ....95 J8
Coulson Cl RLEIW/BBY LE8 ....142 E1
Countesthorpe Rd
RLEIW/BAR LE9 ....142 B5
RLEIW/BBY LE8 ....143 K1
Counting House Rd LEIS LE2 ....131 K5
Countisbury Dr DERBYE DE21 ....44 B5
Countrymans Wy
RLBORO LE12 ....102 A3
RLEINE/SYS LE7 ....115 H7
Countryman Wy COAL LE67 ....116 C7
County Cl BSTN/STPLFD NG9 ....63 L2
WBRGFD NG2 ....51 J5
County Rd CARL NG4 ....38 A4
Coupe St RIPLEY DE5 ....11 K7
Court Cl RLEIW/BAR LE9 ....129 J2
Court Crs WOL/BIL/BRX NG8 ....49 J3
Courtenay Gdns
MAPPK/POR/STA NG3 ....5 J4
Courtenay Rd LEIW LE3 ....125 G6
Court Gdns CFTN/RUD NG11 ....64 D7
Courtland Dr DERBYSE DE24 ....72 E1
Courtland Gdns DERBYE DE24 ....72 E1
Courtland Rd RDERBYSW DE65 ....69 G4
Courtleet Wy BLWL NG6 ....35 M2
Courtney Cl WOL/BIL/BRX NG8 ....49 J2
Courtney Wy BPR/DUF DE56 ....18 B2
The Court DERBYE DE21 ....72 F1
Court Rd LEIS LE2 ....136 F5
RLEINE/SYS LE7 ....133 K3
Court St NOTTE NG7 ....4 B2
Court Yd BSTN/STPLFD NG9 ....48 F7
Covedale Rd LEIE LE5 ....132 B2
Coventry La BSTN/STPLFD NG9 ....48 C4
Coventry Rd BLWL NG6 ....23 M8
BSTN/STPLFD NG9 ....49 L8
RLEIW/BAR LE9 ....140 F8
RLEIW/BAR LE9 ....141 H7
Coventry St LEIW LE3 ....6 A7
Coverdale COAL LE67 ....108 B1
Coverdale Rd WGSTN LE18 ....138 C6
The Covert DERBYE DE21 ....59 J3
Covert Cl CALV/BJ NG14 ....39 J2
COT/KEY/RAD NG12 ....80 D3
HUCK/RAV NG15 ....24 A1
LEIS LE2 ....139 G1
RLEINE/SYS LE7 ....120 C4
Covert La RLEINE/SYS LE7 ....127 L1
Covert Rd WBRGFD NG2 ....65 M1
Covett Wy LEIW LE3 ....130 C2
Cowan St NOTT NG1 ....5 J6
Cowdall Rd LEIW LE3 ....130 B4
Cowdray Cl DERBYSE DE24 ....71 H5
LBORO LE11 ....9 H8
Cowdrey Gdns ARN NG5 ....37 M1
Cowlairs ARN NG5 ....24 C8
Cow La BSTN/STPLFD NG9 ....49 G7
GBY/RBY LE6 ....122 D5
ILK DE7 ....23 M8
DERBYW DE22 ....43 J8
Cowley St BLWL NG6 ....36 B4
Cowley Wy LEIE LE5 ....133 J1
Cowlishaw Cl
BWSH/BRSTN DE72 ....74 C5
Cowper Rd ARN NG5 ....37 J3
EWD/SEL/PNX NG16 ....21 C7
Cowper St DERBYSE DE24 ....71 L2
Cowsley Rd DERBYE DE21 ....44 B8
Cowslip Cl END/NAR LE19 ....135 K7
Coxbench Rd DERBYE DE21 ....30 C3
Cox Green Ct NORM/LIT DE23 ....56 D8
Coxmoor Cl COT/KEY/RAD NG12 .....66 A3
Coxon St DERBYE DE21 ....59 J2
Crabtree Cl CDON/KEG DE74 ....84 E5
DERBYW DE22 ....43 G3
Crabtree Cnr WGSTN LE18 ....137 L2
Crabtree Fld WBRGFD NG2 ....52 B3
Crab Tree Hl DERBYE DE21 ....30 D7
Crabtree Hill Keddleston Rd
DERBYE DE21 ....43 C4
Crabtree Rd BLWL NG6 ....35 L1
Craddock Av DERBYE DE21 ....59 J4
Cradock Dr RLBORO LE12 ....112 D2
Cradock Rd LEIS LE2 ....131 M5
Cradock St LBORO LE11 ....9 K4
LEI LE1 ....7 J4
Crafton St East LEI LE1 ....7 H4
Crafton St West LEI LE1 ....7 G4
Craftsmans Wy
RLEINE/SYS LE7 ....115 H8
Cragdale COAL LE67 ....100 F3
Cragdale Rd ARN NG5 ....37 G2
Cragmoor Rd CALV/BJ NG14 ....39 J4
Craig Gdns LEIW LE3 ....130 B1
Craighill Rd LEIS LE2 ....131 M7
Craiglee Ct DERBYSE DE24 ....71 H4
Craig St LGEAT NG10 ....62 C8
Crammond Cl WBRGFD NG2 ....50 F5
Cramps Cl RLBORO LE12 ....105 G8
Crampton Cft ARN NG5 ....24 E7
Cramworth Dr ARN NG5 ....37 H4
Cranberry Cl CFTN/RUD NG11 ....64 F2
LEIE LE5 ....130 B5
Cranberry Gv NORM/LIT DE23 ....70 D1
Cranbourne Cl
BSTN/STPLFD NG9 ....48 B5
Cranbourne Gdns LEIS LE2 ....132 F7
Cranbourne Gv HUCK/RAV NG15 .....15 J8
Cranbrook Rd RLEINE/SYS LE7 ....133 K1
Cranbrook St NOTT NG1 ....5 J6
Crane-ley Rd GBY/RBY LE6 ....123 J4
Cranesbill Rd LEIE LE5 ....126 F5
Crane St LEI LE1 ....6 F3
Cranfield Wk CFTN/RUD NG11 ....64 D5
Cranfleet Wy LGEAT NG10 ....61 M8
Cranford Gdns WBRGFD NG2 ....65 G3
Cranhill Cl NORM/LIT DE23 ....70 D1

Cranmer Rd RLEIW/BBY LE8 ....142 E1
Cranmer Dr RLEINE/SYS LE7 ....120 D4
Cranmer Gv
MAPPK/POR/STA NG3 ....5 H2
DERBYE DE21 ....3 K3
Cranmer St ILK DE7 ....33 K6
LEIW LE5 ....6 A8
LGEAT NG10 ....62 B6
MAPPK/POR/STA NG3 ....5 H2
Cranmer Wk
MAPPK/POR/STA NG3 ....5 H2
Cranmore Cl ARN NG5 ....25 L5
Cranoe Rd RLEIW/BBY LE8 ....147 M6
Cranshaw Cl RLBORO LE12 ....94 A4
Cransley Av WOL/BIL/BRX NG8 ....49 H5
Cranston Av ARN NG5 ....25 K6
Cranston Crs LEIW LE3 ....124 A6
Cranston Rd BSTN/STPLFD NG9 ....49 G5
Cranthorne Dr
MAPPK/POR/STA NG3 ....52 A1
Crantock Cl LEIE LE5 ....133 G4
Crantock Gdns
COT/KEY/RAD NG12 ....80 D4
Cranwell Cl LEIE LE5 ....132 F5
Cranwell Rd WOL/BIL/BRX NG8 ....35 H5
Craster Dr ARN NG5 ....26 A7
BLWL NG6 ....23 K7
Craven Cl LBORO LE11 ....103 K7
Craven Rd NOTTE NG7 ....36 C8
Craven's Rough COAL LE67 ....116 F3
Craven St LEI LE1 ....6 B7
Crawford Av BSTN/STPLFD NG9 ....48 B7
Crawford Cl WOL/BIL/BRX NG8 ....49 J2
Crawford Ri ARN NG5 ....26 A7
Crawford Rd LEIS LE2 ....130 F1
Crawley Rd DERBYSE DE24 ....72 D2
Crawshaw Cl RLBORO LE12 ....94 A4
Crayford Rd DERBYSE DE24 ....72 E2
Craythorne Wy WGSTN LE18 ....138 C5
Creaton Dr WGSTN LE18 ....138 C5
Creaton Rd WGSTN LE18 ....138 C5
Crecy Cl NORM/LIT DE23 ....57 G4
Crediton Cl WGSTN LE18 ....138 B7
The Crescent ARN NG5 ....37 J3
BSTN/STPLFD NG9 ....48 C6
BSTN/STPLFD NG9 ....62 E5
BSTN/STPLFD NG9 ....63 G4
BWSH/BRSTN DE72 ....61 G8
COT/KEY/RAD NG12 ....80 D5
DERBYE DE21 ....58 D2
DERBYSE DE24 ....72 C1
EWD/SEL/PNX NG16 ....21 C5
ILK DE7 ....19 G8
ILK DE7 ....31 M6
LEI * LE1 ....6 F8
MAPPK/POR/STA NG3 ....37 H7
RLBORO LE12 ....88 D5
RLEIW/BBY LE8 ....136 F8
RLEIW/BBY * LE8 ....139 M7
WGSTN LE18 ....138 A3
Crescent Av CARL NG4 ....38 C6
Crescent Rd COAL LE67 ....108 A8
EWD/SEL/PNX NG16 ....13 H1
Crescent St LEI LE1 ....6 F8
The Cresset DERBYW DE22 ....43 J5
Cressida Pl LEIW * LE3 ....130 C5
Cresswell Av LEIN LE4 ....126 E1
Cresswell Rd BSTN/STPLFD NG9 .....48 E7
The Crest DERBYW DE22 ....43 J5
Cresta Gdns ARN NG5 ....37 H5
Cresta Gv DERBYE DE21 ....44 D6
The Crestway RLEIW/BBY LE8 ....136 D7
Crete Av WGSTN LE18 ....137 J5
Crewe Cl NOTTE NG7 ....4 A4
Crewe St NORM/LIT DE23 ....57 K6
Crewton Wy DERBYSE DE24 ....58 D8
Cribb Cl CFTN/RUD NG11 ....50 F8
Crich Av NORM/LIT DE23 ....56 F5
Crich La BPR/DUF DE56 ....17 L1
Crich Vw ARN NG5 ....37 G5
BPR/DUF DE56 ....10 B7
Cricketers Ct WBRGFD NG2 ....51 K6
Cricket La LBORO LE11 ....103 H7
Cricklewood Rd DERBYW DE22 ....56 F1
Criftin Cl CALV/BJ NG14 ....39 L3
Cringle Ms DERBYE DE21 ....44 C5
Cripps Hl NOTTE NG7 ....55 K6
Critchley St ILK DE7 ....33 K6
Critchlow Rd RLEIW/BAR LE9 ....135 H7
Critch's Flats
EWD/SEL/PNX NG16 ....34 D1
C Rd BSTN/STPLFD NG9 ....50 B8
Crocus Pl WBRGFD * NG2 ....51 G4
Crocus St WBRGFD NG2 ....51 G5
The Croft BPR/DUF DE56 ....10 C6
BPR/DUF DE56 ....18 A6
BWSH/BRSTN DE72 ....74 E1
CDON/KEG DE74 ....86 B5
ILK DE7 ....31 G6
MELB/CHEL DE73 ....82 E7
NORM/LIT DE23 ....57 H7
RLEIW/BAR LE9 ....129 H2
Croft Av HUCK/RAV NG15 ....23 L1
LEIS LE2 ....137 G3
Croft Cl BWSH/BRSTN DE72 ....60 A3
DERBYE DE21 ....59 K1
ILK DE7 ....33 H4
Croft Crs EWD/SEL/PNX NG16 ....34 A2
Croft Dr WGSTN LE18 ....137 M3
Croft End DERBYE DE21 ....30 A7
The Crofters LEIE LE5 ....126 E8
Crofters Cl DERBYE DE21 ....44 B5
Crofters Dr DERBYW DE22 ....43 J5
Croft Hill Rd RLEIW/BAR LE9 ....141 G1
Croft La DERBYE DE21 ....44 B4
RLEIW/BAR LE9 ....134 E7
Crofton Cl BSTN/STPLFD NG9 ....63 H5
WOL/BIL/BRX NG8 ....49 M1
Crofton Rd BSTN/STPLFD NG9 ....48 C7
Croft Rd ARN NG5 ....25 K7
COT/KEY/RAD NG12 ....65 L3
COT/KEY/RAD NG12 ....80 B4
LEIN LE4 ....119 G8
RLEINE/SYS LE7 ....134 C5
RLEIW/BAR LE9 ....141 K3
Croftway COAL LE67 ....116 D7
Cromarty Cl DERBYSE DE24 ....71 J3
LEIN LE4 ....126 A4

Cromarty Ct *WBRGFD* * NG2 ....50 F5
Cromdale La *ARN* NG5 ....26 A6
Cromeford Av *CARL* NG4 ....38 B7
Cromer Cl *MCKLVR* DE3 ....56 A6
Cromer Rd *MAPPK/POR/STA* NG3 ...5 M1
Cromer St *LEIS* LE2 ....132 A4
Cromford Av *WGSTN* LE18 ....137 L6
Cromford Cl
  EWD/SEL/PNX NG16 ....20 F3
  LGEAT NG10 ....75 J2
Cromford Dr *MCKLVR* DE3 ....56 B3
Cromford Rd *DERBYE* DE21 ....44 E7
  EWD/SEL/PNX NG16 ....20 E3
  RIPLEY DE5 ....11 H5
  RLEIW/BAR LE9 ....142 B3
  WBRGFD NG2 ....65 K1
Cromford St *LEIS* LE2 ....7 L5
Cromore Cl *COAL* LE67 ....109 G6
Crompton Rd *ILK* DE7 ....47 M4
Crompton St *DERBY* DE1 ....2 D5
Cromwell Av *ILK* DE7 ....47 L2
  RDERBYSW DE65 ....70 B5
Cromwell Cl *RLBORO* LE12 ....88 C6
Cromwell Crs *CARL* NG4 ....26 F8
Cromwell Rd *BSTN/STPLFD* NG9 ....63 J1
  NORM/LIT DE23 ....2 C9
  RLBORO LE12 ....113 H7
  RLEIW/BBY LE8 ....139 M7
Cromwell St *CARL* NG4 ....38 C8
  EWD/SEL/PNX NG16 ....21 M7
  NOTTE NG7 ....4 C5
Croome Cl *RLBORO* LE11 ....9 L8
Cropston Av *LBORO* LE11 ....102 E5
Cropston Cl *WBRGFD* NG2 ....65 H3
Cropston Dr *COAL* LE67 ....108 F7
Cropston Rd *GBY/RBY* LE6 ....118 C5
  RLEINE/SYS LE7 ....124 C1
Cropthorne Av *LEIE* LE5 ....132 E3
Cropton Cl *DERBYSE* DE24 ....73 G1
Cropton Crs *WOL/BIL/BRX* NG8 ....49 M1
Cropwell Gdns
  COT/KEY/RAD NG12 ....53 L5
Cropwell Gn
  MAPPK/POR/STA NG3 ....51 K1
Cropwell Rd
  COT/KEY/RAD NG12 ....53 K4
Crosby Rd *MAPPK/POR/STA* NG3 ....51 K6
Crosby St *DERBYW* DE22 ....57 H3
The Cross *END/NAR* LE19 ....135 M4
Cross Cl *NORM/LIT* DE23 ....57 G7
Crossdale Dr
  COT/KEY/RAD NG12 ....80 C3
Crossdale Gv *DERBYE* DE21 ....45 G4
Crossdale Wk *ARN* NG5 ....24 C7
Crossfield Dr *ARN* NG5 ....24 E6
Crossgate Dr *WBRGFD* NG2 ....50 E7
Cross Gn *RLEINE/SYS* LE7 ....119 J1
Cross Hedge *RLEINE/SYS* LE7 ....113 J8
Cross Hedge *LEIN* LE4 ....125 G3
Crosshill *COT/KEY/RAD* NG12 ....67 L4
  RIPLEY DE5 ....19 M1
  RLBORO LE12 ....91 H7
Cross Hill Cl *RLBORO* LE12 ....98 A4
Crosshill Dr *ILK* DE7 ....46 F2
Cross Hill La *LBORO* LE11 ....8 F9
Cross Keys Gn *LEIE* LE5 ....127 J8
Crosslands Meadow *CARL* NG4 ....52 D3
Cross La *RIPLEY* DE5 ....11 M8
  RLBORO LE12 ....113 J7
Crossley Cl *RLBORO* LE12 ....105 G8
Crossleys *RLEIW/BBY* LE8 ....145 K8
Crossley St *ARN* NG5 ....36 F5
  LEIW LE3 ....124 A7
  RIPLEY DE5 ....11 H6
Crossman St *ARN* NG5 ....36 F5
Cross Rd *LEIS* LE2 ....132 A5
Cross St *ARN* NG5 ....25 J7
  BSTN/STPLFD NG9 ....49 K8
  CARL NG4 ....38 B8
  CARL NG4 ....38 C8
  DERBYE DE21 ....57 H1
  END/NAR LE19 ....135 M4
  EWD/SEL/PNX NG16 ....21 L5
  LBORO LE11 ....9 L1
  LEIN LE4 ....125 M6
  LEIS LE2 ....132 E8
  LGEAT NG10 ....62 A1
  LGEAT NG10 ....62 C7
  RLBORO LE12 ....94 E6
  RLEINE/SYS LE7 ....120 F4
  RLEIW/BBY LE8 ....136 F7
  WGSTN LE18 ....138 B5
The Crossway *LEIS* LE2 ....137 K1
  LEIW LE3 ....130 E7
The Crossways *LEIN* LE4 ....119 J3
Crosswood Cl *RLBORO* LE11 ....103 G4
Crowan Dr *WGSTN* LE18 ....138 A7
Crowborough Av
  WOL/BIL/BRX NG8 ....49 J5
Crowcroft Wy *LGEAT* NG10 ....61 M5
Crow Hill Rd *CARL* NG4 ....38 C8
Crowhurst Dr *LEIW* LE3 ....130 C7
Crow La *LEIW* LE3 ....131 H4
Crowley Cl *WOL/BIL/BRX* NG8 ....49 G1
Crown Cl *LGEAT* NG10 ....61 L8
Crown Hills Av *LEIE* LE5 ....132 C2
Crown Hills Ri *LEIE* LE5 ....132 C2
Crown Hill Wy *ILK* DE7 ....31 M7
Crownland Dr *MELB/CHEL* DE73 ...72 C6
Crown La *RLBORO* LE12 ....113 H4
Crown Ms *DERBYW* DE22 ....2 B7
Crown St *BPR/DUF* DE56 ....29 J3
  DERBYW DE22 ....2 B7
Crown Ter *BPR/DUF* DE56 ....17 K3
Crown Wk *DERBY* DE1 ....2 F4
Crown Wy *MELB/CHEL* DE73 ....72 C6
Crow Pk Dr *CALV/BJ* NG14 ....39 H4
Crowshaw St *DERBYSE* DE24 ....57 M7
Crowson Cl *RLBORO* LE12 ....101 M6
Crowthorne Av *ARN* NG5 ....24 C6
Crowthorne Gdns *ARN* NG5 ....24 C6
Croxall Cl *CFTN/RUD* NG11 ....64 C3
Croxley Gdns
  EWD/SEL/PNX NG16 ....35 H4
Croydon Rd *NOTTE* NG7 ....50 C2
Croyland Gn *LEIE* LE5 ....133 J1
Crummock Cl
  BSTN/STPLFD NG9 ....49 G7

Crusaders Cl *COAL* LE67 ....108 D2
Cuckmere Cl *DERBYW* DE22 ....43 M2
Cufflin Cl *GBY/RBY* LE6 ....123 H1
Cuffling Cl *LEIW* LE3 ....130 B1
Cuffling Dr *LEIW* LE3 ....130 B1
Cuillin Cl *ARN* NG5 ....24 D5
  LBORO LE11 ....61 L6
Culham Av *LEIE* LE5 ....126 B7
Culver Rd *LEIW* LE3 ....125 G7
Culworth Cl *BPR/DUF* DE56 ....18 B3
Culworth Dr *WGSTN* LE18 ....138 C5
Cumberhills Rd *DERBYW* DE22 ...28 F6
Cumberland Av
  BSTN/STPLFD NG9 ....63 H1
  DERBYE DE21 ....58 C1
Cumberland Cl
  CFTN/RUD NG11 ....65 G8
  EWD/SEL/PNX NG16 ....13 G3
Cumberland Crs
  BWSH/BRSTN DE72 ....59 M6
Cumberland Pl *NOTT* NG1 ....4 F7
Cumberland Rd *LBORO* LE11 ....8 E2
  WGSTN LE18 ....137 J4
Cumberland St *LEI* LE1 ....6 C4
Cumberwell Dr *END/NAR* LE19 ...136 A6
Cumbria Gra *WBRGFD* NG2 ....52 B8
Cumbrian Wy *RLBORO* LE12 ....102 A4
Cumbria Wk *MCKLVR* DE3 ....56 A6
Cummings St *NORM/LIT* DE23 ....2 E9
The Cunnery *ASHB* DE6 ....41 K5
Curborough Dr *DERBYE* DE24 ....73 G1
Curlew Cl *COAL* LE67 ....108 C7
  DERBYE DE24 ....71 H3
  MAPPK/POR/STA NG3 ....52 A2
  RLEINE/SYS LE7 ....120 D3
Curlew Wk *LEIE* * LE5 ....7 L3
Curlew Whf *WBRGFD* * NG2 ....50 D5
Cursley Rd *BSTN/STPLFD* NG9 ....63 C5
Curteys Cl *LEIW* LE3 ....130 F6
Curtis Cl *HUCK/RAV* NG15 ....23 L1
  WGSTN LE18 ....137 L6
Curzon Av *LEIN* LE4 ....125 L1
  WGSTN LE18 ....137 L6
Curzon Cl *DERBYW* DE22 ....43 G3
  RLEINE/SYS LE7 ....121 H2
Curzon Ct *BPR/DUF* * DE56 ....29 K4
  MAPPK/POR/STA NG3 ....5 J5
  MCKLVR * DE3 ....56 B6
Curzon Gdns
  MAPPK/POR/STA NG3 ....5 K4
Curzon La *BPR/DUF* DE56 ....29 H4
  DERBYSE DE24 ....58 E7
Curzon Pl *MAPPK/POR/STA* NG3 ...5 J5
Curzon Rd *DERBYE* DE21 ....44 D8
  LEIS LE2 ....131 J8
Curzon St *CARL* NG4 ....38 E8
  CFTN/RUD NG11 ....77 M6
  DERBY DE1 ....2 D4
  LBORO LE11 ....9 H3
  LEI LE1 ....7 J2
  LGEAT NG10 ....61 M5
  MAPPK/POR/STA NG3 ....5 J5
Cutters Cl *END/NAR* LE19 ....135 L8
The Cuttings *RLEINE/SYS* LE7 ...133 K1
Cuttlebrook Cl *NORM/LIT* DE23 ...71 J1
Cuxton Cl *WOL/BIL/BRX* NG8 ....35 H6
Cycle Rd *NOTTE* NG7 ....50 C5
Cygnet Cl *RLEINE/SYS* LE7 ....120 D3
Cypress Cl *LBORO* LE11 ....103 L8
Cypress Ct *HUCK/RAV* NG15 ....22 F2
Cyprus Av *BSTN/STPLFD* NG9 ....49 K8
Cyprus Dr *BSTN/STPLFD* NG9 ....49 K8
Cyprus Rd *LEIS* LE2 ....137 J1
  MAPPK/POR/STA NG3 ....37 G7
Cyril Av *BSTN/STPLFD* NG9 ....48 B8
  WOL/BIL/BRX NG8 ....36 B7
Cyril Rd *WBRGFD* NG2 ....51 L8
Cyril St *LEIW* LE3 ....130 E7

D

Dabell Av *BLWL* NG6 ....23 J7
Dabey Cl *COAL* LE67 ....116 B7
Dagmar Gv *BSTN/STPLFD* NG9 ....63 J1
  MAPPK/POR/STA NG3 ....37 H6
Dahlia Dr *DERBYE* DE21 ....45 G4
Dairy House Rd *NORM/LIT* DE23 ...57 G6
Daisy Cl *COAL* LE67 ....108 E7
  COT/KEY/RAD NG12 ....67 J5
  GBY/RBY LE6 ....123 L4
Daisy Farm Rd
  EWD/SEL/PNX NG16 ....21 M7
Daisy Rd *MAPPK/POR/STA* NG3 ...37 L6
Dakeyne St
  MAPPK/POR/STA NG3 ....5 M6
Dakota Rd *CDON/KEG* DE74 ....84 F7
Dakyn Rd *LEIE* LE5 ....133 H1
Dalbeattie Cl *ARN* NG5 ....25 M7
Dalby Av *RLEINE/SYS* LE7 ....119M7
  RLEINE/SYS LE7 ....133 K2
Dalby Dr *GBY/RBY* LE6 ....123 K4
Dalby Rd *RLEINE/SYS* LE7 ....118 B9
Dalby Sq *WOL/BIL/BRX* NG8 ....50 A4
Dale Acre *RLEIW/BBY* LE8 ....143 K3
Daleacre Av *CDON/KEG* DE74 ....85 K2
Dale Av *ALFN* DE55 ....12 A1
  CARL NG4 ....38 A8
  LGEAT NG10 ....62 B6
  MAPPK/POR/STA NG3 ....37 L5
  WGSTN LE18 ....137 L3
Dale Brook *RDERBYSW* DE65 ....68 C6
Dalebrook Crs *HUCK/RAV* NG15 ...23 C2
Dale Cl *BWSH/BRSTN* DE72 ....61 H7
  HUCK/RAV NG15 ....23 C1
  WBRGFD NG2 ....51 L8
Dale Ct *BPR/DUF* * DE56 ....18 D7
Dale End Rd *DERBYSW* DE65 ....68 A5
Dale Farm Av
  MAPPK/POR/STA NG3 ....51 L2
Dale Gv *WBRGFD* NG2 ....51 K3
Dalehead Rd *CFTN/RUD* NG11 ....64 B5
Dale La *BSTN/STPLFD* NG9 ....63 J1
Dalemoor Gdns
  WOL/BIL/BRX NG8 ....35 M7
Dale Park Av *BPR/DUF* DE56 ....18 E7

Dale Rd *CARL* NG4 ....38 A8
  COT/KEY/RAD NG12 ....80 C4
  DERBYE DE21 ....59 L1
  DERBYSE DE24 ....59 C8
  EWD/SEL/PNX NG16 ....34 D7
  ILK DE7 ....46 A3
  ILK DE7 ....47 C5
  NORM/LIT DE23 ....57 K5
The Dales *RLEIW/BBY* LE8 ....143 G3
Dalesgate *NORM/LIT* DE23 ....70 D2
Daleside *COT/KEY/RAD* NG12 ....67 K5
Daleside Rd *WBRGFD* NG2 ....51 K8
Daleside Rd East *WBRGFD* NG2 ...52 A3
Dale St *ILK* DE7 ....33 K8
  LEIS LE2 ....7 L6
  WBRGFD NG2 ....5 M8
Dale Ter *WBRGFD* * NG2 ....51 K3
Dale Vw *ILK* DE7 ....47 J1
Dale View Gdns *BPR/DUF* DE56 ...18 D7
Dale View Rd *CARL* NG4 ....37 M8
Dalkeith Av *DERBYSE* DE24 ....72 D2
Dalkeith Rd *LEIE* LE5 ....126 B3
Dalkeith Ter *NOTTE* NG7 ....4 A2
Dallas York Rd
  BSTN/STPLFD NG9 ....63 M1
Dalley Cl *BSTN/STPLFD* NG9 ....48 C7
Dallimore Rd *ILK* DE7 ....47 H3
Dalley La *BPR/DUF* DE56 ....17 C1
Dalness Ct *DERBYSE* DE24 ....71 H4
Dalton Av *DERBYW* DE22 ....57 C4
Dalton Cl *BSTN/STPLFD* NG9 ....62 C2
Daltons Cl *EWD/SEL/PNX* NG16 ...20 E3
Danbury Dr *LEIN* LE4 ....125 H5
Danbury Mt *ARN* NG5 ....37 H5
Dandees Cl *COAL* LE67 ....116 C6
Danebridge Crs *DERBYE* DE21 ....44 E6
Dane Cl *MAPPK/POR/STA* NG3 ...5 J4
Dane Ct *MAPPK/POR/STA* NG3 ...5 J4
Dane Hl *GBY/RBY* LE6 ....123 H7
Danehurst Av *LEIW* LE3 ....130 F1
Danesby Crs *RIPLEY* DE5 ....18 D6
Danesby Ri *RIPLEY* DE5 ....18 E6
Danes Cl *ARN* NG5 ....25 H7
Daneshill Rd *LEIW* LE3 ....131 G2
Dane St *LEIW* LE3 ....6 A6
Danethorpe V *ARN* NG5 ....37 G4
Daniels Wy *HUCK/RAV* NG15 ....23 H1
Dannah Crs *RIPLEY* DE5 ....11 J6
Dannah St *RIPLEY* DE5 ....11 J5
Dan's La *RLEIW/BAR* LE9 ....128 B8
Danvers La *RLBORO* LE12 ....102 A3
Danvers Rd *LEIW* LE3 ....131 C4
  RLBORO LE12 ....113 J6
Darby St *NORM/LIT* DE23 ....2 D9
Darenth Dr *LEIN* LE4 ....124 E4
Darfield Dr *HEANOR* DE75 ....20 E5
Darien Wy *LEIW* LE3 ....130 A5
Darker St *LEIW* LE3 ....6 E4
Darley Cl *BSTN/STPLFD* NG9 ....62 C2
Dark La *BPR/DUF* DE56 ....29 L1
  RLBORO LE12 ....87 K5
Darley Abbey Dr *DERBYW* DE22 ...43 C5
Darley Av *BSTN/STPLFD* NG9 ....63 J4
  CARL NG4 ....38 C6
  NOTTE NG7 ....36 C8
  WGSTN LE18 ....137 L6
Darley Dr *ILK* DE7 ....32 C7
  LGEAT NG10 ....75 L2
  RIPLEY DE5 ....11 C4
Darley Gv *DERBYW* DE22 ....43 L6
Darley La *DERBY* DE1 ....2 E1
Darley Park Dr *DERBYW* DE22 ....43 K6
Darley Park Rd *DERBYW* DE22 ....43 K6
Darley Rd *NOTTE* NG7 ....36 C8
  RLEIW/BBY LE8 ....136 B3
Darley Sq *ILK* DE7 ....33 J2
Darley St *DERBYW* DE22 ....43 L6
  LEI LE1 ....7 L6
Darlington Rd *LEIW* LE3 ....124 E7
Darlton Dr *ARN* NG5 ....25 M8
Darnall Crs *WOL/BIL/BRX* NG8 ....35 H8
Darsway *CDON/KEG* DE74 ....84 E3
Dart Cl *LEIE* LE5 ....139 G2
Dartford Pl *DERBYSE* DE24 ....72 F2
Dartford St *LEIE* LE5 ....131 H6
Dartmeet Ct *NOTTE* NG7 ....36 B8
Darvel Cl *WOL/BIL/BRX* NG8 ....49 M1
Darwen Cl *LEIW* LE3 ....124 F7
Darwin Av *DERBYSE* DE24 ....72 B3
Darwin Cl *ARN* NG5 ....24 C7
  LEIS LE2 ....130 A6
Darwin Rd *LGEAT* NG10 ....75 M2
  MCKLVR DE3 ....56 C4
Dashwood Rd *LEIS* LE2 ....132 A4
Dashwood St *NORM/LIT* DE23 ....2 F8
Datchet Cl *NORM/LIT* DE23 ....56 E7
Dauphine Cl *COAL* LE67 ....109 H6
Davenport Av *LEIS* LE2 ....138 D1
Davenport Rd *DERBYSE* DE24 ....58 A7
  LEIE LE5 ....132 F2
  WGSTN LE18 ....138 B6
Daventry Cl *MCKLVR* DE3 ....56 A4
Davett Cl *LEIE* LE5 ....132 F1
David Av *LEIN* LE4 ....125 J2
David Gv *BSTN/STPLFD* NG9 ....49 H6
David La *BLWL* NG6 ....36 B4
David's Cl *MELB/CHEL* DE73 ....72 C6
Davidson Cl *ARN* NG5 ....26 A8
Davies Rd *WBRGFD* NG2 ....51 L8
Davison Cl *LEIE* LE5 ....132 E1
Davis Rd *BSTN/STPLFD* NG9 ....62 F4
Davy Cl *HUCK/RAV* NG15 ....15M5
Dawlish Cl *HUCK/RAV* NG15 ....23 H1
  LEIE LE5 ....133 H2
Dawlish Ct *DERBYSE* DE24 ....59 G8
  EWD/SEL/PNX NG16 ....21 H4
Dawlish Dr *ARN* NG5 ....37 H4
Dawn Cl *HUCK/RAV* NG15 ....15M6
Dawn's La *BSTN/STPLFD* NG9 ....48 B5
Dawsmere Cl *DERBYE* DE21 ....44 B6
Dawson Cl *EWD/SEL/PNX* NG16 ...21 J3
Dawson's Rd *RLBORO* LE12 ....100 B3
Dawver Rd *EWD/SEL/PNX* NG16 ...34 D2

Daybell Cl *RLEIW/BBY* LE8 ....136 D6
Daybrook Av *ARN* NG5 ....37 G4
Daybrook St *ARN* NG5 ....37 G4
Daylesford Cl *NORM/LIT* DE23 ....56 E7
Days La *BPR/DUF* DE56 ....17 K4
Day St *LEIN* LE4 ....125 L1
Dayton Cl *DERBYSE* DE21 ....59 G2
Deabill St *CARL* NG4 ....52 E1
Deacon Cl *DERBYSE* DE21 ....44 C5
  RLBORO LE12 ....102 A4
Deacon Cottages
  RLEIW/BAR * LE9 ....141 G3
Deacon Rd *LEIN* LE4 ....119 H7
Deacon St *LEIS* LE2 ....6 D9
Dead La *EWD/SEL/PNX* NG16 ....34 B6
Deadman's La *DERBYSE* DE24 ....58 B5
Deakins Pl *NOTTE* NG7 ....50 C2
Dean Av *MAPPK/POR/STA* NG3 ...37 M4
Dean Cl *NORM/LIT* DE23 ....56 E5
  WOL/BIL/BRX NG8 ....49 H2
Deancourt Rd *LEIS* LE2 ....137 M1
Deanery Crs *LEIN* LE4 ....119 H7
Deane Rd *ARN* NG5 ....37 J2
  LEIN LE4 ....126 A6
Deanscourt *COT/KEY/RAD* NG12 ...67 L4
Deans Cft *BSTN/STPLFD* NG9 ....48 F6
Deans Dr *BWSH/BRSTN* DE72 ....59M5
Deanside Dr *LBORO* LE11 ....103 H1
Dean's La *RLBORO* LE12 ....110 F4
Dean St *DERBYW* DE22 ....2 A7
  EWD/SEL/PNX NG16 ....21 C4
  NOTT NG1 ....5 J5
Debdale La *COT/KEY/RAD* NG12 ...80 B3
Deborah Dr *DERBYE* DE21 ....44 E8
Deddington La
  BSTN/STPLFD NG9 ....49 G5
Dee Cl *DERBYSE* DE24 ....71 J4
Dee La *RDERBYSW* DE65 ....55 K8
Deeming Dr *RLBORO* LE12 ....112 D1
Deepdale *EWD/SEL/PNX* NG16 ....12 D3
  LEIE LE5 ....132 D1
Deepdale Av *BSTN/STPLFD* NG9 ...62 B1
Deepdale Cl *WBRGFD* NG2 ....52 A8
Deepdale Ct *HEANOR* * DE75 ....20 C6
Deepdale La *DERBYSE* DE24 ....71 J5
Deepdale Rd *BPR/DUF* DE56 ....17M2
  DERBYE DE21 ....59 K4
  LGEAT NG10 ....75 L1
  WOL/BIL/BRX NG8 ....49 H3
Deepdene Cl *WOL/BIL/BRX* NG8 ...35 L5
Deepdene Wy
  WOL/BIL/BRX NG8 ....35 L5
Deep Furrow Av *CARL* NG4 ....38 B7
The Deepway *RLBORO* LE12 ....112 C2
Deerleap Dr *ARN* NG5 ....25 G8
Deer Pk *WOL/BIL/BRX* NG8 ....49 J3
Deer Park Dr *ARN* NG5 ....24 F7
Deer Park Vw *DERBYE* DE21 ....59 K1
Deers Acre *LBORO* LE11 ....103 M1
De Ferrers Cl *RLBORO* LE12 ....88 C6
De Ferrers Ct *BPR/DUF* * DE56 ....29 J4
Degge St *DERBY* DE1 ....2 E5
Deighton Wy *LBORO* LE11 ....103 G3
Deincourt Cl *DERBYE* DE21 ....59 L1
Delamere Cl *BWSH/BRSTN* DE72 ...61 H7
  DERBYE DE21 ....44 E6
Delaware Rd *LEIE* LE5 ....133 J4
De Lisle Ct *LBORO* LE11 ....102 F5
Dell Wy *CFTN/RUD* NG11 ....64 D5
Dellwood Cl
  MAPPK/POR/STA NG3 ....38 A5
Delta Ct *NOTT* NG1 ....4 F3
Delta St *NOTTE* NG7 ....36 C8
Delven La *CDON/KEG* DE74 ....84 E4
Delves Rd *HEANOR* DE75 ....20 B7
Delville Av *COT/KEY/RAD* NG12 ...80 C3
De Montfort Cl *LBORO* LE11 ....103 G2
De Montfort Ms *LEI* LE1 ....7 H8
De Montfort Sq *LEI* LE1 ....7 G9
De Morgan Cl
  EWD/SEL/PNX NG16 ....13 L5
Denacre Av *LGEAT* NG10 ....62 D6
  WGSTN LE18 ....137 L6
Denarth Av *DERBYSE* DE24 ....72 C4
Denbigh St *DERBYE* DE21 ....44 C8
Denby Common *RIPLEY* DE5 ....19 K5
Denbydale *WGSTN* LE18 ....138 D5
Denby La *RIPLEY* DE5 ....18 F6
Denegate Av *LEIN* LE4 ....119 K7
Denehurst Av
  WOL/BIL/BRX NG8 ....36 A6
Denewood Av
  BSTN/STPLFD NG9 ....49 C5
Denewood Crs
  WOL/BIL/BRX NG8 ....35 J7
Denham Cl *LEIW* LE3 ....130 A1
Denholme Rd
  WOL/BIL/BRX NG8 ....49 H2
Denis Cl *LEIW* LE3 ....130 F2
Denison Ct *NOTTE* * NG7 ....4 A4
Denison Gdns *DERBYE* DE21 ....58 F1
Denison St *BSTN/STPLFD* NG9 ....49 J8
  NOTTE NG7 ....4 A4
Deniston Cl *RLEIW/BAR* LE9 ....141 H3
Denman La *RLEIW/BAR* LE9 ....135 H7
Denman St Central *NOTTE* NG7 ...50 C2
Denman St East *NOTTE* NG7 ....4 B5
Denman St West *NOTTE* NG7 ....50 C2
Denmark Gv
  MAPPK/POR/STA NG3 ....37 H7
Denmark Rd *LEIS* LE2 ....131 J7
Denmead Av *WGSTN* LE18 ....138 A4
Dennett Cl *MAPPK/POR/STA* NG3 ...5 L4
Dennis Av *BSTN/STPLFD* NG9 ....49 J7
Dennis La *NORM/LIT* DE23 ....56 C5
Dennis St *CARL* NG4 ....38 C8
Denstone Dr *DERBYE* DE24 ....72 E3
Denstone Rd
  MAPPK/POR/STA NG3 ....5M6
Dentdale Cl *DERBYSE* DE24 ....73 C1
Dentdale Dr *WOL/BIL/BRX* NG8 ...48 F3
Denton Av *LGEAT* NG10 ....61 L1
Denton Dr *WBRGFD* NG2 ....65 H3
Denton St *LEIW* LE3 ....130 F2
Denver Ct *BSTN/STPLFD* NG9 ....48 C6
Denver Rd *MCKLVR* DE3 ....56 B4

Depedale Av
  BWSH/BRSTN DE72 ....60 A5
  ILK DE7 ....47 H2
Depot St *NORM/LIT* DE23 ....2 E9
Deptford Crs *BLWL* NG6 ....36 A*
Derby Gv *NOTTE* NG7 ....50 C*
Derby La *DERBYE* DE21 ....59 C2
Derby Rd *BPR/DUF* DE56 ....29 K2
  BPR/DUF DE56 ....29 K6
  BSTN/STPLFD NG9 ....48 B5
  BSTN/STPLFD NG9 ....62 A*
  BWSH/BRSTN DE72 ....60 C7
  BWSH/BRSTN DE72 ....73 L4
  CDON/KEG DE74 ....84 A7
  DERBYE DE21 ....30 B2
  DERBYE DE21 ....58 B1
  DERBYE DE21 ....58 F3
  EWD/SEL/PNX NG16 ....34 D*
  HEANOR DE75 ....20 B6
  ILK DE7 ....33 H8
  LGEAT NG10 ....61 M7
  MELB/CHEL DE73 ....72 D5
  MELB/CHEL DE73 ....82 E7
  NOTTE NG7 ....4 B7
  RDERBYSW DE65 ....68 C5
  RIPLEY DE5 ....11 J2
  RLBORO LE12 ....94 D5
Derbyshire Av
  BSTN/STPLFD NG9 ....48 B3
  ILK DE7 ....32 C7
Derbyshire Cl *ILK* DE7 ....32 C7
Derbyshire Dr
  EWD/SEL/PNX NG16 ....13 G3
  ILK DE7 ....47 J1
Derbyshire La *HUCK/RAV* NG15 ...15 L8
Derby St *ARN* NG5 ....25 K8
  BSTN/STPLFD NG9 ....48 B7
  ILK DE7 ....33 K7
  NOTT NG1 ....4 C6
Derby Ter *NOTTE* NG7 ....4 C6
Dereham Dr *ARN* NG5 ....37 K1
Derrington Leys *DERBYSE* DE24 ...73 H1
Derry Dr *ARN* NG5 ....25 K5
Derry Hill Rd *ARN* NG5 ....25 J6
Dersingham Rd *LEIN* LE4 ....125 H5
Derventio Cl *DERBY* DE1 ....43 L8
Derwent Av *BPR/DUF* DE56 ....17 K2
  BWSH/BRSTN DE72 ....60 A4
  DERBYW DE22 ....43M3
  ILK DE7 ....33 C7
Derwent Cl *BSTN/STPLFD* NG9 ...63 J4
  DERBYSE DE24 ....43 J3
  WBRGFD NG2 ....52 A8
Derwent Ct *BPR/DUF* DE56 ....17M3
  DERBY * DE1 ....2 D4
  DERBY DE1 ....2 D4
  NOTTE NG7 ....4 D3
Derwent Crs *ARN* NG5 ....37 L1
Derwent Dr *DERBYSE* DE24 ....71 J3
  HUCK/RAV NG15 ....22 F2
  LBORO LE11 ....8 A8
Derwent Ri *DERBYE* DE21 ....59 K3
  RIPLEY DE5 ....11 C6
  RLBORO LE12 ....105 H6
Derwent St *BPR/DUF* DE56 ....17 K4
  BWSH/BRSTN DE72 ....60 E8
  DERBY DE1 ....3 G3
  LEIS LE2 ....7 L7
Derwent V *BPR/DUF* DE56 ....17 K5
Derwent Vw *BPR/DUF* DE56 ....17 K2
  BPR/DUF * DE56 ....17 L7
Derwent Wk *LEIS* LE2 ....139 G2
Derwent Wy *NOTTE* NG7 ....50 B2
Desborough Rd *ARN* NG5 ....36 E5
Desford Cl *DERBYE* DE21 ....31 M1
Desford La *RLEIW/BAR* LE9 ....128 C2
Desford Rd *END/NAR* LE19 ....135M7
  GBY/RBY LE6 ....129 H1
  RLEIW/BAR LE9 ....129 C2
  RLEIW/BAR LE9 ....134 C2
Devana Av *COAL* LE67 ....108 C7
Devana Rd *LEIS* LE2 ....132 A4
Devas Gdns *DERBYSE* DE21 ....59 H2
Devenports Hl
  RLEINE/SYS LE7 ....133M2
Devenports Wy
  RLEINE/SYS LE7 ....133M2
De Verdun Av *RLBORO* LE12 ....100 F2
De Vere Gdns *ARN* NG5 ....37 K2
Deveron Circ *ARN* NG5 ....25 H6
Devon Cl *DERBYE* DE21 ....31 M1
  EWD/SEL/PNX NG16 ....21M5
  LGEAT NG10 ....61 M2
Devon Dr *ARN* NG5 ....37 C5
  CFTN/RUD NG11 ....65 H7
Devonia Rd *LEIS* LE2 ....139 F3
Devonshire Av
  BSTN/STPLFD NG9 ....63 J8
  BWSH/BRSTN DE72 ....60 A5
  DERBYW DE22 ....43 K4
  LGEAT NG10 ....62 E8
  RIPLEY DE5 ....11 C5
  WGSTN LE18 ....137 L6
Devonshire Cl *ILK* DE7 ....33 J2
Devonshire Crs *ARN* NG5 ....36 F5
Devonshire Dr *BPR/DUF* DE56 ....29 K8
  BSTN/STPLFD NG9 ....48 B5
  HUCK/RAV NG15 ....21 K5
  MCKLVR DE3 ....56 C4
Devonshire La *LBORO* LE11 ....9 M4
Devonshire Prom *NOTTE* * NG7 ...50 C4
Devonshire Rd *ARN* NG5 ....36 F5
  LEIN LE4 ....125 J6
  WBRGFD NG2 ....65 H3
Devonshire Sq *LBORO* LE11 ....9 M4
Devonshire St *LEI* LE1 ....6 E3
Devon St *ILK* DE7 ....47 L2
  MAPPK/POR/STA NG3 ....51 K2
Devon Wy *LEIE* LE5 ....132 D2
Dewberry La
  COT/KEY/RAD NG12 ....53M5
Dewchurch Dr *NORM/LIT* DE23 ...70 F2
  NORM/LIT DE23 ....71 J2
Dexters Cl *RLBORO* LE12 ....104 E8

Dexter St NORM/LIT DE23 3 J9
The Dial COT/KEY/RAD NG12 67 J6
Diamond Dr DERBYE DE21 44 D4
The Dicken RLEIW/BBY LE8 136 D8
Dickens Cl RLBORO LE12 114 B3
Dickens Ct EWD/SEL/PNX NG16 21 M4
LEIW LE3 130 E2
Dickens Sq NORM/LIT DE23 57 K8
Dickinson St DERBYSE DE24 58 B5
Dickinson Wy LEIN LE4 120 D8
Dickson Dr CFTN/RUD NG11 79 H1
Didcot Dr WOL/BIL/BRX NG8 36 B6
Didsbury St LEIW LE3 130 C4
Digby Av MAPPK/POR/STA NG3 37 M4
Digby Cl LEIW LE3 130 F3
Digby Ct NOTTE NG7 4 A9
Digby Hall Dr
MAPPK/POR/STA NG3 38 A4
Digby St EWD/SEL/PNX NG16 34 B1
ILK DE7 33 L6
Dillon Ri LEIW LE3 124 D7
Dillon Rd LEIW LE3 124 D7
Dillon Wy LEIW LE3 124 D6
Dimmingsdale Cl
RLEINE/SYS LE7 118 C8
Dingley Av LEIN LE4 126 A6
Dingley Link WGSTN LE18 138 C4
Diseworth Cl MELB/CHEL DE73 72 D5
Diseworth Rd CDON/KEG DE74 84 E6
Diseworth St LEIS LE2 7 L7
Disney Cl RLEIW/BAR LE9 140 B5
Disraeli Cl RLEIW/BBY LE8 146 D7
Disraeli St LEIS LE2 131 G8
RLBORO LE12 112 E1
Distillery St CFTN/RUD NG11 79 G1
Ditchling Av LEIW LE3 130 E1
Dix Av ILK DE7 31 K1
Dixie St EWD/SEL/PNX NG16 12 F3
Dixon Dr LEIS LE2 132 A4
Dobholes La ILK DE7 31 J1
Dobney Av RLEINE/SYS LE7 121 G2
Dockholm Rd LGEAT NG10 62 A5
Dodburn Ct DERBYSE DE24 71 H3
Dodgeford La RLBORO LE12 100 D2
Dog And Bear La
HUCK/RAV NG15 14 E2
Dog And Gun La
RLEIW/BBY LE8 142 D2
Dogwood Av BLWL NG6 23 K8
Dogwood Ct LEIS LE2 132 E8
Doles La RDERBYSW DE65 70 A4
Dolphin Cl DERBYE DE21 59 L1
Dominion Rd LEIW LE3 124 B7
Domont Cl RLBORO LE12 101 M4
Donald Cl LEIN LE4 126 D3
Donald Hawley Wy
BPR/DUF DE56 29 K4
Donaldson Rd LEIN LE4 125 L7
Donbas Cl BLWL NG6 35 M3
Doncaster Av LGEAT NG10 61 M1
Doncaster Gv LGEAT NG10 62 D6
Doncaster Rd LEIN LE4 125 M6
Doncaster Ter WBRGFD NG2 51 G6
Donington Cl NORM/LIT DE23 71 J2
Donington Dr NORM/LIT DE23 71 J2
Donington La
BWSH/BRSTN DE72 75 G7
Donington Pk
CDON/KEG * DE74 84 A5
Donington Rd CFTN/RUD NG11 64 C6
Donkey La CFTN/RUD NG11 79 J4
Donner Crs ILK DE7 33 J2
Donnett Cl LEIE LE5 132 F1
Donnington St LEIS LE2 7 L7
Dooland Dr
MAPPK/POR/STA NG3 37 K6
Dorchester Av DERBYE DE21 44 C8
Dorchester Cl RLEIW/BBY LE8 143 G1
WGSTN LE18 138 A7
Dorchester Gdns WBRGFD NG2 65 J4
Dorchester Rd
EWD/SEL/PNX NG16 22 D8
LEIW LE3 130 F3
Dore Rd LEIE LE5 7 M9
Doris Rd ILK DE7 33 L8
Dorket Cl ARN NG5 25 L6
Dorket Dr WOL/BIL/BRX NG8 50 A4
Dorking Rd DERBYW DE22 56 F1
NOTTE NG7 50 C1
Dormy Cl BSTN/STPLFD NG9 49 G8
COT/KEY/RAD NG12 53 M4
Dormy Ct BLWL NG6 24 B8
Dornoch Av ARN NG5 37 H5
Dorothy Av
EWD/SEL/PNX NG16 21 L4
HUCK/RAV NG15 15 M6
LEIN LE4 126 B1
LEIS LE2 136 F4
LGEAT NG10 61 M2
Dorothy Gv WOL/BIL/BRX NG8 50 A1
Dorothy Rd LEIE LE5 132 B2
Dorrien Av NORM/LIT DE23 57 K8
Dorset Av LEIW LE3 124 A6
WGSTN LE18 137 K4
Dorset Gdns WBRGFD NG2 65 G2
Dorset St DERBYE DE21 3 M1
LEIN LE4 125 L7
WOL/BIL/BRX NG8 50 B2
Dorterry Crs ILK DE7 47 L2
Double Rail Cl WGSTN LE18 137 L6
Doudney Cl RLEIW/BAR LE9 140 B6
Douglas Av CARL NG4 52 B1
EWD/SEL/PNX NG16 34 A2
HEANOR DE75 20 A5
Douglas Cl COT/KEY/RAD NG12 53 K5
Douglas Crs CARL NG4 52 C1
Douglas Rd LGEAT NG10 61 M6
NOTTE NG7 4 B6
Douglas St DERBY DE1 3 J9
NORM/LIT DE23 57 M5
Douro Dr ARN NG5 25 M6
Dove Cl BPR/DUF DE56 18 E7
MCKLVR DE3 56 E4
The Dovecote DERBYE DE21 30 D1
Dovecote RLBORO LE12 102 A3
Dovecote Cl RLEIW/BAR LE9 140 B8
Dovecote Dr
BWSH/BRSTN DE72 59 L5
WOL/BIL/BRX NG8 49 J3
Dovecote La BSTN/STPLFD NG9 63 K1
RLEIW/BAR LE9 141 G2
Dovecote Rd
EWD/SEL/PNX NG16 21 M5
RLEIW/BAR LE9 141 G2
Dovecote St RLBORO LE12 94 E6
Dovedale Av DERBYSE DE24 59 G8
LGEAT NG10 75 L1
RLEIW/BBY LE8 136 F8
Dovedale Cir ILK DE7 33 J2
Dovedale Cl RIPLEY DE5 19 H1
Dovedale Ct BPR/DUF * DE56 17 M3
LGEAT NG10 75 M1
Dovedale Crs BPR/DUF DE56 17 M2
Dovedale Ri DERBYW DE22 43 H6
Dovedale Rd DERBYE DE21 59 J4
LEIN LE4 120 C8
LEIS LE2 132 C6
MAPPK/POR/STA NG3 37 M8
WBRGFD NG2 65 L2
The Dovedales MCKLVR * DE3 56 B5
Dove La LGEAT NG10 62 A7
Dovenby Rd CFTN/RUD NG11 64 D4
Dover Beck Dr CALV/BJ NG14 27 G3
Dover Cl RLBORO LE12 113 H7
Dover Ct NORM/LIT * DE23 57 L5
Doveridge Av CARL NG4 38 E7
Doveridge Rd CARL NG4 38 D7
Dove Ri LEIS LE2 139 G1
RDERBYSW DE65 68 A5
Dove Rd CDON/KEG DE74 85 G7
COAL LE67 108 E8
RIPLEY DE5 11 G6
Dover St LEI LE1 7 G7
NORM/LIT DE23 57 L6
RLEIW/BBY LE8 146 D7
Dove St BLWL NG6 23 M8
Dower Cl DERBYW DE22 43 L5
Dower House Gdns
RLBORO LE12 112 E1
Downes Cl BLWL NG6 23 L8
Downham Av LEIN LE4 125 J5
Downham Cl ARN NG5 37 L1
MCKLVR DE3 56 C6
Downing Cl BLWL NG6 23 M7
DERBYW DE22 56 D1
Downing Dr LEIE LE5 133 G4
Downing Rd DERBYE DE21 3 M4
Downing St BLWL NG6 23 M7
Downmeadow BPR/DUF DE56 10 C7
The Downs CFTN/RUD NG11 64 E4
Down St LEIN LE4 125 M6
Dowson St
MAPPK/POR/STA NG3 51 K1
Doyle Cl LBORO LE11 103 H1
Drage St DERBY DE1 43 M8
Dragwell CDON/KEG DE74 86 B5
Drakemyre Cl ARN NG5 25 M6
Drake Rd CARL NG4 52 F2
Draper St LEIS LE2 132 A4
Draycott Cl HEANOR DE75 20 A3
Draycott Dr MCKLVR DE3 56 A4
Draycott Rd
BWSH/BRSTN DE72 60 A6
BWSH/BRSTN DE72 61 G8
LGEAT NG10 75 K2
Draymans Ct NOTTE NG7 36 D6
Drayton Av DERBYW DE22 56 D1
Drayton Rd LEIW LE3 124 C8
Drayton St ARN NG5 37 G5
Dresden Cl MCKLVR DE3 56 A5
Drewry Ct DERBYW DE22 2 C4
Drewry La DERBYW DE22 2 B5
Dreyfus Cl DERBYE DE21 59 K2
Dribdale RLEIW/BBY LE8 145 L8
The Drift CFTN/RUD NG11 64 C4
HUCK/RAV NG15 15 M6
Drinkstone Rd LEIE LE5 132 C3
The Drive BPR/DUF DE56 16 D4
BSTN/STPLFD NG9 63 J4
LEIN LE4 125 L1
RLBORO LE12 111 K6
RLEINE/SYS LE7 127 K7
RLEIW/BBY LE8 142 F3
RLEIW/BBY LE8 146 F7
Drome Cl COAL LE67 109 H6
Dronfield Pl ILK DE7 33 J2
Dronfield St LEIS LE2 7 M7
Drovers Wy END/NAR LE19 135 M8
Drumcliff Rd LEIE LE5 133 J1
Drummond Av CARL NG4 38 E6
Drummond Dr
EWD/SEL/PNX NG16 35 J3
Drummond Rd END/NAR LE19 135 L4
ILK DE7 33 H6
LEIN LE4 125 K4
Drury Av DERBYE DE21 59 H3
Drury La LEIS LE2 138 D1
Dryden St LEI LE1 7 G4
NORM/LIT DE23 71 K1
NOTT NG1 4 F4
Dry Pot La RLBORO LE12 93 J5
Drysdale Cl BLWL NG6 35 M2
Drysdale Rd MCKLVR DE3 55 M8
Duchess St BLWL NG6 23 M7
Dudleston Cl LEIE LE5 132 E2
Dudley Av LEIE LE5 133 G1
Dudley Cl LEIE LE5 133 G1
Duesbury Cl DERBYSE DE24 58 C8
Duffield Av WGSTN LE18 137 M3
Duffield Bank BPR/DUF DE56 29 L3
Duffield Cl LGEAT NG10 75 L2
Duffield Ct BPR/DUF * DE56 29 J3
Duffield Rd BPR/DUF DE56 29 M6
DERBYW DE22 43 K8
Duffield St LEIS LE2 7 L6
Duke Cl BLWL NG6 35 K2
Duke Crs EWD/SEL/PNX NG16 22 A6
Dukeries La DERBYE DE21 44 F5
Dukes Cl LEIN LE4 120 D8
WGSTN LE18 137 M4
Dukes Dr LEIS LE2 132 A5
Dukes Pl ILK DE7 33 J3
NOTT NG1 5 K7
Duke St ARN NG5 25 H8
DERBY DE1 2 F1
HUCK/RAV NG15 15 M8
ILK DE7 33 K4
LBORO LE11 9 K1
LEI LE1 6 F8
NOTTE NG7 36 D7
Duke William Mt NOTTE NG7 4 C8
Duluth Av DERBYE DE21 44 E8
Dulverton Av DERBYSE DE24 71 G5
Dulverton Cl LBORO LE11 103 G7
WGSTN LE18 138 B7
Dulverton Rd LEIW LE3 131 G2
Dulverton V WOL/BIL/BRX NG8 35 M4
Dulwich Rd DERBYW DE22 56 C1
NOTTE NG7 50 C1
The Dumbles CARL NG4 26 F7
Dumbles Cl ILK DE7 47 G1
Dumbles La RIPLEY DE5 19 K5
Dumbleton Av LEIW LE3 131 G6
Dumps Rd COAL LE67 108 C1
Dunbar Cl DERBYSE DE24 71 J5
Dunbar Rd COAL LE67 109 G7
LEIN LE4 126 C5
Dunblane Av LEIN LE4 126 B3
Dunblane Rd CFTN/RUD NG11 79 G1
Duncan Av RLEIW/BAR LE9 135 H8
Duncan Cl BPR/DUF DE56 17 M1
Duncan Rd LEIS LE2 131 H8
NORM/LIT DE23 57 K7
Duncan Wy LBORO LE11 103 G1
Duncombe Cl
MAPPK/POR/STA NG3 5 L2
Duncombe Rd LEIW LE3 124 E6
Duncroft Av CARL NG4 38 D6
Dundas Cl NOTT NG1 5 G4
Dundee Rd RLEIW/BBY LE8 142 F1
Dundonald Rd LEIN LE4 125 L6
Dunedin Cl MCKLVR DE3 56 C4
Dungannon Rd CFTN/RUD NG11 64 C7
Dungley Hl BPR/DUF DE56 10 B5
Dunholme Av LBORO LE11 102 F3
Dunholme Cl BLWL NG6 23 M7
Dunholme Rd LEIN LE4 126 C6
Dunire Cl LEIN LE4 125 G4
Dunkery Ct DERBYE DE21 44 E5
Dunkery Rd CFTN/RUD NG11 64 D7
Dunkirk DERBYW DE22 2 D4
Dunkirk Rd NOTTE NG7 50 C6
Dunkirk St LEI LE1 7 G8
Dunlin Rd LEIE LE5 7 L3
Dunlin Whf WBRGFD * NG2 50 E5
Dunlop Av NOTTE NG7 50 C3
Dunnicliffe La MELB/CHEL DE73 82 E8
Dunoon Cl ARN NG5 24 C5
DERBYSE DE24 71 J4
Dunsby Cl CFTN/RUD NG11 64 C6
Dunsford Dr
MAPPK/POR/STA NG3 38 A1
Dunsil Dr WBRGFD NG2 50 F7
Dunsil Rd EWD/SEL/PNX NG16 21 M3
Duns La LEIW LE3 6 C7
Dunsmore Cl
BSTN/STPLFD NG9 63 M3
LBORO LE11 103 H7
Dunsmore Dr DERBYE DE21 44 C5
Dunstall Av LEIW LE3 130 B5
Dunstall Park Rd
DERBYSE DE24 58 B7
Dunstan St CARL NG4 38 D8
Dunster Rd EWD/SEL/PNX NG16 21 M5
RLBORO LE12 113 H6
WBRGFD NG2 65 L1
Dunster St LEIW LE3 130 F2
Dunston Cl LGEAT NG10 62 D8
Dunton Cl DERBYE DE21 3 J3
Dunton St LEIW LE3 6 B3
WGSTN LE18 137 K6
Dunvegan Cl DERBYSE DE24 71 H5
Dunvegan Dr ARN NG5 24 D5
Dupont Gdns LEIW LE3 124 B8
Durban Rd LEIN LE4 119 G8
Durham Av DERBYE DE21 58 C1
WBRGFD NG2 51 K3
Durham Cl WBRGFD * NG2 51 K3
Durham Crs BLWL NG6 36 A1
Durham Dr WGSTN LE18 137 L3
Durham Rd LBORO LE11 103 J1
Durham St ILK DE7 33 K6
Durley Cl DERBYSE DE24 59 G8
Durlston Cl WBRGFD NG2 64 F2
Durnford Rd WGSTN LE18 138 A7
Durnford St NOTTE NG7 36 D5
Durrell Cl LBORO LE11 103 G1
Durris Cl COAL LE67 109 G6
Dursley Cl BLWL NG6 35 M1
Durston Cl LEIE LE5 133 H3
Durward Cl DERBYSE DE24 58 A8
Duxbury Rd LEIE LE5 126 C8
Dylan Thomas Rd ARN NG5 24 F7
Dysart Wy LEI LE1 7 H2

E

Eagle Cl ARN NG5 25 L8
RLEIW/BAR LE9 141 J8
Eagle Ct BLWL NG6 24 B8
Eagle Rd ILK DE7 47 K3
Eagle St BPR/DUF DE56 10 C5
Ealing Cl DERBYW DE22 56 E1
Ealing Rd LEIS LE2 131 K6
Eamont Cl LEIS LE2 137 H4
Eardley Cl DERBYE DE21 58 F2
Eardley Rd ARN NG5 36 C1
Earl Crs CARL NG4 38 D4
Earl Dr EWD/SEL/PNX NG16 22 A6
Earle Smith Cl RLEIW/BBY LE8 136 D8
Earl Howe St LEIS LE2 7 K8
Earl Howe Ter LEIW LE3 6 B7
Earl Russell St LEIS LE2 137 G1
Earls Cl LEIN LE4 120 D8
WOL/BIL/BRX NG8 49 G2
Earls Crs DERBYE DE21 44 F5
Earlsfield Dr ARN NG5 24 B6
Earl Shilton Rd RLEIW/BAR LE9 134 A6
Earl St LEI LE1 7 G4
Earls Wy LEIN LE4 120 D8
Earlswood Cl
BWSH/BRSTN DE72 61 H7
Earlswood Dr
COT/KEY/RAD NG12 65 M3
MCKLVR DE3 56 D3
Earlswood Rd LEIE LE5 133 H4
Easby Cl LBORO LE11 102 F2
Easedale Cl WBRGFD NG2 52 A8
East Acres COT/KEY/RAD NG12 67 K3
East Av LEIS LE2 132 A5
MCKLVR DE3 56 B4
RLEINE/SYS LE7 121 G3
RLEIW/BBY LE8 136 D7
East Bond St LEI LE1 6 E4
Eastbrae Rd NORM/LIT DE23 57 J8
East Circus St NOTT NG1 4 F7
Eastcliffe Av CARL NG4 38 B4
East Cl COT/KEY/RAD NG12 80 C5
DERBYW DE22 43 J5
Eastcote Av BSTN/STPLFD NG9 48 F5
Eastcourt Rd LEIS LE2 138 A1
East Crs BPR/DUF DE56 18 A7
BSTN/STPLFD NG9 63 M2
East Croft Av NORM/LIT DE23 71 H2
Eastdale Rd
MAPPK/POR/STA NG3 52 A1
East Dr NOTTE NG7 50 A6
Eastern Bvd LEIS LE2 131 J4
Eastfield Rd LEIN LE4 120 D7
LEIW LE3 130 F2
RIPLEY DE5 11 L6
Eastglade Rd ARN NG5 36 E1
East Gv NOTTE NG7 36 E7
Eastham Cl
MAPPK/POR/STA NG3 5 L4
Eastham Rd ARN NG5 38 A1
Eastholme Cft WBRGFD NG2 52 B2
Easthorpe St CFTN/RUD NG11 65 H8
East Lawn RDERBYSW DE65 70 B5
Eastleigh Dr MCKLVR DE3 56 C5
Eastleigh Rd LEIW LE3 131 G4
East Link END/NAR LE19 130 B8
Eastmere Rd WGSTN LE18 138 D4
East Moor COT/KEY/RAD NG12 67 L6
Eastmoor Dr CARL NG4 38 D7
East Nelson St HEANOR DE75 20 C5
East Rd LEIN LE4 125 L3
RLBORO LE12 98 B3
East Service Rd DERBYE DE21 58 F5
East St CFTN/RUD NG11 77 M6
DERBY DE1 2 F4
HEANOR DE75 20 E7
ILK DE7 33 K7
LEI LE1 7 G7
LEIS LE2 138 E1
LGEAT NG10 62 D7
NOTT NG1 5 J6
East Vw WBRGFD NG2 65 H1
East View Rd BPR/DUF DE56 10 C6
Eastway CDON/KEG DE74 84 F4
Eastway Rd WGSTN LE18 138 B3
Eastwold COT/KEY/RAD NG12 67 L5
Eastwood Av NORM/LIT DE23 57 G5
Eastwood Cl HUCK/RAV NG15 23 J3
Eastwood Dr NORM/LIT DE23 57 G5
Eastwood Rd
COT/KEY/RAD NG12 53 L4
EWD/SEL/PNX NG16 34 C1
LEIS LE2 137 H2
Eastwood St BLWL NG6 35 M2
Eaton Av ARN NG5 25 L8
DERBYW DE22 43 L2
ILK DE7 47 H1
Eaton Bank BPR/DUF DE56 29 L5
Eaton Cl BSTN/STPLFD NG9 63 M1
DERBYW DE22 43 L2
Eaton Ct BPR/DUF DE56 29 J5
DERBY DE1 2 B1
Eaton Grange Dr LGEAT NG10 61 L7
Eaton Rd CDON/KEG DE74 84 F4
Eatons Rd BSTN/STPLFD NG9 62 B1
Eaton St MAPPK/POR/STA NG3 37 K4
Ebchester Cl LEIS LE2 137 G4
Ebchester Rd LEIS LE2 137 G4
Ebenezer St
EWD/SEL/PNX NG16 20 F4
ILK DE7 33 J4
Ebers Gv MAPPK/POR/STA NG3 37 G7
Ebers Rd MAPPK/POR/STA NG3 37 G7
Ebury Rd ARN NG5 36 F6
Ecclesbourne Av
BPR/DUF DE56 29 J4
Ecclesbourne Cl BPR/DUF DE56 29 J4
Eckington Cl ILK DE7 32 C7
Eckington Ter WBRGFD NG2 51 G6
Ecton Cl ARN NG5 24 D7
Edale Av DERBYSE DE24 58 F8
MCKLVR DE3 56 B5
NORM/LIT DE23 57 J5
Edale Cl DERBYW DE22 43 H6
HUCK/RAV NG15 23 G1
LEIW LE3 130 C4
LGEAT NG10 75 M1
Edale Dr DERBYE DE21 59 K4
Edale Ri BSTN/STPLFD NG9 62 C3
Edale Rd WBRGFD NG2 51 K2
Edale Sq ILK DE7 33 J2
Eddleston Dr CFTN/RUD NG11 64 D6
Eddystone Rd LEIE LE5 127 J8
Edelin Rd LBORO LE11 9 J8
Edenbridge Ct
WOL/BIL/BRX NG8 49 H5
Eden Cl ARN NG5 37 K1
LBORO LE11 103 G1
LEIS LE2 139 G1
Edenhall Cl LEIN LE4 126 B4
LEIS LE2 139 H3
Edenhall Gdns
CFTN/RUD NG11 64 D5
Edenhurst Av LEIW LE3 130 D8
Eden Rd DERBYE DE21 58 F3
LEIS LE2 139 G1
Edensor Dr BPR/DUF DE56 18 A2
Edensor Sq DERBYW DE22 2 C6
Edensor St LEIN LE4 126 A4
Eden St DERBYSE DE24 58 F7
Eden Wy LEIS LE2 137 H5
Edern Cl ARN NG5 24 E8
Edgbaston Cl LEIN LE4 119 H8
Edgbaston Ct NORM/LIT DE23 57 G7
Edgbaston Gdns
WOL/BIL/BRX NG8 36 B7
Edgcote Ct LEIE LE5 126 C7
Edge Hl MELB/CHEL DE73 72 D4
Edgehill Cl RLEIW/BBY LE8 139 M7
Edge Hill Ct LGEAT NG10 76 B3
Edgehill Rd LEIN LE4 126 C6
Edgelaw Ct DERBYSE DE24 71 H4
Edgeley Rd RLEIW/BBY LE8 143 K3
Edge Wy WOL/BIL/BRX NG8 35 H6
Edgewood Dr HUCK/RAV NG15 23 H2
Edgington Cl
COT/KEY/RAD NG12 67 L5
Edginton St
MAPPK/POR/STA NG3 37 K8
Edginton Ter
MAPPK/POR/STA NG3 37 K8
Edgware Rd BLWL NG6 24 B8
DERBYW DE22 56 D1
Edgwood Rd
EWD/SEL/PNX NG16 34 D1
Edinbane Cl ARN NG5 24 D5
Edinburgh Wy RLBORO LE12 113 G6
Edingale Ct BSTN/STPLFD NG9 48 F3
Edingley Av ARN NG5 37 G3
Edingley Sq ARN NG5 36 F3
Edith Av LEIW LE3 130 E8
Edith Ter NOTTE NG7 50 C1
Edith Wood Cl DERBYSE DE24 72 F2
Edlington Dr WOL/BIL/BRX NG8 49 G4
Edmonds Cl ARN NG5 24 E5
Edmonton Ct WBRGFD NG2 65 H1
Edmonton Rd LEI LE1 7 H3
Edmund Rd DERBYE DE21 59 K4
Ednaston Av NORM/LIT DE23 71 H2
Ednaston Rd NOTTE NG7 50 B6
Edwald Rd COT/KEY/RAD NG12 65 M4
Edwalton Cl
COT/KEY/RAD NG12 65 M4
Edwalton Ct BLWL NG6 36 B1
Edwalton Lodge Cl
COT/KEY/RAD NG12 65 L4
Edward Av DERBYE DE21 58 E2
EWD/SEL/PNX NG16 12 F3
LEIW LE3 130 D7
WOL/BIL/BRX NG8 36 B7
Edward Cl HUCK/RAV NG15 23 H3
LEIS LE2 139 G2
Edward Dr LEIS LE2 137 J6
Edward Rd EWD/SEL/PNX NG16 21 L5
EWD/SEL/PNX NG16 35 G2
LEIS LE2 131 M5
LGEAT NG10 62 B7
RLEIW/BBY LE8 145 K8
WBRGFD NG2 51 K7
Edwards Crs BPR/DUF DE56 18 E7
Edwards La ARN NG5 36 F1
Edward St BPR/DUF DE56 17 L2
BSTN/STPLFD NG9 48 B8
DERBY DE1 2 E1
EWD/SEL/PNX NG16 20 F4
LBORO LE11 8 F1
LEIE LE5 7 L3
RLEINE/SYS LE7 124 C1
Edwinstowe Dr ARN NG5 37 G3
Edwinstowe Rd DERBYE DE21 44 E6
Edwin St ARN NG5 37 H1
Eelwood Rd HUCK/RAV NG15 23 H3
Egerton Av LEIN LE4 125 J5
Egerton Dr BSTN/STPLFD NG9 48 B5
Egerton Rd ARN NG5 37 H3
Egerton St MAPPK/POR/STA NG3 5 G2
Egerton Wk
MAPPK/POR/STA NG3 5 H2
Eggesford Rd DERBYSE DE24 71 H5
Eggington Rd RDERBYSW DE65 68 B5
Egginton St LEIE LE5 7 M8
Eglantine Cl LEIS LE2 132 E8
Egling Cft CARL NG4 52 D3
Egmanton Cl DERBYE DE21 44 F6
Egreaves Av HEANOR DE75 20 A3
Egypt Rd NOTTE NG7 36 D6
Eider Cl RLEIW/BBY LE8 142 C3
Eighth Av BSTN/STPLFD NG9 64 A2
Eileen Av LEIN LE4 125 J5
Eisele Cl BLWL NG6 35 K1
Ekowe St NOTTE NG7 36 D5
Eland Cl DERBYE DE21 59 L1
Eland St NOTTE NG7 36 D6
Elbow La LEI LE1 6 D4
Elder Cl ARN NG5 25 L6
Elder Gv HUCK/RAV NG15 23 M3
Eldon Rd BSTN/STPLFD NG9 63 G6
Eldon St LEI LE1 7 G4
Eleanor Av ILK DE7 47 L2
Eleanor Crs BSTN/STPLFD NG9 48 D8
Electric Av WBRGFD NG2 50 E8
Eley Cl ILK DE7 33 G5
Eley Wk DERBY * DE1 2 D6
Elford Ri MAPPK/POR/STA NG3 51 K2
Elgar Dr LGEAT NG10 75 M2
Elgar Gdns
MAPPK/POR/STA NG3 51 K1
Elgin Av LEIW LE3 124 D7
NORM/LIT DE23 56 E6
Eliot Cl LBORO LE11 102 F1
LGEAT NG10 75 M2
Eliot Dr ILK DE7 47 H2
Eliot Rd NORM/LIT DE23 56 F7
Elizabeth Cl DERBYE DE21 58 F2
HUCK/RAV NG15 23 J2
ILK DE7 32 B7
Elizabeth Ct WGSTN LE18 138 A5
Elizabeth Crs WGSTN LE18 137 M3
Elizabeth Dr LEIN LE4 120 C7
LEIS LE2 139 G3
Elizabeth Gdns RLEIW/BBY LE8 136 D8
Elizabeth Gv CARL NG4 38 C5
Elizabeth Pk
EWD/SEL/PNX NG16 12 D3
Elizabeth Rd BSTN/STPLFD NG9 62 E4
RLEIW/BBY LE8 145 K8
Elizabeth St LEIE LE5 132 C2
Elkstone Cl DERBYE DE21 44 F5
Ella Bank Rd HEANOR DE75 20 D6
Ellaby Rd LBORO LE11 103 H1
Elland Rd LEIW LE3 129 M2
Ella Rd WBRGFD NG2 51 K6

Ellastone Av ARN NG5 25 G7
Ellastone Gdns DERBYSE DE24 58 F8
Ellendale Rd DERBYE DE21 44 F8
Ellerby Av CFTN/RUD NG11 64 C5
Ellerslie Gv LGEAT NG10 61 L2
Ellesmere Av DERBYSE DE24 58 B6
Ellesmere Cl ARN NG5 25 M8
Ellesmere Dr BSTN/STPLFD NG9 48 A2
Ellesmere Pl LEIW LE3 130 F5
Ellesmere Rd LEIW LE3 130 F5
WBRGFD NG2 65 K3
Ellington Rd ARN NG5 25 K5
Elliot Cl LEIS LE2 139 J3
RLEIW/BBY LE8 142 E3
RLEIW/BBY LE8 146 E7
Elliott Dr LEIN LE4 126 E1
LEIW LE3 129 M4
Elliott Rd LEIN LE4 125 H3
Elliott St NOTTE NG7 4 D6
Ellis Av HUCK/RAV NG15 23 M1
LEIN LE4 125 L6
Ellis Cl LEIW LE3 123 M7
LGEAT NG10 75 M1
RLBORO LE12 104 D8
RLBORO LE12 105 J7
Ellis Ct MAPPK/POR/STA NG3 5 J3
Ellis Dr LEIW LE3 129 K4
Ellis Flds LEIS LE2 139 J4
Ellis Gv BSTN/STPLFD NG9 63 K2
Ellison Av BWSH/BRSTN DE72 73 L8
Ellison Cl RLEIW/BAR LE9 140 B4
WGSTN LE18 137 K7
Ellis St RLEINE/SYS LE7 124 B1
Ellsworth Ri ARN NG5 36 D1
Ellwood Cl LEIE LE5 132 F3
Ellwood Crs WOL/BIL/BRX NG8 49 L2
Elm Av BPR/DUF DE56 17 L5
BSTN/STPLFD NG9 63 H5
BSTN/STPLFD NG9 63 J1
CARL NG4 38 D8
COT/KEY/RAD NG12 80 D5
EWD/SEL/PNX NG16 34 F1
HUCK/RAV NG15 23 J2
LGEAT NG10 47 M8
LGEAT NG10 62 A6
MAPPK/POR/STA NG3 5 G2
RLBORO LE12 88 D4
Elm Bank MAPPK/POR/STA NG3 37 G7
Elmbridge ARN NG5 24 F8
Elm Cl COT/KEY/RAD NG12 80 D5
GBY/RBY LE6 123 K5
MAPPK/POR/STA NG3 5 G1
RLBORO LE12 113 J5
Elmcroft Av LEIE LE5 126 F8
Elmdale Gdns
WOL/BIL/BRX NG8 35 M7
Elmdale St LEIN LE4 125 L5
Elm Dr CARL NG4 38 D8
RDERBYSW DE65 68 B5
Elmfield Av LEIN LE4 119 K8
LEIS LE2 132 A4
Elm Gv ARN NG5 25 L7
DERBYE DE21 58 F2
DERBYW DE22 43 H2
Elmhurst Av
MAPPK/POR/STA NG3 38 A5
Elmhurst Cl END/NAR LE19 135 L8
Elmore Ct NOTTE NG7 4 C4
The Elms CARL NG4 52 D1
COAL LE67 108 B2
EWD/SEL/PNX NG16 22 D8
RLEIW/BBY LE8 136 F7
RLEIW/BBY LE8 143 J3
Elms Av NORM/LIT DE23 56 F5
RIPLEY DE5 11 H7
Elms Cl CFTN/RUD NG11 79 H1
LEIS LE2 138 E3
RLBORO LE12 97 H2
Elmsdale Gdns CALV/BJ NG14 39 J3
Elms Dr NORM/LIT DE23 56 F6
RLBORO LE12 112 D2
Elmsfield Av HEANOR DE75 20 E5
Elms Gdns CFTN/RUD NG11 79 G1
Elms Gv LBORO LE11 9 L5
RDERBYSW DE65 69 G4
RLBORO LE12 105 H6
Elmsham Av ARN NG5 24 B6
Elmsleigh Av LEIS LE2 132 B6
Elms Pk CFTN/RUD NG11 79 H1
Elms Rd LEIS LE2 132 A7
Elms St DERBY DE1 43 K8
Elmsthorpe Av NOTTE NG7 50 C3
Elmsthorpe Ri LEIW LE3 130 E4
Elm St BWSH/BRSTN DE72 59 M5
Elmswood Gdns ARN NG5 37 H4
Elm Tree Av BPR/DUF DE56 18 E8
LEIW LE3 123 L7
WBRGFD NG2 51 H8
Elmtree Av DERBYSE DE24 57 M8
Elmtree Cl LEIE LE5 127 G5
Elm Tree Rd RLEIW/BAR LE9 142 A5
Elm Vw NOTTE NG7 4 A4
Elmwood Dr DERBYE DE21 44 A5
Elmwood Rw WGSTN LE18 137 L3
Elnor St EWD/SEL/PNX NG16 21 G5
Elsadene Av LEIN LE4 125 M4
Elsalene Dr GBY/RBY LE6 123 G2
Elsdon Cl COAL LE67 108 B2
Elsham Cl LEIW LE3 130 B2
Elson St NOTTE NG7 36 D7
Elston Flds LEIS LE2 137 K1
Elston Gdns CFTN/RUD NG11 64 C3
Elstree Av LEIE LE5 127 J7
Elstree Dr WOL/BIL/BRX NG8 49 L1
Elswick Cl ARN NG5 24 F7
Elswick Dr BSTN/STPLFD NG9 63 M3
Elsworthy Wk LEIW LE3 130 B1
Elterwater Dr WBRGFD NG2 52 A8
Eltham Cl WOL/BIL/BRX NG8 35 K4
Eltham Dr WOL/BIL/BRX NG8 35 L4
Eltham Rd WBRGFD NG2 51 L8
Elton Cl BSTN/STPLFD NG9 48 B7
Elton Rd ARN NG5 36 F6
DERBYSE DE24 57 M8
Elton Rd North ARN NG5 36 E6
Elton Ter NOTTE NG7 4 A1
Elvaston Dr LGEAT NG10 75 K3
Elvaston La DERBYSE DE24 58 F8
DERBYSE DE24 59 G8
Elvaston Rd WOL/BIL/BRX NG8 49 L2
Elvaston St BWSH/BRSTN DE72 60 F8
Elveden Dr ILK DE7 33 G3
Elwin Av WGSTN LE18 138 B3
Embankment Cl DERBYW DE22 42 D8
Emberton Cl WGSTN LE18 138 D4
Emerald Cl DERBYE DE21 44 D5
Emerson Cl LEIN LE4 124 E4
Emerson Sq NORM/LIT DE23 71 K1
Emerys Rd CARL NG4 38 F7
Emmanuel Av ARN NG5 24 E6
MAPPK/POR/STA NG3 37 L6
Emmas Williams Ct RIPLEY DE5 11 H6
Emneth Cl
MAPPK/POR/STA NG3 37 K7
Emperor Wy RLEIW/BBY LE8 142 D3
Empingham Cl
BSTN/STPLFD NG9 62 F5
Empire Rd LEIW LE3 6 A3
Empress Rd LBORO LE11 9 M3
NORM/LIT DE23 2 C8
Emsworth Cl ILK DE7 33 H4
Ena Av WBRGFD NG2 51 K2
Enderby Gdns ARN NG5 25 J6
Enderby Rd RLEIW/BAR LE9 134 E4
RLEIW/BBY LE8 136 C6
Enderby Sq BSTN/STPLFD NG9 49 K7
Endsleigh Gdns
BSTN/STPLFD NG9 49 K8
COT/KEY/RAD NG12 65 L3
DERBYW DE22 56 D1
RLBORO LE12 88 B6
Enfield Cl RDERBYSW DE65 68 C5
Enfield Rd DERBYW DE22 42 F8
Enfield St BSTN/STPLFD NG9 63 J1
Engine La EWD/SEL/PNX NG16 21 M3
England Crs HEANOR DE75 20 E5
Englefield Rd LEIE LE5 133 H2
Ennerdale Cl LEIS LE2 139 H3
WBRGFD NG2 52 A8
Ennerdale Rd ARN NG5 37 H2
LGEAT NG10 61 M5
RLBORO LE12 105 H7
Ennis Cl DERBYE DE21 45 G8
Ennismore Gdns
WOL/BIL/BRX NG8 50 A1
Ennismore Ms CFTN/RUD NG11 65 G5
Enoch Stone Dr DERBYE DE21 58 F3
Ensbury Gdns LEIE LE5 132 F4
Enthorpe St WOL/BIL/BRX NG8 49 M1
Epinal Ct LBORO LE11 103 H2
Epinal Wy LBORO LE11 8 C2
LBORO LE11 9 H8
Epperstone By-Pass
CALV/BJ NG14 27 J2
Epperstone Rd WBRGFD NG2 51 J7
Epping Cl DERBYW DE22 56 C1
Epping Wy LEIS LE2 137 G4
Epsom Rd BSTN/STPLFD NG9 62 C4
LEIN LE4 125 M5
Epworth Dr DERBYSE DE24 72 E3
Equity Rd END/NAR LE19 135 L4
LEIW LE3 6 A9
Erdington Wy
BSTN/STPLFD NG9 62 C4
Erdyngton Rd LEIW LE3 130 D3
Erewash Dr ILK DE7 47 L1
Erewash Gdns ARN NG5 24 E7
Erewash Gv BSTN/STPLFD NG9 62 D6
Erewash Sq ILK DE7 47 L1
Erewash St ALFN DE55 12 E1
Eric Av HUCK/RAV NG15 15 K6
Erith Cl WOL/BIL/BRX NG8 35 H6
Erith Rd LEIS LE2 131 H6
Ernee Cl LEIW LE3 124 B8
Ernest Rd CARL NG4 37 M7
Erskine Rd ARN NG5 36 F6
Erskine St LEI LE1 7 H4
Ervin's Lock WGSTN LE18 137 L7
Ervin Wy RLEINE/SYS LE7 121 J1
Esher Gv MAPPK/POR/STA NG3 37 G6
Eskdale Cl LEIS LE2 139 H3
LGEAT NG10 75 M2
Eskdale Ct WBRGFD NG2 52 A8
Eskdale Dr BSTN/STPLFD NG9 62 E3
WOL/BIL/BRX NG8 35 M7
Eskdale Wk DERBYSE * DE24 73 H1
Esk Hause Cl
COT/KEY/RAD NG12 66 A3
Essex Rd LEIN LE4 126 C5
WGSTN LE18 137 K4
Essex St DERBYE DE21 3 L1
EWD/SEL/PNX NG16 21 K5
Estley Rd RLEIW/BAR LE9 141 J8
Estoril Av WGSTN LE18 138 D4
Estwic Av EWD/SEL/PNX NG16 21 K4
Ethel Av HUCK/RAV NG15 15 M6
MAPPK/POR/STA NG3 37 L6
Ethel Rd LEIE LE5 132 C3
WBRGFD NG2 51 K8
Eton Cl LEIS LE2 131 M7
Eton Ct ILK DE7 32 B7
Eton Gv WOL/BIL/BRX NG8 49 M3
Eton Rd WBRGFD NG2 65 J2
Eton St DERBYSE DE24 58 C6
Etruria Gdns DERBY DE1 43 L8
Etta's Wy RDERBYSW DE65 68 F3
Ettrick Dr DERBYSE DE24 71 J5
Etwall La RDERBYSW DE65 69 H2
Etwall Rd MCKLVR DE3 55 L8
RDERBYSW DE65 69 L8
Etwall St DERBYW DE22 57 H2
Eucalyptus Av CFTN/RUD NG11 64 A6
Eugene Gdns WBRGFD NG2 51 H5
Eugene St WBRGFD NG2 51 H4
Eunice Av RLEIW/BAR LE9 135 H8
Europa Wy CFTN/RUD NG11 65 G4
Euston Dr DERBY DE1 43 M8
Euston St LEIS LE2 131 K6
Evans Av DERBYW DE22 43 L2
Evans Rd BLWL NG6 36 B4
Evanston Gdns DERBYE DE21 58 F1
Evedon Wk ARN NG5 24 F6
Evelyn Dr LEIW LE3 131 G5
Evelyn Gv DERBYE DE21 58 E2
Evelyn Rd LEIW LE3 130 C5
Evelyn St BSTN/STPLFD NG9 63 M1
WBRGFD NG2 5 L8
Everard Wy END/NAR LE19 136 C2
Everest Ct LEI LE1 7 J3
Everett Cl LEIN LE4 126 E1
Evergreen Cl DERBYE DE21 44 E4
Eversley Wk ARN NG5 24 F7
Every St LEI LE1 6 F6
Evesham Cl DERBYE DE21 44 C6
Evesham Ct BSTN/STPLFD NG9 62 E6
Evesham Rd LEIW LE3 131 G5
Evington Cl LEIE LE5 132 C3
Evington Dr LEIE LE5 132 C4
Evington La LEIE LE5 132 D4
Evington Ms LEIE LE5 132 F4
Evington Parks Rd LEIS LE2 132 B4
Evington Pl LEIS LE2 7 L9
Evington Rd LEIS LE2 7 K9
Evington St LEIS LE2 7 K8
Evington Valley Rd LEIE LE5 132 B4
Ewart Rd NOTTE NG7 36 E7
Ewe Lamb Cl BSTN/STPLFD NG9 48 D6
Ewe Lamb La BSTN/STPLFD NG9 48 D6
Ewell Rd WOL/BIL/BRX NG8 49 J2
Exbourne Rd WOL/BIL/BRX NG8 35 K6
Exbury Gdns WBRGFD NG2 64 F3
Excalibur Cl LEIW LE3 129 L5
Excelsior Av DERBYSE DE24 72 D1
Exchange Ar NOTT NG1 5 H7
Exchange Rd WBRGFD NG2 51 K8
Exchange St DERBY DE1 2 F4
Exchange Wk NOTT NG1 5 H7
Exeter Cl CARL NG4 38 D5
RLBORO LE12 88 B6
Exeter Pl DERBY DE1 3 G3
Exeter Rd NOTTE NG7 36 E7
WBRGFD NG2 65 K1
WGSTN LE18 137 M4
Exmoor Av LEIN LE4 125 H7
Exmoor Cl LBORO LE11 103 H7
WGSTN LE18 138 B6
Exploration Dr LEIN LE4 125 K5
Extension St ILK DE7 33 K8
Exton Rd ARN NG5 36 E4
LEIE LE5 126 C8
Eyam Cl BSTN/STPLFD NG9 49 G5
Eye Brook Cl LBORO LE11 102 F5
Eynsford Cl LEIS LE2 132 D7
Eyre's Gdn ILK DE7 33 K5
Eyres La CFTN/RUD NG11 77 L7
Eyre St WBRGFD NG2 5 L7
The Eyrie DERBYSE DE24 71 J5

F

Fabis Dr CFTN/RUD NG11 64 C3
Factory La BSTN/STPLFD NG9 63 J2
ILK DE7 33 J5
Factory St LBORO LE11 9 L4
RLBORO LE12 101 M3
Failsworth Cl CFTN/RUD NG11 64 C4
Fairbank Crs ARN NG5 37 H5
Fairbourne Dr MCKLVR DE3 56 B3
Fairbourne Rd LEIW LE3 130 E6
Fairburn Cl WOL/BIL/BRX NG8 49 G3
Fairburn Wy
EWD/SEL/PNX NG16 22 E8
Faircroft Av LGEAT NG10 61 M2
Fairdale Dr EWD/SEL/PNX NG16 21 M5
Fairdene NORM/LIT DE23 57 K5
Fairefield Crs LEIW LE3 124 B5
Faire Rd LEIW LE3 124 B6
Faires Cl BWSH/BRSTN DE72 60 B6
Fairestone Av LEIW LE3 124 A7
Faire St DERBYW DE22 2 B8
Fairfax Cl LEIN LE4 126 C5
Fairfax Rd LEIN LE4 126 C5
NORM/LIT DE23 2 C9
Fairfield Av BWSH/BRSTN DE72 60 A4
Fairfield Cl CFTN/RUD NG11 64 F2
Fairfield Crs LGEAT NG10 75 L3
Fairfield Rd ILK DE7 19 G8
ILK DE7 33 L6
LEIS LE2 138 F1
NORM/LIT DE23 57 J5
Fairfield St LEIS LE2 7 M7
WGSTN LE18 137 K5
Fairfield Ter
BWSH/BRSTN * DE72 60 B7
Fairford Av LEIE LE5 132 F4
Fairford Gdns NORM/LIT DE23 70 E1
Fairham Av CFTN/RUD NG11 77 M6
Fairham Cl CFTN/RUD NG11 64 F7
Fairham Ct CFTN/RUD * NG11 64 E4
Fairham Dr WOL/BIL/BRX NG8 50 A3
Fairham Rd COT/KEY/RAD NG12 80 B4
Fairhaven Rd RLEINE/SYS LE7 118 C7
Fairholm Ct
MAPPK/POR/STA NG3 5 M4
Fairholme Rd LEIS LE2 137 L1
Fairisle Cl CFTN/RUD NG11 64 E6
DERBYE DE21 45 G4
Fairisle Wy RLEIW/BBY LE8 143 K4
Fairland Crs WBRGFD NG2 65 J3
Fairlawns BPR/DUF DE56 29 H4
Fair Lea Cl LGEAT NG10 76 B1
Fairlight Wy ARN NG5 24 F8
Fairmaid Gv CFTN/RUD NG11 64 C5
Fair Md RLBORO LE12 113 J7
Fairmead Cl
MAPPK/POR/STA NG3 37 K7
Fairmeadows Wy LBORO LE11 103 L8
Fairmount Dr LBORO LE11 8 C7
Fairnley Rd WOL/BIL/BRX NG8 35 H7
Fairstone Hl LEIS LE2 138 F3
Fairview Av
EWD/SEL/PNX NG16 13 K5
RLEIW/BBY LE8 136 D8
Fairview Cl BPR/DUF DE56 18 F8
NORM/LIT DE23 56 E7
Fairview Ct CFTN/RUD NG11 65 H5
Fairview Gra BPR/DUF DE56 18 F8
Fairview Rd ARN NG5 37 J3
The Fairway CARL NG4 38 C4
LEIS LE2 132 D7
LEIS LE2 137 K1
RLEIW/BAR LE9 129 K3
RLEIW/BBY LE8 136 E8
Fairway COT/KEY/RAD NG12 80 E5
RLEIW/BBY LE8 146 F8
Fairway Cl DERBYW DE22 43 H5
Fairway Crs DERBYW DE22 43 H5
Fairway Dr BLWL NG6 24 B8
BSTN/STPLFD NG9 63 H1
Fairway Rd RLBORO LE12 102 A4
Fairway Rd South
RLBORO LE12 102 A6
Fairwood Dr DERBYSE DE24 73 H1
Falaise Wy RDERBYSW DE65 68 C5
Falcon Cl LEIW LE3 129 J5
NOTTE NG7 50 C3
RLEIW/BAR LE9 141 J8
Falconer Crs LEIW LE3 124 C7
Falcon Gv NOTTE NG7 36 E6
Falcon Rd RLEINE/SYS LE7 124 B1
Falcons Ri BPR/DUF DE56 18 A2
Falcon St LBORO LE11 9 M1
NOTTE NG7 36 E6
Falcon Wy DERBYSE DE24 71 J5
Falconwood Gdns
CFTN/RUD NG11 64 A6
Faldo Cl LEIN LE4 126 C2
Fallow Cl CFTN/RUD NG11 64 C5
Fallowfield Rd LEIE LE5 133 H3
Fallow Rd DERBYE DE21 59 K1
Fall Rd HEANOR DE75 20 C4
Falmouth Dr WGSTN LE18 138 A6
Falmouth Rd DERBYSE DE24 73 G2
LEIE LE5 132 D3
Falstaffe Ms NOTTE * NG7 36 E6
Falston Rd WOL/BIL/BRX NG8 49 L1
Faraday Rd NOTTE NG7 50 C3
Far Cft BWSH/BRSTN DE72 61 H7
Farfield Av BSTN/STPLFD NG9 49 J7
Farfield Gv BSTN/STPLFD NG9 49 J7
Far La BWSH/BRSTN DE72 60 B2
RLBORO LE12 95 H4
Far Laund BPR/DUF DE56 17 M1
Farleigh Av WGSTN LE18 138 A4
Farleigh Cl RLEIW/BAR LE9 141 J8
Farley Rd LEIS LE2 132 B7
NORM/LIT DE23 57 H5
Farleys La HUCK/RAV NG15 23 L2
Farley St BLWL NG6 23 M8
Farley Wy RLBORO LE12 104 D8
RLEIW/BAR LE9 129 K1
Farm Av HUCK/RAV NG15 23 H3
Farm Cl BPR/DUF DE56 18 A3
BPR/DUF DE56 18 E7
CFTN/RUD NG11 64 C5
END/NAR LE19 142 A1
ILK DE7 33 L7
LEIN LE4 119 M8
LGEAT NG10 76 C2
RDERBYSW DE65 68 A6
RIPLEY DE5 10 F1
WGSTN LE18 137 K2
Farm Dr DERBYSE DE24 72 E2
Farmers Cl LEIW LE3 123 L7
Farmer St CFTN/RUD NG11 79 K4
Farmhouse Ms
RDERBYSW * DE65 70 B5
Farmhouse Rd DERBYSE DE24 71 J5
Farmlands La NORM/LIT DE23 70 F1
Farm Rd ARN NG5 25 M8
BSTN/STPLFD NG9 63 H2
Farm St DERBYW DE22 2 C7
Farmway LEIW LE3 130 C8
Farnah Green Rd
BPR/DUF DE56 17 H4
Farnborough Gdns
DERBYW DE22 43 M3
Farnborough Rd
CFTN/RUD NG11 64 C7
Farncombe La DERBYE DE21 44 D4
Farndale COAL LE67 108 B1
WGSTN LE18 138 D5
Farndale Cl LGEAT NG10 75 L2
Farndale Dr LBORO LE11 103 K7
WOL/BIL/BRX NG8 48 F3
Farndon Dr BSTN/STPLFD NG9 62 D4
RLEIW/BAR LE9 140 A5
Far New Cl LGEAT NG10 61 M3
Farneworth Rd MCKLVR DE3 56 A5
Farnham Cl MCKLVR DE3 56 A5
Farnham Rd LBORO LE11 9 J9
Farnham St LEIE LE5 7 L4
RLBORO LE12 112 D1
Farningham Cl DERBYE DE21 59 K2
Farnsfield Av CALV/BJ NG14 39 L2
Farnway DERBYW DE22 43 J6
Farnworth Cl LEIN LE4 126 B4
Far Pastures Cl
COT/KEY/RAD NG12 80 C5
Farrier Gdns NORM/LIT DE23 56 E8
Farrier La LEIN LE4 124 F4
Farriers Cft ILK DE7 33 G4
Farriers Gn CFTN/RUD NG11 64 A5
Farriers' Wy RLEINE/SYS LE7 115 H8
Farringdon Cl DERBYW DE22 56 D1
WOL/BIL/BRX NG8 35 H4
Farringdon St LEIE LE5 7 L2
Farr Wood Cl GBY/RBY LE6 123 J4
Far Rye WOL/BIL/BRX NG8 49 K1
Far St CFTN/RUD NG11 79 J4
RLBORO LE12 98 A3
Farthing Ct LGEAT NG10 61 M8
Farthingdale Cl
RLEIW/BAR LE9 142 C4
The Farthings RLBORO LE12 94 E6
Farwells Cl BLWL NG6 36 A4
Fastnet Rd LEIE LE5 127 J8
Faulconbridge Cl BLWL NG6 35 M1
Faversham Cl DERBYSE DE24 72 D2
LEIW LE3 130 A1
Fayrhurst Rd LEIS LE2 137 J1
Fearn Av RIPLEY DE5 11 J6
Fearn Cha CARL NG4 38 C8
Fearn Cl BWSH/BRSTN DE72 61 L8
Fearnleigh Dr BLWL NG6 36 B5
Fearon St LBORO LE11 8 E2
Featherby Dr LEIS LE2 136 E4
Featherstone Cl CARL NG4 38 B4
Featherstone Dr LEIS LE2 137 G5
Feature Rd LEIN LE4 120 C7
Federation St END/NAR LE19 135 L5
Feldspar Cl END/NAR LE19 135 L2
Felen Cl ARN NG5 24 E8
Fellbarrow Cl WBRGFD NG2 66 A2
Felley Wy LEIW LE3 125 G7
Fellow Lands Wy
DERBYSE DE24 71 H4
MELB/CHEL DE73 72 E5
Fellows Rd BSTN/STPLFD NG9 49 J8
Fellows Yd COT/KEY/RAD NG12 66 C8
Fell Side ARN NG5 37 L2
Fellside BPR/DUF DE56 17 L3
DERBYE DE21 59 K2
Fellside Cl WBRGFD NG2 66 A1
Felly Mill La (North)
EWD/SEL/PNX NG16 13 M5
Felly Mill La (South)
EWD/SEL/PNX NG16 13 L6
Felstead Ct BSTN/STPLFD NG9 49 G6
Felstead Rd LEIN LE4 125 H3
WOL/BIL/BRX NG8 49 M1
Felton Cl BSTN/STPLFD NG9 62 F2
Felton Rd WBRGFD NG2 51 H7
Fenchurch Cl ARN NG5 24 E6
Fenchurch Wk DERBYW DE22 56 F1
Fenimore Ct
COT/KEY/RAD * NG12 53 M4
Fennel St LBORO LE11 9 J2
Fenners Cl LEIN LE4 119 G8
Fenroth Cl BLWL NG6 23 K7
Fenton Cl LEIS LE2 138 E4
Fenton Dr BLWL NG6 24 A5
Fenton Rd ARN NG5 36 D3
MCKLVR DE3 56 A5
Fenwick Cl WOL/BIL/BRX NG8 35 K5
Fenwick Rd LEIS LE2 139 J3
WOL/BIL/BRX NG8 35 K5
Fenwick St DERBYSE DE24 58 B8
Fergus Cl CFTN/RUD NG11 64 D7
Ferguson Cl BSTN/STPLFD NG9 63 G5
Fermain Cl LEIE LE5 133 H2
Fern Av ARN NG5 36 F6
Fern Bank LEIE LE5 7 M4
Fern Cl BSTN/STPLFD NG9 48 F8
LEIE LE5 133 J2
Fern Crs EWD/SEL/PNX NG16 21 H4
GBY/RBY LE6 123 H3
Ferndale Cl BSTN/STPLFD NG9 63 H5
Ferndale Dr GBY/RBY LE6 123 H7
Ferndale Rd LEIN LE4 126 C1
LEIS LE2 137 M1
MAPPK/POR/STA NG3 51 M1
Ferndene Dr LGEAT NG10 61 L8
Ferndown Cl LEIW LE3 130 A1
Ferneley Ri RLEINE/SYS LE7 115 K3
Ferngill Cl WBRGFD NG2 50 F6
Fernhill Ct MELB/CHEL DE73 72 E4
Fernhurst Rd LEIW LE3 130 D7
Fernie Cl LEIS LE2 139 G3
Fernie Rd LEIE LE5 126 B8
Fernilee Cl ILK DE7 32 C7
Fernlea END/NAR LE19 135 K6
Fern Lea Av COT/KEY/RAD NG12 67 J5
Fernleigh Av
MAPPK/POR/STA NG3 37 M5
Fernleys Cl LEIN LE4 124 F4
Fern Ri LEIE LE5 127 G6
Fernwood Cl NORM/LIT DE23 57 G7
Fernwood Crs
WOL/BIL/BRX NG8 49 G3
Fernwood Dr
COT/KEY/RAD NG12 53 K3
Ferny Hollow Cl ARN NG5 24 C7
Ferrars Ct LEIW LE3 130 B6
Ferrers Cl CDON/KEG DE74 84 E4
Ferrers Crs BPR/DUF DE56 29 H4
Ferrers Ri GBY/RBY LE6 123 J4
Ferrers Rd COAL LE67 108 D3
Ferrers St LEIS LE2 137 K2
Ferrers Wk
MAPPK/POR/STA NG3 5 L5
Ferrers Wy DERBYW DE22 43 J5
RIPLEY DE5 11 G4
Ferriby Ter WBRGFD NG2 51 G6
Ferrous Cl LEIN LE4 126 A7
Ferryman Rd LBORO LE11 9 L1
Festival Av BWSH/BRSTN DE72 61 G7
LEIN LE4 126 B1
Festival Dr LBORO LE11 103 L1
Festival Rd ILK DE7 47 G2
Festus Cl MAPPK/POR/STA * NG3 5 J3
Festus St CARL NG4 38 E8
Field Av RLBORO LE12 102 A1
Field Cl BSTN/STPLFD NG9 62 F3
BWSH/BRSTN DE72 59 M4
BWSH/BRSTN DE72 61 K8
CARL NG4 38 D5
COAL LE67 100 A8
END/NAR LE19 136 A8
RDERBYSW DE65 68 B5
Field Ct BPR/DUF DE56 18 E8
Field Court Rd GBY/RBY LE6 123 K4
Field Crs DERBYSE DE24 72 E2
Field Crest RLBORO LE12 113 H7
Field Dr DERBYSE DE24 72 E2
Field End Cl RLBORO LE12 88 A6
Fieldfare Ct NORM/LIT DE23 70 E1
Fieldfare Wk LEIE LE5 7 M3
Fieldgate Crs LEIN LE4 119 J7
Fieldgate Dr DERBYE DE21 44 D5
Field Head Wy DERBYE DE21 44 F4
Field House Cl
WOL/BIL/BRX NG8 49 H2
Fieldhouse Rd LEIN LE4 125 L4
Fieldhurst Av LEIW LE3 130 C7
Fielding Rd LEIN LE4 119 K8
Field La BPR/DUF DE56 17 K3
BSTN/STPLFD NG9 62 E3
CALV/BJ NG14 27 G3
DERBYE DE21 44 E8
DERBYSE DE24 72 F1
Fieldon Cl ASHB DE6 41 K5
Field Ri NORM/LIT DE23 57 G8
Field Rd ILK DE7 33 K8
Field Rw BPR/DUF DE56 17 K3
Fields Av CFTN/RUD NG11 79 G2
Fields Farm Rd LGEAT NG10 76 A2
Field St RIPLEY DE5 11 M8
RLBORO LE12 101 M3

Fieldsway Dr *DERBYE* DE21 ....44 B5
Field Ter *RIPLEY* DE5 ....11 H6
Field Vw *LEIW* LE4 ....120 E8
Fieldway *CFTN/RUD* NG11 ....64 F3
Fieldway Crs *RLEINE/SYS* LE7 ...139 M6
Fiennes Crs *NOTTE* NG7 ....4 C9
Fife St *DERBYSE* DE24 ....58 C7
Fifth Av *BSTN/STPLFD* NG9 ....64 B1
Filbert St *LEIS* LE2 ....131 J4
Filbert St East *LEIS* LE2 ....131 K4
Filey St *BLWL* NG6 ....24 A7
Fillingate *RLEINE/SYS* LE7 ......119 M4
Fincham CI *DERBYE* DE21 ....44 B6
Finch CI *LEIE* LE3 ....130 C2
  NOTTE NG7 ....50 D7
Finch Dr *MCKLVR* DE3 ....56 A7
Finchley Av *DERBYW* DE22 ....56 D1
Finchley CI *CFTN/RUD* NG11 ....64 A6
Finch Wy *END/NAR* LE19 ....135 K8
Findern CI *BPR/DUF* DE56 ....17 M1
  DERBYW DE22 ....43 H6
Findern Gn
  MAPPK/POR/STA NG3 ....51 L1
Findern La *RDERBYSW* DE65 ....69 L2
  RDERBYSW DE65 ....70 A8
Findern St *DERBYW* DE22 ....57 H2
Fineshade Av *LEIW* LE3 ....125 G7
Fingal CI *CFTN/RUD* NG11 ....64 D6
Finmere CI *NORM/LIT* DE23 ....56 E7
Finningley Dr *DERBYW* DE22 ....43 J5
Finsbury Av *DERBYW* DE22 ....56 F1
  LBORO LE11 ....9 L5
  RLBORO LE12 ....114 C4
  WBRGFD NG2 ....51 K3
Finsbury Park CI *WBRGFD* NG2 ....65 G2
Finsbury Rd *ARN* NG5 ....24 E5
  BSTN/STPLFD NG9 ....49 L8
  LEIN LE4 ....126 A6
Finson CI *WGSTN* LE18 ....138 B4
Fiona Dr *LEIE* LE5 ....133 J2
Firbank CI *BSTN/STPLFD* NG9 ......62 F3
Firbeck Rd *ARN* NG5 ....25 L7
  WOL/BIL/BRX NG8 ....49 G3
Fir CI *BLWL* NG6 ....23 K8
Fircroft Av *WOL/BIL/BRX* NG8 ....35 J7
Fircroft Dr *HUCK/RAV* NG15 ....23 G2
Fir Di *COT/KEY/RAD* NG12 ....67 L4
Firecrest Wy *BLWL* NG6 ....36 B4
Firestone CI *LEIE* LE3 ....130 A1
Firfield Av *BWSH/BRSTN* DE72 .....61 J7
  LEIN LE4 ....119 L8
The Firs *RLEINE/SYS* LE7 ....120 E5
Firs Av *BSTN/STPLFD* NG9 ....49 K8
  RIPLEY DE5 ....11 H6
Firsby Rd *WOL/BIL/BRX* NG8 ....35 K5
Firs Crs *DERBYW* DE22 ....43 J2
Firs Rd *COT/KEY/RAD* NG12 ....65 M2
Firs St *LGEAT* NG10 ....75 L3
First Av *BLWL* NG6 ....23 M8
  BSTN/STPLFD NG9 ....64 A1
  BWSH/BRSTN DE72 ....61 K2
  CARL NG4 ....38 A7
  CARL NG4 ....38 D6
  CARL NG4 ....52 C2
Firth CI *ARN* NG5 ....26 A6
Firth Dr *BSTN/STPLFD* NG9 ....63 C5
Firth Wy *BLWL* NG6 ....23 L7
Fir Tree CI *RLEIW/BBY* LE8 ......143 J3
Firtree Gv *DERBYE* DE21 ....44 F5
Fir Tree La *GBY/RBY* LE6 ....123 J3
Fisher Av *ARN* NG5 ....37 K2
Fisher CI *RLBORO* LE12 ....88 D5
  RLBORO LE12 ....114 B7
  RLEIW/BAR LE9 ....140 A5
Fisher Ct *ILK* DE7 ....33 K3
Fisher Ga *NOTT* NG1 ....5 K8
Fisher La *BPR/DUF* DE56 ....29 J3
Fisher St *DERBYSE* DE24 ....72 C1
  NOTTE NG7 ....36 D7
Fishley CI *LEIE* LE3 ....123 M8
Fish Pond Dr *NOTTE* NG7 ....4 D9
Fishponds CI *LEIW* LE3 ....123 M7
Fishpond Wy *RLBORO* LE12 ....111 L1
Fishpools *LEIE* LE3 ....130 C8
Fishpool Wy *RLBORO* LE12 ....105 J6
Fiskerton Wy *DERBYE* DE21 ....44 F7
Fitzroy St *LEIW* LE3 ....6 A6
Fitzwilliam CI *LEIS* LE2 ....139 H3
Five Acres *CFTN/RUD* NG11 ....64 E3
Flagholme *COT/KEY/RAD* NG12 .....67 K5
Flagshaw La *ASHB* DE6 ....41 J2
Flake La *ILK* DE7 ....47 J6
Flamborough Rd *LEIE* LE5 ....127 H8
Flamingo Ct *WBRGFD* NG2 ....50 E5
Flamingo Dr *RLEIW/BBY* LE8 ......142 D3
Flamstead Av *CARL* NG4 ....26 F8
  HEANOR DE75 ....19 M3
Flamstead La *RIPLEY* DE5 ....19 H6
Flamstead La *ILK* DE7 ....33 K6
Flamstead St *DERBYSE* DE24 ....72 B1
Flamsteed Rd
  WOL/BIL/BRX NG8 ......35 H6
The Flat *BPR/DUF* DE56 ....18 D7
Flatholme *LEIE* LE5 ....127 J7
The Flatts *BSTN/STPLFD* NG9 .....62 F2
Flatts La *EWD/SEL/PNX* NG16 ......13 H4
Flawborough Ri
  CFTN/RUD NG11 ....65 G4
Flawforth Av *CFTN/RUD* NG11 .....65 H8
Flawforth La
  COT/KEY/RAD NG12 .....65 J8
Flaxendale *COT/KEY/RAD* NG12 ....67 L5
Flaxfield CI *GBY/RBY* LE6 ....123 K4
Flaxholme Av *BPR/DUF* DE56 ....29 K6
Flaxland *RLEINE/SYS* LE7 ....113 J3
Flaxland Crs *RLBORO* LE12 ....112 C4
Flax Rd *LEIN* LE4 ....125 M5
Flaxton Wy *ARN* NG5 ....24 D8
Fleam Rd *CFTN/RUD* NG11 ....64 C3
Fleckney Rd *RLEIW/BBY* LE8 ......144 E5
  RLEIW/BBY LE8 ....146 B7
Fleeman Gv *WBRGFD* NG2 ....51 L6
The Fleet *BPR/DUF* DE56 ....17 K5
  RLEIW/BAR LE9 ....140 C4
Fleet CI *NOTTE* NG7 ....50 B1
Fleet Crs *BPR/DUF* DE56 ....17 K4

Fleet Pk *BPR/DUF* DE56 ....17 L4
Fleet St *NORM/LIT* DE23 ....57 L5
Fleetway CI
  EWD/SEL/PNX NG16 .....21 M6
Fleetwith CI *WBRGFD* NG2 ....66 A2
Fleetwood Rd *LEIS* LE2 ....131 L6
Fleming CI *EWD/SEL/PNX* NG16 ....21 J7
  LBORO LE11 ....103 H1
Fleming Dr *CARL* NG4 ....38 A8
Fleming Gdns *CFTN/RUD* NG11 .....64 A6
Flesh Hovel La *RLBORO* LE12 ....104 E6
Fletcher Ga *NOTT* NG1 ....5 H7
Fletcher Rd *BSTN/STPLFD* NG9 ....49 L8
  RLEIW/BAR LE9 ....140 C4
Fletchers CI *END/NAR* LE19 ......135 M8
Fletcher St *HEANOR* DE75 ....20 C5
Fletchers' Wy *RLEINE/SYS* LE7 ..115 H8
Flewitt Gdns
  MAPPK/POR/STA NG3 .....5 M4
Flintham Dr *ARN* NG5 ....36 F3
Flint St *DERBYSE* DE24 ....72 B1
Flixton Rd *EWD/SEL/PNX* NG16 ....12 D8
Flood St *BWSH/BRSTN* DE72 ....60 A3
Flora St *LEIE* LE4 ....6 A6
Florence Av *LGEAT* NG10 ....62 D6
  WGSTN LE18 ....137 L6
Florence Ct *ILK* * DE7 ....33 K6
Florence Crs *CARL* NG4 ....38 F7
Florence Gv
  CARL NG4 ....37 L8
Florence Rd *CARL* NG4 ....38 F6
  LEIS LE2 ....7 L5
  MAPPK/POR/STA NG3 ....37 L6
  WBRGFD NG2 ....51 L7
Florence St *HUCK/RAV* NG15 ......23 J7
  LEIS LE2 ....131 J8
Florence Wragg Wy *LEIS* LE2 ....139 J3
Florin Gdns *LGEAT* NG10 ....61 M8
Floyd CI *LEIN* LE4 ....126 C2
Flying Horse Wk *NOTT* NG1 ....5 H7
Foljambe Ter
  MAPPK/POR/STA NG3 ....5 K5
Folkestone Dr *DERBYSE* DE24 .....72 E2
Folkton Gdns
  MAPPK/POR/STA NG3 ....37 K6
Folly Br *RLEIW/BBY* LE8 ....143 M8
Folly Rd *DERBYW* DE22 ....43 M6
Folville Ri *LEIW* LE3 ....130 E5
Fontwell Dr *LEIS* LE2 ....136 F2
Forbes CI *LEIW* LE3 ....124 A8
The Ford *RLEIW/BBY* LE8 ....137 G7
Ford Av *HEANOR* DE75 ....20 A3
Ford CI *LEIS* LE2 ....137 G4
  RIPLEY DE5 ....11 G7
Fordham Gn *CFTN/RUD* NG11 ....64 C7
Fordice CI *COAL* LE67 ....108 A8
Ford La *DERBYW* DE22 ....43 M2
Ford Ri *LEIS* LE2 ....137 G4
Ford St *BPR/DUF* DE56 ....17 K3
  DERBY DE1 ....2 D3
  NOTTE NG7 ....36 E6
Ford St North *NOTTE* NG7 ....36 E6
Fordview CI *RLEIW/BBY* LE8 ......139 L6
Fordwells CI *NORM/LIT* DE23 .....56 E7
Foredrift CI *CFTN/RUD* NG11 .....77 L6
Foremark Av *NORM/LIT* DE23 ......57 J7
Forest Av *LEIN* LE4 ....120 B7
  COT/KEY/RAD NG12 .....67 J4
  GBY/RBY LE6 ....123 H4
Forest Ct *LBORO* LE11 ....9 H5
  NOTTE NG7 ....4 C4
Forest Dr *RLBORO* LE12 ....114 A3
  RLEIW/BAR LE9 ....129 J3
Forester CI *BSTN/STPLFD* NG9 ....63 G3
Forester Gv *CARL* NG4 ....38 B8
Forester Rd
  MAPPK/POR/STA NG3 ....37 L7
Foresters CI *LEIW* LE3 ....123 M7
Forester St *CARL* NG4 ....38 E8
  DERBY DE1 ....2 D5
Foresters Wy *RIPLEY* DE5 ....11 G5
Forest Ga *RLEINE/SYS* LE7 ......124 B1
Forest Gv *NOTT* NG1 ....4 F2
  NOTTE NG7 ....4 C3
Forest House La *LEIW* LE3 ......129 K6
Forest La *RLBORO* LE12 ....101 G3
Forest Ri *GBY/RBY* LE6 ....123 H4
  LEIS LE2 ....139 G1
  LEIS LE2 ....129 K4
  RLEINE/SYS LE7 ......133 K2
  RLEIW/BAR LE9 ....128 A4
Forest Rd *COAL* LE67 ....108 B8
  COAL LE67 ....116 A7
  END/NAR LE19 ....135 K2
  LBORO LE11 ....8 B9
  LBORO LE11 ....8 F6
  LEIE LE5 ....7 M2
  RLBORO LE12 ....111 M4
  RLBORO LE12 ....112 C2
  RLEIW/BAR LE9 ....135 H5
Forest Rd East *NOTT* NG1 ....4 E3
Forest Rd West *NOTTE* NG7 ....4 C4
Forest St *RLBORO* LE12 ....102 A4
Forest Vw *GBY/RBY* LE6 ....123 H3
Forest View Dr
  HUCK/RAV NG15 ....15 J8
The Forge *BSTN/STPLFD* NG9 ......47 M2
Forge CI *LEIW* LE3 ....123 L7
  RLBORO LE12 ....94 E6
  RLEIW/BBY LE8 ....145 K7
Forge End *RLEINE/SYS* LE7 ......119 J2
Forge HI *BSTN/STPLFD* NG9 ....63 H3
Forge Mill Gv *HUCK/RAV* NG15 ....24 B2
Forman St *RLBORO* LE12 ....101 M5
Forman St *DERBY* DE1 ....2 D4
  NOTT NG1 ....5 G6
Forrester Av
  BWSH/BRSTN DE72 ......83 K2
Forrester CI *RLEIW/BAR* LE9 ....142 B4
Forryan Rd *RLEIW/BAR* LE9 ......142 B5
Forryans CI *WGSTN* LE18 ....138 C7
Forster St *NOTTE* NG7 ....50 D6
Forsyth CI *RLBORO* LE12 ....102 F1

Forsythia Gdns *NOTTE* NG7 ....50 C5
Forth Av *BSTN/STPLFD* NG9 ....64 A1
Fort Rd *RLBORO* LE12 ....113 H6
Forty Horse CI *RIPLEY* DE5 ....11 L5
Forum CI *DERBYSE* DE24 ....73 H2
Fosbrook Dr *CDON/KEG* DE74 ......84 D3
Fosbrooke Dr *LBORO* LE11 ....76 B2
Fosse CI *BWSH/BRSTN* DE72 ....60 A6
  END/NAR LE19 ....136 B5
Fosse La *LEIW* LE3 ....124 F3
  LEIW LE3 ....125 G8
Fosse Park Av *END/NAR* LE19 ....136 D1
Fosse Pk South
  END/NAR LE19 ....136 D1
Fosse Rd Central *LEIW* LE3 .....131 G2
Fosse Rd North *LEIW* LE3 ....131 G1
Fosse Rd South *LEIW* LE3 ....130 F5
Fosse Wy *RLEINE/SYS* LE7 ....120 D4
Foster Av *BSTN/STPLFD* NG9 ......63 K1
Fosters Dr *ARN* NG5 ....37 H5
Foston Ga *WGSTN* LE18 ....138 C7
Foston La *RLEIW/BBY* LE8 ....143 K3
Foston Rd *RLEIW/BBY* LE8 ....145 G3
Foundry La *BPR/DUF* DE56 ....17 K8
  LEI LE1 ....7 G2
  RLEINE/SYS LE7 ....120 D4
Foundry Sq *LEI* LE1 ....7 G2
Fountain Dale Ct
  MAPPK/POR/STA NG3 ....5 J2
Fountains Av *LEIS* LE2 ....137 H4
Fountains CI *DERBYW* DE22 ....43 L3
  WBRGFD NG2 ....65 M1
Fourth Av *BSTN/STPLFD* NG9 .....64 A1
  CARL NG4 ....37 M7
Fowke St *RLEINE/SYS* LE7 ....119 J1
Fowler Av *DERBYE* DE24 ....59 H3
Fowler CI *LEIW* LE4 ....125 G3
Fowler St *BWSH/BRSTN* DE72 .....60 F8
  DERBYW DE22 ....2 A2
  MAPPK/POR/STA NG3 ....37 H7
Fox CI *DERBYSE* DE24 ....71 H5
  LGEAT NG10 ....76 D7
Foxcote Dr *RLBORO* LE11 ....102 E5
Fox Covert *CARL* NG4 ....52 D3
  LBORO LE11 ....103 M1
  RLEIW/BBY LE8 ....142 D2
Fox Covert La *CFTN/RUD* NG11 ...63 M6
Foxcroft CI *LEIW* LE3 ....131 G1
Foxdell Wy *MELB/CHEL* DE73 .....72 F5
Foxearth Av *CFTN/RUD* NG11 .....64 D5
Foxes CI *NOTTE* NG7 ....4 J3
Foxes Wk *DERBYW* DE22 ....43 J3
Foxfields Dr *DERBYE* DE21 ....44 C5
Foxglove CI *END/NAR* LE19 ......135 L7
  RLBORO LE12 ....113 K5
  RLEINE/SYS LE7 ......115 J8
Foxglove Dr *DERBYE* DE21 ....44 D4
  GBY/RBY LE6 ....123 L4
Foxglove Rd *COAL* LE67 ....108 C7
  EWD/SEL/PNX NG16 ....21 M7
  LEIE LE5 ....127 C5
Fox Gv *BLWL* NG6 ....36 C4
Foxhall Rd *NOTTE* NG7 ....36 E7
Fox HI *COT/KEY/RAD* NG12 ....67 J5
Foxhill Dr *LEIS* LE2 ....136 E4
Foxhill Rd *CALV/BJ* NG14 ....39 J2
  CARL NG4 ....38 A7
Foxhill Rd Central *CARL* NG4 ....37 M7
Foxhill Rd East *CARL* NG4 ....38 B7
Foxhill Rd West *CARL* NG4 ....37 M7
Foxhills *CDON/KEG* DE74 ....86 A6
Foxholes Rd *LEIW* LE3 ....130 A3
Foxhollies Gv *ARN* NG5 ....36 F4
Fox Hollow *LEIS* LE2 ....139 H3
Foxhunter Dr *LEIS* LE2 ....138 C1
Foxlands Av *DERBYW* DE22 ....43 K5
Fox La *LEIS* LE2 ....6 F5
  RLEIW/BAR LE9 ....129 H1
Foxley Ct *DERBYE* DE21 ....44 E5
Fox Meadow *HUCK/RAV* NG15 ......23 K2
Foxon St *LEIW* LE3 ....6 B7
Foxon Wy *LEIW* LE3 ....130 B6
Foxpond La *RLEIW/BBY* LE8 ......139 J6
Fox Rd *CDON/KEG* DE74 ....84 D3
  WBRGFD NG2 ....51 K6
Fox St *DERBY* DE1 ....3 G1
  LEI LE1 ....7 H6
Foxton CI *BLWL* NG6 ....23 K7
  ILK DE7 ....33 G4
Foxton Lock CI *WGSTN* LE18 .....137 L7
Foxwood La *CALV/BJ* NG14 ....26 E2
Foyle Av *DERBYE* DE21 ....58 E3
Fradley CI *BLWL* NG6 ....24 A5
Frampton Av *LEIW* LE3 ....130 F2
Frampton Gdns *NORM/LIT* DE23 ....70 D3
Frampton Rd
  WOL/BIL/BRX NG8 ......35 L8
Frances Gv *HUCK/RAV* NG15 ......15 M6
Frances St *EWD/SEL/PNX* NG16 ...13 H6
Franche Rd *LEIW* LE3 ....131 C1
Franchise St *DERBYW* DE22 ....2 A6
Francis Av *LEIW* LE3 ....130 D8
Francis Dr *LBORO* LE11 ....103 C1
Francis Gv *BLWL* NG6 ....36 C4
Francis Rd *CARL* NG4 ....38 D7
Francis St *DERBYE* DE24 ....3 L2
  LEIS LE2 ....132 B6
  NOTTE NG7 ....4 D4
Franklin CI *ARN* NG5 ....25 C7
Franklin Dr
  COT/KEY/RAD NG12 .....66 B6
Franklin Rd
  EWD/SEL/PNX NG16 .....12 E3
Franklin Wy *RLEIW/BBY* LE8 .....142 D2
Franklyn Dr *DERBYSE* DE24 ....72 E1
Franklyn Gdns
  COT/KEY/RAD NG12 .....80 C3
  WOL/BIL/BRX NG8 ......50 A1
Frankson Av *LEIW* LE3 ....130 E6
Fraser CI *LEI* LE1 ....7 H3
Fraser Crs *CARL* NG4 ....37 M6
Fraser Rd *CARL* NG4 ....37 M6
  WBRGFD NG2 ....51 H7
Fraser Sq *CARL* NG4 ....37 M6
Fraser St *HUCK/RAV* NG15 ....15 H1
Frazer CI *DERBYE* DE21 ....59 J1

Frearson Farm Ct
  EWD/SEL/PNX NG16 .....21 K6
Freckingham St *NOTT* NG1 ....5 K6
Freda Av *CARL* NG4 ....38 B5
Freda CI *CARL* NG4 ....38 B4
Frederic Av *HEANOR* DE75 ....20 D8
Frederick Av *CARL* NG4 ....37 M8
  CDON/KEG DE74 ....86 A4
  DERBYSE DE24 ....72 D1
  ILK DE7 ....47 J2
Frederick Gv *NOTTE* NG7 ....4 A9
Frederick Rd *BSTN/STPLFD* NG9 ...48 B8
  LEIE LE5 ....7 L4
Frederick St *ALFN* DE55 ....12 A2
  DERBYW DE22 ....57 H1
  LBORO LE11 ....9 C4
  LGEAT NG10 ....62 D8
  WGSTN LE18 ....138 B4
Freeland CI *BSTN/STPLFD* NG9 ....62 D4
Freeman Av *NORM/LIT* DE23 ....71 J1
Freeman Rd North *LEIE* LE5 .....126 D8
Freemans Ter *CARL* NG4 ....38 E7
Freemans' Wy *RLEINE/SYS* LE7 ...115 H7
Freemantle Rd *LEIE* LE2 ....132 C6
  MCKLVR DE3 ....56 C4
Freemantle Wk *ARN* NG5 ....24 C7
Freemen's Common Rd
  LEIS LE2 ....131 K5
Freer CI *RLEIW/BBY* LE8 ....136 F7
  WGSTN LE18 ....138 C7
Freeschool La *LEI* LE1 ....6 D5
Freesia CI *MCKLVR* DE3 ....56 C6
Freeston Dr *BLWL* NG6 ....23 K7
Freeth CI *WBRGFD* * NG2 ....51 K5
Freeth St *WBRGFD* * NG2 ....51 K5
Fremount Dr *WOL/BIL/BRX* NG8 ...35 J7
French La *DERBYE* DE21 ....30 D2
French Rd *LEIE* LE5 ....126 C8
French St *ILK* DE7 ....47 L1
  NORM/LIT DE23 ....57 J5
Frensham CI *LEIS* LE2 ....138 E3
Fresco Dr *NORM/LIT* DE23 ....56 D8
Freshwater CI *WGSTN* LE18 ......138 A7
Freshwater Houses
  DERBYSE * DE24 ......59 G8
Fretwell St *NOTTE* NG7 ....36 C8
Frewen Dr *RLEIW/BAR* LE9 ......140 B7
Frewin St *LEIE* LE5 ....126 C8
The Friary *NOTTE* NG7 ....50 C5
Friar Ct *WBRGFD* * NG2 ....50 F6
Friar Ga *DERBY* DE1 ....2 B3
Friar Gate *DERBY* DE1 ....2 C3
Friar La *LEI* LE1 ....4 F8
  NOTT NG1 ....4 D9
Friars Cswy *LEI* LE1 ....6 C5
Friars CI *DERBYW* DE22 ....43 K5
Friars Ct *ILK* DE7 ....47 G1
  NOTTE NG7 ....4 D9
Friar St *LGEAT* NG10 ....62 B8
  NOTTE NG7 ....50 C5
Friary Av *DERBYSE* DE24 ....72 C2
Friary CI *NOTTE* NG7 ....50 C5
Friary St *DERBY* DE1 ....2 C4
Friday La *CARL* NG4 ....38 D6
Friday St *LEI* LE1 ....6 D3
Friesland Dr
  BWSH/BRSTN DE72 ......61 K2
Frinton Av *LEIE* LE5 ....133 H3
Frinton Rd *WOL/BIL/BRX* NG8 ....35 J6
Frisby Av *LGEAT* NG10 ....76 C1
Frisby Rd *LEIE* LE5 ....7 M1
Fritchley CI *RLEIW/BAR* LE9 ....135 J8
Frith CI *LEIW* LE3 ....124 A7
Frizams La *MELB/CHEL* DE73 ......70 D8
Froanes CI *END/NAR* LE19 ....135 L3
Froggatt CI *DERBYW* DE22 ....43 L2
Frog Island *LEIW* LE3 ....5 G3
Frogmore St *NOTT* NG1 ....5 G3
Frolesworth La *LEIW* LE3 ....130 C1
Frolesworth Wy *LEIW* LE3 ....130 C1
Frome Av *LEIS* LE2 ....139 H1
Front St *ARN* NG5 ....25 K8
  LEIS LE2 ....125 M1
Frost Av *EWD/SEL/PNX* NG16 .....20 D5
Fryar Rd *EWD/SEL/PNX* NG16 .....21 K1
Fulbeck Rd *LEIE* LE5 ....133 H3
Fulbrook Rd *NORM/LIT* DE23 ......56 B8
Fulford CI *LEIE* LE5 ....130 A2
Fulforth St *NOTT* NG1 ....5 F4
Fulham Rd *DERBYW* DE22 ....56 F2
Fuller CI *RLEIW/BAR* LE9 ....128 A3
Fullforth CI *CFTN/RUD* NG11 .....79 G1
Fullhurst Av *LEIW* LE3 ....130 F4
Full St *DERBY* DE1 ....2 E2
Fullwood Av *ILK* DE7 ....33 J6
Fullwood CI *BSTN/STPLFD* NG9 ....63 G3
Fullwood St *ILK* DE7 ....33 J6
Fulmar CI *MCKLVR* DE3 ....56 E4
Fulmar Rd *RLEINE/SYS* LE7 .....124 B2
Fulwood Crs *WOL/BIL/BRX* NG8 ...35 L6
Fulwood Dr *LGEAT* NG10 ....61 L8
Furlong Av *ARN* NG5 ....25 J7
Furlong CI *BSTN/STPLFD* NG9 ....48 B7
  RLEINE/SYS * LE7 ....121 G4
Furlongs CI *RLEINE/SYS* LE7 ...121 G4
Furlong St *ARN* NG5 ....25 J8
Furnace La *HEANOR* DE75 ....20 A3
Furnace Rd *ILK* DE7 ....33 M8
Furness CI *WBRGFD* NG2 ....65 M1
Furness Rd *BLWL* NG6 ....36 A4
Furrow CI *RLEINE/SYS* LE7 .....119 J1
Furrows CI *DERBYE* DE21 ....45 J4
Furzebrook Rd *CARL* NG4 ....52 C1
Furze Gdns
  MAPPK/POR/STA NG3 ....5 J2
Fylde CI *BSTN/STPLFD* NG9 ....62 C5

Gable Ct *MCKLVR* DE3 ....56 C7
The Gables *NOTTE* * NG7 ....36 E7
Gables Farm Dr *RLBORO* LE12 ....89 G6
Gables Lea *RLBORO* LE12 ....94 F1
Gabor CI *CFTN/RUD* NG11 ....64 A7
Gabrielle CI *BLWL* NG6 ....36 B3
Gaddesby Av *LEIS* LE2 ....131 G4
Gaddesby La *RLEINE/SYS* LE7 ...115 M7
Gadd St *NOTTE* NG7 ....4 B4
Gadsby CI *ILK* DE7 ....47 L3
Gadsby Ri *BPR/DUF* DE56 ....10 A5
Gadwall Crs *WBRGFD* NG2 ....50 D5
Gainsborough CI
  BSTN/STPLFD NG9 .....62 C1
  DERBYE DE21 ....44 F6
  LGEAT NG10 ....76 C2
Gainsborough Ct
  BSTN/STPLFD * NG9 ...49 L8
Gainsborough Rd *LEIS* LE2 .....131 M7
  LEIE LE5 ....146 E6
Gainsford CI *ARN* NG5 ....36 D2
Gainsford Crs *ARN* NG5 ....36 D2
Gairloch CI *DERBYSE* DE24 ....71 H5
Galahad CI *LEIE* LE3 ....129 L5
Gala Wy *ARN* NG5 ....36 C1
Galby St *LEIE* LE5 ....126 B8
The Galeb *NOTTE* * NG7 ....50 C5
Galena Dr *MAPPK/POR/STA* NG3 ...37 L8
Gallards HI *LEIW* LE3 ....130 C3
Galleywood Dr *LEIN* LE4 ....125 H5
Gallico CI *LBORO* LE11 ....103 H2
Gallimore CI *LEIW* LE3 ....124 C6
Gallows Inn CI *ILK* DE7 ....47 L2
Gallowtree Ga *LEI* LE1 ....6 F5
Galsworthy Ct *LEIW* LE3 ....130 E2
Galway Av *DERBYE* DE21 ....58 F3
Galway Rd *ARN* NG5 ....25 J7
  LEIN LE4 ....125 J2
  NOTTE NG7 ....4 B9
Gamble St *NOTTE* NG7 ....4 C8
Gamble Wy *RLBORO* LE12 ....104 C4
Camel Rd *LEIE* LE5 ....132 F2
Gamston Crs *ARN* NG5 ....37 G4
Gamston Lings Bar Rd
  COT/KEY/RAD NG12 .....65 L6
Ganton CI
  MAPPK/POR/STA NG3 ....37 K6
Ganton Rd *LEIE* LE5 ....130 A1
Garats Hay *RLBORO* * LE12 .....111 M4
Garden Av *ILK* DE7 ....47 K2
Garden City *CARL* NG4 ....38 C7
Garden CI *LEIS* LE3 ....138 E2
Garden Crs *CDON/KEG* DE74 ......84 F4
Gardendale Av
  CFTN/RUD NG11 ....64 B7
Gardeners Wk *ARN* NG5 ....36 D3
Gardenfield Rd *LEIN* LE4 ......126 D3
Gardenia Crs
  MAPPK/POR/STA NG3 ....37 M5
Gardenia Gv
  MAPPK/POR/STA NG3 ....37 M5
Garden Rd *COAL* LE67 ....108 B5
  EWD/SEL/PNX NG16 .....21 L4
  HUCK/RAV NG15 ....15 K8
The Gardens *RIPLEY* DE5 ....11 H8
Gardens CI *WBRGFD* NG2 ....51 L8
Garden St *DERBY* DE1 ....2 D1
  LEI LE1 ....120 C8
  LEIN LE4 ....120 C8
  NOTTE NG7 ....4 B8
  WGSTN LE18 ....137 K6
Gardinia CI *BSTN/STPLFD* NG9 ...62 C5
Gardner CI *LBORO* LE11 ....103 C1
Garendon Av *RLBORO* LE12 ......94 F2
Garendon CI *RLBORO* LE12 ......102 A4
Garendon Gn *LBORO* LE11 ....9 C8
Garendon Rd *COAL* LE67 ....108 F7
  LBORO LE11 ....9 C8
  RLBORO LE12 ....101 M4
Garendon St *LEIS* LE2 ....7 K5
Garendon Wy *GBY/RBY* LE6 ......123 J5
Garfield Av *BWSH/BRSTN* DE72 ...60 E8
Garfield CI *BSTN/STPLFD* NG9 ...48 C8
  NORM/LIT DE23 ....71 G1
Garfield Ct *NOTTE* NG7 ....4 A5
Garfield Pk *RLEIW/BBY* LE8 ....139 M6
Garfield Rd *COAL* LE67 ....108 A8
  NOTTE NG7 ....4 A4
Garfield St *LEIN* LE4 ....125 L7
Garforth CI *WOL/BIL/BRX* NG8 ...36 C7
Garganey CI *COAL* LE67 ....108 C7
The Garland *NOTTE* * NG7 ....50 C5
Garland *RLEINE/SYS* LE7 ....113 J8
Garland Crs *LEIW* LE3 ....124 F7
Garnet Ct *MAPPK/POR/STA* NG3 ...5 M5
Garnet St *CARL* NG4 ....38 D8
Garnett Crs *LEIE* LE2 ....137 G3
Garrett Gv *CFTN/RUD* NG11 ......64 A5
Garrick St *DERBYSE* DE24 ....58 F2
Garry CI *DERBYSE* DE24 ....71 H5
Garsdale *WGSTN* LE18 ....138 D5
Garsdale CI *WBRGFD* NG2 ....66 A1
Garsdale Dr *CFTN/RUD* NG11 .....64 E4
Garth Av *LEIN* LE4 ....125 J3
Garth Crs *DERBYSE* DE24 ....72 F1
Garthorpe Ct *DERBYE* DE21 ......44 D5
Garton CI *BLWL* NG6 ....35 M2
  BSTN/STPLFD NG9 .....62 F2
Garton Rd *LBORO* LE11 ....9 J5
Gartree Rd *LEIS* LE2 ....132 D6
Gary CI *NORM/LIT* DE23 ....71 H2
Gascoigne Av *RLEINE/SYS* LE7 ..121 J2
Gascoigne Dr *DERBYE* DE21 ......59 H3
Gaskell Av *NORM/LIT* DE23 ......57 J8
Gasny Av *CDON/KEG* DE74 ....84 F2
Gas La *WGSTN* LE18 ....138 A5
Gas St *LEI* LE1 ....6 E2
  LGEAT NG10 ....62 A1
Gatcombe CI
  COT/KEY/RAD NG12 .....53 L4
  DERBYE DE21 ....44 E5

Gatcombe Dr COAL LE67 108 E7
Gatcombe Gv LGEAT NG10 61 L4
Gate Brook Cl RIPLEY DE5 11 M7
Gateford Cl BSTN/STPLFD NG9 48 F5
Gateside Rd WBRGFD NG2 50 E6
Gateway St LEIS LE2 6 D8
Gatling St NOTTE NG7 50 C2
Gaulby La LEIS LE2 133 H7
Gaul St BLWL NG6 23 M8
LEIW LE3 6 A9
Gauntley Ct NOTTE * NG7 36 C7
Gauntley St NOTTE NG7 36 C7
Gautries Cl ARN NG5 24 E7
Gavin Cl LEIW LE3 130 A5
Gavin Dr LBORO LE11 103 H1
Gawthorne St NOTTE NG7 36 D6
Gayhurst Cl LEIW LE3 130 D8
WGSTN LE18 138 C5
Gayhurst Rd BLWL NG6 36 C2
Gaynor Ct WOL/BIL/BRX NG8 49 M1
Gayrigg Ct BSTN/STPLFD NG9 62 F2
Gayton Av LEIN LE4 126 A6
NORM/LIT DE23 71 H1
Gayton Cl WOL/BIL/BRX NG8 35 H7
Gayton Hts END/NAR LE19 135 L3
Gayton Thorpe Cl
NORM/LIT DE23 56 D8
Gaywood Cl CFTN/RUD NG11 64 D7
Geary Cl END/NAR LE19 135 M8
GBY/RBY LE6 123 J7
Gedding Rd LEIE LE5 132 C2
Geddington Cl WGSTN LE18 138 C5
Gedge Wy LEIS LE2 137 J1
Gedling Gv ARN NG5 25 K8
NOTTE NG7 4 D4
Gedling Rd ARN NG5 25 K8
CARL NG4 38 D7
Gedling St NOTT NG1 5 K7
Gedney Av
MAPPK/POR/STA NG3 37 K7
Gee Rd COAL LE67 108 C5
Gees Lock Cl LEIS LE2 136 F3
Gelders Hall Rd RLBORO LE12 101 L6
Gelert Av LEIE LE5 133 H1
Gell Rd BSTN/STPLFD NG9 62 E4
Gelscoe La MELB/CHEL DE73 92 B6
Gema Cl DERBYW DE22 43 L3
George Av BSTN/STPLFD NG9 63 K3
LGEAT NG10 62 D7
George Crs ALFN DE55 12 A1
George Green Ct
WBRGFD * NG2 51 K3
Georgeham Cl WGSTN LE18 138 B6
George Hill Cl RLEIW/BAR LE9 140 B4
George Mariott Cl
RLEIW/BAR LE9 140 A6
George Rd CARL NG4 38 C8
WBRGFD NG2 51 J8
George's La CALV/BJ NG14 26 A1
George St ALFN DE55 12 B1
ARN NG5 37 J1
BPR/DUF DE56 17 K3
COAL LE67 108 D3
DERBY DE1 2 D3
END/NAR LE19 135 L4
EWD/SEL/PNX NG16 20 F4
HUCK/RAV NG15 15 L7
LBORO LE11 8 E2
LEI LE1 7 G3
MELB/CHEL DE73 82 E8
NOTT NG1 5 H6
RLEINE/SYS LE7 124 B1
George Toon Ct
RLEINE/SYS * LE7 120 E3
George Yd LBORO LE11 9 J3
Georgia Dr ARN NG5 25 J5
Georgina Rd BSTN/STPLFD NG9 63 K2
Gerard Cl DERBYE DE21 59 K1
Gerard Ct DERBY DE1 2 D5
Gerard Gv RDERBYSW DE65 69 G3
Gerard St DERBY DE1 2 D6
Gerrard Cl ARN NG5 24 E5
Gerrard Crs CDON/KEG DE74 86 B6
Gertrude Rd BWSH/BRSTN DE72 60 E8
DERBYE DE21 44 E7
WBRGFD NG2 51 L7
Gervase Gdns CFTN/RUD NG11 64 B5
Gervas Rd LEIE LE5 127 G8
Ghost House La
BSTN/STPLFD NG9 62 F2
Gibbons Av BSTN/STPLFD NG9 48 B8
Gibbons Cl LEIN LE4 125 L7
Gibbons St NOTTE NG7 50 C7
Gibb St LGEAT NG10 62 C8
Gibfield La BPR/DUF DE56 17 K5
Gibson Cl WGSTN LE18 138 B4
Gibson Rd NOTTE NG7 36 E7
RLBORO LE12 114 B3
Gibson's La RMMWB LE14 99 M6
Gifford Cl LEIE LE5 132 F4
Gilbert Av CFTN/RUD NG11 77 M6
Gilbert Cl DERBYE DE21 59 H3
LEIN LE4 126 C3
Gilbert Crs BPR/DUF DE56 29 J5
Gilbert Gdns
MAPPK/POR/STA NG3 51 L1
Gilbert St DERBYSE DE24 72 F2
Gilderdale Wy DERBYE DE21 44 F4
Gilead St BLWL NG6 23 M8
Giles Av WBRGFD NG2 65 H1
Giles Cl RLBORO LE12 112 F3
Giles Ct WBRGFD * NG2 51 K8
Gillam Butts RLEIW/BBY LE8 143 J4
Gillamoor Ct DERBYSE DE24 73 H1
Gillamore Dr COAL LE67 108 E5
Gillbank Dr GBY/RBY LE6 123 G7
Gillercomb Cl
COT/KEY/RAD NG12 66 B3
Gilliver La COT/KEY/RAD NG12 67 G6
Gilliver St LEIS LE2 131 M7
Gillman Rd LEIW LE3 124 E7
Gillott St HEANOR DE75 20 E7
Gill St EWD/SEL/PNX NG16 13 L1
NOTT NG1 4 F4
Gilmorton Av LEIS LE2 136 F3
Gilmorton Cl LEIS LE2 136 F3
Gilmour Cl LEIN LE4 124 F2
Gilpet Av MAPPK/POR/STA NG3 37 K7
Gilstead Cl RLEINE/SYS LE7 133 K3
Giltbrook Crs
EWD/SEL/PNX NG16 22 A7
Gilt Hl EWD/SEL/PNX NG16 22 B8
Giltway EWD/SEL/PNX NG16 22 A8
Gimson Av RLEIW/BAR LE9 142 B4
Gimson Cl ILK DE7 33 G4
LEIE LE5 126 E6
Gimson Rd LEIW LE3 130 F2
Gin Close Wy
EWD/SEL/PNX NG16 34 A2
Gipsy La LEIN LE4 126 C5
RLEINE/SYS LE7 113 G7
Gipsy Rd LEIN LE4 125 M5
Girton Rd ARN NG5 36 E4
Gisborne Cl MCKLVR DE3 56 C3
Gisborne Crs DERBYW DE22 43 K3
Gisborne Gn DERBY DE1 2 B1
Gisborough Wy RLBORO LE12 102 F2
Gisburn Cl CFTN/RUD NG11 64 E3
The Glade CFTN/RUD NG11 64 C8
LEIW LE3 130 D8
Glade Av WOL/BIL/BRX NG8 50 A2
Gladehill Rd ARN NG5 25 G8
Gladstone Av CFTN/RUD NG11 77 M6
HEANOR DE75 20 C5
LBORO LE11 103 L2
Gladstone Cl MELB/CHEL DE73 72 D4
Gladstone Dr
EWD/SEL/PNX NG16 13 J8
Gladstone Ms RLEIW/BAR * LE9 141 J8
Gladstone Rd DERBYE DE21 59 J2
Gladstone St BSTN/STPLFD NG9 63 J2
CARL NG4 38 B8
EWD/SEL/PNX NG16 21 G4
HEANOR DE75 20 C5
LBORO LE11 9 J1
LEI LE1 7 G4
LGEAT NG10 76 B1
NORM/LIT DE23 57 J6
NOTTE NG7 36 D7
RLBORO LE12 94 E6
RLEINE/SYS LE7 120 A2
RLEIW/BBY LE8 145 K8
RLEIW/BBY LE8 146 D7
WGSTN LE18 138 A4
Gladstone St East ILK DE7 33 K7
Gladstone St West ILK DE7 33 K8
Glaisdale Cl LEIN LE4 125 G4
Glaisdale Dr East
WOL/BIL/BRX NG8 49 J1
Glaisdale Dr West
WOL/BIL/BRX NG8 49 H2
Glaisdale Nook
DERBYSE * DE24 73 H1
Glaisdale Pkwy
WOL/BIL/BRX NG8 49 H2
Glaisdale Rd WGSTN LE18 138 C6
Glamis Cl DERBYE DE21 44 F5
RLBORO LE12 113 G7
Glamis Rd ARN NG5 36 E5
Glamorgan Av WGSTN LE18 137 K5
Glanton Wy ARN NG5 25 L5
Glapton La CFTN/RUD NG11 64 B5
Glapton Rd WBRGFD NG2 51 G6
Glaramara Cl WBRGFD NG2 50 F6
Glasshouse St NOTT NG1 5 H5
Glastonbury Rd DERBYSE DE24 59 G8
Glazebrook Rd LEIW LE3 124 D6
Glazebrook Sq LEIW LE3 124 E7
Gleadmoss La DERBYE DE21 44 E6
The Glebe EWD/SEL/PNX NG16 33 M3
Glebe Av ILK DE7 31 K1
RIPLEY DE5 11 J7
Glebe Cl ASHB DE6 40 C6
LEIS LE2 132 C8
LEIW LE3 123 M7
RLBORO LE12 113 H5
WGSTN LE18 138 B4
Glebe Crs ILK DE7 33 L8
ILK DE7 45 M1
Glebe Dr CALV/BJ NG14 39 H4
RLEIW/BBY LE8 143 H4
Glebe Farm Cl WBRGFD * NG2 65 G3
Glebe Farm Vw CARL NG4 38 D4
Glebeland Cl RLEINE/SYS LE7 115 K5
The Glebelands
RLEIW/BBY LE8 139 L7
Glebelands Rd LEIN LE4 119 H7
Glebe La COT/KEY/RAD NG12 53 K4
Glebe Ri NORM/LIT DE23 57 G6
Glebe Rd CARL NG4 38 A5
COAL LE67 100 A7
EWD/SEL/PNX NG16 35 G1
GBY/RBY LE6 123 J4
LEIS LE2 132 D8
RLEINE/SYS LE7 121 J2
WBRGFD NG2 51 K8
Glebe St BSTN/STPLFD NG9 63 J1
HUCK/RAV NG15 15 L7
LBORO LE11 104 A2
LEIS LE2 7 H8
Glebe Wy RLEINE/SYS LE7 120 C4
The Glen CFTN/RUD NG11 64 C6
Glen Av BPR/DUF DE56 18 A8
EWD/SEL/PNX NG16 21 M6
Glenbarr Av LEIN LE4 6 B1
Glenborne Rd WGSTN LE18 137 L3
Glenbrook COT/KEY/RAD NG12 67 L4
Glenbrook Crs
WOL/BIL/BRX NG8 35 L8
Glencairn Dr WOL/BIL/BRX NG8 35 L7
Glencoe Av LEIN LE4 126 A3
Glencoe Rd CFTN/RUD NG11 64 D6
Glencoyne Rd CFTN/RUD NG11 64 C7
Glencroft Dr DERBYSE DE24 71 H4
Glendale Av LEIW LE3 123 M4
Glendale Cl CARL NG4 38 B5
Glendale Ct BSTN/STPLFD NG9 63 J4
Glendale Dr DERBYE DE21 59 K2
Glendale Gdns ARN NG5 25 K6
Glendon Dr ARN NG5 36 E4
HUCK/RAV NG15 23 L2
Glendon Rd DERBYSE DE24 71 J2
ILK DE7 47 G3
Glendon St ILK DE7 31 L6
LEIN LE4 125 M6
Glendower Cl LEIE LE5 132 F1
Gleneagles Av LEIN LE4 126 B3
Gleneagles Cl MCKLVR DE3 56 D5
Gleneagles Ct COT/KEY/RAD NG12 65 M4
Gleneagles Dr ARN NG5 25 M6
Glenfield Av
EWD/SEL/PNX NG16 22 B8
Glenfield Crs LEIW LE3 124 A7
MCKLVR DE3 56 A5
Glenfield Frith Dr LEIW LE3 124 B6
Glenfield La RLEIW/BAR LE9 129 J1
Glenfield Rd LEIW LE3 124 D8
LGEAT NG10 76 B2
Glenfield Rd East LEIW LE3 131 G2
Glenfields RLBORO LE12 101 L4
Glenfrith Cl LEIW LE3 124 D5
RLBORO LE12 113 K6
Glenfrith Wy LEIW LE3 124 D5
Glengarry Cl LEIW LE3 124 E8
Glengarry Ct LEIW LE3 124 D8
Glengarry Wy DERBYSE DE24 71 H3
LEIW LE3 124 D7
Glen Ga WGSTN LE18 137 K5
Glen Helen CARL NG4 52 D1
Glenhills Bvd LEIS LE2 137 H2
Glenhills Wy LEIS LE2 137 H2
Glenlivet Gdns CFTN/RUD NG11 64 D6
Glenloch Dr CFTN/RUD NG11 64 D7
Glenmore Av RLBORO LE12 101 L3
Glenmore Dr DERBYSE DE24 71 H3
Glenmore Rd LEIN LE4 126 B4
WBRGFD NG2 65 M1
Glenmoy Cl NORM/LIT DE23 57 H8
Glenn Wy BWSH/BRSTN DE72 74 C6
Glenorchy Ct DERBYE DE21 44 F4
Glenorchy Crs ARN NG5 24 C7
Glen Park Av LEIW LE3 123 M5
Glen Park Cl MELB/CHEL DE73 72 D7
Glen Parva Av ARN NG5 25 J6
Glenridding Cl WBRGFD NG2 66 B2
Glen Ri LEIS LE2 136 F4
RLEIW/BBY LE8 139 J5
Glen Rd CALV/BJ NG14 39 J2
LEIS LE2 138 F2
RLEIW/BBY LE8 139 H8
Glenrothes Cl LEIW LE3 130 A2
Glensford Gdns ARN NG5 24 C6
Glenside ARN NG5 37 M2
Glenside Rd BSTN/STPLFD NG9 49 G5
Glenstone Ct NOTTE NG7 4 A1
Glen St LEIN LE4 125 M6
Glentworth Rd NOTTE NG7 50 C1
Glen Vw BPR/DUF DE56 17 K5
Glenville Av LEIS LE2 136 F5
LEIW LE3 124 A5
Glen Vine RIPLEY DE5 11 L6
Glen Wy COAL LE67 108 E8
LEIS LE2 139 G3
Glenwood Av WOL/BIL/BRX NG8 49 H3
Glenwood Rd MELB/CHEL DE73 72 E7
Glins Rd ARN NG5 24 D7
Glossop St DERBYSE DE24 57 M8
LEIS LE2 7 M9
Gloster St DERBYSE DE24 58 C5
Gloucester Av
BSTN/STPLFD NG9 63 J2
EWD/SEL/PNX NG16 35 K3
LGEAT NG10 61 L3
NOTTE NG7 50 C3
RLEINE/SYS LE7 121 G3
Gloucester Crs WGSTN LE18 137 K4
Glover Av WOL/BIL/BRX NG8 49 H3
Goathland Cl ARN NG5 24 F7
Goathland Rd DERBYSE DE24 71 H5
Godber Rd HUCK/RAV NG15 23 J2
Goddard Cl RLEINE/SYS LE7 133 L2
Goddards Cl LEIN LE4 124 F5
WGSTN LE18 144 E4
Godfrey Cl LEIN LE4 124 E1
Godfrey Dr ILK DE7 47 G1
Godfrey St CARL NG4 52 E1
HEANOR DE75 20 C6
Godkin Dr EWD/SEL/PNX NG16 20 E3
Godwin Av WGSTN LE18 138 C5
Godwin Ct WGSTN * LE18 138 B5
Goldcrest Dr DERBYE DE21 59 K1
Goldcrest Rd BLWL NG6 35 M4
Golden Sq RLBORO LE12 94 E7
Golden Va ILK DE7 18 F8
Goldhill WGSTN LE18 137 L3
Goldhill Rd LEIS LE2 132 B8
Golding Cl LBORO LE11 102 F1
Gold La DERBYW DE22 42 C7
Goldsmith Rd LEIW LE3 130 E3
Goldsmith St NOTT NG1 4 F5
Goldstone Ct DERBYE DE21 59 J3
Goldswong Ter
MAPPK/POR/STA NG3 5 H2
Golf Cl NORM/LIT DE23 56 E6
Golf Club Rd ILK DE7 47 L6
Golf Course La LEIW LE3 130 A2
Golf Course Rd
COT/KEY/RAD NG12 80 F5
Golf La BPR/DUF DE56 29 J2
Golf Rd COT/KEY/RAD NG12 53 L4
Goliath Rd COAL LE67 108 B5
Gonalston La CALV/BJ NG14 27 M3
Goodale St NORM/LIT DE23 57 L6
Goodall Crs HUCK/RAV NG15 24 A1
Goodall St NOTTE NG7 4 A2
Goode's Av RLEINE/SYS LE7 120 F5
Goode's La RLEINE/SYS LE7 120 E4
Gooding Av LEIW LE3 130 D4
Gooding Cl LEIW LE3 130 F4
Goodliffe St NOTTE NG7 36 D7
Goodman Cl
EWD/SEL/PNX NG16 22 A7
Goodrington Rd DERBYE DE21 45 G4
Goodsmoor Rd DERBYSE DE24 71 J2
Goods Rd BPR/DUF DE56 17 K5
Goods Yd BPR/DUF DE56 17 K6
Goodwin Cl LGEAT NG10 61 L1
Goodwin Dr
EWD/SEL/PNX NG16 34 B1
Goodwin's La BPR/DUF DE56 17 G6
Goodwin St NOTTE NG7 4 D4
Goodwood Av ARN NG5 25 J7
Goodwood Crs ILK DE7 47 H3
LEIE LE5 132 F3
Goodwood Dr
BSTN/STPLFD NG9 62 D5
DERBYSE DE24 73 G1
Goodwood Rd LEIE LE5 132 F2
WOL/BIL/BRX NG8 49 H3
Goole Av ILK DE7 47 H2
Goose Ga NOTT NG1 5 J7
Goose La EWD/SEL/PNX NG16 12 B7
Gopsall St LEIS LE2 7 K8
Gordon Av LEIS LE2 7 K9
Gordon Cl BSTN/STPLFD NG9 63 H5
Gordon Ri MAPPK/POR/STA NG3 37 J5
Gordon Rd BWSH/BRSTN DE72 59 M6
CALV/BJ NG14 39 L2
LBORO LE11 103 M1
MAPPK/POR/STA NG3 51 K1
NORM/LIT DE23 2 D7
WBRGFD NG2 51 K8
Gordon St ILK DE7 33 K6
Gorham Ri RLEIW/BAR LE9 141 H8
Gorman Ct ARN NG5 25 M8
Gorse Cl EWD/SEL/PNX NG16 21 M6
LGEAT NG10 61 M5
NORM/LIT DE23 70 F1
Gorse Ct ARN NG5 36 C2
Gorse Hl LEIN LE4 124 D2
Gorse La LEIS LE2 139 H4
RLEINE/SYS LE7 120 D4
Gorse Rd COT/KEY/RAD NG12 80 B4
Gorsey Cl BPR/DUF DE56 17 J1
Gorsey Rd
MAPPK/POR/STA NG3 5 J1
Gorsty Cl LEIN LE4 124 F4
Gorsty Leys RDERBYSW DE65 70 B6
Goscote Hall Rd LEIN LE4 125 K1
Gosforth Rd DERBYSE DE24 58 C8
Goshawk Cl RLEIW/BAR LE9 141 J8
Goshawk Rd ILK DE7 47 L4
Gosling St LEIS LE2 6 D8
Gotham La CFTN/RUD NG11 78 F8
Gotham Rd CFTN/RUD NG11 86 E3
RLBORO LE12 88 C3
Gotham St LEIS LE2 7 J8
Gothic Cl BLWL NG6 36 C3
Gough Rd LEIE LE5 132 C1
Goverton Sq BLWL NG6 36 B2
Gowan Cl BSTN/STPLFD NG9 63 G5
Gower St DERBY DE1 2 E5
LEI LE1 7 G3
Goyden Cl ARN NG5 24 E7
Grace Av BSTN/STPLFD NG9 63 M2
Grace Crs HEANOR DE75 20 D6
Gracedieu La RLBORO LE12 100 D5
Grace Dieu Rd COAL LE67 100 B8
Gracedieu Rd LBORO LE11 8 A4
Grace Dr WOL/BIL/BRX NG8 36 B7
Grace Gdns LEIS * LE2 131 J8
Grace Rd LEIS LE2 131 J7
RLEIW/BAR LE9 140 C7
Grafham Cl MELB/CHEL DE73 72 E5
Grafton Av ARN NG5 37 J2
Grafton Ct NOTTE NG7 4 C6
Grafton Dr WGSTN LE18 138 D5
Grafton Pl LEI LE1 6 E3
Grafton Rd LBORO LE11 103 J1
Grafton St NORM/LIT DE23 57 J5
Graham Ri LBORO LE11 103 H1
Graham St ILK DE7 33 K8
LEIE LE5 7 J4
NOTTE NG7 4 A5
Grainger Av WBRGFD NG2 65 J4
Grainger St WBRGFD NG2 51 J5
Grammer St RIPLEY DE5 19 L3
Grampian Cl LEIS LE2 131 K8
Grampian Dr ARN NG5 24 F5
Grampian Wy DERBYSE DE24 71 H4
LGEAT NG10 61 L7
Granary Cl LEIW LE3 123 M8
RLEIW/BBY LE8 146 E8
Granby Av LEIE * LE5 132 B1
Granby Rd LEIS LE2 131 H8
Granby St ILK DE7 33 J5
LBORO LE11 9 H3
LEI LE1 6 F6
Granby Vls WBRGFD * NG2 51 K3
Grandfield Av
COT/KEY/RAD NG12 53 K3
Grandfield Crs
COT/KEY/RAD NG12 53 K3
Grandfield St HEANOR DE75 20 A3
Grandstand Rd DERBYE DE21 3 K1
The Grange HEANOR DE75 20 A7
Grange Av BSTN/STPLFD NG9 63 K1
BWSH/BRSTN DE72 61 H7
CFTN/RUD NG11 64 F7
LEIW LE3 129 L4
NORM/LIT DE23 57 J8
RLEINE/SYS LE7 115 K7
Grange Cl CARL NG4 27 G8
CFTN/RUD NG11 50 F7
GBY/RBY LE6 123 H7
LEIW LE3 123 M7
MELB/CHEL DE73 82 F7
RLEIW/BBY LE8 139 M6
Grange Ct CFTN/RUD NG11 65 G5
Grange Crs CARL NG4 38 D5
Grange Dr CDON/KEG DE74 84 E4
LEIS LE2 136 F4
LGEAT NG10 62 D7
RLEIW/BBY LE8 136 D7
Grange Farm WBRGFD NG2 52 A8
Grange Farm Cl
BSTN/STPLFD NG9 62 E6
CDON/KEG DE74 85 G2
Grangefields Dr
RLEINE/SYS LE7 119 K1
Grange La LEIS LE2 6 E8
RLBORO LE12 113 H7
RLEINE/SYS LE7 133 J3
Grangelea Gdns
BSTN/STPLFD NG9 48 F8
Grange Pk WBRGFD NG2 66 A2
Grange Rd ARN NG5 37 J3
BLWL NG6 36 B4
COT/KEY/RAD NG12 65 L3
DERBYSE DE24 72 F2
LGEAT NG10 62 D7
RLBORO LE12 101 L4
WGSTN LE18 138 B3
Grange St LBORO LE11 9 G1
NORM/LIT DE23 3 H9
Grange Vw EWD/SEL/PNX NG16 21 K4
Grange View Rd CARL NG4 38 D5
Grangeway Rd WGSTN LE18 138 A3
Grangewood Av ILK DE7 33 K8
Grangewood Dr BPR/DUF DE56 17 L8
Grangewood Rd
WOL/BIL/BRX NG8 49 G4
Granite Cl END/NAR LE19 135 L3
Granite Wy RLBORO LE12 113 H3
Grannis Dr WOL/BIL/BRX NG8 35 L7
Grant Av DERBYE DE21 58 F2
Grantham Av DERBYE DE21 44 C6
RLEIW/BAR LE9 141 H7
Grantham Cl
EWD/SEL/PNX NG16 22 A8
Grantham Rd
COT/KEY/RAD NG12 53 G6
COT/KEY/RAD NG12 53 L4
LEIE LE5 127 G7
Granton Av CFTN/RUD NG11 64 D7
Grant St NOTTE NG7 4 B5
Granville Av LEIS LE2 138 D1
LGEAT NG10 62 B6
Granville Cl BPR/DUF DE56 29 J5
Granville Ct
MAPPK/POR/STA * NG3 51 K2
Granville Crs
COT/KEY/RAD NG12 53 J5
WGSTN LE18 137 M2
Granville Rd LEI LE1 131 M4
WGSTN LE18 138 A2
Granville St DERBY DE1 2 A4
LBORO LE11 9 G3
Grape St LEI LE1 6 D4
Grasmere COAL LE67 108 F5
Grasmere Av DERBYE DE21 59 J1
Grasmere Cl HUCK/RAV NG15 15 K7
RLBORO LE12 105 H7
Grasmere Crs DERBYSE DE24 71 J3
Grasmere Gdns
CFTN/RUD NG11 77 M5
Grasmere Rd
BSTN/STPLFD NG9 49 H7
LBORO LE11 103 K8
LGEAT NG10 61 M6
WGSTN LE18 138 D4
Grasmere St LEIS LE2 6 C9
LGEAT NG10 61 M2
Grasmoor Cl
MAPPK/POR/STA NG3 37 J7
Grass Acres LEIW LE3 130 C8
Grassholme Dr LBORO LE11 102 E4
Grassingdale Cl CARL NG4 38 B5
Grassington Cl LEIN LE4 125 G3
Grassington Dr WGSTN LE18 138 C6
Grassington Rd
WOL/BIL/BRX NG8 50 B1
Grassmere COT/KEY/RAD NG12 67 L4
Grass St ILK DE7 33 J4
Grassthorpe Cl DERBYE DE21 44 F6
Grassy La BSTN/STPLFD NG9 63 L2
RDERBYSW DE65 55 L8
Gravel Pit La DERBYE DE21 59 J3
Gravel St LEI LE1 6 E4
Graylands Rd WOL/BIL/BRX NG8 49 J1
Grayling St NORM/LIT DE23 3 H9
Grays Ct END/NAR LE19 135 L4
Graystones Cl WBRGFD NG2 66 A2
Gray St LBORO LE11 9 J6
LEIS LE2 6 C8
Grayswood Dr LEIN LE4 118 E8
Grazingfield CFTN/RUD NG11 64 E3
Greasley Av
EWD/SEL/PNX NG16 22 A5
Greasley St BLWL NG6 35 M1
Great Arler Rd LEIS LE2 131 L7
Great Central Rd LBORO LE11 9 L4
Great Central St LEIW LE3 6 C4
Great Central Wy LEIW LE3 131 H5
Great Freeman St
MAPPK/POR/STA NG3 5 H4
Great Hoggett Dr
BSTN/STPLFD NG9 62 E1
Great Meadow Rd LEIN LE4 124 F5
The Great Northern Cl
WBRGFD NG2 5 K9
Great Northern Rd DERBY DE1 2 A4
EWD/SEL/PNX NG16 21 H5
Great Northern Wy CARL NG4 52 F1
Greatorex Av DERBYSE DE24 72 C2
Greaves Cl ARN NG5 37 M2
WOL/BIL/BRX NG8 35 H6
Greaves St RIPLEY DE5 11 H5
Grebe Cl RLBORO LE12 105 J7
Grebe Wy RLEIW/BBY LE8 142 D3
Greedon Ri RLBORO LE12 114 A3
Greek St NOTTE NG7 4 C6
The Green ASHB DE6 41 G6
BSTN/STPLFD NG9 63 J3
BWSH/BRSTN DE72 73 M8
CALV/BJ NG14 27 K5
CDON/KEG DE74 84 E4
CDON/KEG DE74 92 F2
CFTN/RUD NG11 79 G1
COAL LE67 100 B8
COAL LE67 116 B7
COT/KEY/RAD NG12 53 J4
DERBYW DE22 43 H6
MCKLVR DE3 56 B6
RDERBYSW DE65 70 B6
RLBORO LE12 88 C6
RLBORO LE12 94 A4
RLBORO LE12 94 E6
RLEINE/SYS LE7 115 K3
RLEIW/BAR LE9 135 H8
RLEIW/BAR LE9 141 G2
Green Acre COT/KEY/RAD NG12 65 M3
Greenacre WOL/BIL/BRX NG8 48 F2
Greenacre Av HEANOR DE75 20 E4
Greenacre Dr LEIE LE5 132 F3
Greenacres NORM/LIT DE23 56 F7
Greenacres Cl
EWD/SEL/PNX NG16 22 A5
Green Av CARL NG4 38 E8
MELB/CHEL DE73 72 E6

Greenbank CARL NG4 52 B1
DERBYE DE21 59 H3
Greenbank Dr LEIS LE2 138 F2
Greenbank Rd LEIE LE5 127 H6
Greenburn Cl NORM/LIT DE23 71 G1
WBRGFD NG2 66 A1
Green Cl COT/KEY/RAD NG12 80 D3
HUCK/RAV NG15 24 A2
Greenclose La LBORO LE11 9 H3
Greencoat Rd LEIW LE3 124 C8
Green Crs EWD/SEL/PNX NG16 13 J1
Greencroft CFTN/RUD NG11 64 D5
Greendale Gdns
WOL/BIL/BRX NG8 35 M7
Greendale Rd ARN NG5 37 K1
LEIS LE2 136 F4
MAPPK/POR/STA NG3 52 A1
Green Farm Rd
EWD/SEL/PNX NG16 13 H1
Greenfield Gv CARL NG4 38 A7
Greenfields
EWD/SEL/PNX NG16 20 E3
RLEIW/BBY LE8 136 D8
Greenfields Av NORM/LIT DE23 56 F8
Greenfields Dr COAL LE67 108 E6
COT/KEY/RAD NG12 67 K5
Greenfield St NOTTE NG7 50 B6
Greenfinch Cl DERBYE DE21 59 K1
Greenford Cl WOL/BIL/BRX NG8 35 J4
Greengate La LEIN LE4 119 J8
Greengates Av
MAPPK/POR/STA NG3 37 K4
Green Hl RLBORO LE12 94 E6
Greenhill Av RIPLEY DE5 11 J7
Greenhill Cl END/NAR LE19 135 K8
Greenhill Crs CARL NG4 52 C1
Greenhill Ri CARL NG4 38 C8
Green Hill Ri RLBORO LE12 94 E5
Greenhill Rd CARL NG4 52 C1
COAL LE67 108 F6
LEIS LE2 131 M6
Greenhills Av
EWD/SEL/PNX NG16 21 L4
Greenhills Rd
EWD/SEL/PNX NG16 21 K4
Greenhithe Rd LEIS LE2 131 H6
Greenland Av DERBYW DE22 56 F2
LEIE LE5 126 E7
Greenland Crs
BSTN/STPLFD NG9 63 G3
Greenland Dr LEIE LE5 126 E7
Green La BPR/DUF DE56 17 K3
BWSH/BRSTN DE72 60 A2
CARL NG4 26 F6
CDON/KEG DE74 92 F1
CFTN/RUD NG11 64 B5
COAL LE67 108 C4
DERBY DE1 2 E5
DERBYSE DE24 59 G7
ILK DE7 33 L8
RDERBYSW DE65 69 K3
RLBORO LE12 106 D6
RLEIW/BBY LE8 143 K3
Green Lane Cl LEIE LE5 132 D1
RLBORO LE12 106 D7
Green Lane Rd LEIE LE5 126 B8
Green Leas BWSH/BRSTN DE72 73 L7
Green Leys WBRGFD NG2 65 G3
Greenmount Cl NORM/LIT DE23 70 E1
Green Pk DERBYW DE22 56 E1
Green Platt COT/KEY/RAD NG12 67 J5
Green Rd RLEIW/BAR LE9 141 J8
Green's Farm La CARL NG4 38 E5
Greenside Cl LGEAT NG10 62 C8
Greenside Ct MCKLVR DE3 56 A5
Greenside Pl WGSTN LE18 137 K2
Greens La EWD/SEL/PNX NG16 34 E1
Green St CFTN/RUD NG11 77 K2
WBRGFD NG2 51 H6
Greensward RLEINE/SYS LE7 115 J7
Green Wk LEIW LE3 130 C2
The Greenway DERBYSE DE24 73 H2
LEIN LE4 125 L5
LGEAT NG10 61 M1
Green Wy RDERBYSW DE65 70 B5
Greenway RLEIW/BBY LE8 146 E7
Greenway Cl
BWSH/BRSTN DE72 59 M4
COT/KEY/RAD NG12 53 H4
RLEINE/SYS LE7 119 J1
Greenway Dr NORM/LIT DE23 56 E6
Greenwich Av BLWL NG6 36 A4
Greenwich Cl END/NAR LE19 135 M7
Greenwich Dr North
DERBYW DE22 56 F2
Greenwich Dr South
DERBYW DE22 56 E2
Greenwich Park Cl
WBRGFD * NG2 65 G2
Greenwood Av DERBYE DE21 44 D7
HUCK/RAV NG15 15 K7
ILK DE7 33 L8
MAPPK/POR/STA NG3 52 B2
Greenwood Cl DERBYSE DE24 72 B2
Greenwood Crs CARL NG4 52 B1
Greenwood Gdns
CFTN/RUD NG11 79 H1
Greenwood Rd LEIE LE5 132 D1
MAPPK/POR/STA NG3 51 L2
Greenwood V HUCK/RAV NG15 15 J7
Greetwell Cl WOL/BIL/BRX NG8 49 L1
Gregg Av HEANOR DE75 20 C5
The Gregory NOTTE * NG7 50 C5
Gregory Av BWSH/BRSTN DE72 61 G7
EWD/SEL/PNX NG16 20 E4
MAPPK/POR/STA NG3 37 L5
NOTTE NG7 4 A9
Gregory Bvd NOTTE NG7 4 B2
Gregory Cl BSTN/STPLFD NG9 48 D6
LEIN LE4 120 E8
Gregory Ct BSTN/STPLFD NG9 62 F3
NOTTE NG7 50 C4
Gregorys Cl LEIW LE3 130 B6
Gregory St ILK DE7 33 J6
LBORO LE11 9 K4
NOTTE NG7 50 C4
Gregorys Wy BPR/DUF DE56 18 A2
Gregson Cl LEIN LE4 126 B2
Gregson Gdns
BSTN/STPLFD NG9 62 F6
Gregson Rd BSTN/STPLFD NG9 62 F5
Grendon Cl BPR/DUF DE56 17 M1
WGSTN LE18 138 C4
Grenfell Av NORM/LIT DE23 71 J1
Grenfell Rd LEIS LE2 132 C8
Grenville Dr BSTN/STPLFD NG9 48 C7
ILK DE7 33 K4
Grenville Ri ARN NG5 25 K6
Grenville Rd BSTN/STPLFD NG9 63 M3
Grenvoir Dr RIPLEY DE5 11 L6
Gresham Cl WBRGFD NG2 51 G8
Gresham Gdns ARN NG5 37 L2
WBRGFD NG2 51 H8
Gresham Rd DERBYSE DE24 58 A7
Gresley Cl LEIN LE4 125 G3
RLEINE/SYS LE7 133 K1
Gresley Dr WBRGFD NG2 51 K4
Gresley Rd ILK DE7 33 K6
Gressy Rd CFTN/RUD NG11 64 D5
Gretna Wy LEIE LE5 127 J8
Gretton Rd
MAPPK/POR/STA NG3 37 L3
Grey Cl GBY/RBY LE6 123 K4
Grey Crs GBY/RBY LE6 117 H6
Greyfriar Ga NOTT NG1 5 G9
Grey Friars LEI LE1 6 E6
Greyhound St NOTT NG1 5 H7
Greylag Wy RLEIW/BBY LE8 142 D3
Greyland Paddock
GBY/RBY LE6 123 K4
Greys Dr GBY/RBY LE6 123 J5
Greys Rd ARN NG5 37 K3
Greystoke Cl LEIN LE4 125 J4
Greystoke Dr WOL/BIL/BRX NG8 49 G1
Greystone Av LEIE LE5 132 F1
Grey St DERBYW DE22 2 D6
EWD/SEL/PNX NG16 21 L6
Greythorn Dr WBRGFD NG2 65 H3
Grierson Av ARN NG5 24 F7
Griffin Cl DERBYSE DE24 58 D8
LEIN LE4 126 D2
RLBORO LE12 101 L4
Griffon Rd ILK DE7 47 K3
Griffs Hollow CARL NG4 38 C8
Griggs Rd LBORO LE11 103 M7
Grimes Ga CDON/KEG DE74 85 G8
Grimsby Ter
MAPPK/POR/STA NG3 5 H4
Grimshaw Av DERBYSE DE24 58 F8
Grimston Cl LEIN LE4 126 E3
Grimston Rd NOTTE NG7 50 C1
Grindlow Rd DERBYE DE21 44 E7
Grindon Crs BLWL NG6 24 A5
Grindslow Av ILK DE7 32 C7
Grinsbrook NOTTE NG7 50 C3
Gripps Common
COT/KEY/RAD NG12 67 K6
Grisedale Cl LEIS LE2 131 J4
Grisedale Ct BSTN/STPLFD NG9 62 E3
Gritley Ms WBRGFD NG2 50 F5
Grizedale Gv END/NAR LE19 135 K6
Groby La GBY/RBY LE6 117 H8
Groby Rd GBY/RBY LE6 123 H6
LEIW LE3 123 M4
RLEINE/SYS LE7 124 A2
Grocot Rd LEIE LE5 132 E4
Groombridge Crs
NORM/LIT DE23 70 E1
Groome Av HEANOR DE75 20 A3
The Grove BWSH/BRSTN DE72 61 K7
MCKLVR DE3 56 C5
NOTTE NG7 4 B3
RIPLEY * DE5 11 H7
Grosvenor Av
BWSH/BRSTN DE72 61 K7
LGEAT NG10 75 L3
MAPPK/POR/STA NG3 37 G7
Grosvenor Cl LEIS LE2 137 H6
Grosvenor Crs LEIS LE2 132 D8
Grosvenor Dr NORM/LIT DE23 70 E1
Grosvenor Rd
EWD/SEL/PNX NG16 21 K4
RIPLEY DE5 11 H6
Grosvenor St DERBYSE DE24 58 A6
LEI LE1 7 G3
Grouville Dr ARN NG5 37 L2
Grove Av BSTN/STPLFD NG9 63 J1
NOTTE NG7 4 C3
Grove Bank DERBY * DE1 43 K8
Grovebury Dr NORM/LIT DE23 71 G2
Grovebury Rd LEIN LE4 125 J4
Grove Cl BWSH/BRSTN DE72 73 K3
CALV/BJ NG14 39 K2
Grove Ct RIPLEY DE5 11 K7
Grove La RLBORO LE12 105 H8
Grove Pk RDERBYSW DE65 68 F5
Grove Av MAPPK/POR/STA NG3 37 L4
Grove Rd COAL LE67 108 C3
LBORO LE11 8 D4
LEIE LE5 7 L4
NOTTE NG7 50 D4
RLEIW/BBY LE8 142 D1
Groveside Crs CFTN/RUD NG11 64 A4
Groves Nook MELB/CHEL DE73 72 C6
Grove St BSTN/STPLFD NG9 63 L2
NORM/LIT DE23 2 F8
Grove Wy END/NAR LE19 136 D2
Grundy St NOTTE NG7 36 C8
Guild Cl RLEINE/SYS LE7 118 D4
Guildford Dr WGSTN LE18 137 M2
Guildford Rd LEIS LE2 132 C6
Guildford Wy LBORO LE11 103 G7
Guildhall La LEI LE1 6 D6
Guilford St LEIS LE2 7 L9
Guinea Cl LGEAT NG10 61 L8
Guinevere Wy LEIW LE3 129 L5
Gullet La RLEIW/BAR LE9 129 G2
Gumley Sq END/NAR LE19 135 M4
Gunhills La BPR/DUF DE56 28 C1
Gunn Cl BLWL NG6 23 L8
Gunnersbury Wy
WOL/BIL/BRX NG8 35 H4
Gunthorpe Cl ARN NG5 36 F4
Gunthorpe Dr ARN NG5 37 G3
Gunthorpe Rd CARL NG4 38 B4
LEIW LE3 130 B3
Gurnall Rd LEIN LE4 124 E3
Gurney Av NORM/LIT DE23 71 H1
Gurney Crs END/NAR LE19 142 A1
Guthlaxton Av LEIS LE2 7 J7
Guthlaxton Gap
RLEIW/BAR LE9 141 J3
Guthlaxton St LEIS LE2 7 K7
Guthlaxton Wy WGSTN LE18 138 C7
Guthridge Crs LEIW LE3 130 F4
Gutteridge St COAL LE67 108 A6
Guy Cl BSTN/STPLFD NG9 62 C1
Gwenbrook Av
BSTN/STPLFD NG9 63 J2
Gwenbrook Rd
BSTN/STPLFD NG9 63 H2
Gwencole Av LEIW LE3 130 E7
Gwencole Crs LEIW LE3 130 E8
Gwendolen Rd LEIE LE5 132 B2
Gwendolin Av LEIN LE4 119 M8
Gwendoline Dr RLEIW/BBY LE8 143 H3
Gynsill Cl RLEINE/SYS LE7 124 C2
Gynsill La RLEINE/SYS LE7 124 B4
Gypsum Wy CFTN/RUD NG11 77 L8
Gypsy La BWSH/BRSTN DE72 60 C7

H

Hackett Rd LEIW LE3 124 D7
Hackworth Cl
EWD/SEL/PNX NG16 21 M4
Hadbury Rd ARN NG5 36 D5
Haddenham Rd LEIW LE3 131 G5
Haddon Cl CARL NG4 38 B5
DERBYW DE22 43 H4
ILK DE7 32 C7
RLEINE/SYS LE7 120 D4
Haddon Crs BSTN/STPLFD NG9 63 G5
Haddon Dr DERBYE DE21 59 K3
DERBYW DE22 43 H4
MCKLVR DE3 56 C4
Haddon Nurseries ILK DE7 33 J5
Haddon Rd WBRGFD NG2 65 K1
Haddon St ARN NG5 36 F5
ILK DE7 33 J4
LEIS LE2 7 M5
NORM/LIT DE23 57 J6
Haddon Wy COT/KEY/RAD NG12 53 L3
LGEAT NG10 75 K3
RLBORO LE12 111 L1
Hades La RLBORO LE12 99 G1
RLBORO LE12 99 K5
Hadleigh Cl BSTN/STPLFD NG9 62 C5
Hadley St ILK DE7 47 L2
Hadrian Cl RLEINE/SYS LE7 120 C5
Hadrian Gdns ARN NG5 24 E5
Hadrian Rd LEIN LE4 120 C8
LEIN LE4 125 H2
Hadstock Cl LGEAT NG10 61 M3
Hagg La CALV/BJ NG14 27 M1
ILK DE7 46 B3
Hag La BPR/DUF DE56 16 A5
Hagley Cl MAPPK/POR/STA NG3 51 L1
Haig Pl LEIW * LE3 130 E5
Haig St DERBYSE DE24 58 D7
Hailey Av LBORO LE11 103 G2
Haileybury Crs WBRGFD NG2 65 K3
Haileybury Rd WBRGFD NG2 65 K2
Hailsham Cl MCKLVR DE3 56 B4
Haines Cl DERBYSE DE24 71 K3
Haise Ct BLWL NG6 35 K2
Halberton Dr WBRGFD NG2 65 H3
Halcroft Ri WGSTN LE18 138 B6
Hales Cl COT/KEY/RAD NG12 67 J4
Haley Cl EWD/SEL/PNX NG16 34 B1
The Half Cft RLEINE/SYS LE7 120 E3
Half Moon Crs LEIS LE2 139 G1
Halford Cl RLEIW/BBY LE8 139 M7
RLEIW/BBY LE8 142 D1
Halford Rd RLEIW/BBY LE8 146 D7
Halford St LEI LE1 6 F6
RLEINE/SYS LE7 120 E4
Halifax Cl RDERBYSW DE65 68 C5
Halifax Ct WOL/BIL/BRX NG8 35 H5
Halifax Dr LEIN LE4 125 J4
Halifax Pl NOTT NG1 5 J8
Halkin St LEIN LE4 125 M6
Hallam Av LEIN LE4 119 K8
Hallam Crs East LEIW LE3 130 D5
Hallam Flds CDON/KEG DE74 84 F5
Hallam Fields Rd ILK DE7 47 L3
Hallamford Rd RLBORO LE12 93 K8
Hallam Rd BSTN/STPLFD NG9 63 K1
MAPPK/POR/STA NG3 37 L5
Hallam's La ARN NG5 25 K8
BSTN/STPLFD NG9 63 H2
Hallam Wy ILK DE7 32 B7
Hallaton Rd LEIE LE5 126 D7
Hallaton St LEIS LE2 131 J8
Hall Cl COT/KEY/RAD NG12 53 J4
LEIS LE2 136 F4
RLBORO LE12 114 B7
RLEIW/BBY LE8 146 D6
Hall Ct ILK DE7 47 L1
Hall Cft BSTN/STPLFD NG9 63 K1
RLBORO LE12 101 M3
Hallcroft Av RLEIW/BBY LE8 143 J4
Hallcroft Rd ILK DE7 33 K7
Hall Dr BSTN/STPLFD NG9 63 H2
CFTN/RUD NG11 77 L6
LEIS LE2 138 F1
LGEAT NG10 61 M1
RLBORO LE12 97 K8
WOL/BIL/BRX NG8 49 K3
Hall Dyke DERBYE DE21 59 J2
Halley Cl LEIN LE4 124 E1
Hall Farm Cl CDON/KEG DE74 84 E4
COT/KEY/RAD * NG12 66 B6
RLEINE/SYS LE7 121 K2
Hall Farm Rd BPR/DUF DE56 29 J5
RLEINE/SYS LE7 118 F5
Hallfields COT/KEY/RAD NG12 65 M4
Hallfields La RLEINE/SYS LE7 119 J2
Hall Gdns BSTN/STPLFD NG9 48 F8
RLBORO LE12 88 D7
RLEIW/BBY LE8 139 M7
Hall Ga CDON/KEG DE74 93 G1
COAL LE67 109 G7
Hallgate Cl DERBYE DE21 45 G4
Hallington Dr HEANOR DE75 20 B6
Hall La ASHB DE6 40 E1
BPR/DUF DE56 10 A4
COAL LE67 108 D3
EWD/SEL/PNX NG16 13 H8
LEIS LE2 131 G8
Hall Leys RLBORO LE12 112 E2
Hall Leys La MELB/CHEL DE73 83 H6
Hall Park Cl NORM/LIT DE23 56 F6
Hall Rd EWD/SEL/PNX NG16 21 G3
RLEINE/SYS LE7 127 K7
Halls Brook RLBORO LE12 88 C5
Halls La EWD/SEL/PNX NG16 21 L7
Halls Rd BSTN/STPLFD NG9 62 A1
Hall St ARN NG5 37 H4
DERBYSE DE24 58 E8
Hall View Dr WOL/BIL/BRX NG8 49 H1
Hall Wk END/NAR LE19 135 M3
Halsbury St LEIS LE2 132 B4
Halstead Cl BSTN/STPLFD NG9 63 G3
WOL/BIL/BRX NG8 35 M4
Halstead Rd RLBORO LE12 113 H6
Halstead St LEIE LE5 132 B1
Halstock Dr DERBYSE DE24 59 G7
Halter Slade WGSTN LE18 138 C6
Hambledon Crs LBORO LE11 103 K7
Hambledon Dr DERBYSE DE24 71 H5
WOL/BIL/BRX NG8 49 M2
Hamble Rd LEIS LE2 139 G1
Hambleton Cl LEIW LE3 129 K5
LGEAT NG10 61 L6
Hamblin Crs DERBYSE DE24 71 K3
Hambling Cl BLWL NG6 23 L8
Hamelin Rd LEIW LE3 130 D3
Hamilford Cl LEIE LE5 127 J6
The Hamilton NOTTE * NG7 50 C5
Hamilton Cl ARN NG5 26 A6
BSTN/STPLFD NG9 62 D5
MCKLVR DE3 56 D4
Hamilton Dr
COT/KEY/RAD NG12 53 K3
NOTTE NG7 4 E9
Hamilton La RLEINE/SYS LE7 127 J4
Hamilton Rd ARN NG5 36 F7
COAL LE67 109 G7
DERBYE DE21 59 K1
LGEAT NG10 62 B7
NORM/LIT DE23 2 C9
Hamilton St LEIS LE2 7 K9
Hamilton Wy LEIE LE5 126 F5
The Hamlet HEANOR DE75 20 C5
Hammercliffe Rd LEIE LE5 7 M1
Hammersmith RIPLEY DE5 11 H4
Hammersmith Cl
EWD/SEL/PNX NG16 35 J3
Hampden Gv BSTN/STPLFD NG9 63 J1
Hampden Rd LEIN LE4 126 C5
Hampden St
EWD/SEL/PNX NG16 21 M7
NORM/LIT DE23 57 L7
NOTT NG1 4 F4
Hampshire Ct
EWD/SEL/PNX NG16 12 F3
Hampshire Dr LGEAT NG10 61 M2
Hampshire Rd DERBYE DE21 44 A7
LEIS LE2 131 H8
Hampstead Cl END/NAR LE19 135 M7
Hampstead Dr DERBYW DE22 56 E1
Hampstead Rd
MAPPK/POR/STA NG3 37 J6
Hampton Cl BSTN/STPLFD NG9 62 C4
DERBYE DE21 59 K2
ILK DE7 32 B8
LEIS LE2 137 H6
WGSTN LE18 138 C5
Hampton Ct HEANOR DE75 20 B5
Hampton Rd WBRGFD NG2 65 J1
Hanbury Rd DERBYE DE21 58 C1
LEIE LE5 133 H3
Hand Av LEIW LE3 130 C4
Handel St DERBYSE DE24 58 A7
MAPPK/POR/STA NG3 5 L6
Handford Ct DERBYW * DE22 57 H2
Handford St DERBYW DE22 57 H2
Handley St LEIS LE2 131 J8
Hand's Rd HEANOR DE75 20 D6
Handyside St DERBY DE1 2 E1
Hanford Wy LBORO LE11 103 M2
Hanger Bank
BWSH/BRSTN DE72 73 M7
Hankin Av EWD/SEL/PNX NG16 13 L5
Hankin St HUCK/RAV NG15 24 A1
Hanley Av BSTN/STPLFD NG9 48 F7
Hanley St NOTT NG1 4 F6
Hannah Crs CFTN/RUD NG11 50 F8
Hanover Cl LEIE LE5 126 F6
Hanover Dr RLBORO LE12 114 B4
Hanover Sq DERBYW DE22 56 E1
Hansard Ga DERBYE DE21 3 J3
Hansen Ct WGSTN LE18 137 L5
Hanslope Crs WOL/BIL/BRX NG8 35 H8
Hanslynn BWSH/BRSTN DE72 73 K3
Hanson Crs HUCK/RAV NG15 15 L8
Hanstubbin Rd
EWD/SEL/PNX NG16 13 K1
Hanwell Wy DERBYW DE22 56 F1
Hanworth Gdns ARN NG5 25 H7
Haramead Rd LEI LE1 7 K3
Harberton Cl ARN NG5 25 J6
Harborough Rd LEIS LE2 138 F2
RLEIW/BBY LE8 146 F7
Harby Dr WOL/BIL/BRX NG8 50 A3
Harcourt Cl RLEINE/SYS LE7 120 E3
Harcourt Crs WOL/BIL/BRX NG8 35 K4
Harcourt Pl CDON/KEG DE74 84 F3
Harcourt Rd NOTTE NG7 36 E7
RLEIW/BBY LE8 146 D7
WGSTN LE18 138 C6
Harcourt St BSTN/STPLFD NG9 63 J1
DERBY DE1 2 D6
Harcourt Ter
MAPPK/POR/STA NG3 5 K5
Harcourt Wy END/NAR LE19 136 B1
Hardacre Cl MELB/CHEL DE73 82 E7
Hardhurst Rd DERBYSE DE24 72 F2
Hardie Crs LEIW LE3 130 B5
Harding St LEI LE1 6 C3
Hardstaff Rd WBRGFD NG2 51 L2
Hardwick Av DERBYW DE22 43 H4
ILK DE7 32 C7
Hardwick Cl RIPLEY DE5 11 G4
Hardwick Ct LEIW LE3 131 G4
Hardwick Crs RLEINE/SYS LE7 120 D4
Hardwick Dr MCKLVR DE3 56 C5
Hardwicke Rd
BSTN/STPLFD NG9 63 G4
END/NAR LE19 135 K7
Hardwick Gv NOTTE NG7 4 B8
WBRGFD NG2 51 K6
Hardwick Pl ILK DE7 47 G2
Hardwick Rd ARN NG5 37 G4
LEIE LE5 133 H3
NOTTE NG7 4 C9
Hardwick St DERBYSE DE24 58 A7
Hardwood Cl BLWL NG6 23 K8
Hardy Barn HEANOR DE75 20 E7
Hardy Cl EWD/SEL/PNX NG16 22 D8
LGEAT NG10 76 B1
Hardy Crs RIPLEY DE5 11 M7
Hardy's Av LEIN LE4 126 A3
Hardy's Dr CARL NG4 38 D6
Hardy St EWD/SEL/PNX NG16 22 D8
NOTTE NG7 4 C3
Harebell Cl DERBYE DE21 44 E4
LEIE LE5 126 F5
Harecroft Crs RLEIW/BAR LE9 140 C7
Harefield RLBORO LE12 88 C4
Harefield Av LEIW LE3 130 F7
Harene Crs LEIW LE3 129 J5
Harepit Cl DERBYSE DE24 72 E2
Harewood Av BLWL NG6 36 B2
Harewood Cl BPR/DUF DE56 18 B2
COT/KEY/RAD NG12 53 L4
LGEAT NG10 61 M3
Harewood Rd DERBYW DE22 43 H4
Harewood St LEIE LE5 126 B8
Hargrave Av BWSH/BRSTN DE72 60 A2
Hargreaves Cl NORM/LIT DE23 70 E1
Harkstead Rd ARN NG5 24 F6
Harland Cl RLEIW/BAR LE9 142 B4
Harlaxton Dr LGEAT NG10 62 E6
NOTTE NG7 4 B8
Harlaxton St LEIW LE3 130 F5
Harlaxton Wk
MAPPK/POR/STA NG3 5 H3
Harlech Cl DERBYE DE21 59 L2
ILK DE7 33 G4
LBORO LE11 103 J2
Harlech Ri BSTN/STPLFD NG9 62 F3
Harlequin Cl
COT/KEY/RAD NG12 53 M4
Harlequin Ct
EWD/SEL/PNX NG16 21 H4
Harlequin Wy RLEIW/BBY LE8 142 D3
Harlesden Av DERBYW DE22 42 E8
Harley Cl RLBORO LE12 101 M5
Harley St NOTTE NG7 4 A9
Harlow Cl DERBYSE DE24 72 D3
Harlow Ct ILK DE7 32 B8
Harlow Gv CARL NG4 38 C5
Harmston Ri ARN NG5 36 D3
Harnett Cl NOTT NG1 5 J8
Harold Av EWD/SEL/PNX NG16 20 F3
Harold Ct WBRGFD NG2 5 M7
Harolds La END/NAR LE19 135 M2
Harold St LEIS LE2 131 J7
WBRGFD NG2 5 M7
Harpenden Sq
WOL/BIL/BRX NG8 35 L4
Harpswell Cl DERBYW DE22 43 J5
Harpur Av NORM/LIT DE23 56 F8
Harrier Cl DERBYSE DE24 71 J4
RLEIW/BAR LE9 141 J8
Harrier Gv HUCK/RAV NG15 23 J3
Harrier Rd BPR/DUF DE56 18 A2
Harrier Wy DERBYSE DE24 71 J4
Harriet St NORM/LIT DE23 2 F8
Harriett St BSTN/STPLFD NG9 48 B7
Harriman Cl RLBORO LE12 101 M3
Harrimans Dr
BWSH/BRSTN DE72 61 K7
Harrimans La NOTTE NG7 50 B7
Harringay Gdns DERBYW DE22 57 G1
Harrington Av
BWSH/BRSTN DE72 60 A5
Harrington Cl CARL NG4 38 F6
RLBORO LE12 112 E1
Harrington Dr NOTTE NG7 4 B9
Harrington Rd NORM/LIT DE23 57 G6
RLBORO LE12 102 A4
WGSTN LE18 138 C4
Harrington St
BWSH/BRSTN DE72 60 F8
DERBYSE DE24 72 C1
LEIN LE4 7 L1
LGEAT NG10 75 M2
NORM/LIT DE23 57 L7
Harringworth Rd LEIE LE5 132 F3
Harris Av RIPLEY DE5 11 G5
Harris Cl RIPLEY DE5 11 G6
WOL/BIL/BRX NG8 49 K2
Harrison Cl LEIW LE3 124 A7
RLEIW/BBY LE8 142 E2
WGSTN LE18 137 M6
Harrison Rd BSTN/STPLFD NG9 48 B7
LEIN LE4 125 M6
Harrison St DERBYW DE22 2 A7
LEIN LE4 120 C7
Harris Rd BSTN/STPLFD NG9 63 G2
LEIN LE4 124 F4
Harrogate Crs DERBYE DE21 44 B6
Harrogate Rd LEIN LE4 126 A6
MAPPK/POR/STA NG3 52 A2
Harrogate St CARL NG4 38 D8
Harrogate Wy WGSTN LE18 138 C6
Harrowby Rd NOTTE NG7 4 B8
Harrow Cl LEIW LE3 129 K6
Harrowden Ri LEIE LE5 132 E1
Harrow Dr ILK DE7 47 L3
Harrow Gdns
WOL/BIL/BRX NG8 50 A3
Harrowgate Dr LEIN LE4 119 K7
Harrow Rd HUCK/RAV NG15 23 H2
LEIW LE3 131 G3

WBRGFD NG2 ....**65** J2
WOL/BIL/BRX NG8 ....**49** M3
Harrow St *DERBYSE* DE24 ......**58** C5
Hart Av *LGEAT* NG10 ....**61** L2
Hart Cl *RLEINE/BBY* LE8 ....**142** D2
Hartcroft Rd *ARN* NG5 ....**36** F1
Hartfield Rd *LEIE* LE5 ....**127** H7
Hartford Cl *WBRGFD * *NG2 ....**51** H5
CARL NG4 ....**38** B6
Hartington Cl *ILK* DE7 ....**32** C7
Hartington Pl *ILK* DE7 ....**33** J4
Hartington Rd *ARN* NG5 ....**37** G4
LEIS LE2 ....**7** L5
Hartington St *NORM/LIT* DE23 ..**2** F7
Hartington Wy *MCKLVR* DE3 ...**56** B5
Hartland Dr *NORM/LIT* DE23 ...**71** H1
Hartley Ct *NOTTE* NG7 ....**4** A4
Hartley Dr *BSTN/STPLFD* NG9 ..**63** M1
Hartley Rd *NOTTE* NG7 ....**4** A4
Hartness Rd *CFTN/RUD* NG11 ..**64** A6
Hartopp Cl *RLEINE/SYS* LE7 ...**133** L2
Hartopp Rd *LEIS* LE2 ....**131** M5
Hart Rd *LEIS* LE2 ....**7** L4
Hartshay Hl *RIPLEY* DE5 ....**11** G4
Hartshorn Cl *LEIN* LE4 ....**126** D1
Hartshorne Rd *NORM/LIT* DE23 ..**71** G2
Hartside Cl *WBRGFD* NG2 ....**52** A8
Hartside Gdns *LGEAT* NG10 ....**61** L7
Hartside Wy *HEANOR* DE75 .....**20** F6
Hart St *NOTTE* NG7 ....**4** A9
Hartwell St
MAPPK/POR/STA NG3 ....**5** J3
Hartwood Dr
BSTN/STPLFD NG9 ....**48** B6
Harvard Cl *LEIS* LE2 ....**138** F1
Harvest Cl *ARN* NG5 ....**24** D7
END/NAR LE19 ....**142** B3
LEIN LE4 ....**124** F4
Harvester Cl *LEIW* LE3 ....**129** K6
RIPLEY DE5 ....**11** G5
Harvest Wy *DERBYE* DE21 ......**45** G4
Harvey Cl *LEIS* LE2 ....**138** F1
Harvey Ct *CFTN/RUD* NG11 .....**79** H2
Harvey Cft *BSTN/STPLFD* NG9 ..**48** A3
Harvey Rd *CDON/KEG* DE74 ....**84** F5
DERBYSE DE24 ....**72** D1
WOL/BIL/BRX NG8 ....**35** K8
Harwich Cl *BLWL* NG6 ....**23** L7
Harwill Crs *WOL/BIL/BRX* NG8 ..**35** M5
Harwin Rd *LEIE* LE5 ....**132** F3
Harwood Cl *ARN* NG5 ....**25** M7
Hasgill Cl *DERBYE* DE21 ....**45** G4
Haskell Cl *LEIW* LE3 ....**130** K5
Haslam's La *DERBYW* DE22 .....**43** L5
Haslam St *NOTTE* NG7 ....**4** A4
Haslemere Rd *LGEAT* NG10 ....**61** M7
WOL/BIL/BRX NG8 ....**36** B7
Haslyn Wk *COAL* LE67 ....**108** F7
Hassall Rd *LEIW* LE3 ....**124** C7
Hassock La North
HEANOR DE75 ....**20** F8
Hassock La South
HEANOR DE75 ....**33** G1
Hassocks La *BSTN/STPLFD* NG9 ..**49** M8
Hassop Rd *DERBYE* DE21 ....**44** E7
The Hastings *LEIW* LE3 ....**130** B4
Hastings Av *COAL* LE67 ....**108** E3
Hastings Rd *LEIE* LE5 ....**126** B7
RLBORO LE12 ....**111** K7
RLEINE/BAR LE9 ....**129** J3
Hastings St *CARL* NG4 ....**38** A8
CDON/KEG DE74 ....**84** F5
LBORO LE11 ....**9** C2
NORM/LIT DE23 ....**57** L6
Haswell Rd *BLWL* NG6 ....**35** M2
Hatchmere Cl *DERBYE* DE21 ...**44** E6
Hatfield Rd *LGEAT* NG10 ....**61** M8
Hatfield Dr *WBRGFD* NG2 ......**65** G3
Hatfield Rd *DERBYSE* DE24 ....**72** D2
MAPPK/POR/STA NG3 ....**37** C5
Hathaway Av *LEIW* LE3 ....**130** D6
Hatherleigh Cl
MAPPK/POR/STA NG3 ....**38** A1
Hatherleigh Rd *LEIE* LE5 ......**132** D4
Hathern Cl *LGEAT* NG10 ....**76** B2
NORM/LIT DE23 ....**71** J2
Hathern Dr *RLBORO* LE12 .....**102** D1
Hathern Gn *BSTN/STPLFD* NG9 ..**49** L7
Hathern Rd *RLBORO* LE12 ....**94** B4
RLBORO LE12 ....**102** A2
Hathersage Av *LGEAT* NG10 ...**75** K2
NORM/LIT DE23 ....**57** J7
Hatley Cl *WBRGFD * *NG2 ......**50** F7
Hat Rd *LEIW* LE3 ....**130** C8
Hattern Av *LEIN* LE4 ....**125** H3
Hatton Ct *MELB/CHEL* DE73 ....**82** E8
Hatton Crofts *LGEAT* NG10 .....**76** A1
Hatton Gdns *WOL/BIL/BRX* NG8 ..**35** J4
Haulton Dr *CDON/KEG* DE74 ...**84** E3
Havelock Rd *NORM/LIT* DE23 ..**57** K7
Havelock St *ILK* DE7 ....**33** K8
LBORO LE11 ....**8** F2
LEIS LE2 ....**6** D3
RIPLEY DE5 ....**11** H5
Haven Baulk Av *NORM/LIT* DE23 ..**56** C3
Haven Baulk La *MCKLVR* DE3 ..**56** B8
Haven Cl *LEIW* LE3 ....**129** K5
RLBORO LE12 ....**100** F1
WBRGFD NG2 ....**65** H2
Haven Ct *DERBYSE* DE24 ....**73** H1
Havencrest Dr *LEIE* LE5 ....**126** F8
Havenwood Ri *CFTN/RUD* NG11 ..**64** B7
Haverhill Crs *ARN* NG5 ....**24** B6
Haversham Cl *BLWL* NG6 ....**36** B5
Hawarden Av *LEIE* LE5 ....**126** D8
Hawarden Ter *NOTTE* NG7 ....**4** A2
Hawcliffe Rd *RLBORO* LE12 ...**113** G4
Hawk Cl *RLEINE/BAR* LE9 .....**141** J3
Hawker Rd *LEIS* LE2 ....**139** H3
Hawkesbury Rd *LEIS* LE2 ......**131** J3
Hawkes Hl *LEIS* LE2 ....**137** K2
Hawkes St *DERBYE* DE22 ....**57** G2
Hawkhurst Dr
MAPPK/POR/STA NG3 ....**49** H5
Hawk Ridge Gdns
MAPPK/POR/STA NG3 ....**5** L5
Hawksdale Cl *MELB/CHEL* DE73 ..**72** E6

Hawkshead Av *DERBYE* DE21 ...**44** B6
Hawkshead Cl
COT/KEY/RAD NG12 ....**66** B2
Hawksley Gdns *LEIN* LE4 .....**137** L7
Hawksley Rd *NOTTE* NG7 ....**4** A5
Hawkswood Cl
BSTN/STPLFD NG9 ....**62** F3
Hawksworth Av *ARN* NG5 ......**37** H3
Hawksworth Rd *WBRGFD* NG2 ..**51** K6
Hawksworth St
MAPPK/POR/STA NG3 ....**5** M6
Hawley Cl *RLBORO* LE12 ....**88** D6
Hawthorn Av
BWSH/BRSTN DE72 ....**61** K7
COT/KEY/RAD NG12 ....**66** B5
DERBYSE DE24 ....**58** E8
HUCK/RAV NG15 ....**23** K1
RIPLEY DE5 ....**11** H7
RLEINE/SYS LE7 ....**119** M7
Hawthorn Cl *CALV/BJ* NG14 ....**27** C3
COAL LE67 ....**108** C6
COT/KEY/RAD NG12 ....**65** M3
COT/KEY/RAD NG12 ....**80** C5
LEIW LE3 ....**129** J5
RDERBYSW DE65 ....**68** B6
Hawthorn Crs *ARN* NG5 ....**25** L6
RDERBYSW DE65 ....**70** B5
Hawthorn Dr *RLEINE/BBY* LE8 ..**142** F1
Hawthorne Av
BSTN/STPLFD NG9 ....**62** B1
BWSH/BRSTN DE72 ....**59** M4
LGEAT NG10 ....**62** A8
RLBORO LE12 ....**94** E6
Hawthorne Dr *BPR/DUF* DE56 ..**18** D5
Hawthorne St *LEIW* LE3 ....**130** F1
The Hawthornes
*BPR/DUF * *DE56 ....**18** B2
Hawthorne Dr *LEIE* LE5 ....**132** C4
Hawthorn Gv
BSTN/STPLFD NG9 ....**63** M1
LEIS LE2 ....**132** F8
Hawthorn Ri
EWD/SEL/PNX NG16 ....**33** M3
GBY/RBY LE6 ....**123** H7
Hawthorn Rd *CDON/KEG* DE74 ..**84** F2
RLBORO LE12 ....**113** J6
The Hawthorns *COAL* LE67 ...**116** C7
DERBYE DE21 ....**30** A7
RLEINE/BBY LE8 ....**143** J3
Hawthorn St *DERBYSE* DE24 ...**58** A7
Hawton Crs *WOL/BIL/BRX* NG8 ..**50** A3
Hawtrey Gdns *DERBYSE* DE24 ..**72** E1
Haybarn Cl *END/NAR* LE19 ....**142** B1
Haybrooke Rd *RLBORO* LE12 ..**114** B3
Hayden Av *LEIS* LE2 ....**139** H3
Hayden Cl *LEIN* LE4 ....**125** J4
Hayden La *HUCK/RAV* NG15 ....**15** M5
Haydn Av *ARN* NG5 ....**36** F5
Haydn Rd *ARN* NG5 ....**36** E5
DERBYE DE21 ....**44** D7
Haydock Cl *EWD/SEL/PNX* NG16 ..**22** C8
Haydock Park Rd
DERBYSE DE24 ....**58** C7
Haydon Rd *LBORO* LE11 ....**8** D3
The Hayes *RDERBYSW* DE65 ....**70** A6
Hayes Av *BWSH/BRSTN* DE72 ..**60** F8
NORM/LIT DE23 ....**57** H7
Hayes Cl *COAL* LE67 ....**108** D3
ILK DE7 ....**32** B7
Hayes Crs *ALFN* DE55 ....**11** K1
Hayes Rd *COT/KEY/RAD* NG12 ..**80** B4
WGSTN LE18 ....**138** C4
Hayes Wood Rd *ILK* DE7 ....**31** M6
Hayfield Cl *BPR/DUF* DE56 .....**17** M2
LEIW LE3 ....**123** M7
Hayhill *RLBORO* LE12 ....**113** L2
Hayhill La *RLBORO* LE12 ......**113** K1
Hayles Ct *ARN* NG5 ....**36** F1
Hayley Cft *BPR/DUF* DE56 ......**29** K6
Hayling Cl *ILK* DE7 ....**33** G4
Hayling Crs *LEIE* LE5 ....**126** E7
Hayling Dr *BLWL* NG6 ....**36** B5
Haymarket *LEI* LE1 ....**6** F5
Haynes Av *BSTN/STPLFD* NG9 ..**48** A2
Haynes Cl *CFTN/RUD* NG11 ....**64** D4
Haynes Rd *LEIE* LE5 ....**126** C8
Hays Cl *ILK* DE7 ....**33** H5
Hayward Av *LBORO* LE11 ....**9** M7
Haywood Cl *DERBYSE* DE24 ....**72** E2
LEIE LE5 ....**132** F3
Haywood Ct *WBRGFD* NG2 ....**5** L7
Haywood Rd
MAPPK/POR/STA NG3 ....**37** K5
Haywood St *WBRGFD* NG2 ....**5** L7
Hayworth Rd *LGEAT* NG10 .....**61** M2
Hazel Av *NORM/LIT* DE23 ....**71** H1
Hazelbank Av
MAPPK/POR/STA NG3 ....**37** K6
Hazelbank Rd *RLEINE/BBY* LE8 ..**143** K3
Hazel Cl *END/NAR* LE19 ....**142** A1
HEANOR DE75 ....**20** B6
LEIN LE4 ....**119** M7
RDERBYSW DE65 ....**70** B5
Hazeldene Cl *BPR/DUF* DE56 ...**29** J2
Hazeldene Rd *LEIE* LE5 ....**127** K5
Hazel Dr *DERBYE* DE21 ....**59** L1
EWD/SEL/PNX NG16 ....**34** F7
LEIW LE3 ....**136** D1
Hazel Gv *BPR/DUF* DE56 ....**29** J4
HUCK/RAV NG15 ....**23** L2
MAPPK/POR/STA NG3 ....**37** L3
Hazelhead Rd *RLEINE/SYS* LE7 ..**124** B1
Hazel Hill Crs *ARN* NG5 ....**24** F8
Hazelrigg Cl *CDON/KEG* DE74 ..**84** D3
Hazel Rd *LBORO* LE11 ....**103** J7
Hazel St *BLWL* NG6 ....**23** M8
LEIS LE2 ....**131** K4
Hazeltree Cl *RIPLEY* DE5 ....**11** G7
Hazelwood *COT/KEY/RAD* NG12 ..**67** L4
Hazelwood Av
EWD/SEL/PNX NG16 ....**21** M5
Hazelwood Dr *HUCK/RAV* NG15 ..**23** G1
Hazelwood Hl *BPR/DUF* DE56 ..**16** F7

Hazelwood Rd *BPR/DUF* DE56 ...**17** C8
DERBYE DE21 ....**44** D7
LEIE LE5 ....**132** B4
NOTTE NG7 ....**36** C8
WGSTN LE18 ....**137** L7
Heacham Dr *LEIN* LE4 ....**124** F4
Headingley Cl *COAL* LE67 .....**108** E8
Headingley Ct *NORM/LIT* DE23 ..**57** G7
Headingley Gdns
WOL/BIL/BRX NG8 ....**36** B7
Headingley Rd *LEIE* LE5 ....**119** G8
Headland Rd *LEIE* LE5 ....**132** E4
The Headlands
RLEINE/SYS LE7 ....**115** J7
Headley Rd *LEIW* LE3 ....**130** D8
Heafield Dr *CDON/KEG* DE74 ...**86** B5
Heage Rd *RIPLEY* DE5 ....**10** F6
Healey Cl *WBRGFD* NG2 ....**51** G5
Healey St *WGSTN* LE18 ....**137** K6
Healy Cl *LEIN* LE4 ....**125** H3
Heanor Gate Rd *HEANOR* DE75 ..**20** A6
Heanor Houses *DERBYE * *DE21 ..**59** J4
Heanor Rd *HEANOR* DE75 ......**20** B4
ILK DE7 ....**19** L8
ILK DE7 ....**33** J4
RIPLEY DE5 ....**11** M8
RIPLEY DE5 ....**19** L4
Heanor St *LEI* LE1 ....**6** D3
Heard Crs *BSTN/STPLFD* NG9 ..**49** K7
The Heath *LEIW* LE3 ....**138** C7
Heath Av *END/NAR* LE19 ......**136** C5
NORM/LIT DE23 ....**57** C5
RLEINE/SYS LE7 ....**139** K7
Heathbrook Dr *GBY/RBY* LE6 ..**123** H7
Heathcoat St *LBORO* LE11 ....**9** C3
NOTT NG1 ....**5** J7
Heathcote Cl *DERBYSE* DE24 ..**73** G2
Heathcote Dr *RLBORO* LE12 ..**114** C3
Heathcott Rd *LEIS* LE2 ....**131** K8
Heath Ct *DERBYSE* DE24 ....**71** J4
Heatherbrook Rd *LEIN* LE4 ...**124** D2
Heather Cl *DERBYSE* DE24 .....**71** H5
EWD/SEL/PNX NG16 ....**21** M6
MAPPK/POR/STA NG3 ....**5** L1
Heather Ct *HEANOR* DE75 ......**20** F6
Heather Crs *BWSH/BRSTN* DE72 ..**61** K8
NORM/LIT DE23 ....**71** G1
Heather Dr *WBRGFD* NG2 ....**65** G3
Heatherley Dr *BLWL* NG6 ......**36** D3
Heathermead Cl *DERBYE* DE21 ..**44** D6
Heather Ri *BSTN/STPLFD* NG9 ..**49** J6
Heather Rd *CARL* NG4 ....**38** B6
LEIS LE2 ....**131** L7
Heathervale *CFTN/RUD* NG11 ..**64** F1
Heather Wy *RLEINE/BBY* LE8 ..**143** K4
Heathfield Cl *COAL* LE67 ......**100** B7
Heathfield Av *ILK* DE7 ....**33** L7
Heathfield Gv
BSTN/STPLFD NG9 ....**63** G4
Heathfield Rd *ARN* NG5 ....**36** D3
WGSTN LE18 ....**138** B2
Heath Gdns *BWSH/BRSTN* DE72 ..**61** L7
Heath Rd *LEIW* LE3 ....**119** K7
Heath La *RDERBYSW* DE65 .....**70** B7
Heathley Park Dr *LEIW* LE3 ..**124** E6
Heathrington Gdns *ARN* NG5 ..**24** D6
Heath Rd *RIPLEY* DE5 ....**11** J6
Heaton Cl *MAPPK/POR/STA* NG3 ..**37** K6
Heavenside *RLBORO * *LE12 ....**88** C4
Heawood Wy *LEIE* LE5 ....**130** B6
Heays Cl *LEIW* LE3 ....**124** C7
Hebden Cl *LEIS* LE2 ....**137** G5
NORM/LIT DE23 ....**70** D1
Hebrides Cl *DERBYSE* DE24 ...**71** H4
Heckington Dr
WOL/BIL/BRX NG8 ....**49** M2
Hector Cl *COAL* LE67 ....**108** B5
Hedderley Wk
MAPPK/POR/STA NG3 ....**5** J4
Heddington Cl *WGSTN* LE18 ...**137** L5
Heddington Wy *WGSTN* LE18 ..**137** L2
Hedgebank Cl *DERBYE* DE21 ...**45** G4
Hedge Rd *COAL* LE67 ....**108** A8
Hedgerow Gdns *DERBYE* DE21 ..**45** G4
Hedgerow La *RLEIW/BAR* LE9 ..**129** G2
Hedgerow Rd *LEIW* LE3 ....**130** E3
Hedges Dr *ILK* DE7 ....**47** K3
Hedingham Wy *MCKLVR* DE3 ...**56** M7
Hedley St *NOTTE* NG7 ....**36** E7
Hefford Gdns *LEIN* LE4 ....**125** H3
Heigham Cl *DERBYSE* DE24 ....**72** B4
Heighton Crs *END/NAR* LE19 ..**142** A1
Helena Crs *LEIN* LE4 ....**125** J3
Helen Cl *BSTN/STPLFD * *NG9 ..**63** H1
Hellebore Cl *ARN* NG5 ....**24** C8
Helm Cl *BLWL* NG6 ....**23** K8
Helmsdale Cl *COAL* LE67 .....**109** C7
Helmsdale Gdns *ARN* NG5 .....**24** D6
Helmsley Rd *LEIS* LE2 ....**137** K2
Helston Cl *DERBYSE* DE24 ......**72** F1
WGSTN LE18 ....**138** A6
Helston Dr *WOL/BIL/BRX* NG8 ..**35** H5
Helvellyn Cl *WBRGFD* NG2 .....**51** C5
Helvellyn Wy *LGEAT* NG10 ....**61** M1
Hemington Hl *CDON/KEG* DE74 ..**85** H3
Hemington La *CDON/KEG* DE74 ..**85** J2
Hemington Rd *LEIE* LE5 ....**133** H4
Hemingway Cl *CARL* NG4 ....**38** B8
EWD/SEL/PNX NG16 ....**22** A6
Hemlock Av *BSTN/STPLFD* NG9 ..**48** C7
LGEAT NG10 ....**62** B6
Hemlock Cl *DERBYE* DE21 ......**44** E4
END/NAR LE19 ....**135** K6
Hemlock Gdns *BLWL* NG6 ......**23** K8
Hemsby Gdns *BLWL* NG6 ....**23** K7
Hemscott Cl *BLWL* NG6 ....**23** K7
Hemsley Dr
EWD/SEL/PNX NG16 ....**21** H4
Hemswell Cl
MAPPK/POR/STA NG3 ....**51** L2
Hendon Ri
MAPPK/POR/STA NG3 ....**37** K7
Hendon Wy *DERBYW* DE22 .....**56** F1

Henley Cl *CARL* NG4 ....**52** E1
Henley Crs *LEIW* LE3 ....**130** D6
Henley Gdns *BSTN/STPLFD* NG9 ..**48** C5
Henley Ri *ARN* NG5 ....**36** E4
Henley Rd *LEIW* LE3 ....**131** G1
Henray Av *LEIS* LE2 ....**137** G5
Henrietta St *BLWL* NG6 ....**36** A1
Henry Cl *LEIW* LE3 ....**129** K5
Henry Rd *BSTN/STPLFD* NG9 ..**63** L1
NOTTE NG7 ....**50** C4
WBRGFD NG2 ....**51** J7
Henry St *ARN* NG5 ....**25** J5
DERBY DE1 ....**2** D1
HUCK/RAV NG15 ....**23** M1
RIPLEY DE5 ....**11** H5
WBRGFD NG2 ....**5** M7
Henshaw Av *ILK* DE7 ....**47** H2
Henshaw Pl *ILK* DE7 ....**33** J3
Henshaw St *LEIS* LE2 ....**6** E8
Henson Cl *LEIN* LE4 ....**125** K1
Henson's La *COAL* LE67 ....**100** B7
Henton Rd *LEIW* LE3 ....**131** G2
Hepple Dr *BLWL* NG6 ....**23** J8
Herald Cl *BSTN/STPLFD* NG9 ..**49** M8
Herbert Av *LEIN* LE4 ....**125** M5
Herbert Cl *RLEINE/BBY* LE8 ..**136** D8
Herbert Rd *ARN* NG5 ....**36** E6
Herbert St *LBORO* LE11 ....**103** M2
Herdsmans Cl *END/NAR* LE19 ..**136** A5
Hereford Rd *ARN* NG5 ....**37** J2
CARL NG4 ....**38** D5
DERBY DE21 ....**44** B7
LEIS LE2 ....**131** H8
MAPPK/POR/STA NG3 ....**51** M2
Hereward Dr *RLEINE/SYS* LE7 ..**133** K2
Herle Av *LEIW* LE3 ....**130** D5
Hermitage Av *LEIS* LE2 ....**138** E2
Hermitage Cl *LEIS* LE2 ....**138** E2
Hermitage Ct *DERBYE* DE21 ...**44** F6
Hermitage Rd *COAL* LE67 .....**108** B4
LBORO LE11 ....**102** F5
LEIN LE4 ....**125** L2
Hermitage Wk *ILK* DE7 ....**47** K1
NOTTE NG7 ....**4** D9
Hermon St *NOTTE* NG7 ....**4** C6
Heron Cl *RLBORO* LE12 ....**113** K5
RLEINE/BBY LE8 ....**139** M4
Heron Dr *NOTTE* NG7 ....**50** C3
Herongate Rd *LEIE* LE5 ....**126** D7
Heron Rd *LEIE* LE5 ....**7** M3
RLBORO LE12 ....**105** J7
Herons Ct *WBRGFD* NG2 ....**66** A3
Heronswood Dr *DERBYE* DE21 ..**59** H1
Heron Wy *COAL* LE67 ....**108** D7
END/NAR LE19 ....**136** B5
MCKLVR DE3 ....**56** E5
RLEINE/SYS LE7 ....**120** E3
Heron Whf *WBRGFD* NG2 ....**50** D5
Herrick Cl *END/NAR* LE19 ....**135** L4
RLBORO LE12 ....**113** M4
Herrick Dr *RLEINE/SYS* LE7 ..**133** K2
Herrick Rd *LBORO* LE11 ....**9** H7
LEIS LE2 ....**131** L7
RLBORO LE12 ....**111** K5
Herricks Av *LEIN* LE4 ....**126** D2
Herrick Wy *WGSTN* LE18 .....**138** C6
Herriot Wy *LBORO* LE11 ....**103** H2
Herschell St *LEIS* LE2 ....**132** A4
Hervey Gn *CFTN/RUD* NG11 ...**64** C5
Hervey Woods *COAL* LE67 .....**108** C2
Hesketh Av *LEIS* LE2 ....**137** G4
Hesketh Cl *LEIS* LE2 ....**137** G4
Heskey Cl *MAPPK/POR/STA* NG3 ..**5** J4
Heskey Wk *MAPPK/POR/STA* NG3 ..**5** J4
Heslington Av
WOL/BIL/BRX NG8 ....**36** C7
Hetley Rd *BSTN/STPLFD* NG9 ..**49** K8
Hewes Cl *LEIS* LE2 ....**136** F4
Hewett Cl *RLEINE/BBY* LE8 ...**139** J7
Hewitt Dr *RLEIW/BAR* LE9 ....**129** K3
Hexham Av *ILK* DE7 ....**47** L3
Hexham Rd *WBRGFD* NG2 .....**65** L1
Hextall Rd *LEIE* LE5 ....**132** E4
Hexter Cl *RLEINE/BBY* LE8 ...**142** D3
Heybridge Rd *LEIE* LE5 ....**126** D7
Heybrook Av *RLEINE/BBY* LE8 ..**136** E8
Heydon Cl *BPR/DUF* DE56 .....**17** M1
Heyford Cl *HEANOR* DE75 ......**20** E6
Heyford Rd *LEIW* LE3 ....**130** B3
Hey St *LGEAT* NG10 ....**75** M3
Heythrop Cl *LEIS* LE2 ....**139** H3
Heyworth Rd *LEIW* LE3 ....**131** G6
Heyworth St *DERBYW* DE22 ...**57** G1
Hickings La *BSTN/STPLFD* NG9 ..**48** C7
Hickleton Cl *RIPLEY* DE5 ....**11** C6
Hickling Cl *DERBYE* DE24 ......**72** B4
Hickling Ct *LBORO* LE11 ....**8** F3
Hickling Dr *RLBORO* LE12 ....**114** C3
Hickling Rd
MAPPK/POR/STA NG3 ....**37** L5
Hickling Wy *COT/KEY/RAD* NG12 ..**67** L6
Hickton Dr *RLEINE/BBY* LE8 ...**62** F6
Hickton Rd *ALFN* DE55 ....**11** K1
Hidcote Cl *LEIS* LE2 ....**138** E3
Higgs Cl *LEIE* LE5 ....**132** E2
High Bank *RIPLEY* DE5 ....**19** K5
Highbank Dr *CFTN/RUD* NG11 ..**64** C8
Highbridge *RLBORO* LE12 .....**114** A4
Highbury Av *BLWL* NG6 ....**36** A2
Highbury Cl *DERBYW* DE22 ....**56** D1
WOL/BIL/BRX NG8 ....**35** H4
Highbury Rd *BLWL* NG6 ....**36** A2
COT/KEY/RAD NG12 ....**80** C3
END/NAR LE19 ....**135** K6
High Church St *NOTTE* NG7 ...**36** D6
Highclere Dr *CARL* NG4 ....**38** D7
Highcliffe Rd *LEIN* LE4 ....**126** K4
WBRGFD NG2 ....**51** J2
Highcroft *MAPPK/POR/STA* NG3 ..**37** K3
Highcroft Av *LGEAT* NG10 .....**76** C2
Highcroft Dr *WOL/BIL/BRX* NG8 ..**47** J7
Highcroft Rd *LEIS* LE2 ....**139** H4
High Cross Leys
MAPPK/POR/STA NG3 ....**5** H4

Highcross St *LEIW* LE3 ....**6** C4
High Cross St *NOTT* NG1 ....**5** J6
High Edge Dr *BPR/DUF* DE56 ..**10** M7
Higher Gn *RLEINE/BBY* LE8 ..**139** M7
RLBORO LE12 ....**102** A2
Highfield Cottages
DERBYE DE21 ....**58** C2
Highfield Crs *WGSTN* LE18 ...**138** B3
Highfield Dr *CARL* NG4 ....**37** M7
EWD/SEL/PNX NG16 ....**35** K3
ILK DE7 ....**46** F2
WGSTN LE18 ....**138** B3
Highfield Gdns *DERBYW* DE22 ..**43** K7
Highfield Gv *WBRGFD* NG2 ....**51** K8
Highfield La *LEIS* LE2 ....**58** C2
Highfield Ms *DERBYE * *DE21 ..**58** C2
Highfield Rd *ALFN* DE55 ....**11** H1
BPR/DUF DE56 ....**17** K5
BPR/DUF DE56 ....**18** E7
BSTN/STPLFD NG9 ....**62** B3
COT/KEY/RAD NG12 ....**80** C5
DERBYE DE21 ....**30** A8
DERBYW DE22 ....**43** K8
EWD/SEL/PNX NG16 ....**35** J3
GBY/RBY LE6 ....**123** J5
LBORO LE11 ....**50** B6
NOTTE NG7 ....**50** B6
WBRGFD NG2 ....**51** K8
Highfields *RIPLEY* DE5 ....**11** M7
RLBORO LE12 ....**105** H7
Highfields Dr *LBORO* LE11 ......**8** F3
Highfields Rd *LBORO* LE12 ...**113** H6
Highfield St *LEIS* LE2 ....**7** J3
LGEAT NG10 ....**62** A6
RLEINE/SYS LE7 ....**124** C1
RLEINE/BAR LE9 ....**140** B4
RLEINE/BBY LE8 ....**145** J7
Highfield Wy *RIPLEY* DE5 ....**11** C7
Highgate *WGSTN* LE18 ....**137** L3
Highgate Av *LEIN* LE4 ....**119** J7
Highgate Cl *CARL* NG4 ....**38** A5
Highgate Dr *ILK* DE7 ....**33** C4
WGSTN LE18 ....**137** M2
Highgate Rd *RLBORO* LE12 ...**114** C4
Highgates *DERBY * *DE1 ....**2** D3
High Gv *BPR/DUF* DE56 ....**18** B3
Highgrove Av
BSTN/STPLFD NG9 ....**63** H1
Highgrove Crs *LEIS* LE2 ....**138** F3
Highgrove Dr *MELB/CHEL* DE73 ..**72** D5
Highgrove Gdns
COT/KEY/RAD NG12 ....**65** L4
Highgrove Rd *CARL* NG4 ....**38** C4
High Hazles Rd
COT/KEY/RAD NG12 ....**67** K3
High Holborn *ILK* DE7 ....**33** J4
High Holborn Rd *RIPLEY* DE5 ..**11** L6
Highland Av *LEIW* LE3 ....**129** J5
High Lane Central *ILK* DE7 ....**32** D6
High La East *ILK* DE7 ....**32** F7
High La West *ILK* DE7 ....**32** K7
High Leys Rd *HUCK/RAV* NG15 ..**23** K2
High Meadow
COT/KEY/RAD NG12 ....**66** C6
RLBORO LE12 ....**94** E6
High Meadow Dr *RIPLEY* DE5 ..**11** H7
Highmeres Rd *LEIN* LE4 ....**126** D4
High Pavement
*BPR/DUF * *DE56 ....**17** L4
NOTT NG1 ....**5** J8
High Rd *BSTN/STPLFD* NG9 ...**49** L8
BSTN/STPLFD NG9 ....**62** E6
BSTN/STPLFD NG9 ....**63** H3
High Spania
EWD/SEL/PNX NG16 ....**22** C4
High St *ALFN* DE55 ....**12** C2
ARN NG5 ....**25** K8
BPR/DUF DE56 ....**17** L3
BPR/DUF DE56 ....**18** E7
BSTN/STPLFD NG9 ....**48** C8
CDON/KEG DE74 ....**84** E5
CDON/KEG DE74 ....**86** A5
CFTN/RUD NG11 ....**65** G8
CFTN/RUD NG11 ....**79** J5
COAL LE67 ....**108** A6
END/NAR LE19 ....**135** M4
EWD/SEL/PNX NG16 ....**13** H6
EWD/SEL/PNX NG16 ....**34** D7
HEANOR DE75 ....**20** A3
HEANOR DE75 ....**20** B5
HUCK/RAV NG15 ....**15** M8
ILK DE7 ....**33** K7
LBORO LE11 ....**9** J3
LEI LE1 ....**6** E5
LEIE LE5 ....**132** F5
LEIS LE2 ....**138** E1
LGEAT NG10 ....**62** C7
MELB/CHEL DE73 ....**72** E6
MELB/CHEL DE73 ....**82** E8
NOTT NG1 ....**5** J7
RIPLEY DE5 ....**11** H6
RLBORO LE12 ....**105** H8
RLBORO LE12 ....**112** D1
RLBORO LE12 ....**114** A4
RLEINE/SYS LE7 ....**120** E3
RLEINE/BBY LE8 ....**136** D8
RLEINE/BBY LE8 ....**139** L7
RLEINE/BBY LE8 ....**145** K7
RLEINE/BBY LE8 ....**146** D7
High Street Av *ARN* NG5 ....**25** J8
Highurst St *NOTTE* NG7 ....**4** C5
Hilhurst St *NOTTE* NG7 ....**4** C6
High View Av
COT/KEY/RAD NG12 ....**80** D4
Highway Rd *LEIE* LE5 ....**132** C5
LEIN LE4 ....**120** D7
Highwood Av *BPR/DUF* DE56 ..**17** M6
WOL/BIL/BRX NG8 ....**35** K7
High Wood Bank
BPR/DUF DE56 ....**18** A4
Highwray Gv *CFTN/RUD* NG11 ..**64** B6
Hilary Cl *BPR/DUF* DE56 ....**18** C2
WOL/BIL/BRX NG8 ....**49** H4
Hilary Crs *COAL* LE67 ....**108** E4
GBY/RBY LE6 ....**123** H4
Hilcot Dr *WOL/BIL/BRX* NG8 ...**35** M6
Hilcot Gn *LEIW* LE3 ....**130** M6

Hilders Rd *LEIW* LE3....130 E1
Hilderstone Cl *DERBYSE* DE24....73 H1
Hildyard Rd *LEIN* LE4....125 L6
The Hill *DERBYSE* DE22....43 L6
Hillary Pl *ILK* DE7....46 F2
  LEIW LE3....130 E1
Hillberry *RIPLEY* DE5....11 K6
Hillberry Cl *END/NAR* LE19....135 L7
Hill Brow *DERBY* DE1....2 E5
Hill Cl *DERBYE* DE21....59 J3
  EWD/SEL/PNX NG16....22 A6
  ILK DE7....31 L6
  WBRGFD NG2....65 M1
Hillcrest Av *RLEIW/BBY* LE8....146 D6
Hillcrest Cl *EWD/SEL/PNX* NG16....34 E1
Hillcrest Dr *BPR/DUF* DE56....18 E7
  HUCK/RAV NG15....23 H1
  RIPLEY DE5....11 M7
Hillcreste Dr *MELB/CHEL* DE73....72 D4
Hillcrest Gdns *MAPPK/POR/STA* NG14....39 J2
Hill Crest Gv *ARN* NG5....36 F4
Hill Crest Rd *DERBYE* DE21....44 B8
Hillcrest Rd *COT/KEY/RAD* NG12....80 C3
  WGSTN LE18....137 M2
Hillcrest Vw *CARL* NG4....37 L6
Hillcroft Cl *LEIN* LE4....120 C7
Hill Croft Dr *BWSH/BRSTN* DE72....60 A3
Hillcroft Rd *LEIE* LE2....132 C2
Hill Cross Av *NORM/LIT* DE23....57 G8
Hill Cross Dr *NORM/LIT* DE23....56 F8
Hill Farm Ct *COT/KEY/RAD* NG12....65 L5
Hill Fld *LEIS* LE2....139 J3
Hillfield Gdns *ARN* NG5....24 C6
Hillfield Rd *BSTN/STPLFD* NG9....48 D7
Hillingdon Av
  EWD/SEL/PNX NG16....35 H4
Hillington Ri *ARN* NG5....25 G8
Hill La *COAL* LE67....116 A6
  RLEIW/BBY LE8....142 E4
Hill Lane Cl *COAL* LE67....116 B5
Hillrise Av *LEIW* LE3....130 E1
Hill Rise Rd *NORM/LIT* DE23....57 H8
Hill Rd *BLWL* NG6....24 C3
  BSTN/STPLFD NG9....62 F5
  CFTN/RUD NG11....77 M8
  HEANOR DE75....20 B6
Hillsborough Cl *LEIS* LE2....137 G5
Hillsborough Crs *LEIS* LE2....137 G5
Hillsborough Rd *LEIS* LE2....137 G5
Hillsford Cl *WOL/BIL/BRX* NG8....49 L1
Hill Side *NOTTE* NG5....50 B5
  COAL LE67....86 A6
  EWD/SEL/PNX NG16....20 C4
  RDERBYSW DE65....70 B5
Hillside Av *DERBYSE* DE21....58 E2
  MAPPK/POR/STA NG3....37 L3
  WGSTN LE18....138 B6
Hillside Crs *BSTN/STPLFD* NG9....49 J6
  DERBYSE DE21....59 J3
Hillside Dr *CALV/BJ* NG14....39 K2
  LGEAT NG10....61 M7
Hillside Gv *LGEAT* NG10....61 L1
Hillside Rd *BPR/DUF* DE56....17 K5
Hillside Rd *BSTN/STPLFD* NG9....49 H7
  BSTN/STPLFD NG9....62 F4
  COT/KEY/RAD NG12....53 L4
  DERBYE DE21....59 J3
Hills Rd *ARN* NG5....37 J3
  BWSH/BRSTN DE72....60 F7
Hill St *LEI* LE1....7 G4
  RIPLEY DE5....11 H4
  RLEIW/BAR LE9....141 G3
Hillsway *MELB/CHEL* DE73....72 D4
  NORM/LIT DE23....56 F6
Hill Syke *CALV/BJ* NG14....27 L5
Hill Top *CDON/KEG* DE74....84 D6
  DERBYE DE21....44 B5
Hilltop La *ASHB* DE6....54 B2
  BPR/DUF DE56....18 C5
Hill Top Rd *ALFN* DE55....12 A2
  LBORO LE11....8 D9
Hilltop Rd *LEIN* LE4....126 F4
Hill Vw *BPR/DUF* DE56....29 H4
  END/NAR LE19....136 C4
Hill View Cl *ILK* DE7....18 F8
Hill View Dr *RLEIW/BAR* LE9....142 B4
Hill View Gv *DERBYE* DE21....59 J2
Hill View Rd *BSTN/STPLFD* NG9....62 E5
Hillview Rd
  MAPPK/POR/STA NG3....37 L6
Hill Wy *LEIS* LE2....139 G3
Hilton Cl *LGEAT* NG10....75 K3
  MCKLVR DE3....56 B6
Hilton Crs *WBRGFD* NG2....65 M2
Hilton Rd *MAPPK/POR/STA* NG3....37 L5
  RDERBYSW DE65....68 G8
  RDERBYSW DE65....68 F3
Hinchin Brook *NOTTE* NG7....50 C3
Hinckley Rd *RLEIW/BBY* LE8....128 F7
  RLEIW/BAR LE9....134 C2
  RLEIW/BAR LE9....140 A7
Hind Av *BWSH/BRSTN* DE72....61 G8
Hind Cl *RLEIW/BBY* LE8....142 E1
Hindoostan Av *WGSTN* LE18....137 J4
Hindscarth Crs *MCKLVR* DE3....56 C6
Hinks Av *RLEIW/SYS* LE7....127 K7
Hinsley Cl *ARN* NG5....25 M7
Hipwell Crs *LEIN* LE4....125 J4
Hirst Ct *NOTTE* * NG7....7 J7
Hirst Crs *WOL/BIL/BRX* NG8....49 J5
Hixon's La *ILK* DE7....46 F6
Hoare Rd *BSTN/STPLFD* NG9....62 F5
Hoball Cl *LEIW* LE3....124 C7
Hobart Cl *MCKLVR* DE3....56 D5
  WBRGFD NG2....65 M2
Hobart Dr *BSTN/STPLFD* NG9....48 D6
Hobart St *LEIS* LE2....7 J7
Hobby Cl *RLEIW/BAR* LE9....141 J8
Hob Hl *BPR/DUF* DE56....16 F7
Hobsic Cl *LEIW* LE3....129 M5
  RLEIW/BAR LE9....135 J7
Hobkirk Dr *DERBYSE* DE24....71 J5
Hobsic Cl *EWD/SEL/PNX* NG16....13 H7

Hobson Dr *ILK* DE7....47 J1
Hobson Rd *LEIN* LE4....125 J4
Hoby St *LEIW* LE3....6 A4
Hockerwood *CFTN/RUD* NG11....64 C3
Hockey Cl *LBORO* LE11....95 L8
Hockley *NOTT* NG1....5 K7
Hockley Farm Rd *LEIW* LE3....130 B3
Hodge Beck Cl *DERBYSE* DE24....73 G1
Hodgkin Cl *CFTN/RUD* NG11....64 A6
Hodgkinson St *CARL* NG4....52 E1
Hodson Cl *RLEIW/BBY* LE8....124 E6
Hodson Cl *RLEIW/BBY* LE8....142 D1
Hodson Ct *LBORO* LE11....9 J6
Hodthorpe Cl *DERBYE* DE21....44 E6
Hoefield Crs *BLWL* NG6....35 L1
Hoe Hill Vw *COT/KEY/RAD* NG12....66 B6
Hoewood Rd *BLWL* NG6....23 J8
Hogarth Cl *BSTN/STPLFD* NG9....62 C1
Hogarth Rd *COAL* LE67....108 D2
  LEIN LE4....119 G6
Hogarth St
  MAPPK/POR/STA NG3....51 K1
Hogbarn La *HEANOR* DE75....20 B2
Hoggetts Cl *BSTN/STPLFD* NG9....62 F1
Hogg La *COT/KEY/RAD* NG12....53 J4
Holbeck Rd *HUCK/RAV* NG15....15 L6
  WOL/BIL/BRX NG8....50 A1
Holbein Cl *LBORO* LE11....9 M2
Holborn Av *WBRGFD* NG2....51 K2
Holborn Dr *DERBYW* DE22....42 E8
Holborn Vw *RIPLEY* DE5....11 L7
Holbourne Cl *RLBORO* LE12....105 G8
Holbrook *LEIS* LE2....139 J3
Holbrook Rd *BPR/DUF* DE56....17 K5
  DERBYSE DE24....72 F1
  LEIS LE2....132 C8
Holbrook St *HEANOR* DE75....20 E5
Holbrook Vw *BPR/DUF* DE56....18 A6
Holby Cl *ARN* NG5....24 D7
Holcombe Cl *LEIE* LE67....108 C1
  WOL/BIL/BRX NG8....35 M5
Holcombe St *NORM/LIT* DE23....57 M6
Holdale Rd
  MAPPK/POR/STA NG3....51 M1
Holden Av *BWSH/BRSTN* DE72....73 L7
Holden Cl *RLEIW/BBY* LE8....142 E2
Holden Ct *NOTTE* * NG7....4 C5
Holden Crs *EWD/SEL/PNX* NG16....35 G1
Holden Gdns *BSTN/STPLFD* NG9....49 J8
Holden Rd *BSTN/STPLFD* NG9....49 J8
Holden St *LEIN* LE4....125 L5
  NOTTE NG7....4 C5
Holderness Cl *DERBYSE* DE24....71 H5
Holderness Rd *LEIN* LE4....125 H2
Holgate *CFTN/RUD* NG11....64 A5
Holgate Cl *RLEIW/SYS* LE7....118 C8
Holgate Rd *WBRGFD* NG2....51 G6
Holkham Av *BSTN/STPLFD* NG9....63 G2
  LEIN LE4....126 B6
Holkham Cl *ARN* NG5....37 L1
  ILK DE7....33 G4
Holland Cl *CFTN/RUD* NG11....77 M6
Holland Meadow *LGEAT* NG10....76 B2
Holland Rd *LEIS* LE2....7 K4
Holland St *NOTTE* NG7....4 A2
Holles Crs *NOTTE* NG7....4 D9
Holliers Wy *RLEIW/BAR* LE9....141 G3
The Hollies *BWSH/BRSTN* DE72....61 L2
Hollies Cl *RLEIW/BAR* LE9....134 E4
Hollies Dr *COT/KEY/RAD* NG12....65 L3
Hollies Farm Cl
  MELB/CHEL DE73....82 B4
Hollies Rd *DERBYW* DE22....43 H4
Hollies Wy *RLEIW/SYS* LE7....133 K5
Hollington Cl *DERBYE* DE21....44 C8
Hollington Rd *LEIE* LE5....132 B3
  WOL/BIL/BRX NG8....49 L1
Hollingworth Av *LGEAT* NG10....61 M4
Hollins Cl *LEIS* LE2....138 C3
Hollinwell Av *WOL/BIL/BRX* NG8....50 A2
Hollinwell Cl *LEIW* LE3....130 A2
Hollinwell Ct
  COT/KEY/RAD NG12....65 M4
Hollis Meadow *RLBORO* LE12....88 C4
Hollis St *DERBYSE* DE24....58 E7
  NOTTE NG7....36 E6
The Hollow *CDON/KEG* DE74....84 F3
  LEIE LE5....132 F5
  MCKLVR DE3....56 B7
  NORM/LIT DE23....56 F6
Holloway Rd *BPR/DUF* DE56....29 H3
  DERBYSE DE24....72 D1
Hollow Brooks *DERBYE* DE21....30 A8
Hollowood Av *NORM/LIT* DE23....57 G7
Hollow Rd *RLEIW/SYS* LE7....124 B1
Hollow Station *RLEIW/BBY* LE8....146 E7
The Hollows *CFTN/RUD* NG11....64 E3
  LGEAT NG10....62 E7
Hollow Stone *NOTT* NG1....5 J8
Hollowtree Rd *LEIE* LE5....127 C5
Holly Av *BWSH/BRSTN* DE72....61 K6
  CARL NG4....38 B8
  CFTN/RUD NG11....50 F7
  MAPPK/POR/STA NG3....37 L8
  RIPLEY DE5....11 H7
Holly Bank Cl *LEIE* LE5....127 G5
Hollybrook Cl *LEIN* LE4....126 E1
Hollybrook Gv
  EWD/SEL/PNX NG16....22 F8
Hollybrook Wy *NORM/LIT* DE23....70 D1
Hollybush Cl *LEIS* LE2....127 H8
  RLEIW/SYS LE7....120 D4
Holly Bush La *BPR/DUF* DE56....29 L1
Holly Cl *BWSH/BRSTN* DE72....60 E8
  HUCK/RAV NG15....23 M2
Holly Ct *BSTN/STPLFD* NG9....49 G7
  BWSH/BRSTN DE72....73 L3
  LEIS LE2....132 E8
  MCKLVR DE3....56 B6
Hollycroft *WBRGFD* NG2....65 L3
Hollydale Rd
  MAPPK/POR/STA NG3....51 M1
Hollydene Cl *HUCK/RAV* NG15....22 F7
Hollydene Crs *BLWL* NG6....35 M3
Holly Gdns
  MAPPK/POR/STA NG3....37 K8

Hollygate La
  COT/KEY/RAD NG12....67 M2
Holly Gv *RLEIW/BBY* LE8....136 F7
Holly Hayes Rd *COAL* LE67....108 D3
Holly Hill Rd
  EWD/SEL/PNX NG16....13 K1
Holly House La *BPR/DUF* DE56....17 G3
Holly La *BSTN/STPLFD* NG9....63 J2
Hollymoor Dr *MELB/CHEL* DE73....72 C5
Holly Rd *EWD/SEL/PNX* NG16....22 E8
Holly Tree Av *LEIN* LE4....119 L7
Hollytree Cl *LBORO* LE11....103 L8
  RLBORO LE12....97 G5
Hollywell Av *RIPLEY* DE5....11 M8
Holm Av *DERBYE* DE21....29 M8
Holmdale Rd *RLEINE/SYS* LE7....120 E4
Holmden Av *WGSTN* LE18....137 M5
Holme Av *RLBORO* LE12....88 C4
Holme Cl *CALV/BJ* NG14....27 H3
  ILK DE7....33 H5
Holme Cft *ILK* DE7....32 C8
Holme Dr *LEIS* LE2....132 F8
Holmefield Crs *ILK* DE7....33 L7
Holme Gv *WBRGFD* NG2....51 M5
Holme La *COT/KEY/RAD* NG12....53 L7
  DERBYE DE21....59 G5
Holme Rd *WBRGFD* NG2....51 L6
Holmes Cl *EWD/SEL/PNX* NG16....20 E4
  GBY/RBY DE7....123 J4
Holmesfield Dr *HEANOR* DE75....20 E7
  MCKLVR DE3....56 D5
Holmes Rd *BWSH/BRSTN* DE72....61 H7
Holmes St *HEANOR* DE75....20 B5
  NORM/LIT DE23....2 E9
Holme St *WBRGFD* NG2....51 J5
Holmewood Crs *ARN* NG5....36 F4
Holmewood Dr
  EWD/SEL/PNX NG16....21 M7
  RLEIW/BAR LE9....129 K3
Holmfield *NORM/LIT* DE23....57 J3
Holmfield Av *LBORO* LE11....103 K1
  LEIS LE2....132 B5
Holmfield Av East *LEIW* LE3....130 A4
Holmfield Av West *LEIW* LE3....130 A4
Holmfield Rd *BSTN/STPLFD* NG9....63 G4
  LEIS LE2....132 A5
Holmleigh Gdns
  RLEINE/SYS LE7....133 K5
Holmoak Cl *DERBYE* DE21....44 F4
Holmsfield *COT/KEY/RAD* NG12....80 C5
Holmwood Dr *LEIW* LE3....124 C6
Holroyd Av *WBRGFD* NG2....51 K3
Holt Av *DERBYSE* DE24....73 G1
Holt Crs *RLEIW/BAR* LE9....134 E4
Holt Dr *LBORO* LE11....8 E7
  RLEIW/BAR LE9....129 K3
Holtlands Dr *DERBYSE* DE24....72 D2
Holt Ri *RLBORO* LE12....102 A6
Holt Rd *LEIN* LE4....125 L2
Holts Cl *LEIS* LE2....136 F3
Holyhead Dr *DERBYE* DE21....44 F5
Holyoake Dr *LGEAT* NG10....62 D8
Holyoake Rd
  MAPPK/POR/STA NG3....38 A4
Holyoake St *END/NAR* LE19....135 L5
Holyrood Cl *DERBYE* DE21....59 K2
Holyrood Dr *RLEIW/BBY* LE8....143 H3
Holywell Dr *LBORO* LE11....8 E7
Holywell Rd *ILK* DE7....33 G4
  LEIS LE2....137 G1
Holywell Wy *LBORO* LE11....103 G5
Home Cl *ARN* NG5....25 H7
  RLEIW/BBY LE8....136 F7
  RLEIW/BBY LE8....146 E8
The Home Cft
  BSTN/STPLFD NG9....48 F8
Home Dr *WBRGFD* NG2....65 J3
Homefarm Cl
  BWSH/BRSTN DE72....60 A2
Home Farm Cl *CFTN/RUD* NG11....77 L6
  LEIN LE4....125 G4
  RLBORO LE12....111 M4
Home Farm Dr *DERBYW* DE22....43 L3
Homefield Av *ARN* NG5....25 L6
Homefield La *RLEINE/SYS* LE7....119 K1
Homefield Rd *RLBORO* LE12....114 A3
  WOL/BIL/BRX NG8....36 B8
Homemead Av *LEIN* LE4....125 H5
Homer Dr *END/NAR* LE19....135 L7
The Homestead *RLBORO* LE12....113 H4
Homestead
  EWD/SEL/PNX NG16....20 E3
Homestead Cl *RLBORO* LE12....114 B7
Homestead Dr *WGSTN* LE18....138 B6
Homestead Houses
  RLEIW/BAR * LE9....140 C3
Homestead Rd *COAL* LE67....100 B7
Homestone Gdns *LEIE* LE5....133 J1
Homestone Ri *LEIE* LE5....133 J1
Homeway Rd *RLBORO* LE12....102 A4
Homeway Rd *LEIE* LE5....132 C4
Honeybourne Cl *LEIS* LE2....138 E2
Honeycomb Cl *END/NAR* LE19....135 L7
Honeycroft Cl *BPR/DUF* DE56....17 M5
Honeyfield Dr *RIPLEY* DE5....11 K7
Honeysuckle Cl *COAL* LE67....108 E7
  RLEIW/SYS LE7....115 K8
  WOL/BIL/BRX NG8....35 J6
Honeysuckle Gv *BLWL* NG6....35 M3
Honeysuckle Rd *LEIE* LE5....127 G5
Honeysuckle Wy *RLBORO* LE12....111 L1
Honeywood Dr
  MAPPK/POR/STA NG3....37 L3
Honingham Cl *ARN* NG5....37 K2
Honingham Rd *ILK* DE7....33 G4
Honister Cl *CFTN/RUD* NG11....64 B8
  WBRGFD NG2....52 A8
Honiton Cl *BSTN/STPLFD* NG9....48 A8
  WGSTN LE18....138 A4
Honiton Rd *WOL/BIL/BRX* NG8....35 H5
Hood Cl *ARN* NG5....37 H5
Hooley Cl *LGEAT* NG10....75 M1
Hooley St *EWD/SEL/PNX* NG16....13 K1
Hooton Rd *CARL* NG4....38 A4
Hooton St
  MAPPK/POR/STA NG3....51 K2
Hope Av *MCKLVR* DE3....56 B5
Hope Cl *WBRGFD* NG2....50 F5

Hopedale Cl *NOTTE* NG7....50 C2
Hope Dr *NOTTE* NG7....4 E9
Hopefield Rd *LEIW* LE3....131 G5
Hope St *BSTN/STPLFD* NG9....49 J8
  DERBY DE1....3 G5
  ILK DE7....33 K8
  NORM/LIT DE23....82 D8
Hopetoun St *NORM/LIT* DE23....57 L7
Hopewell Cl *COT/KEY/RAD* NG12....53 L2
Hopewell Wk *ILK* DE7....33 K2
Hopping Hl *BPR/DUF* DE56....17 K7
Hopton Cl *DERBYE* DE21....44 E6
  RIPLEY DE5....11 K6
Hopwell Rd *BWSH/BRSTN* DE72....60 E8
Hopwood Cl *LEIN* LE4....124 F4
Hopyard Cl *LEIS* LE2....136 F3
Horace Av *BSTN/STPLFD* NG9....48 A8
Hornbeam Cl *DERBYE* DE21....44 C5
  END/NAR LE19....135 L7
  LEIS LE2....132 E8
  RLBORO LE12....111 L1
Hornbuckle Ct *NOTTE* NG7....4 B5
Horncastle Rd *DERBYE* DE21....44 B6
Hornchurch Rd
  WOL/BIL/BRX NG8....35 H8
Horndean Av *WGSTN* LE18....138 A4
Hornecroft *RLEINE/SYS* LE7....119 J1
Hornsby Wk *ARN* NG5....24 C7
Hornsea Rd *DERBYE* DE21....44 B6
Horridge St *ILK* DE7....33 K3
Horsecroft Cl *ILK* DE7....33 G5
Horsefair St *LEI* LE1....6 F6
Horsendale Av
  EWD/SEL/PNX NG16....35 K3
Horseshoe Cl *RLEIW/BAR* LE9....142 B3
The Horse Shoes
  CDON/KEG DE74....85 G3
Horsewell La *WGSTN* LE18....138 B7
Horsham Dr *ARN* NG5....24 D7
Horsley Crs *BPR/DUF* DE56....18 A8
  LEIN LE4....126 E4
Horsley Cl *DERBYE* DE21....30 C1
Horsley Rd *DERBYE* DE21....30 D1
Horston Rd *LEIE* LE5....132 C4
Horton Cl *RLEIW/BBY* LE8 * LE8....136 E7
Horton St *NORM/LIT* DE23....3 J9
Horwood Av *NORM/LIT* DE23....57 H5
Horwood Cl *WGSTN* LE18....138 C3
Hoselett Field Rd *LGEAT* NG10....76 C2
Hoskins Cl *WGSTN* LE18....138 C7
Hospital Cl *LEIE* LE5....132 D3
Hospital La *MCKLVR* DE3....55 M8
  RLEIW/BBY LE8....137 H8
Hospital Wy *LBORO* LE11....8 B6
Hotel St *COAL* LE67....108 B6
  LEI LE1....6 E6
Hoten Rd *WBRGFD* NG2....51 K4
Hotoft Rd *LEIE* LE5....126 F7
Hoton Rd *RLBORO* LE12....98 A4
Hotspur Cl *BLWL* NG6....36 C2
Houghton Av *ILK* DE7....33 G4
Houghton Cl
  EWD/SEL/PNX NG16....35 J3
Houghton Ct *DERBYE* DE21....44 D5
Houghton La *LEIS* LE2....133 L6
Houghton St *LEIE* LE5....126 E4
Houlditch Rd *LEIS* LE2....131 M7
Houldsworth Ri *ARN* NG5....25 J5
Hoult St *DERBYW* DE22....57 H3
Hound Rd *WBRGFD* NG2....51 J7
Hounds Ga *NOTT* NG1....5 G8
Hounslow Rd *DERBYW* DE22....56 F1
Houseman Gdns *NOTTE* NG7....4 A2
Housman Wk *LEIN* LE4....125 M7
Houston Cl *ARN* NG5....24 C6
Hovenden Gdns *NOTTE* NG7....4 A2
Hove Rd *ARN* NG5....36 C2
Hoveton Cl *DERBYE* DE24....72 B4
Howard Cl *LBORO* LE11....103 G2
  LGEAT NG10....62 C6
Howard Rd *LEIS* LE2....131 L6
  LEIS LE2....136 F5
Howard St *LBORO* LE11....103 M2
  NORM/LIT DE23....3 H9
  NOTT NG1....5 H6
Howarth Cl *LGEAT* NG10....61 L8
Howbeck Rd *ARN* NG5....25 M6
Howden Cl *LBORO* LE11....102 F4
  MCKLVR DE3....56 A6
Howden Rd *BLWL* NG6....24 A5
  LEIS LE2....137 G3
Howdon Rd *LEIS* LE2....138 F4
Howe Cl *RLEIW/BAR* LE9....140 A5
Howe Ct *COAL* LE67....108 B2
Howe La *RLEINE/SYS* LE7....119 J1
Howell-Jones Rd
  BSTN/STPLFD NG9....62 F4
Howells Cl *ARN* NG5....25 G7
Howe Rd *COAL* LE67....108 B2
  LBORO LE11....9 J9
Howe St *DERBYW* DE22....57 H2
Howick Dr *BLWL* NG6....23 K7
Howitt St *HEANOR* DE75....20 D5
  LGEAT NG10....62 C9
Howth Cl *DERBYE* DE21....58 E3
Hoylake Cl *LEIE* LE5....132 C5
Hoylake Ct *MCKLVR* DE3....56 A4
Hoylake Crs *WOL/BIL/BRX* NG8....35 H8
Hoylake Dr *MCKLVR* DE3....56 A4
Hoyland Av *NOTTE* NG7....50 C5
Hoyland Ct *BPR/DUF* DE56....18 C2
Hslmr Ct *NORM/LIT* DE23....3 H9
Hubbard Cl *RLEIW/BBY* LE8....142 E1
Hubert Shaw Cl *DERBYSE* DE24....72 C3
Hubert St *NOTTE* NG7....33 G5
Huckerby Rd *LEIE* LE5....132 C2
Hucklow Ct *DERBYE* DE21....44 F4
Hucknall Cl *MCKLVR* DE3....56 A4
Hucknall Crs *CARL* NG4....38 C5
Hucknall La *BLWL* NG6....24 A7
Hucknall Rd *ARN* NG5....36 C1
  BLWL NG6....35 M2
  HUCK/RAV NG15....15 H3
Hudson Rd *RLBORO* LE12....114 A3
Hudson St *LBORO* LE11....9 L2
  MAPPK/POR/STA NG3....51 K1
Hudson Wy *DERBYSE* DE24....3 K7

Hufton's Ct *HEANOR* DE75....20 E8
Huggett Cl *LEIN* LE4....126 C3
Hughenden Dr *LEIS* LE2....131 J6
Hulland Cl *DERBY* DE1....3 J7
Hulland Vw *DERBYW* DE22....43 H6
Humber Cl *DERBYSE* DE24....73 G1
  WBRGFD NG2....51 G5
Humber Ldg
  BSTN/STPLFD NG9....49 L8
Humber Rd *BSTN/STPLFD* NG9....49 L8
  LGEAT NG10....62 A6
Humber Rd South
  BSTN/STPLFD NG9....63 M1
Humberstone Cl *LEIS* LE2....126 D7
Humberstone Ga *LEI* LE1....6 F5
Humberstone La *LEIN* LE4....126 C1
Humberstone Rd *LEIE* LE5....7 K2
Humberston Rd
  WOL/BIL/BRX NG8....49 G4
Humble La *RLBORO* LE12....114 B7
Humbleton Dr *DERBYW* DE22....56 E2
Humes Cl *RLEIW/BBY* LE8....142 D3
Humphrey Cl *LBORO* LE11....9 K7
Humphries Cl *LEIS* LE2....132 E2
Huncote Rd *RLEIW/BAR* LE9....135 J8
  RLEIW/BAR LE9....140 B3
  RLEIW/BAR LE9....140 F2
Hungarton Bvd *LEIE* LE5....126 C7
Hungarton Dr *RLEINE/SYS* LE7....121 G4
Hungary La *RLBORO* LE12....94 F1
Hungerhill La *CARL* NG4....26 E5
Hungerhill Rd
  MAPPK/POR/STA NG3....5 K1
Hunston Cl *WOL/BIL/BRX* NG8....35 K4
Hunt Av *HEANOR* DE75....20 C5
Hunter Dr *BPR/DUF* DE56....18 D7
Hunter Rd *ARN* NG5....38 A1
  BPR/DUF DE56....18 B2
  LEIN LE4....125 L6
Hunters Cl *CFTN/RUD* NG11....64 E1
Hunters Cft *DERBYSE* DE24....71 J5
Hunters Rw *RLEIW/BAR* * LE9....142 B7
Hunters Wy *LEIS* LE2....139 H2
  LEIW LE3....130 C2
Huntingdon Cl *RLBORO* LE12....97 L8
Huntingdon Ct
  MELB/CHEL DE73....82 F7
Huntingdon Dr *CDON/KEG* DE74....84 E3
  NOTTE NG7....4 D7
Huntingdon Gn *DERBYE* DE21....3 K2
Huntingdon Rd *LEIN* LE4....126 B5
Huntingdon St *NOTT* NG1....5 G3
Huntingdon Wk *LGEAT* NG10....61 M2
Huntingdon Wy
  BSTN/STPLFD NG9....62 D5
The Huntings *RLEIW/BAR* LE9....129 G2
Huntley Av *DERBYE* DE21....59 L1
Huntly Cl *CFTN/RUD* NG11....64 D6
Hunts Cl *GBY/RBY* DE7....122 A7
Huntsmans Cl *COAL* LE67....116 C7
  RLBORO LE12....104 F8
Huntsman's Dl *RLEINE/SYS* LE7....115 H7
Huntsmans Wy *LEIN* LE4....126 B4
Huntspill Rd *RDERBYSW* DE65....68 C6
Hurcomb St
  MAPPK/POR/STA NG3....37 K8
Hurley Ct *ILK* DE7....32 C7
Hurley Cl *LEIS* LE2....139 G2
Hurst Dr *ILK* DE7....46 A1
Hurst Ri *LEIS* LE2....132 E2
Hurstwood Rd *LBORO* LE11....102 F4
Hurts Cft *BSTN/STPLFD* NG9....63 H3
Hurts Yd *NOTT* NG1....5 G6
Huss's La *LGEAT* NG10....62 D8
Huston Cl *RLBORO* LE12....113 K2
Huston Ct *LBORO* LE11....9 H5
Hutchinson Gn
  MAPPK/POR/STA NG3....5 K4
Hutchinson St *LEIS* LE2....7 J6
Hutton Cl *BSTN/STPLFD* NG9....49 H6
Hutton St *DERBYSE* DE24....72 C1
  WBRGFD NG2....51 K3
Huxley Cl *NORM/LIT* DE23....57 F8
  WOL/BIL/BRX NG8....35 H8
Hyam's La *CDON/KEG* DE74....95 M5
Hyde Cl *CFTN/RUD* NG11....64 D3
  END/NAR LE19....135 M7
  LEIS LE2....139 G4
Hyde Park Cl *WBRGFD* * NG2....51 K3
Hyde Park Rd *DERBYW* DE22....56 E1
Hydra Wk *LEIS* LE2....7 K6
Hylion Rd *LEIS* LE2....137 L1
Hyson Cl *NOTTE* NG7....36 D7
Hyson St *NOTTE* NG7....4 B2

I

Ian Gv *CARL* NG4....38 C7
Ibbetson Av *LEIW* LE3....124 A8
Ibsley Cl *DERBYSE* DE24....73 G1
Ibsley Wy *LEIS* LE2....137 H4
Ickworth Cl *LEIE* LE5....126 C7
Iffley Cl *LEIE* LE5....132 D2
Ilam Sq *ILK* DE7....33 J2
Ilford Cl *ILK* DE7....33 H4
Ilford Rd *DERBYW* DE22....58 D2
Iliffe Av *LEIS* LE2....138 D2
Iliffe Rd *LEIN* LE4....126 C6
Iliffes Cl *RLBORO* LE12....105 J7
Ilkeston Rd *BSTN/STPLFD* NG9....48 A3
  BSTN/STPLFD NG9....48 E6
  HEANOR DE75....20 D7
  ILK DE7....31 J5
  ILK DE7....47 K4
  ILK DE7....48 A7
  NOTTE NG7....4 C6
Illingworth Rd *LEIE* LE5....132 E1
Ilmington Cl *LEIW* LE3....124 A6
Imperial Av *BSTN/STPLFD* NG9....63 J1
  CARL NG4....38 C6
  LEIW LE3....130 F4
Imperial Ct *DERBYW* DE22....43 H2
Imperial Rd *BLWL* NG6....36 B1

BSTN/STPLFD NG9 ....63 J1
RLEIW/BBY LE8 ....146 D7
Inchwood Cl BSTN/STPLFD NG9 ....62 D5
Incinerator Rd WBRGFD NG2......51 J5
Independent St NOTTE NG7.........4 B4
Industrial St NORM/LIT DE23.......2 E1
Infirmary Cl LEI LE1................6 E9
Infirmary Rd LEI LE1...............6 E9
Infirmary Sq LEI LE1...............6 E8
Ingarsby Dr LEIE LE5.............133 G4
Ingham Dr MCKLVR DE3...........56 B7
Ingham Gv NOTTE NG7...........50 C4
Ingham Rd LGEAT NG10..........62 A5
Ingleberry Rd RLBORO LE12.....102 B8
Ingleborough Gdns LGEAT NG10...61 L7
Ingleby Av NORM/LIT DE23.......57 K8
Ingleby Cl COT/KEY/RAD NG12....67 J5
WOL/BIL/BRX NG8...............48 F3
Ingleby Rd LGEAT NG10..........75 K2
WGSTN LE18.................138 A4
Ingle Cl DERBYE DE21.............59 J2
Ingledew Cl DERBYE DE21........44 C6
Ingle Dr GBY/RBY LE6...........123 G7
Inglefield Rd ILK DE7.............47 K1
Ingle's Channel BPR/DUF DE56....17 K3
Ingle St LEIW LE3...............124 F8
Inglewood Av MCKLVR DE3........56 B8
Inglewood Rd CFTN/RUD NG11....64 C6
Ingliston Cl DERBYSE DE24........73 H1
Ingold Av LEIN LE4.............125 H4
Ingram Rd BLWL NG6.............36 B1
Ingrams Wy WGSTN LE18........138 C7
Inham Circ BSTN/STPLFD NG9.....63 G1
Inham Cl BSTN/STPLFD NG9.......62 E2
Inham Rd BSTN/STPLFD NG9......62 E2
Inkerman Rd
EWD/SEL/PNX NG16............13 K2
Inkerman St
EWD/SEL/PNX NG16............13 K2
The Inleys RLBORO LE12.........102 B4
Innes Cl CARL NG4................38 A4
Instow Dr NORM/LIT DE23........42 F1
Instow Ri MAPPK/POR/STA NG3....5 K4
Intake Rd COT/KEY/RAD NG12....80 B4
Inveraray Cl DERBYSE DE24.......71 H4
Invergarry Cl LEIN LE4..........126 E3
Invernia Cl NORM/LIT DE23.......71 J2
Iona Cl DERBYSE DE24............71 J3
LEIN LE4.....................124 F4
Iona Dr BSTN/STPLFD NG9........48 B3
Iona Rd RLEINE/SYS LE7.........120 D3
Iona Wy RLEIW/BBY LE8.........143 K4
Ipswich Circ
MAPPK/POR/STA NG3...........51 L2
Ipswich Cl LEIN LE4.............124 E1
Ireland Av BSTN/STPLFD NG9.....63 J2
Ireland Cl BSTN/STPLFD NG9.....63 L2
Iremonger Rd WBRGFD NG2......51 H4
Ireton Av LEIN LE4..............126 D5
Ireton Gv BSTN/STPLFD NG9......63 H5
Ireton Houses BPR/DUF * DE56...18 C4
Ireton Rd LEIN LE4.............126 C6
Ireton St BSTN/STPLFD NG9......63 J1
NOTTE NG7....................4 D5
Iris Av LEIN LE4...............119 M7
LEIS LE2.....................136 F4
Iris Cl RLBORO LE12............113 K5
Irlam St WGSTN LE18............137 K7
Irmington Gdns LEIE LE5.........133 G4
Iron Ga DERBY DE1................2 E3
Ironworks Rd LEIN LE4..........126 A7
Irvine Cl DERBYSE DE24..........71 H4
Irving Pl DERBYSE DE24..........58 D4
Irwin Av LBORO LE11............103 G1
Irwin Dr BLWL NG6...............35 K2
Isaac's La BSTN/STPLFD NG9......48 B8
Isabella St NOTT NG1..............5 H5
Isandula Rd NOTTE NG7...........36 D5
Isis Cl LEIS LE2................139 H1
Islay Cl ARN NG5................25 K6
BSTN/STPLFD NG9..............48 B5
Islay Rd DERBYSE DE24...........71 J3
Isleworth Dr DERBYW DE22.......56 D1
Islington Dr LEIS LE3...........131 K5
Ismay Rd DERBYE DE21...........58 D1
Isobella Rd LEIW LE3...........130 A6
Ivanhoe Cl LEIN LE4............124 A4
Ivanhoe Rd WGSTN LE18.........137 K5
Ivanhoe St LEIN LE4............131 G1
Ivatt Cl RLEINE/SYS LE7.........133 L2
Ivatt Dr WBRGFD NG2............51 K4
Ives Cl WBRGFD NG2.............65 G3
Iveshead La RLBORO LE12........101 M7
Iveshead Rd RLBORO LE12.......101 L8
Ivybridge Cl DERBYE DE21........45 G4
Ivychurch Crs LEIE LE5..........127 J6
Ivy Cl EWD/SEL/PNX NG16........22 D6
Ivy Ct RDERBYSW DE65...........68 B6
Ivydale Rd LEIN LE4............126 D1
Ivy Gv CARL NG4.................38 B4
NOTTE NG7....................36 E7
RIPLEY DE5....................11 H6
Ivy La EWD/SEL/PNX NG16........21 J3
Ivy Rd LEIN LE4................131 G4
Ivy Sq NORM/LIT DE23.............3 J9

J

Jacklin Dr LEIN LE4.............126 B2
Jacksdale Cl DERBYW DE22.......43 H6
Jackson Av ILK DE7...............33 H6
LGEAT NG10....................61 L1
MCKLVR DE3....................56 E5
Jackson Cl LEIS LE2............139 H2
Jackson's La BPR/DUF DE56.......10 B8
BPR/DUF DE56..................17 J8
RDERBYSW DE65.................69 G5
Jackson St COAL LE67...........108 A7
DERBYSE DE22...................2 B5
LEIN LE4.....................125 M4
Jacob Cl END/NAR LE19..........135 L4
Jacqueline Rd COAL LE67........116 D7
Jacquemart Cl COAL LE67........109 H6
Jacques Cl END/NAR LE19........135 L4
James Av LBORO LE11............103 G1

James Cl DERBY DE1...............2 A3
James Gavin Wy LEIS LE2........139 J3
James St ARN NG5................25 J7
COAL LE67....................108 A7
EWD/SEL/PNX NG16.............34 D1
RLEINE/SYS LE7...............118 B8
RLEIW/BAR LE9................140 B4
RLEIW/BBY LE8................136 E7
Jamesway RLEIW/BAR LE9........142 B3
Janes Wy COAL LE67............116 C7
Japonica Cl LBORO LE11.........103 L8
Japonica Dr BLWL NG6...........35 M3
Jardine Ct BWSH/BRSTN DE72.....60 F8
The Jardines BSTN/STPLFD NG9...49 G6
Jarrett Cl END/NAR LE19........135 L4
Jarrom St LEIS LE2.............131 J4
Jarrow Gdns ARN NG5............24 D5
Jarvey's La RLEIW/BAR LE9......42 C7
Jarvis Av MAPPK/POR/STA NG3....51 M1
Jarvis Dr DERBYSE DE24..........71 J5
Jarvis St LEI LE1................6 C5
Jarvis Wy COAL LE67............108 C2
Jasmine Cl BSTN/STPLFD NG9.....49 H6
CFTN/RUD NG11................64 A6
DERBYE DE21...................58 F2
LBORO LE11...................103 L8
LEIE LE5.....................126 F4
WOL/BIL/BRX NG8...............35 J6
Jasmine Ct END/NAR LE19........135 K6
HEANOR DE75...................20 F6
WGSTN LE18...................137 K5
Jasmine Rd ARN NG5.............36 C5
Jasper Cl COT/KEY/RAD NG12....53 J5
Jawbone La MELB/CHEL DE73.....83 G7
Jayne Cl CARL NG4...............38 E5
WOL/BIL/BRX NG8...............49 J1
Jean Dr LEIN LE4...............125 H6
Jedburgh Cl DERBYSE DE24........71 J5
MAPPK/POR/STA NG3..............5 K4
Jedburgh Wk
MAPPK/POR/STA NG3..............5 K4
Jeffares Cl CDON/KEG DE74.......86 A4
Jefferson Pl DERBYSE DE24.......58 D8
Jellicoe Rd LEIE LE5...........132 C1
Jemison Cl NORM/LIT DE23.......56 C8
Jenned Rd ARN NG5..............25 L5
Jenner St ARN NG5...............36 F7
Jenness Av ARN NG5.............24 C6
Jennett Cl LEIE LE5............133 G1
Jennison St BLWL NG6............24 A8
Jenny Burton Wy
HUCK/RAV NG15................24 A2
Jenny's Ct BPR/DUF DE56........18 A2
Jeremy Cl LEIN LE4.............125 M5
Jermyn Dr ARN NG5..............24 E6
Jermyn St LEIN LE4............125 M5
Jersey Gdns
MAPPK/POR/STA NG3..............5 M4
Jersey Rd LEIN LE4.............125 H3
Jesmond Rd BLWL NG6............36 B1
Jesop Dr DERBYSE DE24..........71 J5
Jessons Cl LEIN LE4...........126 B4
Jessop Av EWD/SEL/PNX NG16....12 D4
Jessop Cl LEIW LE3............124 E7
Jessop Ldg RIPLEY * DE5........11 M8
Jessop's La CARL NG4...........38 C4
Jessop St RIPLEY DE5...........11 M8
Jetcott Av LBORO LE11..........103 L8
Jewsbury Wy LEIW LE3..........130 A5
Joan McHeanor DE75............20 C5
Jodrell Av BPR/DUF DE56.........18 B3
Joe Moore's La RLBORO LE12....111 H6
John Berrysford Cl
DERBYE DE21...................58 D2
John Bold Av RLEIW/BAR LE9....140 C4
John Carroll Ct
MAPPK/POR/STA NG3............51 K1
John F Kennedy Gdns
DERBYE DE21...................59 G1
John Lombe Dr DERBY DE1........43 J8
John O'Gaunts Wy
BPR/DUF DE56..................18 B2
John Phillips Cl LBORO LE11......8 C3
John Port Cl RDERBYSW DE65.....69 G3
Johns Av RLBORO LE12..........113 J6
John's Lee Cl LBORO LE11........8 E9
Johnson Av DERBYSE DE24........58 C8
HUCK/RAV NG15................23 M2
Johnson Cl EWD/SEL/PNX NG16...22 B8
RLEIW/BBY LE8................136 D8
Johnson Dr HEANOR DE75.........20 D5
Johnson Ri RLEIW/BAR LE9.......140 C5
Johnson Rd LEIN LE4...........119 K8
NOTTE NG7....................50 C3
Johnson St LEI LE1...............6 C3
Johns Rd COT/KEY/RAD NG12.....53 L4
John St COAL LE67.............100 B8
DERBY DE1.....................3 H6
END/NAR LE19................135 M5
HEANOR DE75..................20 B5
ILK DE7.......................33 K6
NOTTE NG7....................36 D5
Jolly Farmers La RLBORO LE12...101 L7
Jonathan Cl GBY/RBY LE6........123 L4
Jordan Av WGSTN LE18..........137 L6
Jordan Cl LEIW LE3............124 A7
Joseph St BPR/DUF DE56.........17 K3
NORM/LIT DE23................57 L7
Joseph Wright Ter
DERBY * DE1...................43 L8
Journeyman's Gn
GBY/RBY LE6..................123 H7
Jowett Cl LEIW LE3............124 E6
Joyce Av ARN NG5...............37 H3
BSTN/STPLFD NG9..............62 C4
Joyce Cl ARN NG5...............37 H3
Joyce Rd LEIW LE3............124 F7
Jubalton Cl DERBYSE DE24.......72 C1
Jubilee Av RIPLEY DE5..........11 G6
RLBORO LE12.................114 B2
Jubilee Cl MELB/CHEL DE73......82 F8
Jubilee Ct BPR/DUF DE56........17 L5
Jubilee Crs END/NAR LE19......136 A4
Jubilee Dr LBORO LE11.........103 L1
LEIW LE3.....................124 A4
Jubilee Gdns LEIE LE5..........126 B7
Jubilee Houses
RLEIW/BAR * LE9..............129 H1

Jubilee Rd ARN NG5..............37 J1
DERBYSE DE24..................72 C3
Jubilee St LBORO LE11..........9 M4
Judges St LBORO LE11...........9 M4
Judith Dr LEIE LE5.............132 F3
RLEIW/BBY LE8................143 K3
Judson Av BSTN/STPLFD NG9.....62 D1
Julian Cl ILK DE7...............47 L1
Julian Rd LEIS LE2.............137 G5
WBRGFD NG2...................51 M7
Julie Av HEANOR DE75...........20 F6
Junction Rd LEI LE1..............7 G2
LGEAT NG10....................76 D1
WGSTN LE18...................138 B4
Junction St DERBY DE1..........57 H3
June Av LEIN LE4...............126 E2
Junior St LEI LE1................6 D4
Juniper Cl CFTN/RUD NG11......64 A6
LEIW LE3.....................129 K5
Juniper Ct EWD/SEL/PNX NG16...22 A7
NOTTE NG7.....................4 C4
Juniper Wy RLBORO LE12........111 L1
Juno Cl LEIW LE3..............124 A8
Jupiter Cl LEIS LE2..............7 K6
Jura Av RIPLEY DE5.............11 H5
Jury St DERBY DE1...............2 D3

K

Kamloops Crs LEI LE1.............7 G3
Kappler Cl CARL NG4............38 E8
Karen Gdns BSTN/STPLFD NG9....63 H3
Karen Ri ARN NG5...............25 L6
Kashmir Rd LEI LE1..............7 J2
Kate St LEIW LE3..............129 K5
Katherine Dr BSTN/STPLFD NG9..62 D4
Kayes Wk NOTT * NG1............5 J8
Kay Rd LEIW LE3...............124 D7
Kean Pl DERBYSE DE24...........58 D8
Keats Av NORM/LIT DE23.........56 E6
Keats Cl ARN NG5...............25 H8
END/NAR LE19.................135 L4
EWD/SEL/PNX NG16.............34 F1
LGEAT NG10....................75 M2
Keats Dr HUCK/RAV NG15........23 H1
Keats Wk LEIN LE4.............125 M7
Keays Wy RLEINE/SYS LE7.......127 K7
Keble Cl DERBY DE1..............3 H8
Keble Dr RLEINE/SYS LE7.......120 F8
Keble Rd LEIS LE2.............131 L6
Kedleston Av LEIN LE4.........125 L2
Kedleston Cl BSTN/STPLFD NG9...43 H6
DERBYW DE22...................43 H6
LGEAT NG10....................75 L3
RIPLEY DE5....................11 G4
Kedleston Gdns DERBY * DE1.....2 D1
Kedleston Old Rd
DERBYW DE22...................43 H7
Kedleston Rd DERBYW DE22......28 B8
DERBYW DE22...................43 G3
LEIE LE5.....................132 B3
Kedleston St DERBY DE1..........2 C1
Keeling Cl EWD/SEL/PNX NG16...21 M6
Keenan Cl LEIS LE2.............136 F2
The Keep RLBORO LE12...........88 D7
RLEIW/BAR LE9................129 H2
Keepers Cl BLWL NG6............24 C3
Keepers' Cft RLEINE/SYS LE7....115 J8
Kegworth Av LEIE LE5..........132 D2
Kegworth La RLBORO LE12........93 M3
Kegworth Rd CFTN/RUD NG11.....79 G1
Keightley Rd LEIW LE3.........124 C6
Keighton Hl NOTTE NG7..........50 A6
Kelbrook Cl LEIN LE4..........125 G3
Keldholme La DERBYSE DE24......59 G8
Kelfield Cl BLWL NG6...........36 C2
Kelham Gn
MAPPK/POR/STA NG3............51 K1
Kelham Wy EWD/SEL/PNX NG16...21 J4
Kelling Cl ARN NG5.............36 E1
Kelmarsh Av WGSTN LE18........138 B5
Kelmoor Rd DERBYSE DE24.......58 F8
Kelsey Cl BSTN/STPLFD NG9......63 J4
Kelso Cl COAL LE67............100 B7
Kelso Gdns WBRGFD NG2.........50 F5
Kelso Gn LEIS LE2.............137 H4
Kelstern Rd WOL/BIL/BRX NG8....35 M4
Kelvedon Dr NORM/LIT DE23......70 E1
Kelvedon Gdns
MAPPK/POR/STA NG3..............5 L4
Kelvin Cl BSTN/STPLFD NG9......62 A2
Kelvin Rd MAPPK/POR/STA NG3....37 L8
Kelvon Cl LEIW LE3............124 B6
Kemble Pl DERBYSE DE24.........58 D8
Kemble Sq LEI LE1...............6 F5
Kemmel Rd BLWL NG6............36 B2
Kemp Rd LEIW LE3.............124 C6
Kempsey Cl ARN NG5............24 C7
Kempson Rd LEIS LE2...........131 J7
Kempton Cl
EWD/SEL/PNX NG16.............22 C8
Kempton Dr ARN NG5............25 L6
Kempton Park Rd
DERBYSE DE24..................58 B7
Kendal Cl HUCK/RAV NG15.......15 K7
Kendal Ct WBRGFD NG2..........51 M7
Kendal Dr BSTN/STPLFD NG9.....49 H7
Kendall's Av RLEIW/BAR LE9....141 G3
Kendal Rd LEIN LE4............126 B4
RLBORO LE12.................114 B5
Kendon Av NORM/LIT DE23.......71 J1
Kendray Cl BPR/DUF DE56.......18 B2
Kendrick Dr LEIS LE2..........138 F2
Kenia Cl CARL NG4.............38 B7
Kenilworth Av LBORO LE11......103 G3
NORM/LIT DE23................57 K7
Kenilworth Cl RLBORO LE12.....113 H6
RLEIW/BAR LE9................141 J7
Kenilworth Ct
BSTN/STPLFD NG9..............49 L7
NOTTE NG7.....................4 B1

Kenilworth Dr ILK DE7..........47 G2
LEIS LE2.....................138 D2
Kenilworth Rd
BSTN/STPLFD NG9..............49 L6
NOTTE NG7.....................4 E9
RIPLEY DE5....................11 G6
WGSTN LE18...................137 K4
Kenmore Gdns
MAPPK/POR/STA NG3..............5 K4
Kennedy Av LGEAT NG10..........76 A2
Kennedy Cl ARN NG5.............25 H8
DERBYE DE21...................44 E8
Kennedy Dr BSTN/STPLFD NG9....48 C6
Kennedy Wy LEIW LE3..........129 L5
Kennel La HUCK/RAV NG15........14 C6
Kenneth Gamble Ct
WGSTN LE18..................137 M3
Kenneth Rd ARN NG5............25 K5
Kennington Rd
WOL/BIL/BRX NG8..............50 B2
Kenny Cl RLEIW/BBY LE8........142 E1
Kenrick Rd
MAPPK/POR/STA NG3............37 L6
Kenrick St CARL NG4............38 D8
Kensal Ri DERBYW DE22..........56 F1
Kensington Av HEANOR DE75.....20 A6
LBORO LE11...................103 G2
Kensington Cl
BSTN/STPLFD NG9..............62 E6
LEIS LE2.....................137 H6
LEIS LE2.....................139 G4
Kensington Dr WGSTN LE18......138 D2
Kensington Gdns CARL NG4......38 C8
ILK DE7.......................33 K8
Kensington Park Cl
WBRGFD * NG2.................65 G2
Kensington Rd COAL LE67......108 E7
LGEAT NG10....................61 M3
Kensington St DERBYW DE22......2 C4
ILK DE7.......................47 K1
LEIN LE4.....................125 L6
Kenslow Av NOTTE NG7..........36 C8
Kent Av BSTN/STPLFD NG9.......63 K3
EWD/SEL/PNX NG16.............12 E9
Kent Crs WGSTN LE18..........137 K5
Kent Dr LEIS LE2..............139 G2
Kentish Ct DERBYE DE21.........43 M8
Kentmere Cl WBRGFD NG2........52 A8
Kenton Av EWD/SEL/PNX NG16....35 H4
WGSTN LE18...................138 A6
Kent Rd EWD/SEL/PNX NG16......22 A6
MAPPK/POR/STA NG3............37 L5
Kent St DERBYE DE21............44 B8
LEIE LE5......................7 J4
NOTT NG1......................5 J6
Kentwood Rd WBRGFD NG2.......51 K3
Kenwood Rd LEIS LE2..........132 A8
Kenyon Rd NOTTE NG7...........50 A4
Kepple Ga RIPLEY DE5...........11 K7
Kepston Cl LEIS LE2...........137 H3
Kernan Dr LBORO LE11...........95 K8
Kernel Cl NORM/LIT DE23........56 E7
Kerrial Rd LEIN LE4...........124 C8
Kerry Dr ILK DE7...............31 K1
Kerrysdale Av LEIN LE4........126 B5
Kerry St DERBYE DE21...........44 B8
Kerry's Yd BPR/DUF DE56........18 D7
Kersall Cl BLWL NG6............36 B1
Kersall Dr BLWL NG6............36 B2
Kersall Gdns HUCK/RAV NG15....15 M8
Kershope Dr DERBYE DE21........44 F4
Kertley RLEIW/BBY LE8.........145 K7
Kestrel Cl CARL NG4............37 M6
ILK DE7.......................47 K3
LEIE LE5.....................127 M3
LEIW LE3.....................129 J5
MCKLVR * DE3..................55 L8
RLEINE/SYS LE7...............120 D3
RLEIW/BAR LE9................141 J8
Kestrel Hts EWD/SEL/PNX NG16..12 D4
Kestrel La RLBORO LE12.........113 K5
Kestrels Cft DERBYSE DE24......71 H4
Keswick Av LBORO LE11...........8 A8
NORM/LIT DE23................71 J1
Keswick Cl EWD/SEL/PNX NG16...49 H7
ILK DE7.......................47 H2
WBRGFD NG2...................52 A8
Keswick Ct LGEAT NG10.........61 M5
WBRGFD NG2....................5 L7
Keswick Rd RLEIW/BBY LE8.....136 E8
Keswick St WBRGFD NG2..........5 L7
Kett St BLWL NG6..............35 M1
Keverne Cl WGSTN LE18........138 A6
Keverne Cl WOL/BIL/BRX NG8....35 M5
Kevin Cl DERBYE DE21...........44 F7
Kevin Rd WOL/BIL/BRX NG8......49 H5
Kew Cl CFTN/RUD NG11..........65 G4
Kew Crs HEANOR DE75...........20 F6
Kew Dr LEIS LE2...............139 G4
WGSTN LE18...................137 M2
Kew Gdns DERBYW DE22..........56 F2
WOL/BIL/BRX NG8..............35 J4
Keyham Cl LEIS LE2............126 F6
Keyham La East
RLEINE/SYS LE7...............127 M5
Keyham La West LEIE LE5.......127 H6
Keynsham Cl DERBYSE DE24......58 C7
Keys Cl BLWL NG6..............36 A1
Keys St DERBY DE1..............3 G2
Key St MAPPK/POR/STA NG3......51 K2
Keythorpe St LEIS LE2...........7 K5
Keyworth La
COT/KEY/RAD NG12.............79 K6
Keyworth Rd CARL NG4..........38 B4
COT/KEY/RAD NG12.............91 G2
Kibworth Br RLEIW/BBY LE8.....146 A5
Kibworth Cl ARN NG5............36 D3
Kibworth Rd RLEIW/BBY LE8.....145 J3
RLEIW/BBY LE8................146 A8
RLEIW/BBY LE8................147 G5
RLEIW/BBY LE8................147 J3
Kiddier Av ARN NG5.............25 M8

Kielder Cl END/NAR LE19.......135 K5
Kilbourne Cl RLBORO LE12......114 A5
Kilbourne Rd ARN NG5..........25 M6
Kilbourn St
MAPPK/POR/STA NG3..............5 G3
Kilburn Av LEIS LE2...........138 D1
Kilburn Cl BSTN/STPLFD NG9.....48 F5
Kilburn Dr ILK DE7.............33 H4
Kilburn La BPR/DUF DE56.........18 B4
Kilburn Rd BPR/DUF DE56.......17 M3
Kilby Av LEIN LE4.............125 L2
MAPPK/POR/STA NG3............51 L1
Kilby Dr WGSTN LE18..........138 C6
Kilby Rd RLEIW/BBY LE8.......145 G3
RLEIW/BBY LE8................145 H7
Kildare Rd DERBYE DE21.........58 F3
MAPPK/POR/STA NG3............37 K7
Kildare St LEI LE1..............6 F3
Kildonan Cl WOL/BIL/BRX NG8...35 H5
Killerton Gn CFTN/RUD NG11....64 C3
Killerton Park Dr
CFTN/RUD NG11................64 F3
Killingworth Av DERBYSE DE24...71 K3
Killisick Rd ARN NG5...........25 M7
Killis La BPR/DUF DE56.........18 B7
Kilmelford Cl LEIN LE4........126 B3
Kiln Av LEIN LE4..............126 D1
Kiln Cl ILK DE7................32 C6
Kiln Cft RDERBYSW DE65........69 G3
Kiln Garth RLBORO LE12........113 K7
Kilnsey Ct NORM/LIT DE23......70 D7
Kilnwood Cl
MAPPK/POR/STA NG3............51 L1
Kilsby Rd CFTN/RUD NG11.......64 C5
Kilverstone Av LEIE LE5.......133 H4
Kilverston Rd LGEAT NG10......47 L8
Kilverton Cl WOL/BIL/BRX NG8...50 A2
Kilvington Rd ARN NG5.........25 M8
Kilworth Dr LEIE LE5..........132 C4
Kimber Cl WOL/BIL/BRX NG8.....49 H1
Kimberley Cl
EWD/SEL/PNX NG16.............34 D2
Kimberley Rd
BWSH/BRSTN DE72..............59 M5
EWD/SEL/PNX NG16.............34 F2
LEIS LE2......................7 M9
WBRGFD NG2...................51 J3
Kimberley St RLEIW/BBY LE8....146 D7
Kimbolton Av NOTTE NG7.........4 E6
Kincaple Rd LEIN LE4..........126 B3
Kinchley La RLEINE/SYS LE7....112 F6
Kincraig Rd LEIN LE4..........126 B3
Kinder Cl RLEIW/BBY LE8......142 E2
Kinder Wk DERBYW * DE22........2 A5
Kindlewood Dr
BSTN/STPLFD NG9..............62 F6
King Alfred St DERBYW DE22......2 C4
King Charles St NOTT * NG1......4 F8
Kingcup Cl LEIW LE3..........129 K5
King Edward Av
END/NAR LE19................136 A4
King Edward Ct NOTT NG1........5 J4
King Edward Rd LBORO LE11......9 M5
LEIE LE5.....................126 F4
King Edward St
HUCK/RAV NG15................23 L1
LGEAT NG10...................61 M1
NOTT NG1......................5 J6
Kingfisher Av LEIE LE5..........7 M3
Kingfisher Cl BSTN/STPLFD NG9..63 M2
COAL LE67....................108 F5
LEIW LE3.....................129 J5
MCKLVR DE3....................55 M8
RLBORO LE12..................105 J7
RLEINE/SYS LE7...............120 D3
RLEIW/BBY LE8................139 M6
Kingfisher Rd RLBORO LE12.....113 K5
Kingfishers Ct
COT/KEY/RAD NG12.............66 A3
Kingfisher Wk LEIE * LE5........7 L3
Kingfisher Wy LBORO LE11........9 G6
Kingfisher Whf WBRGFD NG2.....50 D5
King George Av ILK DE7.........33 G7
King George Rd LBORO LE11....104 B4
Kinglake Pl WBRGFD NG2.........51 G5
King John's Rd COAL LE67......108 D1
King Richards Rd LEIE LE3.....131 G2
Kingrove Av BSTN/STPLFD NG9...63 H1
Kings Av CARL NG4..............38 C5
LBORO LE11...................103 K1
Kingsbridge Av
MAPPK/POR/STA NG3............38 C3
Kingsbridge Cl END/NAR LE19...135 L4
Kingsbridge Crs LEIN LE4......118 F8
Kingsbridge Wy
BSTN/STPLFD NG9..............63 G1
Kings Brook Cl RLBORO LE12.....97 H1
Kingsbury Av LEIE LE5.........133 G3
Kingsbury Dr WOL/BIL/BRX NG8..35 L7
Kingsbury Rd DERBYW DE22......56 E1
Kingsclere Av DERBYE DE21......44 F5
Kingscliffe Crs LEIE LE5......133 H3
Kings Cl HEANOR DE75..........20 A5
Kings Cft DERBYW DE22..........43 K3
Kingsdale Cl LGEAT NG10........75 L2
Kingsdale Gv MELB/CHEL DE73...72 C7
Kingsdown Mt
WOL/BIL/BRX NG8..............49 J5
Kings Dr EWD/SEL/PNX NG16.....13 J8
LEIW LE3.....................129 L4
MCKLVR DE3....................56 F5
WGSTN LE18...................138 A4
Kingsfield Rd RLEIW/BAR LE9...142 A5
Kingsford Av NOTTE NG7.........50 C1
Kings Ga CDON/KEG DE74.........85 K3
Kingsgate Av LEIN LE4........119 K7
Kingsland Cl DERBYE DE21......44 D5
Kingsley Cl END/NAR LE19.....135 L6
Kingsley Crs LGEAT NG10........75 M3
Kingsley Dr CARL NG4...........38 E8
Kingsley Rd DERBYW DE22.......43 H4
WBRGFD NG2...................51 J3
Kingsley St DERBYSE DE24......71 K2
LEIS LE2.....................131 L7
Kingsmead Av
BSTN/STPLFD NG9..............48 B5
King's Mead Cl DERBY DE1......2 D1

King's Meadow Rd
  WBRGFD NG2 ....50 E5
Kingsmead Rd LEIS LE2 ....138 A1
Kingsmead Wk DERBY DE1 ....2 C1
King's Mill La
  BWSH/BRSTN DE72 ....83 K3
Kings Moor ARN NG5 ....24 C8
Kingsmuir Rd MCKLVR DE3 ....56 A4
Kings Newton St LEIS LE2 ....7 L3
King's Pl NOTT NG1 ....5 J7
Kings Rd LGEAT NG10 ....61 M1
  RLBORO LE12 ....101 M5
Kingsthorpe Cl LEIN LE4 ....125 K4
  MAPPK/POR/STA NG3 ....37 K6
Kingston Av ILK DE7 ....47 L3
  WCGSTN LE18 ....137 M3
Kingston Ct
  COT/KEY/RAD * NG12 ....53 K4
  ILK DE7 ....32 B7
  WBRGFD NG2 ....5 M7
Kingston La CDON/KEG DE74 ....86 D4
Kingston Rd LEIS LE2 ....132 A4
  WBRGFD NG2 ....65 J1
Kingston St DERBY DE1 ....43 K8
King St BPR/DUF DE56 ....17 K4
  BPR/DUF DE56 ....29 J3
  BSTN/STPLFD NG9 ....63 L1
  COAL LE67 ....108 B7
  DERBY DE1 ....2 D1
  END/NAR LE19 ....135 M4
  EWD/SEL/PNX NG16 ....21 K5
  ILK DE7 ....33 K6
  LBORO LE11 ....9 L5
  LEI LE1 ....6 F8
  LEIS LE2 ....138 F2
  LGEAT NG10 ....62 B7
  NOTT NG1 ....5 G7
  RLBORO LE12 ....106 D7
  RLBORO LE12 ....114 A4
  RLEINE/SYS LE7 ....127 H1
  RLEIW/BBY LE8 ....136 D8
Kings Wk LEIW LE3 ....129 L5
Kings Wy GBY/RBY LE6 ....123 K5
Kingsway COT/KEY/RAD NG12 ...53 J5
  DERBYW DE75 ....57 G3
  HEANOR DE75 ....20 B5
  ILK DE7 ....47 L2
  LEIW LE3 ....130 D7
Kingsway Crs BPR/DUF DE56 ....18 E7
Kingsway Gdns
  HUCK/RAV NG15 ....23 J3
Kingsway North LEIW LE3 ....130 C5
Kingsway Park Cl
  DERBYW DE22 ....57 G2
  LEIE LE5 ....132 C5
Kingswell Rd ARN NG5 ....25 K8
Kingswood Av BPR/DUF DE56 .....18 A2
  LEIW LE3 ....130 T3
  RLBORO LE12 ....102 E2
Kingswood Rd WBRGFD NG2 ......65 H2
  WOL/BIL/BRX NG8 ....49 M2
King William St
  EWD/SEL/PNX NG16 ....12 D3
King Williams Wy
  RLEINE/SYS LE7 ....118 C8
Kinlet Rd ARN NG5 ....36 E1
Kinley Rd LEIN LE4 ....125 J3
Kinoulton La
  COT/KEY/RAD NG12 ....81 M7
Kinross Av DERBYE DE21 ....44 A7
  LEIE LE5 ....133 J1
Kinross Crs LBORO LE11 ....103 H2
  WOL/BIL/BRX NG8 ....49 L1
Kinsdale Dr LEIE LE5 ....133 K1
Kintyre Dr DERBYSE DE24 ....71 H4
  LEIN LE4 ....126 A3
Kiplin Dr END/NAR LE19 ....135 L5
Kipling Cl CFTN/RUD NC11 ....64 A7
Kipling Dr MCKLVR DE3 ....56 B6
Kipling Gv LEIN LE4 ....124 E5
Kipps St NOTT NG1 ....5 J6
Kirby Cl EWD/SEL/PNX NG16 ....21 L4
  RLBORO LE12 ....113 H7
  RLEIW/BAR LE9 ....140 B7
Kirby Dr CDON/KEG DE74 ....86 A6
Kirby La LEIW LE3 ....129 K4
Kirby Rd EWD/SEL/PNX NG16 .....21 L4
  GBY/RBY LE6 ....123 K8
  LEIW LE3 ....131 G2
Kirk CDON/KEG DE74 ....86 B5
Kirkbride Cl BSTN/STPLFD NG9 ...62 F1
Kirkby Av ILK DE7 ....47 K1
Kirkby Gdns WBRGFD NG2 ....51 H5
Kirk Cl BSTN/STPLFD NG9 ....63 H4
  RIPLEY DE5 ....11 G7
Kirk Dale Av DERBYE DE21 ....59 K4
Kirkdale Cl WOL/BIL/BRX * NG8 ..48 F3
Kirkdale Gdns LGEAT NG10 ....75 M1
Kirkdale Rd LGEAT NG10 ....75 M1
  WCGSTN LE18 ....137 K5
Kirkewhite Av LGEAT NG10 ....62 B8
Kirkewhite Ct WBRGFD NG2 ....51 H5
Kirkfell Cl WBRGFD NG2 ....66 A2
Kirkfield Dr BWSH/BRSTN DE72 ..61 H7
Kirkfield Rd RLEIW/BBY LE8 .....143 K3
Kirkham Cl HEANOR DE75 ....20 B6
Kirkham Dr BSTN/STPLFD NG9 ...62 E2
Kirkhill RLBORO LE12 ....102 A3
Kirkhill Cl COAL LE67 ....109 G6
Kirkistown Cl DERBYSE DE24 ......73 G1
Kirkland Cl CDON/KEG DE74 ....84 D4
Kirkland Dr BSTN/STPLFD NG9 ...62 F5
Kirkland Rd LEIW LE3 ....130 D7
Kirkland Wy DERBYSE DE24 ....71 H4
Kirk La CFTN/RUD NC11 ....65 H8
  END/NAR LE19 ....136 A4
Kirkley Dr HEANOR DE75 ....20 A6
Kirkleys Gdns ARN NG5 ....24 E5
Kirk Ley Rd RLBORO LE12 ....88 B7
Kirk Leys Av North
  DERBYE DE21 ....59 J3
Kirk Leys Av South
  DERBYE DE21 ....59 J3
Kirkman Rd HEANOR DE75 ....19 M8
Kirk Rd MAPPK/POR/STA NG3 .....37 L5
Kirk's La BPR/DUF DE56 ....17 M4
Kirkstead CI DERBY DE21 ....44 F6

Kirkstead Gdns NOTTE NG7 ....4 A1
Kirkstead St NOTTE NG7 ....4 A1
Kirkstone Av HEANOR DE75 ....20 F6
Kirkstone Cl LEIW LE3 ....124 B6
Kirkstone Ct LGEAT NG10 ....61 M5
Kirkstone Dr LBORO LE11 ....8 A9
  WBRGFD NG2 ....52 A8
Kirk St DERBY DE1 ....43 L7
Kirkwall Crs LEIE LE5 ....127 J8
Kirloe Av LEIE LE5 ....129 K4
Kirtle Cl WOL/BIL/BRX NG8 ....35 M8
Kirtley Dr WBRGFD NG2 ....50 E5
Kirton Av LGEAT NG10 ....62 B8
Kirton Rd COAL LE67 ....109 H6
Kitchener Av NORM/LIT DE23 ......57 K8
Kitchener Rd LEIE LE5 ....132 C2
  RLEINE/SYS LE7 ....118 C8
Kite Cl RLEIW/BAR LE9 ....141 J7
Kitson Av EWD/SEL/PNX NG16 ....13 G3
Kittiwake Ms NOTTE NG7 ....50 C3
Kiwi Cl HUCK/RAV NG15 ....21 K6
Knapp Cl EWD/SEL/PNX NG16 .....21 K6
Kneesall Gv HUCK/RAV NG15 ....15 M8
Kneeton Cl ARN NG5 ....37 G3
  CARL NG4 ....38 B3
Kneeton V ARN NG5 ....37 G3
Knight Cl LEIN LE4 ....120 D8
Knighton Church Rd LEIS LE2 .....132 A8
Knighton Dr LEIS LE2 ....132 A7
Knighton Fields Rd East
  LEIS LE2 ....131 K7
Knighton Fields Rd West
  LEIS * LE2 ....131 K7
Knighton Grange Rd LEIS LE2 .....132 C7
Knighton Junction La LEIS LE2 ...131 L7
Knighton La CARL LE67 ....131 J7
Knighton La East LEIS LE2 ....131 K7
Knighton Park Rd LEIS LE2 ....132 A5
Knighton Ri LEIS LE2 ....132 C6
Knighton Rd ARN NG5 ....37 H2
  LEIS LE2 ....131 M7
Knighton St LEIS LE2 ....6 E1
Knightsbridge DERBYW DE22 ......56 E1
Knightsbridge Dr WBRGFD NG2 ..65 G3
  WOL/BIL/BRX NG8 ....35 J4
Knightsbridge Gdns
  HUCK/RAV NG15 ....15 K5
  COT/KEY/RAD NG12 ....53 H4
Knights Cl ARN NG5 ....24 D7
  BSTN/STPLFD NG9 ....62 D5
  DERBYSE DE24 ....71 J5
  RLEIW/BAR LE9 ....140 B4
  WBRGFD NG2 ....65 G4
Knight's Crs RLEINE/SYS LE7 .....119 J1
Knight's Garth COAL LE67 ....108 D2
Knights Rd LEIN LE4 ....125 L1
Knight St CARL NG4 ....52 E1
Knightthorpe Rd LBORO LE11 ....8 A2
Knightwood Dr ARN NG5 ....24 F2
Knipton Dr LBORO LE11 ....102 F4
Kniveton Pk ILK DE7 ....33 H8
Knole Rd WOL/BIL/BRX NG8 ....49 J2
Knoll Av HUCK/RAV NG15 ....23 H2
Knoll Cl NORM/LIT DE23 ....56 E7
Knollgate Cl LEIN LE4 ....119 J7
Knowl Av BPR/DUF DE56 ....17 J1
Knowle Hl EWD/SEL/PNX NG16 ...34 E2
Knowle La EWD/SEL/PNX NG16 ..34 B3
Knowle Pk EWD/SEL/PNX NG16 ..34 E2
Knowles Rd LEIW LE3 ....124 C8
Krebs Cl CFTN/RUD NC11 ....64 A6
Krefeld Wy LEIN LE4 ....124 E4
Kyle Gv DERBYE DE21 ....44 F4
Kyle Vw ARN NG5 ....24 E6
Kyme St NOTTE NG7 ....4 B5
Kynance Cl DERBYSE DE24 ....73 G2
Kynance Gdns CFTN/RUD NC11 ..64 F2

L

Labrador Cl LEI LE1 ....7 H3
Laburnam Cl RLBORO LE12 ....111 L1
Laburnam Wy RLBORO LE12 ......111 L1
Laburnum Av
  COT/KEY/RAD NG12 ....80 E5
Laburnum Cl LGEAT NG10 ....47 M8
  RLBORO LE12 ....94 E6
Laburnum Crs DERBYW DE22 ......43 H2
Laburnum Gv
  BSTN/STPLFD NG9 ....63 M2
  DERBYW DE22 ....56 E2
Laburnum Rd LEIE LE5 ....127 G6
Laburnum St
  MAPPK/POR/STA NG3 ....5 J1
Lace Av BSTN/STPLFD NG9 ....49 K8
Lace St NOTTE NG7 ....50 B6
Lacey Av HUCK/RAV NG15 ....23 K2
Lacey Cl ILK DE7 ....33 C4
Lacey Ct RLBORO LE12 ....101 M4
Lacey Fields Rd HEANOR DE75 ...20 E6
Ladbroke Gdns DERBYW DE22 ....56 D1
Ladbroke Gv RLEIW/BBY LE8 .....143 K5
Ladbrooke Crs BLWL NG6 ....36 A4
Ladybank Ri ARN NG5 ....26 A7
Ladybank Rd MCKLVR DE3 ....56 A4
Lady Bay Av WBRGFD * NG2 ....51 K6
Lady Bay Br WBRGFD NG2 ....51 J5
Lady Bay Rd WBRGFD NG2 ....51 L6
Ladybower Rd DERBYE DE21 ....59 K3
  LBORO LE11 ....102 F5
Ladybridge Cl
  BSTN/STPLFD NG9 ....63 J4
Ladycroft Av HUCK/RAV NG15 .....15 L8
Ladycroft Paddock
  DERBYW DE22 ....43 J3
Lady Ga CDON/KEG DE74 ....93 G2
Ladygrove Cottages
  NORM/LIT DE23 ....3 G8
Ladygrove Ter DERBYSE * DE24 ..58 B8
Lady La RIPLEY DE5 ....19 H6
Lady Lea Hl DERBYE DE21 ....30 E1
Lady Lea Rd ILK DE7 ....30 E2
Ladylea Rd LGEAT NG10 ....75 L3
Lady Leys RLEIW/BAR LE9 ....142 B4
Lady Mantle Cl
  MELB/CHEL DE73 ....72 C5

Ladysmith Rd
  BWSH/BRSTN DE72 ....59 M5
  RLEIW/BAR LE9 ....129 H5
  WCGSTN LE18 ....137 J4
Ladysmith St WBRGFD NG2 ....51 L3
Ladysmock Gdns WBRGFD NG2 ..51 H5
Ladywood Rd ILK DE7 ....46 D3
Laithwaite Cl LEIN LE4 ....124 F1
Lake Av HEANOR DE75 ....20 A3
Lake Dr NORM/LIT DE23 ....57 K7
Lakeland Dr HUCK/RAV NG15 ......24 A2
Lakeside Av LGEAT NG10 ....76 A3
Lakeside Cl RLEINE/SYS LE7 ......133 J5
Lakeside Crs LGEAT NG10 ....76 A2
Lakeside Dr NORM/LIT DE23 ....56 D8
Lake St NOTTE NG7 ....4 B5
Lake View Pl HUCK/RAV NG15 .....14 D1
Lamartine St
  MAPPK/POR/STA NG3 ....5 K5
Lamb Close Dr
  EWD/SEL/PNX NG16 ....21 L3
Lamb Crs RIPLEY DE5 ....11 K6
Lambert Av RLBORO LE12 ....101 M4
Lambert Gdns
  WOL/BIL/BRX NG8 ....36 A7
Lambert Rd LEIW LE3 ....131 G5
Lambert St NOTTE NG7 ....36 C8
Lambeth Rd ARN NG5 ....24 E5
Lambhouse La BPR/DUF DE56 ....16 C2
Lambie Cl WOL/BIL/BRX NG8 ......50 A2
Lambley Av
  MAPPK/POR/STA NG3 ....37 M4
Lambley Bridle Rd
  CALV/BJ NG14 ....39 H1
Lambley Dr DERBYW DE22 ....43 G5
Lambley La CARL NG4 ....38 D4
Lambley Rd CALV/BJ NG14 ....27 L7
Lamborne Rd LEIN LE4 ....137 L1
Lambourn Cl DERBYW DE22 ....43 L4
Lambourn Dr DERBYW DE22 ....43 L3
Lambourne Dr
  WOL/BIL/BRX NG8 ....49 K2
Lambourne Gdns ARN NG5 ....37 L2
Lambourne Rd LEIN LE4 ....119 M7
Lambrook Cl MCKLVR DE3 ....56 A5
Lambton Cl ILK DE7 ....33 J4
Lamcote Gdns
  COT/KEY/RAD NG12 ....53 H4
Lamcote Gv WBRGFD NG2 ....51 H6
Lamcote Ms
  COT/KEY/RAD NG12 ....53 H4
Lamcote St WBRGFD NG2 ....51 H6
Lamen Rd LEIE LE3 ....124 C6
Laming Gap La
  COT/KEY/RAD NG12 ....81 H3
Lamins La ARN NG5 ....25 H3
Lammas Gdns WBRGFD NG2 ....51 H5
Lamorna Gv CFTN/RUD NC11 ......64 F1
Lampad Cl MELB/CHEL DE73 ....82 E7
Lampeter Cl DERBYW DE21 ....44 A7
Lamplands
  COT/KEY/RAD * NG12 ....67 J4
Lamplighters RLEIW/BBY LE8 ....145 K8
Lamport Cl LBORO LE11 ....103 G3
  WCGSTN LE18 ....138 D5
Lanark Cl WOL/BIL/BRX NG8 ....50 A4
Lanark St DERBYE DE21 ....44 C8
Lancashire St LEIN LE4 ....125 M4
Lancaster Av BSTN/STPLFD NG9 ..62 C1
  LGEAT NG10 ....61 L3
Lancaster Cl COAL LE67 ....109 H6
Lancaster Ct RLEIW/BAR LE9 .....124 B2
Lancaster Dr RDERBYSW DE65 ...68 C5
  HUCK/RAV NG15 ....23 H5
  LEI LE1 ....6 F9
  MAPPK/POR/STA NG3 ....37 L8
Lancaster St LEIE LE5 ....132 B1
Lancaster Wk DERBYE DE21 ....59 L1
Lancaster Wy LEIS LE2 ....129 L1
  WOL/BIL/BRX NG8 ....35 H5
Lancelot Cl LEIW LE3 ....129 L5
Lancelot Dr
  EWD/SEL/PNX NG16 ....22 D6
Lancelyn Gdns WBRGFD NG2 ......65 J3
Lancing Av LEIW LE3 ....130 E1
Landcroft Crs ARN NG5 ....36 E1
Landcroft La RLBORO LE12 ....86 F7
Lander La BPR/DUF DE56 ....17 L3
Landmere Cl ILK DE7 ....33 C4
Landmere Gdns
  MAPPK/POR/STA NG3 ....37 K6
Landmere La CFTN/RUD NC11 .....64 F4
  COT/KEY/RAD NG12 ....65 K6
Landscape Dr LEIE LE5 ....133 G3
Landsdowne Av RLBORO LE12 ...101 M2
Landsdowne Rd LEIS LE2 ....131 J7
Landsdown Gv LGEAT NG10 ....62 D6
Landseer Cl NOTTE * NG7 ....50 C1
Landseer Rd LEIS LE2 ....131 M6
Landseer St NOTTE * NG7 ....50 C1
The Lane EWD/SEL/PNX NG16 ....34 A3
Lane Cl LEIE LE3 ....124 C4
Laneham Av ARN NG5 ....25 L8
Lanesborough Cl
  RLEINE/SYS LE7 ....118 F4
Lanesborough Ct LBORO LE11 ......9 J6
Lanesborough Dr
  RLEINE/SYS LE7 ....118 F4
Lanesborough Rd LEIN LE4 ....125 M3
Lanes Cl RLBORO LE12 ....114 B3
Laneshaw Rd LBORO LE11 ....102 F5
Lanes Hill Gv RLEIW/BAR LE9 ....140 C8
Laneside Av BSTN/STPLFD NG9 ..62 C5
Laneward Cl ILK DE7 ....33 G3
Langabeer Ct LBORO * LE11 ....9 L3
Langar Cl ARN NG5 ....37 G3
Langbank Av ARN NG5 ....24 C5
Langdale RLEIW/BBY LE8 ....145 K7
Langdale Dr DERBYE DE21 ....44 B5
  LGEAT NG10 ....75 L1
Langdale Rd LEIN LE4 ....120 D8
  MAPPK/POR/STA NG3 ....51 M2
Langdon Cl LGEAT NG10 ....61 L6
Langdown Cl BLWL NG6 ....23 L7
Langford Rd ARN NG5 ....25 M8
  MCKLVR DE3 ....56 B4

Langham Av
  MAPPK/POR/STA NG3 ....51 L1
Langham Dr CALV/BJ NG14 ....39 K2
  END/NAR LE19 ....135 M7
Langham Rd LEIN LE4 ....126 D4
The Langhill LEIE LE5 ....132 D1
Langholm Rd LEIE LE5 ....133 J1
Langley Av ARN NG5 ....37 K1
  ILK DE7 ....33 H2
  LEIN LE4 ....125 K4
Langley Cl RLEIW/BAR LE9 ....135 H7
Langley Dr CDON/KEG DE74 ....86 A5
Langley St DERBYE DE21 ....59 J4
Lang Rd DERBYSE DE24 ....72 D1
Langsett Dr MELB/CHEL DE73 ....72 E5
Langstrath Dr
  COT/KEY/RAD NG12 ....66 A2
Langstrath Rd CFTN/RUD NC11 ...64 C6
Langton Cl CARL NG4 ....52 C1
  COAL LE67 ....108 C1
Langton Hollow
  EWD/SEL/PNX NG16 ....13 H1
Langton Rd RLEIW/BBY LE8 ....146 F6
  WCGSTN LE18 ....138 B6
Langton St LEI LE1 ....6 F4
Langtry Gv NOTTE NG7 ....36 E7
Lanscombe Park Rd
  DERBYW DE22 ....43 H4
Lansdown Cl BSTN/STPLFD NG9 ..62 F3
Lansdowne Av DERBYSE DE24 ....72 C6
Lansdowne Dr LBORO LE11 ....9 H8
  WBRGFD NG2 ....65 H3
Lansdowne Gv WCGSTN LE18 ....137 L7
Lansdowne Rd BLWL NG6 ....36 C3
  RLBORO LE12 ....101 M2
Lansing Cl CFTN/RUD NC11 ....64 D7
Lansing Gdns DERBYE DE21 ....58 F1
The Lant RLBORO LE12 ....102 A3
Lantern La RLBORO LE12 ....88 D5
Lanthwaite Cl CFTN/RUD NC11 ...64 C6
Lanthwaite Rd CFTN/RUD NC11 ..64 C6
Lapford Cl
  MAPPK/POR/STA NG3 ....38 B1
Lapwing Cl DERBYSE DE24 ....71 J5
  LEIN LE4 ....124 F1
Lapwing Ct END/NAR LE19 ....135 L8
Larch Av RIPLEY DE5 ....11 H6
Larch Cl ARN NG5 ....25 C7
  DERBYW DE22 ....43 H4
  EWD/SEL/PNX NG16 ....13 M4
  HUCK/RAV NG15 ....23 M7
Larch Crs BSTN/STPLFD NG9 ....49 H8
  EWD/SEL/PNX NG16 ....21 J5
Larchdene Av
  WOL/BIL/BRX NG8 ....49 H4
Larch Dr LGEAT NG10 ....47 M8
Larch Gv LEIE LE5 ....130 A4
Larch Rd BPR/DUF DE56 ....18 F8
Larch St LEIE LE5 ....7 M2
Larch Wy COT/KEY/RAD NG12 .....80 E5
Larchwood RLEIW/BBY LE8 ....143 J3
Larchwood Av GBY/RBY LE6 ......123 K4
Larchwood Cl LEIN LE4 ....131 L8
Larges St DERBY DE1 ....2 B3
Largs Cl ARN NG5 ....24 C6
Lark Cl BSTN/STPLFD NG9 ....62 E2
  LEIW LE3 ....129 K5
  NORM/LIT DE23 ....71 G1
Larkdale St NOTTE NG7 ....4 C4
Larkfield Rd
  EWD/SEL/PNX NG16 ....34 F2
Larkhill Crs DERBYSE DE24 ....71 K3
Larkland's Av ILK DE7 ....33 L8
Lark Ri RLBORO LE12 ....111 L1
Larkspur Av ARN NG5 ....25 J5
Larkspur Cl LEIE LE5 ....126 F4
Larkspur Ct DERBYE DE21 ....44 E4
Larkswood RLEIW/BBY LE8 ....146 F7
Larwood Gv ARN NG5 ....37 G3
Lascelles Av CARL NG4 ....38 B5
Lashley Gdns DERBYE DE21 ....44 D5
Lastingham Cl LEIS LE2 ....137 L1
Latham St BLWL NG6 ....23 M8
Lathbury Cl DERBYE DE21 ....44 B6
Lathkill Av DERBYSE DE24 ....59 G8
  ILK DE7 ....33 J2
Lathkill Cl BLWL NG6 ....23 M8
  ILK DE7 ....32 C7
Lathkilldale Crs LGEAT NG10 ....75 L2
Lathkill Dr RIPLEY DE5 ....19 H1
Lathkill Rd DERBYE DE21 ....44 D7
Latimer Cl BLWL NG6 ....36 A1
  NORM/LIT DE23 ....56 C8
  RLEIW/BBY LE8 ....142 E1
Latimer Ct RLEINE/SYS LE7 ....124 B2
Latimer Dr BSTN/STPLFD NG9 ....48 F1
Latimer Pl LEIN * LE4 ....125 L7
Latimer St DERBYSE DE24 ....72 B1
  LEI LE1 ....6 A8
  LEIW LE3 ....124 C2
Latrigg Cl MCKLVR DE3 ....56 C2
Lauder Cl DERBYSE DE24 ....71 J5
Laughton Av WBRGFD NG2 ....51 K6
Laughton Crs HUCK/RAV NG15 ...23 J3
Launceston Crs
  CFTN/RUD NC11 ....64 E3
Launceston Dr COAL LE67 ....108 A8
Launde Rd DERBYSE DE24 ....72 F2
  WCGSTN LE18 ....138 A7
Laund Av BPR/DUF DE56 ....17 M1
Laund Cl BPR/DUF DE56 ....17 L2
Launde Rd COAL LE67 ....116 C9
  LEIS LE2 ....133 G8
Launder St WBRGFD NG2 ....51 G5
Laund HI BPR/DUF DE56 ....17 L2
Laund Nook BPR/DUF DE56 ....17 L2
Laundon Cl GBY/RBY LE6 ....123 K5
Laundon Wy GBY/RBY LE6 ....123 J6
  LEIS LE2 ....142 E2
Laundry La LEIN LE4 ....125 M5
The Laurels COAL LE67 ....122 C4
Laurel Av COT/KEY/RAD NG12 ....11 H6
  RIPLEY DE5 ....11 H6
Laurel Bank NORM/LIT * DE23 ....57 L8
Laurel Cl LEIW LE3 ....124 C7
  RLBORO LE12 ....113 J5

Laurel Crs EWD/SEL/PNX NG16 ...34 F1
  ILK DE7 ....31 K2
  LGEAT NG10 ....62 A8
Laurel Dr BWSH/BRSTN DE72 .....73 L8
  LEIS LE2 ....139 H4
  RLEIW/BBY LE8 ....143 J3
Laurel Rd CARL NG4 ....38 A7
  LEIE LE5 ....7 M8
  RLBORO LE12 ....111 L1
  RLEIW/BBY LE8 ....136 F8
Laureston Dr LEIS LE2 ....132 B5
Laurie Cl NOTTE NG7 ....36 E7
Laurie Pl DERBYSE DE24 ....58 C8
Lavender Cl RLBORO LE12 ....111 L1
  RLEIW/BBY LE8 ....136 E7
  WOL/BIL/BRX NG8 ....50 B2
Lavender Gdns HEANOR DE75 .....20 B6
Lavender Gv BSTN/STPLFD NG9 ..63 M2
Lavender Rw DERBYW DE22 ....43 K6
Lavender Wk
  MAPPK/POR/STA NG3 ....5 K2
Laver Cl ARN NG5 ....25 M8
Laverick Rd
  EWD/SEL/PNX NG16 ....12 E3
Laverstock Rd WCGSTN LE18 ....138 A3
Laverstoke Ct DERBYW DE22 ......2 B5
Lawdon Rd ARN NG5 ....25 L6
Lawford Rd LEIS LE2 ....137 H3
Lawley Av DERBYW DE22 ....43 H5
  LEIN LE4 ....119 M8
  RDERBYSW DE65 ....69 G2
Lawn Cl HEANOR DE75 ....20 D6
Lawn Heads Av NORM/LIT DE23 ..57 C5
Lawnlea Cl NORM/LIT DE23 ....71 J2
Lawn Mill Rd
  EWD/SEL/PNX NG16 ....22 B8
Lawnside DERBYE DE21 ....59 K2
The Lawns BWSH/BRSTN DE72 ...73 M7
  LEIS * LE2 ....132 A3
Lawnswood Cl NORM/LIT DE23 ...57 C2
Lawnwood Rd GBY/RBY LE6 ......123 H4
Lawrence Av
  BWSH/BRSTN DE72 ....61 H7
  CARL NG4 ....52 C2
  DERBYE DE21 ....44 F8
  EWD/SEL/PNX NG16 ....21 K5
  EWD/SEL/PNX NG16 ....34 A2
  RIPLEY DE5 ....11 G7
Lawrence Cl
  COT/KEY/RAD NG12 ....67 K4
  LEIN LE4 ....119 C6
Lawrence Dr
  EWD/SEL/PNX NG16 ....13 H7
Lawrence Ms
  EWD/SEL/PNX * NG16 ....21 L4
Lawrence Pk
  EWD/SEL/PNX NG16 ....13 M4
Lawrence St LGEAT NG10 ....47 M8
  LGEAT NG10 ....62 B7
  NORM/LIT DE23 ....57 K7
Lawrence Wy LBORO LE11 ....95 C8
  WBRGFD NG2 ....50 E5
Lawson Av LGEAT NG10 ....62 C8
Lawson St NOTTE NG7 ....4 C3
Law St LEIN LE4 ....125 L4
Lawton Dr BLWL NG6 ....24 A6
Lawyers La LEIS LE2 ....138 E2
Laxford Cl LEIN LE4 ....125 G5
Laxton Av BLWL NG6 ....36 B2
Laxton Cl LEIN LE4 ....119 M7
  WCGSTN LE18 ....138 B5
Laxton Dr HUCK/RAV NG15 ....23 J1
Layton Rd LEIE LE5 ....126 C8
The Lea RLEIW/BBY LE8 ....146 F7
Leabrook Cl CFTN/RUD NC11 .....64 A4
Lea Cl DERBYW DE55 ....43 J4
  LEIN LE4 ....120 B8
Lea Crs ALFN DE55 ....12 A1
Leacroft Rd NORM/LIT DE23 ....57 M6
  WOL/BIL/BRX NG8 ....36 B7
Lea Dr DERBYE DE21 ....58 D1
  MCKLVR DE3 ....56 C4
Leafe Cl BSTN/STPLFD NG9 ....63 G5
Leafenden Cl DERBYW DE22 ....43 J5
Leafgreen Cl NORM/LIT DE23 ......71 G1
Leafgreen La NORM/LIT DE23 .....71 G1
Leafield Gn CFTN/RUD NC11 ....64 C5
Leafy La HEANOR DE75 ....20 B6
Leahurst Gdns WBRGFD NG2 .....65 M1
Leahurst Rd WBRGFD NG2 ....65 M2
Leake La RLBORO LE12 ....96 A6
Leake Rd CFTN/RUD NC11 ....77 M6
  CFTN/RUD NC11 ....88 B1
  RLBORO LE12 ....88 F6
Leake St DERBYW DE22 ....57 H2
  EWD/SEL/PNX NG16 ....13 K1
Lea Ch COAL LE67 ....116 C3
Leamington Cl NORM/LIT DE23 ...57 H6
Leamington Dr
  BSTN/STPLFD NG9 ....63 G3
  RLEIW/BBY LE8 ....142 F1
Leamington St RIPLEY DE5 ....11 J5
Leander Cl CFTN/RUD NC11 ....64 F1
  NORM/LIT DE23 ....57 H8
Leaper St DERBY DE1 ....2 B1
The Leas CALV/BJ NG14 ....39 M2
Leas Cl RLEINE/SYS LE7 ....133 K1
Leatherlands CDON/KEG DE74 ....86 B5
Leawood Gdns DERBYE DE21 ......44 F4
Leche Cft BPR/DUF DE56 ....17 L2
Lechlade Cl ILK DE7 ....32 B7
Lechlade Rd ARN NG5 ....36 E1
Leckhampton Rd LBORO LE11 ...103 G3
Leconfield Rd LBORO LE11 ....103 G7
Ledbury Cha DERBYSE DE24 ....71 H5
Ledbury Cl LEIS LE2 ....139 H3
Ledbury Gn LEIN LE4 ....125 K7
Ledbury Rd LBORO LE11 ....103 K8
Ledbury V WOL/BIL/BRX NG8 ......35 J4
Ledo Av RIPLEY DE5 ....11 H5
Ledwell Dr LEIW LE3 ....124 A6
Lee Cir LEI LE1 ....7 G4
Lee Cl RLEINE/BAR LE9 ....140 C4
Lee Crs ILK DE7 ....33 M7
Leeds Pl DERBY DE1 ....3 G6

Lee Farm Cl MELB/CHEL DE73 .....72 D6
Lee La HEANOR DE75 .....20 F6
Leen Cl BLWL NG6 .....24 D3
Leen Dr BLWL NG6 .....24 A6
  HUCK/RAV NG15 .....15 M7
Leen Ga NOTTE NG7 .....50 C5
Leen Mills La HUCK/RAV NG15 .....15 M6
Leen Pl NOTTE NG7 .....50 C2
Leen Valley Wy HUCK/RAV NG15 .....24 A2
Leen Ri GBY/RBY LE6 .....123 H7
Lee Rd CALV/BJ NG14 .....39 L2
Lees Barn Rd
  COT/KEY/RAD NG12 .....53 H5
Lees Crs COAL LE67 .....108 C2
Lees Hill St WBRGFD NG2 .....5 M8
Leeson St LEIS LE2 .....131 J8
The Lees DERBYSE DE24 .....73 H3
Lees Rd MAPPK/POR/STA NG3 .....37 L6
Lee St LEI LE1 .....7 G4
Leeway DERBYE DE21 .....59 H5
Legion Wy END/NAR LE19 .....130 B7
Leicester St END/NAR LE19 .....135 M4
  RLBORO LE12 .....118 B3
  RLEIW/BAR LE9 .....128 B4
Leicester Rd COAL LE67 .....108 C5
  COAL LE67 .....116 D6
  END/NAR LE19 .....136 A7
  GBY/RBY LE6 .....123 K4
  LBORO LE11 .....9 K5
  LEIN LE4 .....119 H7
  LEIS LE2 .....132 D8
  LEIS LE2 .....136 F5
  LEIW LE18 .....124 B5
  RLBORO LE12 .....102 A5
  RLBORO LE12 .....112 E2
  RLBORO LE12 .....113 J5
  RLEINE/SYS LE7 .....118 E4
  RLEINE/SYS LE7 .....124 C1
  RLEIW/BAR LE9 .....140 C8
  RLEIW/BBY LE8 .....141 H6
  RLEIW/BBY LE8 .....136 F6
  RLEIW/BBY LE8 .....143 K3
  RLEIW/BBY LE8 .....145 K6
  RLEIW/BBY LE8 .....146 B2
  WGSTN LE18 .....138 A3
Leicestershire Round
  COAL LE67 .....116 C4
Leicestershire Wy
  RLBORO LE12 .....114 A7
Leicester Wy DERBYW DE22 .....2 A7
  LEIE LE5 .....132 B1
  LGEAT NG10 .....76 C1
Leigh Rd BSTN/STPLFD NG9 .....62 D4
Leighton Av LBORO LE11 .....102 F4
Leighton St
  MAPPK/POR/STA NG3 .....51 K1
Leire St LEIN LE4 .....125 M5
Leiston Gdns ARN NG5 .....24 E7
Leivers Av ARN NG5 .....25 K7
Leivers Cl RLBORO LE12 .....88 B6
  LEIN LE4 .....126 C2
Lema Cl BLWL NG6 .....24 B7
Lemontree La RLBORO LE12 .....103 L8
Lemyngton St LBORO LE11 .....9 J2
Lena Dr GBY/RBY LE6 .....123 G2
Lendal Ct NOTTE NG7 .....4 C5
Lendrum Ct CALV/BJ NG14 .....39 K3
Leniscar Av HEANOR DE75 .....20 A3
Lennox St NOTT NG1 .....5 K6
Lens Rd DERBYW DE22 .....43 G5
Lenton Av COT/KEY/RAD NG12 .....66 A6
  DERBYE DE21 .....58 D1
  NOTTE NG7 .....4 C8
Lenton Bvd NOTTE NG7 .....4 A9
Lenton Cl NOTTE NG7 .....4 A8
Lenton Hall Dr NOTTE NG7 .....49 M6
Lenton La NOTTE NG7 .....50 D5
Lenton Mnr NOTTE NG7 .....50 C4
Lenton St LGEAT NG10 .....62 A1
Leominster Dr DERBYE DE21 .....44 F5
Leonard Av ARN NG5 .....36 F5
Leonard Cheshire Cl
  HEANOR DE75 .....20 F6
Leonard Cl NORM/LIT DE23 .....2 F7
  NORM/LIT DE23 .....3 G7
Leonard St BLWL NG6 .....35 M2
Leopold Cl RLEIW/BBY LE8 .....143 H3
Leopold Rd LEIS LE2 .....131 L6
Leopold St DERBY DE1 .....2 F6
  LBORO LE11 .....8 F2
  LGEAT NG10 .....62 B7
  WGSTN LE18 .....137 K5
Leroy Wallace Av NOTTE NG7 .....4 A5
Lerwick Cl CFTN/RUD NG11 .....64 E6
Leslie Av BSTN/STPLFD NG9 .....63 K2
  EWD/SEL/PNX NG16 .....34 D2
  NOTTE NG7 .....4 C7
Leslie Cl LBORO LE11 .....103 H1
  NORM/LIT DE23 .....56 C7
Leslie Rd NOTTE NG7 .....36 F7
Letchworth Crs
  BSTN/STPLFD NG9 .....63 G3
Letchworth Rd LEIW LE3 .....130 E1
Letcombe Rd CFTN/RUD NG11 .....64 C4
Lethbridge Cl LEI LE1 .....7 G3
Leven Cl DERBYSE DE24 .....71 K5
Levens Wk WBRGFD NG2 .....66 A2
Leveret Cl MELB/CHEL DE73 .....72 F5
Leveret Dr RLEIW/BBY LE8 .....142 F1
Leveric Rd LEIN LE4 .....126 C7
Leverton Gn CFTN/RUD NG11 .....64 C5
Lewcote La ILK DE7 .....32 E6
Lewett Cl LEIN LE4 .....125 H5
Lewin Br RLEINE/SYS LE7 .....120 E1
Lewindon Ct ARN NG5 .....37 J3
Lewis Cl LEIN LE4 .....124 F5
  MAPPK/POR/STA NG3 .....5 J4
Lewisher Rd LEIN LE4 .....126 C4
Lewis Rd LBORO LE11 .....103 H2
Lewis Wy RLEIW/BBY LE8 .....143 K4
Lexham St LEIN LE4 .....125 M5
Lexington Rd DERBYE DE21 .....58 F2
Leybourne Dr ARN NG5 .....36 C1

Leybury Wy RLEINE/SYS LE7 .....127 K8
Leycroft Rd LEIN LE4 .....124 F1
Leyland Cl BSTN/STPLFD NG9 .....62 D5
Leyland Gdns DERBY DE1 .....43 J8
Leyland Rd LEIW LE3 .....130 D8
Leylands DERBYW * DE22 .....43 J7
Leylands DERBYW DE22 .....43 J7
The Leys CFTN/RUD NG11 .....64 B5
  COT/KEY/RAD NG12 .....66 D8
  DERBYE DE21 .....30 B5
  RLEIW/BBY LE8 .....143 G4
  RLEIW/BBY LE8 .....146 E6
Leys Ct BPR/DUF * DE56 .....18 B3
Leysdale Cl LEIN LE4 .....124 F4
Leys Dr LEIS LE2 .....138 E3
Leys Field Gdns
  MELB/CHEL DE73 .....72 E5
Leysland Av RLEIW/BBY LE8 .....143 G3
Leys Rd CFTN/RUD NG11 .....79 G1
Ley St CARL NG4 .....63 M2
Leyton Crs BSTN/STPLFD NG9 .....63 M2
Leytonstone Dr DERBYW DE22 .....56 E2
Liberty Rd BLWL NG6 .....35 K5
Library Rd NOTTE NG7 .....50 A6
Lichfield Av CARL NG4 .....141 H7
Lichfield Cl BSTN/STPLFD NG9 .....62 C4
Lichfield Dr DERBYSE DE24 .....58 B8
  RLEIW/BBY LE8 .....142 F1
Lichfield Rd RLEIW/BAR LE9 .....140 C8
Lichfield St LEI LE1 .....6 E3
Liddell Gv WOL/BIL/BRX NG8 .....49 K2
Liddington St NOTTE NG7 .....36 D6
Lidgate Cl MCKLVR DE3 .....56 A6
Lidster Cl LEIS LE2 .....126 F7
Lilac Av CARL NG4 .....38 E8
  DERBYW DE22 .....56 E2
  LEIE LE5 .....127 G6
Lilac Cl COT/KEY/RAD NG12 .....80 E5
  DERBYE DE24 .....72 E1
  LBORO LE11 .....103 L8
  WOL/BIL/BRX NG8 .....35 J6
Lilac Ct DERBYSE * DE24 .....72 E1
Lilac Crs BSTN/STPLFD NG9 .....63 M2
Lilac Gv BSTN/STPLFD NG9 .....63 M2
  HEANOR DE75 .....20 C6
Lilac Ms ILK DE7 .....33 H4
Lilac Wy HUCK/RAV NG15 .....23 M2
Lilac Wy RLEINE/SYS LE7 .....115 J8
Lilleker Ri ARN NG5 .....25 J6
Lilleshall Wy LBORO LE11 .....102 F2
Lilley St DERBYSE DE24 .....72 F1
Lillingstone Cl COAL LE67 .....116 C6
Lillington Rd BLWL NG6 .....35 M1
Lily Av CARL NG4 .....38 E8
Lily Bank Cl LEIS LE2 .....100 A6
Lily Gv BSTN/STPLFD NG9 .....63 M2
Lime Av BPR/DUF DE56 .....29 J3
  DERBY DE1 .....2 D7
  DERBYE DE21 .....44 B3
  EWD/SEL/PNX NG16 .....21 G5
  GBY/RBY LE6 .....123 J6
  LBORO LE11 .....9 G5
  RIPLEY DE5 .....11 H6
Lime Crs BPR/DUF DE56 .....17M5
Lime Cft DERBYW DE22 .....43 K3
Limedale Av DERBYE DE21 .....44 F4
Lime Dr RLEINE/SYS LE7 .....120 F5
Lime Gv BSTN/STPLFD NG9 .....62 B2
  BWSH/BRSTN DE72 .....60 D8
  DERBYE DE21 .....58 F2
  LGEAT NG10 .....61M1
  LGEAT NG10 .....62 A1
  RLEIW/BAR LE9 .....129 H2
  RLEIW/BBY LE8 .....136 F7
Lime Grove Av
  BSTN/STPLFD NG9 .....63 J2
Lime Grove Cl LEIN LE4 .....125 G3
Limehurst Av LBORO LE11 .....9 H1
Limehurst Rd LEIE LE5 .....127 H6
The Lime Kilns RLBORO LE12 .....105 H7
Lime Kilns WGSTN LE18 .....138 C7
Lime La ARN NG5 .....25 K3
  DERBYE DE24 .....44 E4
  ILK DE7 .....45 H2
Limerick Rd DERBYE DE21 .....58 F3
The Limes ILK DE7 .....32 C4
Limes Av MCKLVR DE3 .....56 B6
Limes Pk RIPLEY DE5 .....11 G6
Lime St BLWL NG6 .....23 M8
  ILK DE7 .....33 K8
Lime Ter LGEAT NG10 .....62 B7
Lime Tree Av RLEINE/SYS LE7 .....119 L7
  WOL/BIL/BRX NG8 .....36 A4
  WOL/BIL/BRX NG8 .....49 L4
Limetree Cl COT/KEY/RAD NG12 .....80 D5
Limetree Ct ILK * DE7 .....47 G1
Limetree Ri ILK DE7 .....47 G1
Lime Tree La END/NAR LE19 .....136 B5
  HUCK/RAV NG15 .....23 M3
Lime Wk NORM/LIT DE23 .....57 H6
Limmen Gdns
  MAPPK/POR/STA NG3 .....5M4
Limpenny St NOTTE NG7 .....4 B4
Linacres Dr MELB/CHEL DE73 .....72 E5
Linacres St LEIN LE4 .....130 B5
Linby Av HUCK/RAV NG15 .....15 M8
Linby Cl ARN NG5 .....37 H5
  CARL NG4 .....38 C5
Linby Dr WOL/BIL/BRX NG8 .....35 H5
Linby Gv HUCK/RAV NG15 .....15 M7
Linby La HUCK/RAV NG15 .....15 M4
Linby Rd HUCK/RAV NG15 .....15 M7
Linby St BLWL NG6 .....24 A7
Lincoln Av DERBYSE DE24 .....58 E7
  LGEAT NG10 .....61 L3
Lincoln Circ NOTTE NG7 .....4 C8
Lincoln Cl BSTN/STPLFD NG9 .....48 C5
Lincoln Dr RLEINE/SYS LE7 .....121 G5
  RLEIW/BBY LE8 .....142 F1
  WGSTN LE18 .....137 K5
Lincoln Gn MELB/CHEL DE73 .....72 D5
Lincoln Gv COT/KEY/RAD NG12 .....53 K4

Lincoln St BLWL NG6 .....36 C4
  LEIS LE2 .....7 J7
  NOTT NG1 .....5 H6
Lindale Cl WBRGFD NG2 .....66 A1
Lindale Wy MELB/CHEL DE73 .....72 E5
Lindbridge Rd
  WOL/BIL/BRX NG8 .....35 K5
Linden Av CFTN/RUD NG11 .....64 A6
  RLEIW/BBY LE8 .....143 G3
Linden Cl BPR/DUF DE56 .....18 F7
  DER DE1/E LE5 .....132 D4
Linden Farm Dr
  RLEIW/BBY LE8 .....143 H3
Linden Gv BSTN/STPLFD NG9 .....62 C1
  BSTN/STPLFD NG9 .....63 L2
  CARL NG4 .....38 F6
  LGEAT NG10 .....47 L8
  RLBORO LE12 .....113 J6
Linden La RLEIW/BAR LE9 .....129 K3
Linden St LEIS LE2 .....132 C2
  MAPPK/POR/STA NG3 .....5 J1
Linden Wy COAL LE67 .....108 A5
Lindfield Rd LEIW LE3 .....130 E1
  WOL/BIL/BRX NG8 .....35 K5
Lindford Cl DERBYE DE21 .....44 D4
Lindisfarne Cl DERBYSE DE24 .....71 H4
Lindisfarne Dr RLBORO LE12 .....102 E2
Lindisfarne Ri RLEINE/SYS LE7 .....120 D4
Lindley St EWD/SEL/PNX NG16 .....13 H1
  EWD/SEL/PNX NG16 .....21 M5
Lindon Dr DERBYSE DE24 .....73 G1
Lindrick Cl MCKLVR DE3 .....56 D5
Lindrick Dr LEIE LE5 .....132 C5
Lindsay Rd LEIW LE3 .....130 F6
Lindsey Cl DERBYE DE21 .....58 C1
Lindum Cl RLEINE/SYS LE7 .....120 D5
Lindum Gv WBRGFD NG2 .....51 K4
Lindum Rd BLWL NG6 .....36 A4
Linford Av WGSTN LE18 .....138 C5
Linford Ct BSTN/STPLFD NG9 .....48 F3
Linford Crs COAL LE67 .....108 F6
  COAL LE67 .....116 C7
Linford Rd DERBYE DE21 .....103 J7
Linford St LEIN LE4 .....125 L4
Ling Av WGSTN LE18 .....138 C5
Ling Crs CFTN/RUD NG11 .....65 H8
Ling Di RLEINE/SYS LE7 .....115 J8
Lingdale Cl LBORO LE11 .....9 J9
Lingfield Cl MCKLVR DE3 .....56 A4
Lingford COT/KEY/RAD NG12 .....67 L4
Lingford St HUCK/RAV NG15 .....23 M1
Ling Rd LBORO LE11 .....9 K9
Lings Crs COT/KEY/RAD NG12 .....80 C7
Lingwood La CALV/BJ NG14 .....26 F5
Linkfield Av RLBORO LE12 .....113 J6
Linkfield Rd RLBORO LE12 .....113 J6
Linkin Rd BSTN/STPLFD NG9 .....63 G1
Linkmel Cl WBRGFD NG2 .....50 E6
Linkmell Rd WBRGFD NG2 .....66 A1
Linkmel Rd
  EWD/SEL/PNX NG16 .....21 H4
Link Ri COAL LE67 .....116 D7
Link Rd LEIS LE2 .....132 C8
  RLEINE/SYS LE7 .....118 B8
  RLEINE/SYS LE7 .....121 H7
Links Cl DERBYSE DE24 .....71 K3
Linksfield Ct CFTN/RUD NG11 .....65 G5
Links Rd RLEIW/BAR LE9 .....129 G3
  RLEIW/BBY LE8 .....146 F7
Linkway Gdns LEIW LE3 .....131 G2
Linley Av RLBORO LE12 .....102 A5
Linley Gn RLEIW/BAR LE9 .....142 B4
Linnet Cl DERBYE DE21 .....59 K1
Linnet Hl MCKLVR DE3 .....56 A8
Linnett Cl END/NAR LE19 .....135 L8
Linney Rd LEIN LE4 .....125 G4
Linsdale Cl WOL/BIL/BRX NG8 .....48 F2
Linsdale Gdns CARL NG4 .....38 B3
Lintlaw Cl LEIN LE4 .....125 G4
Linton Ri MAPPK/POR/STA NG3 .....51 L1
Linton St LEIS LE2 .....132 A4
Linwood Crs
  EWD/SEL/PNX NG16 .....21 K6
Linwood La LEIS LE2 .....137 K1
Lion Cl WOL/BIL/BRX NG8 .....36 A5
Lipton Rd LEIN LE4 .....124 E1
Liskeard Dr DERBYW DE22 .....43 H3
Lisle St LBORO LE11 .....103 L2
Lismore Cl NOTTE NG7 .....50 C2
Lismore Ct DERBYSE DE24 .....71 H4
Lissett Av ILK DE7 .....33 J8
Lister Ga NOTT NG1 .....5 G6
Liston Dr DERBYSE DE22 .....43 K7
Listowel Crs CFTN/RUD NG11 .....64 C7
Litchen Cl ILK DE7 .....33 K5
Litchfield Cl LGEAT NG10 .....62 E8
Litchfield Ri ARN NG5 .....25 J5
Litchurch La DERBYSE DE24 .....58 A5
Litchurch St NORM/LIT DE23 .....3 G7
Litelmede LEIE LE5 .....126 C8
Little Av LEIN LE4 .....125 M4
Little Bridge St DERBY DE1 .....2 C2
Little Di WGSTN LE18 .....138 C8
Littledale Cl DERBYE DE21 .....45 G4
Little Derby Hl
  RDERBYSW * DE65 .....69M4
Little Dunmow Rd LEIE LE5 .....126 F7
The Littlefare LEIW LE3 .....130 B5
Littlegarth WGSTN LE18 .....137 K5
Little Glen Rd LEIS LE2 .....137 G6
Littlegreen Rd ARN NG5 .....37 K3
Little Hallam Hl ILK DE7 .....47 J2
Little Hallam La ILK DE7 .....47 K1
Little Haw La RLBORO LE12 .....101 L4
Little Hayes WBRGFD NG2 .....65 G3
Little Holme St LEIW LE3 .....6 E1
Little John Wk
  MAPPK/POR/STA NG3 .....5 J2
Little La COT/KEY/RAD NG12 .....66 C4
  EWD/SEL/PNX NG16 .....34 E2
Little Lime La ARN NG5 .....25 J2
Little Lincoln
  COT/KEY/RAD NG12 .....90 A5
Little London La
  COT/KEY/RAD NG12 .....90 A4

Little Longstone Cl
  MCKLVR DE3 .....56 D5
Little Lunnon
  CFTN/RUD NG11 .....77 J2
Little Masons Cl LEIW LE3 .....130 B6
Little Meadow Rd
  MELB/CHEL DE73 .....72 D5
Littlemeer Cl LEIW LE3 .....130 B6
Little Moor La CFTN/RUD NG11 .....79 J4
  LBORO LE11 .....9 M4
Littlemore Cl LEIW LE5 .....132 D1
Little Oak Wood Dr BLWL NG6 .....24 B5
Littleover Crs NORM/LIT DE23 .....57 H7
Littleover La NORM/LIT DE23 .....57 H7
Little Ox CARL NG4 .....52 D3
Little Tennis St WBRGFD NG2 .....51 L4
Little Tennis St South
  WBRGFD NG2 .....51 L5
Littleton St LEIS LE2 .....6 B2
The Littleway LEIE LE5 .....132 D1
Littlewell La ILK DE7 .....47 K6
Little Woodbury Dr
  NORM/LIT DE23 .....70 D1
Little Wood Cl LEIN LE4 .....125 G3
Litton Cl ARN NG5 .....37 J3
  BPR/DUF DE56 .....17 M2
  ILK DE7 .....33 J3
Litton Dr DERBYE DE21 .....59 K4
  MAPPK/POR/STA NG3 .....5 L6
Liverpool St DERBYE DE21 .....44 C7
  MAPPK/POR/STA NG3 .....5 L6
Liversage Pl DERBY DE1 .....3 G6
Liversage Rd DERBY DE1 .....3 G6
Liversage St DERBY DE1 .....3 G6
Livesey Dr RLEIW/BAR LE9 .....140 D8
Livingstone Rd NORM/LIT DE23 .....57 J6
Livingstone St HUCK/RAV NG15 .....15 M7
  LEIW LE3 .....131 G3
Llanberis Gv WOL/BIL/BRX NG8 .....36 A5
Limekiln Ct BLWL NG6 .....23 L7
Lloyd St ARN NG5 .....37 G5
Lobbs Wood Cl LEIE LE5 .....126 F7
Lobelia Cl END/NAR LE19 .....135 K7
  MAPPK/POR/STA NG3 .....5 A1
Lochinvar Cl DERBYE DE21 .....59 K3
Lock Cl ILK DE7 .....47 G1
Locke Av LEIN LE4 .....126 B2
Lockerbie Av LEIN LE4 .....126 A3
Lockerbie St CARL NG4 .....52 D1
Lockhouse Cl LEIS LE2 .....136 F3
Lockington Cl
  MELB/CHEL DE73 .....72 D5
Lockington Rd
  CDON/KEG DE74 .....85 H2
Lock La LGEAT NG10 .....61M2
  LGEAT NG10 .....75 M3
Lockley Cl GBY/RBY LE6 .....123 H7
Locko Rd DERBYE DE21 .....45 J8
The Locks LBORO LE11 .....103 K1
Locksley La CFTN/RUD NG11 .....64 C3
Lockton Av HEANOR DE75 .....20 C7
Lockwood Cl ARN NG5 .....24 F6
  BSTN/STPLFD NG9 .....64 A3
Lockwood Rd DERBYE DE21 .....43 H3
Locomotive Wy DERBYSE DE24 .....3 J7
Lodge Av ARN NG5 .....25 J5
  BPR/DUF DE56 .....29 J4
  LEIN LE4 .....126 D1
  RDERBYSW DE65 .....69 G3
  RLBORO LE12 .....105 H8
  RLEINE/SYS LE7 .....121 G3
  RLEIW/BAR 135 H7
  RLEIW/BBY LE8 .....146 D5
  WOL/BIL/BRX NG8 .....36 B7
Lodge Cl BPR/DUF DE56 .....17 J2
Lodge Farm La ARN NG5 .....25 J6
Lodge Farm Rd LEIE LE5 .....133 G2
Lodge La ASHB DE6 .....41 L3
  DERBY DE1 .....2 D2
  DERBY DE1 .....59 H4
  EWD/SEL/PNX NG16 .....20 C1
  RLEINE/SYS LE7 .....118 B4
Lodge Ms BWSH/BRSTN * DE72 .....60 E8
Lodge Rd EWD/SEL/PNX NG16 .....21 L7
  ILK DE7 .....32 C4
  LGEAT NG10 .....76 A2
Lodge St BWSH/BRSTN DE72 .....60 E8
Lodgewood Av LEIN LE4 .....119 K8
Lodgewood Cl BLWL NG6 .....35 L1
Lodore Cl WBRGFD NG2 .....66 A1
Logan Av LEIS LE2 .....137 G1
Logan St BLWL NG6 .....36 B1
Lois Av NOTTE NG7 .....4 A8
Lombard Cl NOTTE NG7 .....50 D4
Lombard St DERBYW DE22 .....56 D1
Lombardy Rd LEIE LE5 .....7 M2
Lomond Av DERBYSE DE24 .....71 K5
Lomond Crs LEIN LE4 .....125 G5
London La RLBORO LE12 .....91 H8
  RLBORO LE12 .....97 M4
London Rd BWSH/BRSTN DE72 .....74 C5
  CDON/KEG DE74 .....86 B6
  COAL LE67 .....108 C6
  COAL LE67 .....116 B7
  COT/KEY/RAD NG12 .....91 G4
  DERBY DE1 .....2 F5
  LEI LE1 .....7 H8
  LEIS LE2 .....132 A5
  LEIS LE2 .....132 B7
  LEIS LE2 .....138 F2
  LEIS LE2 .....139 J6
  RLBORO LE12 .....99 J2
  RLEIW/BBY LE8 .....139M8
  WBRGFD NG2 .....51 H4
London St LEIE LE5 .....132 B1
Longacre ARN NG5 .....37 K3
Long Acre HUCK/RAV NG15 .....15 H8
Longbeck Av
  MAPPK/POR/STA NG3 .....37 L6
Long Bridge La DERBYSE DE24 .....58 B7
Longbridge La HEANOR DE75 .....20 B4
Longcliffe Gdns LBORO LE11 .....102 F3
Longcliffe Rd COAL LE67 .....7 M2
  RLBORO LE12 .....101 L4
Longcliff Rd COAL LE67 .....108 F7
Long Cl RLBORO LE12 .....104 D8

Long Cft BWSH/BRSTN DE72 .....73 L7
Longdale Rd ARN NG5 .....37 H1
Longden Cl BSTN/STPLFD NG9 .....48 D5
Longden St NOTT NG1 .....5 L6
Longfellow Dr LEIS LE2 .....131 L7
Longfellows LEIW LE3 .....24 F7
Longfield Crs ILK DE7 .....47 K2
Longfield La ILK DE7 .....47 K2
Longford Cl DERBYW DE22 .....43 H5
  WGSTN LE18 .....138 A7
Longford Crs BLWL NG6 .....24 A5
Longford St DERBYE DE21 .....43 H7
Long Furlong RLBORO LE12 .....113 H7
Long Furrow RLEINE/SYS LE7 .....115 H8
Longgrey RLEIW/BBY LE8 .....145 J6
Longhade Furlong
  .....118 D7
Long Hill Ri HUCK/RAV NG15 .....23 K1
Longhurst Ct LEIN LE4 .....126 C2
Longlands Dr RDERBYSW DE65 .....70 A4
Longlands Rd
  BSTN/STPLFD NG9 .....63 M4
Long La BSTN/STPLFD NG9 .....63 H5
  CDON/KEG DE74 .....86 B1
  EWD/SEL/PNX NG16 .....22 F5
  ILK DE7 .....21 J8
  ILK DE7 .....33 H1
  LEIN LE4 .....6 D4
Longleat Cl LEIE LE5 .....126 B7
Longleat Crs BSTN/STPLFD NG9 .....63 G3
Longley La DERBYE DE21 .....59 H1
Longmead Cl ARN NG5 .....37 G1
Longmead Dr ARN NG5 .....37 G1
Long Meadow WGSTN LE18 .....138 C7
Long Meadow Hl CALV/BJ NG14 .....27 L5
Long Mere La CDON/KEG DE74 .....92 F5
Longmoor Gdns LGEAT NG10 .....61 M5
Longmoor La
  BWSH/BRSTN DE72 .....61 J6
  LGEAT NG10 .....61M1
Longmoor Rd LGEAT NG10 .....61 M3
Longmoor Sq WOL/BIL/BRX NG8 .....50 B3
Longridge Rd ARN NG5 .....37 K3
Long Rw BPR/DUF DE56 .....17 K3
  BWSH/BRSTN DE72 .....74 F5
  NOTT NG1 .....5 G7
Longstock Cl DERBYE DE21 .....44 C6
Longstone Gn LEIE LE5 .....127 J8
Longstone Ri BPR/DUF DE56 .....17M1
Longstone Wk DERBY * DE1 .....2 D7
Long St RLBORO LE12 .....100 F7
  RLEIW/BAR LE9 .....140 C4
  WGSTN LE18 .....138 B5
Longthorpe Ct DERBYE DE23 .....56 E8
Longwall Av WBRGFD NG2 .....50 E6
Longwalls La BPR/DUF DE56 .....17 J5
Lonscale Cl WBRGFD NG2 .....66 A2
Lonsdale Dr BSTN/STPLFD NG9 .....62 C5
Lonsdale Pl DERBYW DE22 .....57 H3
Lonsdale Rd LEIN LE4 .....50 C1
  NOTTE NG7 .....50 C1
Lonsdale St LEIS LE2 .....7 L8
Loom Cl BPR/DUF DE56 .....18 A2
Lord Byron St LEIS LE2 .....131 L7
Lord Cl END/NAR LE19 .....135M8
Lord Haddon Rd ILK DE7 .....33 J6
Lord Nelson St WBRGFD NG2 .....51 K3
Lords Av LEIN LE4 .....119 G8
Lords Cl COAL LE67 .....108 E8
Lord St DERBYSE DE24 .....72 B1
  WBRGFD NG2 .....5 M7
Lorimer Av CARL NG4 .....38 D5
Lorne Cl MAPPK/POR/STA NG3 .....5 J2
Lorne Gv COT/KEY/RAD NG12 .....53 K4
Lorne Rd LEIS LE2 .....131 L6
Lorne St DERBYW DE22 .....2 C8
Lorne Wk MAPPK/POR/STA NG3 .....5 J2
Lorraine Cl DERBYSE DE24 .....72 C4
Lorraine Rd LEIS LE2 .....131 H8
Lorrimer Av CARL NG4 .....38 D5
Lorrimer Wy LBORO LE11 .....103 G2
Lortas Rd ARN NG5 .....36 D5
Loscoe-Denby La RIPLEY DE5 .....19M3
Loscoe Gra HEANOR DE75 .....20 A4
Loscoe Mount Rd ARN NG5 .....37 G5
Loscoe Rd ARN NG5 .....37 G6
  DERBYE DE21 .....44 B6
  HEANOR DE75 .....20 B4
Loseby La LEI LE1 .....6 E6
Lothair Rd LEIS LE2 .....131 J6
Lothian Pl CDON/KEG DE74 .....84 E4
  DERBYE DE21 .....44 B8
Lothian Rd COT/KEY/RAD NG12 .....66 A0
Lothlorien Cl NORM/LIT DE23 .....56 F8
Lothmore Wk WBRGFD * NG2 .....50 F5
Lotus Cl MAPPK/POR/STA NG3 .....5M1
Loudon St NORM/LIT DE23 .....2 F8
Loudoun Pl CDON/KEG DE74 .....84 E3
Loughborough Av
  WBRGFD NG2 .....51 K3
Loughborough Rd
  CFTN/RUD NG11 .....79 J8
  COAL LE67 .....100 B8
  LBORO LE11 .....104 B7
  LEIN LE4 .....125 L1
  RLBORO LE12 .....94 E7
  RLBORO LE12 .....96 C1
  RLBORO LE12 .....96 C3
  RLBORO LE12 .....102 A3
  RLBORO LE12 .....105 J3
  RLBORO LE12 .....105 J1
  RLEINE/SYS LE7 .....113 L7
  WBRGFD NG2 .....51 J8
Loughrigg Cl WBRGFD NG2 .....50 F6
Louis Av BSTN/STPLFD NG9 .....49 J8
Louise Av CARL NG4 .....38 E7
  GBY/RBY LE6 .....123 K5
Lousie Greaves La
  DERBYE DE21 .....59 J1
Louvain Rd NORM/LIT DE23 .....57 G4
Lovelace Wk HUCK/RAV NG15 .....15M7
Lovelace Wy RLEIW/BBY LE8 .....145 K8
Lovell Cl BLWL NG6 .....35 K2
Lowater St CARL NG4 .....37 M8
Lowcroft Dr LEIS LE2 .....139 G3
Lowdham La CALV/BJ NG14 .....27 H3
Lowdham Rd CALV/BJ NG14 .....27 H5

CARL NG4 ....38 A4
Lowdham St
MAPPK/POR/STA NG3 ....5 L6
Lower Bagthorpe
EWD/SEL/PNX NG16 ....13 J4
Lower Beauvale
EWD/SEL/PNX NG16 ....21 J4
Lower Bloomsgrove Rd *ILK* DE7 ...33 K5
Lower Brook St *LGEAT* NG10 ....62 C8
Lower Brown St *LEI* LE1 ....6 E4
Lower Cambridge St
LBORO LE11 ....103 M2
Lower Chapel St *ILK* DE7 ....33 K6
Lower Church St
RLEINE/SYS LE7 ....120 L1
Lower Clara Mount Rd
HEANOR DE75 ....20 E6
Lower Ct *BSTN/STPLFD* NG9 ......49 J8
Lower Dale Rd *NORM/LIT* DE23 ...57 K5
Lower Dunstead Rd
EWD/SEL/PNX NG16 ....20 E4
Lower Eldon St *WBRGFD* NG2 ....5 M8
Lower Eley St *DERBY* DE1 ....2 D7
Lower Gladstone St
HEANOR DE75 ....20 C5
LBORO LE11 ....9 J1
Lower Granby St *ILK* DE7 ....33 K5
Lower Gn *LBORO* LE11 ....103 H7
RDERBYSW DE65 ....70 B6
Lower Hall Cl *BPR/DUF* DE56 ....30 A1
Lower Hastings St *LEI* LE1 ....7 G9
Lower Holme *RLBORO* LE12 .....94 F4
Lower Keyham La *LEIE* LE5 ....126 F6
Lower Lee St *LEI* LE1 ....6 F4
Lower Maples *HEANOR* DE75 ....20 E7
Lower Middleton St *ILK* DE7 .....33 L6
Lower Nelson St *HEANOR* DE75 ...20 D5
Lower Orchard St
BSTN/STPLFD NG9 ....48 B8
Lower Park St
BSTN/STPLFD NG9 ....62 A1
Lower Parliament St *NOTT* NG1 ...5 H6
Lower Regent St
BSTN/STPLFD NG9 ....63 L1
DERBYW DE22 ....42 C7
Lower Stanton Rd *ILK* DE7 ....47 K1
Lower Whitworth Rd *ILK* DE7 ....47 K1
Lower Willow St *LEI* LE1 ....7 G2
Lowes HI *RIPLEY* DE5 ....11 H4
Lowes La *MELB/CHEL* DE73 .....72 B6
Lowe St *DERBYSE* DE24 ....58 C8
Loweswater Cl *RLBORO* LE12 ...105 H6
Loweswater Ct *WBRGFD* NG2 ....52 A8
Loweswater Dr *LBORO* LE11 ....103 G6
Lowick Dr *WGSTN* LE18 ....138 C5
Lowland Av *LEIW* LE3 ....129 L5
Lowlands Dr
COT/KEY/RAD NG12 ....80 D3
Lowlands Lea *HEANOR* DE75 ....20 D5
Lowlands Rd *BPR/DUF* DE56 ....17 M3
Low Pavement *NOTT* NG1 ....5 H8
Lows Cl *MELB/CHEL* DE73 ....72 F5
Low's La *ILK* DE7 ....47 L5
Lowther Wy *LBORO* LE11 ....9 K9
Low Wood Rd *BLWL* NG6 ....35 K2
Low Woods La *RLBORO* LE12 ...100 E4
Loxley Cl *DERBYE* DE21 ....44 F5
Loxley Rd *LEIW* LE3 ....124 A6
Loxton Ct *MCKLVR* DE3 ....56 A4
Loyne Cl *DERBYSE* DE24 ....71 K5
Lubbesthorpe Bridle Rd
LEIW LE3 ....130 C6
Lubbesthorpe Rd *LEIW* LE3 .....130 C8
Lubbesthorpe Wy
END/NAR LE19 ....130 B7
Lucas La *RDERBYSW* DE65 ....68 C5
Luccombe Dr *DERBYSE* DE24 ....73 H2
Lucerne Cl *CFTN/RUD* NG11 ......64 F1
Lucerne Rd *DERBYE* DE21 ....45 G4
Lucknow Av
MAPPK/POR/STA NG3 ....37 H7
Lucknow Ct
MAPPK/POR/STA NG3 ....37 H7
Lucknow Dr
MAPPK/POR/STA NG3 ....37 H7
Lucknow Rd
MAPPK/POR/STA NG3 ....37 H7
Ludford Rd *BLWL* NG6 ....24 A7
Ludgate Cl *ARN* NG5 ....24 E5
LEIN LE4 ....119 J7
Ludgate Wk *DERBYW* DE22 .....56 C2
Ludham Av *BLWL* NG6 ....23 M6
Ludlam Av *EWD/SEL/PNX* NG16 ...21 L8
Ludlam Cl *RLEIW/BBY* LE8 .....143 G3
Ludlow Cl *BSTN/STPLFD* NG9 ....49 H6
DERBYE DE21 ....59 K2
LBORO LE11 ....103 G7
LEIS LE2 ....139 G2
Ludlow Hill Rd *WBRGFD* NG2 ...51 M7
Lulworth Cl *LEIE* LE5 ....132 E3
NORM/LIT DE23 ....71 H1
WBRGFD NG2 ....65 G2
WGSTN LE18 ....138 B8
Lulworth Ct
EWD/SEL/PNX NG16 ....22 D8
BPR/DUF DE56 ....16 A5
Lumb La *BPR/DUF* DE56 ....16 A5
Lundie Cl *DERBYE* DE24 ....71 H5
Lune Cl *BSTN/STPLFD* NG9 ......63 J4
Lunsford Rd *LEIE* LE5 ....126 B7
Lupin Cl *DERBYE* DE21 ....45 G4
MAPPK/POR/STA NG3 ....5 J2
Luther Cl *MAPPK/POR/STA* NG3 ...5 M2
Luther St *LEIW* LE3 ....131 G3
Luton Cl *WOL/BIL/BRX* NG8 .....36 B6
Lutterell Ct *WBRGFD* NG2 ....65 H2
Lutterell Wy *WBRGFD* NG2 .....66 A2
Lutterworth Rd *LEIS* LE2 ....137 G2
RLEIW/BBY LE8 ....142 D7
Lyall Cl *LBORO* LE11 ....103 H1
Lybster Ms *WBRGFD* NG2 ....50 F5
Lychgate Cl *DERBYE* DE21 ......44 B5
GBY/RBY LE6 ....118 C5
Lydall Rd *LEIN* LE4 ....137 H3
Lydford Rd *LEIN* LE4 ....126 C5
Lydia Gdns *EWD/SEL/PNX* NG16 ...21 J6
Lydney Pk *WBRGFD* NG2 ....64 F2

Lydstep Cl *DERBYE* DE21 ....45 G5
Lyle Cl *EWD/SEL/PNX* NG16 ......22 C8
Lyle St *LEIN* LE4 ....126 C2
Lyme Pk *CFTN/RUD* NG11 ....64 F2
Lymington Gdns
MAPPK/POR/STA NG3 ....51 K1
Lymington Rd *LEIE* LE5 ....127 H7
Lymn Av *CARL* NG4 ....38 D5
Lyncombe Gdns
COT/KEY/RAD NG12 ....80 D3
Lyncote Rd *LEIW* LE3 ....130 F7
Lyncroft Av *RIPLEY* DE5 ....11 J5
Lyncroft Leys *LEIE* LE5 ....127 K8
Lyndale Cl *LEIN* LE4 ....126 C1
Lyndale Dr *RIPLEY* DE5 ....11 L7
Lyndale Rd *BSTN/STPLFD* NG9 ...48 E7
LEIW LE3 ....130 D7
Lynden Av *LGEAT* NG10 ....76 B1
Lyndhurst Gdns *WBRGFD* NG2 ...65 H3
Lyndhurst Gv *DERBYE* DE21 .....58 E2
Lyndhurst Rd *LEIS* LE2 ....138 E1
WBRGFD NG2 ....51 L3
Lyndhurst St *NORM/LIT* DE23 ....2 E9
Lyndhurst Ter *NORM/LIT* DE23 ...2 E8
Lyndon Dr *LEIS* LE2 ....138 D1
Lyngate Av *LEIN* LE4 ....119 L7
Lynham Ct *BLWL* NG6 ....23 M8
Lynholme Rd *LEIS* LE2 ....137 M1
Lynmouth Cl *LEIW* LE3 ....124 A4
Lynmouth Crs *NOTTE* NG7 ......36 C8
Lynmouth Dr *ILK* DE7 ....33 H4
WGSTN LE18 ....137 L2
Lynmouth Rd *LEIE* LE5 ....127 H7
Lynncroft *EWD/SEL/PNX* NG16 ...21 L5
Lynstead Dr *HUCK/RAV* NG15 ....23 G5
Lynton Cl *RIPLEY* DE5 ....11 H4
Lynton Gdns *ARN* NG5 ....25 L3
Lynton Rd *BSTN/STPLFD* NG9 ....63 G1
Lynton St *DERBYW* DE22 ....2 B6
Lynwood Rd *DERBYSE* DE24 .....71 K3
Lyon Cl *WGSTN* LE18 ....137 L3
Lyons Cl *CFTN/RUD* NG11 ....64 F7
Lytham Ct *DERBYE* DE21 ....44 B6
Lytham Dr *COT/KEY/RAD* NG12 ...66 A4
Lytham Gdns *ARN* NG5 ....24 E6
Lytham Rd *LEIS* LE2 ....131 L6
Lythe Cl *CFTN/RUD* NG11 ....64 E2
Lyttelton St *DERBYW* DE22 ......56 F2
Lytton Cl *MAPPK/POR/STA* NG3 ...5 L5
Lytton Rd *LEIS* LE2 ....131 M6

M

Mabel Gv *WBRGFD* NG2 ....51 L7
Mabel St *WBRGFD* NG2 ....51 H5
Mablowe Fld *WGSTN* LE18 ......138 C7
Macaulay Rd *RLEINE/SYS* LE7 ...119 J1
Macaulay St *DERBYSE* DE24 .....71 J2
LEIS LE2 ....131 K6
Macdonald Rd *LEIN* LE4 ....125 L6
Macdonald Sq *ILK* DE7 ....47 H2
Mackenzie St *DERBYW* DE22 ....57 G1
Mackenzie Wy *LEI* LE1 ....7 H3
Mackinley Av *BSTN/STPLFD* NG9 ...48 B6
Macklin St *DERBY* DE1 ....2 D4
Mackworth Rd *DERBYW* DE22 ....2 A1
Maclaren Gdns *CFTN/RUD* NG11 ...79 H2
Maclean Av *LBORO* LE11 ....103 G1
Maclean Rd *CARL* NG4 ....38 A8
Macready Pl *DERBYSE* DE24 .....58 D8
Madeley Cl *MCKLVR* DE3 ....56 B6
Madeley St *NORM/LIT* DE23 .....57 L5
Madeline Rd *LEIN* LE4 ....125 G1
Madison Av *DERBYE* DE24 ....44 C8
Madras Rd *LEI* LE1 ....7 J4
Mafeking St *WBRGFD* NG2 ....51 L3
Magdala Rd
MAPPK/POR/STA NG3 ....37 G7
Magna Rd *WGSTN* LE18 ....137 L6
Magnolia Av *RLBORO* LE12 .....103 L8
Magnolia Cl *LEIS* LE2 ....137 G2
LEIW LE3 ....129 L3
WOL/BIL/BRX NG8 ....35 J6
Magnolia St *BSTN/STPLFD* NG9 ...49 H6
Magnolia Gv *HUCK/RAV* NG15 ...23 M3
Magnus Rd *LEIN* LE4 ....126 A5
Magson Cl *MAPPK/POR/STA* NG3 ...5 M5
Maiden La *NOTT* NG1 ....5 K7
Maidens Dl *ARN* NG5 ....25 H7
Maiden St *RLEINE/SYS* LE7 .....120 C1
Maidenwell Av *LEIE* LE5 ....127 G6
Maidstone Dr
BSTN/STPLFD NG9 ....49 H5
DERBYSE DE24 ....72 D2
Maidstone Rd *LEIS* LE2 ....7 J7
Maidwell Cl *BPR/DUF* DE56 .....17 M2
WGSTN LE18 ....138 D5
Main Av *DERBYW* DE22 ....43 K2
Maine Dr *DERBYE* DE21 ....58 E1
Main St *ALFN* DE55 ....12 E1
BSTN/STPLFD NG9 ....64 A1
BWSH/BRSTN DE72 ....73 L1
CARL NG4 ....38 D6
CFTN/RUD NG11 ....50 F8
COT/KEY/RAD NG12 ....53 J4
COT/KEY/RAD NG12 ....66 C8
COT/KEY/RAD NG12 ....67 J3
EWD/SEL/PNX NG16 ....12 F3
EWD/SEL/PNX NG16 ....13 G4
EWD/SEL/PNX NG16 ....13 J4
EWD/SEL/PNX NG16 ....22 D6
ILK DE7 ....31 K4
RIPLEY DE5 ....10 E4
RIPLEY DE5 ....10 F2
Mainside Crs
WOL/BIL/BRX NG8 ....49 G4
Main St *BLWL* NG6 ....61 H8
RIPLEY DE5 ....24 A8
BWSH/BRSTN DE72 ....61 H8
BWSH/BRSTN DE72 ....74 B1
BWSH/BRSTN DE72 ....83 J3
CALV/BJ NG14 ....26 F3
CALV/BJ NG14 ....39 K3
CALV/BJ NG14 ....41 K1
CARL NG4 ....26 F8
CDON/KEG DE74 ....85 H3

CDON/KEG DE74 ....85 K1
CFTN/RUD NG11 ....79 J3
CFTN/RUD NG11 ....79 J4
COAL LE67 ....100 B7
COAL LE67 ....100 B8
COT/KEY/RAD NG12 ....80 C5
COT/KEY/RAD NG12 ....90 A4
EWD/SEL/PNX NG16 ....13 H6
EWD/SEL/PNX NG16 ....21 K6
EWD/SEL/PNX NG16 ....22 A5
EWD/SEL/PNX NG16 ....34 A2
EWD/SEL/PNX NG16 ....34 A3
GBY/RBY LE6 ....117 H6
GBY/RBY LE6 ....123 C7
HUCK/RAV NG15 ....15 L4
ILK DE7 ....18 F8
ILK DE7 ....32 C4
ILK DE7 ....47 K7
LEIE LE5 ....126 E7
LEIE LE5 ....132 F4
LEIW LE3 ....123 M6
LEIW LE3 ....130 D5
LGEAT NG10 ....62 D8
MELB/CHEL DE73 ....82 F6
RDERBYSW DE65 ....68 A5
RDERBYSW DE65 ....68 F3
RDERBYSW DE65 ....69 K2
RDERBYSW DE65 ....70 B6
RLBORO LE12 ....86 E8
RLBORO LE12 ....87 K6
RLBORO LE12 ....88 D6
RLBORO LE12 ....89 G6
RLBORO LE12 ....91 G8
RLBORO LE12 ....93 M3
RLBORO LE12 ....94 F4
RLBORO LE12 ....95 H4
RLBORO LE12 ....97 H2
RLBORO LE12 ....100 A3
RLBORO LE12 ....104 A8
RLBORO LE12 ....111 K5
RLBORO LE12 ....112 A8
RLBORO LE12 ....114 A7
RLEINE/SYS LE7 ....115 G5
RLEINE/SYS LE7 ....121 C7
RLEINE/SYS LE7 ....121 K2
RLEINE/SYS LE7 ....127 K7
RLEINE/SYS LE7 ....133 K3
RLEIW/BAR LE9 ....128 A1
RLEIW/BAR LE9 ....129 H2
RLEIW/BAR LE9 ....134 E4
RLEIW/BAR LE9 ....135 H8
RLEIW/BAR LE9 ....141 J8
RLEIW/BAR LE9 ....142 B5
RLEIW/BBY LE8 ....139 M7
RLEIW/BBY LE8 ....145 K8
RLEIW/BBY LE8 ....146 E5
RLEIW/BBY LE8 ....147 L2
WBRGFD NG2 ....52 A8
WGSTN LE18 ....144 D4
WOL/BIL/BRX NG8 ....34 F6
Maitland *RLBORO* LE12 ....113 J6
Maitland Av *ARN* NG5 ....37 K3
Maitland Rd *ARN* NG5 ....37 K3
Maize Cl *NORM/LIT* DE23 ....70 E1
Major St *NOTT* NG1 ....5 J5
Makeney Rd *BPR/DUF* DE56 ....29 K5
Malabar Rd *LEI* LE1 ....7 J4
Malbon Cl *MAPPK/POR/STA* NG3 ...37 J7
Malcolm Ar *LEI* * LE1 ....6 E5
Malcolm Cl *MAPPK/POR/STA* NG3 ...5 H1
Malcolm Gv *NORM/LIT* DE23 .....56 F8
Malcolm Rd *NORM/LIT* DE23 ....57 M5
Maldon Cl *BSTN/STPLFD* NG9 ....62 F3
Malham Cl *LEIN* LE4 ....124 F4
Malham Rd *NORM/LIT* DE23 .....70 D1
Malham Wy *LEIS* LE2 ....139 H2
Malin Cl *DERBYSE* DE24 ....72 F2
Malin HI *NOTT* NG1 ....5 K8
Malkin Av *COT/KEY/RAD* NG12 ...53 L3
Mallard Av *GBY/RBY* LE6 ....123 J4
Mallard Cl *BSTN/STPLFD* * NG9 ...63 M2
Mallard Dr *RLEINE/SYS* LE7 ....120 D3
Mallard Rd *CARL* NG4 ....52 F1
Mallard St *NOTTE* NG7 ....36 D5
Mallard Wk *MCKLVR* DE3 ....56 A8
Mallard Wy *LEIW* LE3 ....129 J5
Malling Cl *RLEIW/BAR* LE9 .....141 H8
Malling Cl *RLEINE/SYS* LE7 ....119 M6
Mallory Pl *LEIE* LE5 ....126 C7
Mallow Cl *LEIE* LE5 ....127 G4
Malmesbury Rd
MAPPK/POR/STA NG3 ....37 L3
Maltby Cl *DERBYW* DE22 ....43 K5
WOL/BIL/BRX NG8 ....35 M5
Maltby Rd
MAPPK/POR/STA NG3 ....37 L3
Malt Cottages *NOTT* NG7 ....36 D6
Malthouse Cl
EWD/SEL/PNX NG16 ....21 K6
Malthouse Rd *ILK* DE7 ....47 K5
The Maltings
BWSH/BRSTN DE72 ....74 E6
DERBY * DE1 ....2 F6
LEIW LE3 ....123 M6
Malting Cl *CFTN/RUD* NG11 .....79 G1
Maltmill La *NOTT* NG1 ....5 H8
Malton Dr *LEIS* LE2 ....139 G1
Malton Pl *DERBYE* DE21 ....44 B6
Malton Rd *NOTTE* NG7 ....36 D5
Malt St *CFTN/RUD* NG11 ....77 M6
Malvern Av *RLBORO* LE12 ......102 A5
Malvern Cl
MAPPK/POR/STA NG3 ....37 J6
MCKLVR DE3 ....56 B4
Malvern Crs *RLEIW/BAR* LE9 ...142 B4
WBRGFD NG2 ....65 K2
Malvern Gdns *LGEAT* NG10 .....61 L7
Malvern Rd *LEIS* LE2 ....132 B5
WBRGFD NG2 ....65 J2
Malvern Wy *DERBYE* DE21 ......44 B6
Mammoth St *COAL* LE67 ....108 B6
Manchester St *DERBYW* DE22 ...57 H1
LGEAT NG10 ....76 B1
Mandalay St *BLWL* NG6 ....36 B3
Mandarin Wy *RLEIW/BBY* LE8 ..142 D3
Mandervell Rd *LEIS* LE2 ....138 D2
Mandora La *LEIS* LE2 ....7 J9

Manesty Crs *CFTN/RUD* NG11 ...64 C8
Manifold Dr *DERBYSE* DE24 .....58 F7
Manifold Gdns *WBRGFD* NG2 ...51 G5
Manitoba Rd *LEI* LE1 ....7 G3
Manly Cl *ARN* NG5 ....24 C7
Mann Cl *LEIW* LE3 ....130 B5
Manners Av *ILK* DE7 ....33 H6
Manners Rd *ILK* DE7 ....33 J6
LEIS LE2 ....131 J8
Manners St *ILK* DE7 ....47 L1
Manning St
MAPPK/POR/STA NG3 ....5 J1
Manning Vw *ILK* DE7 ....33 K5
Mannion Crs *LGEAT* NG10 ......75 M2
Manns Leys *COT/KEY/RAD* NG12 ...67 J5
Mann St *NOTTE* NG7 ....36 D7
Manor Av *BSTN/STPLFD* NG9 ....48 B7
BSTN/STPLFD NG9 ....63 J4
BSTN/STPLFD NG9 ....63 K1
DERBYW DE22 ....57 G4
WBRGFD NG2 ....5 M8
Manor Brook Cl
RLEIW/BAR LE9 ....140 C4
Manor Cl *COT/KEY/RAD* NG12 ...65 M4
LEIS LE2 ....132 F2
RLBORO LE12 ....89 G6
Manor Ct *ALFN* * DE55 ....12 C1
BWSH/BRSTN DE72 ....61 H7
CARL NG4 ....38 D7
RLBORO LE12 ....91 G8
RLEIW/BBY LE8 ....137 G7
Manor Crs *CARL* NG4 ....38 D7
Manor Cft *RIPLEY* DE5 ....11 H3
Manor Dr *LBORO* LE11 ....103 M7
LEIN LE4 ....124 C2
RLBORO LE12 ....114 A5
Manor Farm Cl *CFTN/RUD* NG11 ...79 J4
Manor Farm La
CFTN/RUD NG11 ....64 C6
Manor Farm Meadow
RLBORO LE12 ....88 C6
Manor Farm Rd
BWSH/BRSTN DE72 ....73 M7
Manor Farm Wy *LEIW* LE3 .....123 M8
Manor Fields Dr *ILK* DE7 ....33 H8
Manor Gdns *LEIW* LE3 ....124 A7
RLBORO LE12 ....101 M3
Manor Green Ct *CARL* NG4 .....38 D7
Manor Green Wk *CARL* NG4 .....38 D7
Manor House Dr
COT/KEY/RAD NG12 ....90 A4
Manor House Gdns *LEIE* LE5 ...126 F7
Manor House Rd *LGEAT* NG10 ...76 D1
Manorleigh *BWSH/BRSTN* DE72 ...61 J7
Manor Pk *BWSH/BRSTN* DE72 ...59 H8
CFTN/RUD NG11 ....64 F8
Manor Park Ct *DERBYE* * DE22 ...56 F4
Manor Park Wy *DERBYW* DE22 ...56 F4
Manor Rd *BPR/DUF* DE56 ....17 K4
BWSH/BRSTN DE72 ....59 L6
CARL NG4 ....38 D7
CFTN/RUD NG11 ....77 J1
COT/KEY/RAD NG12 ....80 C4
EWD/SEL/PNX NG16 ....21 K6
ILK DE7 ....33 J6
LBORO LE11 ....103 M7
LEIN LE4 ....126 B1
LEIS LE2 ....132 D7
MELB/CHEL DE73 ....72 D6
NORM/LIT DE23 ....57 G5
RLBORO LE12 ....88 D4
RLEIW/BAR LE9 ....140 B7
RLEIW/BAR LE9 ....142 B3
RLEIW/BBY LE8 ....145 L8
Manor Rd Extension *LEIS* LE2 ...132 F8
Manor St *WBRGFD* NG2 ....51 K4
WGSTN LE18 ....137 M5
Manorwood Rd
COT/KEY/RAD NG12 ....67 K5
Mansell Cl *EWD/SEL/PNX* NG16 ...21 M6
Mansfield Cl *RLBORO* LE12 ....112 E1
Mansfield Gv *NOTT* NG1 ....4 F4
Mansfield Rd *ARN* NG5 ....37 H3
DERBY DE1 ....2 F1
DERBYE DE21 ....44 C4
EWD/SEL/PNX NG16 ....13 M5
EWD/SEL/PNX NG16 ....21 J2
HEANOR DE75 ....20 D5
HUCK/RAV NG15 ....14 E2
NOTT NG1 ....5 G5
Mansfield Road Arch HI
ARN NG5 ....25 J5
Mansfields Cft *RDERBYSW* DE65 ...68 F3
Mansfield St *ARN* NG5 ....37 G5
DERBY DE1 ....43 L8
LEI LE1 ....6 E4
RLBORO LE12 ....112 E1
Manston Cl *LEIN* LE4 ....126 E2
Manston Ms *NOTTE* NG7 ....4 B4
Manthorpe Crs *ARN* NG5 ....37 K4
Mantle La *COAL* LE67 ....108 A5
Mantle Rd *NOTTE* NG7 ....6 A4
Manton Crs *BSTN/STPLFD* NG9 ...49 K7
Manvers Av *RIPLEY* DE5 ....11 J6
Manvers Ct *WBRGFD* NG2 ....51 L6
Manvers Gv *COT/KEY/RAD* NG12 ...53 K4
Manvers Rd *WBRGFD* NG2 ....65 K1
Manvers St *CARL* NG4 ....52 E1
NOTT NG1 ....5 L7
RIPLEY DE5 ....11 J6
Manville Cl *BSTN/STPLFD* NG9 ...48 F4
WOL/BIL/BRX NG8 ....50 A1
Maori Av *HUCK/RAV* NG15 ......23 H3
Maple Av *BSTN/STPLFD* NG9 ....63 M2
LEIS LE2 ....130 A4
LGEAT NG10 ....47 M8
NORM/LIT DE23 ....71 H1
RIPLEY DE5 ....11 G7
RLEIW/BBY LE8 ....142 F1
RLEIW/BBY LE8 ....143 J3
Maplebeck Ct *ARN* NG5 ....25 L8
Maple Cl *COT/KEY/RAD* NG12 ...53 K5
COT/KEY/RAD NG12 ....80 E5
RLBORO LE12 ....88 D7

Maple Dr *BPR/DUF* DE56 ....17 M5
BWSH/BRSTN DE72 ....73 L8
CARL NG4 ....38 F5
DERBYSE DE24 ....72 E1
EWD/SEL/PNX NG16 ....34 F1
HUCK/RAV NG15 ....23 J2
MELB/CHEL DE73 ....72 E5
Maple Gdns *HEANOR* DE75 .....20 B6
Maple Gv *BWSH/BRSTN* DE72 ...61 K7
DERBYW DE22 ....43 H2
LBORO LE11 ....103 M7
LEIN LE4 ....126 B1
Maple Rd North *LBORO* LE11 ...103 M8
Maple Rd South *LBORO* LE11 ...103 M8
Maples St *NOTTE* NG7 ....4 B2
Maplestead Av *DERBYE* DE21 ...44 D6
Mapleton Av *DERBYE* DE21 .....44 D6
Mapleton Rd
BWSH/BRSTN DE72 ....60 D7
WGSTN LE18 ....138 A4
Mapletree Cl *ARN* NG5 ....24 F8
Maple Tree Wk *END/NAR* LE19 ...136 A8
Maplewell Cl *COAL* LE67 ....108 C7
Maplewell Dr *LEIN* LE4 ....124 E1
Maplewell Rd *RLBORO* LE12 ...111 J3
Maplin Rd *LEIE* LE5 ....127 J3
Mapperley Crs
MAPPK/POR/STA NG3 ....37 J5
Mapperley Hall
MAPPK/POR/STA NG3 ....37 H6
Mapperley Hall Dr
MAPPK/POR/STA NG3 ....37 H6
Mapperley La *ILK* DE7 ....32 C5
Mapperley Orch *ARN* NG5 ....26 A3
Mapperley Plns
MAPPK/POR/STA NG3 ....26 A3
Mapperley Ri *ARN* NG5 ....37 J5
Mapperley St
MAPPK/POR/STA NG3 ....5 G2
Mapperley St *ARN* NG5 ....37 G5
Marble St *LEI* LE1 ....6 E7
March Cl *ARN* NG5 ....24 C8
Marchesi Cl *HUCK/RAV* NG15 ...23 J3
Marchington Cl *DERBYW* DE22 ...43 J6
Marchwood Cl
WOL/BIL/BRX NG8 ....50 B3
Marcus Cl *RLEINE/SYS* LE7 ....120 C5
Marcus St *DERBY* * DE1 ....43 L8
Mardale Cl *WBRGFD* NG2 ....66 A2
Mardale Wy *LBORO* LE11 ......103 H7
Mardle Cl *DERBYSE* DE24 ....71 J3
Marefield Cl *RLEINE/SYS* LE7 ...133 L2
Marfitt St *LEIN* LE4 ....125 M5
Marfleet Cl *MCKLVR* DE3 ....56 A4
Margaret Anne Rd *LEIS* LE2 ...138 F3
Margaret Av *DERBYE* DE21 .....58 C2
ILK DE7 ....33 K7
LGEAT NG10 ....61 M3
LGEAT NG10 ....62 D7
Margaret Cl *LEIN* LE4 ....120 C7
Margaret Crs *CARL* NG4 ....38 C5
WGSTN LE18 ....137 M4
Margaret Rd *LEIE* LE5 ....132 C2
Margaret's Ct
BSTN/STPLFD NG9 ....48 F3
Margaret St *COAL* LE67 ....108 A7
DERBY DE1 ....43 L8
Margreave Rd *DERBYE* DE21 ....44 D8
Marham Cl *WBRGFD* NG2 ....5 M9
Marhill Rd *CARL* NG4 ....38 D8
Maria Ct *NOTTE* NG7 ....4 D9
Marie Gdns *HUCK/RAV* NG15 ...23 J3
Marigold Cl *DERBYE* DE21 ......44 F4
Marigold La *RLBORO* LE12 .....113 J5
Marigold Wy *END/NAR* LE19 ...135 K7
Marina Dr *BSTN/STPLFD* NG9 ...63 G2
DERBYSE DE24 ....72 C2
GBY/RBY LE6 ....123 L4
Marina Rd *HEANOR* DE75 ....19 M7
LEIE LE5 ....132 B3
WBRGFD NG2 ....50 E5
Marion's Wy *RLEIW/BAR* LE9 ...141 H3
Maris Cl *CFTN/RUD* NG11 ....64 A5
Maris Dr *CALV/BJ* NG14 ....39 J4
Marjorie Rd *DERBYE* DE21 ......44 C7
Marjorie St *LEIN* LE4 ....125 L6
Markeaton La *DERBYW* DE22 ...42 F7
Markeaton St *DERBYW* DE22 .....2 A1
Market Head *BPR/DUF* DE56 ....17 K4
Market Pl *ALFN* DE55 ....12 C1
BPR/DUF DE56 ....17 L4
COAL LE67 ....108 C2
DERBY * DE1 ....2 E3
EWD/SEL/PNX NG16 ....12 C3
HEANOR DE75 ....20 C6
ILK DE7 ....33 J7
LBORO LE11 ....9 J3
LEI LE1 ....6 E6
LGEAT NG10 ....62 C7
MELB/CHEL DE73 ....82 F8
RIPLEY DE5 ....19 M1
RLBORO LE12 ....102 A3
RLBORO LE12 ....113 J4
Market Pl South *LEI* LE1 ....6 E6
Market St *BWSH/BRSTN* DE72 ...60 D8
CDON/KEG DE74 ....84 F4
COAL LE67 ....108 A5
HEANOR DE75 ....20 C5
ILK DE7 ....33 K7
LBORO LE11 ....9 H3
LEI LE1 ....6 E6
NOTT NG1 ....5 L5
Markfield La *COAL* LE67 ....116 D6
COAL LE67 ....122 A6
Markfield Rd *COAL* LE67 ....122 C3
GBY/RBY LE6 ....123 H3
Markham Ct *DERBYE* DE21 ......57 G5
Markham Crs *ARN* NG5 ....37 G3
Markham Rd *BSTN/STPLFD* NG9 ...49 K8
Markham St *HUCK/RAV* NG15 ...15 H1
Markland Ct *LEIS* LE2 ....137 G3
Mark's Cl *NORM/LIT* DE23 ......71 H1
Mark St *LGEAT* NG10 ....76 B1
Marlborough Dr *BPR/DUF* DE56 ...18 A2
Marlborough Rd *ARN* NG5 ....37 H8
BSTN/STPLFD NG9 ....49 K8
BWSH/BRSTN DE72 ....61 H8

DERBYSE DE24 ....57 M8
LGEAT NG10 ....62 D7
Marlborough Sq *COAL* LE67 ....108 A6
Marlborough St *LEI* LE1 ....6 F7
NOTTE NG7 ....50 C6
Marldon Cl *WOL/BIL/BRX* NG8 ....48 F2
Marle Pit Hl *RLBORO* LE12 ....86 E7
Marl Flds *RLBORO* LE12 ....113 K6
Marlow Av *BLWL* NG6 ....36 C5
Marlow Crs *ILK* DE7 ....32 B7
Marlowe Ct *NORM/LIT* * DE23 ....71 K1
Marlow Rd *LEIW* LE3 ....131 H5
Marl Rd *COT/KEY/RAD* NG12 ......67 L5
Marlwood *COT/KEY/RAD* NG12 ....67 L5
Marmion Rd
  MAPPK/POR/STA NG3 ....51 J1
Marnham Dr
  MAPPK/POR/STA NG3 ....37 J6
Maromme Sq *WGSTN* LE18.......138 B4
Marple Sq
  MAPPK/POR/STA * NG3 ....5 H3
Marquis St *LEI* LE1 ....6 F8
Marriott Av *BSTN/STPLFD* NG9 ....62 E2
Marriott Cl *BSTN/STPLFD* NG9 ....62 E2
Marriott Dr *RLEIW/BBY* LE8 ....146 F7
Marriott Rd *LEIS* LE2 ....137 J2
Marsden Av *BSTN/STPLFD* NG9 ..62 E2
Marsden Cl *BPR/DUF* DE56 ....29 J4
Marsden La *LEIS* LE2 ....136 F1
Marsden St *DERBYSE* DE24 ....58 C8
Marshall Av *RLBORO* LE12 ....114 B3
Marshall Dr *BSTN/STPLFD* NG9 ..48 E1
Marshall Hill Dr
  MAPPK/POR/STA NG3 ....37 M6
Marshall Rd *CARL* NG4 ....37 G5
  HEANOR DE75 ....20 D5
  LEIW LE3 ....6 A2
Marsh Av *RLEIW/BBY* LE8 ....146 F6
Marshaw Cl *MCKLVR* DE3 ....56 C6
Marsh Cl *LEIN* LE4 ....126 D2
Marsh Dr *RLEIW/BBY* LE8 ....146 E6
Marshgreen Cl *DERBYSE* DE24 ....73 H2
Marsh La *BPR/DUF* DE56 ....17 M2
Marsh Lane *BPR/DUF* DE56......17 M3
Marsh Rd *RLBORO* LE12 ....113 J6
Marston Brook
  RDERBYSW DE65 ....68 C6
Marston Cl *BPR/DUF* DE56 ....18 A1
  LEIS LE2 ....138 E4
  NORM/LIT DE23 ....71 H2
Marston Crs *RLEIW/BBY* LE8 ......143 J4
Marston Dr *GBY/RBY* LE6 ....123 K4
Marston Rd *LEIN* LE4 ....126 C5
  MAPPK/POR/STA NG3 ....37 M8
  RLEIW/BAR LE9 ....140 F2
Marstown Av *WGSTN* LE18.......137 K5
Martin Av *LEIS* LE2 ....138 F2
  LEIW LE3 ....129 K4
  RLBORO LE12 ....105 H8
  RLBORO LE12 ....113 H6
Martin Cl *BLWL* NG6 ....23 K7
  COAL LE67 ....108 B1
  LEIN LE4 ....125 M7
  RLEIW/BAR LE9 ....140 B6
Martindale Cl *LBORO* LE11 ....8 B8
  LEIS LE2 ....131 K4
  WBRGFD NG2 ....52 A8
Martindale Ct *BPR/DUF* DE56 .....18 B2
Martin Dr *DERBYE* DE21 ....56 B4
  RLEINE/SYS LE7 ....120 C3
Martinmass Ct *NOTTE* NG7 ....50 C5
Martinshaw La *GBY/RBY* LE6 .....123 J4
Martins Hl *CARL* NG4 ....38 A5
Martin St *LEIN* LE4 ....126 A7
Martival *LEIE* LE5 ....126 C4
Marton Rd *BLWL* NG6 ....24 A6
  BSTN/STPLFD NG9 ....63 G4
Marvin Cl *LEIW* LE3 ....124 F8
Marvin Rd *BSTN/STPLFD* NG9 .....63 K1
Marwell Cl *LEIN* LE4 ....125 K3
Marwood Crs *CARL* NG4 ....38 A5
Marwood Rd *CARL* NG4 ....38 A6
  LEIN LE4 ....125 H3
Marydene Ct *LEIE* LE5 ....133 G4
Marydene Dr *LEIE* LE5 ....133 G4
Maryland Ct *BSTN/STPLFD* NG9 ..48 C6
Maryland Rd *DERBYE* DE21 ....58 F1
Marylebone Crs *DERBYE* DE22 ....56 D2
Mary Rd *EWD/SEL/PNX* NG16 .....21 M6
  LEIW LE3 ....124 F7
Mary's Cl *RLBORO* LE12 ....98 A4
Masefield Av *END/NAR* LE19 ......135 L5
  NORM/LIT DE23 ....57 J8
Masonic Pl *NOTT* NG1 ....4 F6
Mason Rd *ILK* DE7 ....33 H5
Masons Cl *END/NAR* LE19 ....135 M8
Massey Cl *CALV/BJ* NG14..............39 J4
Massey Gdns
  MAPPK/POR/STA NG3 ....5 M3
Masson Wk *DERBYW* DE22 ....2 A6
Matlock Av *WGSTN* LE18.............137 L6
Matlock Ct *NOTT* NG1 ....5 C5
Matlock Houses *DERBY* * DE21 ...59 J4
Matlock Rd *BPR/DUF* DE56 ....17 K2
  DERBYE DE21 ....44 D6
Matlock St *CARL* NG4 ....38 D8
  LEIS LE2 ....7 L5
Matthew Arnold Ct *LBORO* LE11....8 B1
Matthew St *DERBYSE* DE24 ....72 D1
Matthew Wy *NORM/LIT* DE23 ......56 C8
Mattingly Rd *BLWL* NG6 ....35 L1
Matts Cl *LEIS* LE2 ....137 H2
Maud Rd *NOTTE* NG7 ....36 E6
Maun Av *NOTTE* NG7 ....50 B1
Maura Cl *RLEIW/BBY* LE8 ....142 D2
Maurice Dr
  MAPPK/POR/STA NG3 ....37 J5
  RLEIW/BBY LE8 ....143 H4
Mavis Av *CARL* NG4 ....31 G5
Mawby Cl *RLEIW/BBY* LE8 ....142 E2
Maws Cl *EWD/SEL/PNX* NG16 .....22 C8
Max Rd *DERBYE* DE21 ....44 C7
Maxtoke Rd *NOTTE* NG7 ....4 C9
Maxwell Av *DERBYW* DE22 ....43 H7
Maxwell Cl *NOTTE* NG7 ....50 F6
Maxwell Dr *LBORO* LE11 ....102 F1
Maxwell St *BWSH/BRSTN* DE72 ..61 K7

Maycroft Gdns
  MAPPK/POR/STA NG3 ....37 L8
Maydene Cl *CFTN/RUD* NG11......64 B6
Mayes Ri *BLWL* NG6 ....24 C3
Mayfair Crs *DERBYW* DE22 ....56 C1
Mayfair Gdns *ARN* NG5 ....36 D2
Mayfield Av *BPR/DUF* DE56 ....18 E7
  CALV/BJ NG14 ....39 K2
Mayfield Dr *BSTN/STPLFD* NG9 ...48 D5
  LBORO LE11 ....9 H7
  WGSTN LE18 ....138 B3
Mayfield Gv *LGEAT* NG10 ....62 C6
Mayfield Rd *CARL* NG4 ....37 M8
  DERBYE DE21 ....44 C8
  LEIS LE2 ....132 A4
Mayflower Cl *COAL* LE67 ....116 C7
Mayflower Ct *WBRGFD* NG2 ....51 L8
Mayflower Rd
  EWD/SEL/PNX NG16 ....21 M7
  LEIE LE5 ....132 C4
Maylands Av
  BWSH/BRSTN DE72 ....59 M6
Maynard Rd *LEIS* LE2 ....7 K5
Mayns La *RLEIW/BBY* LE8 ....146 B1
Mayo Cl *LBORO* LE11 ....103 K8
Mayo Rd *ARN* NG5 ....36 F6
Mayor's Wk *LEI* LE1 ....131 L4
Maypole *CFTN/RUD* NG11 ....64 C4
Maypole La *NORM/LIT* DE23 ....56 C8
Maypole Yd *NOTT* NG1 ....5 H6
Mays Av *MAPPK/POR/STA* NG3 ....52 B3
Mays Cl *MAPPK/POR/STA* NG3 .....52 A1
Mays Farm Dr *RLEIW/BBY* LE8 ...140 B4
May St *DERBYW* DE22 ....2 C7
  ILK DE7 ....33 J3
Maythorn Cl *CFTN/RUD* NG11......65 G4
Maytree Cl *DERBYE* DE21 ....45 G4
  LEIW LE3 ....129 J4
Maytree Dr *LEIW* LE3 ....129 J4
May Tree La *RLBORO* LE12 ....111 M3
McCarthy Cl *COAL* LE67 ....108 C2
McCarthy Rd *RLBORO* LE12 ....101 L3
McDowell Wy *END/NAR* LE19 ......135 M8
McIntosh Rd *CARL* NG4 ....38 B4
McNeil Gv *BWSH/BRSTN* DE72 .....60 E8
McVicker Cl *LEIE* LE5 ....132 E1
Mead Cl *DERBYSE* DE24 ....71 K3
Meadfoot *BLWL* NG6 ....35 M3
Meadhurst Rd *LEIW* LE3 ....130 E2
Meadow Av *LBORO* LE11 ....103 M1
  RIPLEY DE5 ....11 M7
Meadowbank Ct
  EWD/SEL/PNX NG16 ....21 H4
Meadowbank Wy
  EWD/SEL/PNX NG16 ....21 H4
Meadowbrook Rd
  RLEIW/BBY LE8 ....146 D7
Meadow Cl *BWSH/BRSTN* DE72 ...60 J8
  BWSH/BRSTN DE72 ....59 J3
  DERBYE DE21 ....21 K3
  EWD/SEL/PNX NG16 ....21 K3
  GBY/RBY LE6 ....123 H7
  HUCK/RAV NG15 ....23 H2
  ILK DE7 ....31 H1
  RDERBYSW DE65 ....70 B5
  RLBORO LE12 ....105 J7
  RLEIW/BAR LE9 ....140 B4
  WBRGFD NG2 ....51 J6
Meadow Cottages *CARL* NG4 ......38 D8
Meadow Ct *BPR/DUF* DE56 ....17 K3
  BPR/DUF DE56 ....18 E8
  BWSH/BRSTN DE72 ....74 B1
  END/NAR LE19 ....135 L6
  WBRGFD * NG2 ....51 K5
  WGSTN * LE18 ....138 B5
Meadow Court Rd
  GBY/RBY LE6 ....123 K4
Meadowcourt Rd *LEIS* LE2 ....132 D8
Meadow Crs *CDON/KEG* DE74 ......84 F5
Meadowcroft Cl *LEIW* LE3 ....123 M8
Meadow Dr *COT/KEY/RAD* NG12 ..80 E4
Meadow Edge *END/NAR* LE19 .....135 L5
Meadow End *CFTN/RUD* NG11 ......77 M6
Meadow Gdns
  BSTN/STPLFD NG9 ....63 J3
  HEANOR DE75 ....20 F6
  LEIS LE2 ....137 K2
Meadowgrass Cl
  NORM/LIT DE23 ....70 F1
Meadow Gv *WBRGFD* NG2 ....51 J5
Meadow Hl *RLEIW/BBY* LE8 ....139 L7
Meadow La *BSTN/STPLFD* NG9 ....63 J3
  COAL LE67 ....108 E6
  COAL LE67 ....116 C6
  DERBY DE1 ....3 H3
  DERBYE DE21 ....58 D2
  DERBYSE DE24 ....58 D6
  LBORO LE11 ....9 K1
  LEIN LE4 ....119 M7
  LGEAT NG10 ....76 E1
  RLEINE/SYS LE7 ....120 B2
  WBRGFD NG2 ....51 H5
Meadowlark Gv *DERBYE* DE21 .....44 E6
Meadow Nook *DERBYSE* DE24 .....73 C3
Meadow Ri *EWD/SEL/PNX* NG16 ..35 K1
Meadow Rd *BSTN/STPLFD* NG9 ...63 M7
  CARL NG4 ....52 D1
  DERBY DE1 ....3 G5
  EWD/SEL/PNX NG16 ....34 A7
  RIPLEY DE5 ....11 H6
  RLBORO LE12 ....111 L6
  RLBORO LE12 ....113 H6
The Meadows *CALV/BJ* NG14.......26 F3
  END/NAR LE19 ....136 B8
  HEANOR DE75 ....20 C6
  RLBORO LE12 ....101 L5
  RLEINE/SYS LE7 ....115 J7
Meadow St *EWD/SEL/PNX* NG16 ..12 C2
  ILK DE7 ....33 K6
Meadows Rd *WBRGFD* NG2 ....50 F6
Meadowsweet Rd *LEIE* LE5 ....127 G6
Meadow V *BPR/DUF* DE56 ....29 H4

Meadowvale Crs
  CFTN/RUD NG11 ....64 C6
Meadow Vw *GBY/RBY* LE6 ....122 A6
  LEIS LE2 ....138 F2
  RLEINE/SYS LE7 ....115 K8
Meadow View Cl *DERBYE* DE21 ...44 F4
Meadow Wy *GBY/RBY* LE6 ....123 K4
  MELB/CHEL DE73 ....72 D6
  WGSTN LE18 ....138 D4
Meadwell Cl *LEIS* LE2 ....130 C2
Meadvale Rd *LEIS* LE2 ....132 A8
The Meadway *LEIN* LE4 ....119 L7
  RLEINE/SYS LE7 ....120 D5
Meadway *LEIW* LE3 ....130 E1
Meadwell Rd *LEIW* LE3 ....130 B3
Mear Dr *BWSH/BRSTN* DE72 ....59 M6
The Mease *RDERBYSW* DE65 ....68 C7
Meath Av *DERBYE* DE21 ....58 F3
Medawar Cl *CFTN/RUD* NG11.......44 F4
Meden Cl *CFTN/RUD* NG11 ....64 C4
Medhurst Cl *RLEIW/BBY* LE8 ......142 E2
Medina Cl *DERBYSE* DE24 ....73 H2
Medina Dr *COT/KEY/RAD* NG12 ...66 B6
Medina Rd *LEIW* LE3 ....6 A1
Medway Cl *BSTN/STPLFD* NG9 .....62 F2
Medway Dr *DERBYW* DE22 ....43 L2
Medway St *LEIS* LE2 ....7 L8
  WOL/BIL/BRX NG8 ....50 B2
Meeks Rd *ARN* NG5 ....25 M7
Meerbrook Cl *DERBYE* DE21 ....44 E6
Meerbrook Pl *ILK* DE7 ....47 C2
Meer Rd *BSTN/STPLFD* NG9 ....63 G4
Meeting House Cl *RLBORO* LE12 ..88 D6
Meeting St *RLBORO* LE12 ....112 D2
Megaloughton La *DERBYE* DE21...59 G4
Melba Wy *RLEINE/SYS* LE7 ....119 M6
Melbourn Cl *BPR/DUF* DE56 ....29 J5
Melbourne Cl *BPR/DUF* DE56 ....17 L5
  DERBYW DE22 ....43 H6
  MCKLVR DE3 ....56 D4
  RLEIW/BBY LE8 ....146 D7
Melbourne Houses
  DERBYE * DE21 ....59 J4
Melbourne Rd
  BSTN/STPLFD NG9 ....48 C5
  LEIS LE2 ....7 L8
  WBRGFD NG2 ....50 A6
  WOL/BIL/BRX NG8 ....36 A6
Melbourne St *COAL* LE67 ....108 A6
  DERBY DE1 ....2 F7
  EWD/SEL/PNX NG16 ....13 M1
  LEIS LE2 ....7 K5
Melbreak Av *LBORO* LE11 ....103 J7
Melbreak Cl *MCKLVR* DE3 ....56 C6
Melbury Rd *ARN* NG5 ....37 K3
  WOL/BIL/BRX NG8 ....35 H7
Melcroft Av *LEIW* LE3 ....130 F2
Meldreth Rd
  WOL/BIL/BRX NG8 ....35 J8
Melford Hall Dr *WBRGFD* NG2 .....65 G3
Melford Rd *WOL/BIL/BRX* NG8 .....35 H7
Melford St *LEIS* LE2 ....126 D8
Melfort Cl *DERBYSE* DE24 ....71 K5
Melksham Rd *ARN* NG5 ....25 C7
Melland Pl *LEIS* LE2 ....137 J2
Mellbreak Cl *WBRGFD* NG2 ....66 A1
Mellier Cl *END/NAR* LE19 ....135 L5
Mellor Rd *LEIW* LE3 ....130 E2
Mellor's La *BPR/DUF* DE56 ....30 A1
Mellors Rd *WBRGFD* NG2 ....65 K2
Mellor St *DERBYSE* DE24 ....72 C1
Melrose Av *ARN* NG5 ....37 G4
  BSTN/STPLFD NG9 ....63 J2
Melrose Cl *DERBYSE* DE24 ....71 J5
Melrose Gdns *WBRGFD* * NG2 ......65 J5
Melrose Rd *COAL* LE67 ....100 B8
Melrose St *ARN* NG5 ....37 G5
  LEIN LE4 ....125 M6
Melton Av *LEIW* LE4 ....126 A2
  MELB/CHEL DE73 ....82 E7
  NORM/LIT DE23 ....71 C1
Melton Ct *ALFN* DE55 ....12 A1
  LGEAT NG10 ....61 L2
Melton Dr *RLEIW/BAR* LE9 ....141 J7
Melton Gdns
  COT/KEY/RAD NG12 ....65 J5
Melton Gv *WBRGFD* NG2 ....51 J8
Melton La *RLBORO* LE12 ....86 F6
  RLBORO LE12 ....87 J6
Melton Rd *COT/KEY/RAD* NG12 ...65 L6
  LEIN LE4 ....126 A3
  RLBORO LE12 ....96 B3
  RLBORO LE12 ....97 L8
  RLBORO LE12 ....105 H8
  RLEINE/SYS LE7 ....115 K7
  RLEIW/BBY LE8 ....147 M3
  RMMWB LE14 ....91 L1
  WBRGFD NG2 ....51 J8
Melton St *LEI* LE1 ....7 G2
Melville Cl *LBORO* LE11 ....102 F2
Melville Ct
  MAPPK/POR/STA * NG3 ....37 G7
  RDERBYSW DE65 ....68 F4
Melville Gdns
  MAPPK/POR/STA NG3 ....5 M4
Melville St *NOTT* NG1 ....5 H9
Memorial Rd *DERBYW* DE22 ....43 G5
Memorial Sq *COAL* LE67 ....108 A6
Memory La *LEI* LE1 ....7 G2
Mendip Av *LEIN* LE4......................125 G6
Mendip Cl *LGEAT* NG10 ....61 L9
  RLBORO LE12 ....102 A4
Mendip Ct *DERBYE* DE21 ....44 C5
Menin Rd *DERBYW* DE22 ....43 G5
Mennecy Cl *RLEIW/BBY* LE8 ....143 H4
Mensa Cl *LEIS* LE2 ....7 L6
Mensing Av *COT/KEY/RAD* NG12 ..65 J5
Menzies Cl *LEIN* LE4 ....125 J3
Mercaston La *DERBYE* DE21 ....28 A8
Mercaston Rd *DERBYE* DE21 ....44 D7
Merchant Av *DERBYE* DE21 ....59 H3
Merchant St *BLWL* NG6 ....23 M7
  DERBYE DE21 ....2 A2
Mercia Dr *LEIS* LE2 ....138 D1
Mercian Ms *DERBYE* DE21 ....59 H3
Mercury Cl *ARN* NG5 ....36 C5
  LEIS LE2 ....7 K7
The Mere *RLEIW/BBY* LE8 ....139 L7

Mere Beck *BWSH/BRSTN* DE72 ....74 B1
Mere Cl *LEIS* LE5 ....7 M4
  RLBORO LE12 ....113 J7
Meredith Cl *WBRGFD* NG2 ....50 F6
Meredith Rd *BSTN/STPLFD* NG9 ..48 C5
Meredith Rd *RLEIW/BBY* LE8 ......130 F6
Meregill Cl *ARN* NG5 ....24 D5
Mere La *RLEINE/SYS* LE7 ....121 K2
  RLEIW/BBY LE8 ....139 H5
Mere Rd *LEIE* LE5 ....7 M8
  RLEIW/BBY LE8 ....147 J2
  WGSTN LE18 ....138 C4
Merevale Av *CFTN/RUD* NG11 ......64 D3
Mere Wy *CFTN/RUD* NG11 ....79 H2
Mereworth Cl *ARN* NG5 ....36 E6
Merganster Wy *COAL* LE67 ....108 E7
Meriac St *ARN* NG5 ....24 D7
Meriden Av *BSTN/STPLFD* NG9 ....49 L7
Meridian Cl *ILK* DE7 ....33 J3
Meridian East *END/NAR* LE19 .....130 B7
Meridian North *END/NAR* LE19 ....130 B8
Meridian South *END/NAR* LE19 ...136 B1
Meridian Wy *END/NAR* LE19 ....130 B6
Meridian West *END/NAR* LE19 .....130 B6
Merion Gv *NORM/LIT* DE23 ....56 C6
Merlin Cl *CFTN/RUD* NG11 ....64 B5
  LEIW LE3 ....129 L5
  RLBORO LE12 ....113 K6
  RLEIW/BAR LE9 ....141 J8
Merlin Dr *HUCK/RAV* NG15 ....23 H3
Merlin Gn *DERBYSE* DE24 ....71 H3
Merlin Wy *ILK* DE7 ....47 L4
  MCKLVR DE3 ....55 M8
Merridale Rd *NORM/LIT* DE23 ....57 G8
Merrill Wy *DERBYSE* DE24 ....72 B2
Merrin Cl *RLEINE/SYS* LE7 ....9 K2
Merrivale Ct
  MAPPK/POR/STA NG3 ....37 G7
Merrybower Cl *DERBYSE* DE24 ....71 G4
Mersey St *BLWL* NG6 ....23 M8
Merthull Rd *LEIE* LE5 ....133 G1
Merthyr Ct *DERBYE* DE21 ....44 F5
Merton Av *LEIW* LE3 ....131 G2
  RLEINE/SYS LE7 ....120 F4
Merton Cl *ARN* NG5 ....25 M6
  RLEIW/BAR LE9 ....141 H8
Merton Ct *BSTN/STPLFD* NG9 ......48 C6
Merton Wy *RLEIW/BBY* LE8 ....146 D6
Mervyn Rd *LEIS* LE5 ....132 B3
Messenger Cl *LBORO* LE11 ....95 J8
Metcalf Cl *RLEIW/BAR* LE9 ....140 B5
Metcalfe Cl *DERBYSE* DE24 ....58 F7
Metcalf Rd *EWD/SEL/PNX* NG16 ..21 M4
Methuen Av *LEIN* LE4 ....120 C1
Mettham St *NOTTE* NG7 ....4 A9
The Mews *LGEAT* * NG10 ....61 M2
  MELB/CHEL * DE73 ....82 F8
Meynell Cl *LEIS* LE2 ....139 G3
Meynell Ct *DERBYW* DE22 ....43 G5
Meynell Gv *NOTTE* NG7 ....36 E6
Meynell Rd *LEIE* LE5 ....126 B8
  LGEAT NG10 ....76 B2
  RLBORO LE12 ....104 E8
Meynell St *NORM/LIT* DE23 ....57 K5
Miall Ct *NOTTE* NG7 ....50 C2
Miall St *NOTTE* NG7 ....50 C2
Michael Cl *RLEINE/SYS* LE7 ....121 J1
Michael Ramsey Ct *LEIS* LE2 ....137 G4
Michelle Cl *DERBYSE* DE24 ....71 G4
Michigan Cl *DERBYE* DE21 ....59 G2
Mickleborough Av
  MAPPK/POR/STA NG3 ....37 K7
Mickleborough Wy
  CFTN/RUD NG11 ....65 G4
Micklebring Cl *RIPLEY* DE5 ....11 L5
Micklecroft Gdns
  NORM/LIT DE23 ....56 C8
Mickleden Cl *WBRGFD* NG2 ....50 F5
Mickleden Gn *COAL* LE67 ....108 E5
Mickledon Cl *LGEAT* NG10 ....61 M7
Micklefield Rd *LEIW* LE3 ....44 A3
Mickleross Cl *MCKLVR* DE3 ....132 F4
Mickleton Dr *LEIE* LE5 ....44 A7
  LBORO LE11 ....103 K1
Middlebeck Av *ARN* NG5 ....26 A7
Middlebeck Cl *MELB/CHEL* DE73...72 D6
Middlebeck Dr *ARN* NG5 ....26 A7
Middlebrook Rd
  EWD/SEL/PNX NG16 ....13 L3
Middledale Rd *CARL* NG4 ....52 A1
Middlefell Wy *CFTN/RUD* NG11 ....64 B6
Middlefield Rd *RLEINE/SYS* LE7 ...114 B8
Middle Furlong Gdns
  WBRGFD NG2 ....50 F5
Middle Furlong Ms
  WBRGFD NG2 ....50 F5
Middle Hl *NOTT* NG1 ....5 L5
Middle La *BSTN/STPLFD* * NG9 .....63 J2
Middlemore Cottages *ILK* * DE7 ...47 K6
Middle Nook *WOL/BIL/BRX* NG8 ...49 J2
Middle Orch *RLBORO* LE12 ....114 A6
Middle Pavement *NOTT* NG1 ....5 H7
Middlesex Rd *LEIS* LE2 ....131 H8
Middleton Av *NORM/LIT* DE23 ......57 G5
  RIPLEY DE5 ....19 M2
Middleton Bvd
  WOL/BIL/BRX NG8 ....50 A3
Middleton Cl
  EWD/SEL/PNX NG16 ....35 G1
  RLEIW/BAR LE9 ....140 C1
  WGSTN LE18 ....138 D4
Middleton Crs
  BSTN/STPLFD NG9 ....49 J6
Middleton Dr *NORM/LIT* DE23 ......57 G5
Middleton Pl *LBORO* LE11 ....9 H7
Middleton Rd *ILK* DE7 ....47 L2
Middleton St *BSTN/STPLFD* NG9 ..49 J8
  EWD/SEL/PNX NG16 ....34 A4
  ILK DE7 ....33 L6
  LEIS LE2 ....131 G8
Midhurst Av *LEIW* LE3 ....130 D7
Midhurst Cl *BSTN/STPLFD* NG9 ....49 J6
Midhurst Wy *CFTN/RUD* NG11 ......64 C5
Midlame Gdns *BLWL* NG6 ....23 K8
Midland Av *BSTN/STPLFD* NG9 .....62 A2
  CARL NG4 ....38 E8
  NOTTE NG7 ....50 C4

Midland Crs *CARL* NG4 ....38 D8
Midland Gv *CARL* NG4 ....38 E7
Midland Pl *DERBY* DE1 ....3 J6
Midland Rd *CARL* NG4 ....38 D8
  DERBY DE1 ....3 H7
  EWD/SEL/PNX NG16 ....21 K5
  HEANOR DE75 ....20 C5
Midland St *LEI* LE1 ....7 H5
  LGEAT NG10 ....62 C7
Midshires Wy *BPR/DUF* DE56 ....17 C1
  CDON/KEG DE74 ....76 A8
  COT/KEY/RAD NG12 ....90 A4
  ILK DE7 ....45 K1
  LEIS LE2 ....88 E5
The Midway *NOTTE* NG7 ....50 C7
Midway *DERBYW* DE22 ....43 J5
Midway Rd *LEIE* LE5 ....132 B5
Mikado Rd *LGEAT* NG10 ....76 A2
Milbank Cl *DERBYW* DE22 ....56 C1
Milburn Gdns *DERBYE* DE21 ....44 F4
Milbury Cl *DERBYE* DE21 ....44 D5
Mildenhall Crs *ARN* NG5 ....25 C7
Mildenhall Rd *LBORO* LE11 ....103 C3
Mile Ash La *DERBYW* DE22 ....43 K6
Mile End Rd *CARL* NG4 ....52 C2
Milestone Cl *RLEIW/BBY* LE8 ....147 G7
Milford Av *LGEAT* NG10 ....61 M4
Milford Cl *BLWL* NG6 ....23 L7
  LEIN LE4 ....135 L7
Milford Dr *ILK* DE7 ....33 H4
  MAPPK/POR/STA NG3 ....38 A8
Milford Rd *BPR/DUF* DE56 ....29 J3
  LEIS LE2 ....131 M7
Milford St *DERBY* DE1 ....43 K8
The Mill *BLWL* NG6 ....36 C4
Mill Acre Cl *ILK* DE7 ....33 C5
Millbank Av *BPR/DUF* DE56 ....17 M5
Millbank Cl *DERBYW* DE22 ....33 H4
Millbeck Av *WOL/BIL/BRX* NG8 ....49 J3
Millbeck Cl *WBRGFD* NG2 ....66 A1
Millbrook *LEIN* LE4 ....125 K4
Mill Cl *BPR/DUF* DE56 ....18 E8
  BWSH/BRSTN DE72 ....60 A6
  LEIN LE4 ....125 M1
  RDERBYSW DE65 ....70 B5
  RLBORO LE12 ....102 A2
  RLEIW/BAR LE9 ....140 C7
  WGSTN LE18 ....137 K7
Mill Ct *LGEAT* * NG10 ....62 C8
Mill Crs *ARN* NG5 ....25 J7
Mill Cft *MCKLVR* DE3 ....56 B3
Milldale Cl *CFTN/RUD* NG11 ....64 A5
  RIPLEY DE5 ....19 H1
Milldale Ct *BPR/DUF* DE56 ....17 M4
Milldale Rd *DERBYSE* DE24 ....59 K4
  LGEAT NG10 ....75 M1
Mill Dr *GBY/RBY* LE6 ....123 H8
Millennium Cl *ILK* DE7 ....33 J4
Millennium Wy *DERBYSE* DE24 .....58 E3
Millennium Wy East *BLWL* NG6 .....35 L3
Millennium Wy West
  EWD/SEL/PNX NG16 ....35 L3
Miller Cl *LEIN* LE4 ....126 C2
Miller Hives Cl
  COT/KEY/RAD NG12 ....67 J4
Millers Br *COT/KEY/RAD* NG12 ....67 J5
Millers Cl *LEIW* LE5 ....123 L7
  RLEINE/SYS LE7 ....120 E5
Millers Ct *NOTTE* NG7 ....50 C1
Millersdale Av *ILK* DE7 ....33 J2
  LEIE LE5 ....133 H2
Millersdale Cl *BPR/DUF* DE56.......17 M2
Miller's La *RLBORO* LE12 ....89 G6
Millfield *BWSH/BRSTN* DE72 ....74 F5
Mill Field Cl *CALV/BJ* NG14 ....39 J4
Millfield Cl *ILK* DE7 ....33 G4
  RLEINE/SYS LE7 ....124 B2
Millfield Crs *LEIW* LE3 ....136 D1
Millfield Rd *EWD/SEL/PNX* NG16 ..22 C8
  ILK DE7 ....33 L8
Mill Fleam *RDERBYSW* DE65 ....68 C6
Mill Gn *BWSH/BRSTN* * DE72 ....74 E6
Mill Hl *DERBYSE* DE24 ....73 G3
  END/NAR LE19 ....135 K2
Mill Hill Cl *RIPLEY* DE5 ....11 K6
  RLEIW/BBY LE8 ....156 D8
Mill Hill La *BWSH/BRSTN* DE72 ....61 J6
  COAL LE67 ....116 B6
  LEIS LE2 ....7 J9
  NORM/LIT DE23 ....2 D8
Mill Hill Rd *NORM/LIT* DE23 ....2 D8
Millhouse Ct *BWSH/BRSTN* DE72..60 F8
Millicent Gv *WBRGFD* NG2 ....51 K7
Millicent Rd *WBRGFD* NG2 ....51 J7
Milligan Rd *LEIS* LE2 ....137 J1
The Mill La *GBY/RBY* LE6 ....123 L7
Mill La *BPR/DUF* DE56 ....17 M4
  CARL NG4 ....26 F8
  CDON/KEG DE74 ....86 B5
  COT/KEY/RAD NG12 ....67 J3
  END/NAR LE19 ....135 M4
  EWD/SEL/PNX NG16 ....34 A4
  LBORO LE11 ....120 B7
  LEIN LE4 ....6 C8
  LEIS LE2 ....6 C8
  LGEAT NG10 ....61 M1
  MCKLVR DE3 ....56 B3
  RDERBYSW DE65 ....68 A5
  RIPLEY DE5 ....11 M7
  RLBORO LE12 ....88 D7
  RLBORO LE12 ....91 H7
  RLBORO LE12 ....92 F8
  RLBORO LE12 ....94 A4
  RLBORO LE12 ....113 H1
  RLEIW/BAR LE9 ....134 D8
  RLEIW/BBY LE8 ....137 H7
  RLEIW/BBY LE8 ....146 D8
Mill Meadow Wy
  RDERBYSW DE65 ....68 F3
Mill Moor Cl *MELB/CHEL* DE73 .....72 C5
Millom Pl *DERBYE* DE21 ....44 B6
Mill Rd *BSTN/STPLFD* NG9 ....48 B7
  EWD/SEL/PNX NG16 ....21 M4
  HEANOR DE75 ....20 E7
  RLBORO LE12 ....111 K6
  RLEINE/SYS LE7 ....115 K6
  RLEINE/SYS LE7 ....118 F4
Mill Rw *DERBYE* * DE21 ....59 H2

The Mills *RLBORO* LE12 ....112 E2
Mills Cl *BWSH/BRSTN* DE72.........60 E8
Millstone La *LEI* LE1.....................6 E7
  RLEINE/SYS LE7 ....121 C1
Mill St *BLWL* NG6 ....36 M4
  BPR/DUF DE56 ....17 K3
  DERBY DE1 ....2 B2
  ILK DE7 ....33 K6
  LEI LE1 ....6 F8
Mills Yd *LBORO* LE11 ....9 J4
Mill Vw *RLEIW/BAR* LE9.........135 H8
Mill View Cl *WBRGFD* * NG2 ....51 K3
Millwood Cl *LEIN* LE4 ....125 J2
Milner Av *BWSH/BRSTN* DE72 ...60 E8
  RIPLEY DE5 ....11 M7
Milner Cl *RLBORO* LE12 ....114 A5
Milner Rd *ARN* NG5 ....37 C5
  LGEAT NG10 ....62 B7
Milnhay Rd *HEANOR* DE75.......20 D7
Milnroy Rd *LEIE* LE5................133 J1
Milton Av *ILK* DE7 ....33 J3
Milton Cl *WGSTN* LE18 ....138 C5
Milton Ct *ARN* NG5 ....25 M8
  LBORO * LE11 ....103 H1
Milton Crs *BSTN/STPLFD* NG9 ..63 H5
  LEIN LE4 ....124 F5
Milton Gdns *LEIS* LE2 ....138 C2
Milton Ri *HUCK/RAV* NG15 ......23 H2
Milton Rd *ILK* DE7 ....33 J3
  MCKLVR DE3 ....56 A4
Milton St *DERBYSE* DE22 ....57 H3
  END/NAR LE19 ....135 L6
  ILK DE7 ....33 K3
  LBORO LE11 ....103 J1
  LGEAT NG10 ....62 B8
  NOTT NG1 ....5 H5
Milverton Av *LEIN* LE4 ....125 H6
Milverton Cl *WGSTN* LE18 .....138 A3
Milverton Dr *WGSTN* LE18 .....138 A3
Milverton Dr *ARN* NG5 ....25 G7
Milward Rd *HEANOR* DE75 ......20 A5
Mimosa Cl *CFTN/RUD* NG11 ....64 A6
  RLBORO LE12 ....103 L8
Mimosa Crs *NORM/LIT* DE23 ...71 J2
Minehead St *LEIW* LE3 ....130 F2
Minerva St *BLWL* NG6 ....23 M7
Minster Cl *HUCK/RAV* NG15 ....15 M7
Minster Crs *LEIN* LE4 ....125 H6
Minster Gdns
  EWD/SEL/PNX NG16 ....21 M6
Minster Rd *DERBYE* DE21 ....44 C5
Mint Gv *LGEAT* NG10 ....61 L8
Minton Rd *BSTN/STPLFD* NG9 ..62 F5
Minton Rd *CDON/KEG* DE74 ....84 D3
Mint Rd *LEIS* LE2 ....6 B9
Minver Gv *BLWL* NG6 ....36 M6
Mirberry Ms *NOTTE* * NG7 ....50 A4
Misk Hollows *HUCK/RAV* NG15 ...1 K7
Misk Vw *EWD/SEL/PNX* NG16 ...21 M5
Mission St
  MAPPK/POR/STA NG3 ....37 J5
Misterton Cl *DERBYW* DE22 ......43 J5
Mitchell Av *EWD/SEL/PNX* NG16 ...22 E2
Mitchell Cl *BLWL* NG6 ....35 K1
Mitchell Dr *LBORO* LE11 ....103 C1
Mitchell Rd *END/NAR* LE19 .....135 L4
Mitchell St *LGEAT* NG10 ....62 C8
Mitchell Ter *ILK* DE7 ....47 L2
The Moat *CDON/KEG* DE74 ......84 F4
Moat Cl *RLEIW/BAR* LE9 ....134 D4
Moat Ct *LEIE* LE5 ....127 G2
Moat Rd *LBORO* LE11 ....103 J1
  LEIE LE5 ....132 B2
Moat St *WGSTN* LE18 ....138 A5
Modbury Av *LEIN* LE4 ....125 J3
Model Farm Cl *LBORO* LE11 ....103 J1
Moffat Cl
  MAPPK/POR/STA * NG3 ....37 K8
Moira Cl *DERBYE* DE21 ....44 B8
Moira Dl *CDON/KEG* DE74 ....85 G4
Moira St *LBORO* LE11 ....9 K4
  LEIN LE4 ....125 M6
  MELB/CHEL DE73 ....82 E4
Molineux St *NORM/LIT* DE23 ...57 M5
Mollington Sq *BLWL* NG6 ....35 M3
Molyneux St *RLBORO* LE12 .....114 B6
Monal Cl *RLEIW/BBY* LE8 ....142 D1
Monarch Dr *DERBYE* DE21 ....45 H4
Monarch Wy *HEANOR* DE75 .....20 B5
  LBORO LE11 ....103 L1
Monar Cl *LEIN* LE4 ....126 X3
Mona Rd *WBRGFD* NG2 ....51 L6
Mona St *BSTN/STPLFD* NG9 ......63 L1
Monckton Cl *LEI* LE1 ....7 H2
Moncrieff Crs *DERBYE* DE21 .....44 E7
Mondello Dr *DERBYSE* DE24 .....73 G1
Monica Rd *LEIW* LE3 ....130 D8
Monks Cl *DERBYSE* DE24 ....71 G5
  ILK DE7 ....33 L7
Monks Crs *LEIN* LE4 ....119 C5
Monk's La *CFTN/RUD* NG11 .....77 L6
Monks Meadow *RLBORO* LE12 ..88 D5
Monk St *DERBYW* DE22 ....2 C5
Monksway *CFTN/RUD* NG11 .....64 C5
Monkton Cl *ILK* DE7 ....33 L7
Monkton Dr *WOL/BIL/BRX* NG8 ..35 H1
Monmouth Cl
  WOL/BIL/BRX NG8 ....48 D1
Monmouth Dr *LEIS* LE2 ....137 G5
Monmouth St *DERBYE* DE21 ......3 J1
Monroe Wk *ARN* NG5 ....24 E8
Monsaldale Cl *LGEAT* NG10 .....75 M1
Monsal Dr *DERBYE* DE21 ....59 K4
Monsall Av *ILK* DE7 ....33 J2
Monsall St *NOTT* NG7 ....36 D6
Monsarrat Wy *LBORO* LE11 ....103 H1
Monsell Dr *ARN* NG5 ....25 J6
  LEIS LE2 ....137 G2
Montague Av *RLEIW/SYS* LE7 ..120 F5
Montague Cl *LBORO* LE11 ....103 H1
Montague Rd *HUCK/RAV* NG15 ..15 L7
  LEIS LE2 ....131 M6
  RLEIW/BAR LE9 ....141 K8
Montague St *BLWL* NG6 ....24 A8
  BSTN/STPLFD NG9 ....49 J8
Monteith Pl *CDON/KEG* DE74 ...84 F4
Montfort Ms *CDON/KEG* DE74 ..84 F3
Montfort Crs *ARN* NG5 ....37 H3

Montfort St *NOTTE* NG7 ....4 C6
Montgomery Cl
  BSTN/STPLFD NG9 ....63 G5
  RDERBYSW DE65 ....68 C5
Montgomery St *NOTTE* NG7 ....4 C4
Montpelier *DERBYW* DE22 ....29 H4
Montpelier Rd *NOTTE* NG7 ....50 C6
Montreal Rd *LEI* LE1 ....7 H2
Montrose Ct *NOTT* NG7 ....71 J3
Montrose Ct *BSTN/STPLFD* NG9 ..48 C6
Montrose Rd *LEIS* LE2 ....137 G2
Montrose Rd South *LEIS* LE2 ...137 G2
Montsoreau Wy *RLBORO* LE12 ..113 H7
Monument Hl
  EWD/SEL/PNX NG16 ....12 D4
Monument La
  EWD/SEL/PNX NG16 ....12 C5
  ILK DE7 ....33 J4
Monyash Cl *DERBYE* DE21 ....44 E7
Monyash Wy *BPR/DUF* DE56 .....17 M2
Moon Cl *LEIS* LE2 ....7 J7
The Moor *EWD/SEL/PNX* NG16 ...13 H1
Moor Br *BLWL* NG6 ....24 B6
Moorbridge La
  BSTN/STPLFD NG9 ....48 A6
Moor Dr *DERBYSE* DE24 ....72 E2
Moore Av *CDON/KEG* DE74 ....86 B4
Moore Cl *RLBORO* LE12 ....88 D5
  WBRGFD NG2 ....51 M6
Moor End *DERBYE* DE21 ....59 J2
Moore Rd *MAPPK/POR/STA* NG3 ..37 L5
Moores Av *LGEAT* NG10 ....48 A8
Moores La *END/NAR* LE19 ....135 M4
Moores Rd *LEIN* LE4 ....125 M5
Moor St *NORM/LIT* DE23 ....2 E8
Moor Farm Inn La
  BSTN/STPLFD NG9 ....48 E5
Moorfield Ct *BSTN/STPLFD* NG9 ..48 C6
Moorfield Crs *LGEAT* NG10 ....61 M2
Moorfield Pl *RLBORO* LE12 .....101 H1
Moorfield Rd *BPR/DUF* DE56 ....18 A8
Moorfields *LEIE* LE5 ....127 H7
Moorfields Av
  EWD/SEL/PNX NG16 ....21 K4
Moorgate *DERBYW* DE22 ....56 C1
Moorgate Av *LEIN* LE4 ....119 K7
Moorgate St *LEIN* LE4 ....125 L7
Moorgreen
  NOTTE NG7 ....4 C5
Moorgreen Dr
  WOL/BIL/BRX NG8 ....35 H5
Moorhead Av *DERBYSE* DE24 ...72 D2
Moorhouse Rd
  WOL/BIL/BRX NG8 ....49 J1
Moorland Av *BSTN/STPLFD* NG9 ..62 B1
Moorland Rd *MCKLVR* DE3 ....56 B4
Moorlands Cl *LGEAT* NG10 ....61 M5
Moor La *ASHB* LE 41 K5
  BSTN/STPLFD NG9 ....48 F5
  BWSH/BRSTN DE72 ....46 A8
  BWSH/BRSTN DE72 ....73 M7
  CFTN/RUD NG11 ....77 M6
  CFTN/RUD NG11 ....79 H7
  CFTN/RUD NG11 ....79 J1
  CFTN/RUD NG11 ....79 G1
  DERBYE DE21 ....30 B6
  DERBYSE DE24 ....71 M6
  DERBYSE DE24 ....72 A1
  ILK DE7 ....46 D5
  LBORO LE11 ....9 K3
  MELB/CHEL DE73 ....92 A4
  RLBORO LE12 ....95 G3
Moorpool Crs *BPR/DUF* DE56 ...18 A8
Moor Ri *BPR/DUF* DE56 ....18 A7
Moor Rd *BLWL* NG6 ....24 C2
  EWD/SEL/PNX NG16 ....13 J7
  ILK DE7 ....44 D1
  WOL/BIL/BRX NG8 ....35 H6
Moorsholm Dr
  WOL/BIL/BRX NG8 ....49 H3
Moorside Crs *DERBYE* DE21 ......71 H4
Moorside La *BPR/DUF* DE56 .....18 A7
Moor St *CARL* NG4 ....38 D8
  DERBYE DE21 ....59 J2
Moorway *ILK* DE7 ....44 D3
Moorway Cft *NORM/LIT* DE23 ...56 F8
Moorway La *NORM/LIT* DE23 ....70 E2
Moray Ct *EWD/SEL/PNX* NG16 ..22 D8
Moray Wk *DERBYE* * DE21 ....44 A7
Morban Rd *LEIS* LE2 ....136 F1
Morcote Rd *LEIW* LE3 ....130 C3
Morden Cl *WOL/BIL/BRX* NG8 ..35 H7
Morden Rd *EWD/SEL/PNX* NG16 ..22 A7
Morefern Dr *DERBYE* DE21 ....44 F5
Moreland Ct *WBRGFD* * NG2 ....51 J4
Morello Av *CARL* NG4 ....38 D8
Moreton Dl *RLBORO* LE12 ....114 B3
Moreton Rd *CFTN/RUD* NG11 ...64 C3
Morgan Ms *CFTN/RUD* * NG11 ..64 A5
Morgans Orch *RLBORO* LE12 ...105 H7
Morkinshire La
  COT/KEY/RAD NG12 ....67 J3
Morland Av *LEIS* LE2 ....132 C2
Morledge *DERBY* DE1 ....2 F4
Morledge St *LEI* LE1 ....7 H5
Morleston St *NORM/LIT* DE23 .....3 G8
Morley Av
  MAPPK/POR/STA NG3 ....37 J5
Morley Cl *BPR/DUF* DE56 ....18 C1
Morley Ct *WBRGFD* NG2 ....5 L7
Morley Dr *ILK* DE7 ....33 H4
Morleyfields Cl *RIPLEY* DE5 ......11 K6
Morley La *ILK* DE7 ....30 D7
  ILK DE7 ....45 M1
  RLBORO LE12 ....101 L6
Morley Rd *DERBYE* DE21 ....44 F7
  LEIE LE5 ....7 M5
  MAPPK/POR/STA NG3 ....2 D1
  RLEIW/BAR LE9 ....140 C8
Morley St *ARN* NG5 ....37 H1

  DERBYW DE22 ....57 G1
  LBORO LE11 ....104 A2
Morlich Dr *MCKLVR* DE3 ....71 H3
Morningside Cl *DERBYSE* DE24 ..72 B3
Mornington Cl *LGEAT* NG10 .....61 M1
Mornington Crs *DERBYW* DE22 ..56 F1
  EWD/SEL/PNX NG16 ....35 H4
Mornington La *LEIE* LE5 ....126 B8
Morpeth Av *LEIN* LE4 ....65 J3
Morpeth Dr *LEIS* LE2 ....139 H3
Morpeth Gdns *DERBYE* DE21 ....44 B5
Morrell Bank *ARN* NG5 ....36 D1
Morrell Wood Dr
  BPR/DUF DE56 ....18 C2
Morris Av *BSTN/STPLFD* NG9 ....62 F6
Morris Cl *LBORO* LE11 ....9 M3
  LEIW LE3 ....130 B5
Morrison Ct *RLEIW/BBY* LE8 .....146 E7
Morris Dr *DERBYSE* DE24 ....58 D7
Morris St *CARL* NG4 ....38 E8
Mortiboys Wy *RLEIW/BAR* LE9 ..140 B5
Mortimer Pl *LEIW* LE3 ....130 F6
Mortimer Rd *END/NAR* LE19 ...135 L8
Mortimer St *DERBYSE* DE24 .....57 M8
Mortimer Wy *LBORO* LE11 ......102 F1
  LEIW LE3 ....130 E6
Mortoft Rd *LEIW* LE3 ....125 L4
Morton Wk *LEIE* LE5 ....126 B7
Morval Rd *WOL/BIL/BRX* NG8 ...35 J8
Morven Av *HUCK/RAV* NG15 .....23 M1
The Morwoods *LEIS* LE2 ....138 C2
Moscow Cottages
  BPR/DUF DE56 ....29 K2
Moscow La *RLBORO* LE12 ....101 L6
Mosedale Cl *DERBYSE* DE24 .....58 D7
Moseley St *RIPLEY* DE5 ....11 H5
Moses La *ILK* DE7 ....31 J8
Mosley St *HUCK/RAV* NG15 ......23 L1
  NOTTE NG7 ....36 D7
Moss Cl *ARN* NG5 ....25 G7
Mosscroft Av *CFTN/RUD* NG11 ..64 B6
Mossdale *COAL* LE67 ....108 C1
Mossdale Cl *LEIS* LE2 ....131 J4
Mossdale Rd *ARN* NG5 ....37 G2
  LEIW LE3 ....130 C7
Moss Dr *BSTN/STPLFD* NG9 ......48 F8
Mosse Wy *LEIS* LE2 ....139 G1
Mossgate *LEIW* LE3 ....124 E8
Moss La *RIPLEY* DE5 ....11 H4
Moss Rd *HUCK/RAV* NG15 ....15 K8
  ILK DE7 ....33 J8
Moss Side *CFTN/RUD* NG11 .....64 E4
Moss St *WBRGFD* NG2 ....2 A7
Mossvale Dr *NORM/LIT* DE23 ....70 E1
Mosswood Crs *ARN* NG5 ....24 F8
Mostyn Av *NORM/LIT* DE23 .....57 H6
  RLEINE/SYS LE7 ....121 C3
Mostyn St *LEIW* LE3 ....130 F2
Mottisford Rd *LEIE* LE4 ....125 K3
Mottiste Cl *DERBYSE* DE24 ....73 H2
Mottram St *BSTN/STPLFD* NG9 ..63 C1
Moult Av *DERBYE* DE21 ....59 J3
Moulton Cl *DERBYSE* DE24 ....18 B2
The Mount *ARN* NG5 ....25 H6
  BSTN/STPLFD NG9 ....62 B1
  MAPPK/POR/STA NG3 ....37 M5
  RLEINE/SYS LE7 ....127 K7
Mountain Rd *LEIE* LE4 ....126 E3
Mount Av *LEIE* LE5 ....132 B1
Mountbatten Cl *DERBYSE* DE24 ..72 C3
Mountbatten Gv *CARL* NG4 ....38 C5
Mountbatten Wy
  BSTN/STPLFD NG9 ....62 F5
Mount Carmel St
  NORM/LIT DE23 ....2 D8
Mountcastle Rd *LEIW* LE3 ....131 C5
Mountfield Av *LGEAT* NG10 .....61 L3
Mountfield Dr *ARN* NG5 ....24 E8
Mountfields Dr *LBORO* LE11 ....8 C3
Mountford Cl *DERBYW* DE22 ....44 F5
Mount Grace Rd *LBORO* LE11 ..102 F2
Mount Hooton *NOTT* NG1 ....4 D3
Mount Hooton Rd *NOTTE* NG7 ...4 C2
Mount Pleasant *ALFN* DE55 ......12 B2
  BLWL NG6 ....36 B5
  CARL NG4 ....38 C8
  CDON/KEG DE74 ....84 F4
  CDON/KEG * DE74 ....86 A5
  COT/KEY/RAD NG12 ....53 J4
  COT/KEY/RAD NG12 ....80 D4
  ILK DE7 ....33 J3
  LEIS LE2 ....139 H3
  RIPLEY DE5 ....11 H5
Mount Pleasant Dr
  BPR/DUF DE56 ....17 J2
Mount Rd *LEIE* LE5 ....7 L4
  LEIS LE2 ....138 F2
  RLEIW/BAR LE9 ....142 B4
Mountsorrel *WBRGFD* NG2 ......65 M1
Mountsorrel La *RLBORO* LE12 ..113 J7
  RLBORO LE12 ....113 L4
Mount St *BSTN/STPLFD* NG9 .....48 C8
  BWSH/BRSTN DE72 ....61 K8
  DERBY DE1 ....2 E7
  HEANOR DE75 ....20 C6
  NOTT NG1 ....4 F7
  NOTTE NG7 ....36 D6
Mount Vw *RLEIW/BBY* LE8 ......139 M6
Mowbray Ct
  MAPPK/POR/STA NG3 ....5 K4
Mowbray Dr *RLEINE/SYS* LE7 ...121 C3
Mowbray Gdns *DERBYSE* DE24 ..58 A8
  WBRGFD NG2 ....65 K2
Mowbray Ri *LEIS* LE2 ....25 K7
Mowbray St *DERBYSE* DE24 ......58 A8
Mowmacre Hl *LEIN* LE4 ....125 L7
Mowsley End *WGSTN* LE18 .....138 B5
Moy Av *DERBYSE* DE24 ....71 K5
Moyne Gdns *MELB/CHEL* DE73 ..72 E7
Moyra Dr *ARN* NG5 ....25 G8
Mozart Cl *NOTTE* NG7 ....50 C1
Mozart St *NOTTE* NG7 ....50 C1
Muckle Gate La *RLBORO* LE12 ..106 C6
Mudpie La *WBRGFD* NG2 ....52 A6
Muir Av *COT/KEY/RAD* NG12 ....66 B7
Muirfield Cl *LEIW* LE3 ....130 A1

Muirfield Dr *MCKLVR* DE3 ....56 D6
Muirfield Rd *ARN* NG5 ....24 E6
Mulberries Ct *DERBYSE* DE22 ...43 J3
Mulberry Av *LEIW* LE3 ....130 A5
Mulberry Cl *BPR/DUF* DE56 .....17 M4
  WBRGFD NG2 ....64 F2
Mulberry Gv *HUCK/RAV* NG15 ..23 M3
Mulberry Ms *RIPLEY* DE5 ....19 G1
Mulberry Wy
  BWSH/BRSTN DE72 ....83 L1
  RDERBYSW DE65 ....68 C5
Mull Ct *DERBYSE* DE24 ....71 H4
Mullion Pl *DERBYSE* DE24 ....72 F2
Mull Wy *RLEIW/BBY* LE8 ....143 K4
Mundella Rd *WBRGFD* NG2 ......51 H6
Mundella St *LEIS* LE2 ....132 A4
Mundy Cl *DERBY* DE1 ....2 B1
  RLBORO LE12 ....103 K8
Mundy's Dr *HEANOR* DE75 ....20 D7
Mundy St *DERBY* DE1 ....2 B1
  HEANOR DE75 ....20 C6
  ILK DE7 ....33 J3
Munford Circ *WOL/BIL/BRX* NG8 ..35 L4
Munks Av *HUCK/RAV* NG15 ......15 K8
Munnings Ct *RLEIW/BBY* LE8 ...142 D2
Muntjack Rd *RLEIW/BBY* LE8 ...142 D2
Murby Crs *BLWL* NG6 ....23 M7
Murby Wy *LEIW* LE3 ....130 A6
Murden Wy *BSTN/STPLFD* NG9 ..63 M1
Murdoch Ri *LBORO* LE11 ....103 H1
Muriel Rd *BSTN/STPLFD* NG9 ....49 K8
  LEIW LE3 ....131 G2
Muriel St *BLWL* NG6 ....23 M8
Murrayfield Rd *LEIW* LE3 ....130 A2
Murray Rd *MCKLVR* DE3 ....56 D3
Murray St *DERBYSE* DE24 ....58 D7
  LEIS LE2 ....7 K5
Muscovey Rd *COAL* LE67 ....108 A7
Museum Sq *LEI* LE1 ....7 G8
Musgrove Cl *LEIW* LE3 ....6 A7
Mushill La *RLBORO* LE12 ....98 B2
Muskham Av *ILK* DE7 ....33 K4
Muskham St *WBRGFD* NG2 ....51 H6
Musson Rd *LEIW* LE3 ....124 C8
Musters Crs *WBRGFD* NG2 ....65 K2
Musters Cft *CARL* NG4 ....52 D4
Musters Rd *CFTN/RUD* NG11 ....78 F1
  HUCK/RAV NG15 ....15 H1
  WBRGFD NG2 ....51 J8
Muston Cl *MAPPK/POR/STA* NG3 ..37 J8
Muswell Rd *DERBYW* DE22 ....56 C2
Myers Cl *DERBYSE* DE24 ....71 K3
Myrtle Av *BSTN/STPLFD* NG9 ....62 C1
  LGEAT NG10 ....76 A1
  NOTTE NG7 ....36 F7
  RLEINE/SYS LE7 ....119 L7
Myrtle Gv *BSTN/STPLFD* NG9 ....49 L8
Myrtle Rd *CARL* NG4 ....38 A7
  LEIS LE2 ....7 L9
Myrtus Cl *CFTN/RUD* NG11 ......64 A5

N

Nabbs La *HUCK/RAV* NG15 ....23 H1
Nagle Gv *LEIN* LE4 ....126 B2
Nailers Wy *BPR/DUF* DE56 ....18 A2
Nairn Av *DERBYE* DE21 ....44 B8
  DERBYSE DE24 ....71 H4
Nairn Cl *ARN* NG5 ....25 M6
Namur Cl *DERBYW* DE22 ....57 G4
Namur Rd *WGSTN* LE18 ....137 J4
Nanhill Dr *RLBORO* LE12 ....111 L7
Nanpantan Rd *LBORO* LE11 ....8 B9
  RLBORO LE12 ....110 D2
Nansen Rd *LEIE* LE5 ....132 C3
Nansen St *BLWL* NG6 ....36 A1
Naomi Crs *BLWL* NG6 ....24 A4
Napier Cl *MCKLVR* DE3 ....56 D3
Napier St *DERBYW* DE22 ....57 G2
Narborough Rd *LEIW* LE3 ....6 B7
  RLEIW/BAR LE9 ....135 H8
  RLEIW/BAR LE9 ....142 A2
Narborough Rd North
  LEIW LE3 ....6 B7
Narborough Rd South
  END/NAR LE19 ....136 C2
Narborough Wood Pk
  END/NAR * LE19 ....129 J8
Narrow Boat Cl *WGSTN* LE18 ..137 L4
Narrow La *EWD/SEL/PNX* NG16 ..22 C7
  LEIS LE2 ....137 G1
  RLBORO LE12 ....94 E6
  RLBORO LE12 ....98 A3
Naseby Dr *LBORO* LE11 ....102 E5
  MCKLVR DE3 ....55 M4
  WGSTN LE18 ....138 C5
Naseby Rd *BPR/DUF* DE56 ....18 B3
  LEIN LE4 ....126 C5
Naseby Wy *RLEIW/BBY* LE8 ....139 M7
Nathaniel Rd *LGEAT* NG10 ....62 E8
Nathans Cl *COT/KEY/RAD* NG12 ..52 D8
Navigation St *LEI* LE1 ....7 H5
Navigation Wy *LBORO* LE11 ....103 L2
The Navins *RLBORO* LE12 ....113 J5
Naworth Cl *BLWL* NG6 ....36 B2
Naylor Av *CFTN/RUD* NG11 ......77 M6
  LBORO LE11 ....104 B3
Naylor Rd *RLEINE/SYS* LE7 .....121 G2
Neal Av *LEIW* LE3 ....130 C5
Neal Ct *EWD/SEL/PNX* NG16 ....20 E4
Neale St *LGEAT* NG10 ....62 D8
Neale Rd *LEIW* LE3 ....138 C5
Near Meadow *LGEAT* NG10 ......76 C2
Nearsby Dr *WBRGFD* NG2 ....65 M1
Nearwood Dr *DERBYE* DE21 .....44 C4
Necton St *RLEINE/SYS* LE7 ......120 E4
Nedham St *LEIE* LE5 ....7 L5
Needham Av *LEIS* LE2 ....136 E4
Needham La *LEIS* LE2 ....139 J3
Needham St *RIPLEY* DE5 ....11 M8
Need Wood Av
  BSTN/STPLFD NG9 ....48 B5
Needwood
  Wy *END/NAR* LE19 ....135 K5
Neeps Cft *CALV/BJ* NG14 ....27 J4

Neighwood Cl
  BSTN/STPLFD NG9 ....62 C5
Neilson St *DERBYSE* DE24 ....58 D8
Nell Gwyn Crs *ARN* NG5 ....25 G6
Nelot Wy *LEIS* LE2 ....132 F2
Nelper Crs *ILK* DE7 ....47 L2
Nelson Cl *MCKLVR* DE3 ....56 C4
  RLBORO LE12 ....102 B3
Nelson Flds *COAL* LE67 ....108 E6
Nelson Rd *ARN* NG5 ....25 J8
  BLWL NG6 ....24 A8
  BSTN/STPLFD NG9 ....63 L3
Nelson St *DERBY* DE1 ....2 B7
  ILK DE7 ....33 K3
  LEI LE1 ....7 H8
  LGEAT NG10 ....62 B8
  NOTT NG1 ....5 K7
  RLEINE/SYS LE7 ....120 F4
Nene Cl *HUCK/RAV* NG15 ....23 J4
Nene Dr *LEIS* LE2 ....139 G2
Nene Wy *COAL* LE67 ....108 A3
  RDERBYSW DE65 ....68 B7
Neptune Cl *LEIS* LE2 ....7 L6
Nesfield Cl *DERBYSE* DE24 ....59 G8
Nesfield Ct *ILK* DE7 ....33 J6
Nesfield Rd *ILK* DE7 ....33 J6
Ness Wk *DERBYW* DE22 ....43 J4
Neston Dr *BLWL* NG6 ....35 M3
Neston Gdns *LEIS* LE2 ....137 K1
Neston Rd *LEIS* LE2 ....137 K1
Nether Cl *BPR/DUF* DE56 ....29 H2
  EWD/SEL/PNX NG16 ....21 K4
  MAPPK/POR/STA NG3 ....37 K5
Netherclose St *NORM/LIT* DE23 ..57 L6
Netherfield La *CDON/KEG* DE74 ..75 F4
Netherfield Rd *LGEAT* NG10 ....75 M3
  RLEINE/SYS LE7 ....118 B8
Nether Field Wy *LEIW* LE3 ......130 B6
Netherhall La *LEIN* LE4 ....125 M1
Netherhall Rd *LEIE* LE5 ....127 G7
Nether La *BPR/DUF* DE56 ....16 E7
  BPR/DUF DE56 ....30 B1
Nether Pasture *CARL* NG4 ....52 E1
Netherside Dr *MELB/CHEL* DE73 ..72 E5
Nether St *BSTN/STPLFD* NG9 ....63 L1
Netherwood Ct *DERBYW* DE22 ..43 G4
Nethercliff Wk *ARN* NG5 ....24 C7
Nettlefold Crs *MELB/CHEL* DE73 ..82 F6
Netton Cl *WGSTN* LE18 ....138 A7
Nevanthon Rd *LEIW* LE3 ....130 F2
Neville Cl *RLBORO* LE12 ....101 L3
Neville Dr *COAL* LE67 ....108 E6
  COAL LE67 ....116 B7
Neville Rd *CALV/BJ* NG14 ....26 D1
Neville Smith Cl
  BSTN/STPLFD NG9 ....49 B8
Nevinson Av *NORM/LIT* DE23 ...71 H1
Nevinson Dr *NORM/LIT* DE23 ...57 H5
Nevis Cl *DERBYSE* DE24 ....71 H5
Newall Dr *BSTN/STPLFD* NG9 ...63 G5
Newark Av *WBRGFD* NG2 ....5 M8
Newark Cl *ARN* NG5 ....36 D2
  RLBORO LE12 ....101 K4
Newark Crs *WBRGFD* NG2 ....5 M8
The Newarke *LEIS* LE2 ....6 C7
Newarke Cl *LEIS* LE2 ....6 C7
Newarke St *LEI* LE1 ....6 E5
Newark Rd *DERBYE* DE24 ....44 B5
  LEIE LE4 ....120 C8
Newark St *WBRGFD* NG2 ....5 M8
New Ashby Rd *LBORO* LE11 ....8 B3
New Av *RLEIW/SYS* LE7 ....115 K6
Newbery Av *LGEAT* NG10 ....76 D1
Newbold Av *BWSH/BRSTN* DE72 ..60 A6
Newbold Cl *MELB/CHEL* DE73 ..73 C5
  RLBORO LE12 ....114 B3
Newbold Dr *CDON/KEG* DE74 ...84 F2
Newbon Cl *LBORO* LE11 ....8 C3
New Bond St *LEI* LE1 ....6 E5
Newbound Rd *DERBYSE* DE24 ..73 G1
New Breck Rd *BPR/DUF* DE56 ...17 L4
New Brickyard La
  CDON/KEG DE74 ....86 B6
Newbridge Cl *ILK* DE7 ....32 B7
Newbridge Crs *DERBYSE* DE24 ..72 C3
New Bridge Rd *LEIS* LE2 ....136 F5
New Bridge St *LEIS* LE2 ....131 J4
Newbury Cl
  MAPPK/POR/STA NG3 ....37 L3
  WGSTN LE18 ....138 A3
Newbury Dr
  EWD/SEL/PNX NG16 ....35 H4
Newbury St *DERBYSE* DE24 ......58 C7
Newbury Wy *RLEIW/BBY* LE8 ..136 D7
Newby Gdns *LEIS* LE2 ....139 H3
Newcastle Av
  BSTN/STPLFD NG9 ....63 K1
  CARL NG4 ....38 C6
Newcastle Circ *NOTTE* NG7 ....4 C8
Newcastle Cl *NOTTE* NG7 ....4 C8
Newcastle Farm Dr
  WOL/BIL/BRX NG8 ....36 A6
Newcastle St *BLWL* NG6 ....24 A8
  NOTT NG1 ....4 D6
Newcastle Ter *NOTTE* NG7 ....4 D6
  WOL/BIL/BRX * NG8 ....36 B6
New City Homes
  DERBYSE * DE24 ....58 E7
Newcombe Dr *ARN* NG5 ....26 A8
Newcombe Rd *LEIW* LE3 ....130 F5
New Derby Rd
  EWD/SEL/PNX NG16 ....21 H5
Newdigate Rd
  EWD/SEL/PNX NG16 ....22 E8
Newdigate St
  EWD/SEL/PNX NG16 ....34 E1
  ILK DE7 ....32 A7
  ILK DE7 ....47 L1
  NORM/LIT DE23 ....57 K7
  NOTTE NG7 ....4 C5
Newdigate Vls *NOTTE* NG7 ....4 C5
New Eaton Rd
  BSTN/STPLFD NG9 ....62 B2
New Farm La
  EWD/SEL/PNX NG16 ....35 G1

Newfield Rd ARN NG5......................36 D4
New Fields Av LEIW LE3.................130 F5
New Fields Sq LEIW LE3.................130 F6
New Forest Cl WGSTN LE18.............138 B7
Newgate Cl CARL NG4.....................38 C8
  MELB/CHEL DE73.........................72 F5
Newgate Ct NOTTE * NG7...................4 A8
Newhall Gv WBRGFD NG2................51 K6
Newham Av RIPLEY DE5...................11 G6
Newham Cl HEANOR DE75................20 E6
  LEIN LE4.......................................126 E2
Newhaven Rd DERBYE DE21..............58 F1
  LEIE LE5..133 H4
New Henry St LEIN LE4......................6 C3
Newington St LEIN LE4..................125 M5
New Inn La DERBYE DE21..................30 A8
New King St LBORO LE11....................9 L4
Newland Cl BSTN/STPLFD NG9.........62 E5
  WOL/BIL/BRX NG8...........................50 A2
Newlands Av RLBORO LE12.............102 A5
Newlands Cl
  COT/KEY/RAD NG12.......................66 A3
  RIPLEY DE5...................................11 J6
Newlands Dr ALFN DE55...................12 A2
  CARL NG4......................................38 D6
  HEANOR DE75................................20 D4
Newlands Rd ALFN DE55...................12 A3
Newland St DERBY DE1.......................2 D4
New La RLBORO LE12......................105 K3
New Lawn Rd ILK DE7.......................33 J7
Newlyn Dr NORM/LIT DE23...............57 K7
  WOL/BIL/BRX NG8...........................36 B7
Newlyn Gdns WOL/BIL/BRX NG8......36 A7
Newlyn Pde LEIE LE5......................127 H6
Newmanleys Rd
  EWD/SEL/PNX NG16........................21 J7
Newmanleys Rd (South)
  EWD/SEL/PNX NG16........................21 J6
Newmarket Ct DERBYSE DE24...........58 C7
Newmarket Dr DERBYSE DE24...........58 C7
Newmarket Rd BLWL NG6.................35 M1
Newmarket St LEIS LE2..................131 M7
Newmarket Wy
  BSTN/STPLFD NG9...........................62 D5
New Mount Cl NORM/LIT DE23..........71 H2
New Park Rd LEIS LE2.....................131 J7
New Parks Bvd LEIW LE3.................130 B2
New Parks Crs LEIW LE3.................124 E7
New Park St LEIW LE3.........................6 B7
New Parks Wy LEIW LE3.................130 B2
New Pingle St LEIW LE3..................139 J3
Newpool Bank LEIS LE2..................139 J3
Newport Cl DERBYSE DE24................73 G2
Newport Dr WOL/BIL/BRX NG8.........36 B6
Newport Pl LEIW LE1..........................7 G7
Newport St LEIW LE1.....................131 G1
Newquay Av NOTTE NG7...................36 C8
Newquay Dr LEIW LE3....................124 A6
Newquay Pl DERBYSE DE24...............73 G2
New Rd BPR/DUF DE56.....................10 B8
  BPR/DUF DE56...............................17 K4
  BSTN/STPLFD NG9...........................48 B6
  COT/KEY/RAD NG12.......................53 K4
  DERBYW DE22................................43 L6
  EWD/SEL/PNX NG16..........................6 E4
  LEI LE1..50 B1
  NOTTE NG7...................................68 C5
  RDERBYSW DE65............................12 B5
  RIPLEY DE5...................................11 J5
  RLEIW/BAR LE9............................140 B5
  RLEIW/BBY LE8............................146 F7
New Romney Cl LEIE LE5................127 J7
The Newry WGSTN LE18.................137 K2
New Star Rd LEIN LE4.....................126 D4
Newstead Av
  COT/KEY/RAD NG12.......................53 L3
  DERBYE DE21................................58 D1
  LEIW LE3.....................................125 G6
  MAPPK/POR/STA NG3.....................38 A5
  RLEINE/SYS LE7...........................133 L3
  WGSTN LE18.................................138 A3
Newstead Dr WBRGFD NG2..............51 M8
Newstead Gv NOTT NG1.....................4 F3
Newstead Rd LEIS LE2....................132 A7
  LGEAT NG10...................................61 M4
Newstead Rd North ILK DE7..............33 H4
Newstead Rd South ILK DE7..............33 H4
Newstead St ARN NG5.......................37 G4
Newstead Ter HUCK/RAV NG15.........15 L7
Newstead Wy
  WOL/BIL/BRX NG8...........................35 H5
New St ARN NG5..............................36 F7
  BWSH/BRSTN DE72.........................60 A3
  BWSH/BRSTN DE72.........................60 E8
  CDON/KEG DE74.............................86 B4
  COAL LE67...................................108 B7
  DERBY DE1......................................3 H5
  DERBYE DE21................................30 A7
  LBORO LE11.....................................9 H4
  LEI LE1..6 E6
  LEIS LE2.....................................138 E1
  LGEAT NG10...................................62 C7
  RIPLEY DE5...................................11 J5
  RLBORO LE12...............................105 H8
  RLEINE/SYS LE7...........................121 J1
  RLEIW/BBY LE8............................136 F6
  RLEIW/BBY LE8............................143 K3
New Ter LGEAT NG10........................61 M1
Newthorpe Common
  EWD/SEL/PNX NG16........................21 L7
Newthorpe St WBRGFD NG2.............51 H5
Newton Av COT/KEY/RAD NG12.......53 L3
Newton Cl ARN NG5..........................37 M1
  LBORO LE11.................................103 H1
  RLBORO LE12...............................105 J7
Newtondale Cl
  WOL/BIL/BRX NG8...........................36 B6
Newton Dr BSTN/STPLFD NG9...........62 C8
  WBRGFD NG2.................................65 G3
Newton La RLEIW/BBY LE8.............139 K8
  WGSTN LE18.................................138 D6
Newton Rd CARL NG4.......................38 B4
Newtons La
  EWD/SEL/PNX NG16........................33 L4
  EWD/SEL/PNX NG16........................33 M4
Newton St BSTN/STPLFD NG9...........63 J1
Newton's Wk DERBYW DE22.............43 J7

Newtown Linford La
  GBY/RBY LE6................................123 J2
Newtown St LEI LE1............................6 F9
New Tythe St LGEAT NG10................62 D8
New Vale Rd CARL NG4.......................7 H8
New Wk LEI LE1............................101 M3
  RLBORO LE12...............................140 B8
New Way Rd ILK DE7.......................132 D5
New Zealand La BPR/DUF DE56..........29 J5
  RLEINE/SYS LE7...........................121 G1
New Zealand Sq DERBYW DE22.........57 G2
Nicholas Cl DERBYE DE21..................59 J1
Nicholas Dr GBY/RBY LE6...............123 H7
Nicholas Rd BSTN/STPLFD NG9..........63 J1
Nichols St LEIE LE5.............................7 H5
Nicker Hl COT/KEY/RAD NG12...........80 E4
Nicklaus Rd LEIN LE4......................126 B2
Nicola Gdns NORM/LIT DE23.............71 H3
Nicolson Rd LBORO LE11.................103 G7
Nidderdale WOL/BIL/BRX NG8...........49 G3
Nidderdale Cl
  WOL/BIL/BRX NG8...........................49 G4
Nidderdale Rd WGSTN LE18............138 D5
Nightingale Av RLBORO LE12............94 E6
Nightingale Cl
  EWD/SEL/PNX NG16........................35 H1
  RIPLEY DE5...................................11 H6
Nightingale Crs
  EWD/SEL/PNX NG16........................13 M1
Nightingale Rd DERBYSE DE24...........58 A8
Nile St NOTT NG1...............................5 K6
Nilsson Rd BSTN/STPLFD NG9...........62 F4
Nine Acre Gdns BLWL NG6................23 K8
Nine Acres CDON/KEG DE74..............86 A5
Nine Corners
  EWD/SEL/PNX NG16........................34 D1
Nixon Ri HUCK/RAV NG15.................23 H2
Nixon Wk RLBORO LE12....................64 A7
Nobel Rd CFTN/RUD NG11.................64 A7
Noble St LEIW LE3..........................131 G2
Nock Verges RLEIW/BAR LE9...........140 B5
Noel St DERBYW * DE22....................57 H1
  EWD/SEL/PNX NG16........................34 E1
  LEIW LE3.....................................131 H4
  NOTTE NG7.....................................4 C2
No Man's La ILK DE7.........................46 F7
The Nook BPR/DUF DE56...................18 A8
  BSTN/STPLFD NG9...........................63 J3
  END/NAR LE19..............................135 L4
  HEANOR DE75................................20 A3
  RLBORO LE12..................................88 C6
  RLBORO LE12..................................98 A4
  RLEINE/SYS LE7...........................124 C1
  RLEIW/BAR LE9............................142 B5
  RLEIW/BBY LE8............................136 D8
  RLEIW/BBY LE8............................139 L8
  WGSTN LE18...................................49 J3
Nook Cl GBY/RBY LE6.....................125 G6
  RLBORO LE12...............................102 A5
Nook End Rd HEANOR DE75..............20 B6
Nook St LEIW LE3...........................124 F8
Nooning La BWSH/BRSTN DE72.........60 C1
Norbett Cl BSTN/STPLFD NG9...........62 F4
Norbett Rd ARN NG5.........................25 L7
Norbreck Cl WOL/BIL/BRX NG8........35 M5
Norburn Crs BLWL NG6.....................36 D4
Norbury Av LEIN LE4......................126 A6
Norbury Cl DERBYW DE22.................43 H6
Norbury Ct DERBYW * DE22...............43 H5
Norbury Crs NORM/LIT DE23.............71 G2
Norbury Wy BPR/DUF DE56...............18 A1
  LGEAT NG10...................................61 L1
Nordean Rd ARN NG5........................37 L2
Norfolk Cl HUCK/RAV NG15..............23 H2
Norfolk Gdns DERBYW * DE22...........43 K7
Norfolk Pl NOTT NG1..........................5 G6
Norfolk Rd LGEAT NG10...................62 D6
  WGSTN LE18.................................137 K4
Norfolk St LEIW LE3...........................6 A7
  NORM/LIT DE23................................3 G9
Norfolk Wk LEIW LE1..........................6 A6
  LGEAT NG10...................................61 M2
Norland Cl MAPPK/POR/STA NG3........5 J4
Norman Av NORM/LIT DE23..............57 J7
Normanby Rd
  WOL/BIL/BRX NG8...........................49 G4
Norman Cl BSTN/STPLFD NG9..............5 H3
  MAPPK/POR/STA NG3.....................39 H4
Norman Ct LEIS LE2........................139 H4
Norman Crs ILK DE7..........................33 J4
Norman Dr
  EWD/SEL/PNX NG16........................21 M5
  HUCK/RAV NG15............................23 J3
Normandy Cl LEIW LE3...................124 A4
Normandy Rd
  RDERBYSW DE65............................68 C5
Norman Rd LEIN LE4.......................120 B7
  MAPPK/POR/STA NG3.....................37 L7
  RIPLEY DE5...................................11 G5
Norman St CARL NG4........................52 E1
  EWD/SEL/PNX NG16........................22 D8
  ILK DE7...33 J4
  LEIW LE3...6 A9
Normanton Cl
  RLEIW/BAR LE9............................134 E4
Normanton La
  COT/KEY/RAD NG12.......................80 D3
  NORM/LIT DE23..............................57 G7
  RLBORO LE12..................................95 L5
Normanton Rd DERBY DE1...................2 E6
  LEIE LE5..7 M9
Norris Cl LEIN LE4..........................124 E4
Northacre Rd DERBYE DE21...............44 F5
Northage Cl RLBORO LE12..............112 E3
Northall Av BLWL NG6.....................35 M1
Northam Dr RIPLEY DE5.....................11 G5
Northampton St LEI LE1......................7 H7
  MAPPK/POR/STA NG3.......................5 M3
North Av COAL LE67........................108 B8
  DERBYW DE22................................43 L4
  LEIS LE2......................................132 A5
  LEIW LE1..61 L1
  MCKLVR DE3.................................56 C4
North Bridge Pl LEIW LE3...................6 C5
North Church St NOTT NG1.................5 G5
North Circus St NOTT NG1..................4 E7

Northcliffe Av
  MAPPK/POR/STA NG3.....................37 M5
North Cl MCKLVR DE3.......................56 C4
Northcote St LEIS LE2....................131 M7
Northcote St LGEAT NG10.................62 C8
Northcote Wy BLWL NG6...................36 A2
Northdale Rd
  MAPPK/POR/STA NG3.....................38 A3
Northdene Rd LEIS LE2...................137 M2
Northdown Dr
  BSTN/STPLFD NG9...........................62 F3
  LEIN LE4......................................126 C1
Northdown Rd
  WOL/BIL/BRX NG8...........................50 A1
North Dr BSTN/STPLFD NG9..............63 J1
  LEIE LE5......................................126 E7
North End Cl LEIS LE2....................137 K1
North Dr BSTN/STPLFD NG9..............48 B4
Northern Rd HEANOR DE75...............20 E5
Northfield BPR/DUF DE56...................18 D5
  DERBYE DE24................................71 H4
Northfield Av ILK DE7.......................33 J5
  LEIN LE4......................................119 L7
  LGEAT NG10...................................75 L3
  WGSTN LE18.................................137 M3
Northfield Crs
  BSTN/STPLFD NG9...........................62 E3
Northfield Dr COAL LE67.................108 E6
Northfield Rd
  BSTN/STPLFD NG9...........................62 E3
  LEIN LE4......................................126 C6
  RLEIW/BBY LE8............................136 F6
Northfields LGEAT NG10...................75 M3
  RLEINE/SYS LE7...........................120 F3
Northfields Wy RLBORO LE12............88 C3
Northfold Rd LEIS LE2.....................132 A8
North Ga NOTTE NG7........................36 D6
Northgate St ILK DE7........................33 J6
  LEIW LE3...6 C3
North Hill Av HUCK/RAV NG15..........15 K7
North Hill Crs HUCK/RAV NG15.........15 K8
North La BPR/DUF DE56....................17 H5
Northmead Dr DERBYE DE22.............56 F4
North Mills LEIW * LE3.......................6 B3
Northolme Av BLWL NG6...................24 A8
Northolt Dr WOL/BIL/BRX NG8..........35 H4
North Pde CFTN/RUD NG11................64 F7
  LBORO LE11.................................103 M1
  LGEAT NG10...................................76 A1
  NOTTE NG7.....................................4 C7
  WBRGFD NG2.................................65 J1
North Rw DERBYW DE22....................43 L6
North Sherwood St NOTT NG1..............4 F3
North St ALFN DE55...........................12 B1
  BSTN/STPLFD NG9...........................63 J1
  COAL LE67...................................108 C2
  DERBY DE1....................................43 K8
  EWD/SEL/PNX NG16........................20 F4
  EWD/SEL/PNX NG16........................22 A5
  ILK DE7...33 K6
  MELB/CHEL DE73...........................82 E8
  NORM/LIT DE23..............................57 G5
  RLBORO LE12...............................105 H7
  RLEINE/SYS LE7...........................119 J1
  RLEINE/SYS LE7...........................120 E3
  WBRGFD NG2...................................5 J1
  WGSTN LE18.................................138 B4
North Ter BPR/DUF * DE56................17 L3
Northumberland Cl LEIN LE4.............126 A5
Northumberland Cl
  MAPPK/POR/STA NG3.......................5 J4
Northumberland Rd
  WGSTN LE18.................................137 K4
Northumberland St LEI LE1..................6 D3
  NORM/LIT DE23................................2 D9
Northway Dr DERBY DE1.....................2 A5
Northwold Av WBRGFD NG2.............65 H1
Northwood Av DERBYE DE21.............44 C8
Northwood Crs ARN NG5..................37 G1
Northwood Dr RLBORO LE12...........102 A1
Northwood Rd ARN NG5...................37 G1
Northwood St
  BSTN/STPLFD NG9...........................48 B7
Norton St LEI LE1...............................6 E8
  NOTTE NG7.....................................4 A5
Norwich Cl RLBORO LE12................101 L5
Norwich Gdns BLWL NG6..................23 M6
Norwich Rd LEIN LE4.......................125 H4
Norwich St DERBYE DE21...................44 B8
Norwood Cl DERBYW DE22................56 E2
Norwood Rd LEIE LE5......................132 C4
  NOTTE NG7...................................50 C2
Nointintone St WBRGFD NG2...............5 M8
Nottingham La ALFN DE55.................12 C2
RMMWB LE14..................................99 M1
Nottingham Rd ARN NG5...................37 J1
  BLWL NG6.....................................36 C4
  BPR/DUF DE56...............................17 L4
  BSTN/STPLFD NG9...........................48 A3
  BSTN/STPLFD NG9...........................48 C8
  BWSH/BRSTN DE72.........................59 M6
  CALV/BJ NG14...............................39 H5
  CARL NG4......................................26 B5
  CDON/KEG DE74.............................86 A4
  CFTN/RUD NG11.............................77 M6
  COT/KEY/RAD NG12.......................53 L5
  COT/KEY/RAD NG12.......................80 C5
  DERBY DE1......................................2 F2
  DERBYE DE21................................59 M4
  EWD/SEL/PNX NG16........................13 K1
  EWD/SEL/PNX NG16........................21 K5
  EWD/SEL/PNX NG16........................35 H2
  HUCK/RAV NG15............................24 A2
  ILK DE7...33 K8
  LBORO LE11.....................................9 J4
  LEIE LE5......................................132 B1
  LGEAT NG10...................................62 C7
  NOTTE NG7...................................36 D5
  RIPLEY DE5...................................11 K6
  RLBORO LE12..................................89 H5
  RLBORO LE12................................104 B1
  RLBORO LE12................................105 H1
  RMMWB LE14..................................91 M2
Nowell Cl LEIS LE2.........................137 H6
Nuart Rd BSTN/STPLFD NG9.............49 K8
Nugent Gdns
  MAPPK/POR/STA NG3.......................5 L4

Nugent St LEIW LE3............................6 A4
Nunsfield Dr DERBYSE DE24.............58 F8
Nun's St DERBY DE1............................2 B2
The Nurseries
  EWD/SEL/PNX NG16........................21 L5
Nursery Av BSTN/STPLFD NG9..........63 G2
  BWSH/BRSTN DE72.........................61 K2
  ILK DE7...32 C8
Nursery Cl BWSH/BRSTN DE72..........59 M5
  COT/KEY/RAD NG12.......................53 M4
  HUCK/RAV NG15............................23 L3
  LEIN LE4......................................126 B1
  RLBORO LE12...............................102 A1
  RLEINE/SYS LE7...........................121 J2
  RLEIW/BAR LE9............................134 E5
Nursery Dr CARL NG4.......................38 B7
Nursery End LBORO LE11.................103 H7
Nursery Gv RLBORO LE12................105 J7
Nursery Hollow ILK DE7....................47 J1
  LEIS LE2......................................136 E4
Nursery La BLWL NG6.......................36 C3
  RLBORO LE12...............................112 C1
Nursery Rd ARN NG5........................25 K8
  COT/KEY/RAD NG12.......................53 M4
  LEIE LE5......................................127 H8
Nutbrook Crs ILK DE7.......................47 H3
Nutbrook Trail ILK DE7.....................33 G4
Nutfield Rd LEIW LE3......................131 G4
Nuthall Cir ILK DE7...........................47 G3
Nuthall Gdns WOL/BIL/BRX NG8.......36 B7
Nuthall Gv LEIS LE2........................136 F5
Nuthall Rd WOL/BIL/BRX NG8...........35 M4
Nutkin Cl LBORO LE11........................8 F7
Nutwood Cl DERBYW DE22................43 L4

Oackland Ter LGEAT NG10 ....76 A3
Oadby Hill Dr LEIS LE2....................138 D1
Oadby Ri NORM/LIT DE23..................71 J1
Oadby Rd WGSTN LE18...................138 C4
Oak Acres BSTN/STPLFD NG9...........62 E2
Oak Av COT/KEY/RAD NG12..............53 J3
  EWD/SEL/PNX NG16........................20 F2
  LGEAT NG10...................................47 L8
  RIPLEY DE5...................................11 H8
Oak Cl BPR/DUF DE56.......................29 J5
  BWSH/BRSTN DE72.........................60 A2
  COAL LE67...................................108 E7
  DERBYW DE22................................43 J3
  RLBORO LE12...............................111 L1
Oak Crs NORM/LIT DE23....................56 F7
  RLBORO LE12..................................88 B7
Oakcroft Av RLEIW/BBY LE8............129 J2
Oakdale Cl LEIW LE3.......................130 A1
Oakdale Dr BSTN/STPLFD NG9..........63 G3
Oakdale Gdns DERBYE DE21..............44 F4
Oakdale Rd ARN NG5........................25 M7
  MAPPK/POR/STA NG3.....................51 M7
Oakdene Rd LEIS LE2......................137 L1
Oak Dr DERBYSE DE24......................72 E1
  EWD/SEL/PNX NG16........................21 J5
  EWD/SEL/PNX NG16........................34 F1
  MCKLVR DE3.................................56 C4
  RDERBYSW DE65............................68 B5
  RLEINE/SYS LE7...........................120 F5
Oakenshaw Cl LEIN LE4...................125 J2
Oakfield Av COAL LE67....................116 B7
  LEIN LE4......................................119 K8
  LEIW LE3.....................................124 E3
Oakfield Cl RLEIW/BBY LE8.............139 M6
  WOL/BIL/BRX NG8...........................49 G4
Oakfield Ct ILK DE7...........................31 L6
Oakfield Crs RLEIW/BBY LE8............137 G8
Oakfield Dr LGEAT NG10...................61 M4
Oakfield Rd BSTN/STPLFD NG9..........48 B8
  HUCK/RAV NG15............................23 M1
  LEIS LE2......................................132 A4
  WOL/BIL/BRX NG8...........................49 G4
Oakfields St WBRGFD NG2................51 L6
Oak Flatt BSTN/STPLFD NG9.............62 E2
Oakford Cl WOL/BIL/BRX NG8...........35 L5
Oak Gv HUCK/RAV NG15..................23 M3
Oakham Cl ARN NG5.........................24 D8
  DERBYE DE21................................44 B6
  LBORO LE11.................................103 J1
Oakham Dr COAL LE67....................109 G5
Oakham Rd WBRGFD NG2.................65 H5
Oakham Wy ILK DE7.........................33 H4
Oakhurst Cl BPR/DUF DE56...............17 H1
Oakhurst St LBORO LE11..................103 L3
Oakington Cl ARN NG5......................36 F2
Oakland Av LEIN LE4.......................126 A2
  LGEAT NG10...................................76 A2
Oakland Ct BSTN/STPLFD NG9..........48 E6
Oakland Crs ALFN DE55.....................12 B2
Oakland Rd LEIS LE2.......................131 L6
Oaklands Av HEANOR DE75...............20 E5
  LBORO LE11.....................................8 E6
  NORM/LIT DE23..............................71 G2
Oaklands Cl RIPLEY DE5...................19 G6
Oaklands Rd RDERBYSW DE65..........69 G3
Oakland St NOTTE NG7.....................36 C8
Oaklands Wy MELB/CHEL DE73.........82 F7
Oakleigh Av DERBYE DE21................58 D1
  MAPPK/POR/STA NG3.....................38 A5
  WGSTN LE18.................................137 J6
Oakleigh St BLWL NG6......................36 B3
Oakley Av RLBORO LE12..................101 M3
Oakley Cl RLBORO LE12..................101 M2
Oakley Dr LBORO LE11.......................8 E8
  RLBORO LE12..................................94 B5
Oakley Ms BLWL NG6.......................35 K1
Oakley Rd LEIE LE5.........................126 B8
  RLBORO LE12..................................93 M8
Oakley's Rd LGEAT NG10...................76 C1
Oak Lodge Dr
  WOL/BIL/BRX NG8...........................35 K7
Oakmead Av WOL/BIL/BRX NG8.......35 K7
Oakmeadow LEIW LE3....................123 M8
Oakmeadow Wy GBY/RBY LE6........123 J5
Oakmere Cl COT/KEY/RAD NG12.......66 A3
Oakover Dr DERBYW DE22.................43 H4
Oak Pool Gdns LEIS LE2..................137 H4
Oakridge DERBYE DE21.....................44 F8

Oakridge Cl LEIE LE5.......................127 G4
Oak Rd BWSH/BRSTN DE72................73 K3
  END/NAR LE19..............................141 M1
Oaks Dr RLEIW/BBY LE8..................137 G8
The Oaks DERBYE DE21.....................30 A7
Oakside Crs LEIE LE5.......................133 G2
Oakside Wy DERBYE DE21.................44 F4
Oaks Rd COAL LE67.........................109 G2
  COAL LE67...................................109 L2
  RLEIW/BBY LE8............................139 M7
Oak St LEIE LE5.................................7 M2
  LEI LE23..57 L5
Oaks Wy LEIS LE2...........................132 D7
Oak Tree Av COT/KEY/RAD NG12.......53 K3
Oaktree Av DERBYSE DE24...............57 M8
Oaktree Cl GBY/RBY LE6.................123 J4
  HUCK/RAV NG15............................23 H3
  LEIE LE5......................................127 G5
  RLEIW/BBY LE8............................146 F6
Oak Tree Cl LEIS LE2.......................132 L7
Oak Tree Ct BWSH/BRSTN DE72........60 A6
Oak Tree Dr CARL NG4......................38 E5
Oak Vw NOTTE NG7............................4 A4
Oakwell Crs ILK DE7..........................33 J7
Oakwell Dr ILK DE7...........................33 J7
Oakwood Av WGSTN LE18...............138 B3
Oakwood Cl DERBYSE DE24..............71 H5
  LEIE LE5......................................129 K5
Oakwood Dr DERBYE DE21................44 F5
  LBORO LE11.................................102 F6
  WOL/BIL/BRX NG8...........................36 A8
The Oasis LEIW LE3.......................123 M7
Oban Rd BSTN/STPLFD NG9..............63 G1
Oban St LEIW LE3...........................131 G1
Occupation Rd BLWL NG6.................23 L2
  HUCK/RAV NG15............................23 L2
Ocean Cl LEIE LE5...........................127 G8
Ocean Rd LEIE LE5..........................133 G1
Ockbrook Ct ILK * DE7.......................33 K4
Ockerby St BLWL NG6.......................36 A1
Odam Cl LEIW LE3..........................130 D5
Odeon Ar LEI LE1...............................6 E6
Odesa Dr BLWL NG6.........................35 M3
Offerton Av NORM/LIT DE23..............57 J7
Offranville Cl LEIN LE4....................124 D3
Ogdon Ct MAPPK/POR/STA NG3........51 K1
Ogle Dr NOTTE NG7............................4 A7
Ogle St HUCK/RAV NG15...................15 L8
Ogwen Cl LEIE LE5..........................133 H1
Okehampton Av LEIE LE5................132 D4
Okehampton Crs
  MAPPK/POR/STA NG3.....................38 A1
Oldacres CALV/BJ * NG14..................27 H3
Old Ashby Rd LBORO LE11..............102 F5
Old Barn Cl DERBYE * DE21...............30 A7
Old Blacksmiths Yd DERBY * DE1.........2 E3
Old Brickyard
  EWD/SEL/PNX NG16........................37 L8
Old Bull Farm Cl RLBORO LE12.........86 E5
Oldbury Cl CFTN/RUD NG11..............64 B8
  DERBYE DE21................................44 D5
Old Chapel La
  EWD/SEL/PNX NG16........................13 L5
Old Chester Rd DERBY DE1................43 L7
Old Church Cl DERBYW DE22.............43 G2
Old Church St LEIS LE2...................137 G1
  NOTTE NG7...................................50 C5
Old Coach Rd
  WOL/BIL/BRX NG8...........................49 L6
Old Coppice Side HEANOR DE75........20 C8
Old Derby Rd
  EWD/SEL/PNX NG16........................21 H4
Old Dr BSTN/STPLFD NG9..................49 H7
The Old Engine Yd
  RLBORO LE12..................................97 J2
Old Epperstone Rd
  CALV/BJ NG14...............................27 M3
Oldershaw Av CDON/KEG DE74.........86 A5
Oldershaw Rd RLBORO LE12..............88 D6
Old Farm Rd ARN NG5......................24 D7
Old Field Cl RLEIW/BBY LE8.............143 G3
Oldfield La RDERBYSW DE65.............68 D7
  RLBORO LE12...............................113 K7
Old Gate Av BWSH/BRSTN DE72.........83 J1
Old Gate Rd RLEINE/SYS LE7...........115 K2
Old Hall Dr BPR/DUF DE56................29 H4
  DERBYSE DE24................................58 F8
  NORM/LIT DE23..............................56 F6
Old Hall Cl GBY/RBY LE6.................123 K5
  LEIN LE4......................................120 C7
Old Hall Dr
  MAPPK/POR/STA NG3.....................37 M3
Old Hall Rd NORM/LIT DE23..............57 G6
Old Hartshay Hl RIPLEY DE5..............11 G5
Oldknow St NOTTE NG7......................4 A3
Old La DERBYW DE22.........................43 L5
Old Lenton St NOTT NG1.....................5 J6
Old Lodge Dr ARN NG5......................37 H3
Old Main Rd CALV/BJ NG14...............39 M2
  RLBORO LE12..................................89 H6
Old Manor Cl CALV/BJ NG14..............27 H3
Old Mansfield Rd DERBYE DE21..........44 B4
Old Melton Rd
  COT/KEY/RAD NG12.......................80 C1
  COT/KEY/RAD NG12.......................81 L8
Old Mill Cl BLWL NG6.......................24 B8
  BPR/DUF DE56...............................29 J4
  BSTN/STPLFD NG9...........................62 E5
  NOTTE NG7.....................................4 B5
Old Mill La LEI LE1.............................6 C4
Old Milton St LEI LE1..........................7 G3
Oldoak Rd CFTN/RUD NG11..............64 D5
The Old Pk COT/KEY/RAD NG12.........67 K3
Old Park Cl CFTN/RUD NG11.............86 D1
Old Parsonage La RLBORO LE12.........97 G6
Old Pit La ILK DE7.............................31 L1
The Old Pond HEANOR DE75..............20 E7
Old Rectory Cl RLBORO LE12.............88 C3
Old Rd BPR/DUF DE56........................10 B7
  COT/KEY/RAD NG12.......................80 C1
Old School Cl CFTN/RUD * NG11........64 C7
Old School La
  EWD/SEL/PNX NG16........................34 A2
Old Station Cl COAL LE67................108 B6
  RDERBYSW DE65............................68 F4
  RLBORO LE12...............................101 M5
Old St NOTT NG1...............................5 H5

Old Tollerton Rd *WBRGFD* NG2 ......52 A8
Old Vicarage Cl *NORM/LIT* DE23 ...57 G6
Old Vicarage La *DERBYSE* DE22 .....43 G2
Old Wy *RLBORO* LE12 ....94 E6
The Old Woodyard
RLBORO LE12 ....94 E6
Olga Rd *MAPPK/POR/STA* NG3.....51 K1
Olive Av *LGEAT* NG10 ....62 B6
Olive Gv *CALV/BJ* NG14 ....39 K2
Oliver Cl *HEANOR* DE75 ....20 F5
NOTTE NG7 ....4 C4
Oliver Rd *ILK* DE7 ....47 G2
LBORO LE11 ....9 J7
LEIN LE4 ....126 B5
Oliver St *LEIS* LE2 ....131 J7
NOTTE NG7 ....4 D4
Olive St *DERBYW* DE22 ....2 A6
Olivier St *NORM/LIT* DE23........57 M6
Ollerton Rd *ARN* NG5 ....25 J3
Olphin St *LEIN* LE4 ....125 L7
Olton Av *BSTN/STPLFD* NG9 ....49 K7
Olton Rd *MCKLVR* DE3 ....56 A3
Olympic Cl *LEIW* LE3 ....124 B7
Olympus Ct *HUCK/RAV* NG15 ......23 H4
Onchan Av *CARL* NG4 ....52 C1
Onchan Dr *CARL* NG4 ....52 C1
One Barrow La *RLBORO* LE12 ....109 J1
Onslow Rd *MCKLVR* DE3 ....56 B3
Onslow St *LEIS* LE2 ....7 L9
Ontario Cl *LEI* LE1 ....7 C3
Opal Cl *DERBYE* DE21 ....44 E5
Openacre *EWD/SEL/PNX* NG16 ....12 D3
Openwoodgate *BPR/DUF* DE56 ...18 A3
Openwood Rd *BPR/DUF* DE56 .....18 B4
Orange Gdns *WBRGFD* NG2 ....51 H5
Orange St *WGSTN* LE18 ....137 K7
Orby Cl *MAPPK/POR/STA* NG3 .....51 K1
Orby Wk
MAPPK/POR/STA * NG3 ....51 K1
The Orchard *BPR/DUF* DE56 .....17 L3
GBY/RBY LE6 ....123 J4
ILK DE7 ....31 H1
ILK DE7 ....47 K6
RIPLEY DE5 ....11 M6
RLBORO LE12 ....106 D7
RLEINE/BAR LE9 ....140 C5
Orchard Av *CARL* NG4 ....38 C8
CDON/KEG DE74 ....84 E4
LEIS LE2 ....136 F5
Orchard Cl *BPR/DUF* DE56 ......17 M7
BWSH/BRSTN DE72 ....60 A1
BWSH/BRSTN DE72 ....61 J7
CALV/BJ NG14 ....39 K2
CDON/KEG DE74 ....93 G2
CFTN/RUD NG11 ....64 A5
COT/KEY/RAD NG12 ....53 J4
COT/KEY/RAD NG12 ....66 B7
DERBYSE DE24 ....73 G3
ILK DE7 ....32 B8
ILK DE7 ....44 B3
LEIS LE2 ....138 E3
MELB/CHEL DE73 ....82 E8
NORM/LIT DE23 ....57 G8
RDERBYSW DE65 ....68 B6
RIPLEY DE5 ....11 L8
RLBORO LE12 ....88 B7
RLBORO LE12 ....95 G2
RLBORO LE12 ....100 A3
RLBORO LE12 ....101 M4
WBRGFD NG2 ....51 J5
Orchard Cottages
BPR/DUF * DE56 ....17 L3
Orchard Ct *DERBYSE* DE21 ....59 J2
EWD/SEL/PNX * NG16 ....20 F4
Orchard Crs *BSTN/STPLFD* NG9 ...63 G2
Orchard Est *RLBORO* LE12 ....112 D1
Orchard Gdns *LEIN* LE4 ....126 D1
Orchard Gv *ARN* NG5 ....37 G1
Orchard La *RLEIW/BBY* LE8 .....139 M8
RLEIW/BBY LE8 ....143 K4
Orchard Ri *CARL* NG4 ....26 F8
Orchard Rd *ALFN* DE55 ....12 A1
LEIN LE4 ....119 M8
RLEIW/BAR LE9 ....141 J8
Orchards Dr *WGSTN* LE18 ....137 M5
Orchardson Av *LEI* LE1 ....7 J1
The Orchards *CARL* NG4 ....38 E6
DERBYSE DE22 ....43 H4
LEIE LE7 ....127 H4
Orchard St *BSTN/STPLFD* NG9 ....48 B8
CFTN/RUD NG11 ....77 L6
DERBY DE1 ....2 D2
EWD/SEL/PNX NG16 ....20 F4
EWD/SEL/PNX NG16 ....21 L6
EWD/SEL/PNX NG16 ....34 D1
HUCK/RAV NG15 ....23 L1
ILK DE7 ....33 K8
LBORO LE11 ....9 H3
LEI LE1 ....6 F3
LGEAT NG10 ....62 C8
MCKLVR DE3 ....56 B6
RLEIW/BBY LE8 ....145 K8
Orchard Vw *RLBORO* LE12 ....113 H7
Orchard Wy *LGEAT* NG10 ....61 L4
MELB/CHEL DE73 ....72 D5
RLBORO LE12 ....98 B4
RLEINE/SYS LE7 ....121 G4
Orchid Cl *CFTN/RUD* NG11 ....65 G3
END/NAR LE19 ....135 L6
LEIE LE7 ....127 L5
RLBORO LE12 ....113 K5
Ordish Av *DERBYE* DE21 ....58 D2
Oregon Wy *DERBYE* DE21 ....59 G2
Orford Cl *CFTN/RUD* NG11 ....64 D4
COT/KEY/RAD NG12 ....53 J4
Oriel Ct *DERBY* DE1 ....3 H8
Oriel Dr *RLEINE/SYS* LE7 ....120 F4
Orion Cl *WOL/BIL/BRX* NG8 ....35 J8
Orion Dr *WOL/BIL/BRX* NG8 ......35 J8
Orkney Cl *DERBYSE* DE24 ....71 H4
Orkney Wy *RLEINE/BBY* LE9 ......143 K4
Orlando Dr *CARL* NG4 ....38 C7
Orlando Rd *LEIS* LE2 ....131 M5
Orly Av *CDON/KEG* DE74 ....84 E5
Orme Cl *LEIN* LE4 ....124 E4
Ormen Gn *LEIW* LE3 ....130 B1
Ormonde St
EWD/SEL/PNX NG16 ....20 F3

Ormonde Ter
EWD/SEL/PNX NG16 ....20 F3
Ormskirk Ri *DERBYE* DE21 ....59 K3
Ornsay Cl *ARN* NG5 ....24 C5
Oronsay Rd *LEIN* LE4 ....124 F4
Orpean Wy *BSTN/STPLFD* NG9 ...62 C5
Orpine Cl *LGEAT* NG10 ....126 F5
Orsett Cl *LEIE* LE5 ....126 D7
Orson Dr *WGSTN* LE18 ....137 M4
Orston Av *ARN* NG5 ....25 L8
Orston Dr *WOL/BIL/BRX* NG8 .....50 A3
Orston Gn *WOL/BIL/BRX* NG8 .....50 B4
Orston Rd East *WBRGFD* NG2 .....51 K6
Orston Rd West *WBRGFD* NG2 ....51 J6
Orton Av *BSTN/STPLFD* NG9 ......63 G1
Orton Cl *RLEINE/SYS* LE7 ....115 K6
Orton Rd *LEIN* LE4 ....125 J4
Orton Wy *BPR/DUF* DE56 ....17 M1
Ortzen St *NOTTE* NG7 ....4 B4
Orville Rd *ARN* NG5 ....36 C2
Orwell Cl *LBORO* LE11 ....103 H1
Orwell Dr *LEIN* LE4 ....124 E3
Osborne Cl *LGEAT* NG10 ....61 M3
Osborne Gv *ARN* NG5 ....37 G5
Osborne Rd *LBORO* LE11 ....103 G1
Osborne St *DERBY* DE1 ....3 J8
NOTTE NG7 ....50 C1
Osbourne Cl
EWD/SEL/PNX NG16 ....22 F8
Osgood Rd *ARN* NG5 ....38 A2
The Osiers *CDON/KEG* DE74 ......86 C5
LBORO LE11 ....103 L8
LEIW LE3 ....130 D8
Osier Dr *HUCK/RAV* NG15 ....14 E1
Osman Cl *WBRGFD* NG2 ....50 F6
Osmaston Cl *LGEAT* NG10 ....75 K2
Osmaston Park Rd
DERBYSE DE24 ....58 A8
Osmaston Rd *DERBY* DE1 ....2 F5
LEIE LE5 ....7 M9
Osmaston St *LGEAT* NG10 ....62 A2
NOTTE NG7 ....50 D4
Osnabruck Sq *DERBY* * DE1 ....2 F4
Osprey Cl *CFTN/RUD* NG11 ....64 A6
DERBYSE DE24 ....71 J5
RLEIW/BAR LE9 ....141 J8
Osprey Rd *LEIN* LE4 ....124 E1
Ossington Cl *NOTT* NG1 ....5 G4
Ossington St *NOTTE* NG7 ....4 A4
Osterley Cl *LBORO* LE11 ....103 G3
Osterley Gv *WOL/BIL/BRX* NG8 ...35 H5
Osterly Gn *DERBYW* DE22 ....56 E2
Oswald Cl *RLEINE/SYS* LE7 ....44 F4
Oswin Rd *LEIW* LE3 ....130 D2
Ottawa Rd *LEI* LE1 ....7 H4
Otterburn Dr *DERBYW* DE22 ....43 G5
Otter La *RLBORO* LE12 ....113 K5
Otter St *DERBY* DE1 ....43 L8
Otter Wy *RLEIW/BBY* LE8 ....142 D2
Oulton Cl *ARN* NG5 ....37 K1
DERBYSE DE24 ....72 B3
Oundle Dr *ILK* DE7 ....33 L8
WOL/BIL/BRX NG8 ....50 A4
Ousebridge Crs *CARL* NG4 ....38 E7
Ouse Bridge Dr *CARL* NG4 ....38 E7
Outfields Dr *RLEINE/SYS* LE7 ...118 D5
Outram St *RIPLEY* DE5 ....11 H5
Outram Wy *DERBYSE* DE24 ....71 J5
Outwood Cl *LEIW* LE3 ....130 B2
Outwoods Av *LBORO* LE11 ....8 F4
Outwoods Dr *LBORO* LE11 ....8 E7
Outwoods Rd *LBORO* LE11 ....103 K7
The Oval *COAL* LE67 ....108 B8
LEI LE1 ....7 H4
RLEIW/BAR LE9 ....140 C5
WGSTN LE18 ....138 D3
Oval Ct *NORM/LIT* DE23 ....57 G7
Oval Gdns *WOL/BIL/BRX* NG8 .....36 B7
Overdale Av *LEIW* LE3 ....123 M5
Overdale Cl *LEIW* LE3 ....123 M5
LGEAT NG10 ....75 K1
Overdale Rd *BLWL* NG6 ....36 A4
LEIN LE4 ....126 D1
LEIS LE2 ....138 A1
Overfield Cl *END/NAR* LE19 ......135 L8
GBY/RBY LE6 ....123 H7
Overing Cl *LEIN* LE4 ....125 L4
Over La *BPR/DUF* DE56 ....16 E5
BPR/DUF DE56 ....18 C2
Overpark Av *LEIW* LE3 ....130 D3
Overseal Rd *LEIW* LE3 ....124 C7
Overstone Cl *BPR/DUF* DE56 ......18 B3
Overstrand Cl *ARN* NG5 ....37 K1
Overton Rd *LEIE* LE5 ....126 B8
Owen Av *LGEAT* NG10 ....76 E1
Owen Cl *LEIE* LE7 ....130 B6
LEIW LE3 ....130 B6
Owen St *COAL* LE67 ....108 A6
Owers Av *HEANOR* DE75 ....20 D8
Owlers La *DERBYW* DE22 ....57 G5
Owlston Cl *EWD/SEL/PNX* NG16 ....21 K4
Owlswick Cl *NORM/LIT* DE23 ......56 E7
Owsthorpe Cl *ARN* NG5 ....24 E7
Owston Dr *WGSTN* LE18 ....137 M4
Owthorpe Gv *ARN* NG5 ....36 F5
Owthorpe Rd
COT/KEY/RAD NG12 ....67 K5
Oxborough Rd *ARN* NG5 ....25 G8
Oxbow Cl *WBRGFD* NG2 ....51 G6
Oxburgh Cl *LBORO* LE11 ....103 G2
Oxbury Rd *EWD/SEL/PNX* NG16 ...22 D7
Oxclose La *ARN* NG5 ....36 F1
Oxendale Cl *WBRGFD* NG2 ....66 A1
Oxendon St *LEIS* LE2 ....7 K7
Oxendon Wk *LEIS* LE2 ....7 K7
Oxengate *ARN* NG5 ....36 F1
Oxenhope Cl *NORM/LIT* DE23 .....56 C6
Oxford Av *LEIS* LE2 ....131 M4
Oxford Cl *WBRGFD* NG2 ....66 A1
Oxford Dr *WGSTN* LE18 ....137 K4
Oxford Rd *LEIE* LE5 ....131 M5
WBRGFD NG2 ....51 J8
Oxford St *CARL* NG4 ....38 C6

COAL LE67 ....108 C6
DERBY DE1 ....3 H7
DERBY DE1 ....59 J2
EWD/SEL/PNX NG16 ....21 K5
ILK DE7 ....33 K8
LBORO LE11 ....8 F7
LEI LE1 ....6 F7
LGEAT NG10 ....62 B7
NOTT NG1 ....4 E7
RIPLEY DE5 ....11 H6
RLBORO LE12 ....101 M5
RLEINE/SYS LE7 ....121 C3
Oxley Cl *RLBORO* LE12 ....101 L4
Oxon Wy *LEIE* LE5 ....132 C2
Oxted Ri *LEIE* LE5 ....138 E4
Oxton Av *ARN* NG5 ....37 G3
Ozier Holt *CARL* NG4 ....52 C3
LGEAT NG10 ....76 A1

P

Packer Av *LEIW* LE3 ....129 M3
Packe St *LBORO* LE11 ....9 H3
Packhorse Dr *END/NAR* LE19 ....136 B5
Pack Horse La *LBORO* LE11 ....9 K4
Packhorse Rd *LEIS* LE2 ....137 H4
Pack Horse Rd
MELB/CHEL DE73 ....82 F6
Packington Hl *CDON/KEG* DE74 ....86 A5
Packman Dr *CFTN/RUD* NG11 .....65 H7
Packwood Rd *LEIN* LE4 ....125 J3
Paddington Ms
MAPPK/POR/STA NG3 ....37 L8
The Paddock *BPR/DUF* DE56........30 A1
BSTN/STPLFD NG9 ....63 H5
BWSH/BRSTN DE72 ....60 A3
COAL LE67 ....116 C6
DERBYSE DE24 ....73 H3
RLBORO LE12 ....101 M4
RLEINE/SYS LE7 ....146 F7
Paddock Cft *DERBYE* DE21 ....44 D5
The Paddocks
COT/KEY/RAD NG12 ....65 M4
END/NAR LE19 ....136 A8
EWD/SEL/PNX NG16 ....34 F2
LGEAT NG10 ....61 L2
RLBORO LE12 ....94 F1
Paddock St *WGSTN* LE18 ....138 B5
Paddocks Vw *LGEAT* NG10 ....61 L7
Paddock Vw *RLEINE/SYS* LE7 ...120 F4
Paddy's La *RMMWB* LE14 ....99 L6
Padgate Cl *RLEINE/SYS* LE7 .....133 K1
Padge Rd *BSTN/STPLFD* NG9 ......63 M1
Padley Cl *DERBYW* DE22 ....43 L2
RIPLEY DE5 ....11 G4
Padleys La *CALV/BJ* NG14 ....39 J2
Padstow Cl *DERBYSE* DE24 ....71 H4
Padstow Rd *ARN* NG5 ....36 D1
DERBYSE DE24 ....73 C2
LEIN LE4 ....126 C5
Padwell La *RLEINE/SYS* LE7 .....133 L3
Page La *CDON/KEG* DE74 ....93 C2
Paget Av *LEIN* LE4 ....119 M7
Paget Cl *RLEIW/BBY* LE8 ....146 E7
Paget Crs *CFTN/RUD* NG11 ....65 G7
Paget Rd *LEIS* LE2 ....131 G1
LBORO LE11 ....8 E7
Paget St *LEIS* LE2 ....137 G1
RLEIW/BBY LE8 ....146 E7
Paigle Rd *LEIS* LE2 ....137 G1
Paignton Cl *WOL/BIL/BRX* NG8 ...35 M5
Painter St *LEI* LE1 ....7 G1
Paisley Gv *BSTN/STPLFD* NG9 .....63 G6
Palatine Gv *NORM/LIT* DE23 ....56 D8
Palatine St *NOTTE* NG7 ....4 A2
Palfreyman La *LEIS* LE2 ....139 J3
Palin Ct *NOTTE* NG7 ....4 A2
Palin Gdns *COT/KEY/RAD* NG12 ...53 L4
Palin St *NOTTE* NG7 ....4 A3
Palladium Dr *NORM/LIT* DE23 ....70 E1
Pall Ml *ILK* DE7 ....44 C3
Palm Cl *NORM/LIT* DE23 ....56 E6
Palmer Av *HUCK/RAV* NG15 ....15 L7
LBORO LE11 ....103 K2
Palmer Crs *CARL* NG4 ....38 B8
Palmer Dr *BSTN/STPLFD* NG9 .....62 B2
Palmer Rd *BSTN/STPLFD* NG9 ....62 F5
Palmerston Bvd *WGSTN* LE18 ...138 A1
Palmerston Cl *RLEIW/BBY* LE8 ...146 D7
Palmerston Ct
MELB/CHEL DE73 ....82 F8
Palmerston Gdns
MAPPK/POR/STA NG3 ....5 H4
Palmerston St
EWD/SEL/PNX NG16 ....13 C3
EWD/SEL/PNX NG16 ....13 K5
NORM/LIT DE23 ....57 J6
Palmerston Wy *LEIS* LE2 ....138 B1
Palmer St *LEIN* LE4 ....125 L4
Palm St *NOTTE* NG7 ....36 D7
Pamela Pl *LEIN* LE4 ....125 J3
Pankhurst Rd *LEIN* LE4 ....124 E1
Pantain Rd *LBORO* LE11 ....8 D9
Paper Mill Cl *RLEINE/SYS* LE7 ...44 C5
Papplewick La *HUCK/RAV* NG15 ...15 M8
The Parade *LEIS* * LE2 ....136 E5
LEIS LE2 ....138 E1
MCKLVR * DE3 ....56 B6
Paramore St *RLEIW/BBY* LE8 .....142 E2
Parcel Ter *DERBYW* DE22 ....57 H2
Pares Cl *COAL* LE67 ....108 C2
Pares St *LEI* LE1 ....6 E2
Pares Wy *BWSH/BRSTN* DE72 .....60 A2
Pargate Cl *RIPLEY* DE5 ....19 H1
Parham Cl *LEIN* LE4 ....124 F6
The Park *COT/KEY/RAD* NG12 ....67 K3
EWD/SEL/PNX NG16 ....12 C4
Park Av *ARN* NG5 ....37 J2
CALV/BJ NG14 ....26 A3

CALV/BJ NG14 ....39 J3
CARL NG4 ....38 D7
CDON/KEG DE74 ....84 D4
COAL LE67 ....116 C6
COT/KEY/RAD NG12 ....80 B4
EWD/SEL/PNX NG16 ....21 J5
EWD/SEL/PNX NG16 ....33 M2
EWD/SEL/PNX NG16 ....34 E2
HUCK/RAV NG15 ....15 K8
ILK DE7 ....33 K7
ILK DE7 ....46 A1
LBORO LE11 ....9 J8
LEIS LE2 ....131 J7
MAPPK/POR/STA NG3 ....37 H7
RIPLEY DE5 ....11 K6
RLBORO LE12 ....102 A5
WBRGFD NG2 ....51 K7
Park Av East
COT/KEY/RAD NG12 ....80 B4
Park Av West
COT/KEY/RAD NG12 ....80 B4
Park Cl *BPR/DUF* DE56 ....18 E7
DERBYE DE21 ....29 M7
ILK DE7 ....47 K7
RLBORO LE12 ....101 M3
RLEIW/BAR LE9 ....142 B5
WBRGFD NG2 ....65 G2
Park Ct *HEANOR* * DE75 ....20 D6
Park Crs *BPR/DUF* DE56 ....10 C7
EWD/SEL/PNX NG16 ....21 K3
ILK DE7 ....33 L7
LEIS LE2 ....139 G3
WOL/BIL/BRX NG8 ....49 G3
Parkcroft Rd *WBRGFD* NG2 ....65 K1
Parkdale Rd *LEIN* LE4 ....126 D1
NOTTE NG7 ....52 A1
Park Dr *ALFN* DE55 ....11 K1
HUCK/RAV NG15 ....23 L2
ILK DE7 ....33 K8
LEIW LE3 ....123 M7
LEIN LE4 ....130 A4
LGEAT NG10 ....61 L4
NORM/LIT DE23 ....57 G6
NOTTE NG7 ....4 D8
Parker Cl *ARN* NG5 ....26 A7
DERBY DE1 ....2 C1
Parker Gdns *BSTN/STPLFD* NG9 ...48 B1
Parkers Flds *RLBORO* LE12 ....104 E8
Parker St *DERBY* DE1 ....43 K8
HUCK/RAV NG15 ....15 M8
Park Farm Dr *DERBYE* DE22 ....43 H5
Parkfield Cl *GBY/RBY* LE6 ....123 H7
Parkfields Dr *DERBYW* DE22 ......43 J7
Parkgate *HUCK/RAV* NG15 ....15 M6
Park Gv *DERBYW* DE22 ....43 J7
Park Hall La *ILK* DE7 ....32 B5
Park Hall Rd *RIPLEY* DE5 ....18 E4
Parkham Rd
EWD/SEL/PNX NG16 ....22 D8
Park Hl *EWD/SEL/PNX* NG16 ....33 M2
Parkhill *LEIS* LE2 ....131 H7
Park Hill Av *LEIS* LE2 ....131 H8
Park Hill Dr *LEIS* LE2 ....131 H8
NORM/LIT DE23 ....57 K8
Park Hill La *RLEINE/SYS* LE7 ....106 E8
Park Homes *DERBYSE* * DE24 .....72 B4
Parkhouse Cl *LEIN* LE4 ....125 L2
Park House Gates
MAPPK/POR/STA NG3 ....37 H6
Parkland Cl *CFTN/RUD* NG11 .....64 A4
Parkland Dr *LEIE* LE5 ....138 E1
Parklands Av *ARN* NG5 ....24 F6
Parklands Cl *ARN* NG5 ....24 F6
Parklands Dr *LBORO* LE11 ....103 L7
MELB/CHEL DE73 ....72 E7
Park La *BLWL* NG6 ....36 C3
BPR/DUF DE56 ....10 D7
BWSH/BRSTN DE72 ....83 J3
CALV/BJ NG14 ....27 K7
CDON/KEG DE74 ....84 B4
DERBYW DE22 ....43 K3
LEIS LE2 ....132 B5
NORM/LIT DE23 ....57 G6
Park Leys Ct *DERBYE* DE21 ....59 J3
Park Ms *ALFN* * DE55 ....12 C1
MAPPK/POR/STA NG3 ....37 G7
Park Ravine *NOTTE* NG7 ....4 D9
Park Ri *LEIW* LE3 ....130 C2
RLBORO LE12 ....101 M4
Park Rd *ARN* NG5 ....37 J2
BLWL NG6 ....36 C2
BPR/DUF DE56 ....10 C7
BPR/DUF DE56 ....17 L5
BPR/DUF DE56 ....29 J4
BSTN/STPLFD NG9 ....48 E7
BSTN/STPLFD NG9 ....63 J1
CARL NG4 ....38 D7
COAL LE67 ....108 B6
COT/KEY/RAD NG12 ....53 K3
COT/KEY/RAD NG12 ....80 D3
DERBYE DE21 ....59 H2
END/NAR LE19 ....135 M8
GBY/RBY LE6 ....123 G4
HUCK/RAV NG15 ....15 K8
ILK DE7 ....33 L8
LBORO LE11 ....9 H5
LEIN LE4 ....125 K1
MCKLVR DE3 ....56 B5
NOTTE NG7 ....50 D4
RIPLEY DE5 ....11 J6
RLBORO LE12 ....114 A3
RLEINE/SYS LE7 ....124 E1
RLEIW/BAR LE9 ....140 B8
RLEIW/BBY LE8 ....142 B3
RLEIW/BBY LE8 ....136 E7
WGSTN LE18 ....137 K7
Park Rd North
BSTN/STPLFD NG9 ....63 J1
Park Rw *NOTT* NG1 ....4 E6
Park Side *BPR/DUF* DE56 ....17 L4
Parkside *BPR/DUF* DE56 ....10 C7
COT/KEY/RAD NG12 ....80 D3
GBY/RBY LE6 ....123 K3

WOL/BIL/BRX NG8 ....49 J4
Parkside Av *LGEAT* NG10 ....61 M7
Parkside Cl *EWD/SEL/PNX* NG16 ...12 D3
LEIN LE4 ....124 E1
Parkside Dr
EWD/SEL/PNX NG16 ....12 D3
LGEAT NG10 ....61 M7
Parkside Gdns North
WOL/BIL/BRX NG8 ....49 J4
Parkside Gdns South
WOL/BIL/BRX NG8 ....49 J5
Parkside Ri *WOL/BIL/BRX* NG8 ....49 J5
Parkstone Cl *WBRGFD* NG2 ....64 F2
Parkstone Ct *MCKLVR* DE3 ....56 A5
Parkstone Rd *LEIE* LE5 ....127 H7
RLEINE/SYS LE7 ....120 F2
Park St *BSTN/STPLFD* NG9 ....62 A1
BSTN/STPLFD NG9 ....63 J1
BWSH/BRSTN DE72 ....61 K7
DERBY DE1 ....3 H6
HEANOR DE75 ....20 B5
LBORO LE11 ....9 J5
LEI LE1 ....6 F7
LGEAT NG10 ....62 A6
NOTTE NG7 ....4 A8
RIPLEY DE5 ....11 J6
RLEIW/BBY LE8 ....145 K7
Park Ter *COT/KEY/RAD* NG12 .....80 D2
NOTT NG1 ....4 E7
Park Vale Rd *LEIS* LE2 ....7 M7
Park Va *NOTTE* NG7 ....4 A8
Park Vw *ALFN* DE55 ....12 B2
BWSH/BRSTN DE72 ....30 A7
DERBYE DE21 ....30 A7
HEANOR DE75 ....20 B5
LEIW LE3 ....130 C1
MAPPK/POR/STA NG3 ....37 J5
Park View Cl *DERBYW* DE22.......43 K3
Park View Ct *NOTT* * NG1 ....5 K6
Parkview Rd *ARN* NG5 ....24 D8
Parkway *MELB/CHEL* DE73 ....72 D6
The Parkway *LEIE* LE5 ....126 F8
Park Wy *RDERBYSW* DE65 ....69 G2
Park Whf *NOTTE* NG7 ....4 F9
Parkwood Ct *BLWL* NG6 ....36 C2
Parkyn Rd *ARN* NG5 ....37 H1
Parkyns Piece *RLBORO* LE12 ....88 C5
Parkyns St *CFTN/RUD* NG11 ....79 G1
Parliament Cl *DERBYW* DE22 ....2 A6
Parliament St *DERBYW* DE22 ....2 B6
LEIS LE2 ....6 E9
Parliament Street Mills
DERBYW * 2 B6
Parlour Cl *WGSTN* LE18 ....138 A5
Parr Ga *BSTN/STPLFD* NG9 ....62 E2
Parr La *CALV/BJ* NG14 ....27 L2
The Parrs *BSTN/STPLFD* NG9 ....63 M1
Parry Wy *ARN* NG5 ....25 M7
Parsons Dr *LEIS* LE2 ....136 E4
RLBORO LE12 ....114 C3
Parsons Gv *RIPLEY* DE5 ....19 H5
Parsons Meadow *CARL* NG4 ....52 C3
Parsonwood Hl *COAL* LE67 ....108 C2
Partridge Cl *RLBORO* LE12 ....113 K5
RLEINE/SYS LE7 ....120 D3
Partridge Rd *LEIN* LE4 ....126 D2
Partridge Wy *MCKLVR* DE3 ....56 E4
Parvian Rd *WGSTN* LE18 ....137 L3
Pasley Cl *LEIS* LE2 ....137 H3
Pasley Rd *LEIS* LE2 ....137 H3
Pasteur Av *RIPLEY* DE5 ....11 H5
Pasture Cl *WBRGFD* NG2 ....52 E8
Pasture La *CFTN/RUD* NG11 ....78 D2
LEI LE1 ....6 E3
LGEAT NG10 ....76 E3
RLBORO LE12 ....94 E1
RLBORO LE12 ....94 F5
Pasture Rd *BSTN/STPLFD* NG9 ....48 B6
The Pastures *BPR/DUF* DE56 ......29 J3
END/NAR LE19 ....135 L6
EWD/SEL/PNX NG16 ....21 M7
RLBORO LE12 ....113 J1
RLEINE/SYS LE7 ....120 C4
Pastures Av *CFTN/RUD* NG11 .....64 B7
NORM/LIT DE23 ....56 D8
Pastures Hl *NORM/LIT* DE23 ....56 E7
Pateley Rd *NORM/LIT* DE23 ....58 E1
Paterson Av *DERBYE* DE21 ....58 E1
Paterson Cl *LEIN* LE4 ....124 E1
Paterson Dr *RLBORO* LE12 ....111 K6
Paterson Pl *RLBORO* LE12 ....101 M2
Patmore Sq *NORM/LIT* DE23 ......71 K1
Paton Rd *ARN* NG5 ....36 C2
Paton St *LEIW* LE3 ....6 A9
Patricia Dr *ARN* NG5 ....25 L6
Patrick Rd *WBRGFD* NG2 ....51 J7
Patterdale Cl *WBRGFD* NG2 ....66 A1
Patterdale Dr *LBORO* LE11 ....103 G4
Patterdale Rd *ARN* NG5 ....37 K2
LEIN LE4 ....120 C4
Pattern Yd *BPR/DUF* * DE56 ....17 L4
Paudy La *RLBORO* LE12 ....106 A6
RLBORO LE12 ....106 E3
RMMWB LE14 ....107 H1
Paul Dr *LEIN* LE4 ....126 D3
Pauline Av *LEIS* LE2 ....125 M3
Pavilion Cl *WBRGFD* NG2 ....51 H6
Pavilion Rd *ARN* NG5 ....24 F6
ILK DE7 ....33 G2
NORM/LIT DE23 ....57 G7
WBRGFD NG2 ....51 J6
Pavilion Wy *LBORO* LE11 ....103 L1
Pawley Cl *RLEIW/BBY* LE8 ....142 E1
Pawley Gdns *LEIE* LE5 ....137 H3
Paxton Cl *MCKLVR* DE3 ....56 A6
Paxton Gdns
MAPPK/POR/STA NG3 ....5 L5
Payne Rd *BSTN/STPLFD* NG9 ......62 E4
Payne St *DERBYW* * DE22 ....57 H1
LEIN LE4 ....125 M4
Peach Av *EWD/SEL/PNX* NG16 ...13 K1
Peache Wy *BSTN/STPLFD* NG9 ...48 E5
Peachey St *NOTT* NG1 ....5 G5
Peach St *DERBYW* DE22 ....57 H2
HEANOR DE75 ....20 B6
Peacock Cl *CFTN/RUD* NG11 ....78 F1
Peacock Crs *CFTN/RUD* NG11 .....64 C5

Peacock Dr *RLEIW/BBY* LE8 ......**142** D2
Peacock La *LEI* LE1 ....**6** D6
Peacock Pl *ILK* DE7 ....**33** H3
Peacroft Ct *RDERBYSW* DE65 .....**68** B5
Peacroft La *RDERBYSW* DE65 .....**68** B6
Peak Av *ALFN* DE55 ....**11** M1
Peakdale La *LEIW* LE18 ....**138** D6
Peakdale Cl *LGEAT* NG10 ....**75** L1
  RIPLEY DE5 ....**19** H1
Peak Dr *DERBYSE* DE24 ....**57** L8
Peake Rd *LEIN* LE4 ....**126** B6
Pearce Dr *WOL/BIL/BRX* NG8 .....**49** M1
Pearl Cl *DERBYE* DE21 ....**44** E5
Pearmain Dr
  MAPPK/POR/STA NG3 ....**37** K8
Pearson Av *BSTN/STPLFD* NG9 ....**62** F2
Pearson Ct *ARN* NG5 ....**25** J8
Pearson St *CARL* NG4 ....**52** E1
  NOTTE NG7 ....**36** D5
Pear Tree Av *RIPLEY* DE5 ....**11** G7
Peartree Av *RLBORO* LE12 ....**102** B4
Peartree La *CDON/KEG* DE74 ......**84** E4
  LEIW LE3 ....**123** M8
  RLEINE/SYS LE7 ....**124** B2
Pear Tree Crs *NORM/LIT* DE23 ....**57** L7
Pear Tree La *RLBORO* LE12 ....**102** F1
Peartree Orch *CFTN/RUD* NG11 ....**65** G8
Pear Tree Rd *NORM/LIT* DE23 .....**57** L6
Pear Tree St *NORM/LIT* DE23 .....**57** L7
Peary Cl *ARN* NG5 ....**36** D1
Peasehill *RIPLEY* DE5 ....**11** J7
Peashill Cl *RLBORO* LE12 ....**114** C4
Peas Hill Rd
  MAPPK/POR/STA NG3 ....**5** J3
Peatburn Av *HEANOR* DE75 ....**20** A6
Peatfield Rd *BSTN/STPLFD* NG9 ...**48** B6
Peatling Rd *RLEIW/BBY* LE8 ......**143** L5
Peckham Gdns *DERBYW* DE22 ......**56** E2
Peckleton Common
  RLEIW/BAR LE9 ....**128** A8
Peckleton La *RLEIW/BAR* LE9 .....**128** C7
Pedlars Cl *LEIN* LE4 ....**124** F4
Pedley St *ILK* DE7 ....**33** K8
Pedmore Va *ARN* NG5 ....**24** E8
Peebles Cl *DERBYSE* DE24 ....**71** J5
Peebles Wy *LEIN* LE4 ....**126** B4
Peel Cl *RLEIW/BBY* LE8 ....**146** D7
Peel Dr *LBORO* LE11 ....**9** L7
Peel St *DERBYW* DE22 ....**57** H1
  EWD/SEL/PNX NG16 ....**20** F4
  LGEAT NG10 ....**62** C7
  NOTT NG1 ....**4** F4
Peel Vls *MAPPK/POR/STA* NG3 .....**37** J5
Peers Cl *DERBYE* DE21 ....**44** F5
Peet St *DERBYW* DE22 ....**2** B5
Peewit Cl *LEIS* LE2 ....**136** E4
Pegasus Cl *LEIS* LE2 ....**7** K6
Pegasus Wy *DERBYSE* DE65 ....**68** C5
Peggs La *RLEINE/SYS* LE7 ....**121** K2
Pegwell Cl *NORM/LIT* DE23 ....**57** H8
Peldar Pl *COAL* LE67 ....**108** F7
Peldon Cl *LEIN* LE4 ....**125** H5
Pelham Av *ARN* NG5 ....**36** F7
  ILK DE7 ....**33** J6
Pelham Cottages *NOTTE* * NG7 .....**4** B8
Pelham Crs *BSTN/STPLFD* NG9 ....**49** M8
  NOTTE NG7 ....**4** B7
Pelham Rd *NOTTE* NG7 ....**36** F7
  ILK DE7 ....**33** J6
  LEI LE1 ....**6** E8
  LEIS LE2 ....**138** E1
  NOTT NG1 ....**5** H7
Pelham Wy *LEI* LE1 ....**6** E8
Pell Cl *RLBORO* LE12 ....**105** J7
Pells Cl *RLEIW/BBY* LE8 ....**145** K7
Pemberton St *NOTT* NG1 ....**5** K8
Pembrey Cl *BSTN/STPLFD* NG9 ....**48** B5
Pembridge Cl *BLWL* NG6 ....**36** B5
Pembroke Av *RLEINE/SYS* LE7 ....**120** F5
  WGSTN LE18 ....**137** K5
Pembroke St *DERBYE* DE21 ....**44** B7
  LEI LE1 ....**7** L2
Pembury Cl *RLEIW/BBY* LE8 ......**139** M6
Pembury Rd *WOL/BIL/BRX* NG8 ....**49** J2
Penalton Cl *DERBYSE* DE24 ......**72** C1
Penarth Gdns
  MAPPK/POR/STA NG3 ....**37** J4
Penarth Ri *ARN* NG5 ....**37** J4
Pen Cl *WGSTN* LE18 ....**137** J3
Penclose Rd *RLEIW/BBY* LE8 .....**145** K7
Pendene Rd *LEIS* LE2 ....**132** A6
Pendennis Cl *CARL* NG4 ....**38** F6
  DERBYSE DE24 ....**72** F1
Pendine Cl *ARN* NG5 ....**25** H6
Pendlebury Dr *LEIS* LE2 ....**131** L8
  MCKLVR DE3 ....**56** C6
Pendle Crs
  MAPPK/POR/STA NG3 ....**37** K6
Pendleside Wy *NORM/LIT* DE23 ....**56** C8
Pendock La *COT/KEY/RAD* NG12 ...**79** K5
Pendragon Wy *LEIW* LE3 ....**129** K5
Penfold Cl *RLEIW/BBY* LE8 .....**140** B7
Penfold Dr *RLEIW/BBY* LE8 .....**143** H4
Penge Rd *DERBYW* DE22 ....**42** E8
Penhale Dr *HUCK/RAV* NG15 ......**23** C2
Penhale Rd *LEIW* LE3 ....**130** C7
Penhaligon's Cl
  MELB/CHEL DE73 ....**72** C6
Penhurst Cl *CFTN/RUD* NG11 .....**64** E3
Pen La *COT/KEY/RAD* NG12 ....**91** H3
Penllech Cl *ARN* NG5 ....**24** E8
Penman Wy *END/NAR* LE19 ....**136** C2
Pennant Cl *BLWL* NG6 ....**36** B5
Pennant Rd *BLWL* NG6 ....**36** B5
Pennbury Cl *LEIS* LE2 ....**138** A4
Penney Cl *LGEAT* NG10 ....**76** B3
Pennhome Av *ARN* NG5 ....**37** G5
Pennie Cl *LGEAT* NG10 ....**76** B3
Pennine Cl *ARN* NG5 ....**24** F6
  LEIS LE2 ....**139** H2
  LGEAT NG10 ....**61** L6
  RLBORO LE12 ....**102** A5
Pennine Vw *BPR/DUF* DE56 ....**10** C2
Penn La *MELB/CHEL* DE73 ....**82** E8
Penn Moor Cl *LGEAT* NG10 ....**75** L1
Penn St *BPR/DUF* DE56 ....**17** L3
Pennycress Rd *NORM/LIT* DE23 ...**56** E8

Pennyfields Bvd *LGEAT* NG10 .....**61** L8
Pennyfoot St *NOTT* NG1 ....**5** L8
Penny Long La *DERBYW* DE22 ......**43** J7
  LEIW LE3 ....**129** K4
Penrhyn Av *NORM/LIT* DE23 ....**57** H7
Penrhyn Cl *MAPPK/POR/STA* NG3 ...**5** J4
  RLBORO LE12 ....**101** K5
Penrith Av *COT/KEY/RAD* NG12 ...**53** L3
Penrith Crs *WOL/BIL/BRX* NG8 ....**36** A5
Penrith Cl *DERBYE* DE21 ....**44** B5
Penrith Rd *LEIN* LE4 ....**126** A5
Penryn Dr *WGSTN* LE18 ....**138** A6
Penshore Cl *CFTN/RUD* NG11 .....**64** B6
Pensilva Cl *WGSTN* LE18 ....**138** A6
Pentewen Cl *DERBYW* DE22 ....**43** J5
Pentland Cl *RLBORO* LE12 ......**102** B5
Pentland Gdns *LGEAT* NG10 ......**61** L6
Pentrich Rd *RIPLEY* DE5 ....**11** H5
Pentridge Cl *WGSTN* LE18 ......**138** A7
Pentrip Dr *ILK* DE7 ....**33** C4
Pentwood Av *ARN* NG5 ....**25** K5
Penzance Av *WGSTN* LE18 ....**138** A6
Penzance Rd *DERBYSE* DE24 ......**72** F2
Peoples Hall Cottages
  NOTT * NG1 ....**5** J6
Peppercorn Cl *LEIN* LE4 ....**125** C4
Pepper Dr *RLBORO* LE12 ....**104** D8
Pepper La *ILK* DE7 ....**47** J6
Pepper's Cl *RLBORO* LE12 ......**113** H3
Peppers Dr *CDON/KEG* DE74 ......**85** M5
Percival Rd *ARN* NG5 ....**37** C5
Percival St *LEIE* LE5 ....**126** B8
Percy Rd *LEIS* LE2 ....**131** J8
Percy St *BLWL* NG6 ....**36** B4
  DERBYW DE22 ....**2** B7
  EWD/SEL/PNX NG16 ....**21** L5
  ILK DE7 ....**33** K8
  LEIW LE3 ....**130** E7
Percy Wood Cl
  RDERBYSW DE65 ....**68** A5
  NOTTE NG7 ....**50** C3
Peregrine Ri *LEIN* LE4 ....**124** E1
Peregrine Rd *RLEIW/BAR* LE9 ...**141** J8
Perivale Cl *EWD/SEL/PNX* NG16 ...**35** H4
Perkyn Rd *LEIE* LE5 ....**133** C1
Perlethorpe Av *CARL* NG4 ....**38** B5
  WBRGFD NG2 ....**5** M8
Perlethorpe Cl *CARL* NG4 ....**38** C5
Perlethorpe Crs *CARL* NG4 ......**38** C5
Perlethorpe Dr *CARL* NG4 ....**38** B5
  HUCK/RAV NG15 ....**15** M8
Perran Av *COAL* LE67 ....**108** C5
Perry Cl *RLBORO* LE12 ....**111** K5
Perry Gdns *ARN* NG5 ....**36** F4
Perry Gv *LBORO* LE11 ....**9** L9
Perry Rd *ARN* NG5 ....**36** D4
Perseverance Rd *LEIN* LE4 .....**125** L2
Perth Av *LEIW* LE3 ....**124** E8
Perth Cl *MCKLVR* DE3 ....**56** C3
Perth Dr *BSTN/STPLFD* NG9 .....**48** B6
Perth St *DERBYE* DE21 ....**44** B6
  NOTT NG1 ....**5** H5
Peterborough St *DERBYE* DE21 ...**44** C7
Peterhouse Ter
  NORM/LIT DE23 ....**57** M5
Peterlee Pl *DERBYSE* DE24 ......**72** E1
Peters Cl *ARN* NG5 ....**38** A1
  EWD/SEL/PNX NG16 ....**22** A5
  RLEIW/BAR LE9 ....**140** A5
Peters Dr *LEIE* LE5 ....**126** F8
Petersfield *RLEIW/BAR* LE9 ....**141** J3
Petersfield Cl *ARN* NG5 ....**24** D8
Petersfield Rd *COAL* LE67 .....**108** E4
Petersgate *LGEAT* NG10 ....**61** L6
Petersgate Cl *LGEAT* NG10 ......**61** L5
Petersham Dr *DERBYSE* DE24 .....**73** C1
Petersham Ms *NOTTE* NG7 ....**50** D4
Petersham Rd *LGEAT* NG10 ....**61** L6
Petty Close La *ASHB* DE6 ....**41** C6
Petunia Cl *LEIW* LE3 ....**129** K5
Petworth Av *LEIW* LE3 ....**133** H4
Petworth Dr *ARN* NG5 ....**36** D3
  LBORO LE11 ....**103** C2
  LEIW LE3 ....**130** F1
Pevensey Av *LEIW* LE3 ....**133** H4
Pevensey Rd *LBORO* LE11 ....**103** J2
Peverel Rd *LEIW* LE3 ....**130** E5
Peveril Av *BWSH/BRSTN* DE72 ....**60** A5
Peveril Cl *ALFN* DE55 ....**11** M1
Peveril Cl *RIPLEY* DE5 ....**11** G6
Peveril Crs *ILK* DE7 ....**32** C7
  LGEAT NG10 ....**75** A2
Peveril Dr *ALFN* DE55 ....**12** A1
  ILK DE7 ....**33** H5
  NOTTE NG7 ....**4** E9
  WBRGFD NG2 ....**65** H3
Peveril Ms *NOTTE* * NG7 ....**4** C8
Peveril Rd *BSTN/STPLFD* NG9 ....**49** K7
Peveril St *DERBYSE* DE24 ....**72** B1
  HUCK/RAV NG15 ....**15** L7
  NOTTE NG7 ....**4** B3
Pheasant Field Dr
  DERBYE DE21 ....**59** L1
Philip Av *EWD/SEL/PNX* NG16 ....**35** G1
  EWD/SEL/PNX NG16 ....**21** L6
Philip Gv *CARL* NG4 ....**38** C5
Philips Cft *BPR/DUF* DE56 ......**29** J3
Phillip Dr *LEIS* LE2 ....**137** J6
Phillips Crs *LEIN* LE4 ....**124** E1
Phipps Cl *RLEIW/BBY* LE8 ......**142** E1
Phoenix Av *CARL* NG4 ....**38** C5
Phoenix Cl *LEIE* LE5 ....**124** F8
  WBRGFD NG2 ....**50** F5
Phoenix Dr *RLBORO* LE12 ....**114** B5
Phoenix Pl *BLWL* NG6 ....**35** M3
Phoenix St *DERBY* DE1 ....**2** C7
Phyllis Gv *LGEAT* NG10 ....**62** D8
Piccadilly *BLWL* NG6 ....**36** B1
Piccaver Ri *LEIW* LE3 ....**130** E1
Pickard La *BPR/DUF* DE56 ....**10** B6
Pickering
  EWD/SEL/PNX NG16 ....**21** K5
Pickering Cl *LEIN* LE4 ....**126** B6
Pickering Ri *DERBYE* DE21 ......**44** A6
Pick St *RLBORO* LE12 ....**101** M3

Pickwell Cl *LEIW* LE3 ....**124** C7
Pieris Dr *CFTN/RUD* NG11 ....**64** A6
Pierrepont Av *CARL* NG4 ....**38** B5
Pierrepont Rd *WBRGFD* NG2 ......**51** L7
Piers Rd *LEIW* LE3 ....**124** A6
Pilcher Ga *NOTT* NG1 ....**5** H8
Pilgrims Wy *DERBYSE* DE24 ......**71** C5
Pilkington Rd *LEIW* LE3 ....**130** C4
  MAPPK/POR/STA NG3 ....**37** L6
Pilkington St *BLWL* NG6 ....**23** M8
Pilsley Cl *BPR/DUF* DE56 ....**18** A1
Pimlico *DERBYW* DE22 ....**56** F1
Pimlico Av *BSTN/STPLFD* NG9 ....**48** F4
Pimlico Cl *WBRGFD* NG2 ....**51** J5
Pimm's Rd *ASHB* DE6 ....**41** L7
Pimpernel Cl *END/NAR* LE19 ....**135** K6
Pinchom's Hill Rd
  BPR/DUF DE56 ....**17** M4
Pindar Rd *LEIW* LE3 ....**124** E7
Pinder St *WBRGFD* NG2 ....**5** K8
Pine Av *END/SEL/PNX* NG16 ......**20** A7
Pine Cl *DERBYE* DE21 ....**58** F3
  ILK DE7 ....**31** K2
  RDERBYSW DE65 ....**68** A5
  RIPLEY DE5 ....**11** H6
  RLBORO LE12 ....**88** B7
  RLBORO LE12 ....**103** L8
Pinecroft Ct *DERBYE* DE21 ......**44** F6
Pine Gv *HUCK/RAV* NG15 ....**23** M3
Pine Hill Cl *ARN* NG5 ....**24** D6
Pinehurst Av *HUCK/RAV* NG15 ...**23** C2
Pinehurst Cl *LEIW* LE3 ....**130** A1
The Pines *BWSH/BRSTN* DE72 .....**60** F8
Pine Tree Av *GBY/RBY* LE6 .....**123** K5
  LEIE LE5 ....**126** B8
Pine Tree Cl *LEIS* LE2 ....**138** F3
Pine Tree Gv *LEIW* LE3 ....**129** J5
Pine Vw *NOTTE* NG7 ....**4** A4
Pinewood *RIPLEY* DE5 ....**11** M8
Pinewood Av *ARN* NG5 ....**25** M6
  LEIN LE4 ....**126** C2
Pinewood Cl *LEIN* LE4 ....**124** E2
  RLEIW/BBY LE8 ....**143** J3
Pinewood Dr *COAL* LE67 ....**122** C1
Pinewood Gdns
  CFTN/RUD NG11 ....**64** B7
Pinewood Rd *BPR/DUF* DE56 ......**17** J1
The Pinfold *BPR/DUF* DE56 ......**18** A2
  BWSH/BRSTN DE72 ....**73** K3
  COAL LE67 ....**116** C7
Pinfold *LEIW* LE3 ....**130** C8
Pinfold Cl *CALV/BJ* NG14 ....**27** G3
  COT/KEY/RAD NG12 ....**67** K4
Pinfold Crs *CALV/BJ* NG14 ......**27** G3
Pinfold Gdns *LBORO* LE11 ....**9** K2
Pinfold Ga *LBORO* LE11 ....**9** K3
Pinfold La *BSTN/STPLFD* NG9 ....**48** C8
  LEIN LE4 ....**126** A1
The Pingle *DERBYE* DE21 ....**59** J3
  LGEAT NG10 ....**62** B7
  RLBORO LE12 ....**112** C2
Pingle *DERBYW* DE22 ....**43** J3
Pingle Crs *ARN* NG5 ....**24** D7
  BPR/DUF DE56 ....**17** K2
Pinglehill Wy *MELB/CHEL* DE73 ..**72** F5
Pingle La *BPR/DUF* DE56 ....**10** D5
  BPR/DUF DE56 ....**17** K2
  RLEIW/BAR LE9 ....**134** C8
Pingle St *LEIW* LE3 ....**130** C6
Pingreaves Dr *MELB/CHEL* DE73 ..**72** E5
Pintail Cl *CARL* NG4 ....**52** F2
  RLEIW/BAR LE9 ....**142** C3
Piper Cl *HUCK/RAV* NG15 ....**15** M6
  LBORO LE11 ....**8** C1
  LEIW LE3 ....**124** E8
  RLBORO LE12 ....**94** A5
Piper Dr *RLBORO* LE12 ....**94** A4
Piper Wy *LEIW* LE3 ....**124** E8
Pippin Cl *MAPPK/POR/STA* NG3 ...**37** K8
Pippin Hl *RIPLEY* DE5 ....**19** L8
Pitcairn Cl *WBRGFD* NG2 ....**51** C6
Pitchens Cl *LEIN* LE4 ....**124** D2
Pit Close La *MELB/CHEL* DE73 ...**72** F6
Pithouse La *RLBORO* LE12 ....**87** J6
Pit La *HEANOR* DE75 ....**32** F1
  RIPLEY DE5 ....**11** L8
  RIPLEY DE5 ....**11** J6
Pits Av *LEIW* LE3 ....**130** C8
Pitsford Dr *LBORO* LE11 ....**102** E5
Pittar St *DERBYW* DE22 ....**2** C7
Pitton Cl *WGSTN* LE18 ....**138** A7
Plackett Cl *BSTN/STPLFD* NG9 ...**48** D7
  BWSH/BRSTN DE72 ....**61** H7
Plain Ga *RLEINE/SYS* LE7 .....**113** G7
Plains Farm Cl
  MAPPK/POR/STA NG3 ....**38** A2
Plains Gv *MAPPK/POR/STA* NG3 ...**37** L3
Plains La *BPR/DUF* DE56 ....**16** F3
Plainspot Rd
  EWD/SEL/PNX NG16 ....**13** J5
Plains Rd *MAPPK/POR/STA* NG3 ...**37** L3
Plane Cl *BLWL* NG6 ....**23** K8
Plantagenet Ct
  MAPPK/POR/STA NG3 ....**5** K4
Plantagenet St
  MAPPK/POR/STA NG3 ....**5** K4
Plantain Gdns *NORM/LIT* DE23 ...**71** G2
The Plantation *RLEIW/BBY* LE8 ..**143** J3
Plantation Av *LEIS* LE2 ....**137** G1
Plantation Cl *ARN* NG5 ....**24** F6
Plantation Rd
  COT/KEY/RAD NG12 ....**80** B4
  WOL/BIL/BRX NG8 ....**48** F3
Plantation Side *NOTTE* NG7 .....**36** C7
The Plantations *LGEAT* NG10 ....**61** L7
Plant La *LGEAT* NG10 ....**75** L3
Platt La *COT/KEY/RAD* NG12 .....**80** E3
Platts Av *HEANOR* DE75 ....**20** A6
Platts La *RLBORO* LE12 ....**114** A8
Player Cl *LEIN* LE4 ....**126** B2
Player Ct *NOTTE* * NG7 ....**50** C1
Player St *NOTTE* NG7 ....**50** C1
Plaza Gdns *BLWL* NG6 ....**36** D3

Pleasant Cl *LBORO* LE11 ....**9** G2
  LEIW LE3 ....**129** K5
Pleasant Cl *NOTTE* NG7 ....**4** A2
Pleasant Pl *CDON/KEG* DE74 .....**86** B5
Pleasant Rw *NOTTE* NG7 ....**4** A2
Plimsoll Cl *DERBYW* DE22 ....**57** G1
Plough Cl *LEIW* LE3 ....**129** K6
  RLBORO LE12 ....**113** H7
Ploughfield Cl *NORM/LIT* DE23 ..**70** F1
Plough Ga *DERBYW* DE22 ....**43** K5
Plough La *WBRGFD* NG2 ....**5** L8
Ploughman Av *CALV/BJ* NG14 .....**27** H3
Ploughmans Dr *RLBORO* LE12 ....**102** A2
Ploughman's Lea
  RLEINE/SYS LE7 ....**115** H8
Plover Crs *LEIN* LE4 ....**124** F1
Plover Whf *WBRGFD* NG2 ....**50** E5
Plowman Cl *LEIW* LE3 ....**124** A6
Plowman Ct
  BSTN/STPLFD NG9 ....**62** B1
Plowright Ct
  MAPPK/POR/STA NG3 ....**5** J1
Plowright St
  MAPPK/POR/STA NG3 ....**5** H1
Plumb Rd *HUCK/RAV* NG15 ....**15** K8
Plumptre Cl
  EWD/SEL/PNX NG16 ....**21** K6
Plumptre Flats *NOTT* * NG1 ......**5** J7
Plumptre Pl *NOTT* NG1 ....**5** J7
Plumptre Rd
  EWD/SEL/PNX NG16 ....**20** F2
Plumptre Sq *NOTT* NG1 ....**5** K8
Plumptre St *NOTT* NG1 ....**5** J7
Plumptre Wy
  EWD/SEL/PNX NG16 ....**21** K6
Plumtree *LBORO* LE11 ....**103** K1
Plumtree Rd
  COT/KEY/RAD NG12 ....**67** H5
Plumtree Wy *RLEINE/SYS* LE7 ...**120** F5
Plungar Cl *WOL/BIL/BRX* NG8 ....**49** M1
Pluto Cl *LEIS* LE2 ....**7** K6
Plymouth Dr *LEIW* LE3 ....**132** D4
Plymstock Cl *LEIW* LE3 ....**130** F1
Poachers Cl *LEIW* LE3 ....**123** M7
Poachers Pl *LEIS* LE2 ....**139** H3
Pochin's Bridge Rd
  WGSTN LE18 ....**137** L7
Pochins Cl *WGSTN* LE18 ....**138** A6
Pochin St *RLEIW/BAR* LE9 .....**141** G3
Pochin Wy *RLBORO* LE12 ....**114** B3
Pocket End *LBORO* LE11 ....**103** H7
Pocklingtons Wk *LEI* LE1 ....**6** E6
Podder La
  MAPPK/POR/STA NG3 ....**38** A1
The Point
  MAPPK/POR/STA NG3 ....**37** H7
  WBRGFD * NG2 ....**51** J7
Polaris Cl *LEIS* LE2 ....**7** K6
Polden Cl *RLBORO* LE12 ....**102** A5
Pole's Rd *ASHB* DE6 ....**41** L7
Pollard Rd *LEIW* LE3 ....**130** C4
Pollards Oaks
  BWSH/BRSTN DE72 ....**59** M6
Polly Bott's La or Lea La
  COAL LE67 ....**116** E3
Polperro Wy *HUCK/RAV* NG15 ....**23** G2
Pomeroy Dr *LEIS* LE2 ....**138** D2
Pond Hills La *ARN* NG5 ....**25** K6
Pond Rd *BPR/DUF* DE56 ....**18** A8
Pond St *RLBORO* LE12 ....**106** D8
Ponsonby Ter *DERBY* DE1 ....**2** B4
Pontefract Cl *DERBYSE* DE24 ....**58** B8
Pontypool Cl *DERBYE* DE21 ......**44** F5
Pool Cl *DERBYSE* DE24 ....**73** C3
Poole Meadow *CARL* NG4 ....**52** D3
Pooles Cnr *CALV/BJ* * NG14 .....**39** K3
Pool St *DERBYSE* DE24 ....**72** C1
Pool Rd *LEIW* LE3 ....**130** F1
Pope Crs *END/NAR* LE19 ....**135** L4
Pope St *LEIS* LE2 ....**131** L7
Popham Ct *NOTT* NG1 ....**5** J8
Popham St *NOTT* NG1 ....**5** J8
The Poplars *BSTN/STPLFD* NG9 ...**49** K8
  LEIS LE2 ....**138** E3
Poplar Av *ARN* NG5 ....**36** E6
  COAL LE67 ....**116** B7
  DERBYE DE21 ....**59** J2
  LEIN LE4 ....**119** L7
  LGEAT NG10 ....**47** L8
  RIPLEY DE5 ....**11** H7
  RLBORO LE12 ....**88** B7
  RLEIW/BBY LE8 ....**143** J4
Poplar Cl *CARL* NG4 ....**52** B1
  DERBYSE DE24 ....**58** F8
Poplar Crs *EWD/SEL/PNX* NG16 ...**34** E1
Poplar Hl *RLBORO* LE12 ....**105** L3
Poplar Nook *DERBYW* DE22 ......**43** K3
Poplar Rw *DERBYW* DE22 ....**43** K3
Poplars Av *CALV/BJ* NG14 ......**39** L2
Poplars Cl *COT/KEY/RAD* NG12 ...**80** D3
  GBY/RBY LE6 ....**123** J4
Poplar St *NOTT* NG1 ....**5** K8
Poplar Wy *ILK* DE7 ....**47** H2
The Poppins *LEIN* LE4 ....**124** F1
Poppy Cl *COAL* LE67 ....**108** E7
  GBY/RBY LE6 ....**123** L4
  RLBORO LE12 ....**111** L1
  WGSTN LE18 ....**137** K3
Porchester Rd
  MAPPK/POR/STA NG3 ....**37** L6
Porlock Cl *LGEAT* NG10 ....**61** L7
  RLBORO LE12 ....**102** A5
Porlock St *LEIW* LE3 ....**130** C8
Portage Cl *COT/KEY/RAD* NG12 ...**53** J5
Port Arthur Rd *WBRGFD* NG2 ....**51** L3
Portcullis Rd *LEIE* LE5 ......**127** K4
Porter Cl *CFTN/RUD* NG11 ....**64** A7
Porterhouse Rd *RIPLEY* DE5 .....**11** K6
Porter's La *DERBYE* DE21 ....**44** D4
Porter's Rd *LEIE* LE5 ....**44** D4
Porters Wk
  MAPPK/POR/STA NG3 ....**37** L8
Portgate *WGSTN* LE18 ....**138** C6
Porthcawl Pl *DERBYE* DE21 .....**45** G5

Portico Rd *NORM/LIT* DE23 ......**70** E1
Portinscale Cl *WBRGFD* NG2 .....**66** A3
Portishead Dr *LEIE* LE5 ......**126** C7
Portland Cl *ARN* NG5 ....**56** B5
Portland Ct *ARN* NG5 ....**62** C1
Portland Gra *HUCK/RAV* NG15 ....**15** K8
Portland Hl *NOTTE* NG7 ....**50** A6
Portland Rd *BSTN/STPLFD* NG9 ...**62** A4
  CARL NG4 ....**38** A5
  EWD/SEL/PNX NG16 ....**21** M7
  HUCK/RAV NG15 ....**23** M1
  ILK DE7 ....**33** K4
  LEIS LE2 ....**131** M5
  LGEAT NG10 ....**75** L3
  NOTTE NG7 ....**129** J2
  RLEIW/BAR LE9 ....**129** J2
  WBRGFD NG2 ....**65** K1
Portland St *ARN* NG5 ....**37** H1
  BSTN/STPLFD NG9 ....**49** L8
  NORM/LIT DE23 ....**57** H7
  RDERBYSW DE65 ....**68** F3
  RLEIW/BAR LE9 ....**142** B4
Portland Wk *LEIS* LE2 ....**139** G4
Portloc Dr *LEIW* LE18 ....**138** A7
Portman Cha *DERBYSE* DE24 .....**71** H5
Portman St *LEIN* LE4 ....**125** C5
Portman Wk *LEI* LE4 ....**125** C5
Portreath Dr *DERBYW* DE22 .....**43** J4
Portree Dr *ARN* NG5 ....**24** D5
Portsdown Rd *LEIS* LE2 ....**138** B1
Portsmouth Rd *LEIN* LE4 ......**125** L4
Port Wy *DERBYE* DE21 ....**30** B3
Portway Cl *DERBYW* DE22 ....**43** J3
The Portwey *LEIE* LE5 ....**126** C7
Postern St *NOTT* NG1 ....**4** F7
Post Office La *RLEIW/BBY* LE8 ..**139** H8
Post Rd *RLEINE/SYS* LE7 ......**120** B5
Posy La *BWSH/BRSTN* DE72 ......**73** L8
Potato Pit La *ILK* DE7 ....**46** E6
Potomac Ms *NOTTE* * NG7 ....**4** D8
Pott Acre *RLBORO* LE12 ....**113** K6
Potters Cl *ARN* NG5 ....**24** E8
Potters La *RLBORO* LE12 ....**88** C7
Potter St *DERBYE* DE21 ....**59** H3
  LEI LE1 ....**7** G4
  MELB/CHEL DE73 ....**82** F8
Potterton Rd *LEIE* LE5 ....**125** H3
Pottery Cl *BPR/DUF* DE56 ......**18** A3
Pottery La *RIPLEY* DE5 ....**19** C4
Pougher Cl *RLEIW/BAR* LE9 ....**140** C7
Poulteney Dr *RLBORO* LE12 ....**112** C1
Poulter Cl *NOTTE* NG7 ....**36** B4
Poulton Dr *WBRGFD* NG2 ....**51** K4
The Poultry *NOTT* NG1 ....**5** H7
Powell St *NORM/LIT* DE23 ....**57** J5
Powis St *BLWL* NG6 ....**23** M8
Powtrell Pl *ILK* DE7 ....**47** M1
Powys Av *LEIS* LE2 ....**132** C6
Poynings Av *LEIW* LE3 ....**130** E1
Poynter Cl *HEANOR* DE75 ....**20** A4
Poyser Av *DERBYE* DE21 ....**44** E8
Poyser La *ASHB* DE6 ....**41** L6
Prebend St *LEIS* LE2 ....**7** H3
Premier Rd *NOTTE* NG7 ....**36** E7
Prendwick Gdns *ARN* NG5 ....**24** F7
Prescot Cl *MCKLVR* DE3 ....**56** A6
Presents La *RLBORO* LE12 .....**100** F1
Prestbury Cl *DERBYE* DE21 .....**44** F6
Prestbury Rd *LBORO* LE11 .....**102** F3
Prestbury Rd *LEIE* LE5 ....**126** E6
Preston Cl *GBY/RBY* LE6 ......**123** J7
  RLBORO LE12 ....**114** A5
Preston Ri *LEIE* LE5 ....**127** G6
Prestwich Cl *WOL/BIL/BRX* NG8 ..**35** H5
Prestwold La *RLBORO* LE12 .....**97** G6
Prestwold Rd *LEIE* LE5 ....**126** E7
Prestwood Dr
  WOL/BIL/BRX NG8 ....**35** M4
Pretoria Cl *LEIN* LE4 ....**119** G3
Pretoria Rd *RLEIW/BAR* LE9 ...**129** H1
Previn Gdns
  MAPPK/POR/STA NG3 ....**51** K1
Price Wy *LEIN* LE4 ....**120** D1
Priestland Av *DERBYE* DE21 ....**59** H3
Priestley Rd *LEIW* LE3 ....**130** C3
Priestman Rd *LEIW* LE3 ....**130** A6
Priest Meadow
  RLEIW/BBY LE8 ....**145** K7
Primary Cl *BPR/DUF* DE56 ......**17** L3
Prime Pkwy *DERBY* DE1 ....**3** G1
Primrose Wy *RLEINE/SYS* LE7 ...**121** J1
Primrose Av
  EWD/SEL/PNX NG16 ....**13** K5
Primrose Cl *DERBYE* DE21 ......**44** D4
  END/NAR LE19 ....**135** K2
  MAPPK/POR/STA NG3 ....**5** K2
Primrose Crs *CARL* NG4 ....**38** D8
Primrose Dr *ILK* DE7 ....**31** C7
Primrose Hl *ILK* DE7 ....**33** J4
  LEIS LE2 ....**138** D1
Primrose Ri
  EWD/SEL/PNX NG16 ....**21** L7
Primrose St *CARL* NG4 ....**38** D8
  ILK DE7 ....**33** J4
Primrose Wy *RLEIW/BAR* LE9 ...**129** K1
Primula Cl *CFTN/RUD* NG11 .....**64** A5
Primula Wy *NORM/LIT* DE23 .....**71** H3
Prince Albert Dr *LEIW* LE3 ...**124** A1
Prince Charles Av
  DERBYW DE22 ....**56** C2
Prince Dr *LEIS* LE2 ....**139** C2
Prince Edward Crs
  COT/KEY/RAD NG12 ....**53** H5
Princes Cl *RLEINE/SYS* LE7 ...**124** C1
Princes Dr *NORM/LIT* DE23 .....**56** F5
Princess Av *BSTN/STPLFD* NG9 ...**63** L1
  LEIS LE2 ....**139** C3
Princess Cl *CARL* NG4 ....**38** C5
  HEANOR DE75 ....**20** A6
Princess Dr *BWSH/BRSTN* DE72 ...**59** L6
  LGEAT NG10 ....**61** M3
  RLEIW/BAR LE9 ....**129** H3
Princess Rd Backways *LEI* LE1 ..**6** F8
Princess Rd East *LEI* LE1 ....**7** G9
Princess Rd West *LEI* LE1 ....**6** F8
Princess St *END/NAR* LE19 ....**136** A7
  LBORO LE11 ....**9** J5
  LGEAT NG10 ....**62** B7

Princes St EWD/SEL/PNX NG16 ......21 K4
NORM/LIT DE23 ....57 L6
Prince St COAL LE67 ....108 B7
ILK DE7 ....33 J5
LGEAT NG10 ....62 B7
Prince William Rd LBORO LE11 ....103 L1
Prioridge COT/KEY/RAD NG12 ....67 L5
Prior Rd ARN NG5 ....37 H1
Priors Barn Cl
BWSH/BRSTN DE72 ....60 A5
Priorway Av BWSH/BRSTN DE72...60 A6
Priorway Gdns
BWSH/BRSTN DE72 ....60 A6
Priory Av COT/KEY/RAD NG12 ....66 A6
Priory Circ COT/KEY/RAD NG12 ...66 A6
Priory Cl COAL LE67 ....100 A7
ILK DE7 ....47 G1
MELB/CHEL DE73 ....72 E6
RLEINE/SYS LE7 ....120 D4
Priory Crs CARL NG4 ....38 D6
LEIW LE3 ....130 C2
Priory Gdns DERBYE DE21 ....44 D4
Priory La COAL LE67 ....116 B4
GBY/RBY LE6 ....117 G1
Priory Ms NOTTE NG7 ....50 C5
Priory Rd CARL NG4............38 D6
EWD/SEL/PNX NG16 ....21 K6
HUCK/RAV NG15 ....15 J8
LBORO LE11 ....103 J7
WBRGFD NG2 ....51 L7
Priory St NOTTE NG7 ....50 C5
Priory Wk LEIW LE3 ....129 L4
Pritchard Dr BSTN/STPLFD NG9 ...62 C1
Pritchett Dr NORM/LIT DE23 ....56 C7
Private Rd CALV/BJ NG14 ....26 F2
HUCK/RAV NG15 ....15 J8
MAPPK/POR/STA NG3 ....37 G5
Prize Cl CFTN/RUD NG11 ....64 A6
Progress Wy LEIN LE4 ....126 E4
Promenade
MAPPK/POR/STA NG3 ....5 K3
Prospect Dr BPR/DUF DE56 ....17 K5
Prospect Hl LEIE LE5 ....7 M5
Prospect Pl NOTTE NG7 ....50 D4
Prospect Rd CARL NG4 ....37 L6
HEANOR DE75 ....20 E7
LEIE LE5 ....132 B1
RIPLEY DE5 ....18 E6
RLEIW/BBY LE8 ....146 D1
Prospect St NOTTE NG7 ....50 C1
Providence Pl ILK DE7 ....33 J6
Providence Rd
EWD/SEL/PNX NG16 ....12 E3
Providence St RIPLEY DE5 ....18 F7
Provident St NORM/LIT DE23 ....2 D9
Pryor Rd LBORO LE11 ....114 B3
Pudding Bag La RLBORO LE12 ...101 K7
Pulborough Cl ARN NG5 ....36 D3
Pulborough Gdns
NORM/LIT DE23 ....70 D1
Pulford Dr RLEINE/SYS LE7 ....133 K1
Pullman Rd DERBYE DE21 ....58 D3
WBRGFD NG2 ....51 K3
WGSTN LE18 ....137 M5
Pulteney Av LBORO LE11 ....103 M7
Pulteney Rd LBORO LE11 ....103 M7
Purbeck Av RLBORO LE12 ....102 B4
Purbeck Cl LGEAT NG10 ....61 L7
WGSTN LE18 ....138 B7
Purbeck Dr WBRGFD NG2 ....65 G2
Purcell Rd LEIN LE4 ....125 L7
Purchase Av HEANOR DE75 ....20 A5
Purdy Meadow LGEAT NG10 ....75 K2
Purley Ri RLBORO LE12 ....102 A5
Purley Rd LEIN LE4 ....126 A6
Putney Cl DERBYW DE22 ....56 C2
Putney Rd LEIS LE2 ....131 K5
Putney Rd West LEIS LE2 ....131 J5
Pyatt St WBRGFD NG2 ....51 H6
Pybus St DERBYW DE22 ....57 H1
Pye Hill Rd EWD/SEL/PNX NG16 ..12 E3
Pygall Av CFTN/RUD NG11 ....77 L6
The Pyke RLBORO LE12............113 K6
Pykestone Cl DERBYE DE21 ....44 D5
Pym Leys LGEAT NG10 ....75 K3
Pymm Ley Cl GBY/RBY LE6 ....123 K4
Pymm Ley La GBY/RBY LE6 ....123 K5
Pym St MAPPK/POR/STA NG3 ....51 K1
Pym Wk MAPPK/POR/STA NG3 ....5 M4
Pytchley Cl BPR/DUF DE56 ....18 B3
LEIN LE4 ....125 J7
Pytchley Dr LBORO LE11 ....103 K7

Q

The Quadrangle
HUCK/RAV NG15 ....15 H1
The Quadrant LEIN * LE4 ....125 K5
Quaker Rd RLBORO LE12 ....114 A6
Quantock Cl ARN NG5............24 F5
DERBYSE DE24 ....71 H5
Quantock Ri RLBORO LE12 ....102 A5
Quantock Rd LGEAT NG10 ....61 L6
Quarndon Hts DERBYW DE22 ...43 G5
Quarndon Vw DERBYW DE22 ...43 G5
Quarn Dr DERBYW DE22 ....43 G4
Quarn Gdns DERBY * DE1............43 K8
Quarn St DERBY DE1 ....2 B1
Quarn Wy DERBY DE1 ....2 C1
Quarry Av BLWL NG6 ....35 M1
Quarry Dl HUCK/RAV NG15 ....15 K6
Quarry Hl ILK DE7 ....47 K7
Quarry Hill Rd ILK DE7 ....47 K2
Quarry La END/NAR LE19 ....135 L3
HUCK/RAV NG15 ....15 M3
ILK DE7 ....47 J7
Quay Rd BPR/DUF DE56............17 K5
Quayside Cl WBRGFD NG2 ....51 J6
Quebec Rd LEI LE1 ....7 H4
Queen Elizabeth Wy ILK DE7 ....47 G2
Queen Mary Ct DERBYW DE22 ...43 K8
Queen Mary Rd LEI LE1 ....6 F7
Queen's Av CARL NG4 ....38 C5
HEANOR DE75 ....20 B5
ILK DE7 ....46 A1
ILK DE7 ....47 J7

Queensberry St BLWL NG6............36 C3
Queen's Bower Rd ARN NG5 ....25 G7
Queen's Bridge Rd
WBRGFD NG2 ....51 G4
Queensbury Av WBRGFD NG2...65 H4
Queensbury Cha
NORM/LIT DE23 ....56 E8
Queens Ct BWSH/BRSTN * DE72 ...60 E8
DERBYW * DE22 ....43 J7
Queen's Dr BPR/DUF DE56 ....17 J2
BSTN/STPLFD NG9 ....63 L1
END/NAR LE19 ....136 B5
EWD/SEL/PNX NG16 ....13 J8
EWD/SEL/PNX NG16 ....34 F1
ILK DE7 ....33 J8
LEIS LE2 ....129 L4
LEIW LE3 ....61 M3
LIT DE23 ....57 G5
WBRGFD NG2 ....50 E8
WGSTN LE18 ....137 M5
Queensferry Gdns
DERBYSE DE24 ....72 B3
Queensferry Pde LEIS LE2 ....137 H1
Queensgate Dr LEIN LE4............119 J7
MELB/CHEL DE73 ....72 C7
Queens Gv WBRGFD NG2............51 G4
Queensland Cl MCKLVR DE3 ...56 C3
Queensmead Ct DERBY DE22 ...123 J5
Queens Park Wy LEIS LE2 ....137 H5
Queens Rd BSTN/STPLFD NG9 ...49 M8
CDON/KEG DE74 ....86 B4
COT/KEY/RAD NG12 ....53 K3
LBORO LE11 ....9 L1
LEIS LE2 ....131 M6
RLEIW/BBY LE8 ....136 E8
WBRGFD NG2 ....51 H4
Queens Rd East
BSTN/STPLFD NG9 ....49 M8
Queens Rd North
EWD/SEL/PNX NG16 ....21 K5
Queens Rd South
EWD/SEL/PNX NG16 ....21 K6
Queens Rd West
BSTN/STPLFD NG9 ....63 H3
Queen's Sq
EWD/SEL/PNX NG16 ....21 K5
Queen St ARN NG5 ....21 K6
BPR/DUF DE56 ....17 L4
COAL LE67 ....108 B7
COAL LE67 ....116 B7
DERBY DE1 ....2 E2
EWD/SEL/PNX NG16 ....12 C3
EWD/SEL/PNX NG16 ....21 G4
HUCK/RAV NG15 ....15 K7
ILK DE7 ....33 J7
LBORO LE11 ....9 L4
LEI LE1 ....7 G5
LEIS LE2 ....138 F1
LGEAT NG10 ....62 B8
NOTT NG1 ....5 G6
RIPLEY DE5 ....11 K8
RLBORO LE12 ....102 A3
RLEINE/SYS LE7 ....121 G3
Queensview Dr RIPLEY DE5 ....11 L8
Queen's Wk WBRGFD NG2 ....50 F6
Queensway CDON/KEG DE74...84 D3
DERBYW DE22 ....43 H8
MELB/CHEL DE73 ....82 F7
Quemby Cl LEIN LE4 ....125 L5
Quenby Crs RLEINE/SYS LE7 ...121 G4
Quenby La RIPLEY DE5 ....11 J6
Quenby St LEIE LE5 ....126 B8
Queniborough Rd LEIN LE4 ...126 A6
RLEINE/SYS LE7 ....121 H7
RLEINE/SYS LE7 ....121 J2
Querneby Av
MAPPK/POR/STA NG3 ....37 J5
Querneby Rd
MAPPK/POR/STA NG3 ....37 J5
Quick Cl MELB/CHEL DE73 ....82 E8
Quick Hill Rd DERBYSE DE24 ...71 G5
Quickthorns LEIS LE2 ....132 F8
Quillings Wy BWSH/BRSTN DE72...60 B6
Quiney Wy LEIS LE2 ....139 G1
Quinton Cl LEIN LE4 ....125 L5
Quinton Ri LEIS LE2 ....138 E2
Quorn Av LEIS LE2 ....139 G3
Quorn Cl BSTN/STPLFD NG9 ...63 J4
LBORO LE11 ....9 M7
Quorn Crs COAL LE67 ....108 F7
Quorndon Crs LGEAT NG10 ....76 B2
Quorndon Ri GBY/RBY LE6 ....123 J5
Quorn Gv ARN NG5 ....36 E4
Quorn Pk RLBORO LE12 ....105 M6
Quorn Ri NORM/LIT DE23 ....71 J1
Quorn Rd ARN NG5 ....36 E5
LEIE LE5 ....126 B8

R

Rabown Av NORM/LIT DE23 ....57 H7
Racecourse Rd WBRGFD NG2...51 M3
Radar Rd LEIW LE3 ....130 B2
Radbourne Ga MCKLVR DE3 ...56 B2
Radbourne La ASHB DE6 ....56 A2
DERBYW DE22 ....42 D8
Radbourne Rd MAPPK/POR/STA NG3...51 K4
Radbourne St DERBYW DE22 ...57 G1
Radburn Ct BSTN/STPLFD NG9 ...48 C6
Radcliffe Av DERBYE DE21 ....44 D8
Radcliffe Dr DERBYW DE22 ....57 H4
Radcliffe Gdns CARL NG4 ....38 B7
Radcliffe Mt WBRGFD NG2 ....51 K6
Radcliffe St WBRGFD NG2 ....51 H6
Radcot Lawns LEIS LE2 ....137 H4
Radford Bvd NOTTE NG7 ....50 C1
Radford Bridge Rd
WOL/BIL/BRX NG8............50 A2
Radford Crs CARL NG4 ....38 C5
Radford Dr LEIW LE3 ....130 A4
Radford Grove La NOTTE NG7....50 C1
Radford Rd ILK DE7 ....33 K1
NOTTE NG7 ....4 B1
Radford St DERBYSE DE24 ....58 D8
Radiant Rd LEIE LE5 ....127 G8

NOTTE NG7 ....36 D6
Radley Sq BLWL NG6 ....36 B2
Radmarsh Rd NOTTE NG7 ....50 C4
Rad Mdw LGEAT NG10 ....76 A1
Radmoor Rd LBORO LE11 ....8 F4
Radnor Dr RLBORO LE12 ....101 M2
Radnor Rd WGSTN LE18 ....137 L5
Radstock Rd DERBYE DE21 ....44 C5
Radstone Cl DERBYE DE21 ....44 F5
Radway Dr CFTN/RUD NG11 ...64 E2
Raeburn Dr BSTN/STPLFD NG9 ...62 C5
Raeburn Rd LEIS LE2 ....131 M6
Ragdale Rd BLWL NG6 ....23 M7
LEIN LE4 ....126 B6
Raglan Av DERBYW DE22 ....57 G2
Raglan Ct MAPPK/POR/STA NG3 ...5 J2
Raglan Dr CARL NG4 ....38 F6
Raglan St EWD/SEL/PNX NG16 ...21 L6
Raibank Gdns ARN NG5 ....37 J2
Railway La WGSTN LE18 ....137 K7
Railway Ter DERBY DE1 ....104 A2
Raine Wy LEIS LE2 ....139 H4
Rainham Gdns CFTN/RUD NG11...78 F1
DERBYSE DE24 ....72 E2
Rainier Dr DERBYE DE21 ....58 E1
Rainsford Crs LEIN LE4 ....125 J4
Raithby Cl ARN NG5 ....36 E1
Raleigh Cl CFTN/RUD NG11 ....64 A6
ILK DE7 ....33 K4
Raleigh Sq NOTTE NG7 ....4 C5
Raleigh St DERBYW DE22 ....57 G2
NOTTE NG7 ....4 D5
Ralf Cl WBRGFD NG2 ....65 J3
Ralph Cl LBORO LE11 ....103 H7
Ramblers Cl CARL NG4 ....52 C2
Ramblers Dr DERBYE DE21 ....45 G4
Ramsbury Rd WGSTN LE18 ...137 L2
Ramsdale Crs ARN NG5 ....37 H5
Ramsdale Rd CARL NG4 ....38 C6
Ramsdean Av WGSTN LE18 ...138 A4
Ramsdean Cl DERBYE DE21 ....44 B7
Ramsey Cl BSTN/STPLFD NG9 ...48 C5
Ramsey Dr ARN NG5 ....38 A1
Ramsey Gdns LEIE LE5 ....127 J6
Ramsey Wy LEIE LE5 ....127 G5
Ramshaw Wy DERBYW * DE22 ...2 A6
Ramson Cl LEIE LE5 ....127 G5
Ranby Wk
MAPPK/POR/STA NG3 ....51 K1
Rancliffe Av
COT/KEY/RAD NG12 ....80 B3
Rancliffe Crs LEIW LE3 ....130 E3
Randal Gdns NOTTE NG7 ....4 A1
Randal St NOTTE NG7 ....4 A1
Randles Cl RLEINE/SYS LE7...133 L3
Randolph Rd NORM/LIT DE23 ...57 K7
Ranelagh Gdns DERBYW DE22 ...42 F8
Ranelagh Gv WOL/BIL/BRX NG8 ...49 L2
Rangemore Cl MCKLVR DE3 ...56 C3
Ranmere Rd WOL/BIL/BRX NG8 ...35 L8
Ranmoor Cl BSTN/STPLFD NG9 ...48 F5
Ranmore Cl DERBYE DE21 ....59 K2
Rannerdale Cl WBRGFD NG2 ...66 A1
Rannoch Cl DERBYE DE21 ....59 K2
DERBYW DE22 ....43 J4
LEIN LE4 ....125 G4
Rannoch Ri ARN NG5 ....25 K6
Rannock Gdns
COT/KEY/RAD NG12 ....80 D4
Ranskill Gdns ARN NG5 ....24 E7
Ransom Dr
MAPPK/POR/STA NG3 ....37 J6
Ransom Rd
MAPPK/POR/STA NG3 ....37 J6
Ranson Rd BSTN/STPLFD NG9 ...63 G6
Ranton Wy LEIW LE3 ....125 G7
Ranworth Cl DERBYSE DE24 ...72 B4
Ratby La COAL LE67 ....116 C8
GBY/RBY LE6 ....123 J8
LEIW LE3 ....129 K1
Ratby Meadow La
END/NAR LE19 ....136 C4
Ratby Rd GBY/RBY LE6 ....123 J4
Ratcliffe Cl LEIS LE2 ....132 B7
Ratcliffe Dr RLEIW/BAR LE9 ...135 H4
Ratcliffe La CDON/KEG DE74...75 M8
Ratcliffe Rd LBORO LE11 ....103 M1
LEIS LE2 ....132 A7
RLBORO LE12 ....114 B4
RLEINE/SYS LE7 ....115 K3
Ratcliffe St EWD/SEL/PNX NG16...21 K5
LEIN LE4 ....125 M5
Rathgar Cl WOL/BIL/BRX NG8 ...49 H3
Rathmines Cl NOTTE NG7 ....50 C4
Raven Av ARN NG5 ....36 F3
Raven Cl ALFN DE55 ....12 A1
Ravenhill Cl BSTN/STPLFD NG9 ...62 F3
Ravenhurst Rd LEIW LE3 ....130 D7
Raven Oak Cl BPR/DUF DE56...17 L5
Raven Rd LEIW LE3 ....130 C4
Ravensbridge Dr LEIN LE4 ...125 H7
Ravens Ct LEIS LE2 ....36 F2
Ravenscourt Rd DERBYSE DE22 ...16 K4
Ravenscroft Dr DERBYE DE21 ...58 D1
Ravensdale Av LGEAT NG10 ...61 M5
Ravensdale Dr
WOL/BIL/BRX NG8 ....49 G4
Ravensdale Rd DERBYW DE22...43 G4
Ravensmore Rd ARN NG5 ....36 F5
Ravensthorpe Dr LBORO LE11...102 F5
Ravensthorpe Rd WGSTN LE18...138 B5
Raven St DERBYW DE22 ....2 A7
Ravenswood Rd ARN NG5 ....25 K8
Ravensworth Rd BLWL NG6 ....35 M7
Rawdon Cl CDON/KEG DE74...84 D3
Rawdon St NORM/LIT DE23 ....57 K5
Raw Dykes Rd LEIS LE2 ....131 J5
Rawlings Ct LEIS LE2 ....139 J3
Rawlins Cl RLBORO LE12 ....111 J4
Rawlinson Av NORM/LIT DE23...57 L8
Rawson Gn BPR/DUF DE56 ....18 D6
Rawson St END/NAR LE19 ....135 M4
EWD/SEL/PNX NG16 ....13 L1
LEI LE1 ....6 F8

END/NAR LE19 ....136 A7
EWD/SEL/PNX NG16 ....20 F4
ILK DE7 ....33 K8
LEI LE1 ....7 H8
LEI LE1 ....138 E1
LGEAT NG10 ....62 A2
NOTT NG1 ....4 E7
NOTTE NG7 ....36 E6
RLEINE/SYS LE7 ....115 K3
Regents Wk LEIE LE5 ....129 L4
Regina Cl COT/KEY/RAD NG12 ...53 J5
Reginald Rd North
DERBYE DE21 ....44 D8
Reginald Rd South
DERBYE DE21 ....58 D1
Reginald St NORM/LIT DE23 ....3 G9
Regis Cl DERBYE DE21 ....44 F5
Reid Gdns EWD/SEL/PNX NG16 ...34 F1
Reigate Cl BSTN/STPLFD NG9 ...63 J5
Reigate Dr BSTN/STPLFD NG9 ...63 J5
DERBYW DE22 ....42 D8
Reigate Rd NOTTE NG7 ....36 D5
Rempstone Dr BLWL NG6 ....36 B2
Rempstone Rd RLBORO LE12 ...88 B7
RLBORO LE12 ....95 L1
RLBORO LE12 ....97 L3
Renals St NORM/LIT DE23 ....3 G8
Renals Wy CALV/BJ NG14 ....26 D1
Rendell Rd LEIN LE4 ....125 M6
Rendell St LBORO LE11 ....103 M2
Renfrew Dr WOL/BIL/BRX NG8 ...49 J3
Renfrew Rd LEIE LE5 ....127 J7
Renfrew St DERBYE DE21 ....44 C8
Renishaw Dr LEIE LE5 ....132 C5
Rennie Hogg Rd NOTTE NG7 ...50 D6
Renning End RLBORO LE12 ....113 J7
Repington Rw LEIS LE2 ....137 K2
Repton Av NORM/LIT DE23 ....57 J7
Repton Dr ILK DE7 ....33 M8
Repton Rd BLWL NG6 ....36 B1
LGEAT NG10 ....75 K3
WBRGFD NG2 ....65 J2
WGSTN LE18 ....137 M3
Repton St LEIW LE3 ....6 B3
Reservoir Rd RLEINE/SYS LE7...118 B4
Retford Cl DERBYE DE21 ....44 B5
Retford Rd ARN NG5 ....36 E4
Retlaw Ct BSTN/STPLFD * NG9 ...63 H2
The Retreat LEIE LE5 ....132 D2
RLBORO LE12 ....105 H7
Revell Cl RLBORO LE12 ....112 F1
Revelstoke Av ARN NG5 ....24 B6
Revelstoke Wy ARN NG5 ....24 B6
Revena Cl CARL NG4 ....52 D1
Revesby Gdns
WOL/BIL/BRX NG8 ....36 A8
Revesby Rd ARN NG5 ....37 K2
Revill Cl ILK DE7 ....33 G5
Revill Crs BSTN/STPLFD NG9 ...62 C1
Reydon Dr WOL/BIL/BRX NG8 ...36 B6
Reynolds Av RIPLEY DE5 ....11 K6
Reynolds Dr WOL/BIL/BRX NG8...49 K2
Reynolds Pl LEIW LE3 ....130 C5
Rhyl Crs CARL NG4 ....38 D5
Ribble Av LEIS LE2 ....139 H1
Ribble Dr RLBORO LE12 ....113 H1
Ribblesdale ILK DE7 ....47 G2
Ribblesdale Cl DERBYW DE22 ...43 G5
Ribblesdale Rd ARN NG5 ....37 H2
LGEAT NG10 ....75 L2
Riber Cl ILK DE7 ....32 C7
LGEAT NG10 ....76 B2
Riber Crs ARN NG5 ....36 D2
Richard Cl LEIW LE3 ....130 A4
Richard III Rd LEIW LE3 ....6 B5
Richardson Cl CFTN/RUD NG11...64 A4
RLEIW/BAR LE9 ....140 B6
Richardson Dr ILK DE7 ....31 K1
Richardsons La ALFN DE55 ...12 B2
Richardson St DERBYW DE22...57 H1
Richborough Pl
WOL/BIL/BRX NG8 ....49 H5
Richey Cl ARN NG5 ....25 M8
Richmond Av
BWSH/BRSTN DE72 ....61 L7
EWD/SEL/PNX NG16 ....21 M5
ILK DE7 ....33 K3
LGEAT NG10 ....61 L3
MAPPK/POR/STA NG3 ....37 K8
NORM/LIT DE23 ....57 G7
Richmond Cl ILK DE7 ....32 B7
LEIS LE2 ....131 J7
NORM/LIT DE23 ....56 E8
RLEIW/BAR LE9 ....142 A5
Richmond Dr BPR/DUF DE56...29 J2
BSTN/STPLFD NG9 ....63 J2
COT/KEY/RAD NG12 ....53 K4
LEIS LE2 ....137 J6
MAPPK/POR/STA NG3 ....37 H5
Richmond Gdns ARN NG5 ....25 J4
Richmond Rd DERBYE DE21 ...58 D1
LEIS LE2 ....131 J6
NORM/LIT DE23 ....57 L6
WBRGFD NG2 ....51 L7
Richmond St LEIS LE2 ....6 D8
Richmond Ter
COT/KEY/RAD NG12 ....53 K4
Richmond Wy LEIS LE2 ....139 G4
Rick St NOTT NG1 ....5 J6
Riddings La ASHB DE6 ....40 F5
Riddings St DERBYW DE22 ....2 C7
Ridding Ter
MAPPK/POR/STA NG3 ....5 H4
Riddington Rd END/NAR LE19...142 A1
LEIW LE3 ....130 D8
Ridge La COT/KEY/RAD NG12...53 L2
Ridgemere Cl RLEINE/SYS LE7...121 J4
Ridgemere La RLEINE/SYS LE7...121 J4
The Ridgeway RLEINE/SYS LE7...118 F2
Ridge Wy LEIS LE2 ....138 F4
Ridgeway ARN NG5 ....24 D8
END/NAR LE19 ....142 A1
HEANOR DE75 ....20 D7

MELB/CHEL DE73 ....72 E7
Ridgeway Av NORM/LIT DE23 ....71 G1
Ridgeway Dr ILK DE7 ....46 F2
LEIN LE4 ....126 D1
Ridgeway St
MAPPK/POR/STA NG3 ....5 M3
Ridgewood Ct DERBYE DE21 .....64 C5
Ridgewood Dr
BSTN/STPLFD NG9 ....63 G3
Ridgmont Wk CFTN/RUD NG11 ...64 B7
Ridgway Cl WBRGFD NG2 ....66 A2
Ridgway Rd LEIS LE2 ....132 B2
The Riding LEIN LE4 ....6 A8
Riding Bank MELB/CHEL DE73 ...82 C8
The Ridings BWSH/BRSTN DE72 ..60 A1
CALV/BJ NG14 ....39 L2
COT/KEY/RAD NG12 ....80 E4
RLEINE/SYS LE7 ....112 F8
RLEINE/SYS LE7 ....121 J2
Ridley Cl RLEINE/SYS LE7 ....118 C5
RLEIW/BBY LE8 ....142 E1
Ridley St LEIW LE3 ....6 A8
Ridsdale Rd ARN NG5 ....37 G5
Rifle St NOTTE NG7 ....50 C2
Rigga La BPR/DUF DE56 ....29 L6
Rigley Av ILK DE7 ....33 K6
Rigley Dr ARN NG5 ....24 C8
Rigsby Ct MCKLVR DE3 ....56 A4
Riley Cl RLEIW/BAR LE9 ....140 B6
Riley La RIPLEY DE5 ....10 F1
Rimsdale Cl DERBYSE DE24 ....71 J4
Ringers Cl LEIS LE2 ....132 E7
Ringer's Spinney LEIS LE2 ....132 F7
Ring Fence RLBORO LE12 ....101 M5
Ring Leas COT/KEY/RAD NG12 ...67 K5
Ring Rd LEIS LE2 ....138 B1
Ringstead Cl WBRGFD NG2 ....65 G2
The Ringway RLEINE/SYS LE7 ....121 J1
Ringwood Cl WGSTN LE18 ....138 A4
Ringwood Crs
WOL/BIL/BRX NG8 ....50 A2
Ringwood Rd LEIE LE5 ....127 G5
RLBORO LE12 ....101 M2
Ripley Houses DERBYE * DE21 .....59 J4
Ripley Rd BPR/DUF DE56 ....10 A2
BPR/DUF DE56 ....10 B4
Ripon Crs DERBYSE DE21 ....44 C7
Ripon Dr RLEIW/BBY LE8 ....142 F1
Ripon Rd MAPPK/POR/STA NG3 ..51 M2
Ripon St LEIS LE2 ....132 A4
The Rise ARN NG5 ....37 H4
DERBYW DE22 ....43 J5
END/NAR LE19 ....135 L5
RLEINE/SYS LE7 ....119 L1
Riseborough Wk BLWL NG6 ....23 M6
Risegate COT/KEY/RAD NG12 .....67 K4
Risegate Gdns
COT/KEY/RAD NG12 ....67 K4
Riseholme Av
WOL/BIL/BRX NG8 ....49 G4
Rise Park Rd ARN NG5 ....24 B6
Risley Ct ILK * DE7 ....33 K4
Risley Dr WBRGFD NG2 ....50 F5
Risley La BWSH/BRSTN DE72 .....61 H5
Riste's Pl NOTT NG1 ....5 J7
Riston Cl LEIS LE2 ....138 E4
Ritchie Cl COT/KEY/RAD NG12 ...67 L1
Ritson Cl MAPPK/POR/STA NG3 ...5 K4
Rivenhall Cl NORM/LIT DE23 ......56 D8
Rivergreen CFTN/RUD NG11 ....64 C5
Rivergreen Cl
BSTN/STPLFD * NG9 ....49 G5
Rivergreen Crs
BSTN/STPLFD NG9 ....49 G5
Rivermead COT/KEY/RAD NG12 ...67 K4
WBRGFD * NG2 ....51 H8
River Rd CARL NG4 ....52 C3
Riversdale Cl LEIN LE4 ....119 M8
Riverside Cl DERBYSE DE24 ....3 M6
END/NAR * LE19 ....136 A7
Riverside Dr LEIS LE2 ....136 F1
Riverside Rd BSTN/STPLFD NG9 ..63 L3
DERBYSE DE24 ....3 M6
Riverside Wy END/NAR LE19 .....136 A8
WBRGFD NG2 ....50 F6
Rivers St LEIW LE3 ....6 B5
River St DERBY DE1 ....2 E1
River Vw BPR/DUF DE56 ....17 K8
RLBORO LE12 ....113 J1
WBRGFD NG2 ....51 H6
Rivets Meadow Cl LEIW LE3 ......130 B6
Rivington Dr LBORO LE11 ....102 F5
Rivington St BSTN/STPLFD NG9 ..62 C5
Road No 1 CARL NG4 ....52 D2
Road No 2 CARL NG4 ....52 D2
Road No 3 CARL NG4 ....52 E2
Road No 4 CARL NG4 ....53 G3
Road No 5 CARL NG4 ....52 F2
Road No 7 CARL NG4 ....52 D1
Road No 8 CARL NG4 ....52 D2
Robbie Burns Rd ARN NG5 ....25 G7
Robert Hall St LEIN LE4 ....125 K4
Robert Hardy Whf
LBORO LE11 ....104 B3
Robertsbridge Av LEIN LE4 ....125 J4
Roberts Cl CDON/KEG DE74 ....86 A6
Robert's La HUCK/RAV NG15 ....15 J8
Robertson Cl RLEIW/BAR LE9 ....140 B5
Roberts Rd LEIN LE4 ....125 L6
Roberts St ILK DE7 ....47 L1
WBRGFD NG2 ....5 M7
Robert St DERBY DE1 ....3 G2
Robey Cl HUCK/RAV NG15 ....15 M6
Robey Dr EWD/SEL/PNX NG16 ....21 K4
Robey Ter NOTTE NG7 ....4 A1
Robina Dr EWD/SEL/PNX NG16 ...21 M7
Robin Cl LEIS LE2 ....131 J1
Robin Croft Rd DERBYW DE22 .....43 J4
Robinet Rd BSTN/STPLFD NG9 ...63 K2
Robinettes La
EWD/SEL/PNX NG16 ....34 B6
Robin Hood Cha
MAPPK/POR/STA NG3 ....5 K3
Robin Hood Cl
EWD/SEL/PNX NG16 ....21 K6
Robin Hood Dr HUCK/RAV NG15 ..23 J3
Robin Hood Rd ARN NG5 ....25 G7
Robin Hood St
MAPPK/POR/STA NG3 ....5 L6
Robin Hood Ter
MAPPK/POR/STA NG3 ....5 K5
Robin Hood Wy BLWL NG6 ....24 C5
BSTN/STPLFD NG9 ....48 E5
EWD/SEL/PNX NG16 ....34 D2
HUCK/RAV NG15 ....24 A4
NOTT NG1 ....4 F9
WBRGFD NG2 ....50 F6
Robinia Cl DERBYE DE21 ....45 G4
Robincia Cl WBRGFD NG2 ....65 L2
Robin Ms LBORO LE11 ....8 D7
Robin Rd COAL LE67 ....108 D7
DERBYE DE22 ....43 K8
Robinscross BWSH/BRSTN DE72 .59 M6
Robinson Gdns CFTN/RUD NG11 ..64 A4
LEIS LE5 ....132 C1
MAPPK/POR/STA NG3 ....37 K4
Robin's Wood Rd
WOL/BIL/BRX NG8 ....35 M8
Roborough Gn LEIE LE5 ....133 J1
Robotham Cl END/NAR LE19 .....135 M8
RLEIW/BAR LE9 ....135 H8
Rob Roy Av NOTTE NG7 ....4 A9
Robson Cl DERBYSE DE24 ....58 E3
Roby Lea CDON/KEG DE74 ....84 D3
Rochdale Crs COAL LE67 ....109 H6
Roche Cl ARN NG5 ....38 A1
LEIS LE5 ....137 G3
Rochester Av CARL NG4 ....38 E8
Rochester Cl DERBYSE DE21 ....72 E2
LGEAT NG10 ....61 L8
RLBORO LE12 ....113 G7
RLEIW/BBY LE8 ....146 D5
Rochester Ct
EWD/SEL/PNX NG16 ....35 K1
Rochester Wk CFTN/RUD NG11 ..64 D6
Rochford Ct
COT/KEY/RAD NG12 ....66 A3
Rochley Cl DERBYE DE21 ....44 C7
Rockbourne Cl DERBYSE DE24 ...73 H1
Rockbridge Rd LEIS LE2 ....139 H3
Rock Ct BLWL NG6 ....36 B4
Rocket Cl EWD/SEL/PNX NG16 ..22 E8
The Rockety DERBYE DE21 ....30 C3
Rockford Ct BSTN/STPLFD NG9 ..48 C6
Rockford Rd ARN NG5 ....36 D4
Rockhill Dr RLBORO LE12 ....113 H7
Rockhouse Rd DERBYSE DE24 ....72 E1
Rockingham Cl DERBYE DE22 .....43 L3
LEIE LE5 ....132 F1
RLBORO LE12 ....101 L3
RLEIW/BBY LE8 ....142 F1
Rockingham Rd LBORO LE11 .....103 J1
LEIE LE5 ....132 F1
RLBORO LE12 ....113 G7
Rockland Ri COAL LE67 ....108 D1
Rockley Av COT/KEY/RAD NG12 ..53 K3
EWD/SEL/PNX NG16 ....21 K6
Rockley Cl HUCK/RAV NG15 ....23 C1
Rockley Rd LEIN LE4 ....125 G6
Rock St BLWL NG6 ....23 M7
Rockwood Crs HUCK/RAV NG15 ..23 H1
Rockwood Wk HUCK/RAV NG15 ..23 J1
Rodel Ct MAPPK/POR/STA NG3 ...5 J4
Roden St MAPPK/POR/STA NG3 ...5 K4
Rodney Cl RDERBYSW DE65 ......68 C5
Rodney Rd WBRGFD NG2 ....65 L1
Rodney Wy LEIE LE5 ....33 K3
Rodsley Crs NORM/LIT DE23 ......71 K2
Rodwell Cl WOL/BIL/BRX NG8 ...49 M1
Roebuck Cl ARN NG5 ....24 F6
RLEIW/BBY LE8 ....142 D2
Roecliff Cl COAL LE67 ....116 C7
Roecliffe WBRGFD NG2 ....65 J3
Roecliffe Rd RLBORO LE12 ....117 L2
Roe Farm La DERBYE DE21 ....44 C8
Roehampton Dr
BSTN/STPLFD NG9 ....48 B5
DERBYW DE22 ....42 E8
WGSTN LE18 ....137 M2
Roe Hl CALV/BJ NG14 ....27 C2
Roe La CALV/BJ NG14 ....27 C3
Roesta Cl DERBYSE DE24 ....100 F1
Roe Wk NORM/LIT DE23 ....57 L5
Rogerstone Rd LEIS LE2 ....133 H3
Roker Cl WOL/BIL/BRX NG8 ....35 L6
Roland Av CFTN/RUD NG11 ....50 F8
EWD/SEL/PNX NG16 ....35 J3
Rolleston Cl HUCK/RAV NG15 .....23 H7
Rolleston Crs
EWD/SEL/PNX NG16 ....22 D6
Rolleston Dr ARN NG5 ....25 L8
EWD/SEL/PNX NG16 ....21 L7
NOTTE NG7 ....4 B8
Rolleston Rd WGSTN LE18 ....137 M4
Rolleston St LEIE LE5 ....132 B1
Roman Cl RLEIW/BAR LE9 ....128 A4
Roman Dr BLWL NG6 ....36 C3
Roman Hl WGSTN LE18 ....138 C7
Roman Rd DERBY DE1 ....43 M8
LEIN LE4 ....125 L2
The Romans RLBORO LE12 ....113 J6
Romans Cl BLWL NG6 ....36 C5
Romans Crs COAL LE67 ....109 H6
Roman St LEIW LE3 ....6 A8
Roman Wy BWSH/BRSTN DE72 ..60 A6
RLEINE/SYS LE7 ....120 C5
Romilay Cl BSTN/STPLFD NG9 ...49 L6
Romney Av WOL/BIL/BRX NG8 ...49 H5
Romsley Cl MCKLVR DE3 ....56 B4
Romway Av LEIE LE5 ....132 C5
Romway Rd LEIE LE5 ....132 C5
Rona Cl DERBYSE DE24 ....71 J3
Rona Gdns LEIE LE5 ....127 J8
Ronald St BLWL NG6 ....36 C1
Ronald St NOTTE NG7 ....4 B5
Ronald West Ct LBORO LE11 ....8 B9
The Roods RLEINE/SYS LE7 ....119 J1
The Rookery RLBORO LE12 ....105 C7
Rookery Cl GBY/RBY LE6 ....123 J4
Rookery La RLEIW/BBY LE8 ....146 F7
Rookery Gdns ARN NG5 ....25 K7
Rookery La GBY/RBY LE6 ....123 J4
LEIN LE4 ....126 B1
Rookwood Cl
BSTN/STPLFD * NG9 ....63 J1
Roosa Cl BLWL NG6 ....35 K1
Roosevelt Av DERBYSE DE21 ......58 F1
LGEAT NG10 ....76 A2
Roper Av HEANOR DE75 ....20 D7
Ropewalk CDON/KEG DE74 ....86 A5
Rope Wk RLBORO LE12 ....88 B6
Ropewalk St NOTT * NG1 ....4 E6
Ropsley Crs WBRGFD NG2 ....51 L6
Rosamond's Ride
NORM/LIT DE23 ....57 H7
Rosamund Av LEIE LE3 ....130 E7
Roscoe Av ARN NG5 ....25 J5
Roseacre DERBYE DE21 ....73 H1
Rose Acre Cl LEIE LE5 ....127 K8
Rose Ash La ARN NG5 ....24 F7
Rose Av BWSH/BRSTN DE72 ......60 A6
ILK DE7 ....33 J5
Rosebank DERBYSE DE24 ....25 M6
Rosebank Rd RLEIW/BBY LE8 ...143 K3
Rosebarn Wy LEIE LE5 ....127 H6
Roseberry Ct DERBYE DE21 ....44 F6
Roseberry Gdns
HUCK/RAV NG15 ....24 A1
Rosebery Av RLEIW/BBY LE8 .....146 D7
WBRGFD NG2 ....51 J6
Rosebery Rd RLEINE/SYS LE7 ...118 C3
Rosebery St BLWL NG6 ....36 C3
LBORO LE11 ....8 E2
LEIE LE5 ....132 B1
Rose Cl MAPPK/POR/STA NG3 ....5 J1
Rose Crs LEIW LE3 ....129 K5
Rosecroft Dr ARN NG5 ....37 G1
Rosedale COAL LE67 ....108 C1
Rosedale Av DERBYSE DE24 ....72 E1
LEIN LE4 ....126 B5
Rosedale Cl LGEAT NG10 ....75 M1
LEIN LE4 ....126 B5
Rosedale Dr WOL/BIL/BRX NG8 ..48 F3
Rosedale Rd
MAPPK/POR/STA NG3 ....52 A1
WGSTN LE18 ....138 D5
Rosedene Av LEIN LE4 ....126 C1
Rosedene Cl RLEIW/BAR LE9 ....129 K3
Rose Farm Cl LEIN LE4 ....130 D3
Rosegarth Wk BLWL NG6 ....36 B3
Rose Gv DERBYSE DE24 ....63 M2
COT/KEY/RAD NG12 ....80 D3
Rosegrove Av ARN NG5 ....25 K6
Roseheath Cl NORM/LIT DE23 ....71 J2
Rose Hl COT/KEY/RAD NG12 ......80 C4
Rosehill LBORO LE11 ....103 G3
Rose Hill St NORM/LIT DE23 ....2 F1
Roseland Cl COT/KEY/RAD NG12 .80 B5
Roseleigh Av
MAPPK/POR/STA NG3 ....37 M5
Rosemary Cl WOL/BIL/BRX NG8 ..35 J6
Rosemary Crs COAL LE67 ....108 C3
Rosemary Dr DERBYSE DE24 ......72 E2
Rosemead Dr LEIS LE2 ....138 E3
Rosemoor La DERBYE DE21 ....44 F6
Rosemount Ct DERBYW DE22 ....43 C4
Roseneath Av ARN NG5 ....24 C6
LEIN LE4 ....126 C5
Rosengrave St DERBY DE1 ....2 D6
Rose Rd LEIN LE4 ....125 K5
Rose Tree Av LEIN LE4 ....119 L7
Rosetta Rd NOTTE NG7 ....36 D6
Rosette Ct DERBYE DE21 ....45 G4
Rosewall St ARN NG5 ....25 M8
Roseway LEIN LE4 ....126 B4
Rosewood Cl DERBYSE DE24 ......59 C8
Rosewood Crs HEANOR DE75 .....20 F5
Rosewood Gdns WBRGFD NG2 ...65 G4
Rosewood Wy LBORO LE11 ....9 C8
Roslyn Av CARL NG4 ....38 C6
Roslyn St LEIS LE2 ....72 M8
Rosminian Wy RLBORO LE12 ....114 G3
Rossell Dr BSTN/STPLFD NG9 ....62 C2
Rossendale ILK DE7 ....33 J3
Rossett Cl WBRGFD NG2 ....66 B1
Rossett Dr LEIN LE4 ....125 H5
Rossetti Rd END/NAR LE19 ....135 L4
Rosshill Crs LEIE LE5 ....127 J8
Rossington Dr NORM/LIT DE23 ...70 D1
Rossington Rd WBRGFD NG2 .....51 K2
Ross La CARL NG4 ....27 G8
Rosslyn Av RLBORO LE12 ....113 G6
Rosslyn Dr WOL/BIL/BRX NG8 ...35 L5
Rosslyn Gdns DERBYSE DE24 ....72 E1
Ross Wk LEIN LE4 ....125 L6
LEIN LE4 ....125 L7
Rosthwaite Cl WBRGFD NG2 ......66 A2
Rothbury Av BSTN/STPLFD NG9 ..48 B5
Rothbury Pl DERBYE DE21 ....44 C6
Rotherby Av LEIN LE4 ....126 B6
Rothesay Av NOTTE NG7 ....4 A6
Rothesay Cl DERBYSE DE24 ....71 J3
Rothley Av
MAPPK/POR/STA NG3 ....51 K2
Rothley Rd RLBORO LE12 ....113 J5
Rothley St LEIN LE4 ....125 L6
Rothwell Cl CFTN/RUD NG11 .....64 E3
Rothwell La BPR/DUF DE56 ....17 M3
Rothwell Rd MCKLVR DE3 ....56 B4
Rough Heanor Rd MCKLVR DE3 ..57 J2
Roughs Wood La
HUCK/RAV NG15 ....23 H3
Roughton Cl MCKLVR DE3 ....56 B7
Roulstone Crs RLBORO LE12 ......88 C4
Roundhill RLEIW/BAR LE9 ....129 J3
Roundhay RLEIW/BAR LE9 ....129 J3
Roundhill Rd LEIE LE5 ....132 B4
Roundhill Wy RLEINE/SYS LE7 ...120 D5
Roundhouse Rd DERBYSE DE24 ...3 K6
The Roundway LEIN LE4 ....126 B6
Roundwood Rd ARN NG5 ....25 G8
Routh Av CDON/KEG DE74 ....84 F5
Rowan Av BSTN/STPLFD NG9 .....48 C6
COAL LE67 ....108 F7
RIPLEY DE5 ....11 H7
RLBORO LE12 ....94 E5
Rowanberry Av LEIW LE3 ....130 A1
Rowan Cl DERBYSE DE21 ....58 F2
DERBYSE DE24 ....71 H4
ILK DE7 ....47 K2
Rowan Ct EWD/SEL/PNX NG16 ..34 F1
Rowan Dr BPR/DUF DE56 ....18 F7
CFTN/RUD NG11 ....64 E5
COT/KEY/RAD NG12 ....80 E5
EWD/SEL/PNX NG16 ....13 H1
Rowan Gdns BLWL NG6 ....23 K8
Rowan Park NORM/LIT DE23 ......57 H8
The Rowans RLEIW/BBY LE8 ....143 J3
Rowan St LEIE LE3 ....131 G1
Rowbank Wy RLEINE/SYS LE7 ...102 F4
Rowditch Av DERBYW DE22 ....57 H4
Rowditch Pl DERBYW DE22 ....57 H3
Rowe Gdns BLWL NG6 ....36 B5
Rowe Leyes Furlong
RLBORO LE12 ....113 K6
Rowena Cl DERBYSE DE24 ....58 D8
Rowena Ct RLBORO LE12 ....113 J7
Rowland Av
MAPPK/POR/STA NG3 ....37 L5
Rowland Ms
MAPPK/POR/STA NG3 ....5 L2
Rowland St DERBYSE DE24 ....72 C1
Rowlanson Cl LEIW LE4 ....119 H6
Rowlatts Hill Rd LEIE LE5 ....132 C1
Rowley Fields Av LEIW LE3 ....130 F6
Rowley Gdns NORM/LIT DE23 ....57 C8
Rowley La NORM/LIT DE23 ....57 C8
Rowsley Av LEIE LE5 ....132 B3
NORM/LIT DE23 ....57 H7
Rowsley St LEIE LE5 ....132 B3
Roxburgh Av DERBYE DE21 ....44 C8
Roxton Ct EWD/SEL/PNX NG16 ..22 D2
Royal Ap MELB/CHEL DE73 ....72 D7
Royal Av LGEAT NG10 ....62 B6
Royal Cl BWSH/BRSTN DE72 .....59 M6
Royal Ct END/NAR * LE19 ....136 A7
Royal Ga BPR/DUF DE56 ....18 B4
Royal Gv DERBYE DE21 ....45 H4
Royal Hill Rd DERBYE DE21 ....59 H1
Royal Ms BSTN/STPLFD NG9 .....63 G4
Royal Rd LEIN LE4 ....125 M5
Royal Wy DERBYSE DE24 ....58 C4
Roy Av DERBYSE DE24 ....63 M3
LBORO LE11 ....103 L1
Royce Av HUCK/RAV NG15 ....23 K8
Royce Cl LEIW LE3 ....130 A5
Roy Cl END/NAR LE19 ....136 A7
Roydale Cl LBORO LE11 ....103 J1
Roydene Crs LEIN LE4 ....125 G6
Roydon Cl MCKLVR DE3 ....56 A3
Royland Rd LBORO LE11 ....9 H5
Royston Cl LEIS LE2 ....137 G5
WBRGFD * NG2 ....50 F6
Royston Dr BPR/DUF DE56 ....18 B2
Ruby Paddocks
EWD/SEL/PNX NG16 ....34 D2
Ruby St LEIN LE4 ....125 M4
Ruddington La CFTN/RUD NG11 ..64 F2
Rudge Cl WOL/BIL/BRX NG8 ......49 K2
Ruding Rd LEIW LE3 ....6 B8
Ruding St LEI * LE1 ....6 C5
Rudyard Av DERBYE DE21 ....59 J3
Rudyard Cl LBORO LE11 ....102 F5
Ruffles Av
MAPPK/POR/STA NG3 ....37 M2
Rufford Av BSTN/STPLFD NG9 ....48 E7
CARL NG4 ....38 B5
Rufford Cl HUCK/RAV NG15 ....24 A1
LBORO LE11 ....102 F2
Rufford Rd ARN NG5 ....37 G4
CFTN/RUD NG11 ....65 H8
LGEAT NG10 ....75 M3
Rufford St LEIE LE5 ....132 C1
Rufford Wy WBRGFD NG2 ....65 H1
Ruffs Dr HUCK/RAV NG15 ....23 J7
Ruffstone Cl BPR/DUF DE56 ....18 A8
Rugby Cl BPR/DUF DE56 ....24 C8
Rugby Rd WBRGFD NG2 ....65 G2
Rugby St LEIW LE3 ....6 B2
Rugby Ter NOTTE NG7 ....4 A1
Ruislip Cl EWD/SEL/PNX NG16 ..22 C6
Rumsey Cl COAL LE67 ....100 A7
RLBORO LE12 ....112 C1
Rumsey Dr RLEIW/BBY LE8 ......136 D7
Runcie Cl COT/KEY/RAD NG12 ...67 K5
Runcorn Cl LEIS LE2 ....137 G4
Runcorn Rd LEIS LE2 ....137 H4
Runnymede Ct NOTTE NG7 ....4 D5
Runswick Dr ARN NG5 ....25 K7
WOL/BIL/BRX NG8 ....49 C3
Runton Dr BLWL NG6 ....36 D3
Rupert Brooke Rd LBORO LE11 ...8 A7
Rupert Crs RLEINE/SYS LE7 ......121 J1
Rupert Law RLBORO LE12 ....104 D3
Rupert Rd DERBYE DE21 ....44 E8
Rupert St ILK DE7 ....33 K6
LEI LE1 ....6 E6
Rupert Wy RLEIW/BBY LE8 ....139 M2
Ruscombe Pl
MAPPK/POR/STA NG3 ....5 J3
Rushcliffe Av CARL NG4 ....38 B7
COT/KEY/RAD NG12 ....53 K4
DERBYE DE21 ....58 D1
Rushcliffe Ct BLWL NG6 ....36 B1
Rushcliffe Gdns DERBYE DE21 ...58 D1
Rushcliffe Gv RLBORO LE12 ....88 C3
Rushcliffe Ri ARN NG5 ....37 H5
Rushcliffe Rd HUCK/RAV NG15 ...23 J3
Rushdale Av NORM/LIT DE23 .....71 H4
The Rushes CFTN/RUD NG11 .....77 M6
COAL LE67 ....116 C6
LBORO LE11 ....8 E7
Rushey Cl LEIN LE4 ....126 A3
Rushey La RLEINE/SYS LE7 ......112 F5
Rushford Cl LEIN LE4 ....126 B6
Rushford Dr LEIN LE4 ....126 B6
WOL/BIL/BRX NG8 ....49 C3
Rush Leys LGEAT NG10 ....76 B2
Rushmere Wk LEIW LE3 ....129 L5
Rushton Dr LEIS LE2 ....136 F3
Rushton Gdns
MAPPK/POR/STA NG3 ....5 M2
Rushup Cl DERBYW DE22 ....43 L2
Rushworth Av WBRGFD NG2 ......51 J7
Rushworth Cl
MAPPK/POR/STA NG3 ....5 M2
Rushy Cl WOL/BIL/BRX NG8 ....49 H2
Rushy La LGEAT NG10 ....61 K2
Ruskin Av BSTN/STPLFD NG9 ....63 H3
LGEAT NG10 ....75 M2
RLEINE/SYS LE7 ....121 G5
Ruskington Dr WGSTN LE18 ......138 B2
Ruskin Rd DERBYW DE22 ....43 K8
Ruskin St NOTTE NG7 ....50 C2
Ruskin Wy NORM/LIT DE23 ....56 F7
Russ Cl RLBORO LE12 ....104 D8
Russell Av WOL/BIL/BRX NG8 ....49 K2
Russell Crs WOL/BIL/BRX NG8 ...49 K2
Russell Dr WOL/BIL/BRX NG8 ....49 K2
Russell Gdns BSTN/STPLFD NG9 .63 G5
Russell Rd NOTTE NG7 ....36 D7
Russell Sq LEI LE1 ....7 G2
Russell St DERBYSE DE24 ....58 A6
LBORO LE11 ....9 L3
LGEAT NG10 ....62 B6
NOTTE NG7 ....4 C4
Russell Yd MELB/CHEL * DE73 ...82 B8
Russet Av CARL NG4 ....38 D8
Russet Cl DERBYE DE21 ....44 F6
Russet Wy RLEINE/SYS LE7 ......120 A6
Russley Rd BSTN/STPLFD NG9 ...48 E7
Ruth Dr ARN NG5 ....25 L5
Rutherford Ri DERBYE DE21 ....44 D5
Rutherford Rd LEIN LE4 ....124 E3
Ruthwell Gdns ARN NG5 ....24 E5
Ruthwell Av BSTN/STPLFD NG9 ..62 E5
BWSH/BRSTN DE72 ....60 A5
LEIS LE2 ....131 J6
RIPLEY DE5 ....11 K8
WGSTN LE18 ....137 M4
Rutland Dr LEIW LE3 ....129 L4
MCKLVR DE3 ....56 B4
Rutland Gv LGEAT NG10 ....62 A2
Rutland Rd CARL NG4 ....38 B4
EWD/SEL/PNX NG16 ....21 K6
WBRGFD NG2 ....51 L8
Rutland St ILK DE7 ....33 K6
LBORO LE11 ....9 H4
LEI LE1 ....7 H4
NORM/LIT DE23 ....57 L6
NOTT NG1 ....4 F8
Rutland Ter ILK DE7 ....33 K5
Ryal Cl BWSH/BRSTN DE72 ....60 A2
Ryan Cl DERBYSE DE24 ....71 J4
Rycroft Rd CDON/KEG DE74 ....75 H8
Rydal Av LBORO LE11 ....8 A8
LGEAT NG10 ....61 M5
Rydal Cl DERBYW DE22 ....43 J3
Rydal Dr BSTN/STPLFD NG9 ......49 H7
HUCK/RAV NG15 ....37 G2
Rydal Gv BLWL NG6 ....36 C4
Rydal St LEIS LE2 ....6 C9
Ryde Av LEIS LE2 ....132 B8
Ryde Houses DERBYSE * DE24 ...59 K8
Ryder Rd LEIW LE3 ....130 A1
Rye Butts MELB/CHEL DE73 ....72 C6
Rye Cl DERBYE DE21 ....44 C4
LEIS LE2 ....125 J4
Ryecroft St BSTN/STPLFD NG9 ..48 C7
Ryedale Gdns NORM/LIT DE23 ...74 E3
Ryegate Crs LEIN LE4 ....119 K7
Ryegrass Cl BPR/DUF DE56 ....18 B4
Ryegrass Rd LEIS LE2 ....45 C5
Ryehill Cl WBRGFD NG2 ....51 H5
Ryehill St WBRGFD NG2 ....51 H5
Ryeholm Cl RLBORO LE12 ....88 D4
Ryeland Gdns WBRGFD NG2 ......65 J1
Ryemere Cl EWD/SEL/PNX NG16 ..21 J3
Rye St NOTTE NG7 ....36 D6
Rykneld Cl NORM/LIT DE23 ....70 C1
Rykneld Dr NORM/LIT DE23 ....56 C8
Rykneld Rd NORM/LIT DE23 ......70 C1
Rykneld Wy NORM/LIT DE23 ....70 C1
Rykneld Hl RIPLEY DE5 ....18 F5
Rykneld Rd BPR/DUF DE56 ....18 F8
Rylands Cl BSTN/STPLFD NG9 ...63 M3
Rymill Dr DERBYE DE21 ....44 D6
Ryton Sq WOL/BIL/BRX NG8 ......54 B7
Ryton Wy RDERBYSW DE65 ....68 B7

S

Sacheveral St DERBY * DE1 ....2 F6
Sacheverell Wy GBY/RBY LE6 ....123 J6
Sacheverel St DERBY DE1 ....2 F6
Sackville Gdns LEIS LE2 ....132 A7
Sackville St NORM/LIT DE23 ....57 K7
Saddington Rd RLEIW/BBY LE8 ..145 J3
Saddlers Cl LBORO * LE11 ....103 K1
LEIW LE3 ....123 M7
RLEINE/SYS LE7 ....115 H8
Saddlers Yd COT/KEY/RAD NG12 ..66 C8
Sadler Ga DERBY DE1 ....2 E3
Sadlers Wls RLBORO LE12 ....100 F1
Saffron Dr DERBYE DE21 ....44 E6
Saffron Gdns WBRGFD NG2 ....50 F5
Saffron Hill Rd LEIS LE2 ....131 J7
Saffron La LEIS LE2 ....131 J6
Saffron Rd WGSTN LE18 ....137 J4
Saffron St LEIS LE2 ....137 J1
Sage Rd LEIS LE2 ....6 B8
St Agnes Av DERBYW DE22 ....43 H3
St Aidan's Av RLEINE/SYS LE7 ...120 C5
St Albans Cl LGEAT NG10 ....76 C4
St Albans Ms BLWL NG6 ....36 H1
St Albans Rd ARN NG5 ....25 H8
BLWL NG6 ....24 B8
BLWL NG6 ....24 C4
DERBYW DE22 ....57 C4
LEIS LE2 ....7 K9

St Albans St *ARN* NG5 ....37 G4
St Alkmund's Cl *BPR/DUF* DE56 ..29 J3
St Alkmunds Wy *BPR/DUF* DE56....29 J3
DERBY DE1 ....2 F2
St Andrew Cl *CFTN/RUD* NG11....77 M6
St Andrews Cl *BLWL* NG6 ....24 A8
COAL LE67 ....100 B7
RLBORO LE12 ....97 L8
St Andrew's Dr *ILK* DE7 ....33 J7
LEIS LE2 ....132 C6
St Andrew's Ri *CDON/KEG* DE74....86 A6
St Andrews Rd *LEIS* LE2 ....131 J8
NOTT NG1 ....4 F1
St Andrews Vw *DERBYE* DE21....44 C7
St Anne Dr *LEIS* LE2 ....137 H1
St Annes Cl *DERBY* DE1....2 B1
RLEINE/SYS LE7....121 G5
St Anne's La *CDON/KEG* DE74....84 F4
RLBORO LE12....94 F1
St Ann's HI *MAPPK/POR/STA* NG3 ...5 H1
St Ann's Hill Rd
MAPPK/POR/STA NG3 ....5 H5
St Ann's St *NOTT* NG1 ....5 H5
St Ann's Va
MAPPK/POR/STA NG3 ....5 L3
St Ann's Wy
MAPPK/POR/STA NG3 ....5 G3
St Ann's Well Rd
MAPPK/POR/STA NG3 ....5 J5
St Anthonys Ct *NOTTE* NG7....50 C5
St Augustine Rd *LEIW* LE3....6 A6
St Augustines Cl *NOTTE* NG7....36 E6
St Augustine St *NORM/LIT* DE23....57 K6
St Austell Dr *CFTN/RUD* NG11....64 F2
St Austell Rd *LEIE* LE5 ....127 J8
St Austins Ct *CARL* NG4....38 D7
St Austins Dr *CARL* NG4....38 D7
St Barnabas Rd *LEIE* LE5....132 B1
St Bartholomew's Rd
MAPPK/POR/STA NG3 ....37 K8
St Bernards Av *LEIE* LE5....125 M4
St Bernard's Cl *RLBORO* LE12....101 L5
St Bernard's Rd *COAL* LE67....108 C3
St Bernard St *LEIN* LE1 ....125 M5
St Botolph Rd *RLBORO* LE12....101 M4
St Bride's Wk *DERBYW* DE22....56 F1
Saintbury Rd *LEIW* LE3....124 B6
St Catherines St
COT/KEY/RAD NG12 ....53 J5
St Cecilia Gdns
MAPPK/POR/STA NG3 ....5 J3
St Chad's Rd
MAPPK/POR/STA NG3 ....5 M6
NORM/LIT DE23 ....57 K3
St Christopher St *WBRGFD* NG2....51 K3
St Clare's Cl *NORM/LIT* DE23 ....6 A6
St Clares Ct *COAL* LE67....108 B7
St Columba Wy
RLEINE/SYS LE7....120 D3
St Crispin's Wy *RLEINE/SYS* LE7....120 C6
St Cuthbert's Av
RLEINE/BBY LE8....139 M7
St Cuthbert's Rd *DERBYW* DE22....57 G4
MAPPK/POR/STA NG3 ....5 M5
St David's Cl *DERBYW* DE22....57 H4
LEIS LE2 ....132 C6
LEIW LE3 ....129 K5
St Davids Ct *COAL* LE67....109 G6
St David's Crs *COAL* LE67....109 G5
St Davids Rd *LEIW* LE3....130 A1
St Denys Rd *LEIE* LE5 ....132 F3
St Dunstan Rd *LEIW* LE3....131 G1
St Edmund's Cl *DERBYW* DE22....43 K3
St Edward's Rd
CDON/KEG DE74 ....84 F5
St Ervan Rd *CFTN/RUD* NG11....64 F1
St Faiths Rd *COAL* LE67....108 A4
St George's Dr *WBRGFD* NG2....50 F5
St George's Pl *BPR/DUF* DE56....17 K3
St George St *LEI* LE1 ....7 H6
St Georges Wy *LEI* LE1 ....7 G7
St Giles Rd *NORM/LIT* DE23....57 K6
St Gregory's Dr *RLBORO* LE12....114 A4
St Helens Crs
BSTN/STPLFD NG9....48 A3
CALV/BJ NG14....39 K3
St Helens Dr *LEIN* LE4....125 H7
St Helen's Gv *LEIW* LE3....125 H7
St Helen's Rd *WBRGFD* NG2....65 K1
St Helen's St *DERBY* DE1....2 D2
NOTTE NG7 ....4 D6
St Hildas Cl *RLEINE/SYS* LE7....121 G5
St Hugh's Cl *DERBYW* DE22....43 K5
St Ives *COAL* LE67....108 F7
St Ives Rd *LEIN* LE4....126 C5
WGSTN LE18 ....138 A6
St James Av *ILK* DE7 ....33 L8
St James Chambers *DERBY* * DE1 ...2 E3
St James Cl *BPR/DUF* DE56....18 B3
LEIS LE2 ....139 G4
RLBORO LE12....101 M5
RLEINE/BAR LE9....135 H8
St James' Dr
EWD/SEL/PNX NG16....13 J7
St James Rd *LEIS* LE2....132 A4
NORM/LIT DE23 ....57 K6
RLBORO LE12....101 M4
DERBY DE1 ....2 E4
NOTT * NG1 ....4 F8
St James's Ter *NOTT* NG1 ....4 F8
St James St *DERBY* * DE1 ....2 E4
LEI LE1 ....7 G4
NORM/LIT DE23 ....57 L6
St Johns *END/NAR* LE19....136 C5
St John's Av *DERBYE* DE21....58 F2
RLEINE/SYS LE7....121 G5
St John's Dr *BPR/DUF* DE56....18 E7
St John's Rd *BPR/DUF* DE56....18 F7
CFTN/RUD NG11....65 G8

ILK DE7 ....31 K2
ILK DE7 ....33 L8
LEIS LE2 ....132 A5
St John's St *LGEAT* NG10....62 B8
St John's Ter *DERBY* DE1 ....2 E4
St John St *LEI* LE1 ....6 E3
St Jude's Av
MAPPK/POR/STA NG3 ....37 H5
St Laurence Ct *LGEAT* NG10....76 C1
St Lawrence Bvd
COT/KEY/RAD NG12 ....53 H5
St Lawrence Cl *HEANOR* DE75....20 D5
St Leonards Cl *RLBORO* LE12....97 L8
St Leonard's Dr
WOL/BIL/BRX NG8....49 K3
St Leonards Rd *LEI* LE2....131 M6
St Leven Cl *WOL/BIL/BRX* NG8....35 H7
St Luke's Cl *RLEINE/SYS* LE7....133 K3
WBRGFD * NG2....65 M2
St Luke's St
MAPPK/POR/STA NG3 ....5 L6
St Luke's Wy *CALV/BJ* NG14....39 K7
St Margarets Av
WOL/BIL/BRX NG8....36 A7
St Margaret's St *LEI* LE1 ....6 E3
St Margaret's Wy *LEI* LE1 ....6 E3
LEIN LE4 ....125 J6
St Mark's Rd *DERBYE* DE21....44 B8
St Marks St *LEI* LE1 ....7 G2
NOTT NG1 ....5 J5
St Martins *LEI* LE1 ....6 E6
St Martin's Rd
WOL/BIL/BRX NG8....35 J7
St Martins Sq *LEI* LE1 ....6 E6
St Mary's Av *BWSH/BRSTN* DE72....60 E8
CARL NG4 ....38 C5
LEIE LE5 ....127 G7
LEIW LE3 ....130 A4
St Marys Br *DERBY* * DE1 ....2 B2
St Mary's Cl *ARN* NG5 ....25 K6
BSTN/STPLFD NG9....63 H6
DERBYSE DE24....72 E1
LBORO LE11....8 F2
RLBORO LE12....97 L8
St Mary's Ct *DERBY* DE1....2 B2
LEIW LE3 ....130 A4
St Mary's Crs *CFTN/RUD* NG11....65 G8
RLBORO LE12....88 C4
St Mary's Ga *DERBY* DE1 ....2 E3
NOTT NG1 ....5 J8
St Mary's Pl *NOTT* * NG1 ....5 J7
St Mary's Rd *LEIS* LE2....131 M5
RLBORO LE12....114 A3
St Mary St *ILK* DE7 ....33 J7
St Marys Wk
EWD/SEL/PNX NG16....12 F4
St Mary's Wy *HUCK/RAV* NG15....15 L7
St Marys Wharf Rd *DERBY* DE1....43 M8
St Matthew's Wk
DERBYW DE22....43 K5
St Matthews Wy *LEI* LE1 ....7 G3
St Matthias Rd
MAPPK/POR/STA NG3 ....5 M4
St Mawes Av *CFTN/RUD* NG11....64 F1
St Mawes Cl *DERBYW* DE22....43 H3
St Mellion Av *MCKLVR* DE3....56 D6
St Mellion Cl *LEIN* LE4....118 F8
St Michaels Av *CARL* NG4....38 A7
LEIN LE4 ....125 M4
WOL/BIL/BRX NG8....35 H7
St Michael's Cl *BPR/DUF* DE56....30 A1
COAL LE67 ....116 B6
DERBYSE DE24....59 G8
St Michaels Ct *DERBY* * DE1 ....2 E2
St Michael's La *DERBY* DE1 ....2 E2
St Michael's Sq
BSTN/STPLFD NG9....48 F7
St Michaels Vw *DERBYSE* DE24....59 G8
St Nicholas Cir *ARN* NG5....25 J8
DERBYW DE2....43 H5
St Nicholas Ms *DERBY* * DE1 ....43 K8
St Nicholas Pl *LEI* LE1 ....6 D6
St Nicholas St *NOTT* NG1 ....5 G8
St Norbert Dr *ILK* DE7 ....47 H2
St Olaves Cl *LBORO* LE11....102 F2
St Oswalds Rd *LEIN* LE4....124 D8
St Pancras Wy *DERBY* DE1....43 M8
St Patrick's Dr
EWD/SEL/PNX NG16....34 F1
St Paul's Av *NOTTE* NG7....4 A1
St Pauls Cl *LEIS* LE2....139 H1
St Paul's Dr *RLEINE/SYS* LE7....120 E5
St Pauls Rd *DERBY* * DE1 ....43 L8
LEIW LE3 ....131 G2
St Paul's St *WOL/BIL/BRX* NG8....50 B2
St Paul's Ter *NOTTE* * NG7....4 A1
St Peters Av *RLBORO* LE12....94 E6
St Peter's Churchyard
DERBY DE1 ....2 E4
St Peter's Cl *BPR/DUF* DE56....17 K3
LEIW LE3 ....123 M7
St Peter's Crs *CFTN/RUD* NG11....65 G8
St Peters Cft *BPR/DUF* DE56....17 L3
St Peters Dr *RLEINE/BBY* LE8....136 D7
St Peter's Ga *NOTT* NG1 ....5 H7
St Peters La *LEI* LE1 ....6 E5
St Peters Rd *LEIS* LE2....7 K8
MELB/CHEL DE73....72 E7
St Peter's St *DERBY* DE1....2 E4
NOTTE NG7 ....50 C2
RLEINE/SYS LE7....120 E4
St Peters Wy *DERBY* DE1 ....2 F5
St Philips Rd *LEIE* LE5....132 B4
RLBORO LE12....97 L8
St Quentin Cl *NORM/LIT* DE23....57 G4
St Ronan's Av *BPR/DUF* DE56....29 J4
St Saviour's Gdns *WBRGFD* NG2....51 H5
St Saviour's HI *LEIE* LE5....7 M5
St Saviours Rd *COAL* LE67....108 A7
LEIE LE5 ....7 L6
St Stephen's Av *WBRGFD* * NG2....51 M7
St Stephens Cl
BWSH/BRSTN DE72....59 M6
NORM/LIT DE23 ....71 H1
St Stephens Rd *LEIS* LE2....7 L3
WBRGFD NG2....5 M8

St Swithin's Cl *DERBYW* DE22....57 H4
St Swithin's Rd *LEIE* LE5....133 H2
St Thomas Rd *LEIS* LE2....137 J6
NORM/LIT DE23 ....57 L7
St Vincent Cl *LGEAT* NG10....76 C1
St Vincents Cl *COAL* LE67....108 A8
St Werburgh's Vw
DERBYE DE21....59 H4
St Wilfrid's Cl *RLEIW/BBY* LE8....146 E6
St Wilfrid's Rd *ILK* DE7 ....32 C8
Saint Winefride Rd
RLBORO LE12....101 M4
St Wolstan's Cl *WGSTN* LE18....138 D4
St Wystan's Rd *DERBYW* DE22....57 G4
Salamander Cl *CARL* NG4....38 B5
Salcey Dr *BSTN/STPLFD* NG9....48 B5
Salcombe Circ *ARN* NG5....25 H6
Salcombe Cl
EWD/SEL/PNX NG16....22 A6
WGSTN LE18 ....138 A6
Salcombe Crs *CFTN/RUD* NG11....65 H7
Salcombe Dr *ARN* NG5....25 H6
LEIW LE3 ....124 A7
Salcombe Rd *ARN* NG5....36 D4
Sale St *NORM/LIT* DE23....57 M5
Salford Gdns
MAPPK/POR/STA NG3 ....5 K5
Salisbury Av *LEI* LE1 ....7 J9
RLBORO LE12....88 D6
RLEIW/BAR LE9....141 G3
Salisbury Cl *RLEIW/BBY* LE8....142 H1
Salisbury Dr *BPR/DUF* DE56....18 B2
Salisbury La *MELB/CHEL* DE73....82 F8
Salisbury Sq *NOTTE* NG7....50 C3
Salisbury St *BSTN/STPLFD* NG9....49 M8
LBORO LE11....9 L2
LGEAT NG10....62 C8
NORM/LIT DE23 ....2 B1
NOTT NG7 ....50 C3
Salkeld Rd *LEIS* LE2....137 G5
Sallywood Cl *DERBYSE* DE24....71 H5
Salmon Cl *BLWL* NG6....23 K8
Salop Cl *ARN* NG5....25 H8
Saltash Cl *WGSTN* LE18....138 A6
Saltburn Cl *DERBYE* DE21....44 A6
Saltburn Rd *WOL/BIL/BRX* NG8....35 L8
Saltby Gn *CFTN/RUD* NG11....64 F7
Saltcoates Av *LEIN* LE4....126 A3
Salter Cl *CDON/KEG* DE74....84 D3
Salterford Rd *HUCK/RAV* NG15....23 J2
Saltergate Dr *LEIN* LE4....119 L7
Salford Cl *CARL* NG4....38 A7
Salthouse Cl *DERBYE* DE21....44 F6
Salthouse La *BSTN/STPLFD* NG9....49 L8
Saltney Wy *CFTN/RUD* NG11....64 F7
Salt's Cl *END/NAR* LE19....135 M5
Samantha Ct *DERBYE* DE21....44 F6
Samphire Cl *LEIE* LE5....127 H5
Samson Ct *CFTN/RUD* NG11....64 F7
Samson Rd *COAL* LE67....108 A5
LEIW LE3 ....124 F8
Samuel Ct *RIPLEY* DE5....11 H7
Samuel St *LEI* LE1 ....7 J5
Sancroft Av *DERBYE* DE21....59 J1
Sancroft Rd *DERBYE* DE21....59 K1
Sandacre St *LEI* LE1 ....6 E4
Sandale Cl *WBRGFD* NG2....66 A1
Sandalwood Cl *DERBYSE* DE24....59 G8
Sandalwood Rd *LBORO* LE11....8 C9
Sandays Cl *WBRGFD* NG2....51 G6
Sandbach Cl *DERBYE* DE21....44 E6
Sandbed La *BPR/DUF* DE56....18 A5
Sandby Ct *BSTN/STPLFD* NG9....63 G2
Sanderling Heath *MCKLVR* DE3....55 M8
Sanderson Cl *RLEIW/BBY* LE8....142 E1
Sanderson Rd *DERBYE* DE21....58 F1
Sanders Rd *RLBORO* LE12....112 D2
Sandfield Cl *DERBYE* DE21....44 F7
LEIN LE4 ....126 C2
Sandfield Rd *ARN* NG5....37 K1
BSTN/STPLFD NG9....62 C5
NOTTE NG7 ....4 A8
Sandford Av *LGEAT* NG10....62 C8
Sandford Brook
RDERBYSW DE65....68 C3
Sandford Cl *LEIE* LE5....132 E1
Sandford Rd
MAPPK/POR/STA NG3 ....37 K5
RLEINE/SYS LE7....120 E4
Sandgate *BSTN/STPLFD* NG9....49 H6
Sandgate Av *LEIN* LE4....119 K7
Sandgate Cl *DERBYSE* DE24....72 F1
Sandham Bridge Rd
RLEINE/SYS LE7....118 D4
Sandham La *RIPLEY* DE5....11 J6
Sandhill Dr *END/NAR* LE19....136 B6
Sandhill Rd *EWD/SEL/PNX* NG16....13 M4
The Sandhills *RLBORO* LE12....112 C1
Sandhills Av *LEIE* LE5....126 F4
Sandhills Cl *RLBORO* LE12....100 F1
Sandhole La *RLBORO* LE12....101 H6
Sandhurst Cl *LEIW* LE3....130 A1
Sandhurst Dr *BSTN/STPLFD* NG9....62 F5
CFTN/RUD NG11....78 F1
Sandhurst Gdns *LEIE* LE3....130 F1
Sandhurst St *LEIS* LE2....138 E1
Sandiacre Dr *LEIE* LE4....120 D7
Sandiacre Rd *BSTN/STPLFD* NG9....62 A1
Sandon St *NOTTE* NG7....36 E6
Sandown Av *MCKLVR* DE3....56 A4
Sandown Rd *BSTN/STPLFD* NG9....62 D4
DERBYSE DE24....58 B7
LEIE LE5 ....132 E2
WGSTN LE18 ....138 A3

Sandringham Pl *ILK* DE7....47 H2
Sandringham Ri *RLBORO* LE12....101 K5
Sandringham Rd *COAL* LE67....108 D7
DERBYE DE21....44 A6
LEIS LE2 ....137 J6
LGEAT NG10....61 M3
WBRGFD NG2....51 K3
Sands Cl *CARL* NG4....52 C2
Sandside *COT/KEY/RAD* NG12....67 K5
Sandwell Cl *LGEAT* NG10....75 L7
Sandyford Cl *BLWL* NG6....36 A4
Sandyhill Cl *MELB/CHEL* DE73....72 E5
Sandy La *BSTN/STPLFD* NG9....49 H6
COT/KEY/RAD NG12 ....52 F5
DERBYE DE21....30 D3
HUCK/RAV NG15....15 L3
Sandypits La *RDERBYSW* DE65....69 G3
Sandy Ri *WGSTN* LE18....138 C3
Sanger Cl *CFTN/RUD* NG11....64 A7
Sankey Dr *BLWL* NG6....23 L8
Santolina Dr *DERBYE* DE21....44 D6
Sanvey Ga *LEI* LE1 ....6 D4
Sanvey La *LEIS* LE2....136 F1
Sapcote Rd *RLEINE/BAR* LE9....140 C5
Sapele Cl *CARL* NG4....38 C5
Sapperton Cl *NORM/LIT* DE23....71 H2
Sargent Gdns
MAPPK/POR/STA NG3 ....51 K1
Sarson St *RLBORO* LE12....112 D1
Saskatoon Cl
COT/KEY/RAD NG12 ....53 J5
Saunby Cl *ARN* NG5....36 A4
Saundersfoot Wy *DERBYE* DE21....44 F5
Saunderson Rd *LEIN* LE4....125 H3
Saunton Cl *COT/KEY/RAD* NG12....53 J5
Savage's Rd *CFTN/RUD* NG11....65 G7
Save Penny La *BPR/DUF* DE56....29 L2
Savernake Rd *LEIN* LE4....125 H3
Saville Cl *BSTN/STPLFD* NG9....48 C7
Saville Rd *ARN* NG5....37 K2
RLEIW/BBY LE8....143 G1
Saville St *LEIE* LE5....132 C1
Sawbrook *RLEIW/BBY* LE8....145 L8
Sawday St *LEIS* LE2....131 J4
Sawley Rd *BWSH/BRSTN* DE72....60 F8
BWSH/BRSTN DE72....61 J3
Sawley St *LEIS* LE2....132 B4
Sawmand Cl *LGEAT* NG10....76 A1
Saxby St *LEI* LE2....7 J8
Saxelby Gdns *BLWL* NG6....23 M7
Saxon Dl *LEIS* LE2....137 G5
Saxondale Av *MCKLVR* DE3....56 A3
Saxondale Rd *BLWL* NG6....36 B2
Saxondale Rd *WGSTN* LE18....138 C7
Saxon Gn *NOTTE* NG7....50 C4
Saxons Ri *GBY/RBY* LE6....123 G6
Saxon St *LEIW* LE3....6 C6
Saxon Wy *COT/KEY/RAD* NG12....67 L6
Saxton Cl *BSTN/STPLFD* NG9....48 D3
Saxton Av *HEANOR* DE75....20 C5
Scafell Wy *CFTN/RUD* NG11....64 B8
Scalborough Cl
RLEIW/BBY LE8....143 G3
Scalby Cl *EWD/SEL/PNX* NG16....21 H5
Scalford Dr *WOL/BIL/BRX* NG8....50 A4
Scalpay Cl *LEIN* LE4....124 F4
Scarborough Av *ILK* DE7....33 H7
Scarborough Ri *DERBYE* DE21....44 B6
Scarborough Rd *LEIN* LE4....125 M5
Scarborough St
MAPPK/POR/STA NG3 ....5 K5
Scarcliffe Cl *DERBYSE* DE24....72 C4
Scarfell Cl *WBRGFD* NG2....66 A2
Scargill Av *EWD/SEL/PNX* NG16....21 M6
Scargill Cl *EWD/SEL/PNX* NG16....21 M6
Scargill Rd *ILK* DE7 ....32 C7
Scargill Wk *EWD/SEL/PNX* NG16....21 K6
Scarrington Rd *WBRGFD* NG2....51 K4
Scarsdale Av *DERBYW* DE22....43 G4
NORM/LIT DE23 ....57 G5
Scarsdale Rd *BPR/DUF* DE56....29 J4
Sceptre St *ARN* NG5....37 G5
Schofield Rd *LBORO* LE11....103 G4
School Cl *RLEIW/BAR* LE9....141 G4
WBRGFD NG2....51 H6
School Crs *RLEIW/BAR* LE9....141 J8
School Cft *ALFN* DE55....12 B1
Schoolgate *WGSTN* LE18....137 K3
School Gn *RLBORO* LE12....88 C6
School HI *RLBORO* LE12....105 L3
School House Cl
RLEINE/SYS LE7....124 B2
Schoolhouse HI *BPR/DUF* DE56....10 B6
School La *BPR/DUF* DE56....10 B5
BSTN/STPLFD NG9....63 G3
CDON/KEG DE74....84 E3
COAL LE67 ....108 B1
END/NAR LE19....135 M8
LEIE LE5 ....132 F5
LEIN LE4 ....125 L1
LGEAT NG10....47 K8
MELB/CHEL DE73....72 E6
RIPLEY DE5....11 G6
RLBORO LE12....97 H2
RLBORO LE12....100 F1
RLBORO LE12....111 M5
RLBORO LE12....112 G2
RLEINE/SYS LE7....121 H7
RLEINE/SYS LE7....121 K2
RLEIW/BAR LE9....135 H8
School Rd *EWD/SEL/PNX* NG16....13 L3
RLEIW/BBY LE8....146 F7
School Sq *ILK* DE7 ....32 C8
School St *LBORO* LE11....9 K3
RLEINE/SYS LE7....119 K1
RLEINE/SYS LE7....120 F3
RLEIW/BBY LE8....145 K8
School Wk *BLWL* NG6....146 E7
RLEIW/BBY LE8....146 E7
Science Rd *NOTTE* NG7....4 C6
The Scotches *BPR/DUF* DE56....17 K2
Scotland Av *ARN* NG5....36 D5
Scotlands Dr *COAL* LE67....108 A7
Scotlands Rd *COAL* LE67....108 B7
Scotland Wy *RLEIW/BBY* LE8....143 K4
Scotswood Crs *LEIS* LE2....137 G5
Scott Av *BSTN/STPLFD* NG9....63 K1
Scott Cl *BLWL* NG6....35 K2

Scott Ct *LEIS* LE2....131 L7
Scott Dr *BPR/DUF* DE56....18 C2
Scott St *LEIS* LE2....131 L7
NORM/LIT DE23 ....57 K6
Scotts Yd *RIPLEY* * DE5....11 H5
Scraptoft La *LEIE* LE5....126 E8
Scraptoft Ms *LEIE* LE5....126 E8
Scraptoft Ri *LEIE* LE5....127 K7
Scrimshire La
COT/KEY/RAD NG12 ....67 J4
Script Dr *BLWL* NG6....36 C3
Scrivelsby Gdns
BSTN/STPLFD NG9....63 H3
Scrivener Cl *RLEINE/SYS* LE7....133 L2
Scudamore Rd *LEIW* LE3....129 M2
Seaburn Rd *BSTN/STPLFD* NG9....62 C4
Seacole Cl *LEIE* LE5....130 B5
Seaford Av *WOL/BIL/BRX* NG8....49 M2
Seaford Rd *LEIS* LE2....137 H2
Seaford Wy *ILK* DE7 ....33 K2
Seagrave Cl *COAL* LE67....109 G6
RLBORO LE12....44 F7
Seagrave Ct
WOL/BIL/BRX * NG8....35 H6
Seagrave Dr *LEIS* LE2....138 D1
Seagrave Rd *RLBORO* LE12....114 A3
RLEINE/SYS LE7....115 J2
WOL/BIL/BRX NG8....35 M8
Seale St *DERBY* DE1....43 L8
Seals Cl *RLBORO* LE12....112 D1
Seamer Rd *EWD/SEL/PNX* NG16....22 D8
Searl St *DERBY* DE1....2 B1
Seascale Cl *DERBYE* DE21....44 B6
Seatallan Cl *WBRGFD* NG2....66 A1
Seathwaite Cl
COT/KEY/RAD NG12 ....66 A3
Seatoller Cl *WBRGFD* NG2....66 A3
Seaton Cl *LEIW* LE3....130 A6
MCKLVR DE3....55 L5
Seaton Crs *WOL/BIL/BRX* NG8....35 L6
Seaton Ri *LEIE* LE5....127 J6
Seaton Rd *WGSTN* LE18....138 A6
Second Av *BLWL* NG6....50 M8
BSTN/STPLFD NG9....50 B8
BWSH/BRSTN DE72....61 J3
CARL NG4 ....38 A7
CARL NG4 ....38 A7
MELB/CHEL DE73....72 E7
Seddons Cl *LEIN* LE4....125 H3
Sedgebrook Cl *BLWL* NG6....36 A3
DERBYE DE21....
Sedgebrook Rd *LEIE* LE5....133 H3
Sedgefield Dr *RLEINE/SYS* LE7....120 C4
RLEINE/SYS LE7....133 K1
Sedgeley Rd
COT/KEY/RAD NG12 ....66 B7
Sedgemoor Wy *NORM/LIT* DE23....70 E2
Sedgewood Cv *CFTN/RUD* NG11....64 C4
Sedgley Av *WBRGFD* NG2....51 K2
Sedgwick St
EWD/SEL/PNX NG16....12 F4
Sedley Av *EWD/SEL/PNX* NG16....35 G1
Seely Rd *NOTTE* NG7....4 C6
Sefton Av *BSTN/STPLFD* NG9....48 C7
Sefton Dr
MAPPK/POR/STA NG3 ....37 H6
Sefton Rd *DERBYE* DE21....58 D1
Seine La *END/NAR* LE19....135 K3
Selborne St *DERBYE* DE24....58 B5
Selbourne St *LBORO* LE11....9 L3
Selby Cl *BSTN/STPLFD* NG9....62 C4
Selby La *COT/KEY/RAD* NG12....80 D5
Selby Rd *WBRGFD* NG2....65 K2
Selhurst Ct *NOTTE* NG7....4 A1
Selhurst St *NOTTE* NG7....4 A1
Selina Cl *CDON/KEG* DE74....84 E3
Selina St *MELB/CHEL* DE73....82 E8
Selkirk Cl *LEIN* LE4....126 B4
Selkirk St *DERBYE* DE21....44 C8
Sellars Av *CFTN/RUD* NG11....79 G1
Seller's Wood Dr *BLWL* NG6....35 L1
Seller's Wood Dr West
BLWL NG6....23 J8
Selside Ct *EWD/SEL/PNX* NG16....35 G1
Selston Dr *WOL/BIL/BRX* NG8....50 A4
Selston Rd *EWD/SEL/PNX* NG16....12 F3
Selvester Dr *RLBORO* LE12....112 F2
Selworthy Cl *DERBYE* DE21....44 E5
Selwyn Cl *BLWL* NG6....36 C2
Selwyn St *DERBYW* DE22....57 G1
Sence Crs *RLEIW/BBY* LE8....139 L7
Serina Av *NORM/LIT* DE23....57 H7
Serlby Ri *MAPPK/POR/STA* NG3....51 K1
Serlby Rd *EWD/SEL/PNX* NG16....21 L4
Seton Cl *LBORO* LE11....103 G1
The Settlement
BWSH/BRSTN DE72....60 A2
Sevenlands Dr *DERBYSE* DE24....73 G3
Sevenoaks Av *DERBYW* DE22....56 D2
Seven Oaks Crs
BSTN/STPLFD NG9....48 F6
Seven Oaks Rd *ILK* DE7....47 L6
Seventh Av *BSTN/STPLFD* NG9....64 A2
Severals *BSTN/STPLFD* NG9....48 D8
Severnale Cl *DERBYW* DE22....43 M2
Severn Cl *RLEIW/BAR* LE9....142 B4
Severn Rd *LEIS* LE2....139 H2
Severn St *DERBYSE* DE24....58 D7
LEIS LE2 ....7 K8
Seward St *LBORO* LE11....8 F4
Sextant Rd *LEIE* LE5....127 G8
Seymour Cl *DERBYW* DE22....57 G2
LBORO LE11....102 F2
Seymour Rd
EWD/SEL/PNX NG16....21 K6
HUCK/RAV NG15....23 J2
LEIS LE2 ....131 M5
RLBORO LE12....105 K1
WBRGFD NG2....51 M7
Seymour St *LEIS* LE2....7 J8
MAPPK/POR/STA NG3 ....5 M5
Seymour Wy *LEIW* LE3....129 K5
Shackerdale Rd *WGSTN* LE18....137 M1

Shacklecross Cl
  BWSH/BRSTN DE72............60 A6
Shackleton Cl
  WOL/BIL/BRX NG8............35 H5
Shackleton St *LEI LE1*............7 G2
Shacklock Cl *ARN NG5*............24 E5
Shades Cl *RLEIW/BAR LE9*............141 D3
Shadrack Cl *RLEIW/BAR LE9*............140 B6
Shadwell Gv
  COT/KEY/RAD NG12............53 J4
Shady Gv *RDERBYSW DE65*............68 A5
Shady La *BSTN/STPLFD NG9*............63 H6
  LEIS LE2............132 F6
Shaef Cl *RDERBYSW DE65*............68 C5
Shaeffer Ct *LEIN LE4*............124 F5
Shaftesbury Av *CALV/BJ NG14*............39 L2
  LEIN LE4............125 L5
  LGEAT NG10............61 L2
Shaftesbury Crs
  NORM/LIT DE23............57 M6
Shaftesbury Rd *LEIW LE3*............131 G3
Shaftesbury St *NORM/LIT DE23*............57 M6
  NOTTE NG7............36 E6
Shaftesbury St South
  NORM/LIT DE23............57 M7
Shakespeare Cl *CARL NG4*............52 C2
  CDON/KEG DE74............92 F2
  LEIW LE3............130 C6
Shakespeare Dr *LEIW LE3*............130 D6
Shakespeare Rd
  EWD/SEL/PNX NG16............34 A2
Shakespeare St *DERBYSE DE24*............71 L2
  LBORO LE11............9 H2
  LEIS LE2............131 K7
  LGEAT NG10............62 A6
  NOTT NG1............4 F5
Shakespeare Vls *NOTT NG1*............5 G5
Shaldon Cl *ARN NG5*............24 D6
Shaldon Dr *NORM/LIT DE23*............57 H6
Shalfleet Dr *DERBYSE DE24*............73 G2
Shamrock St *NORM/LIT DE23*............57 J6
Shandwick Ct *DERBYSE* DE24............71 H4
Shangton Rd *RLEIW/BBY LE8*............147 M4
Shanklin Av *LEIS LE2*............132 E8
Shanklin Dr *BSTN/STPLFD NG9*............48 B8
  LEIS LE2............132 E8
Shanklin Gdns *LEIS LE2*............132 E8
Shanklin Houses
  DERBYSE DE24............59 G8
Shannon Cl *NORM/LIT DE23*............71 H1
Shannon Houses
  DERBYSE DE24............72 C2
Shanti Margh *LEIN LE4*............124 F6
Shanwell Cl *WOL/BIL/BRX NG8*............35 H5
Shardlow Rd
  BWSH/BRSTN DE72............73 M8
  DERBYSE DE24............72 F1
  WGSTN LE18............138 A4
Sharmon Crs *LEIW LE3*............130 B3
Sharnford Rd *RLEIW/BAR LE9*............140 C8
Sharnford Wy
  BSTN/STPLFD NG9............48 F3
Sharp Cl *ILK DE7*............47 G1
  LGEAT NG10............76 A1
Sharpes Wy *ARN NG5*............24 F2
Sharpe Wy *END/NAR LE19*............135 M8
Sharphill Rd
  COT/KEY/RAD NG12............65 M3
Sharpland *LEIS LE2*............137 G2
Sharpley Av *COAL LE67*............108 E6
Sharpley Dr *LEIN LE4*............124 E1
  RLBORO LE12............88 D4
Sharpley Rd *LBORO LE11*............102 F5
Sharply Hl *GBY/RBY LE6*............123 H4
Sharrard St *EWD/SEL/PNX NG16*............13 L5
Shaw Cl *RLEIW/BBY LE8*............142 D1
Shaw Crs *HUCK/RAV NG15*............23 J3
Shawcroft Av *ALFN DE55*............12 A4
Shaw La *BPR/DUF DE56*............17 M8
Shaws Gn *DERBYW* DE22............57 H1
Shaw St *ALFN DE55*............12 A1
  CFTN/RUD NG11............79 G1
  DERBYW DE22............2 A2
Shaw St East *ILK DE7*............47 L1
Shaw St West *ILK DE7*............47 L1
Shaw's Yd *BPR/DUF DE56*............18 D7
Shaw Wood Cl *GBY/RBY LE6*............123 J4
Shearer Cl *LEIN LE4*............126 C3
Shearing Cl *CARL NG4*............38 E6
Shearing Hl *CARL NG4*............38 E6
Shearsby Cl *WGSTN LE18*............138 B5
Sheene Rd *LEIN LE4*............124 E3
Sheepcote *RLEINE/SYS LE7*............113 J8
Sheepfold La *CFTN/RUD NG11*............79 G1
Sheffield Pl *DERBY DE1*............3 J6
Sheffield St *LEIW LE3*............131 H4
Shelby Cl *NOTTE NG7*............50 C3
Sheldon Cl *LBORO LE11*............102 F1
  LGEAT NG10............61 M4
Sheldon Rd *HEANOR DE75*............20 D4
Sheldon St *LEIE LE5*............133 G1
  MCKLVR DE3............56 A4
Shelford Crs *CALV/BJ NG14*............39 L2
Shelford Ri
  MAPPK/POR/STA NG3............51 L1
Shelford Rd *CARL NG4*............38 A4
  COT/KEY/RAD NG12............53 K4
Shellduck Cl *RLEIW/BBY LE8*............142 D1
Shelley Av *CFTN/RUD NG11*............64 C4
Shelley Cl *EWD/SEL/PNX NG16*............34 F1
  HUCK/RAV NG15............23 H1
Shelley Dr *DERBYSE DE21*............71 L2
Shelley Rd *ARN NG5*............25 H8
  END/NAR LE19............135 L5
  LBORO LE11............103 H2
  LEIS LE2............131 L7
Shelmory Cl *DERBYSE DE24*............72 B2
Shelt Hl *CALV/BJ NG14*............27 H2
Shelthorpe Av *LBORO LE11*............9 K8
Shelthorpe Rd *LBORO LE11*............9 K8
Shelton Av *HUCK/RAV NG15*............24 B3
Shelton Dr *DERBYSE DE24*............72 D4
Shelton St *MAPPK/POR/STA NG3*...5 L4
Shenfield Gdns *BLWL NG6*............24 B6
Shenington Wy *DERBYW DE21*............44 F5

Shenley Rd *WGSTN LE18*............138 C3
Shenton Cl *LEIN LE4*............126 E1
  RLEIW/BBY LE8............136 D8
Shepard Cl *BLWL NG6*............35 L5
Shepherd Cl *LEIW LE3*............129 H4
Shepherds Cl *LBORO LE11*............8 B8
  RLBORO LE12............95 G2
  RLBORO LE12............102 A2
  WOL/BIL/BRX NG8............35 L8
Shepherd St *NORM/LIT DE23*............57 G6
Shepherds Wood Dr
  WOL/BIL/BRX NG8............36 A8
Shepherd Wk *CDON/KEG DE74*............86 A6
Shepshed Rd *RLBORO LE12*............94 C7
Shepton Cl *ILK DE7*............33 H4
Shepton Crs *WOL/BIL/BRX NG8*............35 M8
Sheran Dr *BPR/DUF DE56*............18 B3
Sherborne Av *WGSTN LE18*............138 A7
Sherborne Rd *WBRGFD NG2*............65 K2
  WOL/BIL/BRX NG8............35 L5
Sherbourne Dr *BPR/DUF DE56*............18 B3
Sheraton Dr *BPR/DUF DE56*............18 B3
Sherbrook Av *ARN NG5*............37 H1
Sherbrooke Rd *ARN NG5*............36 F6
Sherbrook Rd *ARN NG5*............37 G1
Sherbrook Ter *ARN NG5*............37 H1
Sherford Cl *WGSTN LE18*............138 A5
Sheridan Cl *END/NAR LE19*............135 L5
Sheridan St *BSTN/STPLFD NG9*............48 C6
Sheridan St *DERBYSE DE24*............71 K2
Sheriff Cl *LEIS LE2*............131 K7
Sheriff's Lea *BSTN/STPLFD NG9*...62 C5
Sheriffs Wy *WBRGFD NG2*............51 G5
Sheringham Cl *ARN NG5*............37 K1
Sheringham Rd *LEIN LE4*............125 H5
Sherloyd Cl *LEIN LE4*............126 D3
Sherman Dr *BSTN/STPLFD NG9*...64 D3
Sherrard Rd *RLBORO LE12*............114 A6
Sherrard Wy *LEIW LE3*............130 B6
Sherrington Ct *CFTN/RUD NG11*...64 A7
Sherston Cl *DERBYSE DE21*............44 F5
Sherwin Cl *MAPPK/POR/STA NG3*...5 H4
Sherwin Gv *NOTTE* NG7............50 C4
Sherwin Rd *BSTN/STPLFD NG9*...48 B6
  NOTTE NG7............50 C4
Sherwin St *DERBYW DE22*............43 J7
Sherwood Wk *NOTT NG1*............5 G3
Sherwood Av
  BWSH/BRSTN DE72............60 A5
  DERBYE DE21............44 D8
  NORM/LIT DE23............71 H2
Sherwood Ri
  EWD/SEL/PNX NG16............21 K6
  NOTTE NG7............36 F7
Sherwood St *DERBYW DE22*............2 B7
  HUCK/RAV NG15............24 A1
  LEIE LE5............132 C1
Sherwood V *ARN NG5*............37 J4
Sherwood Wk *HUCK/RAV NG15*...15 L5
Shetland Cl *DERBYSE DE21*............44 A8
Shetland Rd *LEIN LE4*............126 A5
Shetland Wy *RLEIW/BBY LE8*...143 K4
Shield Crs *LEIS LE2*............132 C5
Shields Crs *CDON/KEG DE74*............84 D4
Shilling Wy *LGEAT NG10*............61 G3
Shipley Common La *ILK DE7*...33 G3
Shipley La *ILK DE7*............32 D4
Shipley Ri *CARL NG4*............38 C8
Shipley Rd *LEIE LE5*............132 B3
  WOL/BIL/BRX NG8............35 K5
Shipstone St *ILK DE7*............47 M1
  NOTTE NG7............36 D7
Shipston Hl *LEIS LE2*............138 E3
Shipton Cl *WGSTN LE18*............138 D5
Shirebrooke Cl *BLWL NG6*............36 A4
Shire Cl *LEIW LE3*............130 C2
Shiregate Gdns *NORM/LIT DE23*...70 E2
Shireoaks *BPR/DUF DE56*............17 H2
Shireoaks Cl *NORM/LIT DE23*............57 C8
Shires La *LEI LE1*............6 D5
Shires Wk *LEI* LE1............6 E5
Shirley Av *LEIS LE2*............132 B7
Shirley Cl *CDON/KEG DE74*............84 E3
Shirley Crs *BWSH/BRSTN DE72*...61 H7
Shirley Dr *ARN NG5*............25 M8
  RLEINE/SYS LE7............120 F2
Shirley Pk *BWSH/BRSTN DE72*...73 M8
Shirley Rd *DERBYE DE21*............44 C6
  LEIS LE2............132 B7
  MAPPK/POR/STA NG3............37 G7
  RIPLEY DE5............11 H6
Shirley St *LEIS LE2*............125 L5
  LGEAT NG10............75 L3
Shirreffs Cl *RLBORO LE12*............105 J7
Shop La *BPR/DUF DE56*............10 A5
Shop Stones
  BWSH/BRSTN DE72............60 A2
Shoreswood Cl *ARN NG5*............24 F7
Short Av *DERBYW DE22*............43 K2
Short Cl *RLEIW/BBY LE8*............145 K8
Shortcross Av *ARN NG5*............37 K3
Short Hl *NOTT NG1*............5 G8
Short Lands *BPR/DUF DE56*............17 L3
Short La *CDON/KEG DE74*............84 C3
Shortridge La *END/NAR LE19*...135 M4
Short Stairs *NOTT* NG1............5 K8
Short St *BPR/DUF DE56*............17 M3
  LEI LE1............6 E5
Shortwood Av *HUCK/RAV NG15*...23 K2
Shortwood Cl *NOTT NG1*............5 H6
Shorwell Gdns *DERBYSE DE24*...73 G2
Shorwell Rd *CARL NG4*............38 A8
Shottens Cl *LEIN LE4*............124 F5
Shottery Av *LEIE LE5*............130 D6
Shotton Dr *ARN NG5*............25 L1
Shoulbard *RLEIW/BBY LE8*............145 J7
Shrewsbury Av *LEIS LE2*............137 L1
Shrewsbury Cl *DERBYSE DE21*...45 G5
Shrewsbury Rd *WBRGFD NG2*...51 L3
Shrimpton Cl *CFTN/RUD NG11*...79 H1
Shropshire Av *DERBYE DE21*...44 F5
  EWD/SEL/PNX NG16............13 G5
Shropshire Rd *LEIS LE2*............131 H8
The Shrubberies *ARN* NG5............36 F5
  NORM/LIT DE23............2 B7
Shuttleworth La
  RLEIW/BAR LE9............142 B6

Sibson Dr *CDON/KEG DE74*............85 M5
Sibson Rd *LEIN LE4*............119 L8
Sibton La *LEIS LE2*............138 E3
Sickleholm Dr *LEIE LE5*............132 C5
Siddals La *DERBYSE DE22*............43 K3
Siddons Rd *DERBY DE1*............3 H5
Siddons St *DERBYSE DE24*............58 B8
Side Ley *CDON/KEG DE74*............86 A4
The Sidings *DERBYE DE21*............58 B3
Sidlaw Ri *ARN NG5*............24 F6
Sidmouth Av *LEIE LE5*............132 C3
Sidmouth Cl
  COT/KEY/RAD NG12............80 C3
  DERBYSE DE24............59 G8
Sidney Rd *BSTN/STPLFD NG9*...49 J8
  LEIS LE2............132 B8
Sidney St *DERBY DE1*............3 H8
  EWD/SEL/PNX NG16............34 D1
  LGEAT NG10............76 B1
Sidwell St *LEIE LE5*............132 C2
Silbury Cl *CFTN/RUD NG11*............64 B8
Silbury Rd *LEIN LE4*............125 G6
Sileby Rd *RLBORO LE12*............105 H8
  RLBORO LE12............113 J4
Silsden Ri *LEIS LE2*............137 H4
Silver Ar *LEI LE1*............6 E5
Silver Birch Cl *BLWL NG6*............35 M3
Silver Birches *RLBORO LE12*...112 D1
Silverbirch Wy *RLBORO LE12*...111 L1
Silverburn Dr *DERBYE DE21*...44 E5
Silverdale *BSTN/STPLFD NG9*...62 C2
Silverdale Cl *MELB/CHEL DE73*...72 E5
Silverdale Dr *LEIN LE4*............126 D1
Silver Hill Cl *WOL/BIL/BRX NG8*...35 H5
Silverhill Rd *DERBYE DE21*............59 J4
Silver Hill Rd *NORM/LIT DE23*...2 E9
Silverhow Cl *WBRGFD NG2*............66 A2
Silver La *BWSH/BRSTN DE72*...73 K2
Silverstone Dr *LEIN LE4*............126 B2
Silver St *COAL LE67*............108 C3
  LEI LE1............6 E5
Silverton Dr *DERBYSE DE21*............71 G5
Silverton Rd *LBORO LE11*............103 K7
  LEIS LE2............139 G1
Silver Wk *LEI* LE1............6 E5
Silverwood Cl *LEIE LE5*............133 G2
Silverwood Rd
  BSTN/STPLFD NG9............63 J1
Silvey Gv *DERBYE DE21*............59 H3
Simcoe Leys *MELB/CHEL DE73*...72 D5
Simmins Crs *LEIS LE2*............137 H5
Simon Fields Cl *ILK DE7*............31 L5
Simons Cl *WGSTN LE18*............138 C7
Simons Ct *BSTN/STPLFD NG9*...49 H6
Simpson Cl *RLEINE/SYS LE7*...120 C5
Sims Av *DERBY DE1*............2 A3
Sinclair Cl *DERBYSE DE24*............71 J3
  HEANOR DE75............20 B7
Sinfin Av *DERBYSE DE24*............72 B3
Sinfin Fields Crs *DERBYSE DE24*...72 B2
Sinfin La *DERBYSE DE24*............71 K3
  NORM/LIT DE23............57 L8
Sinfin Moor La *DERBYSE DE24*...71 K4
Sir Frank Whittle Rd
  DERBYE DE21............44 A8
Sir John Robinson Wy
  ARN NG5............25 H3
Sir Robert Martin Ct
  LBORO LE11............103 H2
Siskin Cl *MCKLVR DE3*............55 M8
Siskin Dr *DERBYSE DE24*............71 H3
Siskin Hl *LEIS LE2*............138 E3
Sisley Av *BSTN/STPLFD NG9*...62 C1
Sister's La *BWSH/BRSTN DE72*...60 A3
Sitwell Cl *DERBYE DE21*............59 H3
Sitwell Dr *BPR/DUF DE56*............18 B4
Sitwell St *DERBY DE1*............2 F5
  DERBYE DE21............59 J3
Sitwell Wk *LEIE LE5*............132 C5
Six Hills La *RMMWB LE14*............99 L8
Six Hills Rd *RLBORO LE12*...106 A3
  RMMWB LE14............107 M2
Sixth Av *BSTN/STPLFD NG9*...64 A2
Skampton Rd *LEIE LE5*............132 F3
Skeavington's La *ILK DE7*............33 J2
Skelton Dr *LEIS LE2*............137 L1
Skelwith Cl *COT/KEY/RAD NG12*...66 A2
Sketchley Cl *LEIE LE5*............133 H1
Sketchley St
  MAPPK/POR/STA NG3............5 M3
Skevington Av *LBORO LE11*............8 C3
Skiddaw Cl *WBRGFD NG2*............66 A2
Skiddaw Dr *MCKLVR DE3*............56 C6
Skinner's La *COAL LE67*............108 D2
Skipton Circ
  MAPPK/POR/STA NG3............51 L2
Skipton Cl *ILK DE7*............33 H4
Skipworth St *LEIS LE2*............7 L9
Skye Wy *RLEIW/BBY LE8*............143 K4
Skylark Av *RLBORO LE12*............113 K6
Skylark Dr *BLWL NG6*............36 B3
Skylark Wy *DERBYSE DE24*............71 H3
Slack La *ALFN DE55*............11 M3
  BPR/DUF DE56............10 A4
  DERBYW DE22............43 K5
  DERBYW DE22............57 H2
  HEANOR DE75............20 C7
  RIPLEY DE5............11 L5
Slack Rd *ILK DE7*............32 D4
Slade Cl *ILK DE7*............47 K2
  RDERBYSW DE65............69 G3
The Slade Greens *LEIS LE2*...137 G3
Slade Lands Dr
  MELB/CHEL DE73............72 E5
Slade Rd *BSTN/STPLFD NG9*...62 C2
Slaidburn Av *CFTN/RUD NG11*...64 C2
Slaidburn Cl *MCKLVR DE3*............56 C6
Slaney Cl *DERBYSE DE24*............58 C8
Slaney Houses *DERBYSE* DE24...72 B2
Slash La *RLBORO LE12*............113 K3
Slate Brook Cl *GBY/RBY LE6*...123 K4
Slate Cl *LEIW LE3*............123 M7
Slater Av *DERBYW DE22*............2 A3
Slater St *LEIW LE3*............6 C2
Slate St *LEIS LE2*............7 H7
Sledmere Cl *DERBYSE DE24*...59 G8
Sleepy La *MELB/CHEL DE73*...82 F6

Slindon Cft *DERBYSE DE24*............73 H1
Sloan Dr *BSTN/STPLFD NG9*...48 F5
Sloane Cl *END/NAR LE19*............135 L4
Sloane Ct *WBRGFD NG2*............65 G4
Sloane Rd *DERBYW DE22*............56 E1
Smalley Cl *EWD/SEL/PNX NG16*...13 L5
Smalley Dr *DERBYE DE21*............44 F4
Smalley Mill Rd *ILK DE7*............30 F3
Small Meer Cl *MELB/CHEL DE73*...72 D6
Small's Cft *LEIN NG14*............27 G3
Smart Cl *LEIW LE3*............130 B5
Smeath Rd *EWD/SEL/PNX NG16*...13 L5
Smedley Av *ILK DE7*............33 L8
Smedley Cl *WOL/BIL/BRX NG8*...35 M5
Smedley's Av *LGEAT NG10*............61 M2
Smedmore Rd *LEIE LE5*............126 B7
Smeeton Ct *RLEIW/BBY* LE8............146 E7
Smeeton Rd *RLEIW/BBY LE8*...146 E8
Smeeton St *HEANOR DE75*............20 C1
Smith Av *LEIN LE4*............126 D1
  MELB/CHEL DE73............82 F7
  RIPLEY DE5............11 M6
Smith Crs *COAL LE67*............109 G7
Smith Dorrien Rd *LEIE LE5*...126 C8
Smith Dr *EWD/SEL/PNX NG16*...20 E4
Smithfield Av
  BSTN/STPLFD NG9............48 B3
Smithson Dr *WOL/BIL/BRX NG8*...49 J3
Smithurst Rd
  EWD/SEL/PNX NG16............21 H7
Smith Wy *END/NAR LE19*............136 C3
Smithy La *RLBORO LE12*............93 L3
Smithy Crs *ARN NG5*............25 K7
Smithy Farm Dr
  RLEIW/BAR LE9............140 A5
Smithy La *RLBORO LE12*............93 L3
Smithy Rw *NOTT NG1*............5 G7
Smithy Wy *RLBORO LE12*............102 A3
Smore Slade Hills *LEIS LE2*...139 J3
Snake La *BPR/DUF DE56*............29 H4
Snape Wood Rd *BLWL NG6*...23 K8
Snarrow's Rd *RLBORO LE12*...100 C5
Sneinton Bvd *WBRGFD NG2*...51 K3
Sneinton Dl *WBRGFD NG2*............51 K3
Sneinton Hermitage
  WBRGFD NG2............5 M9
Sneinton Hollows
  WBRGFD NG2............51 K3
Sneinton Rd *WBRGFD NG2*............5 L9
Snell's Nook La *LBORO LE11*...102 E6
Snelsmoor La *MELB/CHEL DE73*...72 E6
Snelston Crs *NORM/LIT DE23*...57 C5
Snowberry Av *BPR/DUF DE56*...17 M5
Snowdens End *WGSTN LE18*...138 C6
Snowdon Cl *ARN NG5*............24 F6
  RLBORO LE12............102 A5
Snowdrop Cl *END/NAR LE19*...135 K7
Snow Hl *LEIW LE3*............125 G6
Soarbank Cl
  EWD/SEL/PNX NG16............22 C8
Soar La *LEIW LE3*............6 B4
  RLBORO LE12............86 D7
Soar Rd *RLBORO LE12*............112 F1
  RLEINE/SYS LE7............120 C6
Soar Valley Wy *END/NAR LE19*...136 D3
Sobers Gdns *ARN NG5*............37 M1
Society Pl *NORM/LIT DE23*............2 D9
Softwood Cl *BLWL NG6*............23 K8
Soloman Rd
  EWD/SEL/PNX NG16............33 M5
Solway Cl *BSTN/STPLFD NG9*...63 J2
Somerby Ct *BSTN/STPLFD NG9*...48 F3
Somerby Dr *LEIS LE2*............139 G2
Somerby Rd *RLEINE/SYS LE7*...133 K1
Somerby Wy *DERBYE DE21*............44 D5
Somerfield Wy *LEIW LE3*............129 K5
Somersal Cl *DERBYSE DE24*...72 C4
Somersby Rd *ARN NG5*............37 L2
Somerscales Wk *LEIN LE4*............7 J2
Somerset Av *LGEAT NG10*............62 E7
  RLBORO LE12............97 K8
Somerset Dr *LEIN LE4*............123 M8
Somerset St *DERBYE DE21*............44 B8
Somers Rd *LEIE LE5*............133 G1
Somerton Av *CFTN/RUD NG11*...64 C3
Somerville Rd *LEIW LE3*............130 F6
Somme Rd *DERBYW DE22*............42 F4
Songthrush Av *BLWL NG6*............36 B3
Sonning Wy *LEIS LE2*............136 F5
Sopers Rd *RLEIW/BAR LE9*...141 G4
Sophie Rd *NOTTE NG7*............4 B2
Sorrel Cl *RLBORO* LE12............113 J3
Sorrel Rd *LEIE LE5*............127 G5
Sorrel Wy *END/NAR LE19*............135 K6
Soudan Dr *WBRGFD NG2*............50 F6
South Albion St *LEI LE1*............7 G7
Southampton St *LEI LE1*............7 G5
South Av *COT/KEY/RAD NG12*...53 M3
  DERBYE DE21............59 J3
  DERBYW DE22............43 L4
  LEIW LE3............129 M4
  MELB/CHEL DE73............72 D4
  NORM/LIT DE23............57 H6
  WGSTN LE18............138 A5
South Brae Cl *NORM/LIT DE23*...57 H8
Southchurch Dr
  CFTN/RUD NG11............64 C7
South Church Ga *LEI LE1*............6 D3
Southcliffe Rd *CARL NG4*............38 B8
Southcroft *NORM/LIT DE23*...71 H2
South Croxton Rd
  RLEINE/SYS LE7............121 L3
South Devon Av
  MAPPK/POR/STA NG3............37 M5
Southdown Cl *DERBYSE DE24*...71 G5
Southdown Dr *LEIN LE4*............124 F1
Southdown Rd *LBORO LE11*...103 L8
South Dr *DERBY DE1*............43 K8
  DERBYE DE21............58 E2
  LEIE LE5............126 E7
  MCKLVR DE3............56 C6
  MELB/CHEL DE73............56 M7

RLEIW/BAR LE9*............140 C6
Southernhay Cl *LEIS LE2*............132 A6
Southernhay Rd *LEIS LE2*...132 A6
Southey Cl *END/NAR LE19*...135 L5
  LEIN LE4............7 J1
Southey St *NOTTE NG7*............4 D2
Southfield Av *RLEINE/SYS LE7*...120 F4
Southfield Cl *LEIS LE2*............127 K8
  LEIS LE2............136 E4
Southfield Rd *LBORO LE11*............9 L4
  WOL/BIL/BRX NG8............50 B1
Southfields Av *LEIS LE2*............138 D1
Southfields Dr *LEIS LE2*............137 K2
Southgates *LEI LE1*............6 D6
Southgates U/P *LEI* LE1............6 D6
Southglade Rd *ARN NG5*............36 C1
South Kingsmead Rd
  LEIS LE2............138 A1
South Knighton Rd *LEIS LE2*...132 B8
Southland Rd *LEIS LE2*............138 B1
Southlea Rd *CARL NG4*............38 B8
Southmeads Cl *LEIS LE2*............132 D8
Southmeads Rd *LEIS LE2*............132 E7
Southmead Wy *DERBYW DE22*...56 F4
South Pde *LEIS LE2*............5 G7
South Pl *RIPLEY DE5*............11 H6
South Rd *BSTN/STPLFD NG9*...63 L3
  NOTTE NG7............4 D9
  WBRGFD NG2............65 J1
South Sherwood St *NOTT NG1*...5 H3
Southside *ARN NG5*............26 A8
South Snape Cl *BLWL NG6*...23 K8
South St *ALFN DE55*............11 J1
  ALFN DE55............12 A2
  BWSH/BRSTN DE72............60 E8
  DERBY DE1............2 B3
  EWD/SEL/PNX NG16............21 J5
  EWD/SEL/PNX NG16............22 A7
  HUCK/RAV NG15............15 L8
  ILK DE7............33 J7
  LBORO LE11............9 J4
  LEIS LE2............138 E1
  LGEAT NG10............62 C8
  MELB/CHEL DE73............82 E8
  RLBORO LE12............105 H8
Southview Dr *LEIE LE5*............132 D5
South View Rd *CARL NG4*............38 B5
Southwark Cl *DERBYW DE22*...56 F2
Southway *RLEIW/BBY LE8*............142 F1
South Wy *RLEIW/BBY LE8*............146 F6
Southwell Ri
  EWD/SEL/PNX NG16............21 M8
Southwell Rd *NOTT NG1*............5 K7
Southwold Dr
  WOL/BIL/BRX NG8............50 A2
Southwood St *DERBYSE DE24*...58 C7
Sovereign Gv *LGEAT NG10*............61 M8
Sovereign Wy *DERBYE DE21*...45 H4
  HEANOR DE75............20 B6
Sowbrook La *ILK DE7*............47 J4
Sowter Rd *DERBY DE1*............2 D7
Sowters La *RLBORO LE12*............105 L1
Spa Dr *RLEIW/BAR LE9*............140 B7
Spa La *DERBY DE7*............2 D7
  WGSTN LE18............138 B5
Spalding Rd
  MAPPK/POR/STA NG3............51 K2
Spalding St *LEIE LE5*............132 C1
Spaniel Rw *NOTT NG1*............5 G8
Sparkenhoe Rd *RLEIW/BAR LE9*...141 G4
Sparkenhoe St *LEIS LE2*............7 J7
Sparrow Cl *DERBYSE DE24*...71 H3
  ILK DE7............47 L2
Sparrow Hl *LBORO LE11*............9 G2
Spean Dr *WOL/BIL/BRX NG8*...35 M8
Speeds Pingle *LBORO LE11*...9 G2
Speedwell Cl *DERBYE DE21*...45 G4
  END/NAR LE19............135 L5
Speedwell Dr *LEIE LE5*............126 F4
Speedwell Rd *RLBORO LE12*...113 K6
Speers Rd *LEIW LE3*............124 C7
Spenbeck Dr *DERBYW DE22*...43 L2
Spencefield Dr *LEIE LE5*............132 F4
Spencefield La *LEIE LE5*............133 G4
Spencer Av *BPR/DUF DE56*...17 M3
  DERBYSE DE24............72 B3
  LEIE LE5............120 C8
  LGEAT NG10............47 M8
  MAPPK/POR/STA NG3............38 A2
Spencer Cl *CFTN/RUD NG11*...64 F8
Spencer Crs *BSTN/STPLFD NG9*...48 D7
Spencer Dr *EWD/SEL/PNX NG16*...35 G1
Spencer Rd *BPR/DUF DE56*...17 L3
Spencer St *DERBYSE DE24*...58 E7
  ILK DE7............31 K5
  LEIE LE5............138 E1
Spence St *LEIS LE2*............126 B8
Spendlow Gdns *LEIS LE2*............137 J3
Sperry Cl *EWD/SEL/PNX NG16*...13 K1
Spey Cl *HUCK/RAV NG15*............23 H4
Spicer Cl *BSTN/STPLFD NG9*...63 G5
Spiers St *END/NAR LE19*............135 M8
Spindle Gdns *BLWL NG6*............23 L8
Spindle La *CALV/BJ NG14*............26 B2
Spindle Rd *RLBORO LE12*............111 L1
Spindletree Dr *DERBYE DE21*...44 C5
Spindle Vw *CALV/BJ NG14*...26 A3
Spinners Wy *BPR/DUF DE56*...18 A1
The Spinney *ARN NG5*............37 J3
  BLWL NG6............24 C2
  BPR/DUF DE56............17 L1
  BWSH/BRSTN DE72............60 A6
  CALV/BJ NG14............39 M2
  CDON/KEG DE74............84 E3
  ILK DE7............47 K7
  ILK DE7............47 J3
  RLEINE/SYS LE7............133 J3
Spinney Av *RLEIW/BBY LE8*...143 J3
Spinney Cl *COT/KEY/RAD NG12*...67 G5
  DERBYW DE22............43 L5
  GBY/RBY LE6............123 J5
  LEIS LE2............136 E4
  RLEINE/SYS LE7............120 C4
  WBRGFD NG2............66 A3
Spinney Crs *BSTN/STPLFD NG9*...62 D4
Spinney Dr *GBY/RBY LE6*............123 J5

LGEAT NG10 ....62 A5
RLBORO LE12 ....112 D2
Spinney Halt RLEINE/SYS LE7 ....136 C8
Spinney Hl MELB/CHEL DE73...............82 E8
Spinney Hill Dr LBORO LE11...............8 A7
Spinney Ri BSTN/STPLFD NG9...............7 M3
LEIN LE3 ....119 K8
Spinney Rd COT/KEY/RAD NG12...............80 B4
DERBYE DE21 ....44 D8
DERBYW DE21 ....2 B8
ILK DE7 ....47 J1
LGEAT NG10 ....62 A5
Spinneyside GBY/RBY LE6 ....123 J5
Spinney Wy DERBYSE DE74...............85 K5
Spittal CDON/KEG DE74 ....84 E3
Spondon St ARN NG5 ....37 G5
Sponne Ri WGSTN LE18...............137 J3
Spoonley Wood Ct
NORM/LIT * DE23...............56 D8
Sports Field La RLEIW/BAR LE9...............135 H7
Sports Rd LEIW LE3 ....124 A7
The Spot DERBY * DE1...............2 F5
Spray Cl CARL NG4 ....52 C2
Spridgeon Cl LGEAT NG10...............61 M5
Springbrook Dr
RLEINE/SYS LE7...............133 K1
Spring Cl BPR/DUF DE56...............17 J1
BWSH/BRSTN DE72...............61 G7
GBY/RBY LE6 ....123 H7
Springclose LEIS LE2...............137 H2
Spring Cl RLBORO LE12...............102 A5
Springdale Ct MCKLVR DE3...............56 C6
Spring Dale Gdns
BSTN/STPLFD NG9...............48 B5
Springdale Rd LEIN LE4...............126 C1
COAL LE67 ....100 C7
NORM/LIT DE23 ....56 F7
Springfield Av
EWD/SEL/PNX NG16...............21 L5
HEANOR DE75 ....19 M2
LGEAT NG10 ....61 L4
LGEAT NG10 ....62 D7
Spring Field Cl LEIW LE3...............123 M8
Springfield Cl LBORO LE11...............103 J7
RLBORO LE12 ....97 K8
RLEIW/BBY LE8 ....146 E1
Springfield Crs RLEIW/BBY LE8...............146 E8
Springfield Dr BPR/DUF DE56...............29 H4
EWD/SEL/PNX NG16...............35 K1
Springfield Gdn ILK DE7...............33 K5
Springfield Rd ARN NG5...............25 J6
DERBYE DE21 ....58 F2
HUCK/RAV NG15 ....23 H1
LEIS LE2 ....132 A6
MELB/CHEL DE73...............72 C5
RDERBYSW DE65...............68 F4
RLBORO LE12 ....101 L4
RLBORO LE12 ....114 B3
Springfields WBRGFD NG2...............65 H1
Springfield St NOTTE NG7...............36 D6
Springfield Ter RIPLEY DE5...............11 J6
Springfield Vw RIPLEY DE5...............11 H5
Spring Gdns DERBYE DE21...............44 D8
END/NAR * LE19...............142 A1
Spring Gn CFTN/RUD NG11...............64 C8
Spring Hl EWD/SEL/PNX NG16...............34 D2
Springhill Cl BLWL NG6...............23 M6
Springhill Wy RIPLEY DE5...............11 L7
Spring Hollow BPR/DUF DE56...............17 G8
Spring La CARL NG4 ....38 D2
HEANOR DE75 ....20 C6
RLBORO LE12 ....94 B5
RLBORO LE12 ....101 M5
WGSTN LE18 ....138 B4
Spring Meadow
COT/KEY/RAD NG12...............67 L4
Spring Moor WBRGFD NG2...............52 B2
Spring Rd ALFN DE55...............12 C1
BLWL NG6 ....24 A8
Spring St DERBYW DE22...............2 C6
HUCK/RAV NG15 ....15 L7
Springway LEIS LE3...............133 J2
Springwell Cl RLEIW/BBY LE8...............143 J3
Springwell Dr RLEIW/BBY LE8...............143 H3
Springwell La RLEIW/BBY LE8...............142 D4
Springwood Dr DERBYE DE21...............44 E5
Springwood Gdns ARN NG5...............37 K4
Spruce Av EWD/SEL/PNX NG16...............13 H1
LBORO LE11 ....103 L8
Spruce Gv HUCK/RAV NG15...............23 M2
Sprydon Wk CFTN/RUD NG11...............64 D8
The Square BLWL NG6...............24 C3
CFTN/RUD NG11 ....77 M6
COT/KEY/RAD NG12...............80 C5
DERBYW DE22 ....43 L6
END/NAR LE19 ....142 A1
MCKLVR DE3 ....56 B6
RLEIW/BBY LE8 ....143 K4
RLEIW/BBY LE8 ....145 H1
Squares Dr ARN NG5...............24 F1
Squires Av BLWL NG6...............24 D8
Squire's Ride RLEINE/SYS LE7...............115 H7
Squires Wy NORM/LIT DE23...............70 E1
WBRGFD NG2 ....65 H1
Squirrel Cl END/NAR LE19...............135 L8
Squirrel's Cnr RLEINE/SYS LE7...............115 J7
Squirrel Wy LBORO LE11...............8 F7
Stable Cl END/NAR LE19...............136 A8
Stables St DERBYE DE22...............57 H2
Stacey Av ARN NG5...............24 D8
Stackley Rd RLEIW/BBY LE8...............139 M6
Stadium Pl LEIN LE4...............125 J5
Stadium Ri LEIN * LE4...............125 H6
Stadium Vw DERBYSE DE24...............58 C4
Stadon Rd RLEINE/SYS LE7...............124 B1
Stafford Cl ILK DE7...............31 K1
Stafford Ct BLWL NG6...............35 K1
Stafford Dr WGSTN LE18...............137 K5
Stafford Leys LEIW LE3...............129 K4
Staffords Acre CDON/KEG DE74...............86 A5
Stafford St DERBY DE1...............2 C4
LEIN LE4 ....126 A4
LGEAT NG10 ....62 D7
Stagsden Crs WOL/BIL/BRX NG8...............49 G2

Staindale WGSTN LE18 ....138 D5
Staindale Dr WOL/BIL/BRX NG8...............36 B6
Staines Cl MCKLVR DE3...............56 A6
Stainmore Dr END/NAR LE19...............135 K5
Stainsborough Rd
HUCK/RAV NG15 ....23 G1
Stainsby Av HEANOR DE75...............20 C6
ILK DE7 ....31 J1
Stainsdale Gn COAL LE67...............108 C5
Staker La MCKLVR DE3...............70 B1
Stamford Cl LEIW LE3...............123 M7
LEIN LE4 ....76 B3
Stamford Dr COAL LE67...............109 H5
GBY/RBY LE6 ....123 K5
RLEINE/SYS LE7...............118 D4
Stamford Rd RLEIW/BAR LE9...............129 J3
WBRGFD NG2 ....65 L1
Stamford St DERBYSE DE24...............72 B1
EWD/SEL/PNX NG16...............22 A6
EWD/SEL/PNX NG16...............34 A3
GBY/RBY LE6 ....122 F6
HEANOR DE75 ....20 C5
ILK DE7 ....33 J6
LEI LE1 ....6 F7
LEIW LE3 ....123 M7
Stanage Gn MCKLVR DE3...............56 D5
Stanage Rd RLBORO LE12...............114 C3
Stanbrig WGSTN * LE18...............138 C3
Stancliffe Av BLWL NG6...............24 A8
Stancliff Rd LEIN LE4...............126 D2
Standard Ct NOTT * NG1...............4 F8
Standard Hl NOTT NG1...............4 F8
Standhill Av CARL NG4...............37 M7
Standhill Rd
MAPPK/POR/STA NG3...............37 L6
Stanesby Ri CFTN/RUD NG11...............64 C6
Stanfell Rd LEIS LE2...............131 M7
Stanford Gdns
COT/KEY/RAD NG12...............53 K3
Stanford Hl LBORO LE11...............103 M1
Stanford Rd RLBORO LE12...............95 J5
Stanford St NOTT NG1...............5 G8
Stanhome Dr WBRGFD NG2...............65 H3
Stanhome Sq WBRGFD NG2...............65 H4
Stanhope Crs ARN NG5...............25 J7
CALV/BJ NG14 ....39 K8
Stanhope Rd ARN NG5...............25 J7
CARL NG4 ....38 B3
MCKLVR DE3 ....56 C4
WGSTN LE18 ....138 C6
Stanhope St ILK DE7...............47 J7
ILK DE7 ....47 L1
LEIE LE5 ....132 B2
LGEAT NG10 ....62 A8
NORM/LIT DE23...............57 K6
NOTT NG1 ....5 K7
Stanier Dr LEIN LE4...............126 E3
Stanier Wy DERBYE DE21...............58 E4
EWD/SEL/PNX NG16...............22 B8
Stanley Av NOTTE NG7...............36 E7
RIPLEY DE5 ....11 J5
Stanley Cl DERBYW DE22...............43 K7
ILK DE7 ....33 J8
Stanley Dr BSTN/STPLFD NG9...............48 E7
LEIE LE5 ....126 E7
Stanley Pl NOTT NG1...............4 F6
Stanley Rd DERBYE DE21...............58 E2
DERBYSE DE24 ....72 C1
LEIS LE2 ....132 A4
MAPPK/POR/STA NG3...............37 L5
NOTTE NG7 ....36 D6
WBRGFD NG2 ....65 K1
Stanley St DERBYW DE22...............57 H2
ILK DE7 ....33 K8
LBORO LE11 ....9 J6
LGEAT NG10 ....62 C8
Stanmore Cl WOL/BIL/BRX NG8...............35 J4
Stanmore Gdns ARN NG5...............37 J1
Stansfield St NOTTE NG7...............50 C2
Stanstead Av ARN NG5...............24 B6
COT/KEY/RAD NG12...............66 B7
Stanstead Rd MCKLVR DE3...............56 A3
Stanthorne Cl CFTN/RUD NG11...............64 E3
Stanton Ga ILK DE7...............48 A6
Stanton La
COT/KEY/RAD NG12...............80 F5
RLEIW/BAR LE9...............140 D3
Stanton Rd ILK DE7...............47 K1
LGEAT NG10 ....47 K8
RLEIW/BAR LE9...............140 B7
Stanton Rw LEIS LE2...............137 K1
Stanton St NORM/LIT DE23...............57 K6
Stanway Cl
MAPPK/POR/STA NG3...............52 A1
Stanwick Cl WOL/BIL/BRX NG8...............35 J7
Stanyon Cl RLEIW/BAR LE9...............143 J3
Stapleford La
BSTN/STPLFD NG9...............62 D4
Stapleford Rd
BSTN/STPLFD NG9...............48 A3
LEIN LE4 ....125 H3
Staplehurst Av END/NAR LE19...............130 C7
Staplehurst Dr ARN NG5...............36 E3
Stapleton Rd ILK DE7...............33 J3
Starch La LGEAT NG10...............47 M8
Star Cottages
RLEIW/BAR LE9...............140 B3
Starcross Ct MCKLVR DE3...............56 A4
Starkie Av CDON/KEG DE74...............84 D4
Starmer Cl RLEIW/BAR LE9...............142 C4
Starthe Bank HEANOR DE75...............20 D5
Starth Wood Rd
HUCK/RAV NG15 ....23 H3
Statham St DERBYW DE22...............43 J8
Stathern Wk ARN NG5...............24 F8
Station Ap BPR/DUF DE56...............29 K3
DERBY DE1 ....3 H5
Station Av CARL NG4...............38 C6
HUCK/RAV NG15 ....15 K1
LBORO LE11 ....8 E1
Station Cl MELB/CHEL DE73...............72 D6
RLEIW/BAR LE9...............129 J3
Station Dr RLEIW/BAR LE9...............129 J3
Station La EWD/SEL/PNX NG16...............12 D4
RIPLEY DE5 ....19 M1
RLEINE/SYS LE7...............127 K8

Station Rd BLWL NG6 ....36 A1
BPR/DUF DE56 ....29 K3
BSTN/STPLFD NG9...............63 L1
BWSH/BRSTN DE72...............59 M6
BWSH/BRSTN DE72...............60 F8
CALV/BJ NG14 ....39 K4
CARL NG4 ....38 D8
CDON/KEG DE74...............84 F2
CDON/KEG DE74...............86 C4
COT/KEY/RAD NG12...............80 C5
COT/KEY/RAD NG12...............91 G2
DERBYE DE21 ....30 A8
DERBYE DE21 ....59 H4
END/NAR LE19 ....136 A3
EWD/SEL/PNX NG16...............20 F5
EWD/SEL/PNX NG16...............34 A2
EWD/SEL/PNX NG16...............34 D1
GBY/RBY LE6 ....123 C7
HUCK/RAV NG15 ....15 M8
HUCK/RAV NG15 ....15 J1
ILK DE7 ....32 A7
ILK DE7 ....33 K6
ILK DE7 ....44 B3
ILK DE7 ....45 M2
ILK DE7 ....46 A1
LEIN LE4 ....125 K2
LEIW LE3 ....124 A6
LGEAT NG10 ....61 M2
LGEAT NG10 ....62 D7
MCKLVR DE3 ....56 B5
MELB/CHEL DE73...............72 D6
MELB/CHEL DE73...............82 F7
RIPLEY DE5 ....18 F4
RLBORO LE12 ....88 B6
RLBORO LE12 ....112 E1
RLEINE/SYS LE7...............115 C3
RLEINE/SYS LE7...............118 E4
RLEINE/SYS LE7...............120 E4
RLEINE/SYS LE7...............133 K2
RLEIW/BAR LE9...............128 A4
RLEIW/BAR LE9...............129 H2
RLEIW/BAR LE9...............140 A4
RLEIW/BAR LE9...............141 G3
RLEIW/BBY LE8 ....143 H4
RLEIW/BBY LE8 ....145 L1
RMMWB LE14 ....91 L8
WGSTN LE18 ....137 M5
Station St LBORO LE11...............8 F2
LEI LE1 ....7 H7
LGEAT NG10 ....62 D8
RLEIW/BBY LE8...............136 C7
RLEIW/BBY LE8...............146 E7
WGSTN LE18 ....137 K5
Station Ter COT/KEY/RAD NG12...............53 K4
HUCK/RAV NG15 ....15 M8
Staunton Av NORM/LIT DE23...............71 J1
Staunton Cl CDON/KEG DE74...............84 E3
Staunton Dr ARN NG5...............37 G3
Staveley Cl DERBYSE DE24...............72 C4
RLBORO LE12 ....114 B5
WGSTN LE18 ....138 C5
Staveley Ct LBORO * LE11...............103 M2
Staveley Rd LEIE LE5...............132 B1
Staverton Dr MCKLVR DE3...............56 B3
Staverton Rd WOL/BIL/BRX NG8...............35 J8
Staythorpe Rd LEIN LE4...............126 E2
Steadfold Cl BLWL NG6...............35 M1
Steadman Av RLEIW/BAR LE9...............142 C4
Steads Cl CARL NG4...............38 D8
Steam Mill La RIPLEY DE5...............11 L7
Stebbings Rd LEIS LE2...............137 H2
Steedman Av
MAPPK/POR/STA NG3...............37 L3
Steele Cl LEIE LE5...............132 E2
Steeles Wy CARL NG4...............26 F8
Steeple Cl DERBYE DE21...............44 C5
WGSTN LE18 ....138 C3
Steeple Rw LBORO LE11...............9 J3
Steinbeck Rd CARL NG4...............38 A8
Steins La LEIE LE5...............126 F1
Stella Av COT/KEY/RAD NG12...............66 B7
Stella Gv COT/KEY/RAD NG12...............66 B7
Stelle Wy RLEINE/SYS LE7...............124 B4
Stenor Cl RLEIW/BAR LE9...............145 J7
Stenson Av NORM/LIT DE23...............71 J1
Stenson Ct RIPLEY DE5...............11 K6
Stenson Rd COAL LE67...............108 B5
DERBYSE DE24 ....71 G5
LEIW LE3 ....124 E6
NORM/LIT DE23 ....57 K7
Stephenson Ct LEIW LE3...............124 A5
Stephenson Dr LEIW LE3...............125 G8
Stephensons Wy DERBYE DE21...............58 K4
Stephenson Wy COAL LE67...............108 A4
GBY/RBY LE6 ....123 J4
Stepney Ct WOL/BIL/BRX NG8...............35 K6
Stepping Cl DERBYW DE22...............57 H2
Stepping La DERBYW DE22...............57 H2
Sterling Cl RIPLEY DE5...............18 F5
Sterndale Rd LGEAT NG10...............75 M1
Stevenage Cl DERBYSE DE24...............72 D2
Steven Cl BSTN/STPLFD NG9...............62 D3
Stevenholme Crs ARN NG5...............36 E1
Stevens Cl RLEIW/BAR LE9...............140 C5
Stevens La BWSH/BRSTN DE72...............61 H7
Stevenson Av
BWSH/BRSTN DE72...............60 F7
Stevenson Gdns
CFTN/RUD NG11...............79 H1
RLEIW/BAR LE9...............142 B3
Stevenson Pl NORM/LIT DE23...............56 F7
Stevens Rd LGEAT NG10...............61 L2
Stevenstone Cl LEIS LE2...............139 H2
Stewart Av END/NAR LE19...............135 L6
Stewart Cl DERBYE DE21...............59 J1
Stewart Dr LBORO LE11...............103 C1
Stewart St ALFN DE55...............12 B2
Steyning Crs LEIW LE3...............124 B6
The Stiles RLEINE/SYS LE7...............120 F3
Stiles Rd DERBYE DE24...............58 F8
MAPPK/POR/STA NG3...............38 A2
Stinsford Cl ARN NG5...............25 G7
Stinson Wy COAL LE67...............108 B2
Stirland St RIPLEY DE5...............11 M6
Stirling Av LBORO LE11...............8 A7
Stirling Cl DERBYE DE21...............44 A7
RLBORO LE12 ....104 D3
RLEINE/SYS LE7...............113 G7

Stirling Dr RLEINE/SYS LE7...............133 K1
Stirling Gdns BSTN/STPLFD NG9...............62 F5
Stirling Gv CFTN/RUD NG11...............64 D7
Stockbrook Rd DERBYW DE22...............57 H4
Stockbrook St DERBYW DE22...............2 B6
Stockdale Cl ARN NG5...............24 C5
Stockdove Cl DERBYSE DE24...............71 H3
Stockgill Wy WBRGFD NG2...............66 A1
Stockhill Circ BLWL NG6...............36 A4
Stockhill La BLWL NG6...............36 A4
Stocking La RLBORO LE12...............88 A4
Stockland Rd LEIS LE2...............137 J3
RLEINE/SYS LE7...............127 K7
Stocks Rd EWD/SEL/PNX NG16...............22 C8
Stock Well BLWL NG6...............35 M1
Stockwell Rd LEIS LE2...............138 A1
Stoddard Dr HEANOR DE75...............20 D5
Stoke Cl BPR/DUF DE56...............18 B3
Stoke Ferry La
COT/KEY/RAD NG12...............39 L6
Stoke La CALV/BJ NG14...............39 K4
CARL NG4 ....38 C5
Stokes Dr LEIW LE3...............124 F7
Stolle Cl ARN NG5...............26 A8
Stoneacre ARN NG5...............24 F7
Stonebow Cl RLBORO LE12...............102 F1
Stonebridge Dr RLBORO LE12...............88 D5
Stone Bridge Rd
MAPPK/POR/STA NG3...............5 L3
Stonebridge St LEIE LE5...............132 B1
Stonechat Cl MCKLVR DE3...............56 E4
Stonechat Wk LEIE LE5...............7 M4
Stone Cl DERBYE DE21...............59 J1
LEIN LE4 ....124 E1
Stonecroft RLEIW/BBY LE8...............143 G4
Stonecrop Rd LEIS LE2...............127 G5
Stonehaven Cl ARN NG5...............25 M6
COAL LE67 ....109 G6
Stonehaven Rd LEIN LE4...............126 B3
Stonehill CDON/KEG DE74...............84 F5
Stonehill Av LEIN LE4...............119 L7
Stone Hill Rd NORM/LIT DE23...............2 C9
Stonehills CDON/KEG DE74...............86 A5
Stonehurst La RLBORO LE12...............95 H4
Stonehurst Rd LEIW LE3...............130 D7
Stoneleigh St NOTTE NG7...............4 D5
Stoneleigh Wy LEIW LE3...............124 F7
Stonepit Cl
MAPPK/POR/STA NG3...............37 K7
Stonesby Av WGSTN LE18...............137 J2
Stonesby Cl LEIS LE2...............132 A5
Stonesby V CFTN/RUD NG11...............64 E4
Stoneycroft Rd BLWL NG6...............36 C2
Stoney Cross DERBYSE DE21...............59 J4
Stoneyfield Bank
BPR/DUF DE56...............17 L2
Stoney Flatts Crs
DERBYE DE21...............44 E7
Stoneygate Cl LEIS LE2...............132 A6
Stoneygate Ct LEIS LE2...............132 A5
Stoney Gate Rd DERBYE DE21...............59 H4
Stoneygate Rd LEIS LE2...............132 B5
Stoney Houghton Gdns
BLWL NG6...............23 K7
Stoney La BSTN/STPLFD NG9...............47 M2
DERBYE DE21 ....59 J2
EWD/SEL/PNX NG16...............21 G1
Stoney St NOTT NG1...............5 J7
Stoneywell Rd LEIN LE4...............124 D2
Stonyhurst Ct DERBYSE DE24...............72 C4
Stony La BPR/DUF DE56...............30 A1
Stoodley Pike Gdns
DERBYW DE22...............43 G5
Stoop La RLBORO LE12...............112 E1
Stoppard Cl ILK DE7...............33 H5
Storer Cl RLBORO LE12...............114 B4
Storer Rd LBORO LE11...............8 E2
Stores La RLEIW/BBY LE8...............145 K8
Stores Rd DERBYE DE21...............43 M8
Storey Av CARL NG4...............38 C5
Storey St LEIW LE3...............6 E2
Stornaway Rd LEIE LE5...............127 H8
Stornoway Cl DERBYSE DE24...............71 H4
Storth Av HUCK/RAV NG15...............23 L1
Story Gdns HUCK/RAV NG15...............15 K8
Stotfield Rd WOL/BIL/BRX NG8...............48 F2
Stoughton Av LEIS LE2...............132 B6
Stoughton Cl LEIS LE2...............138 F1
Stoughton Dr LEIS LE2...............132 B4
Stoughton Dr North LEIS LE2...............132 B4
Stoughton Dr South LEIS LE2...............132 B4
Stoughton La LEIS LE2...............133 H6
Stoughton Rd LEIS LE2...............132 B6
LEIS LE2 ....138 E1
RLEINE/SYS LE7...............133 J4
Stoughton St LEIE LE5...............7 K7
Stoughton St South LEIE LE5...............7 K7
Stour Cl LEIS LE2...............139 H1
RDERBYSW DE65...............68 C7
Stourdale Cl LGEAT NG10...............75 L1
Stourport Dr MELB/CHEL DE73...............72 F4
Stowe Av WBRGFD NG2...............65 H2
Stowe Cl LEIW LE3...............124 E6
Stowmarket Dr DERBYE DE21...............44 E7
St Patrick's Rd HUCK/RAV NG15...............15 K8
Strachan Cl RLBORO LE12...............113 K6
Strancliffe La RLBORO LE12...............105 H6
The Strand BSTN/STPLFD NG9...............63 H6
DERBY * DE1...............2 E3
Strand DERBY DE1...............2 E3
Strand Ar DERBY * DE1...............2 E3
Strasbourg Dr LEIN LE4...............124 F4
Stratford Av LEIE LE5...............126 B5
LEIW LE3 ....130 D6
WBRGFD NG2 ....51 K8
Stratford Cl ILK DE7...............33 K3
Strathaven Ct DERBYE DE21...............59 J2
Strathaven Rd LEIE LE5...............126 A5
Strathglen Cl
EWD/SEL/PNX NG16...............22 C8
Strathmore Av DERBYSE DE24...............72 D1
LEIE LE5 ....126 B5
Strathmore Cl COAL LE67...............109 G6
HUCK/RAV NG15 ....23 J2

Stratmore Rd ARN NG5...............25 M6
Streatham Rd DERBYSE DE22...............56 E1
Street La RIPLEY DE5...............18 E1
Strelley Av RIPLEY DE5...............11 G7
Strelley Rd WOL/BIL/BRX NG8...............35 K7
Strelley St BLWL NG6...............23 M8
Strensall Rd LEIE LE5...............127 H4
The Stretton NOTTE * NG7...............50 C5
Stretton Cl MCKLVR DE3...............56 B6
Stretton Dr COAL LE67...............109 G6
Stretton Hall Dr LEIS LE2...............139 K4
Stretton Rd LEIW LE3...............131 G2
RLEIW/BBY LE8 ....139 M5
Striding Edge Cl LGEAT NG10...............61 M5
Stripes Vw CALV/BJ NG14...............26 D1
Stroma Cl DERBYSE DE24...............71 K3
Stroma Wy RLEIW/BBY LE8...............143 K4
Strome Cl WBRGFD NG2...............51 G5
Stroud Rd LEIE LE5...............126 B8
Strudwick Wy RLEIW/BBY LE8...............136 E7
Strutt St BPR/DUF DE56...............17 K4
LBORO LE11 ....8 D4
Stuart Cl ARN NG5...............25 M7
Stuart Rd LEIS LE2...............137 G4
Stuart St DERBY DE1...............2 F2
LEIW LE3 ....131 H4
RLEIW/BBY LE8...............146 E7
Stubbs Rd LEIN LE4...............7 J1
Studbrook Cl CDON/KEG DE74...............84 D4
Studland Wy WBRGFD NG2...............65 K8
Sturdee Cl LEIS LE2...............137 H4
Sturdee Gn LEIS LE2...............137 G3
Sturdee Rd LEIS LE2...............137 H3
Sturgeon Av CFTN/RUD NG11...............64 D3
Sturges La BWSH/BRSTN DE72...............75 J3
Sturrock Cl RLEINE/SYS LE7...............133 K1
Sturton St NOTTE NG7...............36 E7
Styon Rd LEIW LE3...............124 C6
Styring St BSTN/STPLFD NG9...............63 L1
Sudbury Av ILK DE7...............33 L3
LGEAT NG10 ....47 L8
Sudbury Cl DERBY DE1...............2 B4
Sudbury Ms
EWD/SEL/PNX NG16...............21 J6
Sudbury St DERBY DE1...............2 A4
Sudeley Av LEIN LE4...............125 J5
Suez St NOTTE NG7...............36 D6
Suffolk Av BSTN/STPLFD NG9...............64 A3
DERBYE DE21 ....58 D8
HUCK/RAV NG15 ....23 G2
Suffolk Cl WGSTN LE18...............137 L4
Suffolk St LEIE LE5...............132 C2
Sulgrave Rd LEIE LE5...............126 B8
Sulleys Fld DERBYW DE27...............29 H8
Sullington Rd RLBORO LE12...............101 M4
Sullivan Cl
MAPPK/POR/STA NG3...............37 K8
Sullivan St NOTTE NG7...............50 C2
Sumburgh Rd CFTN/RUD NG11...............64 D6
Summerbrook Ct DERBYE DE22...............2 C6
Summerfields Wy ILK DE7...............33 H4
Summerfields Wy South ILK DE7...............33 H5
Summerlea Rd LEIE LE5...............133 G1
Summer Leys La WBRGFD NG2...............51 H4
Summerpool Rd LBORO LE11...............95 K8
Summer Wy
COT/KEY/RAD NG12...............53 J3
Summer Wood Ct
NORM/LIT DE23...............57 H8
Summerwood La
CFTN/RUD NG11...............64 B8
Sunart Cl DERBYSE DE24...............71 K5
Sunbourne Ct NOTTE NG7...............4 B4
Sunbury Gdns ARN NG5...............25 L6
Sunbury Gn LEIE LE5...............127 J8
Sunbury Ri RLEIW/BBY LE8...............143 G3
Sunderland Gv
WOL/BIL/BRX NG8...............35 H5
Sundew Cl DERBYE DE21...............59 K3
Sundew Rd LEIE LE5...............127 G5
Sundown Av NORM/LIT DE23...............71 H1
Sunlea Crs BSTN/STPLFD NG9...............62 D2
Sunningdale Dr
COT/KEY/RAD NG12...............66 B6
HEANOR DE75 ....59 H2
Sunningdale Dr CALV/BJ NG14...............27 G2
ILK DE7 ....46 F2
Sunningdale Rd LEIW LE3...............129 M3
Sunninghill Cl ILK DE7...............32 B2
Sunninghill Dr CFTN/RUD NG11...............64 C4
Sunninghill Ri ARN NG5...............25 L6
Sunny Bank Gdns
BPR/DUF DE56...............17 K5
Sunnycroft Rd LEIW LE3...............130 E2
Sunnydale Rd
MAPPK/POR/STA NG3...............51 M1
Sunnyfield Cl LEIE LE5...............133 G2
Sunny Gv DERBYE DE21...............58 E2
Sunny Hl BPR/DUF DE56...............17 K8
Sunnyhill Av NORM/LIT DE23...............71 J1
Sunnyhill Rd LBORO LE11...............8 E9
Sunny Side LEIS LE2...............139 G3
Sunnyside RLEIW/BBY LE8...............136 D7
Sunnyside Rd
BSTN/STPLFD NG9...............62 F1
Sunrise Av ARN NG5...............36 D2
ARN NG5 ....36 D2
Sun St DERBYW DE22...............2 E3
Sun Wy LEIW LE3...............130 B4
Surbiton Cl DERBYSE DE22...............56 E1
Surbiton Ct ILK DE7...............32 B7
Surbiton Sq WOL/BIL/BRX NG8...............35 M4
Surfleet Cl WOL/BIL/BRX NG8...............49 G4
Surgey's La ARN NG5...............25 L6
Surrey St DERBYW DE22...............57 H1
LEIN LE4 ....125 M6
Susan Av LEIE LE5...............132 F3
Susan Cl HUCK/RAV NG15...............15 M6
Susan Dr BLWL NG6...............36 D2
Sussex Circ DERBYE DE21...............44 C7
Sussex Cl EWD/SEL/PNX NG16...............21 G2
Sussex Rd WGSTN LE18...............137 K4
Sussex St LEIW LE3...............6 C4
Sussex Wy LGEAT NG10...............61 M2
Sutherland Wy
RLEINE/SYS LE7...............118 C8
Sutherland Dr WBRGFD NG2...............65 L3

Sutherland Rd
MAPPK/POR/STA NG3 ....**37** M8
NORM/LIT NG8 ....**57** K7
Sutherland St *LEIS* LE2 ....**7** G3
Suthers Rd *CDON/KEG* DE74 ....**86** A5
Sutton Av *LEIN* LE4 ....**126** A6
MELB/CHEL DE73 ....**72** D4
Sutton CI *DERBYW* DE22 ....**57** G1
LEIS LE2 ....**138** F4
RLBORO LE12 ....**95** G2
RLBORO LE12 ....**112** D2
Sutton Ct *EWD/SEL/PNX* NG16 ....**21** K5
RLEIW/BAR LE9 ....**141** J7
Sutton Dr *DERBYSE* DE24 ....**72** C3
Sutton Gdns *CFTN/RUD* NG11 ....**79** C1
Sutton La *RDERBYSW* DE65 ....**68** A4
RDERBYSW DE65 ....**68** A3
Sutton Passeys Crs
WOL/BIL/BRX NG8 ....**49** M4
Sutton PI *LEIN* LE4 ....**126** A5
Sutton Rd *ARN* NG5 ....**25** K5
CDON/KEG DE74 ....**86** A6
LEIS LE2 ....**131** L8
Swain's Av
MAPPK/POR/STA NG3 ....**51** L1
Swainson Rd *LEIN* LE4 ....**126** C7
Swain St *LEI* LE1 ....**7** H6
Swale CI *LEIS* LE2 ....**139** H1
Swallow CI *BLWL* NG6 ....**36** B4
MCKLVR DE3 ....**56** E4
RLBORO LE12 ....**113** K5
Swallow DI *COAL* LE67 ....**100** B8
Swallowdale Dr *LEIN* LE4 ....**124** F1
Swallowdale Rd *DERBYSE* DE24 ....**71** H3
Swallow Dr *RLEIW/SYS* LE7 ....**120** D3
Swallow Gdns *CARL* NG4 ....**37** M6
Swallows CI *LEIW* LE5 ....**129** J6
Swallow Wk *RLBORO* LE12 ....**94** E6
RLBORO LE12 ....**113** K5
Swan CI *MCKLVR* DE3 ....**69** M1
Swan Meadow *CARL* NG4 ....**52** D3
Swanmote Rd *NORM/LIT* DE23 ....**56** E7
Swannington Rd *LEIW* LE3 ....**125** D3
Swannymote Rd *COAL* LE67 ....**108** L1
Swanscombe Rd *LEIS* LE2 ....**131** K6
Swansdowne Dr
CFTN/RUD NG11 ....**64** D3
Swan St *LBORO* LE11 ....**9** H2
LEIW LE3 ....**6** C4
RLBORO LE12 ....**106** D7
RLBORO LE12 ....**114** A4
Swan Wy *COAL* LE67 ....**108** D7
RLEINE/SYS LE7 ....**120** C3
Swanwick *DERBYE* DE21 ....**44** E6
Swarkestone Br
MELB/CHEL DE73 ....**82** B2
Swarkestone Dr
NORM/LIT DE23 ....**71** G2
Swarkestone Rd
MELB/CHEL DE73 ....**72** D6
Swayfield CI *MCKLVR* DE3 ....**55** M4
Sweetbriar CI *DERBYSE* DE24 ....**72** E2
Sweetbriar Rd *LEIS* LE2 ....**131** G4
Sweet Leys Dr *RLBORO* LE12 ....**88** D3
Sweet Leys Rd *WBRGFD* NG2 ....**50** F6
Swenson Av *NOTTE* NG7 ....**50** C5
Swift CI *MCKLVR* DE3 ....**56** E4
RLEINE/SYS LE7 ....**120** D3
Swift Ct *EWD/SEL/PNX* NG16 ....**21** K5
Swift's CI *RLBORO* LE12 ....**98** A4
Swigert CI *BLWL* NG6 ....**35** K2
MAPPK/POR/STA NG3 ....**51** L1
Swinburne Wy *ARN* NG5 ....**37** G1
Swinderby Dr *DERBYE* DE21 ....**44** M4
Swindon CI *EWD/SEL/PNX* NG16 ..**21** M8
Swiney Wy *BSTN/STPLFD* NG9 ......**62** B5
Swinfield Rd *RLBORO* LE12 ....**112** L1
Swinford Av *LEIS* LE2 ....**137** H5
Swingate *EWD/SEL/PNX* NG16 ......**34** L2
Swingbridge Rd *LBORO* LE11 ....**95** K8
Swiney La *BPR/DUF* DE56 ....**17** L2
Swinstead *WOL/BIL/BRX* NG8 ....**49** K1
Swinstead Rd *LEIS* LE3 ....**133** H3
Swithland Av *LEIN* LE4 ....**125** J6
LBORO LE11 ....**102** F2
Swithland CI *COAL* LE67 ....**116** C7
LBORO LE11 ....**102** F2
Swithland Dr *WBRGFD* NG2 ....**65** J3
Swithland La *RLEINE/SYS* LE7 ......**112** F7
Swithland Rd *COAL* LE67 ....**109** C7
RLEINE/SYS LE7 ....**118** C3
Sword CI *LEIN* LE4 ....**124** A3
Sybil Rd *LEIW* LE3 ....**130** F6
Sycamore Av *DERBYW* DE22 ....**43** H4
RDERBYSW DE65 ....**70** B5
RIPLEY DE5 ....**11** H7
Sycamore CI
COT/KEY/RAD NG12 ....**53** K5
HUCK/RAV NG15 ....**23** J4
LEIS LE2 ....**132** D6
LEIS LE2 ....**139** L4
RDERBYSW DE65 ....**69** G3
RLEINE/SYS LE7 ....**120** F5
Sycamore Ct *DERBYE* DE21 ....**59** J2
Sycamore Crs *LGEAT* NG10 ....**47** L8
GBY/RBY DE6 ....**123** K5
ILK DE7 ....**33** M8
Sycamore Gv *GBY/RBY* LE6 ....**123** K4
Sycamore PI
MAPPK/POR/STA NG3 ....**37** G7
Sycamore Ri *BLWL* NG6 ....**36** A3
Sycamore Rd *CDON/KEG* DE74 ......**84** F2
EWD/SEL/PNX NG16 ....**33** M3
LGEAT NG10 ....**76** A2
RLEINE/SYS LE7 ....**119** L7
The Sycamores
EWD/SEL/PNX NG16 ....**21** J7
Sycamore St *RLEIW/BBY* LE8 ......**136** F7
Sycamore Wy *END/NAR* LE19 ......**141** M1
LBORO LE11 ....**103** L8
Sydenham Rd *DERBYW* DE22 ....**42** E8
Sydney CI *MCKLVR* DE3 ....**56** D4
Sydney Gv *COT/KEY/RAD* NG12 ....**53** J4
Sydney Houses
NORM/LIT * DE23 ....**57** G6
Sydney Rd *BWSH/BRSTN* DE72 ......**60** E8

Sykefield Av *LEIW* LE3 ....**131** G3
Syke Rd *ARN* NG5 ....**24** C7
Sylvan Av *LEIE* LE5 ....**132** B1
Sylvan St *LEIW* LE3 ....**131** G1
Sylvan Wy *LEIW* LE3 ....**129** M3
Synge CI *CFTN/RUD* NG11 ....**64** A7
Syston Av *RLEINE/SYS* LE7 ....**114** A8
RLEINE/SYS LE7 ....**121** H1
Syston St East *LEI* LE1 ....**7** J2
Syston St West *LEI* LE1 ....**7** H1
Sywell Av *LBORO* LE11 ....**102** F4
Sywell Dr *WGSTN* LE18 ....**138** C5

T

Tadcaster Av *LEIS* LE2 ....**137** H4
Taddington Rd *DERBYE* DE21 ....**44** C7
Taft Av *LGEAT* NG10 ....**61** M1
Taft Leys Rd *RLBORO* LE12 ....**88** D5
Tailby Av *LEIE* LE5 ....**126** C7
Talbot Ct *COT/KEY/RAD* NG12 ....**53** J4
Talbot Ct *BSTN/STPLFD* NG9 ....**48** B5
Talbot La *COAL* LE67 ....**100** A8
LEI LE1 ....**6** C6
Talbot St *COAL* LE67 ....**108** B1
DERBYE DE22 ....**2** C4
LEIN LE4 ....**125** L4
NOTT NG1 ....**4** E6
Talgarth CI *DERBYE* DE21 ....**45** C5
Tamar Av *DERBYW* DE22 ....**43** H3
Tamarix CI *CARL* NG4 ....**38** E5
Tamar Rd *LEIN* LE4 ....**126** C5
LEIS LE2 ....**139** H2
Tamerton Rd *LEIS* LE2 ....**137** J3
Tamworth Rd *RLBORO* LE12 ....**101** K5
Tamworth Crs
WOL/BIL/BRX NG8 ....**35** J6
Tanner's La *RLEIW/BAR* LE9 ....**94** E6
Tansey Crs *RLEIW/BAR* LE9 ....**140** A5
Tansley Av *ILK* DE7 ....**31** L6
WGSTN LE18 ....**137** L6
Tansley Ri *DERBYE* DE21 ....**44** D6
Tants Meadow *BPR/DUF* DE56 ......**30** C1
Tantum Av *HEANOR* DE75 ....**20** A3
Tanwood Rd *BSTN/STPLFD* NG9 ....**62** H5
Tanyard *CDON/KEG* DE74 ....**84** F3
Taplow CI *MCKLVR* DE3 ....**56** A5
Tarbat Rd *LEIE* LE5 ....**127** H8
Tarbert CI *WBRGFD* NG2 ....**50** F5
Target St *NOTTE* NG7 ....**50** C2
Tarina CI *MELB/CHEL* DE73 ....**72** E6
Tarragon Rd *LEIS* LE2 ....**6** D1
Tasman CI *MCKLVR* DE3 ....**56** D4
Tatham's La *ILK* DE7 ....**33** J5
Tatlow Rd *LEIN* LE4 ....**130** A1
Tattershall Dr
BSTN/STPLFD NG9 ....**49** M8
NOTTE NG7 ....**4** C7
Tattle HI *ILK* DE7 ....**46** D5
Tatton CI *LEIW* LE3 ....**124** E6
WGSTN LE18 ....**138** A6
Taunton CI *DERBYSE* DE24 ....**59** C7
WGSTN LE18 ....**138** A6
Taunton Rd *LEIW* LE3 ....**130** F2
WBRGFD NG2 ....**65** K1
Taupo Dr *HUCK/RAV* NG15 ....**23** C2
Taurus CI *LEIE* LE5 ....**7** K6
Tavern Av *WOL/BIL/BRX* NG8 ....**36** A5
Taverner Dr *GBY/RBY* LE6 ....**123** H8
Taverners Crs *NORM/LIT* DE23 ......**57** H7
Taverners Rd *LEIN* LE4 ....**119** C8
Tavistock Av
MAPPK/POR/STA NG3 ....**37** C6
RIPLEY DE5 ....**11** C4
Tavistock CI *DERBYSE* DE24 ....**71** H4
HUCK/RAV NG15 ....**23** H2
Tavistock Dr *LEIE* LE5 ....**132** C4
MAPPK/POR/STA NG3 ....**37** C6
Tavistock Rd *WBRGFD* NG2 ....**65** K1
Tawny Wy *NORM/LIT* DE23 ....**56** E8
Tay CI *DERBYSE* DE24 ....**71** H5
Taylor CI *RLBORO* LE12 ....**120** E4
WBRGFD NG2 ....**51** L3
Taylor Crs *BSTN/STPLFD* NG9 ....**48** C7
Taylor La *HEANOR* DE75 ....**20** B4
Taylor Rd *LEI* LE1 ....**7** H2
Taylor's Bridge Rd
WGSTN LE18 ....**137** L6
Taylors CI *RLEIW/BAR* LE9 ....**140** B5
Taylor's Cft *CALV/BJ* NG14 ....**26** F3
Taylor's La *ASHB* DE6 ....**54** C1
Taylor St *DERBYSE* DE24 ....**58** B5
ILK DE7 ....**33** K6
Tayside CI *DERBYSE* DE24 ....**71** H4
Tay Wk *DERBYSE* DE24 ....**43** J4
Teak Rd *MAPPK/POR/STA* NG3 ....**5** K2
Tealby CI *BLWL* NG6 ....**23** K8
Teal CI *CARL* NG4 ....**38** F8
COAL LE67 ....**108** D7
LEIW LE3 ....**129** J5
Teal Wy *RLEINE/SYS* LE7 ....**120** C3
Teal Whf *WBRGFD* * NG2 ....**50** E5
Teasel CI *END/NAR* LE19 ....**135** L7
Tebbs CI *RLEIW/BBY* LE8 ....**143** C3
Technology Rd
BSTN/STPLFD NG9 ....**63** L2
Tedworth Av *DERBYSE* DE24 ....**71** H5
Tedworth Gn *LEIN* LE4 ....**125** H2
Teesbrook Dr
WOL/BIL/BRX NG8 ....**48** F3
Teesdale CI *LEIS* LE2 ....**6** D9
Teesdale Ct *BSTN/STPLFD* NG9 ....**62** E3
Teesdale Rd *ARN* NG5 ....**36** E5
LGEAT NG10 ....**75** L1
Teignmouth CI *LEIE* LE5 ....**132** D4
Telford CI *MCKLVR* DE3 ....**56** C6
Telford Dr *EWD/SEL/PNX* NG16 ....**21** M4
Telford Wy *LEIE* LE5 ....**133** J2
Tempest Rd *LEIN* LE4 ....**125** K1
Templar CI *DERBYSE* DE24 ....**71** C5

Templar Rd *BSTN/STPLFD* NG9 ......**63** M1
Templars Wy *COAL* LE67 ....**108** D2
Templar Wy *RLEINE/SYS* LE7 ......**119** H1
Templebell CI *NORM/LIT* DE23 ......**70** E1
Temple Crs *EWD/SEL/PNX* NG16 ....**35** H3
Temple Dr *EWD/SEL/PNX* NG16 ......**35** H3
Temple HI *COAL* LE67 ....**108** D1
Templemen CI *CFTN/RUD* NG11 ......**64** F7
Templeoak Dr
WOL/BIL/BRX NG8 ....**49** G4
Temple Rd *LEIE* LE5 ....**132** G2
Temple St *NORM/LIT* DE23 ....**2** E8
Tenbury Crs *WOL/BIL/BRX* NG8 ....**35** M6
Tenby Dr *DERBYE* DE21 ....**45** G5
Tendring Dr *WGSTN* LE18 ....**138** D4
Tene CI *ARN* NG5 ....**25** K5
Tennessee Rd *DERBYE* DE21 ....**44** M8
Tennis Court Dr *LEIE* LE5 ....**126** E8
Tennis Ct *NOTTE* NG7 ....**4** D7
Tennis Ms *NOTTE* NG7 ....**4** D7
Tennyson Av *CARL* NG4 ....**38** D6
Tennyson Ct *HUCK/RAV* NG15 ......**23** H1
LBORO LE11 ....**8** B2
Tennyson Dr *BSTN/STPLFD* NG9 ....**48** H1
Tennyson Rd *ARN* NG5 ....**37** J3
Tennyson Sq
EWD/SEL/PNX NG16 ....**34** A3
Tennyson St *DERBYSE* DE24 ....**58** B8
END/NAR LE19 ....**135** L6
ILK DE7 ....**33** J4
LEIS LE2 ....**7** L9
NOTTE NG7 ....**4** D4
Tenter CI *ARN* NG5 ....**24** D7
LGEAT NG10 ....**62** D7
Tentercroft Av *RLEINE/SYS* LE7 ..**121** G3
Tenter La *BPR/DUF* DE56 ....**10** B6
The Terrace *DERBYE* * DE21 ....**44** C8
Terrace St *NOTTE* NG7 ....**4** B1
Terrian Crs *WBRGFD* NG2 ....**51** K3
Terry PI *DERBYSE* DE24 ....**58** D8
Terton Rd *ARN* NG5 ....**24** D7
Tetbury Dr *RLBORO* LE12 ....**101** K5
Tettenbury Rd *ARN* NG5 ....**36** D4
Tetuan Rd *LEIN* LE4 ....**131** C1
Teversal Av *NOTTE* NG7 ....**4** A7
Tevery CI *BSTN/STPLFD* NG9 ....**48** C7
Teviot PI *DERBYE* DE21 ....**44** E5
Teviot Rd *ARN* NG5 ....**36** D2
Tewkesbury CI *WBRGFD* NG2 ....**65** L1
Tewkesbury Crs *DERBYE* DE21 ......**44** B7
Tewkesbury Dr *BLWL* NG6 ....**36** C3
EWD/SEL/PNX NG16 ....**22** C3
Tewkesbury Rd *LGEAT* NG10 ....**76** C3
Tewkesbury St *LEIW* LE3 ....**6** A5
Thackeray's La *ARN* NG5 ....**37** H2
Thackeray St *DERBYSE* DE24 ....**71** L2
LEIS LE2 ....**131** K6
NOTTE NG7 ....**4** B5
Thames CI *DERBYE* DE22 ....**56** D2
Thames St *BLWL* NG6 ....**23** M8
LEI LE1 ....**6** F5
Thane Rd *BSTN/STPLFD* NG9 ....**64** B1
Thanet Dr *DERBYSE* DE24 ....**72** E1
Thatch CI *DERBYW* DE22 ....**43** K5
Thatcher CI *LEIN* LE4 ....**124** F3
Thatchers' Cnr
RLEINE/SYS LE7 ....**115** H8
Thaxted CI *WOL/BIL/BRX* NG8 ......**49** H1
Theatre Sq *NOTT* * NG1 ....**5** G6
Theatre Wk *DERBY* DE21 ....**2** A5
Thelda Av *COT/KEY/RAD* NG12 ......**80** C4
Thetford CI *ARN* NG5 ....**37** L1
Third Av *BLWL* NG6 ....**23** L8
BSTN/STPLFD NG9 ....**64** A1
CARL NG4 ....**37** M7
CARL NG4 ....**38** D6
Thirlbeck *COT/KEY/RAD* NG12 ......**67** L6
Thirlmere *COAL* LE67 ....**109** G6
WBRGFD NG2 ....**66** A2
Thirlmere Av *DERBYW* DE22 ....**43** J4
Thirlmere CI *LGEAT* NG10 ....**61** M5
MAPPK/POR/STA NG3 ....**37** K8
Thirlmere Rd *LGEAT* NG10 ....**61** M5
LBORO LE11 ....**105** H7
WGSTN LE18 ....**138** C4
Thirlestane CI *LEIS* LE2 ....**131** J4
Thirsk PI *DERBYSE* DE24 ....**58** B8
Thistle Bank *RLBORO* LE12 ....**88** C4
Thistle CI *END/NAR* LE19 ....**135** L7
EWD/SEL/PNX NG16 ....**21** M7
RLEINE/SYS LE7 ....**118** D5
Thistledown CI *DERBYW* DE22 ......**43** L5
Thistledown Rd
CFTN/RUD NG11 ....**79** J8
Thistle Green CI *HEANOR* DE75 ....**20** F6
Thistle Rd *ILK* DE7 ....**47** L3
Thomas CI *MAPPK/POR/STA* NG3 ....**5** K3
Thomas Cook CI
MELB/CHEL DE73 ....**82** E8
Thomas Dr *DERBY* DE21 ....**2** A5
Thomas Parkyn CI
CFTN/RUD NG11 ....**79** J8
Thomas Rd *CDON/KEG* DE74 ....**86** A6
COAL LE67 ....**108** B2
Thomasson St *LBORO* LE11 ....**104** B4
Thomas St *RLBORO* LE12 ....**100** F1
Thompson CI
BSTN/STPLFD NG9 ....**63** G4
RLBORO LE12 ....**88** C5
RLBORO LE12 ....**112** D1
Thompson Gdns *ARN* NG5 ....**24** E6
Thompson St
EWD/SEL/PNX NG16 ....**20** F4
Thomson CI *LEIN* LE4 ....**126** B1
Thomson Dr *RIPLEY* DE5 ....**11** M8
Thore CI *DERBYE* DE21 ....**44** E6
Thoresby Av *CARL* NG4 ....**38** B5
WBRGFD NG2 ....**51** K4
Thoresby CI *COT/KEY/RAD* NG12 ....**53** J3
RIPLEY DE5 ....**11** J6
Thoresby Ct
MAPPK/POR/STA NG3 ....**37** H7
Thoresby Crs
BWSH/BRSTN DE72 ....**60** D8
Thoresby DI *HUCK/RAV* NG15 ......**15** M8

Thoresby Rd
BSTN/STPLFD NG9 ....**49** G6
LGEAT NG10 ....**61** M8
Thoresby St *LEIE* LE5 ....**132** C1
Thornborough CI
END/NAR LE19 ....**135** K8
Thornborough Rd *COAL* LE67 ......**108** A4
Thornbury Wy *ARN* NG5 ....**24** D8
Thornby Gdns *WGSTN* LE18 ....**138** C5
Thorncliffe Rd
MAPPK/POR/STA NG3 ....**37** G7
Thorn CI *DERBYW* DE22 ....**43** H3
Thorndale Rd *BLWL* NG6 ....**36** A5
LEIN LE4 ....**126** D1
Thorndike Av *DERBYSE* DE24 ....**58** E8
Thorndike CI *BSTN/STPLFD* NG9 ....**63** M3
Thorndon CI *MCKLVR* DE3 ....**56** B7
Thorn Dr *EWD/SEL/PNX* NG16 ......**21** M7
Thorner CI *BLWL* NG6 ....**36** C2
Thorness *DERBYSE* DE24 ....**73** G2
Thorney HI
MAPPK/POR/STA NG3 ....**37** K8
Thorneywood Mt
MAPPK/POR/STA NG3 ....**37** K8
Thorneywood Ri
MAPPK/POR/STA NG3 ....**37** K8
Thorneywood Rd *LGEAT* NG10 ......**62** D7
Thorn Gv *HUCK/RAV* NG15 ....**23** M3
Thornhill CI *BSTN/STPLFD* NG9 ....**48** F5
Thornhill Rd *NORM/LIT* DE23 ....**57** C6
Thornhills *END/NAR* LE19 ....**135** K5
Thornholme CI *LEIN* LE4 ....**125** C3
Thornley St *NOTTE* NG7 ....**36** C8
Thorn St *NORM/LIT* DE23 ....**57** K5
Thornthwaite CI *WBRGFD* NG2 ......**66** A1
Thornton Av *ARN* NG5 ....**25** H6
Thornton CI *COAL* LE67 ....**109** G6
LEIW LE3 ....**130** B4
Thornton Dr *END/NAR* LE19 ....**136** A7
Thornton La *COAL* LE67 ....**122** A4
Thorntons CI
COT/KEY/RAD NG12 ....**67** L5
Thorntree CI
BWSH/BRSTN DE72 ....**61** K6
Thorn Tree Gdns
EWD/SEL/PNX NG16 ....**21** K3
Thorntree La *DERBY* DE1 ....**2** F4
Thornville CI *LEIN* LE4 ....**126** C6
Thorny CI *LBORO* LE11 ....**103** H1
Thoroton Rd *WBRGFD* NG2 ....**51** K6
Thoroton St *NOTTE* NG7 ....**4** C5
Thorpe Acre Rd *LBORO* LE11 ....**8** A1
Thorpe CI *ARN* NG5 ....**24** E7
BSTN/STPLFD NG9 ....**48** A8
Thorpe Crs
MAPPK/POR/STA NG3 ....**37** M5
Thorpe Dr *MCKLVR* DE3 ....**56** C4
WGSTN LE18 ....**138** B3
Thorpe Field Dr *LEIN* LE4 ....**120** D7
Thorpe HI *LBORO* LE11 ....**103** G4
Thorpe Hill Dr *HEANOR* DE75 ....**20** C8
Thorpelands Dr *DERBYW* DE22 ......**43** H6
Thorpe La *RLEINE/SYS* LE7 ....**121** H8
Thorpe Leys *LGEAT* NG10 ....**76** B2
Thorpe Rd *EWD/SEL/PNX* NG16 ....**21** K3
RLBORO LE12 ....**101** L4
Thorpe's Rd *HEANOR* DE75 ....**20** B6
Thorpe St *ILK* DE7 ....**33** J4
LEIW LE3 ....**6** B7
Thorpe Wy *BPR/DUF* DE56 ....**17** M2
END/NAR LE19 ....**136** B3
Thorpewell *LEIE* LE5 ....**132** D1
Thrapston Av *ARN* NG5 ....**25** K5
Threadgold CI *LEIN* LE4 ....**124** F1
Three Tunes Rd
EWD/SEL/PNX NG16 ....**21** L5
Threlkeld CI *WBRGFD* NG2 ....**66** A1
Thrumpton Av *LGEAT* NG10 ....**62** D8
Thrumpton Dr *WBRGFD* NG2 ....**50** F6
Thrushton CI *RDERBYSW* DE65 ......**70** A5
Thrussington Rd
RLEINE/SYS LE7 ....**115** C5
Thruxton CI *DERBYSE* DE24 ....**73** C1
Thurcaston La *RLEINE/SYS* LE7 ....**118** F3
Thurcaston Rd *LEIN* LE4 ....**119** H8
Thurcroft CI *DERBYW* DE22 ....**57** G1
LEIS LE2 ....**137** H4
Thurgarton Av *WBRGFD* NG2 ....**51** K3
Thurgarton St *WBRGFD* NG2 ....**51** K3
Thurland St *NOTT* NG1 ....**5** H6
Thurlaston La *END/NAR* LE19 ......**135** H3
RLEIW/BAR LE9 ....**134** E8
Thurlby La *COT/KEY/RAD* NG12 ....**80** C5
Thurlby Rd *LEIE* LE5 ....**126** B8
Thurlestone Dr
MAPPK/POR/STA NG3 ....**38** A1
Thurlington Rd *LEIW* LE3 ....**130** E4
Thurloe Ct *CFTN/RUD* NG11 ....**65** C4
Thurlow CI *LEIS* LE2 ....**139** H1
Thurlow Ct *DERBYE* DE21 ....**44** E6
Thurlow Rd *LEIS* LE2 ....**131** L6
Thurman Dr
COT/KEY/RAD NG12 ....**67** L1
Thurman St *ILK* DE7 ....**31** L1
NOTTE NG7 ....**4** B1
Thurmaston Bvd *LEIN* LE4 ....**126** D3
Thurmaston La *LEIN* LE4 ....**126** D4
Thurnby Av *RLEINE/SYS* LE7 ....**133** J2
Thurnby La *LEIE* LE5 ....**133** J6
Thurncourt CI *LEIE* LE5 ....**127** C8
Thurncourt Gdns *LEIE* LE5 ....**127** K8
Thurncourt Rd *LEIE* LE5 ....**127** K8
Thurnview Rd *LEIE* LE5 ....**133** G4
Thursby Rd *CFTN/RUD* NG11 ....**64** C4
Thurstone Furlong
MELB/CHEL DE73 ....**72** C6
Thyme CI *LEIS* LE5 ....**6** B9
Thymus Wk *CFTN/RUD* NG11 ....**64** A6
Thyra Gv *BSTN/STPLFD* NG9 ....**63** L1
MAPPK/POR/STA NG3 ....**37** H6
Tiber CI *DERBYSE* DE24 ....**73** H2
Tickham Av *DERBYSE* DE24 ....**71** C5
Ticknall La *RIPLEY* DE5 ....**18** F6
Tickow La *RLBORO* LE12 ....**101** J5
Tideswell Rd *DERBYE* DE21 ....**44** D6

Tidworth CI *WOL/BIL/BRX* NG8 ......**49** L1
Tigers CI *WGSTN* LE18 ....**137** J5
Tigers CI *WGSTN* LE18 ....**137** J5
Tigers Way *LEI* LE1 ....**131** K4
Tilberthwaite CI *WBRGFD* NG2 ......**66** A1
Tilbury Crs *LEIN* LE4 ....**126** E2
Tilbury PI *DERBYSE* DE24 ....**72** E2
Tilbury Ri *WOL/BIL/BRX* NG8 ....**35** M4
Tilford Crs *LEIS* LE2 ....**137** H5
Tilford Gdns *BSTN/STPLFD* NG9 ....**62** C1
Tilford Rd *HUCK/RAV* NG15 ....**15** H1
Tiller CI *NORM/LIT* DE23 ....**70** F1
Tillett Rd *LEIW* LE3 ....**130** B5
Tilley CI *LEIW* LE5 ....**130** B6
Tillingham Rd *LEIE* LE5 ....**126** D7
Tilling Rd *LEIE* LE5 ....**126** D7
Tilstock CI *EWD/SEL/PNX* NG16 ....**22** E7
Tilton Dr *LEIS* LE2 ....**138** E4
Tilton Gv *ILK* DE7 ....**47** G2
Timbersbrook CI *WBRGFD* NG2 ......**66** A1
Timber St *WGSTN* LE18 ....**137** K6
Timberwood Dr *GBY/RBY* LE25 ....**123** J3
Timsbury Ct *DERBYE* DE21 ....**44** C5
Tinker's Dell *RLEINE/SYS* LE7 ......**115** H7
Tinkersway *WBRGFD* NG2 ....**50** E5
Tinsell Brook *RDERBYSW* DE65 ......**68** B6
Tinsley Ri *EWD/SEL/PNX* NG16 ......**21** H6
Tintagel CI *NORM/LIT* DE23 ....**57** M5
Tintagel Gn *CFTN/RUD* NG11 ....**64** C6
Tintern Dr *WOL/BIL/BRX* NG8 ....**36** B5
Tipnall Rd *CDON/KEG* DE74 ....**84** E4
Tippett Ct *MAPPK/POR/STA* NG3 ....**51** K1
Tip Tree CI *EWD/SEL/PNX* NG16 ....**22** D8
Tiptree CI *LEIN* LE4 ....**125** H5
Tiree CI *BSTN/STPLFD* NG9 ....**48** B5
DERBYSE DE24 ....**71** K3
Tishbite St *BLWL* NG6 ....**23** M8
Tissington Dr *DERBYE* DE21 ....**44** F4
Tissington Rd *NOTTE* NG7 ....**36** E7
Titchfield St *HUCK/RAV* NG15 ......**15** M8
Tithby Dr *ARN* NG5 ....**37** H3
Tithebarn La *ASHB* DE6 ....**54** A2
Tithe CI *COAL* LE67 ....**100** A7
Tithe St *LEIE* LE5 ....**126** C8
The Tithings *RLEIW/BBY* LE8 ......**146** E6
Tiverton Av *COAL* LE67 ....**108** E5
LEIN LE4 ....**126** A5
Tiverton CI *END/NAR* LE19 ....**135** K7
HUCK/RAV NG15 ....**23** H2
LEIS LE2 ....**139** C2
MCKLVR DE3 ....**56** B3
WOL/BIL/BRX NG8 ....**35** M5
Tiverton Rd *LBORO* LE11 ....**103** K8
Tivoli Gdns *DERBYW* DE22 ....**43** J8
Toad La *CALV/BJ* NG14 ....**27** L2
Tobermory Wy *DERBYSE* DE24 ......**71** H4
Tobias CI *ARN* NG5 ....**24** D7
Todd CI *CFTN/RUD* NG11 ....**64** A7
The Toft *RLBORO* LE12 ....**100** F1
Toft CI *COT/KEY/RAD* NG12 ....**67** J5
Toft Rd *BSTN/STPLFD* NG9 ....**62** E4
The Tofts *WGSTN* LE18 ....**138** B6
Tolcarne Rd *LEIE* LE5 ....**127** C7
Tolchard CI *LEIE* LE5 ....**132** E2
Tollemache Av *LEIN* LE4 ....**125** J5
Toller Rd *LEIS* LE2 ....**132** A6
RLBORO LE12 ....**112** C2
Tollerton Gn *BLWL* NG6 ....**36** B2
Tollerton La
COT/KEY/RAD NG12 ....**66** B7
Tollerton Pk
COT/KEY/RAD NG12 ....**66** C2
Tollerton Rd
COT/KEY/RAD NG12 ....**66** B1
Tollhouse HI *NOTT* NG1 ....**4** F6
Tolton Rd *LEIN* LE4 ....**125** H3
Tolwell Rd *LEIN* LE4 ....**125** C1
Tomlin Rd *LEIN* LE4 ....**126** C6
Tomlinson Av *CFTN/RUD* NG11 ......**77** L6
Tomlinsons Cottages
DERBYE * DE21 ....**44** A5
Tom Paine CI *LEIS* LE3 ....**130** B5
Tonbridge Dr *DERBYSE* DE24 ....**72** E2
Tonbridge Mt
WOL/BIL/BRX NG8 ....**49** H5
Tonnelier Rd *NOTTE* NG7 ....**50** C6
Toothill Rd *LBORO* LE11 ....**9** J1
Top CI *LEIW* LE3 ....**130** B6
Top Farm Ct *BPR/DUF* DE56 ....**18** D7
Tophall Dr *RLEIW/BBY* LE8 ....**143** J4
Top Manor CI
BWSH/BRSTN DE72 ....**60** A2
Top Rd *CFTN/RUD* NG11 ....**79** C1
Top Valley Dr *ARN* NG5 ....**24** C7
Top Valley Wy *ARN* NG5 ....**24** C8
Tor Av *ALFN* DE55 ....**11** M1
Torbay Crs *ARN* NG5 ....**36** F2
Torcross CI *LEIW* LE5 ....**124** C7
Torkard Dr *ARN* NG5 ....**24** D7
Toronto CI *LEI* LE1 ....**7** H3
Torridon CI *DERBYSE* DE24 ....**71** J3
Torrington Av *COAL* LE67 ....**108** E5
Torrington CI *WGSTN* LE18 ....**138** B7
Torvill Dr *WOL/BIL/BRX* NG8 ....**49** J2
Toston Dr *WOL/BIL/BRX* NG8 ....**50** A4
Totland Dr *BLWL* NG6 ....**36** B5
Totland Rd *BSTN/STPLFD* NG9 ......**49** C5
LEIW LE3 ....**125** G7
Totley CI *BLWL* NG6 ....**24** A5
Totnes CI *HUCK/RAV* NG15 ....**23** H1
Totnes Rd *MAPPK/POR/STA* NG3 ....**51** M2
Toton La *BSTN/STPLFD* NG9 ....**62** C1
Tottle Gdns *NOTTE* NG7 ....**50** B1
Tottle Rd *NOTTE* NG7 ....**50** E7
Tournament Rd *LEIW* LE18 ....**124** D8
Tovey Crs *LEIS* LE2 ....**137** H3
Tower Crs *EWD/SEL/PNX* NG16 ....**34** C7
Towers CI *RLEIW/BAR* LE9 ....**129** J3
Towers Ri *RLEIW/BAR* LE9 ....**129** J3
Tower St *DERBYSE* DE24 ....**58** B8
LEI LE1 ....**7** J8
Towe's Mt *CARL* NG4 ....**38** C8
Towle CI *BWSH/BRSTN* DE72 ....**59** M6
Towle Rd *LEIW* LE3 ....**124** C7
Towles Flds *RLBORO* LE12 ....**105** K1
Towles Pastures
CDON/KEG DE74 ....**84** E4

Towle St LGEAT NG10 75 L3
Towlsons Cft BLWL NG6 36 B4
The Town DERBYE DE21 30 A8
Town End Rd
BWSH/BRSTN DE72 60 F8
Town Green St RLEINE/SYS LE7 119 J3
Townsend Cl LEIN LE4 126 B2
Townsend Gv MELB/CHEL DE73 72 E5
Townsend Rd END/NAR LE19 135 L4
RLEIW/BAR LE9 140 B6
Townside Cl LGEAT NG10 75 M3
Town St BPR/DUF DE56 29 J4
BPR/DUF DE56 30 A1
BSTN/STPLFD NG9 48 F7
LGEAT NG10 61 M1
Town Vw EWD/SEL/PNX NG16 22 D8
Towpath Cl LBORO LE11 104 A2
Towpath Link WGSTN LE18 137 L7
Towson Av EWD/SEL/PNX NG16 21 G5
Towson Fld RLBORO LE12 88 C5
Trafalgar Cl NOTTE NG7 4 A4
Trafalgar Rd BSTN/STPLFD NG9 63 L3
LGEAT NG10 76 B1
Trafalgar Sq LGEAT NG10 62 C8
Trafalgar Ter LGEAT NG10 62 C8
Trafalgar Wy LEIS LE2 137 H6
Traffic St DERBY DE1 3 G4
WBRGFD NG2 51 G4
Trafford Gdns
WOL/BIL/BRX NG8 36 B8
Trafford Rd LEIE LE5 126 D8
Trafford Wy NORM/LIT DE23 57 G7
Tranby Gdns WOL/BIL/BRX NG8 49 K3
Tranter Pl LEIN LE4 126 B5
Travell's Hl RLBORO LE12 87 L8
Travers Rd LGEAT NG10 61 L1
Treasure Cl LEIW LE3 124 A8
Treaty Rd LEIW LE3 124 B8
Tredegar Dr DERBYE DE21 44 F5
Tredington Rd LEIW LE3 124 B6
Treegarth Sq ARN NG5 24 F6
Treetops Cl LEIE LE5 126 E8
Tree View Cl ARN NG5 25 G6
Trefan Gdns ARN NG5 24 E8
Trefoil Cl LEIE LE5 127 G5
Trefoil Ct NORM/LIT DE23 56 E8
Tregaron Cl DERBYE DE21 45 G5
Tregony Wy DERBYSE DE24 71 H5
Trelawn Cl ARN NG5 37 H5
Trelissick Cl LBORO LE11 102 F2
Tremaine Dr WGSTN LE18 138 A6
Tremayne Rd WOL/BIL/BRX NG8 49 G1
Trenant Rd WGSTN LE18 137 J3
Trenchham Gdns CALV/BJ NG14 39 H4
Trent Av LEIN LE4 119 G8
Trent Bvd WBRGFD NG2 51 L6
Trent Br COAL LE67 108 E8
WBRGFD NG2 51 J6
Trent Bridge Ct NORM/LIT DE23 57 G7
Trent Cl DERBYSE DE24 71 H5
LEIS LE2 139 H2
Trent Crs BSTN/STPLFD NG9 63 J4
Trentdale Rd CARL NG4 52 B1
Trent Dr HUCK/RAV NG15 23 H4
NORM/LIT DE23 71 H2
Trent Gdns CALV/BJ NG14 39 K3
Trentham Dr
WOL/BIL/BRX NG8 36 A8
Trentham Gdns
WOL/BIL/BRX NG8 36 A8
Trent La BWSH/BRSTN DE72 83 J3
CALV/BJ NG14 39 K3
CDON/KEG DE74 84 E2
LGEAT NG10 76 D2
MELB/CHEL DE73 83 G5
WBRGFD NG2 51 K4
Trenton Cl BSTN/STPLFD NG9 48 E6
Trenton Dr LGEAT NG10 62 E7
Trenton Green Dr DERBYE DE21 58 F1
Trent Ri DERBYE DE21 59 K3
Trent Rd BSTN/STPLFD NG9 63 M3
ILK DE7 47 H3
WBRGFD NG2 51 K3
Trentside WBRGFD NG2 51 J7
Trentside North WBRGFD NG2 51 J6
Trent St DERBYSE DE24 58 E8
LGEAT NG10 62 C7
NOTT NG1 5 J9
Trent Vale Rd
BSTN/STPLFD NG9 63 L3
Trent Valley Wy
BSTN/STPLFD NG9 63 G8
COT/KEY/RAD NG12 39 L7
WBRGFD NG2 52 A5
Trentview Ct WBRGFD * NG2 51 K5
Trent View Gdns
COT/KEY/RAD NG12 53 L2
Trescoe Ri LEIW LE3 130 C2
Tresillian Cl DERBYW DE22 43 J5
Tressall Cl ILK DE7 33 L7
Tressall Rd COAL LE67 108 E4
Tressell Wy LEIW LE3 130 B5
Trevanth Rd LEIN LE4 126 D5
Trevelyan Rd WBRGFD NG2 51 K7
Treveris Cl DERBYE DE21 59 J3
Trevino Dr LEIN LE4 126 B2
Trevone Av BSTN/STPLFD NG9 62 C1
Trevor Rd BSTN/STPLFD NG9 63 K2
WBRGFD NG2 65 L1
Trevose Gdns ARN NG5 37 H4
LEIE LE5 127 H8
Treyford Cl CFTN/RUD NG11 64 E3
The Triangle ILK DE7 47 L1
Tricornia Dr BLWL NG6 35 M3
Trigo Cl LEIN LE4 124 E3
Trillium Cl LEIE LE5 127 G4
Tring V ARN NG5 36 E3
The Trinity NOTTE * NG7 50 C5
Trinity Av NOTTE NG7 50 C5
Trinity Cl ILK DE7 33 J4
RLEINE/SYS LE7 120 F4
Trinity Crs CARL NG4 27 G8
RLBORO LE12 97 M4
Trinity La LEI LE1 6 F9
Trinity Rd END/NAR LE19 136 C5
Trinity Sq NOTT NG1 5 H6
Trinity St DERBY DE1 3 H6
LBORO LE11 9 L4
Trinity Wk NOTT NG1 5 H6
Trinstead Wy ARN NG5 25 G8
Tristram Cl LEIW LE3 129 L5
Triumph Rd LEIW LE3 124 A8
NOTTE NG7 50 B3
Trivett Sq NOTT NG1 5 K8
Trocadero Ct DERBY * DE1 2 F7
Trojan Wy RLEINE/SYS LE7 120 C5
Troon Cl EWD/SEL/PNX NG16 22 C8
NORM/LIT DE23 56 E7
Troon Wy LEIN LE4 126 B3
Trough La EWD/SEL/PNX NG16 22 D7
Trough Rd EWD/SEL/PNX NG16 22 E8
Troutbeck COT/KEY/RAD NG12 67 L4
Troutbeck Crs BSTN/STPLFD NG9 49 G7
Troutbeck Gv NORM/LIT DE23 56 E8
Trowbridge Cl DERBYE DE21 44 C5
Trowell Av ILK DE7 47 L2
WOL/BIL/BRX NG8 48 F2
Trowell Gv BSTN/STPLFD NG9 48 B4
LGEAT NG10 61 M6
Trowell La RLBORO LE12 95 J1
Trowell Park Dr
BSTN/STPLFD NG9 48 B5
Trowell Rd BSTN/STPLFD NG9 48 B5
WOL/BIL/BRX NG8 49 G2
Trowels La DERBYW DE22 57 G3
Trueman Gdns ARN NG5 37 M1
Trueman St ILK DE7 33 K3
Trueway Dr RLBORO LE12 102 A5
Trueway Dr South
RLBORO LE12 102 A5
Trueway Rd LEIE LE5 132 C5
Truman Cl MAPPK/POR/STA NG3 5 J4
Truman Dr HUCK/RAV NG15 23 L1
Truman's Rd WBRGFD NG2 51 H6
Truman St EWD/SEL/PNX NG16 22 B8
ILK DE7 33 L6
Truro Cl RLBORO LE12 88 C6
Truro Crs DERBYE DE21 44 C7
NOTTE NG7 36 C8
Truro Dr WGSTN LE18 138 B6
Trusley Gdns NORM/LIT DE23 71 H2
Tuckers Cl LBORO LE11 9 M6
Tuckers Rd LBORO LE11 9 M5
Tuckett Rd RLBORO LE12 111 K5
Tuckey Cl RLEIW/BAR LE9 140 B7
Tudor Cl CARL NG4 52 C2
LEIW LE3 6 B6
LGEAT NG10 62 C6
Tudor Ct HUCK/RAV NG15 23 G2
Tudor Dr LEIS LE2 138 F1
RLEIW/BAR LE9 142 B6
Tudor Falls HEANOR DE75 20 C4
Tudor Field Cl MELB/CHEL DE73 72 E6
Tudor Gv GBY/RBY LE6 123 J6
NOTT NG1 4 F3
Tudor Pl ILK DE7 47 G2
Tudor Rd DERBYE DE21 58 E1
LEIW LE3 6 A4
WBRGFD NG2 51 K8
Tudor Sq WBRGFD NG2 51 K8
Tudwal Cl ARN NG5 24 E8
Tufnell Gdns DERBYW DE22 42 F8
Tulip Av MAPPK/POR/STA NG3 5 K2
Tulip Rd EWD/SEL/PNX NG16 33 M2
Tulla Cl DERBYSE DE24 71 J5
Tumbling Hl BPR/DUF DE56 10 C6
Tunnel Rd NOTTE NG7 4 D7
Tunstall Crs LEIN LE4 126 C7
WOL/BIL/BRX NG8 35 L6
Tunstall Dr BLWL NG6 36 D4
Tunstall Rd ARN NG5 37 K3
Tuphall Cl MELB/CHEL DE73 72 E5
Turnberry Cl BSTN/STPLFD NG9 63 G1
ILK DE7 33 G5
Turnberry Ct COT/KEY/RAD NG12 66 A4
Turnberry Rd BLWL NG6 36 B1
Turnbull Dr LEIW LE3 130 D7
Turnbury Wy LEIE LE5 132 C5
Turner Av EWD/SEL/PNX NG16 20 E4
LBORO LE11 9 H7
Turner Cl BSTN/STPLFD NG9 62 C1
RLBORO LE12 104 D8
Turner Dr EWD/SEL/PNX NG16 21 M8
Turner Ri LEIS LE2 138 F3
Turner Rd LEIE LE5 126 D8
LGEAT NG10 76 A3
Turners La ALFN DE55 11 L1
Turner St DERBYSE DE24 72 B1
HUCK/RAV NG15 15 L8
LEI LE1 6 F9
Turney St WBRGFD NG2 51 H6
Turnpike La BSTN/STPLFD NG9 49 L7
Turnpike Wy COAL LE67 116 C7
Turnstone Wk LEIE LE5 7 M3
Turnstone Whf WBRGFD NG2 50 D5
Turn St RLEINE/SYS LE7 120 E3
Turolough Rd COAL LE67 100 C8
Turpin Av CARL NG4 38 B4
Turton Cl EWD/SEL/PNX NG16 20 E4
Turvey La RLBORO LE12 94 B5
Turville Cl WGSTN LE18 138 C7
Turville Rd LEIW LE3 130 F4
Tuskar Rd LEIE LE5 127 H8
Tuxford Cl DERBYE DE21 44 F6
Tuxford Rd LEIN LE4 126 E4
Tuxford Wk
MAPPK/POR/STA NG3 51 K1
Tweeds Muir Cl DERBYE DE21 44 D5
Twells Cl MAPPK/POR/STA NG3 37 K8
Twelve Houses ILK * DE7 47 J4
Twentylands Dr RLBORO LE12 88 B6
Twickenham Dr DERBYW DE22 56 E1
Twickenham Rd LEIS LE2 137 G5
Twin Oaks Cl NORM/LIT DE23 56 D8
The Twitchell
BSTN/STPLFD NG9 63 J3
Twycross Rd ARN NG5 24 F8
Twycross St LEIS LE2 7 L7
Twyford Cl COAL LE67 109 G6
HEANOR DE75 20 A7
ILK DE7 32 B7
Twyford Gdns CFTN/RUD NG11 64 C3
Twyford Rd LGEAT NG10 75 K3
Twyford St NORM/LIT DE23 2 F8
Tyburn Cl ARN NG5 24 E6
Tyers Cl RLEIW/BAR LE9 134 E4
Tyes End LEIN LE4 124 E4
Tyler Av LBORO LE11 103 K2
Tyler Ct RLBORO LE12 102 A1
Tyler Rd GBY/RBY LE6 123 H7
Tylers Rd RLBORO LE12 100 F1
Tyndale Cha DERBYSE DE24 71 G5
Tyndale St LEIW LE3 6 A8
Tynedale Cl LEIS LE2 139 H2
LGEAT NG10 75 L1
WOL/BIL/BRX NG8 36 B7
Tynedale Rd LBORO LE11 103 G7
Tyne Gdns HUCK/RAV NG15 23 H4
Tyringham Rd WGSTN LE18 138 C5
Tyrrell St LEIW LE3 6 A4
Tysoe Hl LEIW LE3 124 B6
Tythorn Dr WGSTN LE18 137 L2

U

Uffa Magna MCKLVR DE3 56 A7
Ulldale Ct BSTN/STPLFD NG9 62 F3
Ullscarf Cl WBRGFD NG2 66 A2
Ullswater Av RLBORO LE12 105 H6
Ullswater Cl CARL NG4 38 D5
DERBYE DE21 44 B5
WBRGFD NG2 66 B1
Ullswater Crs BSTN/STPLFD NG9 49 G6
Ullswater Dr DERBYE DE21 59 J1
HUCK/RAV NG15 15 K8
LEIS LE2 139 G3
Ullswater St LEIS LE2 6 C9
Ulvers Cft COAL LE67 116 C6
Ulverscroft Dr GBY/RBY LE6 123 K5
Ulverscroft La COAL LE67 116 E2
Ulverscroft Rd LBORO LE11 103 J7
LEIN LE4 7 K1
Una Av LEIW LE3 130 E7
Underhill Av NORM/LIT DE23 57 K8
Underhill Cl NORM/LIT DE23 71 J1
Underwood Crs RLEIW/BAR LE9 140 C7
Underwood Dr RLEIW/BAR LE9 141 A6
Unicorn St LEIN LE4 120 B7
Union Cl HUCK/RAV NG15 15 L5
Union Rd ILK DE7 33 J8
NOTT NG1 5 H5
Union St BSTN/STPLFD NG9 63 K1
LBORO LE11 9 G3
LGEAT NG10 62 C7
MELB/CHEL DE73 82 E8
Unitt Rd RLBORO LE12 112 F3
Unity Crs MAPPK/POR/STA NG3 38 A5
Unity Rd LEIW LE3 124 A7
University Bvd BSTN/STPLFD NG9 49 M7
University Cl RLEINE/SYS LE7 120 F4
University Rd LBORO LE11 8 A6
LEI LE1 131 L4
Upex Cl RLEIW/BBY LE8 142 D3
Upland Dr COAL LE67 116 B6
Uplands Av NORM/LIT DE23 71 G1
Uplands Gdns NORM/LIT DE23 2 B9
Uplands Rd LEIS LE2 137 K2
LEIS LE2 138 F1
Upminster Dr ARN NG5 25 K6
EWD/SEL/PNX NG16 35 H3
Upper Bainbrigge St
NORM/LIT DE23 2 D9
Upper Barn Cl HEANOR DE75 20 D5
Upper Boundary Rd
DERBYW DE22 2 A5
Upper Brown St LEI LE1 6 E7
Upper Canaan CFTN/RUD NG11 65 H7
Upper Charnwood St LEIS LE2 7 K5
Upper Church St
RLEINE/SYS LE7 120 F3
Upper College St NOTT NG1 4 E6
Upper Dale Rd NORM/LIT DE23 57 K6
Upper Dunstead Rd
EWD/SEL/PNX NG16 20 F3
Upper Eldon St WBRGFD NG2 5 M7
Upper George St LEI LE1 7 G3
Upper Gn LBORO LE11 103 H7
Upper Hall Cl BPR/DUF DE56 30 A1
LEIE LE5 127 G7
Upper Hollow NORM/LIT DE23 57 G6
Upper King St LEI LE1 6 F9
Upper Marehay Rd RIPLEY DE5 19 G1
Upper Moor Rd DERBYSE DE24 72 C1
Upper Nelson St HEANOR DE75 20 B5
Upper New Wk LEI LE1 7 J9
Upper Orchard St
BSTN/STPLFD NG9 48 C8
Upper Parliament St NOTT NG1 4 F6
Upper Tichborne St LEIS LE2 7 K8
Upperton Ri LEIW LE3 130 F3
Upperton Rd LEIW LE3 131 G3
Upper Wellington St LGEAT NG10 62 A6
Uppingham Cl LEIE LE5 133 G2
Uppingham Crs WBRGFD NG2 65 H2
Uppingham Dr RLEIW/BAR LE9 141 H7
Uppingham Gdns WBRGFD NG2 51 H5
Uppingham Rd LEIE LE5 126 B8
LEIE LE5 132 F1
RLEINE/SYS LE7 133 K2
Upton Cl HEANOR DE75 20 E6
Upton Dr ARN NG5 37 H2
WGSTN LE18 138 D5
Utah Cl LEIW LE3 124 A8
RDERBYSW DE65 68 C5
Utile Gdns BLWL NG6 23 L8
Uttoxeter Cl LEIN LE4 126 B2
Uttoxeter New Rd
DERBYW DE22 57 G4
Uttoxeter Old Rd
DERBYW DE22 57 H3
Uttoxeter Rd MCKLVR DE3 56 B6
Uxbridge Rd LEIN LE4 125 M3

V

The Vale ILK DE7 33 J4
Vale Cl EWD/SEL/PNX NG16 21 M5
LEIE LE5 127 G8
Vale Crs North WOL/BIL/BRX NG8 50 B1
Vale Crs South
WOL/BIL/BRX NG8 50 B1
Vale Gdns CARL NG4 52 B2
Vale Mills DERBYW * DE22 2 C7
Valence Rd LEIW LE3 130 F3
Valentine Dr LEIS LE2 138 D1
Valentine Rd LEIE LE5 133 H2
Valerie Rd BWSH/BRSTN DE72 73 K8
Vale Rd CARL NG4 52 C1
Valeside Gdns CARL NG4 52 C2
Valetta Rd ARN NG5 25 M8
Valiant Cl LEIW LE3 124 B8
Valjean Crs LEIW LE3 129 J5
Valley Dr EWD/SEL/PNX NG16 21 M6
LEIW LE3 130 B5
Valley Gdns WBRGFD NG2 65 M2
Valley Rd ARN NG5 37 G3
BSTN/STPLFD NG9 62 E2
CARL NG4 37 M6
COAL LE67 116 C7
COT/KEY/RAD NG12 53 L2
COT/KEY/RAD NG12 65 L2
DERBYE DE21 58 F1
EWD/SEL/PNX NG16 22 B8
ILK DE7 47 J2
LBORO LE11 103 J7
LEIN LE4 126 F3
NORM/LIT DE23 57 H6
Valley Vw BPR/DUF DE56 17 L5
ILK DE7 47 J2
Valley View Dr ILK DE7 31 L6
Valley View Rd ALFN DE55 12 A3
Valley Wy COAL LE67 108 B2
Valmont Rd ARN NG5 36 E4
BSTN/STPLFD NG9 48 E8
Vancouver Av
COT/KEY/RAD NG12 53 J4
DERBYE DE21 59 H4
Vancouver Rd LEI LE1 7 H2
Vandyke Rd LEIS LE2 138 F3
Vanguard Rd CDON/KEG DE74 84 E7
LGEAT NG10 76 B2
Varden Av BSTN/STPLFD NG9 49 L6
Varley St DERBYSE DE24 58 B8
Varney Rd CFTN/RUD NG11 64 D4
Vaughan Rd
BSTN/STPLFD NG9 62 E3
LEIS LE2 131 J8
Vaughan St COAL LE67 108 A7
LEIW LE3 6 A5
Vaughan Wy LEI LE1 6 D6
Vauxhall Av DERBYW DE22 42 E8
Vedonis Pk HUCK/RAV NG15 23 L2
Ventnor Ri ARN NG5 36 D3
Ventnor Rd LEIS LE2 132 B8
Ventnor Rd South LEIS LE2 138 B1
Ventnor St LEIE LE5 132 B2
Ventor Houses
DERBYSE * DE24 59 G8
Ventor St LEIE LE5 132 B2
Venus Cl BLWL NG6 36 C2
Verbena Cl MAPPK/POR/STA NG3 5 J1
Verbena Dr NORM/LIT DE23 71 H3
Vercor Cl COAL LE67 109 H6
Verdale Av LEIN LE4 126 D2
Verder Gv ARN NG5 24 C7
Verdon Crs COAL LE67 108 F6
Vere St BLWL NG6 23 M8
Vermont Dr DERBYE DE21 59 G1
Verne Cl CARL NG4 38 A8
Vernon Av BLWL NG6 36 C4
BSTN/STPLFD NG9 63 K1
CARL NG4 38 D7
CFTN/RUD NG11 50 F7
Vernon Ct EWD/SEL/PNX NG16 35 K4
Vernon Dr DERBYE DE21 59 K3
EWD/SEL/PNX NG16 35 K4
Vernongate DERBY DE1 2 B3
Vernon Park Dr BLWL NG6 36 C4
Vernon Pl BLWL * NG6 36 B3
Vernon Rd BLWL NG6 36 B3
LEIS LE2 131 J8
Vernon St DERBY DE1 2 B3
ILK DE7 33 K3
LEIW LE3 6 A4
NOTT NG1 4 E6
Verona Av CARL NG4 52 D1
Veronica Dr CARL NG4 38 B6
EWD/SEL/PNX NG16 22 A7
Vestry Rd DERBYE DE21 44 C5
Vestry St LEI LE1 7 G5
Vetch Cl END/NAR LE19 135 K7
Vetchfield Cl DERBYSE DE24 71 K5
Vicarage Av ILK DE7 33 H3
NORM/LIT DE23 2 B9
Vicarage Cl ARN NG5 36 D4
BPR/DUF DE56 17 L3
GBY/RBY LE6 123 J8
ILK DE7 31 K1
MAPPK/POR/STA NG3 5 G3
RLEINE/SYS LE7 120 F3
Vicarage Ct MCKLVR DE3 56 B6
Vicarage Dr CALV/BJ NG14 39 J3
DERBYE DE21 44 E8
Vicarage Gdns ALFN * DE55 12 C1
HEANOR DE75 20 D6
Vicarage Gn
COT/KEY/RAD NG12 65 M4
Vicarage La BPR/DUF DE56 29 J3
CFTN/RUD NG11 64 F8
COT/KEY/RAD NG12 53 K4
DERBYE DE21 29 M7
EWD/SEL/PNX NG16 12 D3
LEIE LE5 126 F7
LEIN LE4 125 L4
RLBORO LE12 100 F1
RLEINE/SYS LE7 121 H7
RLEIW/BBY LE8 136 D7
Vicarage Ms ALFN DE55 12 C1
Vicarage Rd BPR/DUF DE56 17 K7
MCKLVR DE3 56 A5
MELB/CHEL DE73 72 D5
Vicarage St BSTN/STPLFD NG9 63 J1
COAL LE67 108 D2
ILK DE7 33 H3
Vicarwood Av BPR/DUF DE56 18 A8
DERBYW DE22 43 K6
Vicary La RLBORO LE12 112 A4
Vickers St
MAPPK/POR/STA NG3 37 H7
The Victor NOTTE * NG7 50 C5
Victor Av DERBYW DE22 43 K7
Victor Crs LGEAT NG10 62 A3
Victoria Av BWSH/BRSTN DE72 59 M5
BWSH/BRSTN DE72 60 E8
LEIS LE2 7 J9
WBRGFD NG2 51 K3
Victoria Cl ARN NG5 25 K6
COAL LE67 108 B2
MCKLVR DE3 56 C3
Victoria Ct ILK * DE7 33 J6
Victoria Crs ARN NG5 37 H5
EWD/SEL/PNX NG16 12 D3
Victoria Dr GBY/RBY LE6 123 K5
Victoria Emb WBRGFD NG2 51 G6
Victoria Gdns LEIS LE2 132 A4
Victoria Pde LEI LE1 6 E5
Victoria Park Rd LEIS LE2 131 K5
Victoria Park Wy CARL NG4 52 F1
Victoria Pas LEI LE1 7 J9
Victoria Pl LBORO LE11 9 K5
Victoria Rd ARN NG5 36 F4
BWSH/BRSTN DE72 60 E8
CARL NG4 52 E1
CFTN/RUD NG11 79 J6
COAL LE67 108 B6
EWD/SEL/PNX NG16 13 K1
LGEAT NG10 61 M2
RIPLEY DE5 11 H6
RLBORO LE12 111 K7
RLEIW/BBY LE8 136 D7
WBRGFD NG2 51 J8
Victoria Rd East LEIE LE5 126 C7
Victoria Rd North LEIN LE4 125 L4
Victoria St
BSTN/STPLFD NG9 48 B8
CARL NG4 38 D6
CDON/KEG DE74 84 F2
COT/KEY/RAD NG12 53 K4
DERBY DE1 2 E4
END/NAR LE19 136 A8
EWD/SEL/PNX NG16 12 D3
EWD/SEL/PNX NG16 21 G4
EWD/SEL/PNX NG16 21 K4
EWD/SEL/PNX NG16 34 E1
HUCK/RAV NG15 15 K7
ILK DE7 33 K4
LBORO LE11 9 J5
LEIN LE4 120 C7
LGEAT NG10 75 M2
MELB/CHEL DE73 82 E8
NOTT NG1 5 H7
RIPLEY DE5 11 K5
RLBORO LE12 112 F1
RLEINE/SYS LE7 120 F4
RLEIW/BBY LE8 145 K8
WGSTN LE18 138 B4
Victoria Ter WBRGFD * NG2 5 M7
Victor Rd LEIW LE3 124 B7
Victors Cl LEIS LE2 137 G3
Victory Av RIPLEY DE5 11 K6
Victory Cl LGEAT NG10 76 B2
Victory Rd BSTN/STPLFD NG9 63 L3
DERBYSE DE24 57 M8
Viking Rd WGSTN LE18 137 L3
The Village ILK DE7 32 C8
ILK DE7 46 D5
Village Cl COT/KEY/RAD NG12 65 M4
Village Farm Cl RLBORO LE12 87 K6
Village Rd CFTN/RUD NG11 64 B5
Village St COT/KEY/RAD NG12 65 L4
NORM/LIT DE23 57 K7
Villa Rd COT/KEY/RAD NG12 80 D3
MAPPK/POR/STA NG3 5 G2
Villa St BSTN/STPLFD NG9 49 K8
BWSH/BRSTN DE72 60 F8
Villiers Rd ARN NG5 37 H3
WBRGFD NG2 65 L1
Vincent Av BSTN/STPLFD NG9 63 K2
DERBYE DE21 59 J4
ILK DE7 33 K7
Vincent Cl BPR/DUF DE56 18 E7
LEIW LE3 130 F1
Vincent Gdns NOTTE * NG7 36 C8
Vincent St NORM/LIT DE23 57 K6
Vine Cl NORM/LIT DE23 56 F8
Vine Crs LGEAT NG10 61 M1
Vine Farm Cl
COT/KEY/RAD NG12 67 J4
ILK DE7 47 H1
Vinehouse Cl RLEINE/SYS LE7 118 F4
The Vineries RLEIW/BBY LE8 143 H4
Vines Cross WOL/BIL/BRX NG8 49 J5
Vine St LEI LE1 6 D4
Vine Ter HUCK/RAV NG15 15 M8
Vine Tree Ter RLBORO LE12 97 G5
Viola Cl DERBYE DE21 45 G4
Violet Av EWD/SEL/PNX NG16 21 M6
Violet Cl BLWL NG6 36 B4
Violet Rd CARL NG4 38 B6
WBRGFD NG2 51 L7
Violet St NORM/LIT DE23 57 K6
Viscount Rd CDON/KEG DE74 84 F8
Vivian Av NOTTE NG7 36 F7
Vivian St DERBYE DE21 43 M7
Vostock Cl LEIS LE2 7 K6
Vulcan Cl BLWL NG6 36 C3
Vulcan Ct COAL * LE67 108 B5
Vulcan Rd LEIE LE5 7 K3
Vulcan St NORM/LIT DE23 57 M6
Vulcan Wy COAL LE67 108 B5
Vyner Cl LEIW LE3 130 A5
Vyse Dr LGEAT NG10 76 A1

W

Waddington Dr WBRGFD NG2 65 H3
Wade Av ILK DE7 33 L8
NORM/LIT DE23 57 G5
Wadebridge Gv
DERBYSE DE24 73 G2
Wade Dr MCKLVR DE3 56 C5
Wades Av NOTTE NG7 36 C8
Wade St LEIN LE4 125 K4

NORM/LIT DE23 ....57 G5
Wadham Rd *ARN* NG5 ....37 J2
Wadhurst Gdns
  MAPPK/POR/STA NG3 ....5 K4
Wadhurst Gv *WOL/BIL/BRX* NG8 ....49 H5
Wadkins Wy *RLEINE/SYS* LE7 ......133 L2
Wadsworth Rd
  BSTN/STPLFD NG9 ....48 D7
Wagstaff La
  EWD/SEL/PNX NG16 ....12 F3
Wagtail Cl *DERBYSE* DE24 ....71 H3
Wain Br *RLEIW/BBY* LE8 ....145 H2
Wain Dr *LBORO* LE11 ....95 G8
Wainfleet Cl *ILK* DE7 ....33 G4
Waingrove *CFTN/RUD* NG11 ....64 E4
Waingroves Rd *RIPLEY* DE5 ....11 L7
Wakami Crs *MELB/CHEL* DE73 ....72 C5
Wakefield Av
  COT/KEY/RAD NG12 ....53 L3
Wakefield Cft *ILK* DE7 ....33 G4
Wakefield Pl *LEIN* LE4 ....126 A5
Wakeling Cl *END/NAR* LE19 ....135 L8
Wakelyn Cl *BWSH/BRSTN* DE72 .....74 D6
Wakerley Rd *LEIE* LE5 ....132 D3
Wakes Rd *WGSTN* LE18 ....138 C7
Walbrook Cl *WOL/BIL/BRX* NG8 .....35 L4
Walbrook Rd *NORM/LIT* DE23 ....57 K6
Walcote Cl *BPR/DUF* DE56 ....18 A2
Walcote Dr *WBRGFD* NG2 ....65 G4
Walcote Rd *LEIN* LE4 ....126 C5
Waldale Dr *LEIS* LE2 ....132 A5
Walderk Rd *ARN* NG5 ....36 F6
Waldemar Gv
  BSTN/STPLFD NG9 ....63 L1
Waldene Dr *DERBYSE* DE24 ....72 E1
Waldorf Av *DERBYSE* DE24 ....58 E8
Waldron Cl *WBRGFD* NG2 ....51 H5
Waldron Ct *LBORO* LE11 ....103 L1
Waldron Dr *LEIS* LE2 ....139 G2
Wale Rd *RLEIW/BBY* LE8 ....136 D8
Walesby Crs *WOL/BIL/BRX* NG8 .....50 A1
Walgrave Wk *ARN* NG5 ....24 E8
The Walk *BPR/DUF* DE56 ....18 F7
Walk Cl *BWSH/BRSTN* DE72 ....60 E8
Walker Av *RIPLEY* DE5 ....11 J5
Walker Cl *ILK* DE7 ....47 K3
Walker Gv *BSTN/STPLFD* NG9 ....62 C1
Walker La *DERBY* DE1 ....2 D2
Walker Rd *LEIN* LE4 ....125 L1
  - LEIN LE4 ....126 D1
Walker St *EWD/SEL/PNX* NG16 ......21 L5
  WBRGFD NG2 ....5 L6
Walkers Wy *RLEINE/SYS* LE7 ......120 F3
Walker's Yd *COT/KEY/RAD* NG12 ....53 K4
Walk Mill Dr *HUCK/RAV* NG15 ......15 M6
Wallace Av *LEIE* LE5 ....38 D8
Wallace Dr *GBY/RBY* LE6 ....123 C2
  RLBORO LE12 ....114 A6
Wallace Gdns *BSTN/STPLFD* NG9 ....62 D6
Wallace Rd *LBORO* LE11 ....9 C6
Wallace St *CFTN/RUD* NG11 ....77 M5
  DERBY DE22 ....57 G2
Wallan St *NOTTE* NG7 ....50 C1
Wallet St *CARL* NG4 ....38 E8
  *WBRGFD** NG2 ....51 H5
Wallett Av *BSTN/STPLFD* NG9 ......49 K7
Wallett St *WBRGFD* NG2 ....51 H5
Wallfields Cl *RDERBYSW* DE65 .....70 B4
Wallingford Rd *LEIN* LE4 ....125 K5
  RLEINE/SYS LE7 ....118 F4
Wallis St *BLWL* NG6 ....36 C5
Wall St *RIPLEY* DE5 ....11 H5
Walnut Av *DERBYSE* DE24 ....58 F8
  LEIN LE4 ....119 K7
Walnut Cl *BWSH/BRSTN* DE72 ....73 M7
  COAL LE67 ....116 B7
  ILK DE7 ....33 L8
  LEIS LE2 ....138 E2
  MELB/CHEL DE73 ....72 E7
  RDERBYSW DE65 ....69 K2
Walnut Dr *BSTN/STPLFD* NG9 ....48 F7
Walnut Gv *COT/KEY/RAD* NG12 ......53 K4
  LEIS LE2 ....136 F3
Walnut Leys *RLEIW/BBY* LE8 ......142 B5
Walnut Rd *BPR/DUF* DE56 ....17 M4
  LBORO LE11 ....103 L7
Walnut St *DERBYSE* DE24 ....58 A8
  LEIS LE2 ....131 J4
Walnut Tree Gdns *BLWL* NG6 ....23 K8
Walnut Wy *RLEIW/BBY* LE8 ....142 F1
  RLEIW/BBY LE8 ....143 J3
Walpole Ct *LEIW* LE3 ....130 D2
Walpole St *DERBY* DE21 ....3 M1
Walsgrave Av *LEIE* LE5 ....133 H2
Walsham Cl *BSTN/STPLFD* NG9 ......62 F5
Walsham Ct *DERBY* DE21 ....44 A7
Walshe Rd *LEIE* LE5 ....132 F1
Walsingham Crs *LEIW* LE3 ....129 M4
Walsingham Rd *ARN* NG5 ....37 L2
Walters Av *EWD/SEL/PNX* NG16 .....21 J1
Walters Crs *EWD/SEL/PNX* NG16 ....13 H1
Walter St *BWSH/BRSTN* DE72 ....60 D8
  DERBY DE1 ....43 J8
  NOTTE NG7 ....4 D4
Waltham Av *DERBYSE* DE24 ....71 K3
  LEIW LE3 ....130 C5
Waltham St *WBRGFD* NG2 ....65 M1
Walthamstow Dr *DERBYW* DE22 ......56 F1
Walton Av *DERBYSE* DE24 ....72 C3
  MAPPK/POR/STA NG3 ....51 K2
Walton Cl *RLEIW/BAR* LE9 ....129 K3
Walton Ct *ILK* DE7 ....32 B7
Walton Crs *CARL* NG4 ....38 C8
Walton Dr *COT/KEY/RAD* NG12 ......80 D4
  NORM/LIT DE23 ....57 J3
Walton HI *CDON/KEG* DE74 ....84 B8
  CDON/KEG DE74 ....84 D3
Walton La *RLBORO* LE12 ....105 H3
Walton Rd *ARN* NG5 ....25 L6
  DERBYE DE21 ....58 D2
Walton St *LEIW* LE3 ....131 G4
  LGEAT NG10 ....62 B6
Wand St *NOTTE* NG7 ....50 C1
Wanlip Av *LEIN* LE4 ....119 L8

Wanlip La *RLEINE/SYS* LE7 ......119 M5
Wanlip La *RLEINE/SYS* LE7 ......120 B4
Wanlip Rd *LEI* LE1 ....7 G2
Wanlip St *LEI* LE1 ....7 G2
Wansbeck Cl *NOTTE* NG7 ....4 C5
Wansbeck Gdns *LEIE* LE5 ....127 G7
Wansfell Cl *MCKLVR* DE3 ....56 C6
Wanstead Rd *LEIN* LE4 ....129 L2
Wanstead Wy *ARN* NG5 ....24 C6
Ward Av *HUCK/RAV** NG15 ....23 M1
  MAPPK/POR/STA NG3 ....37 M4
Ward Cl *LEIS* LE2 ....131 G8
Wardens Wk *LEIW* LE3 ....129 M4
Wardle Gv *ARN* NG5 ....25 L7
Wardlow Av *DERBYE* DE21 ....44 E7
Wardlow Rd *ILK* DE7 ....33 H4
Wards Closes *WGSTN* LE18 ....138 C7
Ward's Crs *RLBORO* LE12 ....114 B4
Wards End *LBORO* LE11 ....9 H5
  - LBORO LE11 ....9 J4
Ward St *DERBYW* DE22 ....2 B5
Wardswood Cl
  BRSTN/BRSTN DE72 ....60 B6
Wardwick *DERBY* DE1 ....2 E3
Wareham Rd *RLEIW/BBY* LE8 ....142 F1
Warkton Ct *BSTN/STPLFD* NG9 ......63 C2
Warmsley Av *WGSTN* LE18 ....138 A3
Warmwells La *RIPLEY* DE5 ....11 H8
Warner Av *RLEIW/BBY* LE8 ....142 E2
Warner Pl *LBORO* LE11 ....9 M3
Warners La *LBORO* LE11 ....9 J2
Warner St *DERBYW* DE22 ....2 B8
  MCKLVR DE3 ....56 B6
  RLBORO LE12 ....105 H8
The Warren
  COT/KEY/RAD NG12 ....67 K5
  RLEINE/SYS LE7 ....115 H8
Warren Av *ARN* NG5 ....36 E5
  BSTN/STPLFD NG9 ....48 B8
  LEIN LE4 ....126 E2
Warren Av Extension
  BSTN/STPLFD NG9 ....48 B8
Warren Cl *COAL* LE67 ....116 C7
  LEIE LE5 ....126 E7
Warren Ct *BSTN/STPLFD* NG9 ....48 B8
Warrender Cl
  BSTN/STPLFD NG9 ....49 C6
Warren Dr *LEIN* LE4 ....126 E2
Warrener Gv *ARN* NG5 ....24 C7
Warren HI *GBY/RBY* LE6 ....117 K2
Warren Hills Rd *COAL* LE67 ......109 H5
Warren La *CDON/KEG* DE74 ....75 L5
  COAL LE67 ....100 D8
  LEIW LE3 ....129 J5
Warren Park Wy
  END/NAR LE19 ....135 L2
Warren Rd *END/NAR* LE19 ....136 B6
  HUCK/RAV NG15 ....23 H2
Warren St *DERBYSE* DE24 ....58 D7
  LEIW LE3 ....6 A5
Warren Vw *LEIE* LE5 ....126 E2
Warrington Dr *GBY/RBY* LE6 ......123 J5
Warrington Rd *BLWL* NG6 ....36 C5
Warser Ga *NOTT* NG1 ....5 J7
Warton Av
  MAPPK/POR/STA NG3 ....37 K5
Warwick Av *ARN* NG5 ....37 J2
  BSTN/STPLFD NG9 ....49 K7
  NORM/LIT DE23 ....57 H6
  RLBORO LE12 ....112 C1
Warwick Ct *LBORO* LE11 ....103 H2
Warwick Dr *ILK* DE7 ....33 C4
Warwick Gdns *BPR/DUF* DE56 ....18 B2
  COT/KEY/RAD NG12 ....67 K6
Warwick Rd *END/NAR* LE19 ....142 B1
  LGEAT NG10 ....62 D8
  MAPPK/POR/STA NG3 ....37 H5
  RLEIW/BAR LE9 ....141 H7
  RLEIW/BBY LE8 ....146 B8
  WGSTN LE18 ....137 M4
Warwick St *DERBYSE* DE24 ....58 B5
  LEIW LE3 ....6 A5
  NOTTE NG7 ....50 C5
Warwick Wy *LBORO* LE11 ....103 H2
Wasdale Cl *WBRGFD* NG2 ....66 A2
Wash Br *CALV/BJ* NG14 ....27 L3
Washdyke La *HUCK/RAV* NG15 ....15 J7
Washford Rd *RDERBYSW* DE65 ....68 C7
Washington Av *DERBY* DE21 ....44 F8
Washington Cl
  MELB/CHEL DE73 ....82 E8
Washington Dr
  BSTN/STPLFD NG9 ....48 D6
Wasnidge Cl
  MAPPK/POR/STA NG3 ....5 K5
Wasnidge Wk
  MAPPK/POR/STA NG3 ....5 K4
Watchcrete Av
  RLEINE/SYS LE7 ....121 H2
Watcombe Circ *ARN* NG5 ....36 F5
Watcombe Rd *ARN* NG5 ....37 G6
Watendlath Cl *WBRGFD* NG2 ....66 A2
Waterdown Rd *CFTN/RUD* NG11 ......64 B6
Waterfield Cl *LEIE* LE5 ....132 F2
Waterfield Rd *RLEINE/SYS* LE7 ...118 D5
Waterford Dr *DERBYE* DE21 ....58 E3
Waterford St *BLWL* NG6 ....36 C5
Watergate *RLEINE/SYS* LE7 ......115 J8
Watergate La *END/NAR* LE19 ......130 B8
Watergo La *MCKLVR* DE3 ....56 A8
Waterhouse La *CARL* NG4 ....38 C5
Watering La *BPR/DUF* DE56 ....30 B1
Water La *COT/KEY/RAD* NG12 ....53 J5
  RLBORO LE12 ....106 D7
Waterloo Ct *DERBY* DE1 ....43 M8
Waterloo Crs *NOTTE* NG7 ....4 C3
  RLEIW/BBY LE8 ....143 H4
  WGSTN LE18 ....138 C3
Waterloo La *BSTN/STPLFD* NG9 .....48 C1
Waterloo Prom *NOTTE* NG7 ....4 C4
Waterloo Rd *BSTN/STPLFD* NG9 .....63 L2
  HUCK/RAV NG15 ....15 L5
  NOTTE NG7 ....4 C3

Waterloo Spinney La
  RLBORO LE12 ....111 M3
Waterloo Way *LEI* LE1 ....7 C9
Watermeadow Rd
  DERBYSE DE24 ....72 E2
The Watermeadows
  LGEAT NG10 ....61 M7
The Water Mdw
  MELB/CHEL DE73 ....82 B1
Watermead Wy *LEIN* LE4 ....125 M3
Water Orton Cl
  BSTN/STPLFD NG9 ....62 C4
Waterside *EWD/SEL/PNX* NG16 .....12 D3
Waterside Dr *DERBYSE* DE24 ......43 L5
  LBORO LE11 ....103 M2
  LGEAT NG10 ....61 M4
  WBRGFD NG2 ....66 A1
Waterside Gdns *NOTTE** NG7 ......50 C6
Waterside Rd *LEIN* LE4 ....126 E4
Waterville Cl *LEIW* LE3 ....130 A1
The Waterway *LGEAT* NG10 ....62 A3
Waterway St *WBRGFD* NG2 ....51 H5
Waterway St West
  WBRGFD NG2 ....51 G5
Waterworks Rd *COAL* LE67 ....108 C6
Watery Gate La
  RLEIW/BAR LE9 ....134 C7
Watery La *ASHB* DE6 ....54 B2
Watford Rd *WOL/BIL/BRX* NG8 .....35 M5
Watkinson St *HEANOR* DE75 ....20 D5
Watkin St *MAPPK/POR/STA* NG3 .....5 H4
Watling St *LEI* LE1 ....6 E2
  RLBORO LE12 ....113 H5
Watnall Rd *EWD/SEL/PNX* NG16 ....35 G1
  HUCK/RAV NG15 ....23 J4
Watson Av *HEANOR* DE75 ....20 D5
  MAPPK/POR/STA NG3 ....51 M1
Watson Dr *ILK* DE7 ....33 C5
  LEIN LE4 ....126 A5
Watson St *DERBY* DE1 ....2 B1
  DERBYW DE22 ....43 J8
Watten Cl *DERBYSE* DE24 ....71 K5
Watts Cl *LEIE* LE5 ....124 E4
Waudby Cl *END/NAR* LE19 ....142 A1
Waughs Dr *RLBORO* LE12 ....113 H7
Waveney Cl *ARN* NG5 ....37 L1
  DERBYSE DE24 ....43 M2
Waveney Ri *LEIS* LE2 ....139 H1
Waverley Av
  BSTN/STPLFD NG9 ....63 L1
  CARL NG4 ....38 E6
Waverley Cl *LBORO* LE11 ....102 F2
Waverley Rd *RLEIW/BBY* LE8 .....143 G1
  WGSTN LE18 ....137 K5
Waverley St *DERBYSE* DE24 ....58 A8
  LGEAT NG10 ....62 D6
  NOTTE NG7 ....4 D3
Waverley Ter *NORM/LIT** DE23 .....2 E8
  NOTT NG1 ....4 F5
Wavertree Dr *RLEIW/BAR* LE9 ....142 B3
Wavertree Dr *LEIN* LE4 ....125 M4
Wayfarer Dr *RLEINE/SYS* LE7 ....115 J7
Wayfaring Rd *DERBYE* DE21 ....44 E6
Wayne Cl *CFTN/RUD** NG11 ....64 C6
The Wayne Wy *LEIE* LE5 ....132 D1
  LEIE LE5 ....119 L8
Wayside Dr *LEIE* LE5 ....126 B1
  LEIS LE2 ....139 G2
Wayzgoose Dr *DERBYE* DE21 ....3 K2
Weardale Rd *ARN* NG5 ....36 C5
Weaver Cl *LBORO* LE11 ....9 K9
Weaver Rd *LEIE* LE5 ....127 H8
Weaver's Cl *BPR/DUF* DE56 ....18 A1
  BWSH/BRSTN DE72 ....60 B6
  RLBORO LE12 ....88 D4
Weaver's La
  EWD/SEL/PNX NG16 ....14 D4
  HUCK/RAV NG15 ....14 D4
Weaverthorpe Rd *ARN* NG5 ....37 L2
Webb Cl *LEIW* LE3 ....129 M5
Webb Rd *WOL/BIL/BRX* NG8 ....48 M1
Webb St *HUCK/RAV* NG15 ....15 J1
Webbs Wy *RLEIW/BAR* LE9 ....140 B5
Webster Av
  EWD/SEL/PNX NG16 ....21 K6
Webster Rd *LEIW* LE3 ....130 C3
Webster St *DERBY* DE1 ....2 D6
Weedon Cl
  MAPPK/POR/STA NG3 ....51 L1
Weekday Cross *NOTT* NG1 ....5 H8
Weightman Dr
  EWD/SEL/PNX NG16 ....21 M8
Weirfield Rd *DERBYW* DE22 ....43 L5
Weir Rd *RLEIW/BBY* LE8 ....146 E8
Welbeck Av *CARL* NG4 ....38 B5
  ILK DE7 ....47 H2
  LEIN LE4 ....125 J5
Welbeck Cl *MAPPK/POR/STA* NG3 ....5 H3
  RLEIW/BBY LE8 ....143 C1
Welbeck Gdns
  BSTN/STPLFD NG9 ....62 D4
Welbeck Gv *DERBYW* DE22 ....43 H4
Welbeck Rd *COT/KEY/RAD** NG12 ....53 L3
  LGEAT NG10 ....61 M4
  WBRGFD NG2 ....51 J7
Welbeck Wk
  MAPPK/POR/STA NG3 ....5 G3
Welby Av *NOTTE* NG7 ....4 A8
Welch Av *BSTN/STPLFD* NG9 ....48 C7
Welcombe Av *LEIW* LE3 ....130 C6
Weldbank Cl *BSTN/STPLFD* NG9 .....62 D7
Weldon Cl *RLBORO* LE12 ....114 B3
Weldon Rd *LBORO* LE11 ....95 J8
  LEIE LE5 ....138 B4
Welford Cl *LEIS* LE2 ....131 M8
Welford Pl *LEI* LE1 ....6 E7
Welford Rd *LEI* LE1 ....6 F6
  LEIS LE2 ....131 K5
  LEIS LE2 ....137 M1
  LEIW LE3 ....136 F7
  WGSTN LE18 ....138 A1
  WGSTN LE18 ....138 B6
Welham Crs *ARN* NG5 ....25 L8
Welland Cl *COAL* LE67 ....108 C8
  MCKLVR DE3 ....56 B4
Welland Ct
  MAPPK/POR/STA NG3 ....51 K1
Welland Rd *RDERBYSW* DE65 ....68 B6

  RLBORO LE12 ....113 H1
Welland St *LEIS* LE2 ....7 K8
Welland Vale Rd *LEIE* LE5 ....133 H5
Wellbrook Av *RLBORO* LE12 ....114 B4
Welldon St *RIPLEY* DE5 ....19 L3
Wellesbourne Dr *LEIW* LE3 ....124 B6
Wellesley Av *WOL/BIL/BRX* NG8 ...43 H7
Wellesley Crs *WOL/BIL/BRX* NG8 ..35 H5
Welles St *LEI* LE1 ....6 C6
Wellgate Av *LEIN* LE4 ....119 K7
Wellhouse St *LEIN* LE4 ....138 A7
Wellin Cl *COT/KEY/RAD* NG12 ......65 M4
Wellinger Wy *LEIW* LE3 ....130 C3
Wellington Circ *NOTT* NG1 ....4 E7
Wellington Ct *BPR/DUF* DE56 ......17 K4
Wellington Crs *DERBY** DE1 ....3 J6
  WBRGFD NG2 ....51 K8
Wellington Pl
  EWD/SEL/PNX NG16 ....21 K5
Wellington Rd *CALV/BJ* NG14 ......39 L2
Wellington Sq *NOTTE* NG7 ....4 C6
Wellington St
  BSTN/STPLFD NG9 ....62 A1
  DERBY DE1 ....3 H7
  EWD/SEL/PNX NG16 ....21 K4
  HEANOR DE75 ....20 B5
  LBORO LE11 ....9 K4
  LEI LE1 ....6 E6
  LGEAT NG10 ....62 A5
  MAPPK/POR/STA NG3 ....5 H4
  RIPLEY DE5 ....11 J6
  RLEINE/SYS LE7 ....120 E4
Wellington Ter *NOTTE** NG7 ....4 C5
Wellington Vls *NOTTE* NG7 ....4 C5
Wellin La *COT/KEY/RAD* NG12 ......65 M4
Well La *BPR/DUF* DE56 ....17 K8
Wells Av *WGSTN* LE18 ....144 D4
Wells Ct *NORM/LIT** DE23 ....56 C4
Wellsic La *RLEINE/SYS* LE7 ......119 J1
Wellspring Dl *BSTN/STPLFD* NG9 ...62 C2
Well Spring HI *WGSTN* LE18 ......138 C7
The Wells Rd
  MAPPK/POR/STA NG3 ....37 K5
Wells Rd *MCKLVR* DE3 ....56 C5
Well St *DERBY* DE1 ....43 L8
  RIPLEY DE5 ....11 H6
Well Yd *BPR/DUF** DE56 ....17 L2
Well Yard *RLBORO* LE12 ....102 A4
Welney Cl *MCKLVR* DE3 ....56 B7
Welshpool Rd *DERBYE* DE21 ....44 F8
Welstead Av *WOL/BIL/BRX* NG8 ....35 M5
Welton Gdns *BLWL* NG6 ....23 L7
Welwyn Av *DERBYSE* DE24 ....72 C3
  DERBYW DE22 ....43 H4
Welwyn Rd *WOL/BIL/BRX* NG8 ......49 J2
Wembley Gdns
  BSTN/STPLFD NG9 ....48 F5
  DERBYW DE22 ....56 E1
Wembley Rd *ARN* NG5 ....37 M4
  LEIW LE3 ....129 M2
Wemyss Gdns
  WOL/BIL/BRX NG8 ....50 B5
Wendling Gdns *ARN* NG5 ....24 F7
Wendover Cl *MCKLVR* DE3 ....56 A6
Wendover Dr *WOL/BIL/BRX* NG8 ....35 M5
Wendys Cl *LEIE* LE5 ....127 K8
Wenlock Cl *EWD/SEL/PNX* NG16 ....22 A7
  MCKLVR DE3 ....56 C6
Wenlock Wy *LEIN* LE4 ....126 E4
Wensleydale Cl
  WOL/BIL/BRX NG8 ....36 B6
Wensleydale Rd *LGEAT* NG10 ......75 M1
  WGSTN LE18 ....138 D6
Wensley Dr *DERBYE* DE21 ....59 K4
Wensley Ri *LEIS* LE2 ....137 G5
Wensley Rd *ARN* NG5 ....37 J2
Wensor Av *BSTN/STPLFD* NG9 ....49 K7
Wentbridge Rd *LEIN* LE4 ....126 B4
Went Rd *LEIN* LE4 ....125 L1
Wentworth Cl *MCKLVR* DE3 ....56 B6
  RLEIW/BBY LE8 ....146 F8
Wentworth Ct
  EWD/SEL/PNX NG16 ....34 C1
Wentworth Cft *HEANOR* DE75 ....20 E5
Wentworth Gn *RLEIW/BBY* LE8 ....129 H3
Wentworth Rd *ARN* NG5 ....36 F5
  BSTN/STPLFD NG9 ....63 L1
  COAL LE67 ....108 A7
  LEIW LE3 ....131 G1
  RLEIW/BBY LE8 ....145 L8
Wentworth St *ILK* DE7 ....33 L5
Wentworth Wy
  COT/KEY/RAD NG12 ....65 M4
Werburgh Cl *DERBYE* DE21 ....59 H3
Werburgh St *DERBYW* DE22 ....2 C5
Wesleyan Chapel Wk
  BSTN/STPLFD NG9 ....48 B8
Wesley Cl *GBY/RBY* LE6 ....123 G7
  RLBORO LE12 ....94 E6
Wesley La *BWSH/BRSTN* DE72 ....60 A2
Wesley Pl *BSTN/STPLFD* NG9 ....48 C7
Wesley Rd *DERBYSE* DE24 ....72 F2
Wesley St *ARN* NG5 ....36 F6
  EWD/SEL/PNX NG16 ....21 G4
  ILK DE7 ....33 J3
  LEIN LE4 ....125 K4
Wesley Wy *CFTN/RUD* NG11 ....79 H1
  COAL LE67 ....116 C7
Wessex Dr *EWD/SEL/PNX* NG16 .....21 L7
  LEIW LE3 ....130 C2
Wessington Ms *DERBYW* DE22 ......43 J6
West Av *BSTN/STPLFD* NG9 ....48 C7
  BWSH/BRSTN DE72 ....60 D7
  DERBY DE1 ....3 J2
  LEIS LE2 ....131 M5
  LGEAT NG10 ....61 L1
  MELB/CHEL DE73 ....72 D6
  RDERBYSW DE65 ....68 A5
  RIPLEY DE5 ....11 J6
  WBRGFD NG2 ....51 J8
  WGSTN LE18 ....138 B6
West Bank Av *DERBYW* DE22 ....43 H4
West Bank La *NOTTE* NG7 ....4 A5
West Bank Ms *CDON/KEG* DE74 .....86 A5
West Bank Rd *DERBYW* DE22 ....43 J2
Westbourne Cl *DERBYW* DE22 ......56 D1

Westbourne Rd
  EWD/SEL/PNX NG16 ....13 L5
Westbourne St *LEIN* LE4 ....125 L7
West Br *LEI* LE1 ....6 C6
Westbridge Cl *LEI* LE1 ....6 A6
Westbury Cl *BSTN/STPLFD* NG9 .....63 G3
Westbury Dr *BPR/DUF* DE56 ....18 A2
Westbury Rd *ARN* NG5 ....36 D5
  LEIS LE2 ....131 L6
Westbury St *DERBYW* DE22 ....57 H4
Westcliffe Av *LEIW* LE3 ....38 B4
  COT/KEY/RAD NG12 ....53 L3
Westcliffe Ct *NOTTE** NG7 ....50 E4
West Cl *COT/KEY/RAD* NG12 ....80 C5
  DERBYW DE22 ....43 J5
Westcotes Dr *LEIW* LE3 ....131 G3
West Cottages *DERBYE** DE21 .....43 M6
West Crs *BSTN/STPLFD* NG9 ....63 M3
West Croft Av *NORM/LIT* DE23 .....71 H7
Westcross Av
  BSTN/STPLFD NG9 ....48 C7
West Cross La *RLEINE/SYS* LE7 ...113 C6
Westdale Av *LEIS* LE2 ....136 E5
Westdale Cl *LGEAT* NG10 ....75 L2
Westdale Crs *CARL* NG4 ....38 B5
Westdale La East *CARL* NG4 ....38 C6
Westdale La West
  MAPPK/POR/STA NG3 ....38 A4
Westdale Rd
  EWD/SEL/PNX NG16 ....12 D3
Westdene Av *DERBYSE* DE24 ....72 B2
Westdown Dr *LEIN* LE4 ....126 C2
West Dr *LEIE* LE5 ....126 E7
  MCKLVR DE3 ....56 B5
  NOTTE NG7 ....49 M7
West End *BSTN/STPLFD* NG9 ....63 K2
  RLBORO LE12 ....93 K3
West End Ar *NOTT* NG1 ....4 F7
West End Crs *ILK* DE7 ....33 H7
West End Dr *BWSH/BRSTN* DE72 ....74 C6
  ILK DE7 ....33 H7
West End St *BSTN/STPLFD* NG9 .....62 A1
Westerby Cl *WGSTN* LE18 ....138 B5
Westerdale Rd *WGSTN* LE18 ....138 D6
Westerfield Wy
  CFTN/RUD NG11 ....64 E3
Westerham Cl
  WOL/BIL/BRX NG8 ....35 H8
Westerham Rd
  CFTN/RUD NG11 ....78 F1
Westerhope Cl
  COT/KEY/RAD NG12 ....66 A3
Westerlands *BSTN/STPLFD* NG9 ....62 D2
Western Bvd *LEIS* LE2 ....36 B7
  WOL/BIL/BRX NG8 ....36 B7
Western Dr *HEANOR* DE75 ....20 D7
  RLEIW/BBY LE8 ....136 F5
Western Flds *CFTN/RUD* NG11 ......78 F1
Western Gdns
  WOL/BIL/BRX NG8 ....36 B7
Westernhay Rd *LEIS* LE2 ....132 A6
Western Park Rd *LEIW* LE3 ....130 E2
Western Rd *LEIW* LE3 ....131 H4
  MCKLVR DE3 ....56 C5
  NORM/LIT DE23 ....2 D8
Western St *NOTT* NG1 ....5 H4
Western Ter *NOTTE* NG7 ....4 C6
Westfield Av *HEANOR* DE75 ....20 D7
  RLEIW/BBY LE8 ....143 H3
  WGSTN LE18 ....137 M3
Westfield Cl *ILK* DE7 ....47 G1
  RLEINE/SYS LE7 ....115 F3
Westfield Dr *ILK* DE7 ....33 H5
  LEIW LE3 ....8 E4
Westfield La *RLEINE/SYS* LE7 ....119 G2
Westfield Rd *LEIW* LE3 ....130 E2
Westfields La *CALV/BJ* NG14 ......26 C5
West Furlong
  COT/KEY/RAD NG12 ....67 L6
West Ga *LGEAT* NG10 ....62 C8
Westgate Av *LEIN* LE4 ....119 L7
Westgate Rd *LEIS* LE2 ....137 M1
Westgate St
  MAPPK/POR/STA NG3 ....5 L3
Westgreen Av *DERBYSE* DE24 ......72 B2
Westgv *DERBYSE* DE24 ....72 B2
Westhall Rd *MCKLVR* DE3 ....56 B6
Westhay Ct *WOL/BIL/BRX* NG8 .....50 A2
West HI *RIPLEY* DE5 ....11 M8
Westhill Rd *LEIW* LE3 ....130 E1
Westholme Gdns
  WOL/BIL/BRX NG8 ....50 A1
West Holme St *LEIW* LE3 ....6 C6
Westhorpe Dr *LGEAT* NG10 ....62 A7
Westland Av *HUCK/RAV* NG15 ....23 H3
West Langton Rd
  RLEIW/BBY LE8 ....147 J8
West Lawn *RDERBYSW* DE65 ....70 A5
West Leake La *CFTN/RUD* NG11 .....77 G7
  RLBORO LE12 ....87 J3
West Leake Rd *RLBORO* LE12 ......87 M6
Westleigh Av *DERBYW* DE22 ....57 C1
  LEIW LE3 ....131 G4
Westleigh Rd *LEIW* LE3 ....131 G4
  WGSTN LE18 ....137 J6
  WOL/BIL/BRX NG8 ....35 J5
Westley Crs *DERBYSE* DE24 ....30 B5
Westmeadow La *RLBORO* LE12 ......93 J4
Westmead Av *LEIE* LE5 ....132 F1
Westminster Av *LGEAT* NG10 ......62 A2
Westminster Cl
  MAPPK/POR/STA NG3 ....5 M1
Westminster Dr *LEIS* LE2 ....137 H6
Westminster Rd *LEIE* LE5 ....132 C6
Westminster St *DERBYSE* DE24 ....58 D7
West Moor *WBRGFD* NG2 ....52 B2
Westmorland Av *LBORO* LE11 ....8 B9
  LEIN LE4 ....126 A5
  WGSTN LE18 ....137 K5
Westmorland Cl *DERBYE* DE21 ......3 K1
Westmorland Wy
  EWD/SEL/PNX NG16 ....12 F4
Westoby Cl *RLBORO* LE12 ....102 B4
Weston Av *NOTTE* NG7 ....4 C3
Weston Cl *ARN* NG5 ....37 J3
  LEIS LE2 ....139 J3

RLEINE/SYS LE7 ....115 K6
Weston Crs LGEAT NG10 ....75 K3
Weston Park Av DERBYSE DE24 ...72 B4
Weston Rd DERBYSE DE72 .....83 K1
Weston Spot Cl RIPLEY DE5 ......11 H8
Weston St HEANOR DE75 ....20 E7
West Orch RLBORO LE12 ......114 A6
West Pk WBRGFD NG2 ....51 H8
West Park Rd DERBYW DE22 ....43 J7
Westray Cl BSTN/STPLFD NG9 ....48 F4
West Rd DERBYE DE21 ....59 H2
West Rw DERBYW DE22 ....44 B4
West Service Rd DERBYE DE21 ...58 E5
West St ALFN DE55 ....12 A1
  ARN NG5 ....25 J8
  END/NAR LE19 ....135 L5
  EWD/SEL/PNX NG16 ....20 F4
  HEANOR DE75 ....20 B5
  HUCK/RAV NG15 ....15 L8
  ILK DE7 ....33 J8
  LEI LE1 ....6 F9
  LEIW LE3 ....124 A6
  RLEINE/SYS LE7 ....120 E3
  RLEIW/BBY LE8 ....136 E6
  WBRGFD NG2 ....5 L7
West Ter HUCK/RAV NG15 ......15 L8
  ILK DE7 ....33 K6
West Thorpe RLBORO LE12 .....90 F8
West Vw WBRGFD NG2 ....65 H1
  NORM/LIT DE23 ....56 F8
Westview Ct CARL NG4 ....38 D7
West View Rd CARL NG4 ....38 D7
Westville Dr HUCK/RAV NG15 ...23 J3
Westville Gdns
  MAPPK/POR/STA NG3 ....5 J2
West Wk LEI LE1 ....7 H9
  WBRGFD NG2 ....5 L7
Westway COT/KEY/RAD NG12 ....67 J5
Westwick Rd WOL/BIL/BRX NG8 ..49 G1
Westwick St ILK DE7 ....47 L1
Westwood Dr DERBYSE DE24 ....72 B2
Westwood Rd WBRGFD NG2 ......51 K3
Wetherby Cl
  EWD/SEL/PNX NG16 ....22 C8
  RLEINE/SYS LE7 ....121 J1
  WOL/BIL/BRX NG8 ....35 M7
Wetherby Rd DERBYSE DE24 ....58 B8
  LEIN LE2 ....126 B4
Wetherlam Cl WBRGFD NG2 .....51 G5
Wexford Cl LEIS LE2 ....139 H3
Weyacres BWSH/BRSTN DE72 ....59 M6
Weybridge Cl ILK DE7 ....32 F7
Weymouth Cl LEIW LE18 ......138 B7
Weymouth St LEIN LE4 ....125 M7
Whaddon Dr LGEAT NG10 ....9 L8
Whall Cl RLBORO LE12 ....112 E2
The Wharf BWSH/BRSTN DE72 ...74 E6
Wharfdale Rd WOL/BIL/BRX NG8 ..48 F4
Wharfedale Cl DERBYW DE22 ...43 M3
Wharfedale Rd LGEAT NG10 .....75 L1
Wharf La COT/KEY/RAD NG12 ....53 J4
Wharf Rd NOTTE NG7 ....4 F9
Wharf St LEIN LE4 ....120 D7
Wharf St North LEI LE1 ....7 G3
Wharf St South LEI LE1 ....7 G4
Wharf Wy LEIS LE2 ....136 F5
Wharncliffe Rd ILK DE7 ....33 J7
  LBORO LE12 ....9 L4
Whatton Oaks RLBORO LE12 ...113 J7
Whatton Ri ARN NG5 ....36 F3
Whatton Rd CDON/KEG DE74 ....86 A8
Wheatacre Rd CFTN/RUD NG11 ..64 D6
Wheat Cl WOL/BIL/BRX NG8 .....49 H2
Wheatcroft Vw
  CFTN/RUD NG11 ....65 G4
Wheatcroft Wy DERBYE DE21 ...44 A5
Wheatfield Cl LEIW LE3 ......124 A8
Wheatfields Rd
  MAPPK/POR/STA NG3 ....37 L8
Wheatgrass Rd
  BSTN/STPLFD NG9 ....62 F2
Wheathill Gv NORM/LIT DE23 ...70 E1
Wheatland Cl DERBYSE DE24 ....71 G5
  LEIS LE2 ....139 H4
Wheatland Dr LBORO LE11 ......9 L8
Wheatland Rd LEIN LE4 ......125 H2
Wheatlands Dr RLEIW/BBY LE8 ..143 H3
Wheatley Cl CFTN/RUD NG11 ...79 G3
Wheatley Dr CARL NG4 ....38 A8
Wheatley Rd BSTN/STPLFD NG9 ..63 K3
Wheatley Rd LEIN LE4 ....126 B1
Wheatley's Rd LEIN LE4 ......126 B1
Wheatsheaf Cl DERBYE DE21 ...45 G5
Wheatsheaf Cl CALV/BJ NG14 ..39 K3
Wheat St LEI LE1 ....7 G4
Wheeldale WGSTN LE18 ....138 D5
Wheeldale Cl WOL/BIL/BRX NG8 ..48 F3
Wheeldon Av BPR/DUF DE56 ....17 M7
  DERBYW DE22 ....43 J8
Wheeler Av EWD/SEL/PNX NG16 ..21 M6
Wheeler Ga NOTT NG1 ....5 G7
Wheldon Av CARL NG4 ....38 A5
Whenby Cl MCKLVR DE3 ....56 A5
Whernside Cl DERBYSE DE24 ....73 G1
Whernside Rd ARN NG5 ....37 J2
Whetstone Cl
  WOL/BIL/BRX NG8 ....35 H4
Whetstone Dr COAL LE67 .....108 C6
Whetstone Gorse La
  RLEIW/BBY LE8 ....142 E5
Whiles La LEIN LE4 ....119 M8
Whilton Crs ILK DE7 ....32 B7
Whinbush Av DERBYSE DE24 ....72 C2
Whinchat Rd LEIE LE5 ....94 F5
Whinfell Cl CFTN/RUD NG11 ....64 D5
Whinham Av RLEIW/BAR LE9 ....141 H8
Whinlatter Dr WBRGFD NG2 ....66 A1
Whiston Cl ARN NG5 ....35 L6
Whiston Rd NORM/LIT DE23 ....57 L5
Whitaker Gdns NORM/LIT DE23 ...2 A9
Whitaker Rd NORM/LIT DE23 ....2 A9
Whitaker St NORM/LIT DE23 ....57 L5
Whitbread St NOTTE NG7 ......36 D7
Whitburn Rd BSTN/STPLFD NG9 ..62 C4

Whitby Av DERBY DE21 ....44 A6
Whitby Cl RLBORO LE12 ....102 F2
  RLEIW/BAR LE9 ....141 J7
  WOL/BIL/BRX NG8 ....48 F3
Whitby Crs ARN NG5 ....37 L2
Whitby Rd EWD/SEL/PNX NG16 ..21 L4
Whitcombe Gdns ARN NG5 .....24 E7
Whitcombe Pl RIPLEY DE5 .....11 H5
Whitcroft Cl CFTN/RUD NG11 ..116 C7
Whitcroft's La COAL LE67 ....110 B8
Whiteacres RLEIW/BBY LE8 ....142 B4
White Barn Dr RLEIW/BAR LE9 ..142 B4
Whitebeam Cl END/NAR LE19 ..135 L7
Whitebeam Rd LEIS LE2 ......132 E8
Whitechapel St
  WOL/BIL/BRX NG8 ....36 B5
Whitecross Gdns DERBY DE1 ...43 J8
Whitecross St DERBY DE1 ....2 B2
Whitefield Rd LEIN LE4 ......125 K4
White Furrows
  COT/KEY/RAD NG12 ....67 J5
Whitegate LBORO LE11 ....9 L1
Whitegates Rd LBORO * LE11 ....9 L1
White Gates RIPLEY DE5 ......11 M7
Whitegate V CFTN/RUD NG11 ...64 B6
Whitehall Rd LEIE LE5 ....132 F3
Whitehaven Gv
  MELB/CHEL DE73 ....72 E4
Whitehead Cl DE73 ....33 H5
Whitehead Crs WGSTN LE18 ...137 M4
Whitehead Dr
  EWD/SEL/PNX NG16 ....13 H7
White Horse La LEIN LE4 ....125 M1
Whitehouse Av LBORO LE11 .....9 M6
Whitehouse Cl DERBYSE DE24 ..72 B3
White House Cl GBY/RBY LE6 ..123 J4
Whitehouse Ri BPR/DUF DE56 ..17 J1
Whitehurst St DERBYSE DE24 ..58 B8
Whitelands COT/KEY/RAD NG12 ..67 L5
White La BPR/DUF DE56 ....16 B4
Whiteley Rd RIPLEY DE5 ......11 K8
White Lodge Gdns
  WOL/BIL/BRX NG8 ....35 H8
Whitely Cl BSTN/STPLFD NG9 ..48 C7
Whitemoor Av
  WOL/BIL/BRX NG8 ....36 B7
Whitemoor Hall BPR/DUF DE56 ..18 B2
Whitemoor La BPR/DUF DE56 ...18 B2
Whitemoor Rd BLWL NG6 ......36 B5
Whitemoss Cl
  WOL/BIL/BRX NG8 ....49 J4
Whiteoaks Rd LEIS LE2 ....139 G4
White Rd ARN NG5 ....36 C4
Whitesand Cl LEIW LE3 ......124 B6
White's Av
  MAPPK/POR/STA NG3 ....55 M1
White's Cft CALV/BJ NG14 ....26 F3
White St DERBYW DE22 ....43 J8
  RLBORO LE12 ....112 D1
  RLEIW/BBY LE8 ....146 D7
Whiteway DERBYW DE22 ....43 J5
Whitewell Gdns DERBYSE DE24 ..73 G2
Whitfield Cl CFTN/RUD NG11 ...64 F1
Whiting Av BSTN/STPLFD NG9 ..62 D5
Whitley Cl LEIW LE3 ....124 F7
Whitman Cl LEIW LE3 ....130 B1
Whitmore Rd DERBYE DE21 ....58 D1
Whitstable Cl NORM/LIT DE23 ..57 H8
Whittaker La DERBYE DE21 ....30 B5
Whittaker Rd
  BSTN/STPLFD NG9 ....62 E4
Whitteney Dr LEIS LE2 ....137 H5
Whittier Rd LEIE LE5 ....131 K8
  WBRGFD NG2 ....51 L4
Whittingham Rd
  MAPPK/POR/STA NG3 ....37 L4
Whittington Dr GBY/RBY LE6 ..123 C6
Whittington St DERBYSE DE24 ..72 B2
Whittlebury Dr NORM/LIT DE23 ..56 D8
Whittle Cl RLEIW/BBY LE8 ....142 D1
Whitton Cl ARN NG5 ....24 F6
  BSTN/STPLFD NG9 ....63 G5
Whitwell Cl WOL/BIL/BRX NG8 ..35 J4
Whitwell Rd WOL/BIL/BRX NG8 ..35 J6
Whitwell Rw LEIS LE2 ....137 J2
Whitwick Moor COAL LE67 ....100 B8
Whitwick Rd COAL LE67 ......108 B6
  COAL LE67 ....116 A1
Whitwick Wy LEIW LE3 ....125 G7
Whitworth Dr CALV/BJ NG14 ...39 C5
  COT/KEY/RAD NG12 ....53 J5
Whitworth Ri ARN NG5 ....24 D7
Whitworth Rd ILK DE7 ....47 K1
Whyburn La HUCK/RAV NG15 ...15 G8
Whyburn St HUCK/RAV NG15 ...24 A1
Whysall St HEANOR DE75 ......20 C5
Whyston Ct HUCK/RAV NG15 ...23 G2
Whyteleafe Gv DERBYE DE21 ...44 F6
Wichnor Cl CFTN/RUD NG11 ...64 C3
Wicken Ri WGSTN LE18 ......138 C3
Wickens Wk
  MAPPK/POR/STA NG3 ....5 M3
Wickersley Cl DERBYW DE22 ...43 J5
Wicket Gv NOTTE NG7 ....50 C3
Wickham Rd LEIS LE2 ....138 F3
Wicklow Cl RLBORO LE12 ....102 A5
Wicklow Dr LEIE LE5 ....132 E1
Wickstead Cl
  MAPPK/POR/STA NG3 ....37 K4
Wicksteed Cl BPR/DUF DE56 ..18 B2
Widdowson Cl BLWL NG6 ......23 K7
Widdybank Cl DERBYW DE22 ...43 C5
Widecombe La CFTN/RUD NG11 ..64 B7
Wide La RLBORO LE12 ....94 E6
  RLBORO LE12 ....98 C3
Wide St RLBORO LE12 ....94 E7
Widford St LEIE LE5 ....126 E7
Widmerpool La
  COT/KEY/RAD NG12 ....80 F7
The Widon LBORO LE11 ......103 J2
Wighay Rd HUCK/RAV NG15 ...15 H5
Wightman Cl LBORO LE12 ....101 M4
  RLEIW/BAR LE9 ....140 B4
Wigley Cl WOL/BIL/BRX NG8 ...5 M3
Wigley Rd LEIE LE5 ....127 G2
Wigman Rd WOL/BIL/BRX NG8 ..35 H7
Wigmore Cl MCKLVR DE3 ......56 A4
Wigston La LEIS LE2 ....137 H1

Wigston Rd RLEIW/BBY LE8 ...136 F7
  WGSTN LE18 ....138 D3
Wigston St LEI LE1 ....7 G6
  RLEIW/BBY LE8 ....143 K3
Wilberforce Rd LEIW LE3 ....131 H4
Wilcox Dr EWD/SEL/PNX NG16 ..13 L6
Wilde Crs EWD/SEL/PNX NG16 ..13 L1
Wilden Crs CFTN/RUD NG11 ...64 C4
Wildman St NOTTE NG7 ....4 C4
Wildpark La ASHB DE6 ....41 G1
Wildsmith St DERBYSE DE24 ...58 E7
Wild St DERBYW DE22 ....57 H2
Wilford Crs East WBRGFD NG2 ..51 H6
Wilford Crs West WBRGFD NG2 ..51 G6
Wilford Gv WBRGFD NG2 ......51 H6
Wilford La WBRGFD NG2 ......51 G8
Wilford Rd CFTN/RUD NG11 ...64 F4
  WBRGFD NG2 ....50 F5
Wilfred St NORM/LIT DE23 ....57 M5
Wilfrid Gv WBRGFD NG2 ......65 J4
Wilhallow La
  EWD/SEL/PNX NG16 ....13 J4
Wilkins Dr DERBYSE DE24 .....58 C3
Wilkins Gdns CFTN/RUD NG11 ..64 A6
Wilkinson Av BSTN/STPLFD NG9 ..63 K1
Wilkinson St WOL/BIL/BRX NG8 ..36 B6
Willaston Cl BLWL NG6 ....36 A3
Wilbert Av ARN NG5 ....25 L7
Willerby Rd ARN NG5 ....37 L2
Willersley Dr WBRGFD NG2 ....51 G5
Willesden Av DERBYW DE22 ...42 E8
Willesden Gn
  EWD/SEL/PNX NG16 ....35 H4
Willetts Rd DERBYE DE21 .....44 E8
Willey La EWD/SEL/PNX NG16 ..13 J4
William Av EWD/SEL/PNX NG16 ..21 K5
William Booth Rd WBRGFD NG2 ..51 L3
William Cl CARL NG4 ....38 F7
  RLEINE/SYS LE7 ....121 J1
William Rd BSTN/STPLFD NG9 ..48 B8
  WBRGFD NG2 ....51 J7
Williams Cl ALFN DE55 ....12 B1
  END/NAR LE19 ....141 M1
Williams Rd BSTN/STPLFD NG9 ..62 F4
William St BPR/DUF DE56 .....17 K3
  DERBY DE1 ....2 B1
  END/NAR LE19 ....135 M8
  HUCK/RAV NG15 ....15 L8
  LBORO LE11 ....9 G4
  LEIE LE5 ....7 H5
  LGEAT NG10 ....62 A5
Willington Rd RDERBYSW DE65 ..69 G3
  RDERBYSW DE65 ....70 A7
Willn Cl COAL LE67 ....108 F7
Willn St NORM/LIT DE23 ......57 K6
Willoughby Av LGEAT NG10 ...62 A5
  NOTTE NG7 ....4 A8
Willoughby Cl
  BWSH/BRSTN DE72 ....61 K7
  NOTTE NG7 ....49 M7
Willoughby Ct NOTTE NG7 .....4 A9
Willoughby Gdns LEIW LE3 ...129 L4
Willoughby Rd RLEIW/BBY LE8 ..143 G4
  WBRGFD NG2 ....65 K1
Willoughby St BSTN/STPLFD NG9 ..63 L1
  ILK DE7 ....33 L6
  NOTTE NG7 ....4 A9
Willow Av BSTN/STPLFD NG9 ..62 B1
  CARL NG4 ....38 E7
  HUCK/RAV NG15 ....23 H2
  LGEAT NG10 ....62 B6
  RIPLEY DE5 ....11 H8
Willow Brook
  COT/KEY/RAD NG12 ....80 E5
Willow Brook Cl LEIW LE3 ...124 A5
Willowbrook Cl
  RDERBYSW DE65 ....68 A5
  RLEIW/BAR LE9 ....141 K8
Willowbrook Gra
  MELB/CHEL DE73 ....72 E6
Willowbrook Pk LBORO LE11 ..103 J1
Willow Brook Rd LEIE LE5 .....7 M2
Willowbrook Vw LEIE LE5 ....133 J1
Willow Cl BWSH/BRSTN DE72 ..73 M8
  CALV/BJ NG14 ....39 K2
  COT/KEY/RAD NG12 ....53 K5
  DERBYW DE22 ....43 K5
  END/NAR LE19 ....142 A1
  RLBORO LE12 ....88 B7
Willow Cl LEIS LE2 ....7 J7
Willow Crs CARL NG4 ....27 C8
  CARL NG4 ....38 E5
Willow Cft DERBYSE DE24 .....73 C3
Willowcroft Rd DERBYE DE21 ..45 L4
Willowdene COT/KEY/RAD NG12 ..67 L4
Willow Dr GBY/RBY LE6 ......123 J6
  HUCK/RAV NG15 ....14 D1
  RLEIW/BBY LE8 ....143 J3
Willowfields RDERBYSW DE65 ..68 B5
Willow Gn COAL LE67 ....109 C5
Willow Gv BPR/DUF DE56 .....17 L5
  RLEINE/SYS LE7 ....113 G6
Willowherb Cl DERBYSE DE24 ..71 K5
Willow Hill Cl BLWL NG6 .....35 L1
Willow La CARL NG4 ....38 D5
Willow Park Dr WGSTN LE18 ..138 A4
Willow Park Wy
  BWSH/BRSTN DE72 ....73 L8
Willowpit La RDERBYSW DE65 ..54 B8
Willow Pl WGSTN LE18 ......138 B5
Willow Pool La RLBORO LE12 ..95 G2
Willow Rd CARL NG4 ....38 D7
  CDON/KEG DE74 ....84 F2
  LBORO LE11 ....103 L2
  NOTTE NG7 ....50 D7
  RLEIW/BBY LE8 ....136 F3
Willow Rw DERBY DE1 ....2 D2
Willowsend Cl RDERBYSW DE65 ..70 B6
The Willows RLBORO LE12 ...105 K1
Willowtree Cl LEIE LE5 ......127 G5
Willow Vw NOTTE NG7 ....4 A5
Willow Wk RLEINE/SYS LE7 ...120 D4
Willow Wong CALV/BJ NG14 ...39 K2
Willson Av NORM/LIT DE23 ....57 G7

Willson Dr ALFN DE55 ....11 M1
Willson Rd NORM/LIT DE23 ....57 G7
Wilwell Dr WBRGFD NG2 ......65 G4
Wilmington Av DERBYSE DE24 ..72 C7
Wilmington Ct LBORO LE11 .....9 M6
Wilmore Crs LEIW LE3 ....130 B5
Wilmore Rd DERBYSE DE24 ....71 J2
  DERBYE DE21 ....58 D2
Wilmot Av DERBYSE DE24 .....72 E4
Wilmot Dr ILK DE7 ....31 K2
Wilmot La BSTN/STPLFD NG9 ..63 K3
Wilmot Rd BPR/DUF DE56 .....17 L3
Wilmot St DERBY DE1 ....2 F6
  HEANOR DE75 ....20 C6
  ILK DE7 ....33 J6
  LGEAT NG10 ....75 L2
Wilmslow Dr DERBYE DE21 ....44 F6
Wilne Av LEIS LE2 ....7 M8
Wilne Cl LGEAT NG10 ....75 L3
Wilne La BWSH/BRSTN DE72 ..74 F6
  BWSH/BRSTN DE72 ....75 G3
Wilne Rd BWSH/BRSTN DE72 ..74 E1
  LGEAT NG10 ....75 K3
Wilne St LEIS LE2 ....7 M8
Wilnicott Rd LEIW LE3 ....130 D6
Wilshee Cl WGSTN LE18 .....138 A7
Wilshere Cl RLEIW/BAR LE9 ..129 H2
Wilson Av HEANOR DE75 ......19 M3
Wilson Cl ARN NG5 ....37 M2
  LEIS LE2 ....130 B5
  MCKLVR DE3 ....56 A7
Wilson Rd DERBYE DE21 ......44 D7
  EWD/SEL/PNX NG16 ....21 K6
  WGSTN LE18 ....137 J6
Wilson St DERBY DE1 ....7 L5
  LEIS LE2 ....7 L5
Wilsthorpe Rd
  BSTN/STPLFD NG9 ....61 J7
  DERBYE DE21 ....44 D8
Wilstone Cl LBORO LE11 .....103 G4
Wilton Av LBORO LE11 ....9 M7
Wilton Cl DERBYSE DE24 ......71 G5
  LEIS LE2 ....139 G2
Wilton St BLWL NG6 ....36 C5
  ILK DE7 ....33 K6
  LEI LE1 ....6 F3
Wiltshire Av EWD/SEL/PNX NG16 ..12 F3
Wiltshire Rd DERBYE DE21 ....44 B8
  LEIN LE4 ....125 H5
  WGSTN LE18 ....137 M4
Wimbledon Dr
  EWD/SEL/PNX NG16 ....35 J4
Wimbledon Rd ARN NG5 ......36 E4
  DERBYW DE22 ....43 J4
Wimbledon St LEIE LE5 ....7 G5
Wimborne Cl WBRGFD NG2 ....65 G2
Wimborne Rd LEIS LE2 ......138 B1
Wimbourne Cl
  MELB/CHEL DE73 ....72 E6
Wimbourne Rd NOTTE NG7 .....4 A3
Wimpole Gdns DERBYSE DE24 ..49 H6
Wimpole Rd BSTN/STPLFD NG9 ..49 H6
Wincanton Cl DERBYSE DE24 ..58 B6
Winchcombe Wy DERBYE DE21 ..44 E5
Winchendon Cl LEIE LE5 ....126 C8
Winchester Av
  BSTN/STPLFD NG9 ....49 J7
  LEIW LE3 ....130 F4
  RLEIW/BBY LE8 ....136 E7
Winchester Cl RLBORO LE12 ..68 F3
Winchester Ct ARN NG5 ....37 J4
Winchester Crs DERBYE DE21 ..44 B8
  ILK DE7 ....33 L7
Winchester Rd RLEIW/BBY LE8 ..137 G8
Winchester St ARN NG5 ......37 H4
Windermere Av ILK DE7 ......47 G2
Windermere Cl CARL NG4 .....38 D5
  WBRGFD NG2 ....52 B8
Windermere Crs DERBYW DE22 ..43 J4
Windermere Dr DERBYE DE21 ..44 J2
  RLEIW/BAR LE9 ....141 H3
Windermere Rd
  BSTN/STPLFD NG9 ....49 H6
  HUCK/RAV NG15 ....15 K7
  LGEAT NG10 ....61 L5
  NOTTE NG7 ....36 E7
  WGSTN LE18 ....138 D4
Windermere St LEIS LE2 .....131 J4
Winder's Wy LEIS LE2 ....137 H2
Windlea Rd ALFN DE55 ....12 A1
Windleden Rd LBORO LE11 ...102 F5
Windley Crs DERBYW DE22 ....43 K6
Windley Dr ILK DE7 ....33 H5
Windley La BPR/DUF DE56 ....28 C1
Windmill Av BPR/DUF DE56 ...18 F7
  HUCK/RAV NG15 ....23 L1
  LEIN LE4 ....119 M7
Windmill Bank WGSTN LE18 ..138 C6
Windmill Cl BWSH/BRSTN DE72 ..60 A2
  CDON/KEG DE74 ....84 F5
  DERBYSE DE24 ....73 H3
  GBY/RBY LE6 ....123 H7
  MAPPK/POR/STA NG3 ....51 K2
Windmill Cottages
  DERBY * DE73 ....44 D4
Windmill Ct COT/KEY/RAD NG12 ..80 D5
Windmill End RLEINE/SYS LE7 ..113 J8
Windmill Gdns RLEIW/BBY LE8 ..146 E5
Windmill Gv HUCK/RAV NG15 ..23 L1
Windmill Hill La DERBYW DE22 ..57 G1
Windmill La BPR/DUF DE56 ....17 L3
  MAPPK/POR/STA NG3 ....51 K2
  WBRGFD NG2 ....51 M7
Windmill Rd LBORO LE11 ....104 B4
  RDERBYSW DE65 ....68 F4
Windmill Vw BPR/DUF DE56 ...10 C7
Windmill Wy CDON/KEG DE74 ..85 M5
Windrush Cl BSTN/STPLFD NG9 ..49 H6
  DERBYW DE22 ....43 M2
Windrush Dr LEIS LE2 ....139 H2

Windsmoor Rd
  EWD/SEL/PNX NG16 ....13 H7
Windsor Av GBY/RBY LE6 ....123 J5
  LEIN LE4 ....125 M5
  LEIS LE2 ....137 J6
  MELB/CHEL DE73 ....82 E7
  NORM/LIT DE23 ....57 G7
Windsor Cl BSTN/STPLFD NG9 ..47 M2
  BWSH/BRSTN DE72 ....60 A6
  COAL LE67 ....108 F6
  HEANOR DE75 ....20 E7
  HUCK/RAV NG15 ....15 M7
  LEIS LE2 ....139 G4
  RLBORO LE12 ....112 F1
  RLBORO LE12 ....113 H7
Windsor Ct ILK DE7 ....32 B7
  LGEAT NG10 ....61 M5
  MCKLVR DE3 ....56 B4
Windsor Crs ARN NG5 ....37 M2
  BSTN/STPLFD NG9 ....48 C8
  ILK DE7 ....47 H3
Windsor Dr DERBYE DE21 .....59 K1
  RLBORO LE12 ....101 L5
Windsor Rd LBORO LE11 .....103 H2
  BSTN/STPLFD NG9 ....48 B8
  BSTN/STPLFD NG9 ....63 L1
Windy La DERBYE DE21 ....30 A6
Winforde Crs LEIW LE3 ......130 A4
Wingate Cl WOL/BIL/BRX NG8 ..49 K1
Wingbourne Wk BLWL NG6 ....24 A6
Wingerworth Park Rd
  DERBYE DE21 ....59 J2
Wingfield Dr BSTN/STPLFD NG9 ..49 L6
  DERBYE DE21 ....59 J2
  ILK DE7 ....33 H4
Wingfield St LEIN LE4 ......125 M5
Wings Dr HUCK/RAV NG15 ....23 K1
Wingfield Crs CALV/BJ NG14 ..39 K3
Winifred St HUCK/RAV NG15 ..23 M1
  LEIS LE2 ....6 D9
Winrow Gdns BLWL NG6 ......36 A4
Winscale Av ARN NG5 ....24 E7
Winscombe Mt CFTN/RUD NG11 ..64 B8
Winsford Cl WOL/BIL/BRX NG8 ..35 M5
Winslow Dr WOL/BIL/BRX NG8 ..138 C3
Winslow Gn DERBYE DE21 ....58 F1
  LEIE LE5 ....127 G7
Winstanley Dr LEIW LE3 ....130 D3
Winster Av CARL NG4 ....38 C5
Winster Cl BPR/DUF DE56 ....17 M2
  BSTN/STPLFD NG9 ....49 G4
Winster Dr LEIN LE4 ....120 C7
Winster Rd DERBYE DE21 ....44 C6
Winster Wy LGEAT NG10 .....75 K2
Winston Av RLEIW/BAR LE9 ..141 H3
Winston Cl BSTN/STPLFD NG9 ..47 M2
  MAPPK/POR/STA NG3 ....38 A1
Winterbourne Dr
  BSTN/STPLFD NG9 ....48 C6
Winterburn Gdns
  RLEIW/BBY LE8 ....136 D8
Winterburn Wy LBORO LE11 ..102 F4
Winter Closes
  EWD/SEL/PNX NG16 ....13 K6
Winterfield Cl LEIW LE3 ....123 M8
Wintergreen Cl LEIS LE5 ....127 G4
Wintergreen Dr
  NORM/LIT DE23 ....70 D1
Wintersdale Rd LEIE LE5 ....133 C1
  LEIE LE5 ....133 J2
Winterton Cl ARN NG5 ....37 K1
  LEIN LE4 ....120 D7
Winterton Ri ARN NG5 ....37 K1
Winthorpe Rd ARN NG5 ......25 L8
Winton Av LEIW LE3 ....130 F5
Wintringham Crs ARN NG5 ...37 L2
Wirksworth Rd BPR/DUF DE56 ..16 C6
  BPR/DUF DE56 ....29 H4
  ILK DE7 ....47 G3
Wisgreaves Rd DERBYSE DE24 ..58 D7
Wishford Av NOTTE NG7 ......50 C4
Wisley Cl CFTN/RUD NG11 ....65 G4
Wistow Cl WGSTN LE18 .....144 E4
  WOL/BIL/BRX NG8 ....36 C7
Wistow Rd RLEIW/BBY LE8 ...145 H1
  RLEIW/BBY LE8 ....146 B5
  WGSTN LE18 ....138 B6
  WGSTN LE18 ....138 B6
Witham Cl RDERBYSW DE65 ...68 C5
Witham Dr NORM/LIT DE23 ....71 H1
Withcote Av LEIE LE5 ....133 G2
Withens Cl LEIE LE5 ....124 E8
Witherdell LEIN LE4 ....124 E4
Withern Rd WOL/BIL/BRX NG8 ..35 K6
Withers Wy LEIE LE5 ....130 B6
Withington Cl LEIW LE3 ....130 B5
Witney Cl ARN NG5 ....24 C8
  DERBYSE DE24 ....58 A7
Wittering Cl LGEAT NG10 ....76 C2
Witton Cl DERBYSE DE24 .....71 H3
Wiverton Rd NOTTE NG7 ......36 E7
Woburn Cl COT/KEY/RAD NG12 ..66 A3
  LBORO LE11 ....137 G3
  LEIS LE2 ....137 G3
  WGSTN LE18 ....138 C5
Woburn Cft LGEAT NG10 .....61 L3
Woburn Pl DERBYW DE22 ......56 F2
Woburn Ri ARN NG5 ....37 M2
Wodehouse Av CFTN/RUD NG11 ..77 M5
Wodehouse Rd LEIW LE3 ....130 C3
Wokingham Av LEIS LE2 .....137 H5
The Wolds RLEINE/SYS LE7 ..115 J7
Wolds Dr COT/KEY/RAD NG12 ..80 D4
Wolds La COT/KEY/RAD NG12 ..67 H7
  COT/KEY/RAD NG12 ....80 D7
Wolds Ri COT/KEY/RAD NG12 ..80 D4
Wolfa St DERBY DE22 ....2 C5
Wollacombe Cl
  MAPPK/POR/STA NG3 ....38 B2
Wollaton Av LEIE LE5 ....38 B4
  LBORO LE11 ....103 G3
Wollaton Cl LEIW LE3 ....123 M7
Wollaton Ct BLWL NG6 ....36 C1
Wollaton Crs BSTN/STPLFD NG9 ..49 J7
Wollaton Hall Dr
  WOL/BIL/BRX NG8 ....50 B4
Wollaton Paddocks
  WOL/BIL/BRX NG8 ....49 G3

Wollaton Ri *WOL/BIL/BRX* NG8 ......49 J5
Wollaton Rd *BSTN/STPLFD* NG9 ......49 J7
  DERBYE DE21 ....44 D7
  WOL/BIL/BRX NG8 ....49 L3
Wollaton St *NOTT* NG1 ....4 F6
Wollaton V *WOL/BIL/BRX* NG8 ....48 F3
Wolsey Av *NOTTE* NG7 ....4 B5
Wolsey Cl *GBY/RBY* LE6 ....123 J5
  LEIW LE3 ....129 K5
  RLEIW/BBY LE8 ....145 K7
Wolsey Dr *GBY/RBY* LE6 ....122 F6
Wolsey La *RLEIW/BBY* LE8 ....145 K7
Wolsey Rd *COAL* LE67 ....108 A5
Wolsey St *LEIN* LE4 ....125 J7
Wolsey Wy *LEIW* LE11 ....9 M3
  RLEINE/SYS LE7 ....120 D4
Wolverley Gra *DERBYSE* DE24 ....73 H1
Wolverton Rd *LEIW* LE3 ....131 G5
Woodale Cl *NORM/LIT* DE23 ....70 D1
Wood Av *LGEAT* NG10 ....61 L1
Woodbank Leis LE2 ....136 F5
Woodbank Dr
  WOL/BIL/BRX NG8 ....49 H5
Woodbank Rd *GBY/RBY* LE6 ....123 H4
  WGSTN LE18 ....138 A1
Woodbine Av *LEIS* LE2 ....7 K9
Woodborough La *ARN* NG5 ....25 M4
Woodborough Rd *LEIE* LE5 ....132 E3
  MAPPK/POR/STA NG3 ....5 J2
Woodboy St *LEI* LE1 ....7 G2
Woodbridge Av
  CFTN/RUD NG11 ....64 C4
Woodbridge Cl
  MELB/CHEL DE73 ....72 D6
Woodbridge Rd *LEIN* LE4 ....125 M4
Woodbrook Rd *LBORO* LE11 ....8 D9
Woodchester Dr *DERBYSE* DE24 .....73 H1
Woodchurch Rd *ARN* NG5 ....24 F6
Wood Cl *RLBORO* LE12 ....102 B4
Wood Cl Camp *DERBYE* DE21 ....30 A8
Woodcote Rd *LEIW* LE3 ....130 D8
Woodcote Wy *NORM/LIT* DE23 ....56 B7
Wood Cft *NORM/LIT* DE23 ....57 H7
The Woodcroft
  CDON/KEG DE74 ....93 G2
Woodcroft Av *LEIS* LE2 ....137 L1
Wood End *LEIW* LE3 ....124 E8
Wood End Rd *HEANOR* DE75 ....20 C5
Woodfall La *DERBYW* DE22 ....28 D5
Woodfield Cl *END/NAR* LE19 ....135 M7
Woodfield Rd *LEIS* LE2 ....132 F8
  RLEINE/SYS LE7 ....119 J1
  WOL/BIL/BRX NG8 ....35 J6
Woodford Cl *ARN* NG5 ....24 C6
  WGSTN LE18 ....138 A7
Woodford Rd *ARN* NG5 ....37 L2
  DERBYW DE22 ....42 B8
  HUCK/RAV NG15 ....23 M1
Wood Ga *LBORO* LE11 ....9 J4
Woodgate *LEIW* LE3 ....6 B2
  RLEINE/SYS LE7 ....119 J1
Woodgate Cl
  COT/KEY/RAD NG12 ....67 J4
Woodgate Ct *NOTTE* NG7 ....4 C6
Woodgate Dr *LEIN* LE4 ....119 K7
  MELB/CHEL DE73 ....72 E6
Woodgate La
  COT/KEY/RAD NG12 ....67 H4
Woodgate Rd *RLBORO* LE12 ....88 A7
Woodgon Rd *RLEINE/SYS* LE7 ....124 B1
Woodgreen Rd *LEIN* LE4 ....126 B6
Woodgreen Wk *LEIN* LE4 ....126 B6
Woodhall Cl *LEIW* LE3 ....130 B2
Woodhall Dr *NORM/LIT* DE23 ....56 C7
Woodhall Rd *WOL/BIL/BRX* NG8 ......49 M2
Woodhedge Dr
  MAPPK/POR/STA NG3 ....37 L7
Wood HI *LEIE* LE5 ....7 M4
Woodhouse Cl *COAL* LE67 ....116 C6
Woodhouse La *LBORO* LE11 ....110 F1
Woodhouse Rd *BPR/DUF* DE56 ....18 B8
  COAL LE67 ....108 F7
  END/NAR LE19 ....135 K8
  RLBORO LE12 ....112 C2
Woodhouse St
  MAPPK/POR/STA NG3 ....51 K2
Woodhouse Wy
  EWD/SEL/PNX NG16 ....35 H4
Woodhurst Cl *DERBYE* DE21 ....44 B6
Woodkirk Rd *CFTN/RUD* NG11 ....64 D5

Woodland Av
  BWSH/BRSTN DE72 ....60 A5
  BWSH/BRSTN DE72 ....61 K7
  ILK DE7 ....33 H3
  LEIS LE2 ....132 A6
Woodland Cl *COAL* LE67 ....116 C7
  COT/KEY/RAD NG12 ....53 M4
  COT/KEY/RAD NG12 ....67 K5
Woodland Dr
  EWD/SEL/PNX NG16 ....35 K3
  LEIW LE3 ....130 B5
  MAPPK/POR/STA NG3 ....37 H6
Woodland Gv *ARN* NG5 ....37 H3
  BSTN/STPLFD NG9 ....63 H2
Woodland Rd *DERBYW* DE22 ....43 J7
  LEIE LE5 ....126 B8
  WBRGFD NG2 ....51 K6
The Woodlands *BLWL* NG6 ....36 A2
  COT/KEY/RAD NG12 ....53 J4
  MELB/CHEL DE73 ....82 F7
  WGSTN LE18 ....138 D3
Woodlands Cl *DERBYE* DE21 ....29 M7
  DERBYE DE21 ....58 D1
  LBORO LE11 ....9 K9
Woodlands Dr *GBY/RBY* LE6 ....123 H3
  LBORO LE11 ....9 G7
  RLBORO LE12 ....102 A2
Woodlands Farm Cl
  HUCK/RAV NG15 ....23 H3
Woodlands La *DERBYW* DE22 ....29 H8
  MELB/CHEL DE73 ....72 E7
  RLEIW/BAR LE9 ....129 J1
Woodlands Pk
  BWSH/BRSTN DE72 ....60 E5
Woodlands Rd *DERBYW* DE22 ....43 H1
Woodlands Wy
  MELB/CHEL DE73 ....82 E7
Woodland Wy
  EWD/SEL/PNX NG16 ....21 J5
Wood La *BPR/DUF* DE56 ....29 K1
  CARL NG4 ....38 E6
  CFTN/RUD NG11 ....77 K7
  HUCK/RAV NG15 ....15 K8
  ILK DE7 ....31 H2
  RIPLEY DE5 ....10 E3
  RLBORO LE12 ....112 F3
Woodlane Gdns
  MAPPK/POR/STA NG3 ....37 K8
Woodlea Gv *DERBYE* DE21 ....30 A7
Woodleigh *COT/KEY/RAD* NG12 ......80 C5
Woodley Rd *GBY/RBY* LE6 ....123 G7
Woodley Sq *BLWL* NG6 ....24 A5
Woodley St *CFTN/RUD* NG11 ....65 G8
Wood Link *BLWL* NG6 ....23 J8
Woodman's Cha
  RLEINE/SYS LE7 ....115 H8
Woodmans Wy *RLBORO* LE12 ....102 A2
Woodminton Dr
  MELB/CHEL DE73 ....72 D4
Woodnewton Dr *LEIE* LE5 ....133 H3
Wood Nook Cl
  EWD/SEL/PNX NG16 ....13 K1
Woodpecker Cl *LEIW* LE3 ....129 J5
Woodpecker HI *ILK* DE7 ....46 E5
Woodrising Cl *DERBYE* DE21 ....44 F4
Wood Rd *DERBYE* DE21 ....59 L1
Woodrow Av *WOL/BIL/BRX* NG8 .....35 L7
Woods Cl *LEIS* LE2 ....139 G1
Woodsend Cl *CALV/BJ* NG14 ....39 K3
Woodsford Gv
  CFTN/RUD NG11 ....64 C5
Woodshawe Ri *LEIW* LE3 ....130 C5
Woodshop La *MELB/CHEL* DE73 ......82 B1
Woodside *EWD/SEL/PNX* NG16 ....21 J5
  ILK DE7 ....31 H4
  RLBORO LE12 ....105 C7
Woodside Av
  COT/KEY/RAD NG12 ....53 M4
  EWD/SEL/PNX NG16 ....34 C1
  RIPLEY DE5 ....11 H7
Woodside Cl *LEIN* LE4 ....126 B6
  RLEIW/BAR LE9 ....135 K7
Woodside Crs *ILK* DE7 ....33 H2
  LGEAT NG10 ....61 M7
Woodside Dr *ARN* NG5 ....25 H7
  DERBYW DE22 ....43 L3

Woodside Rd
  BSTN/STPLFD NG9 ....49 K7
  BSTN/STPLFD NG9 ....62 E3
  CALV/BJ NG14 ....39 H4
  COT/KEY/RAD NG12 ....53 M3
  LEIS LE2 ....139 H4
  LGEAT NG10 ....61 L2
Woods La *DERBYW* DE22 ....2 C7
Woods Meadow *DERBYSE* DE24 ......73 H2
Woodsorrel Dr *DERBYE* DE21 ....44 F4
Woodstock Av *NOTTE* NG7 ....50 C1
Woodstock Cl *DERBYW* DE22 ....43 H3
  LEIW LE3 ....125 J3
Woodstock Rd
  BSTN/STPLFD NG9 ....62 C4
  LEIN LE4 ....125 J3
Woodstock St *HUCK/RAV* NG15 ......23 M1
Wood St *DERBY* DE1 ....3 G2
  EWD/SEL/PNX NG16 ....21 K4
  ILK DE7 ....33 K6
  LEI LE1 ....6 F3
  RIPLEY DE5 ....11 H5
  RIPLEY DE5 ....11 M7
Woodthorne Av *DERBYSE* DE24 .....72 C3
Woodthorpe Av *ARN* NG5 ....37 J3
  DERBYE DE21 ....58 D1
  LBORO LE11 ....9 K9
Woodthorpe Ct *ARN* NG5 ....37 J4
Woodthorpe Dr *ARN* NG5 ....37 H3
Woodthorpe Gdns *ARN* NG5 ....37 J4
Woodthorpe Rd *ARN* NG5 ....37 K4
Wood Vw *COT/KEY/RAD* NG12 ....65 M4
Woodview *COT/KEY/RAD* NG12 ....67 L4
Woodville Cl *BSTN/STPLFD* NG9 .....63 G1
Woodville Dr *ARN* NG5 ....37 G4
Woodville Gdns *WGSTN* LE18 ....138 A2
Woodville Rd *ARN* NG5 ....37 G4
  LEIW LE3 ....130 F2
Woodward Av *RLBORO* LE12 ....112 C1
Woodward St *WBRGFD* NG2 ....51 H6
Woodyard La *RLEIW/BBY* LE8 ....136 D7
Wooldale Cl *RLEINE/SYS* LE7 ....118 C8
Wooliscroft Wy *ILK* DE7 ....33 G5
Woollaton St *HUCK/RAV* NG15 ....15 M8
Woolmer Rd *WBRGFD* NG2 ....51 G6
Woolpack La *NOTT* NG1 ....5 K7
Woolrych St *NORM/LIT* DE23 ....57 K5
Woolsington Cl
  WOL/BIL/BRX NG8 ....35 H5
Woolsthorpe Crs *ILK* DE7 ....47 H3
Wootton Cl *RLBORO* LE12 ....88 C5
  RLEIW/BBY LE8 ....142 D1
  WOL/BIL/BRX NG8 ....35 H8
Wootton Ri *LEIS* LE2 ....131 J8
Worcester Av *RLEINE/SYS* LE7 .....119 M6
Worcester Crs *DERBYE* DE21 ....44 B7
Worcester Dr *WGSTN* LE18 ....137 K5
Worcester Gdns *ARN* NG5 ....37 J2
Worcester Rd *ARN* NG5 ....37 J2
  LEIS LE2 ....131 H8
Wordsworth Av *DERBYW* DE22 ....71 J2
  HUCK/RAV NG15 ....23 H1
Wordsworth Crs
  END/NAR LE19 ....135 L6
Wordsworth Dr *DERBYE* DE21 ....71 L2
Wordsworth Rd *ARN* NG5 ....25 H8
  EWD/SEL/PNX NG16 ....34 A2
  LBORO LE11 ....8 A2
  LEIS LE2 ....131 L6
  NOTTE NG7 ....50 C1
  WBRGFD NG2 ....65 J1
Worksop Rd
  MAPPK/POR/STA NG3 ....51 K2
Worrall Av *ARN* NG5 ....25 K8
  LGEAT NG10 ....62 B6
Worrall Cl *LEIW* LE3 ....130 B3
Worrall Rd *LEIW* LE3 ....130 B3
Worsh Cl *RLEIW/BBY* LE8 ....142 D2
Worsley Wy *RLEIW/BBY* LE8 ....142 E1
Worthington St *LEIS* LE2 ....7 L7
Worth St *CARL* NG4 ....38 C7
Wortley Av *BSTN/STPLFD* NG9 ....48 B4
Wortley Cl *COAL* LE67 ....108 C6
  ILK DE7 ....33 L7
  RLBORO LE12 ....102 A1
Wortley Ct *LBORO* LE11 ....9 K2
Wortley Hall Cl *NOTTE* NG7 ....50 A5
Worwood Dr *WBRGFD* NG2 ....65 G2

Wossock La *RLBORO* LE12 ....87 K2
Woulds Fld *COT/KEY/RAD* NG12 .....67 K6
Wragley Wy *DERBYSE* DE24 ....71 G5
The Wranglands
  RLEIW/BBY LE8 ....145 L8
Wray Cl *MAPPK/POR/STA* NG3 ....5 M5
Wreake Dr *RLEINE/SYS* LE7 ....115 L4
Wreake Rd *RLEINE/SYS* LE7 ....120 C7
Wreford Crs *LEIE* LE5 ....127 J8
Wren Cl *LEIS* LE2 ....131 J8
  RLEINE/SYS LE7 ....120 C3
Wren Park Cl *BPR/DUF* DE56 ....17 H1
  RDERBYSW DE65 ....70 B6
Wrenthorpe V *CFTN/RUD* NG11 .....64 C6
Wren Wy *MCKLVR* DE3 ....55 M8
Wretham Cl *MCKLVR* DE3 ....56 B7
Wright Av *RIPLEY* DE5 ....11 K6
Wright Cl *RLEIW/BBY* LE8 ....142 D3
Wright La *LEIS* LE2 ....139 H3
Wrights Acre *RLBORO* LE12 ....113 M3
Wrights Cl *RLBORO* LE12 ....112 D2
Wrights Orch
  COT/KEY/RAD NG12 ....80 C5
Wright St *CARL* NG4 ....38 D8
  RIPLEY DE5 ....11 M8
Wroughton Ct
  EWD/SEL/PNX NG16 ....21 L5
Wroxall Wy *LEIW* LE3 ....125 C7
Wroxham Cl *DERBYSE* DE24 ....72 B3
Wroxham Dr *WOL/BIL/BRX* NG8 .....49 H4
Wyaston Cl *DERBYW* DE22 ....43 J6
Wyatt Cl *LEIW* LE3 ....130 A3
Wyatt Rd *COAL* LE67 ....108 C6
Wyatts Wy *RIPLEY* DE5 ....11 J5
Wych Elm Rd *LEIS* LE2 ....132 E8
Wychwood Dr
  BSTN/STPLFD NG9 ....48 B5
Wychwood Rd *RLEIW/BBY* LE8 ......142 E2
Wycliffe Av *RLBORO* LE12 ....105 H7
Wycliffe Gv
  MAPPK/POR/STA NG3 ....37 J5
Wycliffe St *LEI* LE1 ....6 E6
  NOTTE NG7 ....36 D6
Wycombe Cl *CFTN/RUD* NG11 ....64 B7
Wycombe Rd *LEIE* LE5 ....126 C7
Wye Dean Dr *WGSTN* LE18 ....138 B5
Wye Gdns *NOTTE* NG7 ....50 B1
Wye St *DERBYSE* DE24 ....58 E7
Wyggeston Rd *COAL* LE67 ....108 B7
Wykeham Rd *ARN* NG5 ....37 L2
Wykes Av *CARL* NG4 ....38 D5
Wylam Cl *LEIW* LE3 ....124 E7
Wymar Cl *LEIW* LE4 ....125 G4
Wymeswold La *RLBORO* LE12 ....97 L7
Wymeswold Rd
  COT/KEY/RAD NG12 ....90 A7
  RLBORO LE12 ....97 J2
  RLBORO LE12 ....97 J5
  RLBORO LE12 ....98 A3
Wymondham Cl *ARN* NG5 ....37 L1
Wynbreck Dr
  COT/KEY/RAD NG12 ....80 D4
Wyndale Dr *ILK* DE7 ....47 G1
  RLEINE/SYS LE7 ....120 F2
Wyndale Rd *LEIS* LE2 ....133 G8
Wyndham Cl *LEIS* LE2 ....133 G8
Wyndham Ms *NOTT* NG1 ....4 F1
Wyndham Rd *LBORO* LE11 ....102 F1
Wyndham St *DERBYSE* DE24 ....58 E8
The Wyndings *ARN* NG5 ....37 K3
Wynfield Rd *LEIW* LE3 ....130 F2
Wyngate Dr *LEIW* LE3 ....130 F2
Wynndale Dr *ARN* NG5 ....36 E4
Wynthorpe Ri *LEIW* LE3 ....130 E3
Wynton Av *DERBYSE* DE24 ....58 D7
Wynton Cl *RLEIW/BBY* LE8 ....143 G1
Wynward Cl *ILK* DE7 ....33 G4
Wynwood Cl *BSTN/STPLFD* NG9 ....62 F5
Wynwood Rd
  BSTN/STPLFD NG9 ....62 F5
Wyrale Dr *WOL/BIL/BRX* NG8 ....35 J6
Wysall La *COT/KEY/RAD* NG12 ....90 A2
Wysall Rd *COT/KEY/RAD* NG12 ....79 M7
  COT/KEY/RAD NG12 ....90 F3
  RLBORO LE12 ....97 J2
Wyston Brook
  RDERBYSW DE65 ....68 B6

Wyvelle Crs *CDON/KEG* DE74 ....86 A4
Wyvern Av *LEIN* LE4 ....126 B5
  LGEAT NG10 ....76 B7
Wyvern Cl *EWD/SEL/PNX* NG16 ......21 K4
Wyvern Rd *RLBORO* LE12 ....112 C2
Wyvernside *DERBY* * DE21 ....58 D3
Wyvern Wy *DERBYE* DE21 ....58 D3
Wyville Cl *NOTTE* NG7 ....50 C2
Wyville Rw *LEIW* LE3 ....130 E6

Y

Yalding Dr *WOL/BIL/BRX* NG8 ....49 G3
Yalding Gdns *WOL/BIL/BRX* NG8 ....49 G3
Yardley Dr *WGSTN* LE18 ....137 M2
Yardley Wy *BPR/DUF* DE56 ....18 C3
Yarmouth St *LEI* LE1 ....6 F3
Yarrow Cl *DERBYSE* DE24 ....71 J5
  LEIE LE5 ....127 G6
Yarwell Cl *DERBYE* DE21 ....44 B6
  MAPPK/POR/STA NG3 ....38 A5
Yarwell Dr *WGSTN* LE18 ....138 C5
Yatesbury Crs
  WOL/BIL/BRX NG8 ....35 J7
Yates St *NORM/LIT* DE23 ....57 L6
Yaxley Cl *RLEINE/SYS* LE7 ....133 K1
Yeats Cl *LEIW* LE3 ....130 B6
Yelverton Av *LEIE* LE5 ....133 G4
Yeoman *BLWL* NG6 ....24 D3
Yeoman La *LEI* LE1 ....6 F5
Yeoman's Di *RLEINE/SYS* LE7 ....115 H7
Yeoman St *LEI* LE1 ....7 G5
Yeovil Cl *DERBYSE* * DE24 ....59 C8
Yew Barrow Cl *WBRGFD* NG2 ....66 A2
Yew Cl *ARN* NG5 ....37 H5
  LEIW LE3 ....129 K6
  RLBORO LE12 ....88 B7
Yewdale Cl *CFTN/RUD* NG11 ....64 B7
  WBRGFD NG2 ....66 A2
Yewdale Gv *DERBYE* DE21 ....45 G4
The Yews *LEIS* LE2 ....138 F1
Yews Cl *MELB/CHEL* DE73 ....72 E6
Yew Tree Av *ARN* NG5 ....37 G6
  BWSH/BRSTN DE72 ....60 B2
Yew Tree Cl *COT/KEY/RAD* NG12 ...53 B5
  DERBYSE DE24 ....59 C8
Yew Tree Dr *LEIW* LE3 ....130 A1
Yew Tree La *BWSH/BRSTN* DE72 ....73 K3
  CARL NG4 ....38 E5
  CFTN/RUD NG11 ....64 A5
Yew Tree Rd *HUCK/RAV* NG15 ....23 M2
Yonge Cl *COT/KEY/RAD* NG12 ....53 J5
York Av *BSTN/STPLFD* NG9 ....63 K3
  EWD/SEL/PNX NG16 ....12 F3
  LGEAT NG10 ....61 C2
York Cl *CARL* NG4 ....38 D5
  LEIS LE2 ....137 J6
  RLBORO LE12 ....88 B6
  RLBORO LE12 ....113 H7
York Dr *WOL/BIL/BRX* NG8 ....35 H5
Yorke St *HUCK/RAV* NG15 ....23 L1
York Pl *COAL* LE67 ....109 H5
York Rd *DERBYE* DE21 ....44 D8
  LBORO LE11 ....8 F3
  LEI LE1 ....6 E7
  LGEAT NG10 ....62 A6
Yorkshire Rd *LEIN* LE4 ....126 A6
York St *CARL* NG4 ....38 E8
  DERBY DE1 ....2 B3
  LEI LE1 ....6 F7
  NOTT NG1 ....5 H4
Youlgreave Cl *DERBYE* DE21 ....44 D6
Young Cl *BLWL* NG6 ....35 K2
Young St *NORM/LIT* DE23 ....57 K6
Ypres Rd *DERBYW* DE22 ....43 G5
Yukon Wy *LEI* LE1 ....7 H3
Yvonne Crs *CARL* NG4 ....38 D8

Z

Zetland Cl *COAL* LE67 ....108 A7
Zetland Crs *DERBYSE* DE24 ....71 G5
Zouch Rd *RLBORO* LE12 ....94 E4
Zulla Rd *MAPPK/POR/STA* NG3 ....37 G7
Zulu Rd *NOTTE* NG7 ....36 D5

Index - featured places

Abbey Business Park
  LEI LE1 ....6 E2
Abbey Primary School
  LEIN LE4 ....125 L5
Abbey Pumping Station
  LEIN LE4 ....125 K5
Abbey Road Primary School
  WBRGFD NG2 ....65 L1
The Abingdon Business Centre
  DERBYSE DE24 ....58 A6
Abington High School
  WGSTN LE18 ....138 A5
Acton Road Industrial Estate
  LGEAT NG10 ....76 C1
Adam House Medical Centre
  LGEAT NG10 ....61 M2
Adco Business Centre
  NOTTE NG7 ....36 C8
Air Cargo Terminal
  CDON/KEG DE74 ....85 J7
Albany Infant School
  BSTN/STPLFD NG9 ....48 C7
Albany Junior School
  BSTN/STPLFD NG9 ....48 C7
Albert Hall
  NOTT NG1 ....4 F7
Albion Leisure Centre
  ILK DE7 ....33 K7
Aldercar Infant School
  EWD/SEL/PNX NG16 ....20 E3
Aldercar School
  EWD/SEL/PNX NG16 ....20 E3

Alderman Richard Hallam
  Primary School
  LEIN LE4 ....125 G6
Alderman White Lower School
  BSTN/STPLFD NG9 ....49 K7
Alderman White School
  BSTN/STPLFD NG9 ....63 G1
Allenpark Infant School
  DERBYSE DE24 ....72 C2
Allestree Park Golf Club
  DERBYW DE22 ....43 K1
All Hallows CE Primary School
  CARL NG4 ....38 D6
All Saints CE Primary School
  RLEIW/BAR LE9 ....140 B8
  WGSTN LE18 ....138 A5
Alvaston & Boulton Sports Club
  DERBYSE DE24 ....72 B1
Alvaston Infant School
  DERBYSE DE24 ....59 G4
Alvaston Junior School
  DERBYSE DE24 ....72 F1
Amber Business Centre
  RIPLEY DE5 ....11 M2
Amber Trading Estate
  EWD/SEL/PNX NG16 ....22 B8
The American Adventure
  Theme Park
  HEANOR DE75 ....32 F2

Annie Holgate Junior School
  HUCK/RAV NG15 ....23 K1
Anstey Nomads FC
  RLEINE/SYS LE7 ....118 D8
Apex Business Park
  CFTN/RUD NG11 ....64 E7
Arboretum
  NOTT NG1 ....4 E6
Arboretum Primary School
  NORM/LIT DE23 ....57 L5
Arkwright Primary School
  WBRGFD NG2 ....51 H6
Army Training Corps
  COAL LE67 ....108 B8
Arnold & Carlton College
  ARN NG5 ....25 K8
Arnold Health Centre
  ARN NG5 ....25 K7
Arnold Hill School
  ARN NG5 ....37 L1
Arnold Leisure Centre
  ARN NG5 ....25 K7
Arts Centre
  NOTT NG1 ....4 E7
Arts Theatre
  NOTT NG1 ....5 H7
Ascot Industrial Estate
  LGEAT NG10 ....62 A1
Ashbrook J & I School
  BWSH/BRSTN DE72 ....59 M5
Ash Croft Primary School
  DERBYSE DE24 ....71 J5

Ash Field School
  LEIE LE5 ....132 D3
Ashforth Business Centre
  MAPPK/POR/STA NG3 ....5 J3
Ashgate Primary School
  DERBYW DE22 ....2 A2
Ash Lea Special School
  COT/KEY/RAD NG12 ....67 K5
Ashmount School
  LBORO LE11 ....9 G8
Aspen Business Centre
  DERBYE DE21 ....58 F3
Assarts Farm Medical Centre
  EWD/SEL/PNX NG16 ....35 H3
Assembly Rooms
  DERBY DE1 ....2 E3
Asterdale Leisure Centre
  DERBYE DE21 ....59 L5
Asterdale Primary School
  DERBYE DE21 ....59 K4
Aston Hall Hospital
  BWSH/BRSTN DE72 ....83 L1
Aston on Trent Primary School
  BWSH/BRSTN DE72 ....73 L7
Attenborough Nature Reserve
  BSTN/STPLFD NG9 ....63 K4
Attenborough
  Preparatory School
  BSTN/STPLFD NG9 ....63 J5
Audley Centre
  DERBY DE1 ....2 F4

Auster Industrial Estate
  LEIN LE4 ....126 D1
Avenue Infant School
  LEIS LE2 ....131 M6
Awsworth Junior School
  EWD/SEL/PNX NG16 ....34 A3
Awsworth Trading Estate
  ILK DE7 ....33 K5
Aylestone Leisure Centre
  LEIS LE2 ....131 K7
Babington Community
  Technology College
  LEIN LE4 ....124 F4
Babington Hospital
  BPR/DUF DE56 ....17 J4
Badgerbrook County
  Primary School
  RLEIS/BBY LE8 ....142 D2
Bailey Brook Industrial Estate
  HEANOR DE75 ....20 F5
Bakersfield Medical Centre
  MAPPK/POR/STA NG3 ....52 A1
Balloon Wood Industrial Estate
  BSTN/STPLFD NG9 ....48 F5
Bar Lane Industrial Estate
  BLWL NG6 ....36 B5
Barley Croft Primary School
  LEIN LE4 ....125 G4
Barrington Park
  Industrial Estate
  LEIN LE4 ....124 F2

Barrow Health Centre
RLBORO LE12 .... 105 G8
Barrow Road Business Park
RLBORO LE12 .... 113 M4
Beacon Hill Country Park
LGEAT NG10 .... 111 G5
Beardall Street
Primary School
HUCK/RAV NG15 .... 15 M8
Beauchamp College
LEIS LE2 .... 138 E4
Beaufort Street
Business Centre
DERBYE DE21 .... 3 L1
Beaumont Leys Health Centre
LEIN LE4 .... 125 G4
Beaumont Leys School
LEIN LE4 .... 124 F5
Beaumont Lodge
Primary School
LEIN LE4 .... 124 F1
Becket Primary School
DERBYW DE22 .... 2 C6
Beckett RC School
CFTN/RUD NG11 .... 64 E2
Bede Island Business Park
LEIS LE2 .... 6 B8
Beechdale Swimming Centre
WOL/BIL/BRX NG8 .... 50 A1
Beedles Lake Golf Centre
RLEINE/SYS LE7 .... 115 G7
Beeston Clinic
BSTN/STPLFD NG9 .... 63 K1
Beeston Fields Golf Club
BSTN/STPLFD NG9 .... 49 H7
Beeston Primary School
BSTN/STPLFD NG9 .... 49 K7
Belgrave & Birstall Station
LEIN LE4 .... 125 K2
Belgrave Cemetery
LEIN LE4 .... 125 K3
Belgrave Hall
LEIN LE4 .... 125 L4
Belgrave Industrial Centre
LEIN LE4 .... 125 L5
Belgrave RFC
LEIN LE4 .... 125 K3
Belgrave St Peters CE
Primary School
LEIN LE4 .... 125 K3
Bell Foundry Museum
LBORO LE11 .... 9 L2
Belper Meadows Sports Club
BPR/DUF DE56 .... 17 J3
Belper Natural Health Centre
BPR/DUF DE56 .... 17 J4
Belper School
BPR/DUF DE56 .... 18 A3
Belper Sports Centre
BPR/DUF DE56 .... 18 B3
Belton CE Primary School
RLBORO LE12 .... 100 F1
Belvoirdale Primary School
COAL LE67 .... 108 B7
Belvoir Shopping Centre
COAL LE67 .... 108 A6
Bemrose Community School
DERBYW DE22 .... 57 H3
Bendbow Rise Infant School
LEIW LE3 .... 130 B4
The Benjamin Outram
Business Centre
RIPLEY DE5 .... 11 J8
Bennerley School
ILK DE7 .... 33 K3
Bennnerley Fields
Special School
ILK DE7 .... 33 K3
Bentinck Primary School
NOTTE NG7 .... 4 B3
Berridge Infant School
NOTTE NG7 .... 36 C7
Berridge Junior School
NOTTE NG7 .... 36 C8
Bestwood Business Park
BLWL NG6 .... 24 C3
Bestwood Country Park
ARN NG5 .... 24 E4
Bestwood Park Health Centre
ARN NG5 .... 24 F8
Bestwood Swimming Pool
ARN NG5 .... 36 F1
Bilborough Sixth Form College
WOL/BIL/BRX NG8 .... 35 G8
Birstall Golf Club
LEIN LE4 .... 125 K2
Bishop Ellis RC Primary School
RLEINE/SYS LE7 .... 120 D7
Bishop Lonsdale CE
Primary School
DERBYW DE22 .... 2 A8
Bispham Drive Junior School
BSTN/STPLFD NG9 .... 62 C4
Blaby Industrial Park
RLEIW/BBY LE8 .... 136 E6
Blenheim Industrial Estate
BLWL NG6 .... 23 J7
Blessed Robert RC
Primary School
CFTN/RUD NG11 .... 64 C7
Bloomsgrove Industrial Estate
NOTTE NG7 .... 4 A5
Blue Bell Hill Infant School
MAPPK/POR/STA NG3 .... 51 K1
Boars Head Industrial Estate
DERBYE DE21 .... 3 H2
Bonington Junior School
BLWL NG6 .... 35 M1
Borrow Wood Infant School
DERBYE DE21 .... 59 K2
Borrow Wood Junior School
DERBYE DE21 .... 59 K2
The Bosworth College
RLEIW/BAR LE9 .... 128 A4
Bosworth Primary School
WBRGFD NG2 .... 50 F6
Boulevard Industrial Park
BSTN/STPLFD NG9 .... 49 M8

Boulton Clinic
DERBYSE DE24 .... 72 E1
Boulton Primary School
DERBYSE DE24 .... 72 E1
Brackenfield Special School
LGEAT NG10 .... 61 M6
Brackensdale J & I School
DERBYW DE22 .... 56 F1
Bradbury-Midway
Industrial Estate
NOTTE NG7 .... 50 B8
Bradgate Park Country Park
GBY/RBY LE6 .... 117 M4
Bradshaw Retail Park
DERBY DE1 .... 2 F6
Bramble Business Centre
DERBY DE1 .... 2 E4
Bramcote CE Primary School
BSTN/STPLFD NG9 .... 48 F7
Bramcote Crematorium
BSTN/STPLFD NG9 .... 48 E4
Bramcote Hill
Comprehensive School
BSTN/STPLFD NG9 .... 48 F5
Bramcote Hills Golf Club
BSTN/STPLFD NG9 .... 49 G5
Bramcote Hills Primary School
BSTN/STPLFD NG9 .... 48 F6
Bramcote Leisure Centre
BSTN/STPLFD NG9 .... 48 E6
Bramcote Park
Comprehensive School
BSTN/STPLFD NG9 .... 48 E6
Braunstone Frith
Industrial Estate
LEIW LE3 .... 129 M2
LEIW LE3 .... 130 B2
Braunstone Frith J & I School
LEIW LE3 .... 130 B1
Breadsall CE Primary School
ILK DE7 .... 44 C3
Breadsall Hilltop J & I School
DERBYE DE21 .... 44 C4
Brewhouse Yard Museum
NOTTE NG7 .... 4 F9
Breydon Industrial Centre
LGEAT NG10 .... 62 D8
Bridge Business Park
LEIN LE4 .... 120 B8
Bridge Junior School
LEIE LE5 .... 7 M3
Brinkhill Primary School
CFTN/RUD NG11 .... 64 D4
Brinsley Primary School
EWD/SEL/PNX NG16 .... 13 J7
British Gypsum Business Park
CFTN/RUD NG11 .... 77 M8
Broad Marsh Shopping Centre
NOTT NG1 .... 5 H8
Broadway Cinema
NOTT NG1 .... 5 J7
Brockington College
END/NAR LE19 .... 136 A5
Brocks Hill Primary School
LEIS LE2 .... 138 F4
Brookfield Primary School
MCKLVR DE3 .... 56 B7
Brookhill Leys Infant School
EWD/SEL/PNX NG16 .... 21 L6
Brookhill Leys Junior School
EWD/SEL/PNX NG16 .... 21 L5
Brooklands Infant School
LGEAT NG10 .... 76 B1
Brooklands Junior School
LGEAT NG10 .... 62 B8
Brooksby Primary School
CFTN/RUD NG11 .... 64 D4
Brookside Industrial Units
BSTN/STPLFD NG9 .... 48 B7
Brookside Primary School
LEIS LE2 .... 139 H1
RLBORO LE12 .... 88 C6
Brookside Special School
ILK DE7 .... 44 C3
Brookvale High School
GBY/RBY LE6 .... 123 H5
Broomfield College
ILK DE7 .... 44 F2
Broomfield Primary School
RLEINE/SYS LE7 .... 115 J8
Broom Leys Primary School
COAL LE67 .... 108 E6
Browns Lane Business Park
COT/KEY/RAD NG12 .... 81 G5
Broxtowe College
BSTN/STPLFD NG9 .... 63 J2
Bulwell Business Centre
BLWL NG6 .... 23 L8
Bulwell Forest Golf Club
BLWL NG6 .... 24 B8
Bulwell Health Centre
BLWL NG6 .... 35 M1
Bunny CE Primary School
CFTN/RUD NG11 .... 79 J7
Burford Primary School
ARN NG5 .... 37 G1
The Burleigh College
LBORO LE11 .... 103 G4
Burton Joyce Primary School
CALV/BJ NG14 .... 39 K2
Burton on the Wolds
Primary School
RLBORO LE12 .... 105 K1
Bushloe High School
WGSTN LE18 .... 137 M6
Busm Business Park
LEIN LE4 .... 125 L6
Buswells Lodge
Primary School
LEIN LE4 .... 124 E4
Butterley Station
RIPLEY DE5 .... 11 J3
Byron Cinema
HUCK/RAV NG15 .... 15 M8
Caldecote Primary School
LEIE LE3 .... 130 E6
Canal Museum
NOTT NG1 .... 5 G9

Canalside Industrial Estate
LGEAT NG10 .... 48 A8
Cargo Terminal
CDON/KEG DE74 .... 85 G7
Carillon Shopping Centre
LBORO LE11 .... 9 J3
The Carillon War Memorial Tower
LBORO LE11 .... 9 H4
Carlton Business Centre
CARL NG4 .... 38 D7
Carlton Cemetery
CARL NG4 .... 38 C7
Carlton Digby Special School
MAPPK/POR/STA NG3 .... 38 A4
Carlton Le Willows
Comprehensive School
CARL NG4 .... 38 F6
Carlyle Infant School
NORM/LIT DE23 .... 56 F7
Carrington Court Industrial Park
DERBY DE1 .... 2 B4
Carrington Primary School
ARN NG5 .... 36 F7
Castle
LEI LE1 .... 6 C7
Castle Clinic
NOTT NG1 .... 4 D6
Castle Donington
Community College
CDON/KEG DE74 .... 84 F4
Castle Hill Country Park
LEIN LE4 .... 118 E8
Castle Industrial Park
HUCK/RAV NG15 .... 23 J1
Castle Meadow Retail Park
WBRGFD NG2 .... 50 F4
Castle Museum & Art Gallery
NOTTE NG7 .... 4 F8
Castle Park Industrial Estate
WBRGFD NG2 .... 50 F6
Castle Rock High School
COAL LE67 .... 109 H5
Cathedral
DERBY DE1 .... 2 E2
LEI LE1 .... 6 D6
Cathedral Road Clinic
DERBY DE1 .... 2 D2
Catherine Junior School
LEIN LE4 .... 125 M7
Catherine Street
Industrial Estate
LEIN LE4 .... 126 B5
Cavendish Close Infant School
DERBYE DE21 .... 44 E7
Cavendish Close Junior School
DERBYE DE21 .... 44 E7
Caves of Nottingham
NOTT NG1 .... 5 H8
Central Bus Station
DERBY DE1 .... 3 G4
Central Infant School
CARL NG4 .... 38 B7
Centurion Business Park
BLWL NG6 .... 23 J6
Centurion Way Business Park
DERBYE DE21 .... 43 M7
Chaddesden Medical Centre
DERBYE DE21 .... 58 C1
Chaddesden Park Infant School
DERBYE DE21 .... 44 F8
Charlotte Infant School
ILK DE7 .... 33 J5
Charlton House Medical Centre
LGEAT NG10 .... 62 D7
Charnwood Forest Golf Club
RLBORO LE12 .... 111 J5
Charnwood Health Centre
LEIE LE5 .... 7 M3
Charnwood Leisure Centre
LBORO LE11 .... 9 H5
Charnwood Primary School
LEIS LE2 .... 7 K4
Chartwell Drive
Industrial Estate
WGSTN LE18 .... 137 L4
Chaucer Infant School
ILK DE7 .... 33 K7
Chaucer Junior School
ILK DE7 .... 33 K6
Chellaston Infant School
MELB/CHEL DE73 .... 72 E5
Chellaston Junior School
MELB/CHEL DE73 .... 72 D6
Chellaston School
MELB/CHEL DE73 .... 72 D6
Cherry Tree Hill Infant School
DERBYE DE21 .... 58 F2
Cherry Tree Hill Junior School
DERBYE DE21 .... 58 E2
Chettles Industrial Estate
NOTTE NG7 .... 50 B2
Chetwynd Road
Primary School
BSTN/STPLFD NG9 .... 62 E5
Chevin Golf Club
BPR/DUF DE56 .... 29 J2
The Chilwell Alderman Pounder
Infant School
BSTN/STPLFD NG9 .... 62 F2
Chilwell College House
Junior School
BSTN/STPLFD NG9 .... 63 H2
Chilwell Manor Golf Club
BSTN/STPLFD NG9 .... 63 J3
Chilwell Retail Park
BSTN/STPLFD NG9 .... 62 F1
Chilwell School
BSTN/STPLFD NG9 .... 63 H4
Christ the King RC
Comprehensive School
ARN NG5 .... 25 M8
Christ the King RC
Primary School
LEIW LE3 .... 130 F1
Church Cemetery
NOTTE NG7 .... 4 F2
Church Hill CE Infant School
LEIN LE4 .... 120 D8

Churchview Business Park
BLWL NG6 .... 36 C5
Church Wilne Water
Sports Club
BWSH/BRSTN DE72 .... 75 H2
City Farm
MAPPK/POR/STA NG3 .... 5 M5
City Gallery
LEI LE1 .... 7 G6
City Gate Business Park
DERBYSE DE24 .... 58 B6
City Golf Course
BLWL NG6 .... 23 L6
City of Leicester School
LEIE LE5 .... 133 H3
City Road Industrial Park
DERBY DE1 .... 43 L8
Civil Service Sports Ground
WBRGFD NG2 .... 65 G1
Claremont Primary School
ARN NG5 .... 36 F6
Clarendon City College
NOTT NG1 .... 5 J7
Clarendon College
ARN NG5 .... 36 F7
Clarendon Park
Medical Centre
LEIS LE2 .... 131 L6
Clifton Leisure Centre
CFTN/RUD NG11 .... 64 D6
Clifton Medical Centre
CFTN/RUD NG11 .... 64 C7
Cloudside Junior School
LGEAT NG10 .... 61 M1
Clyde Street Medical Centre
LEI LE1 .... 7 H4
Coalville Business Park
COAL LE67 .... 108 A6
Coalville Community Hospital
COAL LE67 .... 108 E6
Cobden Primary School
LBORO LE11 .... 9 L3
Cobden Street Industrial Estate
LEIN LE4 .... 7 K2
The Cockpit
DERBY DE1 .... 3 G4
Cockshut Lane Business Centre
MELB/CHEL DE73 .... 82 D7
Codnor CE Primary School
RIPLEY DE5 .... 11 M7
Codnor Gate Industrial Estate
RIPLEY DE5 .... 11 L5
Coleman Primary School
LEIE LE5 .... 132 C3
College of Continuing Education
HUCK/RAV NG15 .... 15 M8
College of Further Education
NOTT NG1 .... 5 K6
College Street Health Centre
LGEAT NG10 .... 62 A6
The College
DERBY DE1 .... 2 A5
Colwick Business Park
CARL NG4 .... 52 D2
Colwick Country Park
WBRGFD NG2 .... 52 B3
Colwick Industrial Estate
CARL NG4 .... 52 D3
CARL NG4 .... 52 F2
CARL NG4 .... 52 D1
Concordia Industrial Estate
LGEAT NG10 .... 76 A2
Coppice Primary School
HEANOR DE75 .... 20 C7
Corfield CE Infant School
HEANOR DE75 .... 20 B6
Cornerhouse
NOTT NG1 .... 5 G6
Cosby Golf Club
RLEIW/BAR LE9 .... 142 B6
Cosby Primary School
RLEIW/BAR LE9 .... 142 B3
Cossall Industrial Estate
EWD/SEL/PNX NG16 .... 33 M5
Cossington CE Primary School
RLBORO LE12 .... 114 B7
Cossington Street
Sports Centre
LEIN LE4 .... 125 M6
Costock CE Primary School
RLBORO LE12 .... 89 G6
Costume Museum
NOTT NG1 .... 5 G8
Cotgrave CE Primary School
COT/KEY/RAD NG12 .... 67 J4
Cotgrave Infant School
COT/KEY/RAD NG12 .... 67 K4
Cotgrave Place Golf &
Country Club
COT/KEY/RAD NG12 .... 67 G1
Cotgrave Shopping Centre
COT/KEY/RAD NG12 .... 67 K4
Cotmanhay County
Junior School
ILK DE7 .... 33 J2
Cotmanhay Infant School
ILK DE7 .... 33 J2
Countesthorpe College
RLEIS/BBY LE8 .... 143 G4
County Archives
WBRGFD NG2 .... 5 G9
County Business Park
WBRGFD NG2 .... 51 J5
Court Industrial Estate
DERBYE DE21 .... 44 A7
Covenant College
NOTT NG1 .... 4 F3
Crescent Junior School
LEIW LE3 .... 130 C3
Cricket Club
RLEIS/BBY LE8 .... 146 C1
The Croft Medical Centre
LEIS LE2 .... 139 G3
Cromford Road
Industrial Estate
EWD/SEL/PNX NG16 .... 20 D7

Crompton Road
Industrial Estate
ILK DE7 .... 47 L3
Crossdale Drive
Primary School
COT/KEY/RAD NG12 .... 80 C3
Crown Hills Community College
LEIE LE5 .... 132 D3
Cumberland Trading Estate
LBORO LE11 .... 8 D2
Curzon Cinema
LBORO LE11 .... 9 J3
The Curzon Primary School
DERBYW DE22 .... 43 G1
Cycle Track
LEIS LE2 .... 131 K6
Dagfa House School
BSTN/STPLFD NG9 .... 49 L7
Dale Medical Centre
NORM/LIT DE23 .... 2 D9
Dale Primary School
NORM/LIT DE23 .... 57 J5
The Dales Medical Centre
ILK DE7 .... 32 C8
Dallimore Primary School
ILK DE7 .... 47 H3
Danemill Primary School
END/NAR LE19 .... 135 M5
Darul Uloom School
LEIN LE4 .... 125 L1
David Lloyd Club
DERBYSE DE24 .... 3 L6
Daybrook Business Centre
ARN NG5 .... 37 H1
Dayncourt School
COT/KEY/RAD NG12 .... 53 L4
Deaf Society
NOTTE NG7 .... 4 D3
De Lisle RC School
LBORO LE11 .... 8 A3
The Delves School
ALFN DE55 .... 11 K1
De Montfort Hall
LEI LE1 .... 131 L4
De Montfort University
LEIS LE2 .... 6 D8
RLEINE/SYS LE7 .... 127 L7
Denby Free CE Primary School
RIPLEY DE5 .... 19 M5
Denby Potter & Visitors Centre
RIPLEY DE5 .... 19 G4
Derby Airfield
RDERBYSW DE65 .... 68 D3
Derby Business
Development Centre
DERBYE DE21 .... 3 L1
The Derby Chest Clinic
DERBY DE1 .... 2 E5
Derby City General Hospital
DERBYW DE22 .... 56 F5
Derby College Wilmorton
DERBYSE DE24 .... 58 D5
Derby County FC (Pride Park)
DERBYSE DE24 .... 58 C4
Derby Crown & County Courts
DERBY DE1 .... 3 G3
Derby Independant
Grammar School
NORM/LIT DE23 .... 56 B8
Derby Moor Community School
NORM/LIT DE23 .... 56 F8
Derby Museum & Art Gallery
DERBY DE1 .... 2 E3
Derby Playhouse Theatre
DERBY DE1 .... 3 G5
Derby Road Industrial Estate
HEANOR DE75 .... 20 B6
LGEAT NG10 .... 61 M2
Derby Rowing Club
DERBY DE1 .... 43 L8
Derbyshire Ccc (County Ground)
DERBYE DE21 .... 3 J1
Derbyshire Royal Infirmary
DERBY DE1 .... 3 G6
DERBYSE DE24 .... 58 B7
Derby Small Business Centre
DERBY DE1 .... 3 H6
Derby & South Derbyshire
Magistrates Court
DERBY DE1 .... 2 F3
Derby Superbowl
NORM/LIT DE23 .... 57 L8
Derby Trading Estate
DERBYE DE21 .... 43 M8
Derrymount School
ARN NG5 .... 25 K6
Derwent Bus Centre
DERBY DE1 .... 3 H1
Derwent Business Park
RIPLEY DE5 .... 11 H6
Derwent Community School
DERBYE DE21 .... 44 A8
Derwent Medical Centre
DERBY DE1 .... 2 E1
Derwentside Industrial Estate
BPR/DUF DE56 .... 17 K6
Derwentside Industrial Park
BPR/DUF DE56 .... 17 K4
Derwent Street
Industrial Estate
LGEAT NG10 .... 75 M1
Digby Industrial Estate
EWD/SEL/PNX NG16 .... 22 B8
Disabled Driving Centre
DERBYW DE22 .... 56 F3
Diseworth CE Primary School
CDON/KEG DE74 .... 93 G1
Djanogly City
Technology College
NOTTE NG7 .... 36 E6
The Donington Grand
Prix Collection
CDON/KEG DE74 .... 84 B7
Donington Park Farmhouse
CDON/KEG DE74 .... 83 M7
Donington Park Motor
Racing Circuit
CDON/KEG DE74 .... 84 A6

Douglas Primary School
NOTTE NG7 .... 4 B6
Dovedale Primary School
LGEAT NG10 .... 75 L1
Dovelands Primary School
LEIW LE3 .... 130 F2
Draycott Primary School
BWSH/BRSTN DE72 .... 60 E7
Duffield Road Industrial Estate
DERBYE DE21 .... 44 A1
Dunkirk Primary School
NOTTE NG7 .... 50 C6
Durban House Heritage Centre
EWD/SEL/PNX NG16 .... 21 K4
Eagle Centre Market
DERBY DE1 .... 2 F5
Earls Close Industrial Estate
LEIN LE4 .... 120 C8
East Derbyshire Magistrates
ILK DE7 .... 33 J7
Eastfield Primary School
LEIN LE4 .... 120 D7
East Midlands
International Airport
CDON/KEG DE74 .... 84 F7
East Midlands Nuffield Hospital
NORM/LIT DE23 .... 70 D1
Eastwood Comprehensive
Lower School
EWD/SEL/PNX NG16 .... 21 L4
Eastwood
Comprehensive School
EWD/SEL/PNX NG16 .... 21 J4
Eastwood Health Centre
EWD/SEL/PNX NG16 .... 21 L5
Eastwood Infant School
EWD/SEL/PNX NG16 .... 21 K5
Eastwood & Kimberley
Community College
EWD/SEL/PNX NG16 .... 21 K4
EWD/SEL/PNX NG16 .... 34 D1
Eastwood Town Cricket Club
EWD/SEL/PNX NG16 .... 21 L4
Ecclesbourne School
BPR/DUF DE56 .... 29 J4
Edgewood Primary School
HUCK/RAV NG15 .... 23 H3
Edna G Olds Primary School
NOTTE NG7 .... 4 A9
Edwalton Municipal Golf Club
COT/KEY/RAD NG12 .... 66 A4
Edwalton Primary School
COT/KEY/RAD NG12 .... 66 A3
Eis Loughborough Pool
LBORO LE11 .... 8 B6
The Elizabeth Woodville
Primary School
GBY/RBY LE6 .... 123 J5
Ellerslie Cricket Club
WBRGFD NG2 .... 51 J7
Ellesmere Business Park
ARN NG5 .... 36 F5
Ellesmere College
LEIW LE3 .... 130 F5
Elliot Durham Swimming Pool
MAPPK/POR/STA NG3 .... 37 J6
Elliott Durham
Comprehensive School
MAPPK/POR/STA NG3 .... 37 H4
Ellis Guilford
Comprehensive School
WOL/BIL/BRX NG8 .... 36 A5
Elms Primary School
MAPPK/POR/STA NG3 .... 5 H1
Elvaston Castle
BWSH/BRSTN DE72 .... 59 K8
Elvaston Castle Country Park
BWSH/BRSTN DE72 .... 73 K1
Elvaston Castle Working Estate
Museum
BWSH/BRSTN DE72 .... 73 L1
Elvaston Cricket Club
BWSH/BRSTN DE72 .... 59 K8
Emily Fortey School
LEIW LE3 .... 130 D1
Enderby Golf Club
END/NAR LE19 .... 136 A5
Enderby Leisure Centre
END/NAR LE19 .... 135 M4
END/NAR LE19 .... 135 M5
Enderby Road Industrial Estate
RLEIS/BBY LE8 .... 136 C6
Endland Industrial Estate
DERBYW DE22 .... 57 H3
English Martyrs RC
Primary School
LGEAT NG10 .... 61 M6
English Martyrs RC School
LEIW LE3 .... 124 F6
Erewash Museum
ILK DE7 .... 33 K7
Erewash Valley Golf Club
ILK DE7 .... 47 M6
Ernehale Infant School
ARN NG5 .... 37 L1
Eskdale Junior School
BSTN/STPLFD NG9 .... 62 F2
Etwall Leisure Centre
RDERBYSW DE65 .... 68 F3
Etwall Primary School
RDERBYSW DE65 .... 68 F3
Evington Pool
EVIE LE5 .... 133 G4
Evington Valley
Primary School
LEIE LE5 .... 132 B4
Exchange Arcade
NOTT NG1 .... 5 H7
Exhibition Centre
CDON/KEG DE74 .... 84 A7
Eyres Monsell Primary School
LEIS LE2 .... 137 H3
Faircharm Industrial Estate
LEIS LE2 .... 131 H5
Fairfield Primary School
BSTN/STPLFD NG9 .... 62 B1

The Fairfield Primary School
LEIW LE18 .... 137 K4
Fairfield School
LBORO LE11 .... 9 K5
Fairham Community College
CFTN/RUD NG11 .... 64 D8
Family Medical Centre
DERBYSE DE24 .... 58 E7
Farnborough
Comprehensive School
CFTN/RUD NG11 .... 64 E4
Feller Priory
EWD/SEL/PNX NG16 .... 14 A4
Fernvale Primary School
RLEINE/SYS LE7 .... 133 K1
Fernwood
Comprehensive School
WOL/BIL/BRX NG8 .... 49 H3
Fernwood J & I School
WOL/BIL/BRX NG8 .... 49 H3
Field House Infant School
ILK DE7 .... 47 K1
Findern County
Primary School
RDERBYSW DE65 .... 70 C8
Firbeck Primary School
WOL/BIL/BRX NG8 .... 48 F3
Fire Station Training Centre
DERBYW DE22 .... 56 F4
Firfield Primary School
BWSH/BRSTN DE72 .... 61 J7
Firs Estate Primary School
DERBYW DE22 .... 2 B8
Fleckney CE Primary School
RLEIS/BBY LE8 .... 145 J7
Fleckney Industrial Estate
RLEIS/BBY LE8 .... 145 L8
Fleckney Leisure Centre
RLEIS/BBY LE8 .... 145 K6
Folville Junior School
LEIW LE3 .... 130 E5
Forest Fields Primary School
NOTTE NG7 .... 36 D7
Forest Hill Golf Club
COAL LE67 .... 122 A6
Forest Lodge Primary School
LEIW LE3 .... 124 C7
Forest School
NOTTE NG7 .... 4 C1
Fosse Medical Centre
LEIW LE3 .... 131 G1
Fosse Park Shopping Centre
END/NAR LE19 .... 136 D2
Fosse Primary School
LEIW LE3 .... 6 A2
Foxbank Industrial Estate
RLEIW/BAR LE9 .... 140 B4
Foxwood GM School
BSTN/STPLFD NG9 .... 48 F6
Framework Knitters Museum
CFTN/RUD NG11 .... 79 G1
Frederick Harrison
Infant School
BSTN/STPLFD NG9 .... 48 D7
Freemens Common
Trading Estate
LEIS LE2 .... 131 K5
Friar Gate House School
DERBY DE1 .... 2 B2
Friar Lane FC
LEIS LE2 .... 131 K7
Friesland School
LGEAT NG10 .... 61 K2
Fullhurst Community College
LEIW LE3 .... 130 F4
The Galleries of Justice
NOTT NG1 .... 5 H8
Garendon High School
LBORO LE11 .... 103 G3
Gartree High School
LEIS LE2 .... 138 F4
Gas Research Centre
LBORO LE11 .... 102 F6
Gateway Christian School
ILK DE7 .... 46 D4
Gateway 6th Form College
LEIS LE2 .... 6 D7
Gayton Community
Junior School
NORM/LIT DE23 .... 71 H1
Gelders Hall Industrial Estate
RLBORO LE12 .... 101 K5
The George Spencer School
BSTN/STPLFD NG9 .... 62 C2
Gilbros Business Centre
LEI LE1 .... 7 G4
Gilroes Cemetery
LEIW LE3 .... 124 E5
Gilroes Crematorium
LEIW LE3 .... 124 E5
Gilthill Primary School
EWD/SEL/PNX NG16 .... 22 B8
Glaisdale Business Centre
WOL/BIL/BRX NG8 .... 49 H2
Glaisdale Park Industrial Estate
WOL/BIL/BRX NG8 .... 49 H1
Glapton Primary School
CFTN/RUD NG11 .... 64 B5
Glebelands Primary School
LEIN LE4 .... 119 G7
Glenbrook Primary School
WOL/BIL/BRX NG8 .... 35 K8
Glenfield Hospital
LEIW LE3 .... 124 C5
Glenfield Primary School
LEIW LE3 .... 123 M7
Glen Gorse Golf Club
WGSTN LE18 .... 139 H4
Glen Hills Primary School
LEIS LE2 .... 136 E4
Glenmere Primary School
WGSTN LE18 .... 138 D4
Golden Valley Railway
ALFN DE55 .... 11 M3
Goodsmoor Road
Industrial Estate
DERBYSE DE24 .... 71 J2

Gorse Hill Hospital
LEIW LE3 .... 124 D3
Gotham Cricket Club
CFTN/RUD NG11 .... 77 M5
Gotham Primary School
CFTN/RUD NG11 .... 77 L6
Grace Dieu Manor School
COAL LE67 .... 100 D7
Grace Dieu Priory
COAL LE67 .... 100 D6
Grampian Primary School
DERBYSE DE24 .... 71 H3
Granby Junior School
ILK DE7 .... 33 J5
Granby Primary School
LEIS LE2 .... 131 H8
Grange Business Park
RLEIS/BBY LE8 .... 136 D6
Grange Primary School
LGEAT NG10 .... 62 D7
Greasley Beauvale DH Lawrence
Infant School
EWD/SEL/PNX NG16 .... 21 M4
Greasley Beau Vale
Junior School
EWD/SEL/PNX NG16 .... 21 M5
Greasley Sports Centre
EWD/SEL/PNX NG16 .... 21 M5
Great Central Railway
CFTN/RUD NG11 .... 78 E3
LBORO LE11 .... 9 M7
RLBORO LE12 .... 112 C4
Greencroft Junior &
Primary School
CFTN/RUD NG11 .... 64 D4
Greengate Medical Centre
LEIN LE4 .... 119 L7
Greenhill Lane Industrial Estate
ALFN DE55 .... 12 A1
Greenholme School
NOTTE NG7 .... 50 C3
Green Lane Infant School
LEIE LE5 .... 7 M3
The Green Surgery
COAL LE67 .... 116 B7
Greenwood Dale
Technology School
WBRGFD NG2 .... 51 L3
Greenwood Infant School
WBRGFD NG2 .... 51 L2
Greenwood Junior School
WBRGFD NG2 .... 51 L3
Greenwood & Sneinton Family
Medical Centre
WBRGFD NG2 .... 51 L2
Greystoke Primary School
END/NAR LE19 .... 136 A7
Greythorn Primary School
WBRGFD NG2 .... 65 G2
Groby Community College
GBY/RBY LE6 .... 123 H5
Group Surgery & Clinic
DERBYW DE22 .... 43 H5
The Grove Hospital
BWSH/BRSTN DE72 .... 74 B6
Guthlaxton College
WGSTN LE18 .... 137 M6
GX Superbowl
NOTTE NG7 .... 50 C6
Hadden Park High School
WOL/BIL/BRX NG8 .... 35 K8
Haddon Primary School
CARL NG4 .... 38 B5
Hallam Fields Junior School
ILK DE7 .... 47 K2
Hall Orchard CE
Primary School
RLBORO LE12 .... 105 H8
The Hall Primary School
LEIW LE3 .... 124 C6
The Hall
COT/KEY/RAD NG12 .... 52 A6
Hamilton Business Park
LEIN LE4 .... 126 F4
Hamilton Community College
LEIE LE5 .... 127 J5
Hamilton - Site of
Medieval Village
RLEINE/SYS LE7 .... 127 J4
Hammersmith Station
RIPLEY DE5 .... 11 H3
Haramead Business Centre
LEI LE1 .... 7 H3
Hardwick J & I School
NORM/LIT DE23 .... 57 K6
Harrington Junior School
LGEAT NG10 .... 61 M6
Harry Carlton School
RLBORO LE12 .... 88 D5
Harvey Hadden Sports Centre
WOL/BIL/BRX NG8 .... 35 J8
Harvey Hadden Stadium
WOL/BIL/BRX NG8 .... 35 K8
Hathern CE Primary School
RLBORO LE12 .... 94 B4
Hathernware Industrial Estate
RLBORO LE12 .... 95 G2
Hawthorne Primary School
BLWL NG6 .... 24 C3
Haydn Primary School
ARN NG5 .... 37 G5
Haymarket Shopping Centre
LEI LE1 .... 6 F4
Haymarket Theatre
LEI LE1 .... 6 F4
Haywood
Comprehensive School
ARN NG5 .... 37 G2
Hazel Primary School
LEIS LE2 .... 131 K4
Heage Primary School
BPR/DUF DE56 .... 10 B5
The Health Centre
WBRGFD NG2 .... 51 J8
Heanor Gate Industrial Estate
HEANOR DE75 .... 20 A7
Heanor Gate School
HEANOR DE75 .... 20 A6

Heanor Health Centre
HEANOR DE75 .... 20 C6
Heanor Langley Infant School
HEANOR DE75 .... 20 C6
Heanor & Langley Mill District
Memorial Hospital
HEANOR DE75 .... 20 D6
Heanor Leisure Centre
HEANOR DE75 .... 20 D6
Heanor Town Sports Ground
HEANOR DE75 .... 20 C6
Heatherbrook Primary School
LEIN LE4 .... 124 D1
Heathfield Primary School
ARN NG5 .... 36 D4
Hemington Primary School
CDON/KEG DE74 .... 85 H2
Henry Mellish
Comprehensive School
BLWL NG6 .... 36 A2
Herbert Strutt Primary School
BPR/DUF DE56 .... 17 J5
Heritage Centre
CFTN/RUD NG11 .... 79 G2
Herrick Primary School
LEIN LE4 .... 126 B3
Heymann Primary School
WBRGFD NG2 .... 65 H3
Highbank Primary School
CFTN/RUD NG11 .... 64 B8
Highbury Hospital
BLWL NG6 .... 36 A2
Highcliffe Primary School
LEIN LE4 .... 119 K8
Highfield Primary School
LGEAT NG10 .... 62 A5
Highfield Rangers FC
LEIN LE4 .... 126 C3
Highfields Medical Centre
LEIS LE2 .... 7 L6
Highgate Primary School
RLBORO LE12 .... 114 B3
Highgate Primary School
LEIW LE3 .... 6 C6
High Pavement
Sixth Form College
ARN NG5 .... 36 D2
High School Sports Ground
ARN NG5 .... 36 E5
High View Secondary School
DERBYE DE21 .... 44 C6
High View Technology Centre
DERBYE DE21 .... 44 C6
Hill Lane Industrial Estate
COAL LE67 .... 116 B5
Hillside Medical Centre
BSTN/STPLFD NG9 .... 48 D8
Hilton Industrial Estate
RDERBYSW DE65 .... 68 B4
Hilton Primary School
RDERBYSW DE65 .... 68 B5
Hind Leys Community College
RLBORO LE12 .... 102 B3
HM Prison
ARN NG5 .... 36 F4
CALV/BJ NG14 .... 27 J5
LEI LE1 .... 6 F9
HM Young Offenders Institution
& Remand Centre
(Glen Parva)
LEIS LE2 .... 137 H5
Hogarth Primary &
Nursery School
MAPPK/POR/STA NG3 .... 37 L8
Holbrook CE Primary School
BPR/DUF DE56 .... 18 A8
Holgate School
HUCK/RAV NG15 .... 23 J1
Hollybrook Medical Centre
NORM/LIT DE23 .... 70 C1
Hollygate Industrial Park
COT/KEY/RAD NG12 .... 67 L3
Hollygirt School
MAPPK/POR/STA NG3 .... 5 G2
Hollywell Primary School
EWD/SEL/PNX NG16 .... 22 C8
Holme Pierrepont
Country Park
COT/KEY/RAD NG12 .... 52 D4
Holmfield Primary School
LEIW LE3 .... 129 M4
Holy Cross RC School
HUCK/RAV NG15 .... 15 M6
Holywell Primary School
LBORO LE11 .... 103 G7
Horsendale Primary School
EWD/SEL/PNX NG16 .... 35 J4
Horsley CE Primary School
DERBYE DE21 .... 30 D1
Horsley Lodge Golf Club
ILK DE7 .... 30 F3
Horsley Woodhouse
Primary School
ILK DE7 .... 31 H1
Hucknall Airfield
HUCK/RAV NG15 .... 23 K5
Hucknall Industrial Park
HUCK/RAV NG15 .... 23 J3
Hucknall Leisure Centre
HUCK/RAV NG15 .... 15 M7
Hucknall National
Junior School
HUCK/RAV NG15 .... 15 L7
Hucknall Town FC
HUCK/RAV NG15 .... 23 K2
Humberstone Heights
Golf Club
LEIE LE5 .... 126 E6
Humberstone Infant School
LEIE LE5 .... 126 F6
Humphrey Perkins
High School
RLBORO LE12 .... 105 G7
Huncote Cemetery
RLEIW/BAR LE9 .... 135 H7
Huncote Community
Primary School
RLEIW/BAR LE9 .... 135 H7
Huncote Leisure Centre
RLEIW/BAR LE9 .... 135 G7

Hunters Lodge Medical Centre
LEIW LE3 .... 129 K5
Huntingdon Primary &
Nursery School
MAPPK/POR/STA NG3 .... 5 H3
Ilkeston Bowl
ILK DE7 .... 33 J8
Ilkeston Community Hospital
ILK DE7 .... 33 H3
Ilkeston School
ILK DE7 .... 33 H7
Ilkeston Swimming Pool
ILK DE7 .... 33 J6
Imperial Avenue Infant School
LEIW LE3 .... 130 F4
Industrial Museum
DERBY DE1 .... 2 F2
Inglehurst Primary School
LEIW LE3 .... 124 F8
Interchange 25 Business Park
BWSH/BRSTN DE72 .... 61 K3
Iona School
MAPPK/POR/STA NG3 .... 51 L2
Ironville & Codnor Park
Primary School
EWD/SEL/PNX NG16 .... 12 D3
Irwin College
LEIS LE2 .... 7 K9
Ivy Grove Surgery
RIPLEY DE5 .... 11 H6
Ivy House Special School
NORM/LIT DE23 .... 3 J8
Jacksdale Primary School
EWD/SEL/PNX NG16 .... 12 F4
James Peacock Infant School
CFTN/RUD NG11 .... 64 F8
Jesse Gray Primary School
WBRGFD NG2 .... 65 J2
Jewish Cemetery
WBRGFD NG2 .... 65 J4
Jewry Wall Museum & Site
LEIW LE3 .... 6 C6
John Carrol Leisure Centre
NOTTE NG7 .... 4 A5
John Clifford Primary School
BSTN/STPLFD NG9 .... 63 L1
John Doran Gas Museum
LEIS LE2 .... 131 J5
John Flamsteed
Community School
RIPLEY DE5 .... 18 E5
John Port School
RDERBYSW DE65 .... 68 F3
John Ryle Health Centre
CFTN/RUD NG11 .... 64 C6
John Storer Clinic
NOTT NG1 .... 4 E1
John Storer House
(Community Centre)
LBORO LE11 .... 9 H4
Judgemeadow
Community College
LEIE LE5 .... 133 G4
Kedleston Hall (NT)
DERBYW DE22 .... 42 C2
Kedleston Park Golf Club
DERBYW DE22 .... 42 E1
Kegworth Museum
CDON/KEG DE74 .... 86 A5
Kegworth Primary School
CDON/KEG DE74 .... 86 A5
Kegworth Squash Club
CDON/KEG DE74 .... 86 A5
Ken Martin Swimming Pool
BLWL NG6 .... 24 A6
Kensington Junior School
ILK DE7 .... 33 L8
Kestrel Business Park
CARL NG4 .... 52 E2
Keyworth Health Centre
COT/KEY/RAD NG12 .... 80 C5
Keyworth Primary School
COT/KEY/RAD NG12 .... 80 C5
Kibworth CE Primary School
RLEIS/BBY LE8 .... 146 D6
Kibworth Golf Club
RLEIS/BBY LE8 .... 146 F8
Kibworth High School
RLEIS/BBY LE8 .... 146 D7
Kilburn J & I School
BPR/DUF DE56 .... 18 E7
Kilby CE Primary School
WGSTN LE18 .... 144 D3
Kilby CE Primary School
NORM/LIT DE23 .... 57 K6
Killisick Junior School
ARN NG5 .... 25 M6
Kimberley Leisure Centre
EWD/SEL/PNX NG16 .... 34 E1
Kimberley Primary School
EWD/SEL/PNX NG16 .... 34 D1
Kimberley School
EWD/SEL/PNX NG16 .... 34 E1
King Edward Park
Primary School
MAPPK/POR/STA NG3 .... 5 M6
King Edward VII College
COAL LE67 .... 109 G5
King Richard III Infant School
LEIW LE3 .... 6 A7
Kings Mead Clinic
DERBY DE1 .... 2 C1
Kingsmead Industrial Estate
DERBYW DE22 .... 57 H1
The Kings School
WBRGFD NG2 .... 51 G6
Kingsway Hospital
DERBYW DE22 .... 56 F3
Kingsway Hospital
School of Nursing
DERBYW DE22 .... 56 F3
Kingsway Industrial Park
DERBYW DE22 .... 56 F2
Kingsway Primary School
LEIW LE3 .... 130 C5
Kingsway Retail Park
DERBYW DE22 .... 57 G2
Kirby Muxloe Castle
RLEIW/BAR LE9 .... 129 J1

Kirby Muxloe Golf Club
RLEIW/BAR LE9 .... 129 H3
Kirby Muxloe Primary School
RLEIW/BAR LE9 .... 129 J2
Kirby Muxloe Sports Club
RLEIW/BAR LE9 .... 129 J1
Kirk Hallam Community
Technology College
ILK DE7 .... 47 H1
Kirk Hallam Ladywood School
ILK DE7 .... 47 H1
Kirk Langley CE Primary School
ASHB DE6 .... 41 K5
Knighton Fields
Primary School
LEIS LE2 .... 131 K7
Lace Centre
NOTT NG1 .... 4 F8
Lace Market Theatre
NOTT NG1 .... 5 H8
Lady Bay Primary School
WBRGFD NG2 .... 51 L6
Ladycross Infant School
LGEAT NG10 .... 61 M1
Lady Jane Grey
Primary School
GBY/RBY LE6 .... 123 J5
Ladylea Industrial Estate
ILK DE7 .... 18 F3
Lakeside Business Park
LEIN LE4 .... 120 B8
Lakeside Infant School
LGEAT NG10 .... 75 M2
Lambley Primary School
CARL NG4 .... 26 F8
The Lancaster School
LEIS LE2 .... 131 L8
Lancaster Sports Centre
DERBY DE1 .... 2 E2
Landau Forte College
City Technical College
DERBY DE1 .... 2 F1
Langley Business Park
EWD/SEL/PNX NG16 .... 20 E1
Langley Mill CE Infant School
EWD/SEL/PNX NG16 .... 20 F4
Langley Mill Junior School
EWD/SEL/PNX NG16 .... 20 E3
Langley Park Industrial Estate
EWD/SEL/PNX NG16 .... 20 F4
Langmoor Primary School
LEIS LE2 .... 138 D2
Lantern Lane Primary School
RLBORO LE12 .... 88 D5
Larkfields Junior School
EWD/SEL/PNX NG16 .... 34 F1
Larklands Infant School
ILK DE7 .... 33 L7
Latimer Primary School
RLEINE/SYS LE7 .... 124 C2
Launde Primary School
LEIS LE2 .... 138 F1
Lawn Primary School
DERBYW DE22 .... 43 H6
The Lawrence Museum
EWD/SEL/PNX NG16 .... 21 K4
Law School
NOTT NG1 .... 4 F5
Leen Mills Primary School
HUCK/RAV NG15 .... 15 M7
Lees Brook Community School
DERBYE DE21 .... 44 F7
Leeson Clinic
LEIW LE3 .... 131 G4
Leicester Airport
LEIS LE2 .... 133 L8
Leicester College
LEI LE1 .... 6 E2
LEI LE1 .... 7 G1
LEIS LE2 .... 131 K4
LEIW LE3 .... 131 H4
Leicester Exhibition Centre
LEI LE1 .... 7 G5
Leicester FC (Walkers Stadium)
LEIS LE2 .... 131 J5
Leicester Frith Hospital
LEIW LE3 .... 124 D5
Leicester General Hospital
LEIE LE5 .... 132 E2
Leicester Grammar
Junior School
LEIE LE5 .... 133 G3
Leicester Grammar School
LEI LE1 .... 6 D6
Leicester High School
For Girls
LEIS LE2 .... 132 C7
Leicester Ivanhoe CC
LEIW LE3 .... 129 H5
Leicester Leys Leisure Centre
LEIN LE4 .... 124 E2
Leicester Montessori
Grammar School
LEI LE1 .... 131 M4
Leicester Montessori School
LEI LE1 .... 131 M4
LEIS LE2 .... 132 B5
Leicester Racecourse
LEIS LE2 .... 138 C1
Leicester Royal Infirmary
LEI LE1 .... 6 E9
Leicestershire CCC (Grace Road)
LEIS LE2 .... 131 J7
Leicestershire Golf Club
LEIE LE5 .... 132 D5
Leicester Tigers RFC
(Welford Road Ground)
LEIS LE2 .... 131 K4
Leics Museum of Technology
LEIN LE4 .... 125 K5
Lenton Business Centre
NOTTE NG7 .... 50 C3
Lenton Health Centre
NOTTE NG7 .... 4 A7
Lenton Industrial Estate (East)
NOTTE NG7 .... 50 D7
Lenton Industrial Estate (West)
NOTTE NG7 .... 50 C8

Lenton Leisure Centre
NOTTE NG7 .... 4 A9
Lenton Primary School
NOTTE NG7 .... 50 D4
Leysland Clinic
RLEIS/BBY LE8 .... 143 G3
Leysland High School
RLEIS/BBY LE8 .... 143 G3
Limehurst High School
LBORO LE11 .... 9 H1
Lime Leigh Medical Centre
LEIW LE3 .... 131 G4
Linby Cum Papplewick CE
Primary School
HUCK/RAV NG15 .... 15 M4
Linden Junior School
RLEIS/BBY LE8 .... 143 J3
Linden Primary School
LEIE LE5 .... 132 E4
Lingdale Golf Club
RLBORO LE12 .... 117 J1
Lings Bar Hospital
WBRGFD NG2 .... 66 A1
Little Eaton Primary School
DERBYE DE21 .... 30 A8
Little Hill Primary School
WGSTN LE18 .... 138 A5
Littleover Community School
NORM/LIT DE23 .... 56 D7
Littleover Medical Centre
NORM/LIT DE23 .... 56 F6
The Little Theatre
LEI LE1 .... 7 G7
London Road Private Hospital
LEIS LE2 .... 132 B6
Longcliffe Golf Club
RLBORO LE12 .... 102 D7
Long Eaton Community School
LGEAT NG10 .... 62 B8
The Long Eaton & District
Arts Council
LGEAT NG10 .... 62 B8
Long Eaton Stadium
LGEAT NG10 .... 62 D7
Long Lane CE Primary School
ASHB DE6 .... 40 C6
Longmoor Primary School
LGEAT NG10 .... 61 M4
Long Row Primary School
BPR/DUF DE56 .... 17 K3
Longslade Community College
RLEINE/SYS LE7 .... 119 M6
Long Street Surgery
WGSTN LE18 .... 138 A5
Long Whatton CE
Primary School
RLBORO LE12 .... 94 A4
Lons Infant School
RIPLEY DE5 .... 11 H5
Loscoe CE Primary School
HEANOR DE75 .... 19 M3
Loughborough Cemetery
LBORO LE11 .... 9 L9
Loughborough Central Station
LBORO LE11 .... 9 M4
Loughborough CE
Primary School
LBORO LE11 .... 8 F4
Loughborough College of
Further Education
LBORO LE11 .... 8 F5
Loughborough Crematorium
LBORO LE11 .... 9 M9
Loughborough General Hospital
LBORO LE11 .... 9 K3
Loughborough Health Centre
LBORO LE11 .... 9 K3
Loughborough High School
LBORO LE11 .... 9 K5
Loughborough Hospital
LBORO LE11 .... 8 D2
Loughborough Motorway
Trading Estate
RLBORO LE12 .... 101 L5
Loughborough University
LBORO LE11 .... 8 E6
LBORO LE11 .... 8 B5
Loughborough University
School of Art & Design
LBORO LE11 .... 9 H3
Lum Farm Leisure Centre
RIPLEY DE5 .... 19 J2
Lynncroft Primary School
EWD/SEL/PNX NG16 .... 21 L4
Mackworth College
DERBYW DE22 .... 56 D2
Madford Business Park
ARN NG5 .... 37 H1
Magazine Gatehouse
LEIS LE2 .... 6 D7
Main Shopping Centre
DERBY DE1 .... 3 G5
Manners Industrial Estate
ILK DE7 .... 33 H5
Manorfield CE Primary School
RLEIW/BAR LE9 .... 140 B5
Manor High School
LEIS LE2 .... 133 H8
The Manor Surgery
BSTN/STPLFD NG9 .... 63 K1
Manvers Junior School
COT/KEY/RAD NG12 .... 67 K4
Mapleweli Hall School
RLBORO LE12 .... 111 J8
Mapperley CE Primary School
ILK DE7 .... 32 D5
Mapperley Plains
Primary School
MAPPK/POR/STA NG3 .... 37 M4
Margaret Glen-Bott
Comprehensive School
WOL/BIL/BRX NG8 .... 49 M3
Markeaton Crematorium
DERBYW DE22 .... 42 F8
Markeaton Primary School
DERBYW DE22 .... 43 J8
Markets & Corn Exchange
LEI LE1 .... 6 F6

Marlow Road Industrial Estate
LEIS LE2 .... 131 H5
Maripool Junior School
HEANOR DE75 .... 20 E6
Marriott Primary School
LEIS LE2 .... 137 J1
Martin High School
RLEINE/SYS LE7 .... 118 B8
Martinshaw Primary School
GBY/RBY LE6 .... 123 H3
Mayflower Primary School
LEIE LE5 .... 132 D3
Maywood Golf Club
BWSH/BRSTN DE72 .... 61 H1
Meadowbank Day Hospital
WBRGFD NG2 .... 50 F6
Meadow Brookes
Business Park
LGEAT NG10 .... 76 A3
Meadow Farm Primary School
DERBYE DE21 .... 58 E3
Meadow Lane Industrial Estate
LBORO LE11 .... 104 A1
Meadow Lane Infant School
BSTN/STPLFD NG9 .... 63 H3
The Meadow Primary School
WGSTN LE18 .... 138 C4
The Meadows Industrial Estate
DERBYE DE21 .... 3 L3
DERBYE DE21 .... 3 J3
Meadows Primary School
WBRGFD NG2 .... 51 G5
The Meadows Primary School
BPR/DUF DE56 .... 29 H1
Meadow Trading Estate
WBRGFD NG2 .... 51 J5
Media Centre
NOTT NG1 .... 5 J7
Medway Community
Primary School
LEIS LE2 .... 7 K8
Medway Infants School
LEIS LE2 .... 7 L9
Melbourne Halland Gardens
MELB/CHEL DE73 .... 83 G8
Melbourne J & I School
MELB/CHEL DE73 .... 82 F7
Melbourne Park Medical Centre
MELB/CHEL DE73 .... 36 A4
Melbury Primary School
WOL/BIL/BRX NG8 .... 35 H7
Mellers Primary School
NOTTE NG7 .... 4 A5
Mellor Primary School
LEIN LE4 .... 125 M4
Memorial Hall
RLEINE/SYS LE7 .... 118 F5
Mental Health Clinic
BSTN/STPLFD NG9 .... 63 K2
Meridian Business Park
END/NAR LE19 .... 130 B7
Meridian Leisure Park
LEIW LE3 .... 130 C6
Merridale Medical Centre
LEIW LE3 .... 130 F6
Merrill College
DERBYSE DE24 .... 72 D3
DERBYSE DE24 .... 72 C1
Merrydale J & I School
LEIE LE5 .... 126 C7
The Merton Primary School
RLEINE/SYS LE7 .... 120 F5
Meteor Business Park
DERBY DE1 .... 43 M8
Metro Cinema
DERBY DE1 .... 2 E5
Michael House School
HEANOR DE75 .... 32 E1
Mickleover Golf Club
NORM/LIT DE23 .... 56 D6
Mickleover Primary School
MCKLVR DE3 .... 56 B5
Mickleover Surgery
MCKLVR DE3 .... 56 C6
Middleton Primary School
WOL/BIL/BRX NG8 .... 50 A3
Midland Railway Centre
RIPLEY DE5 .... 11 J3
Milford Primary School
BPR/DUF DE56 .... 17 L8
Millennium Business Centre
CFTN/RUD NG11 .... 64 C7
Millennium Business Centre
DERBYE DE21 .... 58 C3
Millfield Community
School Centre
LEIW LE3 .... 130 C7
Millgate Centre
LEIS LE2 .... 131 L7
Mill Hill Industrial Estate
END/NAR LE19 .... 135 L3
Mill Hill School
RIPLEY DE5 .... 11 K7
Mill Lane Industrial Estate
GBY/RBY LE6 .... 123 L6
Moat Community College
LEIS LE2 .... 7 J6
Moderns RFC
CFTN/RUD NG11 .... 50 F7
Montrose Primary School
LEIS LE2 .... 137 H1
The Moore Clinic
BPR/DUF DE56 .... 17 K3
Moorgreen Industrial Park
EWD/SEL/PNX NG16 .... 21 M2
Moorhead Primary School
DERBYSE DE24 .... 72 D1
Moorways Primary School
DERBYSE DE24 .... 72 A1
Moorways Sports Centre
DERBYSE DE24 .... 72 B1
Morley Hayes Golf Club
ILK DE7 .... 31 J6
Morley Primary School
ILK DE7 .... 31 G8
Mornington Primary School
EWD/SEL/PNX NG16 .... 35 H3
Mountford House School
ARN NG5 .... 37 G6

Mount St Bernard Abbey
COAL LE67 .... 109 H2
Mountsorrel CE Primary School
RLBORO LE12 .... 113 H5
Mountsorrel Health Centre
RLBORO LE12 .... 113 J6
Mowacre Community &
Sports Centre
LEIN LE4 .... 125 J1
Mowmacre Hill Primary School
LEIN LE4 .... 125 J1
Mundy CE Junior School
HEANOR DE75 .... 20 C6
Murray Park
Community School
MCKLVR DE3 .... 56 D3
Museum of Nottingham Lace
NOTT NG1 .... 5 H8
Narborough Health Centre
END/NAR LE19 .... 136 A7
National Ice Centre
NOTT NG1 .... 5 K7
The National School
HUCK/RAV NG15 .... 15 K6
National Space Centre
LEIN LE4 .... 125 K3
National Water Sports Centre
COT/KEY/RAD NG12 .... 52 C5
Natural History Museum
WOL/BIL/BRX NG8 .... 49 L4
Nature Care Clinic
LEI LE1 .... 6 E7
Netherfield Infant School
CARL NG4 .... 52 D1
Netherfield Junior School
CARL NG4 .... 38 E8
Netherfield Medical Centre
CARL NG4 .... 38 E8
Nethergate Special School
CFTN/RUD NG11 .... 64 D6
Nether Hall School
LEIE LE5 .... 127 H6
Newarke Houses
LEI LE1 .... 6 D7
Newbridge High School
COAL LE67 .... 108 B8
Newchase Business Park
DERBYSE DE24 .... 58 A6
New College Nottingham
BLWL NG6 .... 36 A3
New Croft Primary School
RLBORO LE11 .... 102 A4
New Parks Leisure Centre
LEIW LE3 .... 124 C8
Newry Junior School
WGSTN LE18 .... 137 K2
Newstead Industrial Estate
ARN NG5 .... 25 L8
Newstead Primary School
HUCK/RAV NG15 .... 15 H1
New Swannington
Primary School
COAL LE67 .... 108 A2
Newtown Linford
Primary School
GBY/RBY LE6 .... 117 H7
New Walk Centre
LEI LE1 .... 6 E7
New Walk Museum &
Art Gallery
LEI LE1 .... 7 G8
Nightingale Business Park
DERBYSE DE24 .... 58 B7
Nightingale Infant School
DERBYSE DE24 .... 58 A8
Nightingale Junior School
DERBYSE DE24 .... 58 A7
Noel Baker Community School
DERBYSE DE24 .... 72 D3
Normanton Junior School
NORM/LIT DE23 .... 57 J8
Normanton on Soar
Primary School
RLBORO LE12 .... 95 H4
Normanton Village
Infant School
NORM/LIT DE23 .... 57 J8
Northfield House
Primary School
LEIN LE4 .... 126 B6
Northgate Primary School
NOTTE NG7 .... 36 C1
Nottingham Airport
COT/KEY/RAD NG12 .... 66 D2
The Nottingham
Bluecoat School
WOL/BIL/BRX NG8 .... 36 B2
Nottingham City Hospital
ARN NG5 .... 36 E2
Nottingham City Hospital
Mobility Centre
ARN NG5 .... 36 F3
Nottingham Community College
MAPPK/POR/STA NG3 .... 5 L6
Nottingham Forest FC
(City Ground)
WBRGFD NG2 .... 51 J6
Nottingham General Hospital
NOTTE NG7 .... 4 E8
Nottingham High School
NOTT NG1 .... 4 D3
Nottingham High School for Girls
NOTT NG1 .... 4 D3
Nottingham Industrial Museum
WOL/BIL/BRX NG8 .... 49 L4
Nottingham Magistrates Court
WBRGFD NG2 .... 51 G4
Nottingham Nuffield Hospital
ARN NG5 .... 37 H2
Nottingham Racecourse
WBRGFD NG2 .... 52 A4
Nottingham RFC
BSTN/STPLFD NG9 .... 63 K3
Nottinghamshire County
Cricket Club (Trent Bridge)
WBRGFD NG2 .... 51 J6

Nottingham South & Wilford
Industrial Estate
CFTN/RUD NG11 .... 64 F3
Nottingham Trent University
CFTN/RUD NG11 .... 63 M5
CFTN/RUD NG11 .... 64 B4
NOTT NG1 .... 4 E4
NOTT NG1 .... 5 G5
Nottingham University Hospital
NOTTE NG7 .... 50 B5
Notts County Football Club
(Meadow Lane)
WBRGFD NG2 .... 51 J5
Nuffield Hospital
LEIE LE5 .... 126 F7
Nutbrook Cricket Club
ILK DE7 .... 32 F7
Oadby Golf Club
LEIS LE2 .... 138 C1
Oadby Health Centre
LEIS LE2 .... 138 E2
Oadby Industrial Estate
LEIS LE2 .... 138 D2
Oadby Town FC
WGSTN LE18 .... 138 D3
Oak & Ash Business Park
LEI LE1 .... 7 L2
Oaks Industrial Estate
END/NAR LE19 .... 135 L8
LBORO LE11 .... 103 L1
The Oaks Medical Centre
BSTN/STPLFD NG9 .... 49 K8
Oakwood Infant School
DERBYSE DE24 .... 72 E1
Oakwood Junior School
DERBYSE DE24 .... 72 E1
Oakwood Leisure Centre
DERBYE DE21 .... 44 E5
Oakwood Medical Centre
DERBYE DE21 .... 44 E6
Ockbrook School
BWSH/BRSTN DE72 .... 60 A2
Odeon Multiplex
LEIS LE2 .... 131 K5
Old Basford Health Centre
BLWL NG6 .... 36 C5
Old Hall Mill Business Park
DERBYE DE21 .... 30 A8
Old John Tower
GBY/RBY LE6 .... 117 K4
Old Rectory Museum
LBORO LE11 .... 9 J1
The Old Vicarage School
DERBYW DE22 .... 43 L5
Old Wyggestonians
Sports Club
WGSTN LE18 .... 138 D3
The Open University
ARN NG5 .... 36 F7
NOTTE NG7 .... 4 B8
Orchard Business Park
ILK DE7 .... 33 H6
LGEAT NG10 .... 61 M1
Orchard Park Industrial Estate
LGEAT NG10 .... 62 A1
Orchard Primary School
CDON/KEG DE74 .... 84 E3
Ormonde Fields Golf &
Country Club
RIPLEY DE5 .... 12 B7
Orton Industrial Estate
COAL LE67 .... 108 B6
The Osiers Business Centre
LEIW LE3 .... 136 C1
Osmaston Park
Industrial Estate
DERBYSE DE24 .... 58 B6
Our Lady of Perpetual Succour
RC Primary School
BLWL NG6 .... 36 B1
Our Ladys Convent School
LBORO LE11 .... 9 J5
Outwoods Edge
Primary School
RLBORO LE12 .... 103 L8
Overdale J & I School
LEIS LE2 .... 138 A1
Oxley Primary School
RLBORO LE12 .... 101 L4
Palm Court Industrial Centre
NOTTE NG7 .... 36 D6
Parkdale Primary School
CARL NG4 .... 52 B1
Parker Industrial Estate
DERBYE DE21 .... 43 M7
Park Farm Medical Centre
DERBYW DE22 .... 43 H5
Park Hill Golf Club
RLEINE/SYS LE7 .... 114 F1
Park House Medical Centre
CARL NG4 .... 38 D7
Parklands Infant School
LGEAT NG10 .... 61 M6
The Parklands Primary School
LEIS LE2 .... 137 J6
Parks Primary School
LEIW LE3 .... 124 E7
Parkview Primary School
DERBYE DE21 .... 44 E5
Pasley Road Health Centre
LEIS LE2 .... 137 H3
Passenger Terminal
CDON/KEG DE74 .... 85 G7
The Pastures Primary School
END/NAR LE19 .... 135 K5
Peartree Clinic
NORM/LIT DE23 .... 57 L6
Pear Tree Infant School
NORM/LIT DE23 .... 57 L6
Pear Tree Medical Centre
NORM/LIT DE23 .... 57 L6
Peckieton Lane Business Park
LEIS LE2 .... 128 A8
Pegasus Business Park
CDON/KEG DE74 .... 85 K7
Peoples College of
Tertiary Education
NOTT NG1 .... 5 G8

Perkins Industrial Estate
 DERBYE DE21 .... **44** A7
Peter Baines Industrial Estate
 DERBYW DE22 .... **2** D6
Phoenix Arts Centre
 LEI LE1 .... **6** E7
Phoenix Infant School
 CARL NG4 .... **38** D5
Piccadilly Cinema
 LEI LE1 .... **6** F4
Pickfords House Museum of
 Georgian Life & Costume
 DERBY DE1 .... **2** C3
Picture House
 LEI LE1 .... **6** E5
Pierrepont Gamston
 Primary School
 WBRGFD NG2 .... **66** A1
Pilkington Library
 LBORO LE11 .... **8** A7
Pilling's Lock
 RLBORO LE12 .... **104** E6
Pinewood Infant School
 ARN NG5 .... **25** M6
Pinfold Trading Estate
 BSTN/STPLFD NG9 ..... **48** C7
Playhouse Theatre
 NOTT NG1 .... **4** F7
Playworld
 CARL NG4 .... **26** C6
Plumtree School
 COT/KEY/RAD NG12 .... **80** C1
Pochin Primary School
 RLEINE/SYS LE7 .... **121** H7
Police Museum
 DERBY DE1 .... **2** E2
Portland Leisure Centre
 WBRGFD NG2 .... **51** H6
Portland Primary School
 WOL/BIL/BRX NG8 ..... **49** C1
Portway Infant School
 DERBYW DE22 .... **43** J3
Portway Junior School
 DERBYW DE22 .... **43** J3
Pottery Primary School
 BPR/DUF DE56 .... **18** A3
Prime Industrial Estate
 NORM/LIT DE23 .... **58** A5
Priory Junior School
 CARL NG4 .... **38** C6
The Priory RC Primary School
 EWD/SEL/PNX NG16 ... **21** M6
Puppets Theatre
 MAPPK/POR/STA NG3 .... **5** J3
Pye Bridge Industrial Estate
 ALFN DE55 .... **12** D1
Quarry Hill Industrial Estate
 ILK DE7 .... **47** K2
Quarry Hill Industrial Park
 ILK DE7 .... **47** K2
Queen St Baths
 DERBY DE1 .... **2** E2
Queens Drive Industrial Estate
 WBRGFD NG2 .... **50** E6
Queens Hall
 LBORO LE11 .... **9** H4
Queens Leisure Centre
 DERBY DE1 .... **2** E2
Queensmead Infant School
 LEIW LE3 .... **130** D2
Queen's Medical Centre
 NOTTE NG7 .... **50** B4
Queniborough
 Industrial Estate
 RLEINE/SYS LE7 .... **121** H2
Quorn & Woodhouse Station
 RLBORO LE12 .... **112** B2
Racecourse Industrial Park
 DERBYE DE21 .... **44** A7
Radcliffe on Trent Golf Club
 COT/KEY/RAD NG12 .... **53** M5
Radcliffe on Trent
 Infant School
 COT/KEY/RAD NG12 .... **53** L4
Radcliffe on Trent
 Junior School
 COT/KEY/RAD NG12 .... **53** K5
Radford Court
 Industrial Estate
 NOTTE NG7 .... **4** A6
Radford Primary School
 NOTTE NG7 .... **50** C2
RAF Building
 COAL LE67 .... **108** E7
Rail Museum
 ALFN DE55 .... **11** L3
Ratby Primary School
 GBY/RBY LE6 .... **122** F6
Ratby Sports Club
 GBY/RBY LE6 .... **123** G7
Ratcliffe College
 RLEINE/SYS LE7 .... **114** E5
Ravensdale Infant School
 MCKLVR DE3 .... **56** C4
The Rawlins
 Community College
 RLBORO LE12 .... **112** E1
Rearsby St Michael
 & All Angels CE
 Primary School
 RLEINE/SYS LE7 .... **115** L6
The Record Office
 for Leicestershire,
 Leicester & Rutland
 WGSTN LE18 .... **138** A4
Redhill Leisure Centre
 ARN NG5 .... **25** J5
Redhill Primary School
 BWSH/BRSTN DE72 .... **60** B2
Redhill School
 ARN NG5 .... **25** J6
Redlands Community
 Primary School
 RLBORO LE12 .... **114** A3
Redwood J & I School
 DERBYSE DE24 .... **71** J4
Regent College
 LEI LE1 .... **131** L4

Regent Place Retail Park
 LBORO LE11 .... **9** G2
Regent Street
 Industrial Estate
 END/NAR LE19 .... **136** A7
Reigate Primary School
 DERBYW DE22 .... **42** D8
Richard Bonnington
 Primary School
 ARN NG5 .... **25** K6
Richard Herrod Leisure Centre
 CARL NG4 .... **38** A7
Richard Hill CE Primary School
 RLEINE/SYS LE7 .... **118** F5
Richardson Endowed
 Primary School
 ILK DE7 .... **31** K1
Riddings Infant School
 ALFN DE55 .... **12** B1
Riddings Junior School
 ALFN DE55 .... **12** B1
Ridgeway Infant School
 NORM/LIT DE23 .... **57** H8
Ripley Hospital
 RIPLEY DE5 .... **11** G6
Ripley Infant School
 RIPLEY DE5 .... **11** H7
Ripley Junior School
 RIPLEY DE5 .... **11** G7
Ripley Leisure Centre
 RIPLEY DE5 .... **11** H6
Rise Park Junior School
 ARN NG5 .... **24** D6
Rise Park Shopping Centre
 ARN NG5 .... **24** D6
Risley Lower Grammar CE
 Primary School
 BWSH/BRSTN DE72 .... **61** J3
Riverlyn Medical Centre
 BLWL NG6 .... **36** A1
Riversdale Surgery
 BPR/DUF DE56 .... **17** K3
Riverside Community College
 LEIW LE3 .... **130** F7
Riverside Primary School
 LEIN LE4 .... **119** M8
Riverside Retail Park
 NOTTE NG7 .... **50** E7
Robert Bakewell
 Primary School
 LBORO LE11 .... **103** H1
Robert Mellors
 Primary School
 ARN NG5 .... **25** L7
Robert Shaw Primary School
 WOL/BIL/BRX NG8 ..... **50** B1
Robin Hood Industrial Estate
 MAPPK/POR/STA NG3 .... **5** L6
Robin Hood Primary School
 ARN NG5 .... **36** E1
Robin Hood Statue
 NOTT NG7 .... **4** F9
Robinsons Industrial Estate
 NORM/LIT DE23 .... **58** A5
Roddington Country Park
 CFTN/RUD NG11 .... **79** G3
Roehill Infant School
 NORM/LIT DE23 .... **3** D1
Rolleston Infant School
 LEIS LE2 .... **137** H5
Rolleston Junior School
 LEIS LE2 .... **137** H5
Ropewalk Industrial Centre
 ILK DE7 .... **33** L6
Rosebery Primary School
 LBORO LE11 .... **8** E2
Rose Hill Business Centre
 NORM/LIT DE23 .... **2** F9
Rosehill Clinic
 MAPPK/POR/STA NG3 .... **5** M4
Rosehill Special School
 MAPPK/POR/STA NG3 .... **5** M4
Rothley CE Primary School
 RLEINE/SYS LE7 .... **113** J8
Rothley Park Club House
 RLEINE/SYS LE7 .... **119** H3
Rothley Park Golf Club
 RLEINE/SYS LE7 .... **119** G2
Rothley Station
 RLEINE/SYS LE7 .... **118** F2
Roundhill College
 RLEINE/SYS LE7 .... **120** D6
Round Hill Primary School
 BSTN/STPLFD NG9 ..... **49** K8
Rowlatts Hill Primary School
 LEIE LE5 .... **132** E1
Royal Crown Derby
 Visitor Centre
 NORM/LIT DE23 .... **3** G8
Royal School for the Deaf
 DERBYW DE22 .... **57** H1
RTC Business Park
 NORM/LIT DE23 .... **57** M7
Ruddington Fields
 Business Park
 CFTN/RUD NG11 .... **79** H2
Ruddington Grange Golf Club
 CFTN/RUD NG11 .... **65** G5
Ruddington Medical Centre
 CFTN/RUD NG11 .... **65** G8
Rushcliffe Arena
 WBRGFD NG2 .... **65** H1
Rushcliffe Golf Club
 RLBORO LE12 .... **88** B3
Rushcliffe Leisure Centre
 WBRGFD NG2 .... **65** K3
Rushcliffe School
 WBRGFD NG2 .... **65** K3
Rushey Mead Health Centre
 LEIN LE4 .... **126** B3
Rushey Mead Primary School
 LEIN LE4 .... **126** A5
Rushey Mead
 Recreation Centre
 LEIN LE4 .... **126** A3
Rushey Mead School
 LEIN LE4 .... **126** A3

Rylands Junior School
 BSTN/STPLFD NG9 ..... **63** L3
Sacred Heart RC Primary School
 LBORO LE11 .... **8** F8
Sacred Heart RC School
 WOL/BIL/BRX NG8 ...... **7** M4
Saffron Hill Cemetery
 WGSTN LE18 .... **137** K3
Saffron Lane Sports Centre
 LEIS LE2 .... **131** K6
Saffron Lane Stadium
 LEIS LE2 .... **131** K6
St Albans RC Primary School
 DERBYE DE21 .... **58** D1
St Andrews CE Primary School
 ILK DE7 .... **45** M2
St Andrews Special School
 DERBYE DE21 .... **44** C5
St Anns Well Infant School
 MAPPK/POR/STA NG3 .... **5** L2
St Augustines RC
 Primary School
 MAPPK/POR/STA NG3 .... **5** H1
St Barnabas Catholic Cathedral
 NOTT NG1 .... **4** E6
St Barnabas Primary School
 LEIE LE5 .... **126** C8
St Bartholomews CE
 Primary School
 RLBORO LE12 .... **112** C2
St Benedict RC School
 DERBYW DE22 .... **43** K6
St Botolphs CE Primary School
 RLBORO LE12 .... **102** A3
St Chads CE Infant School
 NORM/LIT DE23 .... **2** D9
St Clare RC Primary School
 COAL LE67 .... **108** B7
St Clares Special School
 MCKLVR DE3 .... **56** D5
St Crispins School
 LEI LE1 .... **131** M5
St Edwards CE Primary School
 CDON/KEG DE74 .... **84** F4
St Edwards' RC School
 MAPPK/POR/STA NG3 .... **51** K1
St Elizabeths RC
 Primary School
 BPR/DUF DE56 .... **17** K2
St Georges Catholic
 Primary School
 NORM/LIT DE23 .... **57** G8
St George's Retail Park
 LEIE LE5 .... **7** J5
St Giles Special School
 DERBYE DE21 .... **44** A6
St Helens Business Centre
 DERBY DE1 .... **2** D1
St James CE Infant School
 DERBY DE1 .... **3** G7
St John Fisher RC
 Primary School
 DERBYSE DE24 .... **59** G7
 WGSTN LE18 .... **138** C3
St John Houghton
 Catholic School
 ILK DE7 .... **47** G1
St Johns CE Primary School
 BPR/DUF DE56 .... **17** L2
 BSTN/STPLFD NG9 ..... **48** C3
 CARL NG4 .... **52** C2
 RIPLEY DE5 .... **11** K5
St Johns College
 BSTN/STPLFD NG9 ..... **48** F8
St Johns Primary School
 LEIS LE2 .... **132** A5
St Josephs RC Primary School
 LEIE LE5 .... **127** H7
 NORM/LIT DE23 .... **2** D7
St Josephs School
 NOTT NG1 .... **4** E6
St Laurence CE Primary School
 LGEAT NG10 .... **76** C1
St Lukes CE Primary School
 RLEINE/SYS LE7 .... **133** K2
St Margarets Baths
 LEI LE1 .... **6** D4
St Margarets Business Centre
 LEI LE1 .... **6** E3
St Margarets Bus Station
 LEI LE1 .... **6** E4
St Margarets Sports Centre
 LEI LE1 .... **6** D2
St Martins Shopping Centre
 LEI LE1 .... **6** E6
St Mary De Castro Church
 LEI LE1 .... **6** C7
St Mary RC Primary School
 NOTTE NG7 .... **36** D7
St Marys CE Primary School
 BLWL NG6 .... **24** A7
St Marys Fields Infant School
 LEIW LE3 .... **131** G5
St Marys Primary School
 LBORO LE11 .... **8** F2
St Marys RC Primary School
 DERBY DE1 .... **2** E1
St Mathews Sports Hall
 LEI LE1 .... **7** H3
St Matthews Business Centre
 LEI LE1 .... **6** F3
St Patricks RC Primary School
 CFTN/RUD NG11 .... **50** F7
 LEIN LE4 .... **125** M5
St Pauls CE Primary School &
 Community Centre
 RLBORO LE12 .... **111** L6
St Pauls RC School
 LEIE LE5 .... **133** G3
St Peter & St Paul CE
 Primary School
 RLEINE/SYS LE7 .... **120** E2
St Peters CE Junior School
 CFTN/RUD NG11 .... **65** H6
 NORM/LIT DE23 .... **56** F6
St Peters CE Primary School
 RLEIS/BBY LE8 .... **136** D8

St Peters Health Centre
 LEIS LE2 .... **7** J7
St Teresas RC Primary School
 WOL/BIL/BRX NG8 ..... **35** L7
St Thomas Catholic
 Primary School
 ILK DE7 .... **33** J8
St Thomas More RC School
 LEIS LE2 .... **132** A7
St Werburghs CE
 Primary School
 DERBYE DE21 .... **59** H2
St Winefrides RC
 Primary School
 RLBORO LE12 .... **101** M3
Salutation Inn
 NOTT NG1 .... **5** G8
Sandfield Close
 Primary School
 LEIN LE4 .... **126** C2
Sandiacre Friesland
 Sports Centre
 BWSH/BRSTN DE72 .... **61** K2
Savoy Cinema
 NOTT NG7 .... **4** A8
Sawley J & I School
 LGEAT NG10 .... **75** L3
Sawmills Industrial Park
 HEANOR DE75 .... **20** B4
Scala Cinema
 ILK DE7 .... **33** J7
Scargill CE Primary School
 ILK DE7 .... **32** B8
Scotholme Primary School
 NOTTE NG7 .... **36** D7
Scotlands Industrial Estate
 COAL LE67 .... **108** C7
Scraptoft Golf Club
 RLEINE/SYS LE7 .... **127** L5
Scraptoft Valley
 Primary School
 LEIE LE5 .... **127** H7
Screen Room Cinema
 NOTT NG1 .... **5** J6
Seagrave Primary School
 RLBORO LE12 .... **106** D7
 WOL/BIL/BRX NG8 ..... **35** H5
Selston Bagthorpe
 Primary School
 EWD/SEL/PNX NG16 .... **13** L3
Sgcs Business Park
 BSTN/STPLFD NG9 ..... **63** L3
Shaftesbury Junior School
 LEIW LE3 .... **131** G3
Shardlow Business Park
 BWSH/BRSTN DE72 .... **74** B6
Shardlow Marina Caravan Park
 BWSH/BRSTN DE72 .... **74** F6
Shardlow Primary School
 BWSH/BRSTN DE72 .... **74** C6
Sheet Stores Industrial Estate
 LGEAT NG10 .... **76** B2
Shelthorpe Primary School
 LBORO LE11 .... **9** L8
Shenton Primary School
 LEIE LE5 .... **7** L3
Shepshed Dynamo FC
 RLBORO LE12 .... **102** A3
Sherwin Sports Centre
 NORM/LIT DE23 .... **57** M7
Shipley Country Park
 HEANOR DE75 .... **32** D2
Shipstones Business Centre
 NOTTE NG7 .... **36** C6
Shires Shopping Centre
 LEI LE1 .... **6** E5
Shonki Business Centre
 LEI LE1 .... **6** F2
Showcase Cinema
 NORM/LIT DE23 .... **2** D7
 NOTTE NG7 .... **50** C7
Sidney Robinson Business Park
 DERBYSE DE24 .... **59** H4
Silverhill Primary School
 MCKLVR DE3 .... **56** A4
Sinfin Central Business Park
 DERBYSE DE24 .... **71** K6
Sinfin Community School
 DERBYSE DE24 .... **71** J4
Sinfin Golf Club
 DERBYSE DE24 .... **71** L2
Sinfin Primary School
 DERBYSE DE24 .... **71** K2
Sir Francis Ley Industrial Park
 NORM/LIT DE23 .... **58** A6
Sir Jonathan North
 Community College
 LEIS LE2 .... **131** L8
Slater Primary School
 LEIW LE3 .... **6** C2
Snape Wood Medical Centre
 BLWL NG6 .... **23** K7
Snape Wood Primary School
 BLWL NG6 .... **23** L8
S N College
 NOTT NG1 .... **5** G7
Sneinton CE Primary School
 MAPPK/POR/STA NG3 .... **51** K3
Sneinton Health Centre
 WBRGFD NG2 .... **5** L7
Soar Valley College
 LEIN LE4 .... **126** A4
South East Derbyshire College
 HEANOR DE75 .... **20** D6
 ILK DE7 .... **47** K1
Southern Cemetery
 WBRGFD NG2 .... **65** H4
Southgate Infant School
 DERBYSE DE24 .... **58** D7
Southgate Retail Park
 NORM/LIT DE23 .... **2** D9
South Leicester RFC
 WGSTN LE18 .... **138** B7
South Nottingham College
 WBRGFD NG2 .... **65** H2
Southwark Infant School
 BLWL NG6 .... **36** B3

Southwark Junior School
 BLWL NG6 .... **36** C4
South Wigston Health Centre
 WGSTN LE18 .... **137** L3
South Wigston High School
 LEIS LE2 .... **137** J8
South Wilford Endowed
 Primary School
 CFTN/RUD NG11 .... **50** F8
Southwold Primary School
 WOL/BIL/BRX NG8 ..... **50** B2
South Wolds School
 COT/KEY/RAD NG12 .... **80** D5
Sparkenhoe Community
 Primary School
 LEIS LE2 .... **7** K3
Spence Street Sports Centre
 LEIE LE5 .... **126** B3
Spinney Hill Primary School
 LEIE LE5 .... **132** B2
Springfield Primary School
 BLWL NG6 .... **24** A6
 DERBYE DE21 .... **59** H1
Springfield Road
 Health Centre
 LEIS LE2 .... **132** A5
Spring St Primary School
 HUCK/RAV NG15 .... **15** K8
Springwater Golf Club
 CALV/BJ NG14 .... **27** C1
Stadium Business Court
 DERBYSE DE24 .... **58** C7
Stadium Industrial Park
 LGEAT NG10 .... **62** D7
Stafford Leys Community
 Primary School
 LEIW LE3 .... **129** K5
Standhill Infant School
 MAPPK/POR/STA NG3 .... **37** M3
Stanhope Primary School
 CARL NG4 .... **38** B4
Stanley Common CE
 Primary School
 ILK DE7 .... **31** K4
Stanstead Primary School
 ARN NG5 .... **24** C7
Stanton-on-the-Wolds
 Golf Club
 COT/KEY/RAD NG12 .... **80** F5
Stanton Vale Special School
 ILK DE7 .... **47** K1
Stapleford Health Centre
 BSTN/STPLFD NG9 ..... **62** B1
Stenhouse Medical Centre
 ARN NG5 .... **25** J7
Stenson Fields Primary School
 DERBYSE DE24 .... **71** H8
Stephenson College
 COAL LE67 .... **108** A7
Stevenson Junior School
 BSTN/STPLFD NG9 ..... **48** D7
Stokes Wood Primary School
 LEIW LE3 .... **124** F7
Stonebow Primary School
 RLBORO LE12 .... **102** F1
Stonebridge Court
 Industrial Estate
 MAPPK/POR/STA NG3 .... **5** M5
Stonebridge Mental
 Health Centre
 MAPPK/POR/STA NG3 .... **5** M5
Stonehill High School
 RLEINE/SYS LE7 .... **119** L6
Stoneygate College
 LEIS LE2 .... **132** B5
Stoneygate Football Club
 RLEINE/SYS LE7 .... **127** L7
Stoneygate School
 LEIS LE2 .... **132** A5
 RLEIS/BBY LE8 .... **146** A1
Stoughton Grange Farm
 LEIS LE2 .... **132** F6
Street Industrial Estate
 LEIN LE4 .... **7** L1
Street Lane Primary School
 RIPLEY DE5 .... **18** F2
Strelley Health Centre
 WOL/BIL/BRX NG8 ..... **35** H6
Stretton Hall (Hospital)
 LEIS LE2 .... **139** L3
Sunney Hill Infant School
 NORM/LIT DE23 .... **57** J9
Sunningdale Industrial Park
 LEIW LE3 .... **130** A4
Sunnyside Primary School
 BSTN/STPLFD NG9 ..... **62** F1
Swanwick Junction
 ALFN DE55 .... **11** L2
Swanwick Primary School
 ALFN DE55 .... **11** H1
Swarkestone Boat Club
 MELB/CHEL DE73 .... **82** B3
Swithland St Leonard CE
 Primary School
 RLBORO LE12 .... **112** C8
Sycamore J & I School
 MAPPK/POR/STA NG3 .... **5** L3
Syston Health Centre
 RLEINE/SYS LE7 .... **120** F3
Tales of Robin Hood
 NOTT NG1 .... **4** F7
Taylor Primary School
 LEI LE1 .... **7** J2
Temple House Clinic
 NORM/LIT DE23 .... **2** E7
Temple of Venus
 RLBORO LE12 .... **102** D4
Tennis Court Industrial Estate
 WBRGFD NG2 .... **51** L4
Theatre Royal & Concert Hall
 NOTT NG1 .... **4** F6
Thistly Meadow
 Primary School
 RLEIS/BBY LE8 .... **137** G8
Thornfield Industrial Estate
 MAPPK/POR/STA NG3 .... **51** K2
Thornhill Day Hospital
 DERBYW DE22 .... **56** F3

Thornton's Holt Camping Park
  COT/KEY/RAD NG12 .... 53 H7
Thorpes Road Industrial Estate
  HEANOR DE75 .... 20 B6
Thringstone Primary School
  COAL LE67 .... 100 B6
Thurlaston CE Primary School
  RLEIW/BAR LE9 .... 134 E4
Thurmaston Cemetery
  LEIN LE4 .... 120 C8
Thurnby Lodge
  Primary School
  LEIE LE5 .... 133 H1
Thythorn Field
  Primary School
  WGSTN LE18 .... 138 B8
Tollerton Primary School
  COT/KEY/RAD NG12 .... 66 B6
Tomlinson Industrial Estate
  DERBYE DE21 .... 43 M5
Top Valley Health Centre
  ARN NG5 .... 24 D7
Top Valley School
  ARN NG5 .... 24 C7
Torkard Hill Medical Centre
  HUCK/RAV NG15 .... 23 L1
Totan Banks Road
  Infant School
  BSTN/STPLFD NG9 .... 62 D5
The Towers Hospital
  LEIE LE5 .... 126 D6
Town Hall & Theatre
  LBORO LE11 .... 9 J3
Trading Estate
  LEIS LE2 .... 7 J5
Trent Bridge Primary School
  WBRGFD NG2 .... 51 H7
Trent Business Centre
  LGEAT NG10 .... 62 A5
Trent College
  LGEAT NG10 .... 62 A6
Trent Lane Industrial Estate
  CDON/KEG DE74 .... 84 F1
Trent Lock Golf Centre
  LGEAT NG10 .... 76 A4
Trent Pool Sports Centre
  WBRGFD NG2 .... 51 K5
Trent South Industrial Park
  WBRGFD NG2 .... 51 L4
Trent Vale Infant School
  BSTN/STPLFD NG9 .... 63 M3
Trinity Hospital
  LEI LE1 .... 6 C7
The Trinity School
  WOL/BIL/BRX NG8 .... 35 L7
Troon Industrial Estate
  LEIN LE4 .... 126 E3
Troon Way Business Centre
  LEIN LE4 .... 126 D3
Trowell CE Primary School
  BSTN/STPLFD NG9 .... 48 B3
UCI Cinemas
  DERBYE DE21 .... 44 A6

Underwood CE Primary School
  EWD/SEL/PNX NG16 .... 13 K6
Unity Primary & Nursery School
  NOTTE NG7 .... 4 C4
University Chaplaincy
  BSTN/STPLFD NG9 .... 49 L8
University Exhibition Centre
  LEI LE1 .... 6 C6
University of Derby
  DERBY DE1 .... 2 C2
  DERBYW DE22 .... 2 A2
  MCKLVR DE3 .... 56 D4
University of Leicester
  LEI LE1 .... 131 L4
  LEIS LE2 .... 132 A7
University of Leicester
  Harold Martin
  Botanic Garden
  LEIS LE2 .... 132 D7
University of Leicester
  Sports Ground
  LEIS LE2 .... 132 E7
University of Nottingham
  NOTTE NG7 .... 49 M6
  NOTTE NG7 .... 50 B3
Uplands Infant School
  LEIS LE2 .... 7 L7
Uplands Primary School
  LEIS LE2 .... 7 L7
Uppingham Road
  Health Centre
  LEIE LE5 .... 126 C8
Vernon Park Trading Estate
  BLWL NG6 .... 36 C4
Vernon Street Medical Centre
  DERBY DE1 .... 2 B3
Victoria Business Park
  CARL NG4 .... 52 F1
Victoria Clinic
  LEIS LE2 .... 131 M5
Victoria Health Centre
  NOTT NG1 .... 5 H5
Victoria Leisure Centre
  NOTT NG1 .... 5 K6
Victorian Market Hall
  DERBY DE1 .... 2 F4
Victoria Shopping Centre
  NOTT NG1 .... 5 H5
Vidya Medical Centre
  DERBY DE1 .... 2 F7
Virgin Active - Derby
  DERBYE DE21 .... 3 J2
Vulcan Business Centre
  LEIS LE2 .... 7 K3
Waingroves Primary School
  RIPLEY DE5 .... 11 L7
Walnut Street Medical Centre
  LEIS LE2 .... 131 J4
Walter Evans CE
  Primary School
  DERBYW DE22 .... 43 K5
Walter Halls Primary School
  MAPPK/POR/STA NG3 .... 37 J5

Wanstead Industrial Park
  LEIW LE3 .... 129 M2
Warner Village
  LEIW LE3 .... 130 C6
Warren Primary School
  ARN NG5 .... 24 E5
Water Leys Primary School
  WGSTN LE18 .... 137 M3
Watermead Country Park
  LEIN LE4 .... 120 B7
  RLEINE/SYS LE7 .... 120 B5
Waterside Retail Park
  ILK DE7 .... 33 L6
Waverley Street Clinic
  DERBYSE DE24 .... 58 A8
Welbeck Primary School
  WBRGFD NG2 .... 51 G5
Wellside Medical Centre
  DERBY DE1 .... 2 E6
Westbridge Industrial Park
  LEIW LE3 .... 6 C6
West Bridgford School
  WBRGFD NG2 .... 65 H2
Westbrook Special School
  LGEAT NG10 .... 62 A8
Westcotes Health Centre
  LEIW LE3 .... 131 G3
Westdale J & I School
  MAPPK/POR/STA NG3 .... 38 A4
Western Golf Club
  LEIW LE3 .... 129 M1
Western Park School
  LEIW LE3 .... 130 D1
Westglade Junior School
  ARN NG5 .... 24 D7
West Hallam Cricket Club
  ILK DE7 .... 32 B8
West Hallam Medical Centre
  ILK DE7 .... 32 C8
Westleigh Business Park
  RLEIS/BBY LE8 .... 136 F6
Westleigh RFC
  RLEIS/BBY LE8 .... 136 E8
  RLEIS/BBY LE8 .... 142 E2
West Park Community School
  DERBYSE DE21 .... 59 C2
West Park Leisure Centre
  LGEAT NG10 .... 61 M8
The Wheldon School
  LEIN LE4 .... 38 A6
Whetstone Golf Club
  RLEIW/BAR LE9 .... 142 C3
Whitegate Primary School
  CFTN/RUD NG11 .... 64 B7
Whitehall Primary School
  LEIE LE5 .... 132 F3
Whitemoor Court
  Industrial Estate
  NOTTE NG7 .... 36 C7
Whitemoor Primary School
  WOL/BIL/BRX NG8 .... 36 B6
Whitwick Business Park
  COAL LE67 .... 108 B5

Whitwick Cemetery
  COAL LE67 .... 108 C3
Whitwick Health Centre
  COAL LE67 .... 108 C2
Whitwick St John the Baptist
  CE Primary
  COAL LE67 .... 108 C1
Wholesale Fruit &
  Flower Market
  WBRGFD NG2 .... 51 J4
Whyburn Primary School
  HUCK/RAV NG15 .... 15 K8
Wigston College of
  Further Education
  WGSTN LE18 .... 137 M5
Wigston Swimming Pool
  WGSTN LE18 .... 137 M6
Wilberforce Road Surgery
  LEIW LE3 .... 6 A9
Wilford Business Park
  CFTN/RUD NG11 .... 64 F3
Wilford Hill Crematorium
  WBRGFD NG2 .... 65 H4
William Booth
  Birthplace Museum
  WBRGFD NG2 .... 5 M7
William Booth Infant School
  WBRGFD NG2 .... 5 M8
William Crane School
  WOL/BIL/BRX NG8 .... 35 M4
William Gilbert
  Endowed Primary School
  BPR/DUF DE56 .... 29 J3
William Howitt Junior School
  HEANOR DE75 .... 20 B5
William Lilley Infant School
  BSTN/STPLFD NG9 .... 62 B1
William Sharp School
  WOL/BIL/BRX NG8 .... 35 G8
Willoughby Primary School
  RLBORO LE12 .... 91 G8
Willow Brook
  Primary School
  COT/KEY/RAD NG12 .... 80 F5
Willowbrook Primary School
  LEIE LE5 .... 133 J1
Willow Farm Business Park
  CDON/KEG DE74 .... 84 F1
Willow Farm Primary School
  CARL NG4 .... 38 E5
Willow Industrial Estate
  BLWL NG6 .... 24 A7
Willow Sports Centre
  DERBY DE1 .... 2 D2
Wilmorton Community
  Primary School
  DERBYSE DE24 .... 58 B6
Windmill Road
  Industrial Estate
  LBORO LE11 .... 104 B4
Winstanley High School
  LEIW LE3 .... 130 C6

Wollaton Cricket Club
  WOL/BIL/BRX NG8 .... 49 J3
Wollaton Park Golf Club
  WOL/BIL/BRX NG8 .... 49 M4
Wollaton Vale Health Centre
  WOL/BIL/BRX NG8 .... 49 H4
Wolsey House
  Primary School
  LEIN LE4 .... 125 J4
Woodborough Road Clinic
  ARN NG5 .... 37 H5
Woodbrook Vale High School
  RLBORO LE12 .... 103 K8
Woodland Grange
  Primary School
  LEIS LE2 .... 139 H3
Woodlands Community School
  DERBYW DE22 .... 43 H3
Woodlands Day Hospital
  LEIW LE3 .... 135 M7
Woods Foundation School
  ARN NG5 .... 27 G3
Woodstock Primary School
  LEIN LE4 .... 125 J3
Woodview Business Centre
  ARN NG5 .... 24 E6
Woolden Hill CP School
  RLEINE/SYS LE7 .... 118 C7
Wreake Valley
  Community College
  RLEINE/SYS LE7 .... 121 G2
Wren Park Primary School
  MCKLVR DE3 .... 56 E5
Wyggeston Hospital
  LEIW LE3 .... 131 G3
Wyggeston & Queen
  Elizabeth I College
  LEI LE1 .... 131 L5
Wygston's House
  Museum of Costume
  LEI LE1 .... 6 D6
Wymeswold Airfield (Disused)
  RLBORO LE12 .... 97 K6
Wymeswold CE
  Primary School
  RLBORO LE12 .... 98 A4
Wymeswold Industrial Park
  RLBORO LE12 .... 97 L6
Wyvern Business Park
  DERBYE DE21 .... 58 E4
Wyvern County
  Primary School
  LEIN LE4 .... 126 B5
Ye Old Trip To Jerusalem Inn
  NOTT NG1 .... 5 G9

Notes

 **Street by Street** QUESTIONNAIRE

Dear Atlas User
Your comments, opinions and recommendations are very important to us. So please help us to improve our street atlases by taking a few minutes to complete this simple questionnaire.

You do NOT need a stamp (unless posted outside the UK). If you do not want to remove this page from your street atlas, then photocopy it or write your answers on a plain sheet of paper.

Send to: The Editor, AA Street by Street, FREEPOST SCE 4598, Basingstoke RG21 4GY

ABOUT THE ATLAS...

Which city/town/county did you buy?
_____

Are there any features of the atlas or mapping that you find particularly useful?
_____
_____
_____

Is there anything we could have done better?
_____
_____
_____

Why did you choose an AA Street by Street atlas?
_____
_____
_____

Did it meet your expectations?

Exceeded ☐   **Met all** ☐   **Met most** ☐   **Fell below** ☐

Please give your reasons
_____
_____
_____
_____
_____
_____

 MX

continued overleaf

Where did you buy it?

For what purpose? (please tick all applicable)

To use in your own local area ☐ **To use on business or at work** ☐

Visiting a strange place ☐ **In the car** ☐ **On foot** ☐

Other (please state)

LOCAL KNOWLEDGE...

Local knowledge is invaluable. Whilst every attempt has been made to make the information contained in this atlas as accurate as possible, should you notice any inaccuracies, please detail them below (if necessary, use a blank piece of paper) or e-mail us at *streetbystreet@theAA.com*

ABOUT YOU...

Name (Mr/Mrs/Ms)

Address

Postcode

Daytime tel no

E-mail address

Which age group are you in?

Under 25 ☐ **25-34** ☐ **35-44** ☐ **45-54** ☐ **55-64** ☐ **65+** ☐

Are you an AA member? **YES** ☐ **NO** ☐

Do you have Internet access? **YES** ☐ **NO** ☐

Thank you for taking the time to complete this questionnaire. Please send it to us as soon as possible, and remember, you do not need a stamp (unless posted outside the UK).